£5.99

PENGUIN

MARLBOROUGH AS MI.

Dr David G. Chandler was educated at Marlborough College, and Keble College, Oxford. He served four years in the Army, two spent in Nigeria as a captain in the Royal Army Educational Corps. He taught at the Royal Military Academy Sandhurst, for over thirty-three years, and became Head of the Department of War Studies. He retired in 1994. He has been a Visiting Professor at Ohio State University, the Virginia Military Institute and the US Marine Corps University, Quantico, and has lectured all over the world. He is Honorary President of the British Commission for Military History, Fellow of the Royal Historical Society, Honorary Founding President of the European Union Re-Enactments Society and Special Historical Consultant to the International Napoleonic Society. For six years he was a Trustee of the Royal Armouries at HM Tower of London and Leeds. He was awarded an honorary degree of D.Litt. at Oxford University in 1991, one of only four military historians to have been so honoured since the end of the First World War.

David Chandler is well known for his writing on Napoleon and Marlborough, and has brought this period of history alive through his many books. His books include *Marlborough as Military Commander*, *The Campaigns of Napoleon* and *Waterloo: The Hundred Days*. He has been a military consultant and adviser on a number of television programmes, notably to the BBC during the production of the twenty-part serialization of Tolstoy's *War and Peace* (1971–3), and for the Channel Four series *Great Commanders* (1992–3).

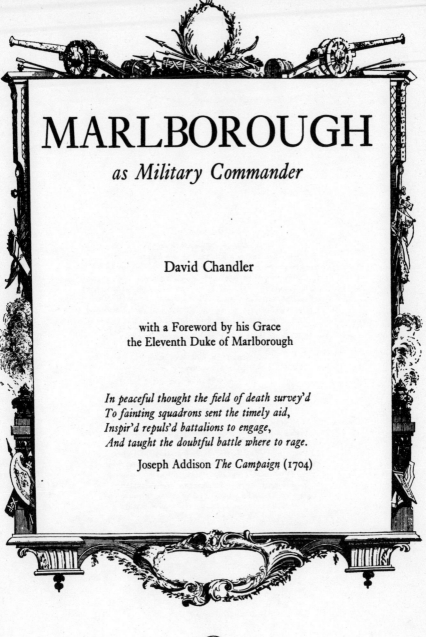

MARLBOROUGH

as Military Commander

David Chandler

with a Foreword by his Grace
the Eleventh Duke of Marlborough

In peaceful thought the field of death survey'd
To fainting squadrons sent the timely aid,
Inspir'd repuls'd battalions to engage,
And taught the doubtful battle where to rage.

Joseph Addison *The Campaign* (1704)

PENGUIN BOOKS

Dedicated to my Mother
J. M. C.
with love and respect

PENGUIN BOOKS

Published by the Penguin Group
Penguin Books Ltd, 27 Wrights Lane, London w8 5tz, England
Penguin Putnam Inc., 375 Hudson Street, New York, New York 10014, USA
Penguin Books Australia Ltd, Ringwood, Victoria, Australia
Penguin Books Canada Ltd, 10 Alcorn Avenue, Toronto, Ontario, Canada m4v 3b2
Penguin Books India (P) Ltd, 11, Community Centre, Panchsheel Park, New Delhi – 110 017, India
Penguin Books (NZ) Ltd, Private Bag 102902, NSMC, Auckland, New Zealand
Penguin Books (South Africa) (Pty) Ltd, 5 Watkins Street, Denver Ext 4, Johannesburg 2094, South Africa

Penguin Books Ltd, Registered Offices: Harmondsworth, Middlesex, England

First published by B. T. Batsford Ltd 1973
Published as a Classic Penguin 2000

1

Copyright © David Chandler, 1973
All rights reserved

Printed and bound in Great Britain by The Bath Press, Bath

Contents

List of Illustrations

Maps and Diagrams

ACKNOWLEDGEMENTS

I would first like to express my gratitude to His Grace the Eleventh Duke of Marlborough for consenting to write the Foreword and for permission for the inclusion of quotations from the Column of Victory and the Blenheim Archives; also for allowing reproduction of certain tapestries and paintings at Blenheim Palace. I owe a similar debt to Earl Cadogan for Pl. 32.

My thanks are due to the following for permission to reproduce maps: the Director-General and M. G. Coets of the *Institut Géographique*

Militaire, Abbaye de la Cambre, Brussels (Pls. 20, 22, 24, 26); Dr. Appelt
of the Bavarian *Landesvermessungsamt* (Pls. 13 & 15); Ordnance Survey
and H.M. Stationery Office (Pl. 5) and the Directors of Hoare's Bank
(Pl. 5 inset). For paintings and prints I thank: National Portrait Gallery
(Pls. 12, 16 & 17); National Maritime Museum (Pl. 2); British Museum
(Pls. 7 & 8); Parker Gallery (Pls. 14 & 21); Oranje Nassau Museum,
Delft (Pl. 18); Rijksmuseum, Amsterdam (Pl. 19); Radio Hulton Picture
Library (Pl. 25) and the Musée de l'Armée, Paris (Pls. 28–30).

I am also grateful to Mr. Peter Carson and Messrs. Longmans for
permission to include an amended version of the 'Analysis of Selected
Sieges' which first appeared in my edited version of *Robert Parker and
the Comte de Mérode-Westerloo*. Mr. Alan Hodge and Mr Peter Quennell,
editors of *History Today* gave permission to use parts of an article which
appeared in 1964.

The Trustees of the British Museum have allowed me to cite passages
from various volumes in the Additional Manuscripts collection. I would
like to thank Geo. Harrap Ltd. and Charles Scribner's Sons for direct
quotation from Winston S. Churchill's *Marlborough, His Life and Times*
(British & American editions) and Martinus Nijhoff of the Hague for
quotes from B. van 'T. Hoff, *The Correspondence of John Churchill and
Anthonie Heinsius*. The Public Record Office authorities also kindly
approved my use of certain manuscript material.

I would also like to express my thanks to the Director and Staff of the
Ohio State University Library, to Lt.-Col. G. A. Shepherd and his Staff
of the R.M.A.S. Central Library, and to Mr. D. W. King O.B.E., F.L.A., Chief
Librarian M.O.D. Library (Central and Army) and his assistants for much
help in the finding of books. Without the aid and encouragement of
Mr. Samuel Carr of Batsford it is doubtful whether this volume would
have seen the light of day, nor could I have dispensed with the services of
Mrs. Denyse Marples, Mrs. Myra Wright and Miss Pat Deans who
between them typed the manuscript. Mrs. Helen Wace and the Headmaster
of Culford School kindly helped me trace an elusive painting. Mr. David
Green and Mr. W. Parncutt have invariably made my visits to Blenheim
Palace both pleasant and instructive. Mr. Arthur Banks kindly drew the
maps from my design, and I am grateful to B. T. Batsford Ltd. and Mr.
Peter Kemmis Betty for publishing this second edition, six years after the
original publication.

Lastly, I owe an immense debt of gratitude to my wife, assisted by my
sons, for undertaking the thankless chore of indexing and to all my
family for tolerating the many occasions when my vacant or preoccupied
expression revealed that I was far away, 'following the drum' along the
dusty roads of eighteenth-century Flanders.

D.G.C.

Foreword *by His Grace the Eleventh Duke of Marlborough*

Towards the close of his biography of Marlborough, Sir Winston Churchill marvels that a general who never rode off a battlefield except as a victor should have failed, in retirement, to have set down some record of his astonishing campaigns. 'He was by no means indifferent to his fame. His desire "to leave a good name to history" had always been strong within him; but as he looked back over his life he seems to have felt sure that the facts would tell their tale and that he need not stir himself to do so. He looked to the great stones rising round him into a noble pile as one answer which would repeat itself with the generations.'

Certainly here at Blenheim there can be no risk whatever of a fading of Marlborough's fame. Wherever one looks—at the tapestries, at the Column of Victory, at the chapel tomb where Fame flourishes her trumpet and History her quill—the message is driven home: this was no ordinary man. On the ceiling of the Saloon, Laguerre shows him in his chariot at the zenith of victory, a demi-god among the gods of Olympus. And yet of course there was another side. We have but to read his letters to know of his troubles, of all those worries and disappointments ranging from the intransigence of the Dutch to the terrible headaches which were later to lead to cerebral strokes. So that when to the casual onlooker Marlborough appeared to be at the height of his triumphal progress from Ramillies to Oudenarde he, sick at heart and sick in head, was writing to his wife, 'I am so disheartened that when I shall have done my duty I shall submit to Providence'; and again, 'There is no happiness but in retirement.'

Indeed, only too often when one picks up a letter of his written at the time of Blenheim one reads of despondency; and yet there too one applauds his courage as he rises above it to declare, 'My greatest concern is for the Queen. . . . England will take care of itself and not be ruined because a few men are not pleased'.

In my view, as in Sir Winston's, Marlborough was not only a great commander of men but a great man, to be admired as much for his patience and self-discipline as for his victories at Blenheim, at Ramillies, at Oudenarde. . . . From time to time, during the two and a half centuries which have elapsed since his death, distinguished writers have dealt with various aspects of his career, the most recent of them being Mr. David Chandler, an expert in military tactics and in military history. I welcome this study, based as it is on many months of research.

Blenheim Palace
19 June 1972 *Marlborough*

Inscription on the Column of Victory, Blenheim Palace*

'The Castle of Blenheim was founded by Queen Anne in the fourth year of her reign in the year of the Christian era one thousand seven hundred and five. A monument designed to perpetuate the memory of the signal victory obtained over the French and the Bavarians near the village of Blenheim on the banks of the Danube by JOHN, DUKE OF MARLBOROUGH, the hero not only of his nation, but his age: whose glory was equal in the Council and in the Field: who by wisdom, justice, candour and address, reconciled various and even opposite interests, acquired an influence which no rank, no authority can give, nor any force but that of superior virtue, became the fixed, important centre, which united in one common cause, the principal states of Europe. Who by military knowledge, and irresistible valour, in a long series of uninterrupted triumphs, broke the power of *France*: when raised the highest, when exerted the most, rescued the *Empire* from desolation, asserted and confirmed the liberties of Europe. . . .'

Reproduced here, and at the head of later chapters, by kind permission of His Grace the Duke of Marlborough.

John Churchill, first Duke of Marlborough, was the greatest soldier produced by the British Isles in modern history. Many famous commanders have paid tribute to his transcendent qualities. Although Napoleon did not include his name in his list of seven greatest commanders

---

* The author of this celebrated panegyric was Henry St. John, Viscount Bolingbroke. As will appear in later chapters of this work, his relationship with the First Duke of Marlborough was not unclouded, particularly in later years. However, following her widowhood, Duchess Sarah could find no statesman, soldier or scholar with an apter or more polished style, than her husband's late adversary. Lord Bolingbroke was consequently entrusted with the composition, which is acknowledged to be a masterpiece in its conciseness, completeness and expression. It is reproduced here and at the head of subsequent chapters with the original spelling and punctuation, only '[os]' being added to certain dates to denote 'Old Style'. (See note, p. 3). The arrangement of certain passages has, however, been slightly adjusted to produce a continuous passage of prose. The Column was erected in 1730.

of history,* there is ample evidence that the Emperor held his name in respect. On 14 April 1821, for example, Surgeon Arnott of the 20th Regiment of Foot visited Longwood on St. Helena, and subsequently recorded his conversation with Napoleon. 'He began talking about English armies, and particularly praised the Duke of Marlborough, whom he described as a man whose mind was not narrowly confined to the field of battle; he fought and negotiated; he was at once a captain and a diplomatist.'[1] The Emperor went on to present a copy of Archdeacon Coxe's recently-published *Memoirs of the Duke of Marlborough* to the officers of Arnott's regiment.

Equally interesting is the first Duke of Wellington's reply when asked 'whether he thought Napoleon or Marlborough the greater general. "It is difficult to answer that," he replied. "I used to say that the presence of Napoleon at a battle was equal to a reinforcement of 40,000 men. But I can conceive nothing greater than Marlborough at the head of an English army. He had greater difficulties than I had with his allies; the Dutch were worse to manage than the Spaniards or the Portuguese. But, on the other hand, I think I had most difficulties at home." '[2]

More recently, Field-Marshal Montgomery has described the Duke as 'a military genius, capable, when he was given the chance, of transcending the contemporary limitations of warfare ... Marlborough absorbs the attention of the military historian as the giant of his times.'[3]

Not unnaturally, so important a figure has attracted a great deal of attention from historians as well as from soldiers. Thomas Lediard, Archdeacon Coxe, General Murray, Lords Macaulay and Wolseley, Frank Taylor, C. T. Atkinson and Hilaire Belloc, all have made, in their various generations, important contributions. Their work paved the way for the writing of the two definitive works on the subject and the period, namely Winston S. Churchill's epic *Marlborough, his Life and Times*, and Professor G. M. Trevelyan's masterpiece, *England under Queen Anne*. Small wonder if the appearance of two such famous works caused a pause in the production of further volumes, but the moratorium was broken in 1956 by the publication of Professor A. L. Rowse's notable study on *The Early Churchills*, and recent years have seen the appearance of valuable and stimulating volumes by Dr. Ivor F. Burton and J. H. Crockatt, not to forget the related studies by Alan Wace, Nicholas Henderson, Major R. E. Scouller, Henry Kamen, Dr. H. T. Dickinson, David Green and Iris Butler.

With so many distinguished predecessors it has been an act of some

---

* Alexander, Hannibal, Caesar, Gustavus Adolphus, Turenne, Eugene and Frederick.
[1] C. Ray, *The Lancashire Fusiliers*, London 1971, p. 72.
[2] Lord Stanhope, *Miscellanies*, London 1872, p. 87.
[3] Montgomery of Alamein, *A History of Warfare*, London 1968, pp. 295 and 311.

temerity to write a further monograph devoted to an examination of Marlborough the soldier. Yet it would have been impossible for any list of the 'Great Captains' of History to exclude so prominent a commander, and it would have been equally unfitting if the 250th anniversary of the great Duke's death had not elicited a respectful salute from one who has felt the greatest fascination for the man and his times, and who has spent much of his spare time during a dozen years on the faculty of the Royal Military Academy Sandhurst delving into the military affairs of the early 18th century.

The two and a half centuries since Marlborough's passing have seen immense changes in both world and military affairs, and yet in certain respects the present day has more in common with his generation than the more immediate past. Both periods have been typified by a 'limited' rather than a 'total' approach to the conduct of war, and a strong popular revulsion on an international scale against the horrors of unrestricted warfare. These respective rejections of totality in favour of limitation differ widely in terms of motivation, but they both indubitably share basic humanitarian considerations, and the generals of both epochs have felt the effects of 'restraining orders'. These moral and physical restraints were experienced as fully by General Douglas MacArthur in Korea as by Duke John in Western Europe some eight generations earlier.

How Marlborough faced up to these limitations and still achieved a notable degree of success in the field forms one constantly recurring theme in the chapters that follow. A second, and even more topical issue in these troubled days of continuing international tensions and struggles, will be the inability of the Duke, for all his military greatness, to 'win the peace' his successes seemed to have merited. Attention will be devoted to the ever-shifting kaleidoscope of politico-military relationships, although considerations of length and the avowed objective of the present series have necessarily curtailed the amount of space available for the treatment of these no less vital aspects of eighteenth-century warfare. For it was on the political plane that Marlborough ultimately failed.

A third theme of some contemporary relevance is the complex tale of the Duke's—and England's—relations with the member-states of the Second Grand Alliance, for no period has been more dominated by the convoluted problems of international agreements and associations— whether for peace or war—than our own. The tact with which he handled the national differences with the Dutch in particular repay study, for the contribution of the United Provinces to the struggle was of central importance at every stage (a fact that some commentators have tended to underrate, mainly because of the large amount of anti-Dutch sentiment generated by the Tory 'peace-party' at the time). Marlborough's skill at first creating and then preserving the Alliance until his dismissal was notable by any standards of diplomacy, but this entailed important modifications in the strategy of the war which eventually had fateful repercussions upon its outcome. This subject alone deserves a volume of its own, but it is hoped that sufficient information has been incorporated in the pages that follow to keep the reader orientated, although Thomas Carlyle was probably correct when he described eighteenth-century diplomacy as 'a balance of power delirium not to be comprehended by any man'.

In attempting to assess any great military leader, it is essential to set him firmly within his military context. If this is overlooked, as is sometimes the case in military biographies, a very distorted image can emerge. Space has been devoted, therefore, to analyses of Marlborough's military education and of the contemporary art of warfare. There can be no denying that his true greatness rests in his showing as a general. If in terms of British politics and European diplomacy he ultimately failed, his military record remains unique and unimpaired.

The publication in 1951 of the full correspondence between Marlborough and his most important ally (with Prince Eugene), Grand Pensionary Anthonie Heinsius of the United Provinces, has thrown a great deal of light upon the Duke's day-to-day work as both statesman and soldier, and has done much to complement the mass of material to be found in Coxe and Murray, and above all in the Blenheim archives. The British Museum manuscripts have also yielded some virtually unused material—including the correspondence between Cadogan, Marlborough's trusted aide, and Lord Raby, Queen Anne's ambassador to the court of Prussia for many years.[4] On a lower level, the Diary of Ensign Cramond illuminates the Irish episodes in Marlborough's earlier career, as seen and recorded by a junior officer.[5] A number of further minor discoveries have cast a little more light onto certain controversies surrounding the conduct of the battle of Malplaquet, and full use has been made of the documentation to be found in the 12 volumes of Pelet and Le Vault, which reveal much of the thinking of the French high command during the ten campaigns. For the rest, the task has mainly been a question of incorporating the fruits of modern scholarship and published works into the retelling of the well-known but nonetheless fascinating story of Marlborough's turbulent and eventful military career, set against the rich tapestry of his times. In the process, it is hoped that some indication of the man's complicated but basically benign personality will emerge. It must be admitted that in some ways 'Corporal John' remains something of an enigma. His unwillingness to set down on paper any account of his

[4] Additional Manuscript 22,196 (British Museum)
[5] Ibid. 29,878 (British Museum).

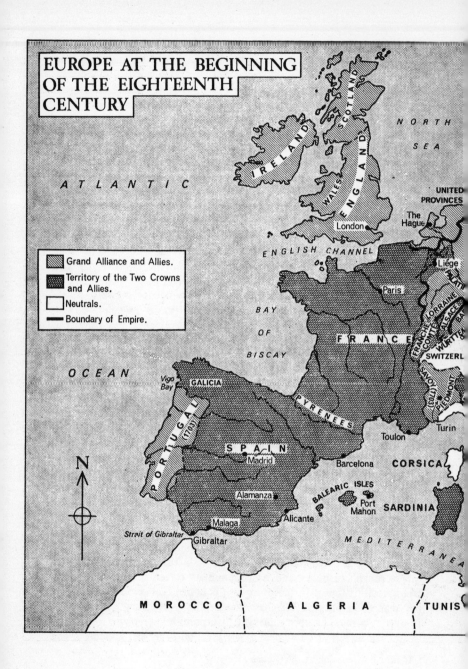

EUROPE AT THE BEGINNING OF THE EIGHTEENTH CENTURY

Grand Alliance and Allies.

Territory of the Two Crowns and Allies.

Neutrals.

Boundary of Empire.

ATLANTIC

OCEAN

NORTH SEA

IRELAND

SCOTLAND

WALES

ENGLAND

London

ENGLISH CHANNEL

UNITED PROVINCES

The Hague

Liège

Paris

FRANCE

FRANCHE-COMTÉ

LORRAINE

ALSACE

WÜRTT

BA

SWITZERL

SAVOY

DUCHY

PIEDMONT

BAY

OF

BISCAY

PYRENEES

Vigo Bay

GALICIA

PORTUGAL (1703)

SPAIN

Madrid

Alamanza

Malaga

Strait of Gibraltar

Gibraltar

N

Barcelona

Alicante

BALEARIC ISLES

Port Mahon

Toulon

Turin

CORSICA

SARDINIA

MEDITERRANEA

MOROCCO

ALGERIA

TUNIS

actions has often been regretted, but this reticence has at least posed a fascinating challenge to later historians. Much about the man can be culled from reading between the lines of his stately and courteous correspondence, and from the recorded impressions of the men and women who knew him. The picture that emerges is of a man cast in no common mould who played a major role in raising his country to the status of a major European power for the first time since the reign of Henry V, and thus heralded and facilitated the great imperial adventure that would dominate British and world history for the following two centuries. His memory deserves to be perpetuated in the hearts of his countrymen.

Author's note. The spelling of the proper and place names presents problems. In the case of the former, the most commonly accepted format has been adopted: thus 'Tallard' instead of 'Tallart', which was the correct early eighteenth-century form, although it was invariably spelt as 'Tallard' from at least the 1760s. In the case of place names the same convention has been employed in most instances: thus 'Nimwegen' rather than 'Nymegen', and 'Liége' instead of 'Liège' (a relatively recent change).

The Royal Military Academy, Sandhurst

June 1972

I

First Emergence, 1650-1684

'A certain French lieutenant-colonel, being commanded to defend a
pass, was so disheartened at the approach of a detachment of the
Dutch ... that he immediately quitted his post. Advice being
brought of it to Mons. de Turenne, he turn'd to another General
who stood near him, and offered to lay a wager, that his handsome
Englishman should retake the pass with half the number of men the
other had lost it. And he was not deceived in his opinion; Captain
Churchill regain'd the post, won the Marshal his wager, and gain'd
for himself the applause of the whole army.'

M. de Rousset, cited by Thomas Lediard.

Human Destiny moves in mysterious and unpredictable ways. Whilst a number
of History's 'Great Captains' emerged onto the world stage in early manhood—
Alexander the Great, Prince Eugene of Savoy and Napoleon Bonaparte are the
obvious examples—others, almost equally famous, only grasped the baton of
high command and the concomitant opportunities and responsibilities in middle
or later life. Prominent on any list of the latter, alongside such men as Julius
Caesar, Oliver Cromwell, Ulysses Grant and Field-Marshal Blücher, must be
placed the name of John Churchill, First Duke of Marlborough, probably the
greatest soldier-statesman produced by the British. Indeed, he was all of 50
before his first real chance of martial fame materialised, an age of considerable
maturity in the seventeenth and eighteenth centuries when relatively few men
survived to reach the traditional lifespan of three score years and ten, so great
were the hazards presented by sickness, crude surgery, over-indulgence (for
those wealthy enough to afford it) and a score of other pitfalls. Consequently
it was all the more remarkable that John Churchill proved capable of withstanding the rigours of ten successive major campaigns with never a break of more than
a few short winter months in which to recover from them, and even these brief
intervals were dominated by the needs of diplomacy and home politics. His
military record was almost unique: 'He never fought a battle he did not win, nor
besieged a town he did not take', wrote an early biographer in just summary.[1]

Few soldiers have inspired a greater degree of devotion in the men they led, or a greater measure of grudging admiration from those he outwitted and defeated time after time: perhaps only Napoleon and Rommel in relatively modern times shared such a *mystique*, but their military careers terminated at the ages of 46 and 53 respectively, whilst Marlborough's extended well into his sixty-second year.

Even when the end to active military service came to Marlborough early in 1712, it was due to political intrigue and the machinations of jealous foes rather than to any marked deterioration in his powers of command; although physical ailments had multiplied in his later years under the strain of the enormous responsibilities he bore so unflinchingly, his record of success in the field had reached a new height in 1711, his last campaign.

The thread of his career, like that of his great descendant, and most famous biographer, Sir Winston Churchill, did not run evenly. Both men suffered their share of misfortunes, including periods of complete eclipse in public life, as well as the sweets of fame and acknowledged achievement—but from first to last both proved men of dynamic power and ability. Like most great men in high position, John Churchill made many enemies during his years of greatness, and possibly because the ablest of these ultimately brought about his fall from royal favour and office, their partisan calumnies and insinuations have received considerable credence amongst certain historians of later generations, including the great Macaulay. In the words of Sir John Creasey, 'There are few successful commanders on whom fame has shone so unwillingly as upon John Churchill, Duke of Marlborough.'[2] Marlborough's political record and private character were certainly not *sans reproche*, and even his showing as a commander of genius had its darker moments, but on balance he was the foremost Englishman of his day as well as one of the greatest soldiers of all time. In the sense that he directly inspired the emergence of the British Army to international stature and less directly influenced the related development of the Royal Navy, it can be asserted that Marlborough made possible the expansion of the British Empire during the eighteenth century, for without such finely-forged instruments the conquest of French Canada, French India or the French West Indies would never have been possible. Therefore it can be said of Marlborough's work, as Octave Aubrey said of Napoleon's, 'when an achievement lasts so long and bears such fruit, it provides its own justification.'[3]

*   *   *

A half century of accumulated and varied experience lay behind John Churchill before he became widely recognised as a leading soldier. As is the case with many another historical figure, the details of his earliest years lie largely obscured by the mists of over three centuries. The Duke unfortunately never saw fit to record his memories of either his upbringing or his years of triumph and tribulation for the benefit of posterity—and his reticence was being regretted even during his own lifetime. In 1719, Dr. Felton surmised that 'if the Duke of Marlborough would give us his own Memoirs we should find he could write as well as fight like Caesar.'[4] Nevertheless, it is possible to piece together the most important details of his birth and formative influences.

He was born at Asche House in Devonshire on or about 26 May 1650 (O.S.)* the eldest surviving son of that prolific pair, the former Cavalier cavalry commander Winston Churchill and his wife Elizabeth (née Drake). On his father's side he came from a line of solid countrymen of local worth, most probably farmers for the most part (attempts by biographers and apologists to prove a more illustrious ancestry are not very convicing), but both his father and grandfather and several close relatives had entered various branches of the legal profession. Such social distinction as there was in his lineage came rather from his mother's family. The Drakes were the senior branch of the family that had produced the great Elizabethan sea-dog and circumnavigator, Sir Francis, and more recently Elizabeth's maternal grandfather, John, Lord Boteler had married the sister of George Villiers, first Duke of Buckingham, the ill-fated favourite of King Charles I. The young John may have inherited his sound common sense and sharp mind from his father's line, and his dashing good looks, urbanity and gifts as a courtier from his mother's side.

His earliest years were spent under genteel, but in many respects awkward family circumstances. Both his father and grandfather (John Churchill of Wooton Glanville) suffered for their loyalty to the crown during the Great Civil War. The former had fought for the King at both Lansdown Hill and Roundway Down, attaining the rank of Captain of Horse; the latter had served as sometime royal commissioner for the Sherborne district. These activities incurred Commonwealth fines of £446 and £448 respectively, and Winston Churchill was further debarred from legal practice.[5] The fines were heavy in terms of contemporary values, and so poverty was not unknown to Asche House, whence Winston transferred his young wife to live with his mother-in-law, Lady Drake, in 1647. This in itself must have proved a trying situation, for the old lady and her son had been staunch Parliamentarians throughout the troubles, and Asche House itself had received the rude attentions of Royalist forces (its owner eventually being awarded £1,500 compensation towards its repair). Clearly, however, ties of blood proved stronger than those of political conviction, so the near-penniless Winston found a haven for his burgeoning family. In all his wife

* The 'Old Style' calendar, as used in England, differed by ten days in the seventeenth century from the 'New Style' dating in vogue on the Continent. Thus John Churchill's birth date can be variously represented as 26 May (O.S.) or 5 June (N.S.). For convenience, all dates that follow will be 'New Style' unless otherwise indicated. From 1700 the difference became 11 days.

bore him 12 children, of whom 5 survived infancy, namely Arabella (1649–1730), John (1650–1722), George (1653–1710), Charles (1656–1715) and Theobald (1663–85). Thus from a tender age young Churchill learnt the need for financial care, political tact, and respect for the Stuart monarchy and the established religion—characteristics that remained parts of his personality for life and determined his actions at several critical junctures, as will be seen.

As for his father, he spent the long days of the Interregnum in sad reflection, a little heraldic and genealogical research (he ultimately published a book in 1675 entitled *Divi Britannici* on the Divine Right of Kings), and in the not unrewarding task of educating his family. It would also have been strange if, in the long winter evenings, he had not refought his old battles and campaigns for the benefit of his eldest son (at least when Lady Drake was not present), and thereby possibly first attracted the boy's interest to the profession of arms, and at the same time inculcated a little tactical lore about the proper handling of cavalry in action.

The Restoration of Charles II in 1660 caused the family fortunes to take a decided turn for the better. Winston was returned to the Convention Parliament early in 1661 as MP for Weymouth, and soon made his mark. Besides membership of several important committees, he received the *entrée* at Court, and in late 1661 was granted an 'augmentation of arms' by his grateful monarch. This was a cheap way of gratifying loyal servants, and whilst it satisfied Winston's heraldic and social aspirations, we can surmise that he (like many other erstwhile Cavalier who hoped that the New Elysium had dawned) was somewhat disappointed by the material improvement in his position: at any rate he adopted for his motto *Fiel pero despichado* ('Faithful but Unfortunate').

Eventually a more substantial mark of royal favour was bestowed, and Winston found himself appointed a Commissioner for Irish Land Claims. The family moved to Dublin, where John attended the City Free School. A year later (1663) his studies were transferred to St. Paul's School after his father's temporary recall to London, and there he continued his education until 1665. Details of his life and doings at this period are almost non-existent—but a book survives which carries a manuscript note alongside a reference to Vegetius's tome *De Re Militari*: 'From this very book John Churchill, scholar of this school, afterwards the celebrated Duke of Marlborough, first learnt the elements of the art of War, as was told to me, George North, on St. Paul's Day 1724/5 by an old clergyman who said he was a contemporary scholar....'[6] A further brief reference to the *alumnus* was included in the Apposition Speech of 1702: '*Hic Marlburius denique ab ipso Caesare Gallos domare et a Gallorum injuriis vicinas gentes tueri didicit.*'[7]*

Whilst John was expounding the exploits of Caesar fighting the Gauls, other members of the family were continuing to advance themselves by various means,

---

* Trans. 'Here Marlborough learnt from Caesar himself, how to tame the Gauls, and protect neighbouring peoples from Gallic iniquities.'

conventional and unconventional. The year 1663 brought a knighthood for his hardworking but somewhat lugubrious lawyer-father who continued his duties in London and Dublin alternately, and another 12 months found him appointed to a minor court position in the King's Household. That same year saw the eldest child of the family, Arabella, secure a coveted post in the household of the Duchess of York, where she soon caught the Duke's roving eye—some accounts say following a hunting accident near York, where the King's brother gallantly rescued a damsel in distress and became intimately aware of her not inconsiderable physical attractions. Whatever the truth of that story, Arabella was later capably combining the roles of maid-of-honour to the Duchess and *maîtresse-en-titre* to the Duke, to whom she bore several children, the most notable of whom, James Fitz-James, eventually became Duke of Berwick and a Marshal of France—and proved no insignificant opponent of his greater uncle in the campaigns of later years. The liaison was over by 1677, for in that year the wayward Arabella subsided into respectable matrimony with Colonel Charles Godfrey.

Arabella's influence in her early days at Court, however, was one factor in securing the post of page to the Duke of York for her younger brother just aged 16. His good-looks and affable charm stood him in good stead in that very permissive society, and soon he was making his mark in Court circles and (rather less officially) in certain influential boudoirs.

Other events of moment for his future career were his meeting with another royal page, Sidney Godolphin, destined to become a lifelong friend, and his securing 'a pair of colours' in the Foot Guards (14 September 1667 O.S.) as a result of a direct appeal to his good-natured master, the Duke of York. These various preferments, military and courtly, had placed John Churchill's foot on to the first rung of the ladder leading to future distinction, but as yet there was little to single him out from other aspiring young courtiers practicing their bows at Westminster or St. James's Palace. Very soon, however, he was to experience a radical change of scene; with it would begin his serious military education.

In 1668 John Churchill joined the Tangier garrison* as a 'volunteer'. History has left us no details of his skirmishes with the Moors, but the garrison was kept busy. Not all its members were credits to the military profession. 'The firemaster (an Ordnance officer responsible for mortars) is certainly a most ignorant person,' runs one near contemporary report, 'as to the knowledge of any ingredient except brandy.'[8] Yet it was valuable experience and a rude contrast with court life. Here, then, the young officer learnt the first rudiments of his chosen profession. Similarly, he also came to appreciate the role of the fleet. Once again we have no details, but in 1670 it is surmised that he served aboard ship in operations against the pirate-den of Algiers, his father being paid the sum of £140

* Part of the dowry of Catherine of Braganza, abandoned in 1683.

at the King's command towards defraying the charges of his son's 'equipage and other expenses in the employment he is now forthwith to undertake aboard our fleet in the Mediterranean Seas.'[9] He may also have travelled in Spain.*

After a three years absence the young man returned to Court, aged almost 21. He was soon noted for two conflicting attributes—his friendly advocacy of moderation when asked for advice, and a growing reputation as a dashing, not to say rash, lover. Among the several ladies whose 'sleepy eye bespoke the melting soul' for the handsome young officer was Barbara Villiers, Duchess of Cleveland, his second cousin once removed. For a number of years he intermittently enjoyed the favours of this temperamental beauty, perhaps drawing extra excitement from the knowledge that he was trespassing on royal preserves. There is no doubt that the monarch knew all about the liaison. It seems Charles II once caught the pair *en flagrant délit* but in his easy-going way overlooked the matter on the grounds that 'you do it to get your bread.' Indeed, material gratification was attendant upon the sensual, for in 1674 the Duchess presented her admirer with a present of some £4,500 which he cannily invested in an annuity which reputedly produced an income of £500 for life. Two years earlier the lady had presented Churchill with a daughter—a further addition to her numerous progeny of bastards. The young man was also involved in two duels during this period, coming off slightly the worse in both cases; he does not seem to have been a very expert swordsman at this juncture, but his valour was never in doubt.

The perils he faced were not exclusively those of a man-about-court. During the Third Dutch War, he was present aboard the Duke of York's flagship, *The Prince*, in the hard-fought but indecisive action of Solebay (June 1672). It would seem he served with distinction for later the same month we learn that 'Mr. Churchill that was ensigne to the King's Company was promoted Captain.'[10] This appointment,† for which his highly-connected mistress probably found the fee, was in the Duke of York's Admiralty Regiment (later the 24th of Foot).

The same year King Charles appointed his bastard, James Scott, Duke of Monmouth, to command an English contingent fighting for Louis XIV against the Dutch, newly under the leadership of William of Orange. A composite regiment included a detachment from the Admiralty Regiment, commanded by Churchill, and after wintering at Court, as was now his wont, he travelled to Flanders, destined to be the scene of his later glories, and proceeded to distinguish himself at the siege of Maastricht (17 June–8 July 1673). He was a member of a 'forlorn hope' led by Monmouth to capture part of the covered-way‡ on 24 June, but ended in taking a complete *demi-lune* in addition. Next day, when the Dutch made a sortie to retake the position, he was again a member of a small band of 30 soldiers—Claude-Hector de Villars (a name we shall meet again)

* See below p. 196.
† The commission is dated 13 June (O.S.) 1672.
‡ See fortification diagram, p. 79.

was another—who beat back the attempt after a bold charge over fire-swept ground. During this same incident he was credited with saving Monmouth's life, and received a slight wound for his pains. This deed brought him public recognition and commendation from the French King in person. From this time on, 'Mr. Cherchelle' (as Lord Alington called him) bore an enviable and established reputation for physical courage, earning the esteem of the common soldier which he never lost.

The ceaseless, feckless shifts of Stuart foreign policy brought peace to England in 1674, but a number of English regiments continued to serve in the French pay, and Churchill along with them. In early April he was appointed to the colonelcy of an English regiment by Louis XIV, and thereafter served with the great Marshal Turenne in his advance into the Palatinate that year. Now he was learning the military art from the hands of a master, and many authorities—including Wolseley and Atkinson—regard this as the most vital stage of his martial education, at least in the realm of grand tactics. Others, most notably Sir Winston Churchill, are less convinced, although none deny the ultimate value of the experience.

Churchill was present at the battles of Sinzheim (16 June) and Entzheim (4 October), both fought under difficult conditions. On the second occasion Turenne and 22,000 men were faced by an Imperialist army of over 40,000, which was awaiting further reinforcement by 20,000 Brandenburgers. Unless forestalled, this concentration would inevitably lead to the French loss of parts of Alsace, Lorraine, Franche Comté, and even the Champagne area, so the Marshal gambled all on a surprise attack. Advancing under cover of night (2/3 October)— a feature of many a Marlburian operation of later years, as will be seen—Turenne crossed the River Breusch and forthwith engaged 35,000 of de Bournonville's command at great risk on the 4th, using a thick mist to shield his final moves.

The key to the position was the 'Little Wood' on the Imperialist left, and it was towards this sector that Churchill inevitably gravitated. The objective was taken—lost—and retaken at heavy cost—and in the end the Imperialists withdrew. So exhausted were the French, however, that they, too, had to retire but the strategic danger was for the time averted. 'No-one in the world could possibly have done better than Mr. Churchill . . .' reported Louis Duras, Earl of Feversham (destined in a later year to be a thorn in the side of his subject), '. . . and M. de Turenne is very well pleased with all our nation.'[11] Another participant who earned credit that day was a certain Colonel of French Dragoons, the Duc de Boufflers of whom we shall again hear more in another context. Churchill himself proved somewhat critical of Turenne's handling of the infantry, part of whom saw no action of any significance. Yet there is something to be said for Viscount Wolseley's view that 'Marlborough learnt from a French general how to destroy French armies.'[12] One can learn as much, if not more, from the mistakes and oversights of war as from the glamorous successes. Turenne, for his part, prophesied distinction for the 'handsome Englishman,' who was clearly something of a favourite.

It is still uncertain whether John Churchill took part in the very celebrated Winter campaign of 1674–5 under Turenne's orders—his great descendant believes so emphatically; other scholars are not so sure, and there is no decisive proof either way. At any rate, he was back at Court early in January 1675, for in that month he was appointed Master of the Robes to the Duke of York and promoted (from 16 January N.S.) Lieutenant-Colonel in the Duke of York's Regiment of Foot, formerly the Admiralty Regiment, the bill once more being footed by the helpful Barbara—probably shortly before the liaison came to an end.

The next years (1675–7) are very obscure; some sources believe he was present at Sasbach (June 1675) where Turenne was killed at the age of 64. That August he was certainly sent on a mission to Paris on his master's business; in October he was allowed to import into England his personal effects and silver plate which might seem to imply the end of his campaigning services overseas. All is very uncertain, except that he was a member of an army court-martial held in September 1676.

Then the mists begin to lift a little. Our subject's fortunes were still improving step by step. Late in 1677 he was appointed to the colonelcy of 'a Regiment of Foot' in the English (as opposed to the French) army, and at some unknown date the following Spring he married in secret the love of his life, Sarah Jennings.

This tempestuous love-affair dates in its origins from at least 1676, for Honoré Courtin, French Ambassador, reported on 29 November of that year to his master that 'Mr. Churchill prefers to serve the very pretty sister of Lady Hamilton (née Frances Jennings) than to be lieutenant-colonel in Monmouth's regiment.'[13]: Sarah, a daughter of a sometime MP for St. Albans, had since child-hood been friend and confidant to the Duke of York's daughter by Mary of Modena, the Princess Anne. For a number of years Sarah had been overshadowed at court by her brilliant sister 'la belle Jenyns', who married twice, first to Lord Hamilton, and after his death to 'Lying Dick Talbot', subsequently Duke of Tyrconnel (destined to be killed at the siege of Limerick in 1691). Sarah's ascendancy over Princess Anne increased with the passing of time, and by the mid-1670s she was a favourite sans pareil and a Lady in Waiting.

Miss Jennings was a handsome, fair-haired, highly intelligent but very self-willed young woman, endowed with an almost legendary reputation for virtue (at least, within the context of her very easy-going companions and surroundings) and hot temper. The courtship was stormy and difficult; on the one hand Sarah used to drive her suitor almost to distraction with her changing moods (although Barbara must have taken some explaining away), and it is possible that the migraines that were to plague him at critical moments for the rest of his life took root during this extensive period of emotional strain. Then again, once both parties knew their own minds, both families opposed the match on financial grounds, as neither had the prospect of a substantial fortune. The young people, however, aided by the Duchess of York, eventually had their way, and launched forth into a marriage that was to prove a genuine love-match for all of its 44 year duration.

Sarah was to prove both the blessing and the bane of John Churchill's life. The contented homelife and her useful political connections of the early years were greatly to assist the rise of her husband to the highest responsibilities and dignities in the land. The key to all was the special relationship with Anne. Churchill's talents, great as they were, would not alone have brought him so high as he was to attain. Indeed, it has been suggested that William III's selection of Marlborough for the highest command in 1701, and his use of him to negotiate the Second Grand Alliance, stemmed as much from his awareness of the family's likely position in the next reign as from his appreciation of his intrinsic merits. In the seventeenth and eighteenth centuries, connections and patronage were of the utmost significance and the future Duke was liberally provided with both, thanks in large part to his wife.

Unfortunately there was another side to Sarah. Her volatile and waspish temperament caused truly monumental rows within her own immediate family, and her husband was not immune from them. There can be no doubt that Sarah ruled her husband in all domestic matters (*pace* Miss Iris Butler)*; in 1706, for instance, at the very height of his fame, we find him anxiously consulting her about the purchase of a series of tapestries on 'the Art of War' which he had found, going cheap, in Belgium; 'Wou'd you have mee bye them?' he asked.[14] Clearly, he cared not to make the decision on his own, and indeed left much of the responsibility for building and furnishing Blenheim Palace to her—a rare responsibility for a woman in that unemancipated age.

If Sarah's domineering ways occasionally disturbed the marital calm they were potentially far more disruptive in public life. With increasing rank and station the Duchess's quarrelsomeness, haughtiness and Whig partisanship became almost unbearable, and made her husband many a foe. In the end poor, bullied 'Brandy Nell' could stand her 'Mrs. Freeman' no longer, and turned to an easier and more prosaic relationship with Mrs Masham—an event which marked the fatal waning of the Marlborough influence. As one contemporary described it, Sarah made 'all her life one warfare upon earth,' and Sir John Vanbrugh, the unfortunate architect of Blenheim Palace, would later call her 'that B.B.B. old B., the Dutchess of Marlbh' (*sic*).[15] This, however, is to anticipate developments that still lay many years ahead in 1678. It is more relevant here to record that the couple, after spending a difficult Winter living

* In *The Rule of Three*, London, (1966) Miss Butler described the marriage with considerable insight and sympathy, but is a trifle too generous to Sarah. Mr. David Green's representation is possibly more accurate in this respect. See Bibliography p. 355.

with Sir Winston and his family, set up house near the Cockpit in Whitehall under somewhat impecunious circumstances, and set about raising a considerable family that eventually numbered seven daughters and two sons, of whom six of the former survived childhood.

The strong possibility of war against France in 1678 caused Churchill and his friend Sidney Godolphin (now a coming politician) to be sent to the Hague to negotiate a treaty with the Dutch and Spaniards. This represents his first nationally-important mission, and brought him into touch with 'Dutch William'. It would seem he made a good impression on the Stadtholder. Barillon, the observant French ambassador, reported to Louis some time later (1680) that although 'he is not a man with any experience in public affairs . . . it is also said that the Prince of Orange wishes to have him and wants no other man as English minister.'[16] Perhaps William's wife Mary, sister of Anne, helped smooth the young diplomat's first essay at international statecraft. The mission ultimately proved abortive, however, as Charles II was at the same time in secret negotiations with Louis, and matters were still not resolved one way or the other when Churchill returned to England.

Early in May Churchill was appointed to the temporary rank of Brigadier-General of Foot, and on 13 September he received orders from Monmouth which promised active employment: 'You are forthwith to repair to the army in Flanders, to command there as eldest Brigadier of Foot, and your brigade is to consist of two battalions of Guards, one battalion of the Holland Regiment; and the regiments of Her Royal Highness and Colonel Legge.'[17]

The prospects of war proved illusory, and the warring powers were persuaded to compromise on their difficulties and sign the Peace of Nimwegen. The English battalions returned home early the next year and a number were disbanded. Churchill would have to wait six more years for an active command as Brigadier-General.

Domestic crises now became the focal points of national attention. The details of the Popish Plot and the many attempts to exclude the Duke of York from the succession on account of his Catholic faith do not concern us here. Suffice it to record that Churchill accompanied his master into temporary exile in Brussels in 1679, and thereafter served as a confidential emissary between the two royal brothers—and Louis XIV—on a number of occasions. In due course the Duke of York was permitted to move to Scotland, Churchill again accompanying him as a member of his suite. It was not until 1682, however, that Charles II felt strong enough to allow his brother back into England. After a conference at Newmarket the royal ban was lifted, and James travelled back to Scotland for the last time to collect his wife and household.

This journey proved unexpectedly perilous to both Duke and his servant. On 15 May the frigate *Gloucester* in which the party was travelling was driven aground off the Lincolnshire coast, and began to sink. With typical stubborness,

James refused to order 'abandon ship' until almost too late. In the event the royal party narrowly managed to escape in the long-boat, but by then it was too late to save the crew, 130 of whom were drowned. Churchill kept his counsel to himself, but he was privately highly critical of James' behaviour on this occasion which resulted in the unnecessary tragedy. Perhaps for the first time he began to draw apart from his patron and master; at least Duchess Sarah would have it so.[18]

A less dangerous duty for Colonel Churchill was the task of travelling to Denmark to escort Prince George to his wedding with Princess Anne (July 1683). The Princess promptly appointed her bosom friend, Sarah, to be a Lady of the Bedchamber at a salary of £200 a year. As for John, he had undergone several disappointments in recent years when coveted appointments (including that of Master-General of the Ordnance) had eluded his grasp, but now the good offices of the Duke of York found him raised to the Scottish peerage as Baron Aysmouth (December 1682). Next year he also secured the Colonelcy of the Royal Regiment of Dragoons (19 November 1683, O.S.) and thus became closely associated with the mounted arm, complementing his earlier experiences as an officer of Foot Guards, Marines and infantry of the line. The choicest appointments, however, had still to come his way.

It is suitable to close this introductory chapter on a happy family note which highlights the intensely human side of the man who would soon be swept up in the high affairs of state. The passage from a letter to an absent Sarah reveals the very real bonds of love and affection binding Churchill to his wife and children. 'My Lady Sunderland's maid by her ladyship's order brought a bottle of cordial (? indistinct) for the children to drink, but I think it is too hot for their stomachs, so that I kept it for my own drinking, unless you send me word that they may drink it. You cannot imagine how I am pleased with the children, for they having nobody but their maid, they are so fond of me that when I am at home they will be always with me, and kissing and hugging me. Their heats (spots) are quite gone, so that against you come home they will be in beauty . . . Miss is pulling me by the arm that she may write to her dear Mamma, so that I will so no more, only beg that you will love me always so well as I love you, and then we cannot but be happy.'[19]

Royal Champion and Betrayer, 1685-1688

'SIR—Since men are seldom suspected of sincerity, when they act contrary to their interests, and though my dutiful behaviour to Your Majesty in the worst of times . . . may not be sufficient to incline you to a charitable interpretation of my actions, yet I hope the great advantage I enjoy under Your Majesty, which I own I never can expect in any other change of government, may reasonably convince Your Majesty and the world that I am actuated by a higher principle, when I offer that violence to my inclination and interest as to desert Your Majesty at a time when your affairs seem to challenge the strictest obedience from all your subjects, much more from one who lies under the greatest personal obligations to Your Majesty. This, Sir, could proceed from nothing but the inviolable dictates of my conscience, and a necessary concern for my religion. . . .'
Churchill's letter to James II, 23 November 1688 (O.S.), cited *inter alia* by Thomas Lediard in *The Life of John* (1736).

The New Year of 1685 found John Churchill in high favour with the Duke of York, and his wife Sarah firmly established as reigning favourite of the Princess Anne. This double-insurance appeared to augur well for the family's future, although as yet few of the more lucrative perquisites of royal favour had been bestowed.

In mid-February all court intrigues were suddenly transcended by the rapidly deteriorating health of the King. Charles II's last illness was short, and he breathed his last on the 16th, commending Nell Gwynn's welfare—his sometime mistress —to the assembled notables crowding the royal bedchamber. On the accession of his Catholic brother, James, to the throne, young Churchill was sent off to Versailles to inform Louis XIV of these important developments. It would seem, however, that Churchill was already anxious about the possible religious policies of his master. 'If the King should attempt to change our religion', he is reputed to have remarked to Lord Galway in Paris, 'I will instantly quit his service.'[1] This statement is of some significance in view of events three years later.

Nevertheless, there were few outward signs of tension between master and man in the first year of James's short and catastrophic reign. The King was still delighted to confer favours on his one-time page, and Churchill to receive them. In quick succession he was appointed a Lord of the Bedchamber, and admitted to the English peerage as 'Baron Churchill of Sandridge in the County of Herefordshire'. His appointment as Colonel of the King's Own Regiment of Dragoons was also confirmed.[2] The Churchill star seemed to be rising in court and national circles.

Without a doubt, Churchill served James well in 1685. His important role in the Sedgemoor campaign, to which we now must turn, proved both his loyalty and his martial skill. During it we find him entrusted with an independent command for the first time, although he was destined to be superceded—to his dismay and chagrin—as the climax approached.

The Duke of Monmouth's arrival in the West Country to stir up rebellion was ill-timed and even worse executed. In its timing, it was paradoxically both too late and too early: too late in the sense that the long initial delays in mounting the expedition (due to the inbred indecisiveness of Charles II's natural son by Lucy Walters, the enticements of Lady Henrietta Wentworth, and unfavourable weather, in roughly equal proportions) allowed some warning of what was afoot to reach the Court of St. James; too early in that the venture was mounted prematurely before the King had out-lived the brief burst of popularity with his people which accompanied his accession. Had Monmouth but held his hand one short year the outcome might have been very different.

Planning to rally the staunch Protestantism of the West, and to exploit the current economic recession crippling the Cornish tin industry, Monmouth sent his supporter, Archibald Campbell, Earl of Argyle, to raise the Lowlands of Scotland as a distraction whilst he in person embarked with a few followers in a small convoy of hired vessels and left the Texel in Holland for Lyme Regis to play his main gamble—the prize being his uncle's crown, the stake his own head. Egged on by such sinister and unreliable confidants as Lord Grey of Wark ('Cold Caleb' to Alexander Pope) the weak-willed and hesitant Monmouth now dreamed of a rapturous welcome in the shires, a rapid march to capture Bristol, whose wealth and shipping would enable the rebels to open sea links with their confederates in Scotland and more sympathisers in Cheshire, and thereafter a triumphant triple advance towards London to topple James from his throne. Such was the plan—hopelessly over-optimistic and ill-conceived as events were soon to prove.

On 11 June (O.S.) Monmouth landed at Lyme, fully three weeks after Argyle's arrival in Scotland, following a stormy voyage. With him he brought four cannon and a few hundred stand of arms. His arrival was indeed welcomed by the local peasantry, but the local gentry significantly refused their support. News of the invasion reached London two days later by the hand of the hard-riding Mayor of Weymouth—being conveyed to the King by Sir Winston Churchill, MP for Lyme Regis, and his warrior son. On this occasion James did not hesitate a single hour. The militias of the West were ordered to mobilise, a compliant Parliament declared Monmouth an outlaw, and all available regular troops were ordered to Salisbury. Urgent orders of recall were sent to the six English regiments serving William of Orange on contract in the United Provinces, four companies of Irish Guards were ordered from Ireland, and within a day John Churchill—appointed Brigadier-General for the second time in his career—was covering the roads towards the West at the head of six troops of horse and dragoons, followed hot-foot by five companies of Colonel Kirke's Regiment newly returned from Tangier.

Lord Churchill's column made rapid progress; he had not been Turenne's pupil for nothing, and he was clearly determined to make the most of this opportunity to establish his standing as an independent commander. Marching by way of Salisbury, Blandford and Dorchester, the 17 June (O.S.) found him at Bridport, where he added to his meagre force the Dorset Militia—currently very shaken by the rough handling it had received from part of the rebel array three days before. The next day he moved forward to Axminster—as Monmouth marched into distant Taunton at the head of possibly 3,000 armed peasantry.

Churchill was now hard on the heels of the rebels, but it behoved him to move with caution. Monmouth's army was increasing every day—shortly after proclaiming himself the rightful King at Taunton on the 18th it had swollen to 7,000 men. The Royal force at this stage comprised only 300 regular troopers and an indeterminate number of local militia, whose military value was far from certain. A number of desertions to join Monmouth had taken place, and Churchill was rightly cautious about the Somersetshire Militia which was soon due to join him. Referring to their flight from Axminster on the 17th at the mere rumour of Monmouth's approach, Churchill reported that 'there is not any relying on these regiments that are left unless we had (sic) some of your Majesty's standing forces to lead them on and encourage them.'[3] He warned James that the safety of the whole West Country was in danger unless larger numbers of troops were made immediately available.

Under the circumstances the commander was right to restrict his activities to shadowing Monmouth's slow and clumsy movements and harrassing isolated parties of rebels, 'which I think is the only way for me to join you or to do the King's service'[4] as he wrote to the Duke of Somerset from Chard on 19 June (O.S.). The next day saw a sharp skirmish at Ashill which firmly established Monmouth's presence at Taunton. Churchill meanwhile was busying himself like the good soldier he was in improving the administrative arrangements for his troops. 'Paid for four carts to go to Chard and attend on the Lord Churchill, and guides, and other expenses—£1–11–0' runs one local entry in the Axminster records.[5] We shall have occasion on a later page to note the personal interest he took in such matters on a far grander scale.*

Whilst Churchill carefully observed the rebels, other matters of military moment were taking place as James mobilised and deployed his remaining standing forces. A train of artillery was ordered from the Tower of London consisting of 16 brass cannon and many waggons of stores, and began to make its ponderous way down the Great West Road towards Marlborough town escorted by five more companies of Kirke's Regiment. On 16 June (O.S.) a bye-train was ordered to set out from Portsmouth—eight guns strong—to be accompanied by waggons bearing spare weapons and tentage for the use of the army as a whole, commanded by Churchill's brother Charles. The Board of Ordnance had fulfilled both these requirements by the 19th, whilst 150 Horse Guards, 60 Horse Grenadiers, and three battalions of Foot Guards (commanded by the Duke of Grafton—another of Charles II's 'indiscretions') stood ready to leave the capital. Finally, James decided to entrust the entire army to Louis Duras, the Huguenot Earl of Feversham. He was promoted Lieutenant-General and appointed 'General-in-Chief' on 19 June.

Churchill's various biographers have loudly criticised the unfairness of this appointment, but on the whole it may be considered to have constituted a reasonable royal decision. It is true that Feversham was a glutton and no great soldier, but he was a nephew of the great Turenne, and his loyalty to James survived even the testing days of 1688 despite the religious issue. Moreover, there were good reasons why James might hesitate to retain John Churchill in overall command. His strong family ties with the West country could have laid him open to local pressures. Further, he had served under the command of Monmouth in earlier days, and this too, might constitute a complication in certain circumstances. Indeed, it is known that Monmouth made at least one insidious approach to his former comrade. It is also possible, of course, in that age of continuous intrigue and gossip, that Churchill's remarks in Paris earlier the same year had reached the royal ear. Lastly, Churchill—for all his undoubted popularity in the army—was still untried as an independent commander-in-chief, so Feversham was hardly more of an unknown quantity than his second-in-command, and as we shall see, the latter's showing in this campaign was not quite so poor as has sometimes been represented by his many detractors.

Naturally enough, John Churchill was bitterly disappointed when news of his supercession reached him on or about the 22nd. 'I see plainly that I am to have the trouble and that the honour will be another's', he complained.[6] To his credit, however, he was to co-operate with the Earl most conscientiously if

* See below p. 130.

a little critically, and doubtless his promotion to Major-General (3 July O.S.) eventually helped to soften the blow. A hint of strain remained, as is shown in a letter written from Somerton on the eve of Sedgemoor: 'Of this and all other things you will here (*sic*) more at large from my Lord Feversham, who has the sole command here, soe that I know nothing but what is his pleasure to tell me, soe that I am afraid of giving my opinion freely.'[7]

For all his supposed reputation for being 'slow and infirm of purpose', Feversham's initial energy and determination were commendable. Leaving London on the 20th, he forced-marched his men westwards, reaching Bristol at the head of his cavalry just three and a half days later after covering 115 miles of road. He thus forestalled Monmouth at the major strategic objective, and made Bristol safe by ordering the immediate destruction of the bridge over the Avon at Keynsham, whither came the rebels on the 24th after a leisurely and confused march from Taunton by way of Bridgwater, Shepton Mallet and Pensford. Churchill, meantime, after being reinforced by Kirke's infantry and some more cavalry (21st), had dogged Monmouth's heels, moving along a shorter route through Langport, Somerton, Wells and Pensford, where he paused on the 26th to hang one 'James the Feltmaker' (a rare example of Churchill instituting summary justice against civilians—perhaps we may deduce that the poor man was unfortunate to encounter him in an ill-mood on account of his imminent rendezvous with his new General-in-Chief) before riding on to Bath that same evening. There the royal generals now concentrated some 2,500 regular troops. The guns, of course, were still some days distant near the Kennet.

The rebels, perhaps 8,000 foot armed with a wide variety of weapons and 1,000 horse mounted on a motley collection of steeds, had turned away from Keynsham in great disappointment, realising that Bristol and all it entailed now lay beyond their grasp. On the 26th, parts of the two armies ran into each other near Norton St. Philip. The rebels emerged from a confused action with the honours of the day—the Duke of Grafton having obligingly blundered into an ambush in a narrow-lane enclosed by high hedges, thereby incurring some 50 casualties. Somewhat chastened by this experience, the royal forces fell back to Bradford-on-Avon to reconsider their next move, whilst Monmouth marched on towards Frome and Shepton Mallet.

The minor success at Norton St. Philip could not disguise from either Monmouth or his men that they had lost the initiative, and were in retreat. Soon news of setback after setback began to arrive with depressing regularity. The 28th brought grave tidings from far-off Scotland: Argyle's revolt had failed and its leader already lay beheaded. Next, a vital convoy of munitions was lost to royal cavalry at Frome. Monmouth's disheartened army began to melt away— first by tens, then by hundreds, and it was at the head of only 4,000 dispirited men that the Pretender limped back into Bridgwater on 3 July. The citizenry were now notably cool in their welcome, and the footsore peasants were required to camp out in the Castle Field beyond the town. The current spate of wet weather had done nothing to improve their morale.

The rain falls on the just and the unjust with impartiality, and the royal army found its movements equally hindered by the inclement weather. Feversham had at last joined up with his cannon at Westbury on the 29th, but the arrival of the tentage was delayed. 'We have had abundance of rain which has very much tried our soldiers', wrote John to Sarah a little earlier, 'which I think is ill because it makes us not press the Duke of Monmouth so much as I think he should be. . . .'[8] The militia was also becoming restive, and had to be offered regular rates of pay to dissuade it from disbanding. Acts of indiscipline by the soldiery against the local population were on the increase, but Feversham pressed on through Frome, Shepton Mallet, Glastonbury and Somerton, and finally fetched up at the little village of Weston Zoyland—only four miles from Bridgwater—on 5 July (O.S.). The royal army—which was now perhaps 3,000 men and 16 guns strong (the less reliable militia were quartered out of harm's way at Middlezoy and Othery)— gratefully pitched its recently-received tents in the area of ground behind the Bussex Rhine (a dry drainage-ditch) on the edge of Sedgemoor, and began to console itself for its recent exertions with the aid of the local cider and (no doubt) the local damsels.

The story of what followed is well known, and need not be recounted at length here. Certain misconceptions and misrepresentations, however, need to be corrected, and the role of John Churchill in the battle of Sedgemoor described. Monmouth, emboldened by despair to seize a fleeting opportunity to win or lose all in one last gamble, was led to believe by a local sympathiser from Chedzoy that the royal army had neglected to take the least precautions to secure its camp and was roaring drunk into the bargain. Consequently, Monmouth, after a brief look at the scene from the turret of St. Mary's church-tower (which cannot have told him much as a modern visit to that vantage point will prove) decided to lead his army over the Moor at dead of night in an attempt to surprise the royal troops in their tents, snatch an easy victory, and then march triumphantly back towards Bristol. Such was the plan—a bold one by any standards but not wholly unreasonable given the degree of local knowledge available to him and the desperation of the general situation, had he but checked his intelligence reports.

However, Feversham and Churchill (the General-Officer-of-the-Day), were not in fact guilty of such breaches of field security as Monmouth had been led to believe—and had failed to ascertain personally. Indeed a comprehensive set of precautions had been put into effect. The artillery was parked on the left of the camp to command the road to Bridgwater which constituted the most probable line of attack. A detachment had been told off to hold Burrow Bridge over the Parrett to secure the left and rear. Colonel Oglethorpe and the Blues were similarly sent off at dusk to patrol the further side of the Black Ditch (today approximately the King's Sedgemoor Drain) and the approaches to the Polden Hills

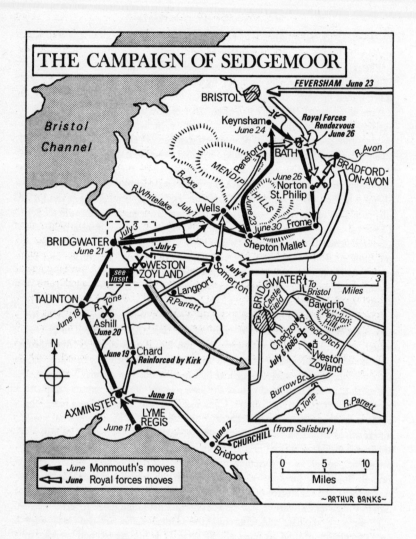

THE CAMPAIGN OF SEDGEMOOR

Bristol Channel

FEVERSHAM June 23

BRISTOL

Keynsham
June 24

*Royal Forces
Rendezvous
June 26*

Pensford

BATH

R.Avon

R.Axe

MENDIP
HILLS

June 26
Norton
St. Philip

BRADFORD-
ON-AVON

R.Whitelake

July 1 Wells

June 23

June 30 Frome

Shepton Mallet

BRIDGWATER
June 21

July 3

July 5

WESTON
ZOYLAND

Somerton

July 4

*see
inset*

Langport

R.Parrett

TAUNTON

June 18

R. Tone

Ashill
June 20

June 19 Chard
Reinforced by Kirk

June 18

AXMINSTER

LYME
REGIS

June 11

June 17

CHURCHILL

(from Salisbury)

Bridport

Inset map

BRIDGWATER

To
Bristol

0   3
Miles

Castle
Field

Bawdrip

Pendon
Hill

Chedzoy

Black Ditch

July 6 1685

WESTON
ZOYLAND

Burrow Br.

R.Tone

R.Parrett

N

0   5   10
Miles

◄━━ *June* Monmouth's moves
◄═══ *June* Royal forces moves

~ARTHUR BANKS~

so as to safeguard the right flank against surprise and also to give early warning of any attempt by the rebels to slip away under cover of darkness. In front of the royal position, Captain Compton and a party of horse were placed in Chedzoy village to watch the Moor, and the usual series of sentry posts and main guards were established along the Bussex Rhine and in the camp. The horses of the remaining cavalrymen were left ready-saddled in their lines in the village for the night.

That Monmouth's projected night attack was not detected at the start was due to a dense seasonal mist rising from the Moor. This served to disguise his five-mile approach march for about half its length—and at one moment the rebels stood breathlessly silent in their ranks whilst Oglethorpe's cavalry jingled past only a few yards and a single drain away. However, this same mist also proved Monmouth's downfall. At a critical moment the local guide lost his way to a crossing over another dyke—the Langmoor Rhine—and a royal trooper near Chedzoy heard the confusion as the rebel column crowded up. He discharged his pistol, and rode off at full speed to alert Captain Compton and then the camp. Reaching the Bussex Rhine, this intelligent trooper rode up and down crying out 'with all imaginable earnestness, twenty times at least, "Beat your Drums, the Enemy is come; for ye Lord's sake beat your Drums!" ' as the Rector of Chedzoy recorded the next day in a unique description of the battle. 'Now the drums beat', he graphically continues, 'the drummers running to it even barefoot for haste. All fly to arms. All are drawn out of their tents, and in five battalions stand in the open space between the tents and the Dike (*sic*), fronting (i.e. facing) the Dike, not having their clothes or arms all on and ready. Thus were they expecting the enemy.'[9]

From this moment, Monmouth was doomed to failure. Lord Grey of Warke and the horse spurred off ahead of the seven regiments of rebel foot in an attempt to seize the Upper Plungeon (or crossing-place) over the Bussex Rhine, only to be forestalled by Compton and his retiring patrol. The 800 rebel horsemen then rode down the line of the dyke receiving the fire of the royal infantry, now stood-to on the further bank. A few volleys, and the untrained horses were bolting back over the Moor in headlong flight, crashing through the anxious ranks of their dismounted confederates as they tramped stolidly towards the firing, and panicked the rebel ammunition carts in the rear near Peasey Farm. This notwithstanding, Monmouth succeeded in bringing his infantry and their three guns up to the Bussex Rhine, where they took up a position facing the extreme right of the royal line. Soon a brisk firefight was in progress, punctuated by the periodic flash and thunder of the rebel cannon, the rebels causing heavy losses to Dumbarton's Regiment (later the Royal Scots) on the exposed end of the line. The exact position of this unfortunate formation was clearly delineated in the darkness by the glowing matches of the musketeers.

Long before this juncture (about 3 a.m.) Major-General Churchill had assumed effective control of the royal army, as was proper for the General Officer-of-the-Day. There was still no sign of Feversham—a point that has been seized upon by many writers to prove his incapacity or even downright cowardice—and it would appear that he was indeed still abed in Weston Zoyland. This does not prove anything, however; it is known that the Earl had been a heavy sleeper ever since sustaining a serious injury to his head some years earlier, and in any case he had good reason to have faith in his defensive arrangements and in the abilities of his second-in-command. Nevertheless, a rather prompter arrival on the field of battle might have been expected: in the event, Feversham seems to have appeared there shortly after four o'clock.

Some time before the General's arrival, Churchill had taken the necessary steps to gain control over the situation. With the aid of Bishop Mew of Winchester, a visitor to the camp who gallantly lent his coach-horses and servants to help Churchill drag several cannon from the left of the line (it seems that most of the artillerymen and their civilian team-drivers had fled at the first alarm), the three rebel guns were soon silenced by superior fire. Some time later a Sergeant Weems of Dumbarton's Foot was awarded a royal grant of £40 for his skill in helping handle the guns. Next, Churchill ordered the two left-hand battalions of the royal line (presently unengaged) to march behind their colleagues and take post to the right of Dumbarton's decimated companies. This brought the royal infantry exactly face to face with their opponents and soon the better-disciplined and directed fire of the regulars—most of whom were armed with flintlocks—was wreaking havoc with the rebels, whose ammunition at this point began to give out.

Such was the situation that Feversham found awaiting him when he at last took over command. Any doubts about his capacity as a soldier are finally disproved by the orders he proceeded to issue. After making a reconnaissance of the further bank through the Lower Plungeon, he wisely ordered his infantry to maintain a desultory fire but on no account to attempt to scramble over the Rhine until first light. Oglethorpe's mystified cavalry rode up at this juncture along the Bridgwater road to report that they had found the town completely devoid of any signs of the enemy. This enabled Feversham to fashion a two-pronged cavalry attack, ready to charge the enemy flanks when he gave the word; another sensible concept. Then, as first light began to tinge the Eastern horizon, Feversham slipped the leash, and the triple attack began. Churchill in person leading one of the cavalry wings. Soon all was over. Monmouth deserted his army, and most of his men turned and fled; the 'Red' regiment, led by Colonel Wade refused to budge from a neighbouring meadow full of corn where many gallantly died trying to cover the flight of the remainder. 'Here ye flight and pursuit, 42 killed' laconically noted the Rector of Chedzoy on his map.

By full daylight the royal army was in full cry after their discomfited opponents, butchering and hanging as many as they could catch, 'Kirke's Lambs' earning a particularly cruel reputation, seconded only by that of the Militia, which had taken no part in the battle itself—the last ever to be fought on English soil. Losses are hard to calculate with any certainty, but the following approximations may not be very far from the mark: the royal army suffered perhaps 300 casualties (the brunt of them borne by Dumbarton's); the rebels lost some 1,000 killed in hot blood (including 'slain in ye Moor and buried in one pit, 195') besides many more hunted down and strung-up over the succeeding weeks. About 500 prisoners were taken that morning, over 350 of them, including many wounded, being crowded into Weston Zoyland Church to await summary justice or even the worse judicial murder at the hands of the infamous Judge Jeffreys during his notorious 'Bloody Assize'. Monmouth himself was captured in a ditch, taken to London and executed on Tower Hill on the 15 July, the incompetent headsman needing all of five strokes to sever the handsome head from its unfortunate body.

Churchill commanded the troops that rode forward to occupy Bridgwater later on the 6th, but it seems that he had nothing to do with the wreaking of the royal vengeance on the hapless West Country, for he soon returned to London bearing Feversham's jubilant despatch to the King. As he had anticipated, the lion's share of the rewards were lavished on Feversham, who received the Garter and other marks of royal favour. But Churchill was not forgotten; in August he was awarded the lucrative colonelcy of the Third Troop of Life Guards in succession to Feversham and the London Gazette of 18 July (O.S.) duly described how he had 'performed his part with all the courage and gallantry imaginable.'[10]

This was a just summary of Churchill's role throughout the Sedgemoor campaign. His skill in shadowing Monmouth, his ability at dealing with administrative problems, his tactical skill in battle and 'three o'clock in the morning courage', his promising showing in his first essay at independent command and his preparedness (however grudging) to give up the first place and serve as loyal and competent subordinate to a man he disliked—all these attributes of John Churchill as man and soldier are worthy of notice. But this is not to imply that Feversham was a ninny, wet-nursed by his brilliant subordinate. If at times he moved more cautiously than many thought necessary he nevertheless achieved both major objectives of the campaign—namely the securing of Bristol and the destruction of the rebel army. And, as General Hindenburg reputedly remarked to a lady enquiring whether it was he or von Francis who really won the battle of Tannenburg in 1914—'Madam, I do not exactly know who won the battle, but I am quite certain who would have lost it'—the ultimate responsibility for victory or defeat rested, from 19 June, with the Earl and not the Baron. Feversham was fortunate to be blessed with such a capable and conscientious subordinate, but the ultimate outcome of the Sedgemoor Campaign was essentially a team effort for which both men deserve a share of the credit. For Churchill the episode marks the first emergence of the commander. For James, it offered encouragement for him to proceed with his politico-religious ambitions.

*   *   *

It is quite possible that this campaign and its aftermath were instrumental in setting in train the processes of disillusion which resulted, three short years later, in Churchill abandoning his long-time patron and friend in favour of William of Orange. On the one hand, his supercession in the highest post must have rankled long after the affair was over; on the other, it is certain that Churchill strongly disapproved of the witch-hunt and persecution that followed the collapse of Monmouth's rebellion. His sense of justice was outraged as he heard of Judge Jeffreys' badgering of witnesses as he handed out wholesale sentences of death or transportation to the West Indies during the circuits in the West. His sense of propriety was sickened by the heartless way in which batches of convicts sentenced to transportation, were given to courtiers by the King to sell as virtual slaves for the best price they could fetch—included in their number being the 40-odd school-girls of Taunton—awarded as prizes of war to the Maids of Honour—whose only crime had been to make colours (reputedly from their petticoats) for Monmouth's regiments.* The execution of the aged Dame Alice Lisle for harbouring fugitives was another *cause célèbre* of the time. Churchill would not be a party to judicial murder, and he accused James of having a heart of marble; and when Henry Booth, Lord Delamere, was hauled before the House of Lords on trial for treason (January 1686), it was Churchill who, as junior member of the court of peers presided over by Jeffreys, had to give the first verdict. He firmly called out 'Not Guilty', thus setting off a chain reaction which resulted in an acquittal—to James's undisguised fury.[11]

The political history of the remainder of James's short reign can only be summarised here. Suffice it to say that Churchill took an ever graver view as James packed an enlarged army with Roman Catholic officers, dismissed Parliament in a pique, announced the repeal of the Test Acts, purged the Universities, attempted to browbeat and control the Anglican clergy, and gave clear evidence of his intention of re-establishing Popery in the land, with the help, if need be, of Louis XIV, upon whose generous subsidies the King was determined to rely for as long as necessary. Churchill's personal career seemed at a standstill although he remained in favour at court. To his credit, he never dissimulated over the religious issue, and this may well account for his lack of further advancement.

The Churchills drew still closer to Princess Anne during these unsettled times, and step by step became involved in intrigue with William of Orange

* In the end, the erring girls were sold back to their fathers for a lump sum of about £3,000.

whose wife, Mary, was another of James's daughters. William's emissary, Everard van Weede, Heer van Dykevelt was soon in touch, and by May 1687 Churchill was bold enough to write a frankly treasonable letter to the Prince of Orange. 'I thought it my duty to your Highness and the Princess Royal ... to give you assurances in my own hand that my places and the King's favour I set at naught in comparison of the being true to my religion. In all things but this the King may command me. . . .'[12] His strongly rooted Protestant beliefs were fast turning James's erstwhile favourite into a traitor.

The complex manœuvrings of 1688 cannot concern us here as James piled blunder upon blunder, and then, too late, saw his danger and began quite unconvincingly to redress some public grievances. The birth of a Prince of Wales in June 1688 and the acquittal of the Seven Bishops the following month forced the plotters to expedite their schemes for opposite—yet related—reasons: the first threatened a lasting Catholic occupancy of the throne, the second (or rather the popular enthusiasm it evoked) proved the mood of London and the people. So the secret invitation to William III was dispatched. Churchill was not a signatory, but within a few weeks he had clarified his position: 'Mr. Sidney will lett you know how I intend to behave myself. I think it is what I owe to God and my Country; my honour I take leave to put in your Royalle Hignesses (*sic*) hands in which I think it safe; if you think there is any thing else that I ought to doe, you have but to command me. . . .'[13]: The revelation of the breach with James could not now long be delayed.

By mid-October James had fully mobilised his forces. 'For as much as We have received undoubtable advice that a great and sudden invasion, with an armed force of foreigners, will speedily be made in a hostile manner upon this our kingdom,' ran the preamble to a royal order dated 15 October (O.S.) directing Lord Dartmouth, Master-General of the Ordnance to form a 'marching train' of 254 and men equipped with 20 cannon and all other necessaries.[14] The King could not decide where the blow might fall, but tended to favour the East Coast, and garrisoned Hull, Colchester and Ipswich accordingly. Dutch William, however, after waiting for 'the Protestant Wind', chose Torbay in the West, and made a safe landing there on Guy Fawkes' Day (O.S.)—an ambiguous omen. With him he brought a substantial force of experienced troops—3,600 cavalry and 10,600 foot (mostly Dutch but including six battalions of English troops under General Mackay), besides 20,000 spare muskets for his sympathisers. All this while the Royal Navy remained inactive—influenced amongst others by Captain George Churchill, yet another member of the clan.

James now ordered a concentration of force around Salisbury; leaving out the 7,000 men he left in unruly and unreliable London, the distant Scottish and Irish contingents, it would seem that Lord Feversham collected at least 20,490 men and perhaps 26 guns there, and another 5,000 men near Warminster. Such a force, properly handled, should have proved sufficient for its purpose, but in the event it lacked firm leadership at the highest level—that of the King himself. Churchill was still at the King's side, and indeed was promoted a Lieutenant-General, but his loyalty must by now have been suspect for he had recently been seen 'to loll out his tongue and laugh at the whole proceedings' at a royal review held in Hyde Park.[15] But James seems to have deliberately shut his eyes to these omens.

The King moved to Windsor *en route* for Salisbury, but he soon learnt of the desertion to the enemy of Lord Cornbury and two other cavalry colonels with part of their men. James reached Salisbury on 19 November, and took such steps as lay in his power to stop the rot. Feversham begged his master to order Churchill's arrest—he had been observed to gloat over the news of the first desertions, and he had openly advised certain colonels to follow Cornbury's example—but James continued to prevaricate. Then it was too late. After vainly advising his master at a council of war held on the morning of 23 November to attack William forthwith, Churchill slipped away from the royal camp that same night and rode off with 400 others to join the Prince of Orange at Axminster. At last the mask was fully off, and Churchill had the grace and propriety (and also the prudence) to send a letter explaining his action to his former master. 'I am actuated by a higher principle when I offer that violence to my inclination and interest as to desert Your Majesty at a time when your affairs seem to challenge the strictest obedience from all your subjects, much more (from) one who lies under the greatest obligation to Your Majesty. This, Sir, could proceed from nothing but the inviolable dictates of my conscience, and a necessary concern for my religion.'[16] It had clearly been no easy decision, but Churchill seems to have squared off his conscience about his reiterated promises of continued loyalty to James by casuistically asserting that he still intended no disrespect for or physical violence against his person.

Following this important defection, the rot really set in for James. The trickle of army officers and other dignitaries joining William became a flood. Hard on Churchill's heels went Prince George of Denmark, Anne's rather ineffectual husband, but James passed off this event with the observation that the 'loss of a stout trooper would have been greater.' A more telling blow was the whisking away of Anne herself from London—an operation conducted with great efficiency by the strong-willed Sarah aided by the Bishop of London late at night on 26 November. Soon revolts were being reported from every corner of the realm as Williamites revealed their true colours. William's advance towards London was both leisurely and triumphant, and after a few weeks of hesitation James finally made up his mind and left Rochester for exile in France. The news reached William on the 23 December (O.S.), and the next day he entered London, sending Churchill off to restore order amongst a horde of royal soldiers who had been disbanded by Feversham without pay. The first, critical, stage of the Glorious Revolution had been accomplished—for hardly any loss of life.

John Churchill's apologists—including his great descendant, as well as Field Marshal Lord Wolseley and (more recently), Dr. A. L. Rowse—have asserted that this desirable and almost bloodless outcome was largely due to the skilfully-timed defection by James's Lieutenant-General, claiming that he snatched the fuse, as it were, from a highly explosive situation. They have also been at pains to attribute patriotic, religious and even moral motives to his action, arguing that he had a special loyalty to Princess Anne and an even higher duty to the people as a whole. No doubt there is some truth in these assertions, although the subject of these relentless, scholarly *apologia* never saw fit to reveal his motives beyond the religious issue we have already noted. In the final analysis, however, it must be plainly asserted that Churchill was also motivated by ambition and self-interest. He was determined to be on the winning side—and indeed, helped guarantee success to William by effectively taking over much of the royal army with him. In this he was a typical seventeenth-century politician with an eye to the main chance, and it is probably wrong to give his more altruistic motives undue significance; he had learnt the need to 'trim' in order to survive, first as a child during the Commonwealth upheavals, and later throughout his long association with the intrigue-dominated court-life of the later Stuarts. But beyond this there is also the unpleasant element of personal betrayal involved in his desertion of James in his hour of supreme need. That ill-advised and stubborn monarch probably deserved his eclipse, being, in the unkind if realistic words of one French contemporary, 'a silly, weak man who has given up three kingdoms for a Mass', but if Marlborough is to be commended for his stalwart stand on the religious issue, his former master was similarly loyal to his own convictions, whatever the constitutional issues at stake, and what is hailed as virtue in the one man can hardly with justice be damned as bigotry in the other. Both were stubborn men, but it was Churchill who in the event ratted on his former friend and benefactor, and in view of his later behaviour towards him and William III which we shall have occasion to notice in the next chapter, it is difficult if not impossible to absolve Churchill of ruthlessness, ingratitude, intrigue and treachery against a man to whom he owed virtually everything in his life and career to date.

Nevertheless, 'the moving finger writes, and having writ moves on' and subsequent events would seem to show that Churchill's actions, however questionable and even indefensible in the immediate context of 1688, were nevertheless to the ultimate advantage of the country that he was destined to serve so long and well. Yet a bitter taste lingers; the slur must always remain.

3

William's General, 1689-1691

'Kirke hath fire, Lanier thought, Mackay skill and Colchester bravery; but there is something inexpressible about the Earl of Marlborough. All their virtues seem to be united in his single person. I have lost my wonted skill in physiognomy, if any subject of your Majesty can ever attain such a height of military glory as that to which this combination of sublime perfections must raise him.'

The Prince de Vaudemont, in a letter to William III, 1691.
Lives of the Two Illustrious Generals, London 1713, p. 30.

The early months of the new regime were dominated by complex constitutional and political questions as the Prince of Orange and his consort felt their way through the labyrinthine complexities of English politics towards the establishment of a dual monarchy. At first William hoped to secure a unique title to the throne, but the Earl of Danby and a substantial part of the Convention Parliament championed the blood-claim of Mary. There was also friction between the House of Lords and the Commons as to whether James II had merely deserted his throne or could be regarded as having fully and irrevocably abdicated. A further faction only favoured the establishment of a regency, and in the final analysis William was fortunate to be offered the compromise of a shared throne. So it was that William III and Mary II were jointly proclaimed. John Churchill trod a careful *via media* in these prickly debates, but played no unimportant background role by influencing Princess Anne (James II's younger daughter) through Sarah, to surrender her immediate rights of succession to William in the event of her sister Mary predeceasing her husband.

At first it seemed that William and Churchill would cooperate well enough. The King gave his new servant the most important role in reorganising the lamentably backward English army—'My Lord Churchill proposes all' as old Marshal Schomberg somewhat laconically remarked[1]—and further confirmed his rank of Lieutenant-General. In the coronation honours (April 1689) he was created Earl of Marlborough, resuscitating a title that had once been linked to his mother's family. His financial fortunes were also improving. Since 1685 he had been Governor of the Hudson Bay Company, and his energetic interest had reaped substantial benefits. His military posts were also lucrative, but despite this relative prosperity he was still the poorest Earl in the country and he would soon come to resent being passed over for such rich plums as the Master-Generalship of the Ordnance.

Barely six months divided master and man in age, Churchill being slightly the elder. In physical appearance they were very different. Dutch William was short in stature, ugly of countenance through the ravages of smallpox, hunch-backed and asthmatic, plagued with a persistent hacking cough; years of responsibility and grave problems had prematurely aged the King. Marlborough—as we may now call him—was a very Adonis by comparison. The best first-hand description dates from 1707. Churchill, Sicco van Goslinga wrote, was 'about the middle height, and the best figure in the world: his features without fault, fine, sparkling eyes, good teeth, and his complexion such a mixture of white and red as the fairer sex might envy: in brief, except for his legs, which are too thin, one of the handsomest men ever seen.'[2]

In terms of character, the two men had more in common although there were also important differences. Both were intensely ambitious. 'William cared for nothing but politics and power, writes Dr. A. L. Rowse, the 'convolutions and combinations of states, the army and action.'[3] Such a description might almost have fitted Marlborough in his prime. Both were intensely devoted to the Protestant religion, and William's lifelong crusade against the ambitions of France would in due course be passed on to his military successor in large measure. Except where his Dutch favourites were concerned, William was an extremely frugal man; Marlborough's carefulness with money—and the lives of his troops—would become legendary. Both had experienced difficult up-bringings under very different circumstances, but whereas this had reinforced William's innate shyness, making him highly introspective, and at times both vindictive and sly, Marlborough had become urbane, charming to a fault and extraordinarily persuasive, although he was also as crafty and dissimulating as any man when it was necessary to his purposes. Both were also men of intellect capable of vision who could see beyond immediate interests and concerns, and most of their actions were based upon sound common sense. William's military gifts lay in the realms of policy and strategy rather than grand tactics, and in the fullness of time Marlborough would far outshine him in every branch of generalship—but then he would prove superior to every soldier of his day and merit inclusion amongst the greatest military men of all time. John Churchill was a model husband and father, utterly devoted to his wife and children his whole life. William, also, was greatly—if less demonstrably—attached to his Queen, as his terrible grief after her death in 1694 would bear witness. Allegations of homosexual relationships with certain of his favourites—in particular Arnold Joost van Keppel, first Earl of

Albemarle—can be dismissed as propaganda fabrications by his enemies, although inevitably some of the mud stuck to his reputation, however unjustly. Charges of corruption would similarly sully Marlborough's name and bring about his fall.

On the other hand, Marlborough was in some ways far more open-minded than William. For example he never shared the King's distrust of mankind in general, nor his disinterest in (almost distaste for) the fairer sex—Mary and a single mistress excepted. Churchill might envy and dislike the Dutch favourites for very human reasons, but he never formed a permanent aversion to any individual, country or people as his later showing as the head of a highly discordant multinational coalition would amply prove. For his part, William never liked or courted popularity with the English. It can be said that he regarded his royal duties as the not inconsiderable price he had to pay for the advantages of detaching the British Isles from the French alliance and of redeploying his adopted kingdom's resources of men, ships and money in support of his feud with Louis xiv. He saw everything from the European or Dutch points of view. The King quite rightly had grave reservations about the military value of the generals and army he had inherited from James ii, however hurtful this attitude was to prove to such men as Marlborough, but by 1696 he had wrought such a transformation that he could justly describe his English infantry as the best troops he had ever commanded. He would also eventually come to realise the full potential of Marlborough as a commander and diplomat of the greatest promise.

Yet for a number of years William was to prove extremely wary of the Marlborough family. In politics, William well knew, there is scant place for gratitude. If Marlborough had deserted one master in 1688, who could say that he would not turn his coat a second time? His clandestine links with James ii's court in exile were soon well-known to William. Although the tenuous link was condoned, if not tacitly encouraged for his own ends by the reigning monarch—Lord Ailesbury, in his Memoirs (Vol. i, p. 391) declares that William used such pseudo-Jacobites, as Marlborough, to trade useless or false information in return for full and reliable news of what was afoot at the Court of St. Germain, Lord Middleton being particularly forthcoming—it could never be wholly ignored as a possible source of future danger. In the second place there was the question of the Marlborough influence over Princess Anne. The childless Queen Mary envied her sister's ever-increasing (though short-lived) family, whilst Anne's reversionary rights to the throne inevitably made her the focal point of some intrigue despite the fact that her sister's health was for many years far superior. William and Mary, however, soon came to resent and distrust John's and Sarah's positions as trusted advisers to the princess. A further source of potential friction was Marlborough's great popularity within the English army. By continental standards (*pace* Sir Winston Churchill) the Earl could at best be regarded as a promising amateur at this time, and consequently it is understandable why

William was hesitant to appoint him to the more important commands whatever the political advantages of such a move. William's Dutch generals are often criticised—and with justice—but it is not always appreciated that the hated Solms, aged Waldeck, the Prince of Nassau and General Overkirk received their various high commands on the double basis of their experience in continental warfare and of their relationship (by birth or marriage) to the House of Orange. The same was true of Henry Butler, first Duke of Ormonde, Marlborough's chief native rival for preferment. It was also natural for William to regard with favour those officers who had served under him in Flanders prior to 1688—for instance Mackay and Tollemache. In William's view Marlborough was still a soldier of unproved quality and a subject of uncertain loyalty. Small wonder, therefore, that he waited for proof of both attributes before committing himself. Unfortunately Marlborough's growing sense of frustration and of being slighted would lead to a further deterioration in his personal relations with his new sovereign before many years were out.

In May 1689 England declared war on France and joined the major struggle which had been escalating since the previous November. To trace its causes would require a survey of half a century's history for which there is hardly space here.[4] After virtually ten years of peace, France was still casting hungry eyes on various choice territories along her eastern frontiers. Her armies and fleets —although rapidly passing their prime—were being refurbished by Louvois. The Revocation of the Edict of Nantes (1685) had driven much French-influenced talent into exile and provided France's Protestant foes—particularly William of Orange—with a religious motive for renewed suspicion, leading in part to the formation of the League of Augsburg in 1686. By 1688, England, the United Provinces and France were engaged in a tariff war with colonial undertones, as competition in New France, the West Indies and distant India grew more open. The ancient rivalry between the House of Bourbon and the House of Habsburg (Austrian and Spanish branches) had only been temporarily alleviated by the Truce of Ratisbon (1684), although this was supposed to last for 20 years.

The general European situation was decidedly war-prone, and three interconnected chains of events hastened the actual outbreak of hostilities. First there was the contested election of a successor to the Bishopric of Cologne, a prize which would include the strategic fortresses of Bonn, Rheinberg, Kaiserwerth, and the Bishopric of Liége to the successful claimant. The Austrian Emperor and the Pope favoured the claim of Joseph Clement of Bavaria (brother of Elector Max Emmanuel of that country); Louis XIV desired to see Cardinal Fürstenburg installed. The climax to this dispute came in August 1688 when French troops marched into much of the bishopric's territory, but were forestalled at Cologne by Prussian troops mobilised by the Emperor as head of the Holy Roman Empire. By late September large French forces were advancing into Germany intent on securing Philippsburg and other key towns. It was not until 11 December, however, that the Empire declared war on France. The unanimous reaction of the states of the Empire to French moves had come as something of a surprise to Louis XIV whose response was to devastate the Palatinate for the second time in a brutal demonstration of power.

The second strand of motivation centred around the perennial Habsburg-Turkish struggle on the Middle Danube. In summer 1688 fortune was acting to Austria's advantage, and when the Emperor was successful the princes of the Holy Roman Empire were generally and illogically at their most intractable and disloyal—hence the original French belief that the omens were favourable for their moves on the Rhine, a major miscalculation as events proved.

Thirdly there had been France's attempt to foster ill-will between the Houses of Orange and Stuart. Hoping to drive James II into France's arms once and for all, Louis put no obstacles in the way of William's expedition to England in November. This, it was calculated by French diplomats, would either plunge England into a protracted civil war, which would absorb Dutch resources, or result in England drawing closer to France in reaction to William's revealed ambitions. This plot also misfired disastrously. There was no civil war, William was welcomed, and James became a fugitive within less than two months. The House of Orange had thus made a major strategic acquisition in time of peace. This was playing Louis' own game with a vengeance, and he reacted in pique by declaring war on the United Provinces on 26 November.

Soon after this the German situation exploded into open war as has already been described, and Prince Waldeck led a Dutch army into the Spanish Netherlands to allay Spain's growing fears of French intentions as Louis' troops ravaged the Palatinate to the South. War was declared between France and Spain the following 15 April. Louis' attempts to find allies in the Baltic and Poland failed abysmally, and even the Turks, driven onto the defensive in Hungary, could promise no more diversionary aid. In other words Louis' brash and ill-considered diplomacy had resulted in a resounding failure and plunged the whole of Europe into what is best described as the Nine Years War. The ring was about closed when Austria and the United Provinces concluded an alliance on 12 May, and the seal was set upon it when William—as King of England—fully joined the struggle in September 1689.

Such in broad outline was the overall political background. We must now return to May 1689, for in that month the Earl of Marlborough received an active military command very much to his taste. Preoccupied with political matters in England and a Jacobite rebellion in Scotland, William entrusted overall command of his forces in Flanders to the 69-year-old Prince of Waldeck, but appointed Marlborough to command the 8,000 strong English contingent included in his army of 35,000 men. The Earl hastened to Maastricht to attend an Allied conference (23 May–2 June) and was soon bombarding the King and William Blathwayt, Secretary-at-War with requests for clarification of policy regarding tactical training (was the Dutch or the English manual to be adopted ?) and other matters.

William's scepticism about the overall value of English troops was well founded at this period. Compared to the strictly-disciplined Dutch, the English army in Flanders was little better than a rabble. In the words of Walton, 'although there were regiments of men there was no army. There was no organisation, no field administration, in fact none of that fitness for immediate service to be found at that time in continental armies. There was no transport train, indeed scarcely any commissariat of any sort.'[5] Even worse, the army included disaffected elements—and the year 1689 was to see a number of minor mutinies. '*Le Roi Jacques est encore trop considéré parmi ces troupes*' reported Waldeck on 26 June.

Marlborough's first task was to bring some measure of order and organisation to his command. Prince Waldeck watched his efforts with sympathetic interest. 'I wish that these troops, who are believed to be very brave, were as disciplined as they are brave,' the commander-in-chief wrote on 28 June, 'M. de Marlbrouck (*sic*) has much trouble with them.' By mid-July a change for the better was to be noticed, but in September Waldeck was still lamenting that 'The English suffer from sickness, temperament, nonchallance, wretched clothing and the worst of shoes,' adding, however, 'The Earl of Marlborough does his best.'[6] The English bore an evil record for looting friendly inhabitants, and for stripping the clothes off their own wounded comrades. Fortunately, their reputation was greatly redeemed by their valorous conduct in actual battle.

Administrative problems and late arrival of contingents delayed the opening of the Allied offensive in the region until late June. Then at last Waldeck moved from near Tirlemont and headed towards Fleurus. His chief opponent was Marshal d'Humières at the head of some 24,000 French troops. Two months of standard march and counter-march followed as each army manœuvred for the advantage, but the period was not without exciting incidents. On 6 August, for example, Marlborough almost fell into an ambush. 'My Lord Malburra (*sic*) and several of the Dutch generals,' recorded Ensign William Cramond of Collier's Regiment in his informative diary, 'being going from the Spanish camp near Dendermond to Brussels, were waited for by a thousand French hors whose vanguard got between them and a small party of their hors. . . .' Fortunately a stalwart lieutenant of this cavalry fought his way back through the French to give '. . . timely notice to ye generalls who gott off.'[7] An even closer scrape would be experienced in 1702.*

At length Prince Waldeck brought his army over the River Sambre and camped near the walled-town of Walcourt. Early on the 25 August, the Allied foragers were sent out into the surrounding country, escorted by 600 English soldiers of Colonel Hodges' Regiment (the 16th Foot, later the Bedfordshire and

* See below p. 106. This incident in 1689 is not mentioned by W. S. Churchill or Wolseley.

Hertfordshire Regiment). There they were suddenly attacked by the vanguard of d'Humières' army. To cover the retreat of the surprised foragers, Hodges 'behaved extremely well' and succeeded in delaying the development of the French attack for several vital hours. He steadily retired his men to a neighbouring mill where they comported themselves 'with the same resolution.' By this time (about 11 a.m.) Marlborough had arrived within sight of the engagement. Perceiving that Hodges was coming under fire from several French batteries, he ordered him to withdraw again to a hill East of the town, behind which the main Allied battle-line was fast forming.

Stung by his men's inability to overcome the cool resistance of Hodges' vastly outnumbered regiment, d'Humières unwisely ordered his men to assault Walcourt itself. Several attacks were pressed home 'with more resolution in their conduct considering it had walls round it and 600 men within', but heavy casualties were sustained from Marlborough's enfilading guns. The French counter-bombardment does not seem to have been very effective. 'A bomb fell among the officers of Colonell Hale's Regiment without doing any harm, the Fuzze (sic) being stifled,' recalled an anonymous participant. 'Two more fell in a meadow near our Guards, with the same success.'⁸ Still the impetuous French commander chose to escalate the fighting. A party of *Gardes Françaises* fought their way to the gates of Walcourt but failed to set them alight, and the safety of the hard-pressed garrison was assured when Brigadier-General Tollemache brought the Coldstream Guards and a German battalion into the town about 2 p.m. Thwarted again, d'Humières flung his men in a desperate attack against the right of the main Allied battle-line beyond the town, but by this time the initiative was fast passing into Waldeck's hands. At six o'clock, judging the timing with nicety, Waldeck unleashed a double attack against the tiring French. Against their left advanced General Slangenberg's Dutch; against their right spurred Malborough at the head of the Life Guards and the Blues, supported by two regiments of foot.

This double-blow decided the day. The French infantry reeled back in total disarray, but thanks to the stalwart services of Colonel Villars at the head of the French cavalry, d'Humières was able to extricate his men and beat a retreat. French losses are variously put at 600 or 2,000. Allied casualties were very slight, being put by Cramond at 'about 60 or 70 soldiers and 4 or 5 officers' besides 30 men captured from the foragers at the outset of the action. 'This fortunate success gave great encouragement to our army,' continues the Ensign, 'and doubtless much the contrary to the French, it being the flower of their army that was ruffeld.'⁹ D'Humières', dubbed *le maréchal sans lumière* by his colleagues, found himself disgraced.

Owing to administrative problems, Waldeck made little attempt to follow-up this success in 'ruffling' the French army, and within two weeks he was ordering the British contingent into winter quarters. Nevertheless he was highly pleased with the outcome of this, the only notable incident of the entire campaign. To William he reported of the English part in glowing terms. 'Mons. the Colonel Hotzes (Hodges) and the English, who are with him, have accomplished miracles, and I could never have believed that so many of the English would show such a *joie de combattre* . . . M. the Count Marlbaroy (*sic*) is certainly one of the most gallant men I know. . . .'[10] In another letter the Prince further commended the 39-year-old Marlborough, who, 'in spite of his youth' had displayed, the veteran general claimed, greater military aptitude in this single campaign than many generals achieved in a lifetime.

Marlborough had indeed deserved well of both Waldeck and William, and on 26 August (O.S.) the latter awarded him the lucrative colonelcy of the 7th Foot, (later the Royal Fusiliers) in recognition of his skill and valour. The King was prepared to concede that the handsome Earl was shaping well, but he still doubted he possessed the administrative experience to justify the highest commands.

*   *   *

For some months prior to Walcourt, William's attentions had been increasingly directed towards Ireland. His first preoccupations after assuming the crown had been directed towards home affairs and Scotland, where William Claverhouse, Earl of Dundee, had defeated General Hugh Mackay at Killiekrankie (27 July 1689) at the cost of his own life. William's relative neglect of Irish affairs afforded James II with an opportunity. In late March the former King had landed at Kinsale from a French squadron, accompanied by the Duke of Berwick (Marlborough's kinsman) and other supporters including French advisers. By the end of the month James had been joined by his appointee as Lord Deputy, Richard Talbot, Earl of Tyrconnel (Sarah's brother-in-law), and had reached Dublin without encountering serious opposition. Apart from a few isolated pockets of resistance in Ulster, James's control over the country was virtually complete within a month.[11]

Ireland had long constituted the Achilles' heel of the mother country. Many problems went back to the reign of Elizabeth I, if not to the distant days of Strongbow, but the most intractable dated from Cromwell's conquest in the mid-seventeenth century. After the Restoration, a degree of *de facto* religious co-existence had grown up, (until James II's accession) but the land problem remained unsolved. Despite the return of one third of sequestered properties to their original owners under Charles II, many injustices remained unrepaired, and the problem of absentee landlords was endemic.

James's first plan seems to have been to complete the occupation of Ireland and then send an army of 35,000 Irishmen into Scotland to assist Dundee and the loyal clans. Several serious obstacles, however, stood in his way. First, his most influential Irish supporters were divided over the desirability of 'liberating' Scotland and England from the Williamite yoke; a number wished to break the English connection once and for all. Second, Louis XIV controlled the purse-strings, and proved slow in honouring his agreements to provide a corps of veteran troops, the naval reverse sustained at Bantry Bay (11 May) providing an excuse. Thus in many ways James was little more than a puppet with scant control over his own destiny. And thirdly, there was the unexpectedly stubborn resistance of the last Protestant refuges—Londonderry and Enniskillen—which absorbed practically all his military resources. The famous siege of London-derry began in mid-April, and lasted all of 105 days. James's French commander, the ruthless Conrad von Rosen—whose attempts to treat Ulster to the fate of the Palatinate were with difficulty restrained—proved incapable of pressing the siege to a successful conclusion despite the desperate condition of the defenders. This gallant defence gave William time to devise counter-measures.

Despite his many preoccupations and problems, not the least of which was Parliamentary unwillingness to vote money for new forces, William managed to find another army. Negotiations with Denmark produced several fine regiments. A naval convoy of food and munitions was assembled to attempt the relief of Londonderry—the most pressing necessity if a bridgehead was to be maintained in Ireland—and on 10 August Colonel Kirke boldly broke through the boom blocking Lough Foyle and resupplied the city. Three days later, the aged Marshal Schomberg landed near Bangor with 14,000 Dutch, English and Danish troops, and William's attempt to conquer Ireland had begun.

The early months of the invasion were not particularly dynamic. Schomberg methodically moved to take Carrickfergus and Belfast, and then marched to Dundalk (9 September). There he stayed for long weeks, whilst a combination of bad weather and ill-administration (particularly amongst the English troops who made no attempt to build shelters or obey any sanitary regulations) resulted in much fatal sickness—'a violent lax'—which reduced many English regiments to merely 60 men with the colours. The Dutch and Danes fared somewhat better, but Schomberg was prepared to make no further aggressive moves until the following Spring. In sum, therefore, the campaign had got off to a parlous start.

During the winter William prepared to cross over to Ireland and lead his army in person. This suggestion met many protests, but by proroguing the Convention Parliament William out-manoeuvred his loudest critics and pressed ahead with his preparations. Ignoring continental complications, he devoted all his attention to Ireland, where James had at last received the 5,000 promised French troops and a new commander, the Duc de Lauzun (March 1690). In exchange, however, Louis insisted on Irish regiments being sent to France.

After being delayed for aggravating weeks by the slowness of the new (more favourable) Parliament in granting revenues, in mid-June William landed in

Ireland with reinforcements, bringing his army to a total paper-strength of almost 44,000 men; James's army was computed to muster about 39,000 in all. The King immediately set out to seek a decisive battle, which was duly fought at the Boyne (1 July O.S.).

Marlborough took no direct part in these military activities. To his probable disappointment he was not offered a field command. Since Walcourt, indeed, his popularity with William and Mary had considerably waned. During the campaign of 1689 his wife had inevitably become involved in disputes between the joint-sovereigns and the Princess Anne over the provision of an adequate and independent Parliamentary revenue for the latter. In the end the Commons voted Anne £50,000 p.a., but this victory infuriated Mary, who included the Earl in her disfavour as well as his scheming wife, whose influence over the Princess was now confirmed once and for all.

When William departed for Ireland he left the management of the realm in the hands of his Queen, assisted by a Council of Nine. Marlborough found himself included in the number of what were popularly known as 'the Nine Kings' in the role of principal military adviser with the rank of Lieutenant-General (from 3 June O.S.) This was doubtless a sop to his pride, but Mary made scant effort to disguise her distaste at his appointment. 'I can never either trust or esteem him,' she wrote to William. The Earl busied himself finding new recruits for the forces, but soon major crises arose calling for the most careful attention. Whilst William busied himself regaining the military initiative in Ireland, a series of disasters took place elsewhere. In Flanders, Waldeck was severely beaten at the battle of Fleurus (1 July) by the great Luxembourg—a setback threatening grave international complications which minor siege successes on the Rhine front could not obliterate. Even worse, nine days later, the French fleet beat the joint-Allied navies off Beachy Head, thus gaining control of the Channel and, theoretically at least, isolating William in Ireland. This naval disaster, 'the most conspicuous single success the French have ever gained at sea over the English',[12] at once threatened the possibility of a French invasion of England and of limitless French reinforcement of Ireland. The first consideration was deemed the most grave. The shire militias were mobilised, and Marlborough busied himself with plans for the defence of the South coast.

William's victory at the Boyne was thus overshadowed, and he felt compelled to order five regiments back to England from Ireland and to summon as many more from Flanders. Fortunately for England, Louis and his ministers did not choose to make the most of their undoubted strategic advantage. Despite the pleas of James II (who had returned to France with all speed after the Boyne), Louis would neither send more troops into Ireland nor mount an immediate invasion of England; a small French landing was made at Teignmouth to burn the town in July by way of a demonstration of future attentions in store, but that was all. Slowly the invasion fever subsided in England, and life returned to normal. In Ireland, meantime, William and his Dutch generals strove to set the seal on their earlier battle-success. Dublin and Waterford were duly occupied and the line of the River Shannon crossed, but the defenders of Limerick proved unexpectedly stubborn. When Patrick Sarsfield successfully raided and partially destroyed William's siege train in a brilliant operation, and the notorious Irish weather took a turn for the worse, it became evident that the siege would not be successfully concluded that year, so William regretfully began to consider its abandonment and prepared to return in person to London to deal with the many pressing matters awaiting his attention.

Meanwhile Marlborough's fertile mind had been weighing up the overall strategic situation as it affected Ireland. He came to the conclusion that a bold attempt to seize the vital southern Irish ports of Cork and Kinsale before the weather became impossible would confer decided advantages. He had obtained information from spies that neither place was particularly well defended and if successful, such a double-blow would sever French communications with Lauzun, Tyrconnel and Berwick, and thus effectively isolate the remaining Jacobite forces in Ireland ready for the *coup de grâce* the following year. Accordingly he prepared a plan along these lines, proposing that he should implement it in person, and on 17 August submitted it to the Council of Nine. To his bitter disappointment the Queen and a majority rejected the proposal as too foolhardy at so late a season of the year; above all, given the recent invasion scare, there was a marked disinclination to send the greater part of the regular forces out of the country on what appeared to many of the noble Lords-in-Council as a hare-brained scheme.

Fortunately, the Queen referred the plan to the King, presently besieging Limerick. He consulted the Dutch generals, who also advised rejection. But William was pre-eminent as a strategist, and he appreciated the underlying soundness of the scheme. Marlborough argued on paper that it would only need some 5,000 men from England, and these could be found by allocating for the purpose the five regiments switched from Flanders, two of those transferred from Ireland, and a single regiment of marines. Accordingly, William unexpectedly approved the plan, and placed Marlborough in command. Writing on 14/24 August the King indicated his full consent. 'I strongly approve of your plan to embark with 4,000 infantry and the marines, which together make 4,900 men, and is a sufficient force to capture Cork and Kinsale. You will have to take enough munitions with you, and use the ship's guns, for we can send you none from here.* But for cavalry I will send you enough, and will take good care that the (enemy) army shall not be a burden upon you. It is only time which must be saved, and you must hasten as quickly as you can. . . .'[13]

Here was the opportunity for Marlborough's first essay at independent

* Munitions and cannon were in short supply after Sarsfeld's effective raid already referred to.

command: his plan was now accepted, and he had been given a virtual *carte blanche* to implement it. He seized his chance with the greatest imaginable enthusiasm. Any doubts that William might retain concerning Marlborough's administrative capacity should have been dispelled by the speed and efficiency with which he now prepared the expedition. Munitions and weapons were requisitioned from the Tower of London and the arsenals of Portsmouth and Plymouth, including 12,931 'granados' and even some suits of obsolete half-armour. Supplies and shipping were requested from the relevant authorities, and the five battalions from Flanders were marched to Portsmouth. There, despite the failure of the shipping to appear for a number of days, they were eventually embarked by the 9 September (N.S.). To achieve as much as this in only 14 days—even allowing for the ready availability of the troops—was amazing by seventeenth-century standards, and it is surprising that few historians seem to have noted it.

Marlborough and his staff reached Portsmouth on 5 September, the day after receiving his definitive orders from the Queen, whereby he was enjoined '. . . to repair on board of our fleete and to endeavour with the forces under your command to reduce the townes of Cork and Kinsale. . . .'[14] Mary was still far from enthusiastic about the project, and wrote somewhat spitefully to her husband that 'If the wind continues fair, I hope this business will succeed; though I find, if it do not, those who have advised it will have an ill time, all except Lord Nottingham being very much against it . . . thinking it too great a hazard.'[15]

Unfortunately the weather did not remain fair, and the expedition remained tossing at anchor for 18 weary days, many of its members, including the commander, becoming very seasick. Great precautions had been taken to conceal the eventual destination of the armada. It was 'hinted' that the purpose was a retributory raid against the French coast to avenge Teignmouth, and even the Admiralty were not let into the secret, hence no doubt, their slowness in providing the necessary vessels. It is doubtful whether the French were fooled for one moment. Somewhat too coincidentally, perhaps, Lauzun and Tyrconnel left Ireland for France on 12 September, taking the French troops with them. Even in England, there was considerable speculation that Ireland was the true destination.

William had returned to London on 10 September, after handing over the senior command to Godart de Ginkel (later Earl of Athlone). The siege of Limerick had meanwhile been raised (30 August) and the main army withdrawn to the East, towards Tipperary, but the King left Ginkel with orders that he was to assist the sea-borne project to the tune of 5,000 men once it had landed, and as the siege of Limerick was abandoned, a number of heavy guns were also to be provided.

At last it was possible for the 82 sail to leave Spithead, and on 27 September the anchors were raised. The wind remained difficult, however, and the voyage

to the mouth of Cork harbour took five storm-tossed days. After silencing and
occupying a battery of eight cannon situated in Prince Rupert's Tower, the
fleet anchored at Passage West. On the 3 October, 'aboute one o'clocke in the
morning we began to land at Passage,' recorded Ensign Cramond, 'and had a great
part of our troopes landed by 12 o'clocke and before night wee encamped
theare.' Some 6,345 men (including a contingent of sailors) were put ashore,
and next day the force advanced towards Cork. Meantime a train of eight large
guns was wending its slow way from Waterford, escorted by 1100 horse and
dragoons and almost 4,000 foot under Generals Schravemor and Tettau respectively. Although Marlborough had specifically requested the services of the
English generals Mackay and Kirke and a number of English battalions, General
Ginkel pointedly provided him with Dutch, Huguenots and Danes under the
overall command of the proud Frederick William, Duke of Württemberg. 'I
am sure he will make no difficulty in the point of command,'[16] the Commander-
in-Chief optimistically forecast.

The city of Cork stands some ten miles from the sea on the banks of the
River Lee amidst several marshes. In 1690 it was surrounded by a strong though
ancient rectangular town wall, strengthened by a dozen flanking towers, of which
four were of bastion design. In the centre of the Eastern face was the water-
gate with its defences. The main city gates were to the North and South, also
fairly well protected. Beyond the Lee to the North on a low hill overlooking the
town stood Shandon Castle, and over the South Channel were two more detached fortifications, the incomplete Cat Fort standing 90 feet above the town,
and the more massive, complete and modern Fort Elizabeth overlooking the
south-western corner of the city-wall. The eastern and western approaches were
largely obstructed by a network of tidal waterways and marshland. To hold this
city Colonel Macgillicuddy, known locally as 'rude and boisterous', had seven
Irish Catholic regiments totalling almost 6,000 men.

Marlborough's first independent siege operation was therefore not of the
easiest, although from his spies he knew that the defence's impression of solid
strength was more apparent than real, and that many of the garrison were raw
levies of little military experience. By the evening of 5 October, the English
advance guard was within cannon-shot of the south gate when a party of dragoons
supported by some foot briefly sallied forth. A short skirmish drove them back
and a second enemy sortie at midnight was similarly repulsed. By this time
General Schravemor's horse had approached to within half-a-mile of the north
gate, but for a while there was some anxiety that Berwick might interpose his
8,000 men (who were advancing on Buttevant from Kilmarnock) between the
newly-arrived cavalry and the more distant foot and guns commanded by
Tettau. In fact there was no danger of this as Berwick had already concluded that
Cork was doomed. The 20-year-old general ordered Macgillicuddy to evacuate
and fire the town, doubting his aptitude on account of his earlier craven flight

from Waterford, but the 'boisterous' colonel was determined to redeem his reputation by a stalwart defence, so stood his ground.[17]

The morning of the next day saw the arrival of Tettau's battalions north of the city, whilst the English busied themselves landing stores and guns from the fleet. In the afternoon Marlborough ordered 2,000 men to occupy the southern suburbs, but the enemy set fire to the houses and retired into the forts. 'Wee had some popping from the hedges, but without loss,' recalled Cramond. That same evening General Tettau launched 1,000 Danes against the northern suburbs and Shandon castle; once again, the enemy fired the buildings and withdrew. Guided by Sir Richard Davies, Dean of Ross (another redoubtable cleric in the tradition of Bishop Mew whom we met at Sedgemoor*), 200 troopers were transferred over the Lee some three miles above Cork and brought into the main camp, which Marlborough had moved forward to within a mile of the city.

Early on the 5th, Marlborough had conducted a detailed reconnaissance of the defences. Concluding that the two gates were too strongly defended, he settled for making a breach in the eastern curtain some 60 yards north of the south-east tower. The approach to this breach, once made by the artillery, would be difficult, the Lee only being fordable at low tide, but it appeared the best solution. Ten naval pinnaces helped bring up guns and stores, and soon four batteries were being established to engage Fort Elizabeth and sweep the eastern curtain walls which would have to be dominated before the breaching battery proper could be installed close to the objective.

By a stroke of good fortune, an excellent site for one of these batteries was found in Fort Cat. Two exploring sailors had discovered early that morning that the post was unoccupied. 'Coll. Hales detachment ware ordered to martch with all expedition from theare severall postes to possess it,' Cramond continues, 'about 200 of which enter'd the Fort at a gun port . . . Wee lodged ourselves in Ditches and other places convenient nere the Forte (Elizabeth) as well to prevent a sally and to cover ourselves from theare small-shot.'[18]

By late evening eight 24 pdrs and a dozen 18 pdrs had been established to engage the southern and eastern defences, whilst the Danes completed a fifth battery at Shandon Castle on the northern side. The profusion of dykes, ditches and sunken lanes referred to by Cramond made it unnecessary to dig parallel or approach trenches.

The 6th saw the batteries in full action, pounding the defences and also dropping a number of mortar bombs into the city. By the late evening the English had managed to infiltrate a party between Fort Elizabeth and the South Channel, whilst more men took possession of neighbouring St. Finbarre Cathedral. The same hour saw the arrival of the peppery Duke of Württemberg who at once challenged Marlborough's right to command the joint-army. With a display of that masterly tact that would always be a feature of his handling of

* See above, p. 20.

difficult allied commanders*, Marlborough agreed to share the command on an alternate daily basis, and further chose 'Württemberg' as the password for the next day. The general was so charmed that he selected 'Marlborough' for his first day of command, and in effect left complete control of the operation in the Earl's competent hands.

Midday on the 7th saw the arrival of more large artillery pieces, destined to form the breaching battery. These were emplaced in a position 500 yards from the eastern curtain wall, and soon a systematic fire was being brought to bear on the single point.

Elsewhere activity centred around Fort Elizabeth. The spire of the cathedral had been manned by a detachment of sharpshooters under a Lieutenant Townsend. From this eminence, they were able to overlook the defences of the fort, and bring an aggravating sniper fire to bear. In turn the tower came in for much enemy attention, and when his men showed signs of wishing to quit their eyrie, Lieutenant Townsend kept them at their duty by having the men below remove the ladder. One prominent casualty caused by this fire was Colonel O'Neill, commandant of Fort Elizabeth. Meanwhile, at the suggestion of the 'fighting Dean', parties were busy diverting the stream which supplied power to the city's main mill. On the eastern side, the wall was seen to be beginning to crumble by 4 p.m., and three English regiments were ordered to prepare to cross into the eastern marsh at low water, ready to launch an assault once the breach was ready, but at the last moment this order was countermanded. The reason was that the Governor had beat a parley. With considerable cunning, Colonel Macgillicuddy sent out separate emissaries to both Marlborough and Württemberg. The former demanded unconditional surrender; the latter offered honourable terms. By the time this *contretemps* had been resolved, the ebb-tibe had passed, and the Governor had won half a day's grace.

The following night part of the garrison tried to escape over the western marshes, but were detected and driven back with heavy loss. Early on Sunday 8 October, the sloop-of-war *Salamander* was brought up to anchor near the northeast corner of the defences, and added its fire to that of the breaching forces. When the water level was passable, a double column of Allied troops broke out from cover and rushed over the main Lee and the South Channel into the marshes. From the north came 1,000 Danes, who 'beat a party of 100 out of sum (*sic*) houses they were lodged in by the side of the Marrsh. . . .' From the south, 'at one o'clocke, the battalions of Churchill, Marlburrow, Collier, the Granadiers (*sic*) of Trallany (Trelawny), a parte of the detachment of Munmuth (Monmouth) and Boulton† past into the Marrsh' after fording the Channel.

* See below, p. 132.

† In all 1,500 men under Brigadier-General Charles Churchill, Marlborough's brother. The Monmouth referred to was Charles Mordaunt Earl Monmouth, later Earl of Peterborough.

'The Towne fireing on them all the time but with small damage, all the Gran-
adeers and sum detachments marcht on and lodged themselves within pistole
shote of the wall in a Ditch. All this time our batteries inlarg'd the breatch wch.
was about fit for a storm.'[19] Among the casualties was the Duke of Grafton,
Charles II's natural son, who was mortally wounded.

Before the order to storm could be issued, at 3 p.m. the garrison beat a parley
once more. The Governor again sought terms, but Marlborough was inflexible
despite his desire to finish matters at Cork and proceed against Kinsale before
the weather broke. The talks came to an end. Once more the guns spoke, but after
half an hour the white flag was seen again. With no more ado the Governor
agreed to surrender himself and his officers and men as prisoners of war, 'the
Generall promising to intercede for the King's Mercy for them.' Fort Elizabeth
was to be handed over immediately, and all Protestant prisoners within the town
set at liberty. The town was to be handed over the next morning; all arms and
munitions would be accounted for; in return the inhabitants not to 'be damnified
in their goodes or persons or ye Clergie anyway mollested.'

There was some infringement of this last clause. Before the regiments could
enter the town to occupy it the next morning (the southern bridge had to be
repaired), the Danes got in ahead and ran amok for a time before order could be
restored. As soon as the garrison had been evacuated and disarmed,* Marlborough
ordered all troops out of the city except for Colonel Hale's regiment which was
appointed as garrison. So, for a loss of 50 English lives and perhaps 30 Danes and
Dutchmen, ended the siege of Cork.

Marlborough had no time to savour his success. Even while the final terms
were being negotiated, his cavalry was covering the 17 miles to Kinsale which was
reached that afternoon. The defender, Colonel Sir Edward Scott, made no
attempt to hold the unwalled town, but retired into the two forts, the 'Old' and
the 'New' with his 2,000 men, and cried defiance when summoned to capitulate
by Brigadier-General Villiers. The town was recovered intact despite an attempt
to fire it by the garrison. Villiers applied for three guns and as many regiments of
foot to enable him to tackle the Old Fort on a peninsula jutting into the Bandon
River, but these made slow progress from Cork owing to the atrocious roads,
and only reached the scene of action on 11 October.

The same day found Marlborough conducting a careful reconnaissance of the
two forts, which were situated to command Kinsale's excellent harbour. The
'New Fort' (or Fort Charles) was a modern, well-designed position, standing
about 100 feet above sea level on the northern side of the Bandon River estuary.
An agent, contacted some time before by Villiers, computed the garrison of this
fort at near 1,300 men and its armament at almost 100 cannon, ranging from

* They were subsequently massed on a small island. Their plight was tragic during the
hard winter that followed, and Marlborough (from London) was induced to pay £100
for the relief of 'the poor Irish prisoners'.

24- to 42-pounders. Clearly the capture of Fort Charles would present the major problem. The 'Old Fort' was very dilapidated, and manned by some 450 men under a Colonel O'Driscoll. Given the delay in the arrival of the guns, Marlborough determined to grasp the lesser nettle first.

Rejecting the idea of a seven-mile night march to surprise the fort (a resolve probably strengthened by memories of Monmouth's disaster in 1695)*, the Earl asked the fleet to provide a flotilla of ships' boats to convey the assault force by water. At dawn on the 13th Major-General Tettau (the Dane) accordingly stormed ashore at the head of nearly 1,000 men; then, feinting against the weakest sector of the defences, Tettau led his main attack against the strongest part, catching the foe off-balance. The explosion of a magazine killed 40 Irishmen; some 60 more were killed in the assault, and the rest 'found mercy'. This coup cost the lives of one officer and 15 soldiers.

Scott's reply to a renewed summons to surrender was that 'it would be time enough to capitulate a month hence.'[20] Marlborough therefore had no alternative but to set about a methodical siege, opening regular trench lines to north and south of the objective. Eight days hard digging followed, 'without the helpe of cannon', bringing the trenches to within a dozen paces of the covered way. The first heavy guns at last made their appearance late on the 21st, and two days later six were in action on the Danish side, and five 24 pdrs. and two mortars were emplaced in positions amidst the English trench lines. The Danish battery in particular made good practice, 'beating down theare defences and dismounting moste of theare guns. Sum shots were made from the other side of the watter but had smaller effect by reason of the distance.'[21] Each evening the mortars 'threwe in a few bombes' to keep the garrison apprehensive, and late on the 24th the breach was deemed practicable and a general storm was ordered for the next day. Marlborough was eager to complete matters; many of his men were going sick from the cold, whilst Sarsfield's cavalry was hovering not too far away.

As in the case of Cork, the assault was forestalled at noon on the 25th, when the Governor sought terms. These Marlborough was willing to give, considering the progressive deterioration in the weather. 'Hostages were exchanged and a treatty bigun which towards night ended in Artickels to this effect, that the garrison should continue in the forte the 26th (O.S.) and march out on the 27th with bag and baggage, drumes beating, Colours flying, lighted matches and bullets in mouth, and to have a safe convoy to Limrike. Which was all accordingly perform'd. The garrison consisted of three regiments. Our loss before the place was very inconsiderable in respect of the service.'[22] Marlborough's casualties are computed to have been about 250 killed and wounded, besides many more sick.

Appointing his brother Charles governor of the conquest, Marlborough hastened back to London where his welcome was predictably cordial. William

* See above, p. 18.

typically qualified his expressions of approval. 'No officer living, who has seen so little service as my Lord Marlborough, is so fit for great commands.'[23] Churchill's sanguine hopes that he might receive the overall Irish command rather than Ginkel were soon dashed, William intimating that he expected him to perform further recruiting duties in 1691 before accompanying him to Flanders.

The campaign of 1691 in the Low Countries was a failure militarily. Although the formation of the First Grand Alliance between England, the Empire and the United Provinces on 9 March was a diplomatic success for William, his subordinate resented his exclusion from the inner councils and in London proved dilatory in attending meetings, picked a quarrel with Lord President Carmarthen, and generally sulked. Called over into Flanders in May, he participated as an observer on William's staff during the short course of a campaign in which, in Sir Winston Churchill's words, the King had 'entered the field too late and quitted it too soon.' The results were inconclusive, but included the loss of Mons to the French at the very start and a humiliating rebuff at Leuze at the very close. Nevertheless, it is evident that Marlborough's talents were being recognised in some quarters. The Prince de Vaudemont, asked by William to evaluate the British generals in the field, replied with the famous, oft-repeated eulogy of the 43-year-old soldier which provides the quotation at the head of this chapter. William seems to have received this encomium with equanimity and even approval, but it may have stimulated a sense of jealousy for his gifted subordinate.

If it can be stated that Marlborough learnt the first rudiments of his profession during the reigns of Kings Charles II and James II, it can be claimed with equal authority that the first three years of the reign of William III saw his emergence as a commander. His experience was ever broadening. To first-hand knowledge of how the French made war, he now added an appreciation of conditions pertaining to fighting against them alongside the Dutch, destined to be his most important Allies for the remainder of his active career as a general. The English regiments— and John Churchill—had much to learn from the generals and troops of the United Provinces, who had been much engaged in wars against France since 1672, and there is good reason to suppose that the future Captain-General made full use of his opportunities, however riled he would eventually become over the preference for Dutch generals shown by his new monarch.

During the period covered by this chapter we have seen Marlborough maturing as a soldier. In 1689 he is deeply involved in the movement of an English force across the Channel, and in inspiring some sort of order amongst its disordered and indisciplined ranks before the opening of the campaign. At Walcourt he commands a wing of the Allied army—a far more testing occasion than the similar command at Sedgemoor in 1685—and emerged with Waldeck's golden opinion of his worth as a soldier.

The Irish campaign of 1690–91 marks a new departure for the emerging soldier. Here he demonstrates for the first time his keen strategic sense and his ability to plan a minor campaign in all its administrative and tactical aspects, and then convert precept into successful practice. If the operations in southern Ireland afforded no opportunity for a pitched battle, they gave Marlborough the chance to command his first sieges and develop those aspects of the military art associated with Vauban's name. Future years would see the skills first demonstrated before Cork and Kinsale put many times to the test before the fortresses of Flanders—and always with equal success. Perhaps even more important, this campaign reveals Marlborough's personal grasp of the influence of sea power acting in conjunction with land forces. His appreciation of the role of combined operations would underlie many plans during the War of the Spanish Succession as we shall have occasion to note in later chapters.   .

This campaign also taught Marlborough two further lessons of great value. The first was the need for sound military administration and care for the *minutiae* of logistics. The second was the importance of tact in handling senior Allied commanders. His handling of the command crisis after the appearance of Württemberg was masterly and foreshadows similar problems in future years associated with the names of the Margrave of Baden and the Elector of Hanover.

Lastly, the abortive campaign of 1691 in Flanders provided the emerging general with an excellent example of how not to wage a continental campaign. All this was grist to the mill, and by the end of the year we may assert that Marlborough's military education was well-nigh complete. Be that as it may, it is a matter of historical fact that it would be another ten weary years before Marlborough enjoyed another command in the field. The reasons for this will be described in the next chapter.

Disgrace and Reinstatement, 1692-1701

'Philip, a grandson of the House of France, united to the interests, directed by the policy, supported by the Arms of the Crown, was placed on the throne of Spain. King William the Third beheld this formidable union of two great, and once rival monarchies. At the end of a life spent in defending liberties of Europe, he saw them in their greatest danger. He provided for their security in the most effectual manner. He took the Duke of Marlborough into his service—Ambassador Extraordinary Plenipotentiary to the States General of the United Provinces. The Duke contracted several alliances before the death of King William. He confirmed and improved these. He contracted others after the accession of Queen Anne, and re-united the Confederacy, which had been dissolved at the end of a former war, in a stricter and firmer league—Captain General Commander-in-Chief of the Forces of Great Britain. . . .'

From the inscription on the Column of Victory,
Blenheim Palace (continued).

From 1692 until 1698, the Marlborough fortunes suffered almost total eclipse. Fortune, indeed, appeared to have turned away its face. The greater part of this period can receive only the barest mention in these pages. Sir Winston Churchill has so exhaustively examined and analysed every nuance of Marlborough's period of disgrace that there is little to be added, except to suggest, with the utmost respect, that this eminent scholar and statesman was more than a little *parti pris* in his examination of the evidence. It must suffice here to relate the historical facts, and draw such conclusions from them as may have a bearing on Marlborough's later military career.

William, it must be admitted, was probably as much sinned against as sinning in the matter of the Marlboroughs. There is no doubt that John and Sarah had their grievances, and that William was guilty of ingratitude and even stupidity towards them. The refusal of a dukedom and the Order of the Garter (once promised), and the failure to appoint the Earl to the Master-Generalship of the Ordnance (the eventual recipient in 1693 being the lightweight Henry Sidney, Earl of Romney) amounted to slights that could but rankle in a deserving and ambitious subject's breast. Such resentment may help explain, but can hardly condone, some of Marlborough's subsequent actions. It may well be that Church-ill's almost abject attempts to gain James II's forgiveness for his actions in 1688 were largely insincere, but his meetings with Jacobite agents—even if in part condoned by William III—must have left an underlying suspicion of his good intentions in the royal mind. The Marlboroughs' championing of Princess Anne in the 'family quarrel' was hardly disinterested; Sarah took £1,000 a year from Anne at the latter's entreaty, and when 'Mr. Freeman' pressed Anne to seek her father's forgiveness in the December of 1691 there can be little doubt that he was using both James and Anne as levers in his disagreements with William. Here was an over-mighty subject indeed, who clearly felt that his ser-vices were indispensable. When Marlborough took it upon himself to criticise publicly William's gifts to his favourites, and then refused a military position in Flanders for 1692 unless he was given command over all the English troops, it was clear that an explosion was imminent. What made it certain was Marl-borough's attempts, both in Parliament and in the army, to hamper William's conduct of the war and spread disaffection amongst the officers, as an 'exercise in collective bargaining' designed to force the King's hand. That this was done partially in the name of English pride does not substantially mitigate the offence of rank insubordination, and William was a soldier (albeit not a particularly good one) before anything else. By this time Queen Mary was also the Churchill family's most implacable foe.

On 20 January, Lord Nottingham on the King's order required the Earl to dispose of all his posts and offices, nominally on account of bribery and extortion. He was permitted to sell-out, but was banned the Court. Tollemache succeeded to his Lieutenant-Generalcy; the Troop of the Life Guards went to Lord Colchester, and Lord George Hamilton took the colonelcy of the Royal Fusiliers. The Hudson Bay Company Governorship eventually went to Sir Stephen Evance. Five lean years of unemployment had begun.

The nadir of the Marlborough fortunes had not yet been reached, however. Although Princess Anne stood staunchly by her friends, and left the court for Syon House, the family situation passed from bad to worse. The spring of 1692 brought a renewed invasion scare and new accusations against Marlborough and others, which caused William III, from Flanders, to order the arrest of the suspects. After an appearance before the Council, where the specific charges of one Robert Young were considered, Marlborough was sent to the Tower of London on 14 May. There he languished for five weeks, an incarceration made even sadder by the death of his younger son, Charles Churchill. The invasion danger passed its crisis point with the Anglo-Dutch naval victory of La Hogue (29 May), and Sarah employed all her wiles to secure her husband's release. Charges of high treason were not to be lightly set aside however—given the hostility of Queen Mary—despite the rapid discrediting of Young as a witness, and the proving that supposedly incriminating letters were in fact forgeries. Nevertheless, in the long run there was no denying the legal rights of the individual subject and on 25 June the Earl was released after bringing a writ of *habeas Corpus*, on recognisances totalling £6,000. Lords Halifax and Shrewsbury stood as sureties for part of this sum, and were promptly removed from the Privy Council on the spiteful Queen's order as a result. Although the prospect of block and axe had receded, there was absolutely no question of a return to royal favour. Marlborough therefore could take no part in the military setback of the loss of Namur, or the defeats of Steinkirk (3 August 1692) and Landen (29 July 1693). Whether his presence with the army might have averted these disasters—as some commentators avow—is incapable of proof, but at least he can in no way be blamed for them. More significantly, the reverses increased the clamour of Parliament against the placing of English troops under Dutch officers.(Count Solms becoming a particular object of popular wrath).

Marlborough remained very much a spectator of these events, although he continued to attend the House of Lords as was his right. He also continued his correspondence with France. This led, in 1694, to the celebrated incident of the Camaret Bay letter. Marlborough's detractors claim that it was he who alerted the French to the mounting of a combined operation against Brest in June of that year. It is practically certain that Marlborough did indeed send a message on or about the 3 May (O.S.) describing what was afoot; although the original letter has never been produced, there is considerable evidence to support this assertion.* However, as Sir Winston has been at great pains to demonstrate, it is equally certain that the French authorities had already learned of the expedition from another source—possibly Godolphin, Danby or other malcontents who were as deeply involved in cross-Channel correspondence as Marlborough himself—as early as April. Marlborough's defenders assert that at worst the Earl was indulging in his old pastime of passing on information that Versailles had already received—*knowing* this to be the case. Without a doubt he stands absolved of originating this treacherous leak; on the other hand, although William III later declared that he was long aware that the French knew the secret, but hoped that Tollemache's discretionary orders would suffice, there is no evidence that Marlborough took steps to warn the English government that their expedition was in great jeopardy as the secret was out. This would have been the course of honour, and the disaster that ultimately befell General Tollemache (who was killed with 2,000 of his 7,000 men) may possibly be laid to some small degree at the Earl's

* See Winston S. Churchill, Vol. 1, ch. 25, passim. His claim that this letter may have been a forgery seems more plausible than real.

door, although Tollemache bears the brunt of the responsibility for pressing home a patently impossible attack. However, it was at worst an error of omission rather than one of commission, and the whole episode is so obscure and inconclusive that it is still not possible to make a definite ruling. In sum, perhaps we should award Marlborough the benefit of the doubt.

Pleas by his friends, including Lord Shrewsbury, for the restoration of royal favour were wholly unavailing until after the sudden death of Queen Mary from smallpox on 7 January 1695. This opened the way for some improvement in the situation, as it eventually entailed the reconciliation of William with his sister-in-law, the Princess Anne, now without question heir to the throne. There was no immediate proferring of royal forgiveness to the Marlboroughs, however; they were allowed to return to court (in March) but John received no offer of employment. To his credit, William never believed the alleged involvement of Marlborough in the plot that led to the famous trial, attainder and execution of Sir John Fenwick (1695–97), although the House of Commons was harder to convince of his complete innocence.

It was not until 1698 that the corner was turned in the two men's relationship. An important preliminary step in that direction was the restoration of Lord Sunderland, the notorious 'manager' of public affairs, to the Privy Council in June 1697 and his appointment as Lord Chamberlain some months before the Treaty of Ryswick brought the Nine Years' War to an unmourned conclusion (October); Marlborough and Sunderland had long been associated in politics, and Sarah and Lady Sunderland were also close friends. This helped pave the way to reconciliation. The occasion was the decision to create a household for the young Duke of Gloucester (born 1689), Anne's eldest son. The post of governor to the Duke would be one of high consequence. William would have preferred to see his trusted Shrewsbury in the role, but the offer was declined. After further hesitation (and no little discreet prompting in all likelihood from the scheming Sunderland, who realised how popular the appointment would be to Princess Anne, heir to the throne, and her husband), William ultimately offered the position to Marlborough. It was unhesitatingly accepted with both relief and gratitude, and the news was announced in the *London Gazette* of 16 June (O.S.) 1698. 'My Lord,' quoth the King with rare amiability, 'teach him to know what you are, and my nephew cannot want for accomplishments'. At last the long years in the wilderness were ending. Before very long, William and Marlborough would be working together in exemplary fashion, their joint-task being to prepare the ground for a still greater struggle against the wiles and ambitions of France.

To the uninformed outsider, it must have appeared in summer 1698 that the Earl of Malborough was fully restored to royal favour. His seat on the Privy Council was restored, together with his regiment and military rank. His name was on the list of nine Lord Justices for the Council of Regency promulgated in July. His children and relations were soon seen to be granted posts and favours: the surviving son, aged 12, became Master of Horse to the nine-year-old Duke of Gloucester (at £500 a year), and a needy relative of Sarah's was appointed his laundress (with a stipend of £200).* The Princess Anne provided a generous dowry for the Earl's daughter, Lady Henrietta, when she married Francis Godolphin that same spring (a gesture to be repeated in January 1700 to mark the nuptials of Lady Anne and Charles, Lord Spencer, heir to the influential Sunderland). Marlborough's brother George gained a coveted seat on the Board of Admiralty in October 1699, and brother Charles was short-listed (though in vain) for the Governorship of Kingston-upon-Hull. The warm sun of patronage therefore did not ignore the Churchill kith and kin.

Yet appearances were to a large degree deceptive, at least so far as the King's feelings for the Marlboroughs were concerned. Although the English Earl's private influence continued to wax strong, he was still not entrusted with any post of really major significance beyond the Royal Governorship. 'The King's coldness to me still continues . . .'[2] he wrote lugubriously in May. No doubt his open support of the Tory position in the Lords over the burning political issues of Prince George of Denmark's remuneration and the rescinding of Irish land grants made to Dutch favourites could not have recommended him unduly to William, although Marlborough stoutly opposed the crippling military reductions that Parliament demanded and ultimately obtained. Thus our trimmer continued on his way along the tightrope of English politics, striving to reconcile the status of royal servant with his close Tory connections. This was not easy to achieve.

So matters stood until early August 1700, when the sudden tragic death of the young Gloucester from smallpox hastened the process of drawing master and servant closer together into a more profitable relationship. The death of the heir-apparent to Anne had three important effects. First, it made the constitutional issue of the succession more urgent than ever, leading eventually to the Act of Settlement and the granting of reversionary rights to the Protestant rulers of Hanover. Second, the need to gain Tory support for this induced William to trim his ministry, dropping several die-hard Whigs in favour of such men as Godolphin, Marlborough's staunch friend and ally. Third, it meant for Marlborough 'with a non-party outlook, a Whig foreign policy, and a rather faded Tory coat,'[3] another brief period of unemployment. But very soon thereafter the omens began to indicate that the wily King was at last undergoing a change of heart; the call to Marlborough could not now be long delayed.

Perhaps the most important reason for this improvement in his prospects was the growing international concern over a problem that had underlain much European diplomacy for several decades, namely the Spanish Succession. The

* An elder sister, Abigail Hill, was found a place in the Marlborough household—a charitable act that would be bitterly regretted in the fullness of time. Her brother Jack Hill, was made a Groom of the Bedchamber to the Duke of Gloucester.

appalling state of health of the inbred, childless and disease-ravaged King
Charles II of Spain had given rise to much speculation and intrigue over what
would follow his demise, which had been continuously considered imminent for
almost 40 years. The Spanish inheritance, despite the financial insolvency of the
corruption-dominated and Inquisition-bound state and empire, was both vast
and highly prestigious. Despite the loss of the United Provinces and the waning
of influence over Portugal, Spain's European domains still included the
Milanese, Naples, Sicily and Sardinia, the strategically-placed Spanish Netherlands, and a number of important naval bases in the Mediterranean. Her overseas possessions included Mexico, Peru, Florida and the Phillipines.

The question of who would succeed the impotent Charles had taxed all the
major European powers. Several wars had already been fought at least in part
over the reversionary issue. Now, in the late seventeenth century, Louis XIV,
the Emperor Leopold and William III, were all disposed to seek out a mutually-
acceptable heir through collective bargaining in order to maintain, it was rather
piously hoped, both the balance of power and the peace of Europe.

Scant heed was paid to considering what might, or might not, be the desires
of the present wearer of the Spanish crown; there was much secret talk of
compensation and adjustments as the major powers plotted the partition of the
Spanish inheritance. In 1698 there were three claimants. The one with the strongest legal claim was indubitably the French Dauphin, the 'heir-in-blood' through
his mother, Maria Theresa (sister of Charles II), and grand-mother, Anne of
Austria, (sister of Philip IV of Spain). Both ladies on marriage into the House of
Bourbon had been required formally to renounce their hereditary rights, but in
the case of Maria Theresa the legality of this was questionable as the Spanish
government had failed to implement a number of other financial undertakings
in the marriage treaty; it could thus be argued that the renunciation was null and
void. A further advantage of the Dauphin was the existence of his father's
strong army, for Louis had kept his forces in being after the Peace of Ryswick.
However, *Le Roi Soleil* at this time acknowledged that such an aggregation of
power to the French cause would be fatal to the peace of Europe, and he was in
consequence prepared to bargain for a part of the inheritance only. This attitude
would ultimately change, as we shall see.

The second claimant was the Emperor Leopold I of Austria, or rather (on
transfer) his younger son the Archduke Charles.* This claim was complex in the
extreme. Leopold's mother had been another Spanish princess, Maria Anna, and
his first wife, Margaret Theresa, had been another of Charles II's sisters. However, Leopold, with devious logic, was trying to establish that the right of

---

* The reason for this was to prevent (or so it was intended) all possibility of the Spanish
and Austrian Empires becoming re-united, a principle accepted at Charles V's death.
However, the death of Emperor Joseph I (childless) in 1711 made the Archduke
Emperor after all, as Charles VI.

succession to the Spanish throne could pass through his body (from his mother) to the child of a later (third) marriage to Eleanor of Neuburg, to wit the Archduke. This was a contentious proposition (at least until all other claimants had been eliminated), but fear of French aggrandisement in Europe strengthened the Emperor's claim, although the First Grand Alliance of 1689 (and its renewal of 1695) had bound the signatories to support 'the lawful heir to the Spanish throne' without specifically nominating that fortunate individual. Thus Leopold had attempted to hedge his bet. Ultimately, however, the Austrian claim would emerge strongly.

The third candidate for consideration was Joseph Ferdinand, Electoral Prince of Bavaria. His mother, Maria Antonia, the daughter of the Emperor Leopold I's first marriage to Margaret Theresa, had been required by the Emperor to renounce *her* claim upon marriage to Max Emmanuel, Elector of Bavaria. This 'voluntary' renunciation by Maria Antonia was not valid in Spanish law, so everything depended on the validity, or otherwise, of her elder sister's, Maria Theresa's, renunciation of the inheritance on marriage to Louis XIV after the Treaty of the Pyrenees. If this, too, was invalid, then the succession would legally descend to the off-spring of the elder daughter, in other words to the Dauphin. As we have seen, there were sound grounds for supporting his claim. However, the strength of Joseph Ferdinand's position lay in the fact that he was the heir to a relatively minor electorate, and thus could be deemed a compromise candidate, acceptable to both the Bourbon and the Austrian Habsburg powers if due compensation was forthcoming for their own candidates.

This forms the background to the First Partition Treaty negotiated by William III with Louis XIV (through their intermediaries, Portland and Count Tallard respectively) in September 1698. William's interest was by any means to avert the danger of a successful French claim to the entire succession. Aware that England's military power was minimal after the reductions forced through by Parliament whilst the United Provinces and Austria had little chance to withstand France in the field alone, and realising that vital English interests were bound up with the matters of trade with the Indies and above all in the keeping in 'friendly hands' of the key naval posts of Gibraltar, Ceuta, Minorca and Oran in the Mediterranean and of Havana in the West Indies, William set out to persuade Louis to accept the compromise candidate in return for an Anglo-Dutch guarantee of proper territorial compensation. The Dauphin would receive Naples, Sicily, Finale and other Italian lands; the Archduke Charles would be handed the Milanese and Luxembourg; the remainder would go to the Electoral Prince. The Emperor, however, was not willing to agree to this scale of compensation, and when the secret leaked out, the ailing Charles II, in fury, made a first will (published 14 November) leaving everything to the Electoral Prince. This last complication worried neither William nor Louis; Bavaria would never be able to enforce the will, but would be glad to receive the greater part of the inheritance under the guarantee of the great powers. The Austrian opposition was a more serious obstacle but some semblance of a balance of power might have been maintained along these lines. However, on 6 February 1699 the Electoral Prince suddenly died. This unforeseen event returned the issue into the melting pot, with the added complication that the Emperor, thanks to the Peace of Carlowitz with the Turks (signed 7 February) was now free to turn all his attention to west-European affairs.

Nevertheless, despite the lack of a compromise candidate, William doggedly set about creating a new agreement with France. The Second Partition Treaty, a protocol signed by England and France on 11 June 1699, was destined to be, in the words of a distinguished modern historian, 'a still-born child'.[4] By this instrument, the lion's share of the Spanish inheritance was to go to the Archduke Charles, but the Milanese would be added to the French portion (to be ruled by the Duke of Lorraine in exchange for his Duchy). However the Emperor, afforded two month's grace to consider and adhere, refused absolutely to countenance the suggestions. Leopold's attitude was (with some justification) that Louis' negotiation of the First Partition was tantamount to his admitting the validity of the crucial renunciation by Maria Theresa, and that since the only other claimant was dead, the succession must revert in its entirety to himself, and through him to the Archduke Charles. Neither the English Parliament nor the Dutch States-General were enamoured of the new proposal, and so it was virtually a dead-letter from the outset, but William hoped against hope that Charles' death, now really imminent, would cause a more general acceptance. But once again, the signatories had neglected to consider the reaction in Madrid to this further blatant, if well-intentioned, infringement of Spanish sovereignty.

The bombshell exploded in November, when news arrived in London, the Hague and Vienna, that Charles II had signed a second will on his deathbed, leaving all to the 16-year-old Philip of Anjou, on sole condition that the crowns of France and Spain should never be united. The expiring monarch, much beset by court factions, had one final desire: to leave his patrimony intact to a successor of his own choosing—and this he felt he had achieved before breathing his last (one suspects gratefully) on 1 November 1700. Versailles had been secretly notified of the new will during October, but for once a confidence had been kept, due to no small extent to the fact that Louis found himself in something of a quandary. European reaction to the news was mixed; there was jubilation in Madrid, Brussels and Paris; in London and the Hague opinion was more restrained, but there was widespread relief that at least the Dauphin had been passed over, thus somewhat reducing the dread possibility of a future union of the French and Spanish crowns; only in Vienna was there downright fury as the Emperor forthwith prepared for war against France; Leopold still regarded himself and his heirs as the only justifiable recipients of the entire inheritance.

At the Court of St. James, the sickly William III was secretly near despair. All his machinations had failed, and unless Louis decided to honour the Second Partition besides persuading Spain to override the will and accept its terms, there could be no avoiding a further large-scale war. Any lingering doubts about Louis' decision were swept away on 16 November, when he, after considerable mental wrestling, publicly acknowledged his grandson as Philip V of Spain and the Indies. It was widely noted that no specific guarantee that Anjou would forfeit his reversionary rights to the French throne was included in the announcement, and the statesmen of Europe anxiously realised there might be more than hyperbole in the Spanish ambassador's famous exclamation, 'the Pyrenees have ceased to exist.'[5]

Although in William's view Louis XIV had broken his pledges, he was further mortified to note that influential sections of both Dutch and English opinion were clamorous for the formal recognition of Philip V. The King and Grand Pensionary Anthonie Heinsius came to recognise that they would have to bow to pressure, at least for the time being, in order to gain a little time in which to educate influential opinion, seek alliances, and rearm. Thanks to a number of blunders by Louis XIV, these processes were expedited. First, in February 1701, the French King sent troops into the Spanish Netherlands to occupy—in the name of his grandson—some 20 fortresses (three of them in Liége) that had been handed to the Dutch by the Peace of Ryswick. As he had been appointed temporary Viceroy by the Spanish Regency Council, Louis was technically within his rights, but the sweeping away of the measures designed to assure the safety of the Dutch frontiers in one fell swoop (only Maastricht was saved) could only have grave repercussions. Not immediately, however; the States-General, on the motion of the Amsterdam deputies, decided that appeasement was in order, and despite their fear of the implicit threats posed by the French army, voted in favour of recognising the new King of Spain; the excuse was the immediate repatriation of the Dutch garrison-troops by the French. But, given a little time for the shock to sink in, the United Provinces would turn to a more war-like mood.

In Britain, too, the first reactions were muted. The Commons offered to honour the agreement of 1678 and send 10,000 troops to Holland *if* and when the French attacked; they further gave William leave to seek allies. But the Tory price for these helpful concessions, together with the passing of the Act of Settlement, proclaiming Sophia of Hanover ('the old strumpet') the constitutional heir to the Princess Anne, was an insulting reduction of the King's civil list and the impeachment of a number of his most trusted servants for their parts in negotiating the abortive Second Partition Treaty. William, guessing that he had but a few short months to live, was forced to trim, and woo the Tories by agreeing to a formal recognition of Philip V. In return, the Commons confirmed their defensive undertakings, for no 'war-party' existed at this time.

Thus the stage was set for the full emergence of the Earl of Marlborough into the centre of European affairs. He was the only conceivable choice for the command of the English contingent, should it be mobilised, and with an eye to his undoubted importance in the reign-to-come, William decided that the Earl should also play a large part in England's search for allies. On 31 May (O.S.) he was accordingly appointed commander of all English foot serving in Holland, and the next month (28 June) he was further proclaimed Ambassador-Extraordinary and Plenipotentiary, with the right to 'conceive treaties without reference, if need be, to King or Parliament.'[6] If the words were more impressive than the reality in respect of the powers, the remuneration was considerable: £2,000 p.a., a further staff and entertainment allowance of £1,500 and a set of gold and silver-gilt plate from the Jewel House weighing 5,893 ounces.

Meantime, Louis was still further exacerbating the situation with consummate lack of tact. His envoys appeared to be dictating to the world. 'Their haughtiness inspired resentment, not fear, while their territorial gains aroused the hatred of Europe without giving France real protection.'[7] The same February that saw the Netherlands crisis found Louis specifically reserving the rights of his grandson to succeed to the French throne. The speedy granting of monopolistic trading privileges to a French trading company for the 'assiento' (or supply of slaves and thus, owing to the unofficial opportunities this opened, of many more commodities to the Spanish Americas) was not calculated to cheer the money-conscious merchants of London or the Hague who had hoped for a share in the market. Step by step, the United Provinces and England awoke to their peril. 'Our all is now at stake,' proclaimed Daniel Defoe, 'and perhaps in as great a danger as at any time since we were a nation.'[8] The politicians were slower to awaken, but behind them the peoples were stirring.

Marlborough accompanied William to Holland in early July, and threw himself with immense energy and *bonhomie* into his new duties. The ailing King soon retired to Het Loo, leaving the Earl and Heinsius to negotiate on his behalf, but he kept his finger on the pulse of the talks through couriers. Initially, their task was to try to persuade the French to evacuate the Spanish Netherlands, and to induce the Empire to come to some accord over the Succession issue. Marlborough was further charged with trying to gain the adherence of Portugal, but his pre-eminent duty was to secure the safety of the United Provinces, by peaceful means if possible. Be it noted there was no mention of dethroning Philip v.

The mission was no easy matter, but Marlborough's skills, so long neglected, were equal to the challenge. The Emperor's emissaries arrived full of old resentments concerning the Second Partition Treaty. The French ambassador, d'Avaux, was stiff and unbending. Portugal was on the point of concluding a (temporary) alliance with France. The German princelings also were most concerned with the main chance, and indeed some states were being wooed into

the French camp, including Bavaria, Liége and Cologne, the seats of the Wittelsbach family. The situation was not improved by the outbreak of major operations
in North Italy, where Prince Eugene of Savoy advanced from the Tyrol with
30,000 Austrian troops to win the battles of Carpi (9 July), Novara and Peschiera
against the Franco-Spanish forces of Marshal Catinat, and later held-off his
successor, Villeroi, at the hard-fought field of Chiari (1 September).

The need to reach agreements that would be mutually acceptable to William
III, to the Tories in the House of Commons, to the Dutch, to the Emperor, and
to the minor powers, was both pressing and difficult, but the Earl, aided by his
new staff members, Adam Cardonnel and William Cadogan, was both tireless
and tactful, earning golden opinions from Heinsius and others, and little by
little progress was made through the maze of protocol and conflicting interests.
However, it was soon evident that an alliance for war would be the outcome,
for on 5 August the French mission to the Hague was permanently recalled to
France.

From that date the main duty was to form an effective alliance; as Marlborough
wrote to Sarah, '. . . our actions now must be governed by what the French will
think fit to do.'[9] Ominous French staff talks took place at Namur, to Marlborough's concern, for he well knew the unpreparedness of the English forces
slowly assembling over the Channel. 'The English have orders to be in readiness
to march, but I hope His Majesty will have the goodness not to draw them into
the field, unless there is an absolute necessity, the greatest part of the men being
newly raised.'[10] The immediate crisis passed, however, when it was learnt that
Marshal Villeroi had departed for the Italian front; Flanders might expect
a short further breathing-space before being plunged into war.

The work of finding allies was slow at first. Apart from the now thoroughly-
alarmed and cooperative United Provinces, only the Elector Palatine was willing
to reveal his hand at the start. However, on 7 September it proved possible to
sign the Treaty of the Second Grand Alliance, binding England, the United
Provinces and Austria to the following undertakings: the Emperor was to receive
the Milanese, Naples, Sicily, the Spanish Mediterranean islands, the Spanish
Netherlands and Luxembourg—if he could take them; it was stipulated, however,
that a barrier of fortresses would be established in both the last two areas for the
security of the United Provinces. The Maritime Powers were to be given a free
hand in the West Indies, and the German states were to be wooed into a co-
operative mood by the offer of Anglo-Dutch subsidies, whilst the Emperor
grudgingly agreed to recognise the Elector of Brandenburg as King of Prussia
as the price of his wholehearted support. Far from demanding the removal of
Philip V the treaty accepted in principle his retention of the throne of both Spain
and the Indies subject to guarantees that the crowns of France and Spain would
never be united. The clauses dealing with the quotas of armed forces each
signatory was to provide were left vague, and became the subject of further

negotiation and haggling, Marlborough being very well aware, probably more so than the King who by this time was completely disillusioned with English political forms, that the Tories would be highly critical if careful economy was not observed. 'If the King should be prevailed upon to settle this by his own authority,' wrote the astute Earl, 'that (then) we shall never see a quiet day more in England, and consequently not only ruin ourselves but also undo the liberties of Europe; for if the King and Parliament begin with a dispute, France will give what law she pleases.'[11] For this same reason, Marlborough was most anxious to obtain full Parliamentary approval for all his actions and tentative agreements, a limit date of 24 November being originally set for the ratification of the main treaty. One by one, over the following months, the states of the Empire, including Prussia, Hesse, Hanover, Celle, the Palatinate, Munster and Berlin, together with Denmark, came to terms, agreeing to provide men for the coming struggle, and in October Sweden (as she refused to join the Alliance) was prevailed upon to keep out of the dispute, and thus not distract Prussia or Saxony. The 'oil of diplomacy' was occasionally administered in the hope of hastening matters a little. On 14 February 1702 Marlborough wrote to Grand Pensionary Heinsius that '. . . by this post there is care taken to let M. Lillenroot (Swedish ambassador to the Hague) know that if he has power and will hasten the finishing of this treaty for the 10,000 men, that he shall have a present of 15,000 crowns.'[12] Doubtless to the considerable regret of the would-be beneficiary the treaty fell through owing to Sweden's even deeper involvement in the Great Northern War.

The question of the *dénombrement*, the allocation of men and ships expected from the various signatories, dragged on from month to month, as each power for varied motives tried to escape as lightly as possible. A measure of preliminary agreement was reached in November, the details being presented to the House of Commons the following January. It was tentatively agreed (the matter did not amount to a formal undertaking even then) that England would provide two soldiers for every five recruited or paid for by the Dutch, together with five ships of war out of every eight the Maritime Powers would bring into commission. Austria—acknowledged to be in difficult financial straits which the ending of Turkish preoccupations seemed to have done nothing to ease—was to provide a force of 90,000 men for operations in western Europe.

The main bones of contention involved the Anglo-Dutch ratios. For their part, the Dutch could not understand why England, whose level of prosperity had reputedly risen by 20 per cent since 1695, was only prepared to provide a field army of 40,000 men to the Dutch 60,000, the English representing only 55 per cent of the forces the country had sustained eight years before. The States-General were also expected to find all siege artillery for both armies, and be responsible for the costs of any sieges undertaken. In England, much resentment would be felt at the war-long failure of the United Provinces to honour the naval side of the agreements or to break off their lucrative trades with France through third parties.[13] But the Dutch replied that as they were forced to bear the brunt of the land war in the Flanders region and to finance it by means of loans bearing high rates of interest, they were in no position to honour their naval undertakings to the letter nor to restrict their commerce. It was for long believed that the Dutch put all of 102,000 troops into the war, thus making the situation still more disproportionate, but the researches of a recent British historian have firmly established that this figure included 42,000 garrison troops which were not the subject of the agreement, which was restricted to forces for use in the field.[14] These figures, it should be noted, would be greatly increased by both parties as the struggle developed, and further English contingents would be sent to the West Indies and later to Portugal as the war spread. The overall situation was not, therefore, quite so one-sided as some historians have claimed.

There were still a few lingering hopes that peace might be preserved until 16 September 1701. On that date the former King James II of England died in France, and in an emotional reaction Louis XIV rashly recognised his son as the lawful King of England. This further error of judgment crystalised the English opposition to France as nothing else could have been expected to do, involving as it did significant constitutional and religious issues. In the furore which followed, Louis recalled Count Tallard, his ambassador, but William (who had returned to England without Marlborough on 18 September) seized the opportunity to dissolve Parliament, presumably in the hope of weakening the Tory grip on its deliberations. This action also, of course, held up the ratification of both the treaties and the *dénombrement*, and when the new Parliament met in January 1702 it was still narrowly Tory-dominated, although a number of Jacobite-Tories had lost their seats, and William was able to dispense with the ministerial services of both Godolphin and Rochester. So grave was the sense of the European emergency, however, that little time was spent in factious infighting. The Tories unexpectedly insisted on the insertion of an eighth article in the agreements, denouncing as void any claims to the English throne by the *praetensus* or Pretender James III. This move, which the Whigs were delighted to support for very different reasons, was really a manœuvre designed to *prevent* or delay the ratification of the Second Grand Alliance, for the Tories were convinced that the Emperor, a stickler for legitimism, would never concede the new article.

Dutch William throughout remained extremely anxious for the safety of the United Provinces. Together with Marlborough he laid plans for the coming year, which everybody realised must hold the opening of a general war. Marlborough took a cooler view of the overall situation, potentially grave though it was on all sectors, arguing that a set-back or two in Flanders would be preferable to denying aid to the Emperor, as this might cause the overthrow of Prince Eugene in Italy. For at least the first time, therefore, he showed himself to be a sounder strategist and realist than his master and mentor. All in all, though, William and Marlborough saw eye-to-eye about the adoption of an English continental strategy for the coming struggle; some of the Tories were already enamoured of a maritime approach—concentrating national resources on naval strength associated with expeditions to capture enemy colonies, subsidising allies with money, but with only a token commitment of force to the Continent. Such a strategy was not in accordance with William's concept of England's role in any war against France.

In fact William was not destined to see even the declaration of the great struggle he had tried so hard to avert, and more recently worked so hard to prepare for. His health had been giving considerable alarm for several months, and on 21 February, (O.S.) while out riding, his horse stumbled on a mole-hill and threw its rider, who sustained a broken collar-bone. At first it seemed that this might mend, but eventually graver symptoms manifested themselves, and on 8/19 March 1702, William III died, aged 52.

A brief period of stunned disbelief settled over English and Dutch affairs. Could the Alliance survive the blow? Queen Anne was immediately proclaimed. Now Marlborough's real moment had come. She lost no time in lavishing the fullest royal favour on her faithful friends of long-standing. John was confirmed as a matter of course in his chief command over English troops at home and in Flanders (9 March) (O.S.), and also made a Knight of the Garter, a long-desired honour. Another long-frustrated ambition was fulfilled when he was made Master-General of the Ordnance shortly after (14 March). Within two years Marlborough would be receiving emoluments in excess of £60,000 p.a., besides gifts and the percentage on the army bread contracts that was also his less official due as commander-in-chief. Nor, of course, was 'dear Mrs. Freeman' or 'Mr. Montgomery' forgotten. Sarah was immediately appointed Groom of the Stole, Mistress of the Robes and Keeper of the Privy Purse to the Queen, which earned her a private income of over £5,000 a year, whilst in May, a new Tory Ministry centred around Godolphin as Lord High Treasurer came into existence.* George Churchill would shortly move to the head of the Board of Admiralty.

---

* Sidney Godolphin, for all his brilliance as Lord Treasurer, was basically a man o very simple and unassuming character. He was more of a public servant than a politician, and was well described by Mrs. Manley as '. . . the greatest genius of his age with the least of it in his aspect . . . .'He was a compulsive gambler and yet an astute financier. He was also a breeder of race-horses. As Lord Treasurer from May 1702 until August 1710, he was virtual chief minister of England, but the ministry would totally change its complexion over the years, moving from Tory to Whig. Its basis was the team of Godolphin and Marlborough, neither of them having much time for faction or party strife. A lifelong friend of Marlborough and his Duchess, Godolphin died a poor man in 1712, proof of his probity whilst in office. However, he is suspected of having rather

Suddenly the sun shone brightly on the name of Churchill; after 50 years of alternate prosperity and vicissitude, he had at last come into his own; Marlborough was the most important grandee in the land. The next ten years would prove or disprove how much he deserved his preferment. But now the opportunity to show his full worth had indubitably come, with a crisis of confidence in English intentions being manifested in the States General and the Emperor still delaying his agreement to the *praetensus* clause. All Marlborough's skills as a statesman and politician were more immediately in demand than his abilities as a general.

The very first task was to constitute a credible Ministry. The Queen, for all of Sarah's great personal influence over her, was already known for her stubborn Tory proclivities and above all for her steadfast loyalty to High Church Anglicanism. These circumstances, together with Marlborough's wishes, determined in large measure the cabinet's composition, and it was soon clear that the Whig heyday was truly over. As secretaries of State for the Southern and Northern Departments were appointed the veteran Tory, the Earl of Nottingham, and the amiable Sir Charles Hedges. Lord Jersey became Lord Chamberlain, Lord Normanby received the Privy Seal, and Sir Edward Seymour was appointed the Comptroller—Tories one and all. The Queen's uncle, the highly influential Lord Rochester, coveted the post of Lord Treasurer, but this Marlborough would not countenance, being aware of the importance of the holder of that post in seconding his forthcoming military endeavours, and so a disgruntled Rochester was reappointed Lord Lieutenant of Ireland. For the key post Marlborough was determined to gain the services of his trusted friend of 40 years' standing, Sidney Godolphin. This experienced public servant was a genuinely modest and unambitious man of great experience and brilliance in handling the ponderous machinery of late-Stuart government; furthermore, he was second only to the Marlboroughs in the estimation of the Queen. In the end he bowed to royal pressure, and accepted the white staff of office on 17 May. The level-headed moderate Tory, Robert Harley was Speaker of the Commons and *ipso facto* Leader of the House, and for a number of years he formed with Marlborough and Godolphin an inner group of the Ministry known as the 'triumvirate'; although the day would come when 'Tricky-Dicky' would abandon and bring down his erstwhile friends, he never forfeited the trust of his sovereign until 1714. For the rest, a few minor posts went to reliable Whigs—for the Queen and her advisers, posed on the brink of a major war, desired to see as broad-based an administration as circumstances would allow. Thus Lord Devonshire remained Lord

devious relationships with the Jacobites, and was sensitive to ridicule and misrepresentation (see Sacheverell incident p. 271 below). Sarah described him after his death as 'the finest man that ever lived.' He proved the steadiest and most trust-worthy of Marlborough's associates, and did much to prepare the way for his great campaigns by using his influence and the public purse to good effect.

Steward, and Henry Boyle retained the Chancellorship of the Exchequer (a subordinate government post in the early eighteenth century), whilst the Duke of Somerset became Master of Horse. Marlborough's wish to see the great Whig grandee, the Duke of Shrewsbury, included in the Ministry, was politely rebuffed.

Of key importance was the personality of the Queen herself. Anne, in her 38th year, was neither highly intelligent nor very dynamic. She was a loving wife to her husband George of Denmark and a devoted (though very unfortunate) mother to her children. Never of very strong health or personality, she was capable of a few devoted friendships and a matching number of strong antipathies, in both of which the Marlborough clan would come to share. 'Brandy Nan', as her uncharitable Jacobite critics dubbed her, was generally a very sensible woman whose governing skills have tended to be over-easily discounted. Her committment to her demanding task was total and unswerving, and if she tended to be strongly influenced by key friends she was never wholly ruled by them once she had become Queen of England. As Queen, Anne was determined to be 'above party'. Although a woman of limited intellect and conversation, she was nobody's fool. Strongly attached to the Anglican Church, she utterly distrusted the Whigs and was suspicious of the House of Hanover. An intensely lonely woman after the death of Prince George in 1708, with no child to comfort her later years, Anne proved a ruler of above-average ability and would see her country emerge to a position of prominence in the 18th century world.[14] She might share the Stuart traits of stubborness and ingratitude, but she also possessed qualities of true statesmanship.

On 15 May 1702, England formally declared war on France.

5

The Art of War

'Every Art and Science has its peculiar terms, which are obscure to all who are not vers'd in it, or at least have not made it their business to be acquainted with them. The Art of War, like all the rest, has many words unknown, or at least not familiar to any but those whose profession and duty obliges to be masters of them. Yet there are but few men who do not eagerly hearken after, or read news, and at this time, when all Europe is embroiled in war, there can be little news without some account of martial exploits, where there always occur some terms of art not intelligible to persons unskill'd in military affairs. These difficulties are generally pass'd by unregarded, as if not material for the understanding of what is read; and yet in reality, they are as necessary and proper to be known as any other part of the relation, which without them becomes but a confus'd notion of something done or acted, without any distinct judicious knowledge of the methods, parts and circumstances of the action.... Here they are all explain'd, not in obscure words, as if they were designed for artists only, but in such a plain familiar method as may render them easy to all capacities.'

From the introduction to *A Military Dictionary*, London 1702,
'By an Officer, who served several years abroad.'

Before any valid judgement can be passed on the qualities or weaknesses of any military commander, it is necessary to consider the major aspects of the contemporary art of war. The basic criteria of success or failure are intimately bound up with the individual general's ability to measure up to the military circumstances of his time.

The Duke of Marlborough was unique in the way he adjusted to, and even largely overcame, the obstacles placed in the way of waging effective warfare under the prevalent conditions of his day. This chapter will review the salient points, indicating Marlborough's attitudes and improvements, but no attempt will be made at this stage to provide a full assessment of his generalship.* The
* See below, Chapter 15, for a full appraisal.

object, rather, is to set the scene for the campaigns to be described in the following chapters, noting the differences of attitude and method that distinguished the armies of the various contestants.

General Conceptions of Warfare

In certain respects, the period of Marlborough's campaigns (and the decades immediately before and after) form a watershed in the history of the development of warfare. The previous generations had witnessed the long-drawn horrors of the Wars of Religion, when regions in Central Europe had been ruthlessly laid waste in the name of either a Catholic or a Protestant deity. It has been estimated that the population of what is now known as Central Germany dropped by one third during the Thirty Years War,[1] through the interaction of the sword, pestilence and famine. As for the future, it held the grim prospect of nationalistic and empire-building conflicts on an hitherto undreamed-of scale, involving whole peoples, economies and continents, but in Marlborough's day the impact and scale of wars was considerably limited by both mental and physical restrictions and the resultant widespread observance of firm military conventions, at least in western Europe.

Some of the reasons for this were psychological. The ruthlessness of such generals as Wallenstein and Tilly, the sacker of Magdeburg in 1631, had bred a revulsion against military excess in a large section of influential European opinion. This widespread attitude coincided with the onset of the Age of Reason which taught the virtues of moderation and tolerance, whilst the teaching of such seventeenth century jurists as Vattel and Grotius, who had attempted to bring wars within the scope of concepts of international law, enjoyed an increased vogue. Of course the occasional atrocity was still perpetrated—for example the two sackings of the Palatinate by French forces in 1674 and 1688, or Marlborough's and Baden's ravaging of Bavaria in July 1704—but the outcry these incidents provoked shows that they offended the conscience of the age, at least in the West. Matters were somewhat different in both northern and south-eastern Europe, where the Russo-Swedish and Habsburg-Ottoman feuds were at times prosecuted with a ferocity reminiscent of the earlier Age. In the West, however, generals were constantly being reminded of the virtures of moderation by economy-minded governments. This trend indubitably encouraged military mediocrity, and only a few commanders of the calibre of Marlborough and Prince Eugene were bold enough to insist on returning a measure of effectiveness and decision to the conduct of warfare by constantly seeking for situations favouring a major engagement, or what Clausewitz in the next century would term 'the bloody solution of the crisis'. The Duke regarded a field success as 'of far greater advantage to the common cause than the taking of twenty towns.'[2]

Practical considerations also underlay the contemporary preference for siege wars and campaigns of chess-board manœuvring, with generally-speaking limited short-term objectives. In the first place, almost all wars were seasonal in nature. Campaigns were fought between the months of April and October, and then armies entered winter quarters until the following spring. The odd siege might be pushed through to a conclusion, and very occasionally a bold commander (like Turenne in December 1674) might 'steal a march' and surprise his opponent by an unseasonal offensive, but such occasions were rare. One main reason was lack of food and kindling wood for men and of fodder for horses during winter months; another was the appalling state of most European roads from the onset of the autumnal rains to the recession of the spring floods. In the intervening period the earthern tracks became either impassable quagmires or frozen-rutted, virtually precluding the movement of artillery and military vehicles, whilst rivers and canals—the alternative means of movement—became raging torrents or ice-bound for the same months of the year. As will be seen, even at the right time of the year, marches could be extremely hazardous and delay-prone. The campaigning season varied in different parts of Europe. In Spain, for example, it was the heat of summer rather than the cold of winter that brought operations to a standstill. Such seasonal limitations discouraged bold schemes of long-term operations and encouraged military stalemate.

Marlborough, for once, was decidedly conventional in at least this respect; the period between November and March was habitually reserved for liaison visits to Allied courts or for political activities in England, although in 1708, unusually, the campaign only came to a final close in January 1709. The Duke did not, however, approve of campaigns given wholly over to sieges or elaborate manœuvrings. From first to last he was the proponent of the major battle as the sole means to break an enemy's military power and thus his will to resist. In this he was following the advice given by Turenne to Condé in the preceding generation: 'Make few sieges and fight plenty of battles; when you are master of the countryside the villages will give us the towns.'[3] Most French commanders chose to ignore this concept, and even Marlborough, as will be seen, was often forced by his Allies or overall circumstances into undertaking numerous sieges in the Flanders theatre. His record as a commander during the forthcoming struggle would hold four major battles, two actions and over 30 important sieges.* He proved uniquely successful in whatever he put his hand to. His first major biographer, Thomas Lediard, could justly claim that '. . . he passed all the rivers and lines he attempted, took all the towns he invested, won all the battles he fought (this often with inferior, rarely with superior force) was never surprised by his enemy . . . was ever beloved by his own soldiers and dreaded by those of the enemy.'[4]

Marlborough's *penchant* for seeking decisive battles was not shared by any

* See Appendix, p. 336.

European government save that of Sweden, whose soldier-king, Charles XII, was even more renowned for his boldness (which often verged on rashness) and singleness of purpose. Battles were widely considered to be unjustifiably expensive in manpower and military material, both hard to replace. As armies grew slowly larger as governments improved their administrative machinery, so too they grew rapidly more costly. By 1711 Queen Anne would be employing 75,000 native-born troops and perhaps half as many more mercenaries and other forces 'in pay'.[5] At the height of the wars, Louis XIV deployed 250,000 soldiers, Austria perhaps 110,000, whilst the United Provinces could call on over 100,000 men. Of the major countries, only Spain's native land forces barely reached 30,000 in 1703, but subsequently grew. Nevertheless, the cost of even this small arrangement amounted to about 18 million *reales*.[6] Armed forces, therefore, in most instances represented a sizeable investment of national capital, and were not to be squandered in heedless actions.

Certain changes in weaponry had made battles more expensive in terms of casualties than formerly. The development and issue of the flintlock-musket in place of the older matchlock considerably increased regimental fire-power. The flintlock was several pounds lighter than its predecessor, only misfired twice in ten shots on average, and could be discharged eight times faster (a good foot soldier being capable of firing two shots a minute). The introduction of pre-packed paper cartridges (containing powder and one-ounce ball) and of simplified reloading drills were the main reasons for this. 'Firearms and not cold-steel now decide battles,' observed Puységur (1655–1743).[7] Associated with this change was the almost equally-important switch from pike to socket bayonet. Although the number of pikes had greatly shrunk during the late seventeenth century (to a proportion of one to every five musketeers), in the 1690s 'the Queen of Weapons' still employed numbers of men who might otherwise have carried death-dealing muskets. Their 14 to 18 foot length made pikes into exceedingly unwieldy weapons. The development of the socket bayonet—through the intermediate stages of the less satisfactory 'plug' and 'ring' varieties—effectively banned the pike from the battlefield, and in consequence increased the potential firepower of the battalion as well as its tactical flexibility, at least for those commanders, like Marlborough, who possessed sufficient imagination to appreciate the new possibilities. The French were somewhat slower than their English or Dutch neighbours in abandoning their last pikes, but by 1703 practically every west-European army were equipped with these improved weapons: only the Russians and Turks still clung to the match-lock for a further period.

This changeover brought with it a rise in battle-casualties, which in turn reinforced the caution of governments and many generals. At the battle of Steinkirk (1692), regarded by many contemporaries as 'the severest infantry battle ever fought' before the change in weapons, each side lost some 4,000 casualties out of a joint-total of 90,000 troops actually engaged (there being

150,000 men present in all). A mere 12 years later, at Blenheim, after the transition in weaponry, the Allied victors lost 12,500 casualties out of 52,000 (24 per cent) and the vanquished suffered 20,000 killed and wounded (without regard to prisoners) out of 56,000 (40 per cent). Five years later at Malplaquet the boot would be on the other foot, the French inflicting a 23 per cent overall casualty rate on their far-stronger opponents before grudgingly conceding the ground.* Losses on this scale were exceptional and caused a bitter outcry, but such statistics undoubtedly encouraged monarchies and republics to discourage their generals from fighting on any but the most advantageous terms. 'Conduct yourself in such a way as not to compromise the reputation of my army' wrote Louis XIV on one occasion,[8] a theme constantly repeated in one form or another in the latter years of his reign. Small wonder that wars of sieges and manœuvres were favoured, although in fact major sieges could also be very costly. To capture Lille in 1708†, for example, cost the Allies all of 15,000 men—but this considerable loss was spread over a period of four months which to many seemed more acceptable than a single day's bloodletting.

Since the Thirty Years War the profession of common soldier had become so discredited that it proved most difficult to replace from the customary sources such horrendous losses, to which should be added the equally large number who succumbed to sickness in insanitary billets over the long winter months. All armies recruited their men from a variety of sources, which included native peasantry (the basis), sizeable contingents of mercenaries and regiments of exiles, a considerable proportion of the criminal classes and a necessary leavening of genuine volunteers and adventurers of the type of Captain Robert Parker, Sergeant Millner or Private Deane, but even in this class of soldiery motives of insolvency or family trouble were often decisive in inducing them 'to entertain a high opinion of a military life'.

There was no universal form of conscription for standing armies at this time (although in the Spanish Netherlands, Count Bergeyck instituted a form of selective service by lot for his country's expanded forces in 1702–3). In the case of the Militias the situation was somewhat different, but militiamen could not usually be required to serve outside their country or provincial boundaries, although in France this restriction was increasingly ignored from 1708, large numbers of militiamen being selected by lottery for service with the front-line formations. The only forms of compulsory military service in Great Britain related to ne'er-do-wells and vagabonds (admittedly terms capable of liberal interpretation) and certain classes of criminals. Justices of the Peace were empowered to direct that felons should 'go for a soldier' in place of prison, or even death sentences.

The onus for recruiting was largely laid on the shoulders of the regimental

* See below, pp. 240–72.
† See pp. 223–39.

colonels. These officers were still very much the owners of their formations. The government would approve a petition from a well-to-do personage to raise a new regiment, and the new colonel-proprietor would proceed to sell companies or troops to other aspirants after a military life. These officers would in turn seek out recruits to fill the ranks, aided by monetary grants on a *per capita* basis from the Treasury; this bounty-money had reached a level of 80/- a recruit in England by 1708.[9] The government also provided firearms (but not sidearms) and made a grant towards the cost of initially uniforming a formation, although this remained basically a regimental responsibility.

Between campaigns, every regiment would send back parties of officers and trusted soldiers 'to beat for recruits' to make good the losses of the previous season. The lengths to which these recruiters would go to fill their quotas sometimes included barefaced fraud and even kidnapping, and although the government never set up a legal press-gang system such as operated for the Navy, many misdemeanours were tacitly overlooked. Recruiting was slightly easier in hard times than in good, for as Defoe percipiently noted, in times of distress 'the poor starve, thieve or turn soldier,' as was certainly the case in France after the dreadful winter of 1708–9.* but as wars progressed a sufficiency of manpower became increasingly hard to procure. Recourse was therefore had to the prisons and work-houses, and the periodic jail-deliveries became an important source of recruits.[10] The presence in the army of criminal elements did little to improve the repute of a military life in general, and made necessary the harsh and brutalising concepts of discipline which often affected the innocent as well as the guilty, and this in turn made the finding of men genuinely willing to 'take the Queen's Shilling' and bounty all the more difficult for the Captain Kites and Sergeant Plumes of the recruiting parties.[11]

Abuses were not all one-sided. A whole class of 'bounty-jumpers' appeared— men prepared to join a regiment, receive their bounties and then desert to repeat the process with another unit. Official penalties were severe, but many hard-pressed officers were prepared to turn a blind eye and ask no questions. Some, like Peter Drake, made their living in this way, and even moved from army to army at the height of the war with complete impunity.[12]

A substantial part of every army was made up of foreigners. Queen Anne employed regiments of Huguenot exiles and Louis XIV employed Irish formations —the famous 'Wild Geese'. All countries also hired mercenary forces from European princelings; thus the British used Hanoverians and Hessians, the Dutch hired Danes and Prussians, and the French employed Swiss and Bavarians. Most of these forces were contracted for one campaign at a time in return for a substantial subsidy. In 1709, 81,000 out of a total 150,000 British forces came from Allied sources and subsidies totalled over £600,000. Such hybrid and multi-national forces rarely evinced much enthusiasm for a particular cause

* See below, p. 245.

(another factor limiting the impact of warfare) but they could be inspired by a particular commander, as Marlborough would soon demonstrate.

Another limitation was the supply-system of the age. It proved very difficult to feed and move armies without vast preparations—and this placed yet further restrictions on the conduct of effective campaigns. It was out of the question to permit the rank and file to forage for themselves or 'live off the countryside', even in enemy territory. Such activities were stridently denounced by 'civilised' opinion, and were in any case deemed wholly impracticable because they could well encourage mass desertions amongst the unwilling soldiery. The conduct of the formal 'grand forages' involved almost as many security precautions as the proximity of an enemy army. Armies therefore could march and fight over the distance they could carry their bread, habitually halting every fourth day to set up field ovens and bake a further supply, and this reliance on pre-stocked arsenals and large convoys of slow-moving waggons placed severe trammels on even the more gifted commanders, making surprise and rapid movement very hard to achieve. Under these conditions it was almost impossible to force battle on an alert, unwilling opponent.

Marlborough, however, was outstandingly successful at most aspects of field administration (as witness his march to the Danube in 1704) and he forced action on his foes on at least three occasions. Aided by such trusted subordinates as Quartermaster-General Cadogan and Henry Davenant, his financial agent, the Duke again and again pulled off great *coups* and surprises, using night marches and a careful regard for administrative detail to fool his less-enterprising opponents. The results were seen at Donauwörth, Blenheim and Oudenarde. Such achievements were not paralleled in the Spanish theatre, however, where the Duke's mandate did not run. The British forces—and their Allies in the Peninsula—suffered hideously from maladministration and governmental neglect and defeat was the ultimate result. But it cannot be denied that Marlborough used his immense influence to ensure that Flanders received the lion's share of whatever supplies or reinforcements were available.

The amount of direct suffering occasioned by these wars varied according to geographical as well as political considerations. Campaigns tended to be channelled time after time into certain areas where the existence of reasonable roads and waterways, a relatively high level of fertility, and the presence of rich towns, attracted the attention of both statesmen and generals. In western Europe at this period wars centred around five main regions. The 'Cockpit of Europe' (N.E. France, the Spanish Netherlands, and parts of the southern United Provinces) was much fought over on account of the assistance its resources provided for military movement and subsistence, and above all its geographical location athwart the 'invasion route' linking the North German Plain with the approaches to Paris and Versailles. Second only to the 'Cockpit' was North Italy, where the Po Valley's communications and general fertility were also favourable, whilst the area's proximity to the Alpine passes guarding the southern approaches to the Tyrol and Austria, and, conversely, the westerly route (along the narrow Ligurian coast) from Piedmont and Genoa towards Toulon and ultimately Lyons, assured its strategic importance. Interposed between these two war-areas was the Central and Upper Rhine region, stretching from the much-ravaged Palatinate to the recently acquired French Alsatian possessions around Strasbourg, and eastwards into the inhospitable Black Forest region. This obstacle guarded the approaches to the fourth zone—that of the Upper Danube, extending from Ulm down the great river to Vienna, the Austrian capital. This front would see much activity in 1703, 1704 and again be subject to scares in both 1707 and 1711. Lastly, much fighting would take place along the eastern seaboard of Spain through Catalonia and Valencia, Barcelona providing the focal point. The strongly particularist and anti-Bourbon sentiments of these areas and the comparatively-high (for the Iberian Peninsula) level of fertility, together with their general accessability to the Allied fleets operating in the Mediterranean, turned these provinces into a major war front from 1705 to 1714, ill-advisedly for the Grand Alliance though it was to prove.

For much of the rest of western Europe (although there were minor campaigns and 'raids' in other areas), the drums of war beat only distantly, although the economic repercussions were widely felt—particularly in Spain, France and the United Provinces which were at different dates reduced to a state of near bank-ruptcy by the harsh exigencies of the far-flung war.

Such then were the general conditions affecting warfare at the turn of the century. Taken in combination, they were sufficiently complex to encourage if not dictate a 'limited' conduct of operations and the cautious handling of armies. To a description of those armies in general and of the British army in particular we must next turn our attention.

The Control, Organisation and Equipment of Armies

The administrative control of the English army evolved in a typically haphazard and almost inconsequential way. Constitutionally the ultimate authority remained the monarch, but since the Glorious Revolution Parliament had abrogated to itself much power through control of the annual army estimates and Mutiny Act; without the one, the army could not be paid and without the other, military discipline could not be imposed. Both William III and Queen Anne, therefore, had to be at some pains to build and maintain generally favourable Parliamentary majorities in both houses; this was partly done by the use of placemen and organisation of caucuses, but the shifting political scene caused several adjust-ments in Queen Anne's ministries and as will be seen these had no small effect on Marlborough's military and political fortunes.

The monarchy exerted its authority over the army through a number of high officials. The most important were the two Secretaries of State (for the Northern and Southern Departments), one of whose signatures or countersignatures was required on many commissions and other executive orders. Next came the Secretary-at-War, a somewhat nebulous post whose occupant was responsible for much administrative detail and inter-departmental liaison duty, and often served as the Ministry's 'front' in the Commons; and lastly the Paymaster-General, a functionary much exposed (justly or not) to charges of malversation and fraud.

Military administration was divided between two authorities; the army's general headquarters in Whitehall, controlled by the commander-in-chief, which overlooked most matters pertaining to the horse and foot; and the Board of Ordnance (virtually a quasi-independent Department of State), under its Master-General—which controlled all matters respecting artillery, munitions and several other support functions. Friction between these authorities was not unknown, but by a happy chance Marlborough held both key positions between 1701 and 1711 and forged stronger bonds between the two than formerly. Boards of Commissioners of Supply and Transportation overlooked the farming-out of contracts for most supplies, cartage and shipping with varying reliability, and Queen Anne's reign saw the creation of a 'Comptroller of Army and Accounts' (1703) and later the Board of General Officers (1707), which investigated corrupt and fraudulent practices, and was used, later, to reduce or circumvent Marlborough's personal influence over military appointments. The Treasury loomed over all.

On the Continent, broadly similar hierarchies existed. Only in the United Provinces was any form of 'popular' (or rather oligarchical) control exerted over the armed forces, in this case by the States-General, which, like the British Parliament, could refuse the vote of vital funds. This institution also appointed the so-called Field-Deputies to serve alongside every field commander, virtual 'political commissars' who could veto Dutch participation in operations they disapproved of. Such men as Colonel Goslinga, Geldermaison or Hop were to prove considerable thorns in Marlborough's flesh (though less so than some of their senior serving officers), but it was a considerable point that the Dutch were prepared to acknowledge his authority at all. All other countries engaged in the Spanish Succession War were strongly autocratic monarchies. Louis XIV controlled his armies through his Secretary for War, a whole array of *bureaux* and departments, the inspectors-general (the name of one of whom, Martinet, has entered the English language), and not least the military *intendants* who were appointed to each army to relieve the commander of many administrative responsibilities, and, rather less popularly, to report back to Versailles independently on the progress of operations. *Cahiers* of instructions were issued each campaign, and generals had scant initiative. A body of war commissaries supervised commissariat, remount, transport and ambulance services, whilst the artillery and engineer services came under the *Grand Maître de l'Artillerie*. The

Emperor of Austria was advised on military matters by the *Hokriegsrat*, the principal medium of orders between the Emperor and his generals from 1675. Supply was the responsibility of the *Generalkriegskommissariat* (from 1650) and *Generalproviantamt*, whilst the *Feldzeugmeister* oversaw the artillery arm.

Such were some of the major authorities charged with the direction and support of field armies. The organisation of troops in the field into large formations remained undeveloped. There were no corps or divisional organisations and even the brigades of four and more battalions, or a dozen or so squadrons, were *ad hoc* organisations of temporary duration, the regiment or battalion remaining the vital operational and administrative unit. It is true—as C. T. Atkinson was the first to point out—that the organisation of armies into 'wings' and the twin lines of battle did constitute higher formations of a sort, but not until late in the century would permanent organisations come into existence, each endowed with its own staff. In Marlborough's day staffs were very rudimentary. No general staff existed in any country (although Louvois had vainly attempted to found an approximation in the late seventeenth century), and in consequence it was often left to the discretion of individual commanders to select their assistants. There were no chiefs of staff at this period, but in many cases the Quartermaster-General in addition to his logistical functions (exercised through the regimental quarter-masters) performed the duties. Other staff positions included Adjutants-General, Chief Engineers and other senior arms representatives. At a lower level, Brigade-Majors were beginning to appear—responsible for coordinating the employment of the battalions and squadrons through their majors and adjutants. Every important general would also employ a number of Aides-de-Camp, usually young officers of known talent, needy relatives, or sons of political acquaintances.

Marlborough relied on a relatively small staff of hand-picked men. He was very skilled at choosing the right officers. The burly Irishman William Cadogan served him loyally and superlatively well as Quartermaster-General from 1701 to 1712, an officer whose talent for *minutiae* transformed the Duke's broad concepts into practicable orders and carried out a myriad ancillary duties and special missions in addition.* A second key figure was the Duke's Secretary, Adam Cardonnel, who handled much of the endless diplomatic correspondence which the Duke conducted both in and out of campaign. Third for a number of years was Henry Davenant, the financial agent, whose monetary arrangements with the Exchequer and with continental bankers underwrote the immense charges of war. Dr. Hare, the Chaplain, cared for Marlborough's spiritual welfare and doubled as an unofficial historian, keeping a useful *Journal* of events.† Colonel John Armstrong, Marlborough's senior engineer for a number

* He also had his faults. Van den Bergh called him 'the greatest thief of the whole army' in a letter to Heinsius dated 21 March 1709. See the article by A. J. Veenendaal in *History*, 1950, pp. 34–47.

† The authenticity of parts of Hare's *Journal* is now somewhat suspect, however.

of years, was the guiding inspiration behind many important siege successes, whilst Colonel (later Brigadier) Holcroft Blood served him well as senior gunner and engineering consultant until his death in 1707.

The Duke also took more than usual care in choosing his aides. Men like Colonels Parke and Bingham or Major John Richards were expected to be able to assess local situations and report back accurately and independently on them as well as carry messages. They thus served as Marlborough's eyes—a truly vital function on days of battle when both distance and dense clouds of blackpowder smoke made it impossible for any one man to keep full control over every sector. Marlborough's much noticed knack of appearing at points of the greatest crisis and danger was frequently due to information brought back by his aides.

Orders were often relayed direct from Captain-General to regimental commander. We must next turn to a brief examination of regimental organisation.

Cavalry regiments included several categories. The 'Horse' comprised the Household Cavalry (the French *Maison du Roi*) other *élite* regiments of heavy cavalry (such as the English 'Blues' or the French *Gendarmerie*) and considerable numbers of line formations, many of which were raised at the onset of a war and disbanded at its close. Secondly there were the Dragoons—still essentially mounted infantrymen but becoming increasingly used in cavalry roles. Except in France this type of mounted soldier tended to be despised by the regular cavalry, and was indeed paid less. Thirdly, the Austrian, Polish and Russian armies (slowly imitated by France) employed numbers of irregular light horsemen, hussars and cossacks. Contemporary opinion regarded these as 'properly speaking, little more than brigands on horse-back,'[13] and their tendency towards indiscipline restricted their use to mainly raiding and reconnoitring operations.

Mounted regiments were divided into some nine troops or *compagnies* of approximately 50 troopers or dragoons apiece. Household formations had special, larger establishments (the Life Guards, for instance, had 156 'gentlemen' besides officers in each troop) and Dragoon regiments also tended to hold more men (perhaps 540) than their line cavalry equivalents. A troop was commanded by a captain, a lieutenant, a cornet and a quartermaster, aided by two or three Corporals of Horse (Sergeants of Dragoons) and a trumpeter or hautbois player. Above the troop, the regimental headquarters comprised a colonel, a lieutenant-colonel, a major, adjutant, chaplain, surgeon and kettle-drummer. A trooper of horse received 2/6 a day to the dragoon's 1/6. For action, two or three troops would be grouped into *ad hoc* squadrons under the senior captain, but these formations were tactical rather than administrative at this period. British clothing included long red-coats, sword belt and heavy thigh-boots, and tricorne hats. Dragoons were coming to wear white cross-belts. Armour had almost disappeared, but in 1707 Marlborough ordered the reissue of breastplates to the heavy cavalry (to be worn beneath the coat). Cavalry weapons were basically the straight-sword and pistols, but dragoons and light cavalry also carried a carbine or musketoon and bayonet for dismounted action, and a proportion also carried axes or hatchets for use in pioneering roles.

The infantry of Marlborough's army comprised four battalions of Guards, a fluctuating number of line regiments (all, save the Royal Scots, consisting of a single battalion,* and all identified by their colonels' names although numbering was coming in), and a group of foreign units (including a number of Huguenot formations) in addition to mercenary formations in the Queen's pay hired from year to year from such countries as Hanover, Hesse, Denmark and Prussia. The average regiment consisted of a headquarters and 12 companies—making a full strength of about 820 officers and men (some on paper were supposed to read 938), although few would muster more than 500 on campaign—and the end of a war meant either complete disbandment or ruthless reductions to near skeletal cadres. Each company held between 40 and 60 rank and file, and was commanded by a captain, lieutenant and ensign, assisted by two sergeants, as many corporals and a drummer. Each battalion included one grenadier company of picked soldiers (there were no regiments of this nature in the British service although for special attacks numbers of grenadier companies were often brigaded together). Regimental headquarters comprised a colonel, lieutenant-colonel, a major, adjutant, surgeon and his mate, quartermaster, solicitor (or agent), a drum-major and a deputy marshal. The three senior officers were invariably also company commanders, drawing pay in both capacities. Thus a colonel of foot drew 12/- a day as battalion commander and about 10/- a day as a company officer (equivalent rates in the Guards were 20/- and 14/- respectively), and all officers were entitled to further allowances for servants. At the bottom of the scale, the humble private 'sentinell' drew 8d a day—sixpence subsistence and twopence 'off-reckonings', from which a number of standard army and regimental deductions were made. As in the horse, details of organisation varied considerably.

In the case of both the Horse and Foot, the colonel was frequently an officer holding higher army rank and responsibilities. On days of battle, therefore, the regiment or battalion was often commanded by the lieutenant-colonel or even the major. A regiment's seniority was determined by its number in the Army list—an important consideration when formations were disbanded at the end of a war.

The infantryman wore a tricorned hat, leather shoes, white or grey breeches with gaiters and a red coat embellished with linings and facings of varying hue according to regiment. He also wore cross-belts and carried a flintlock† and bayonet, a sword, 24 cartridges, a knap-sack, cloak and cooking-pot, weighing in all about 50 lbs.[14] Officers carried swords and pistols, sergeants the half-pike

* Larger multi-battalion regiments were more popular in the French, Spanish and Dutch armies.

† A version of the William III Land-Musket, often erroneously called the 'Brown Bess'— in fact a later weapon.

or spontoon. Standards of clothing varied until 1707 when a Royal Warrant regulated quality—at least officially. Clothing was issued according to a two-year cycle, and part of the soldier's off-reckonings were stopped to reimburse the cost. Unscrupulous colonels (responsible for clothing their men) made profits through sharp practice, but they were a minority. Firearms were issued to a unit by the government, but bayonets and side-arms were frequently chargeable to regimental funds.

As has already been noted, the artillery was provided and administered by the Board of Ordnance, a world unto itself. The personnel were fractionally better paid and clothed than their cavalry or infantry equivalents. Their coats were of blue cloth with red facings. The guns, pontoons, engineering and munition services, together with the pioneers, were massed together into the Trains of Artillery. In the field, these formations were only answerable to the Captain-General and their own hierarchy—and this was one sore bone of contention between the Ordnance and the army as a whole. It was only gradually, therefore, that professional gunners and engineers were accorded army ranks, but Marlborough was careful to continue the processes of integration.* He also encouraged the widespread adoption of a light, sprung, two-wheeled cart (drawn by two horses) as the standard army train supply vehicle—an example of the Duke's eye for important detail.

Nevertheless, the artillery as a whole constituted a serious drag on field operations. The field guns were very heavy, weighing three tons dead weight or more. They required many horses to draw them—eight or ten apiece—and the continuing practice of harnessing these in tandem doubled the extent of road they might otherwise have taken up. A third disadvantage lay in the fact that most draught horses and their drivers were provided on short-term contracts by civilian contractors. Most of these were local, often operating on a two-day march which caused endless problems of replacement. To move 25 siege guns and all equipment needed 470 horses. Although commanders could, in emergency, requisition both transport and horses, the civilian drivers proved most unwilling to court a glorious death for their temporary employers, and often deserted their cumbersome charges and fled at the first hint of action.

Maximum effective range was about 600 yards for ball and 250 yards for grape or 'partridge shot', although greater use was being made of ricochet fire to increase destructiveness and distance of overall carry. Field guns varied in size, including the tiny 1½-pounder 'regimental' guns which could be drawn by one horse or four men, the standard nine-pounder demi-culverin, and the great 24-pounder (the largest gun that habitually accompanied field armies). The more powerful cannons that were required for siege-work—the 36- and 48-pounders and siege-mortars—were placed in separate 'heavy trains' and were brought up

* In 1716 Marlborough was instrumental in securing the formation of what would become the Royal Regiment of Artillery.

(by water in 'well-boats' whenever possible) under separate escort as and when required. Both field and siege trains also included a number of howitzers ('haubitzers') in care of 'fire-masters', but their projectiles were difficult to fire with any great degree of accuracy, the shell-fuses of varying length having to be lit separately. When the battlefield was reached, the pieces were usually grouped in rough batteries of six or eight guns apiece. Marlborough was well known for taking great personal interest in the siting of his guns—a rarity amongst contemporary commanders—and through the valiant inspiration of men like Holcroft Blood and the Richards brothers it was even feasible to move some of the pieces to new sites during action—an unheard of refinement which made the employment of the guns more flexible and effective.

To maintain, supply and repair these monsters of brass and iron required the services of a myriad of craftsmen together with vast amounts of munitions and stores. An army's trains comprised many hundred waggons in addition to the guns, hampering movement still further. On occasion (as in 1704) the Duke would be constrained to leave the heavier guns behind in the interests of speed and mobility, but this constituted a bold risk.

The provision of bread and bulk forage was usually entrusted to civilian contractors through the agency of Commissioners of Supply and Transport appointed by the government, and their representatives, the field commissaries. Although carefully-controlled 'grand forages' were quite regularly undertaken, most rations and forage were provided by slow-moving convoys trundling ponderously after the army, and by pre-stocked depots. Most armies halted every fourth day to establish field-ovens and bake bread. In times of peace or winter quarters, however, the troops were left to fend for themselves to a greater extent, hence the importance of placing forces in fertile hostile countryside at the end of the campaigning season so that 'contributions' could be levied from an enemy, rather than a friendly, population. Friend or foe, however, tended to suffer equally, but in the Duke's campaigns there was usually enough money available (thanks to the close cooperation of Godolphin, the Lord Treasurer) for the purchase of necessaries—which assured a maximum of willing local co-operation, and, often, much useful information.

The bulk bread contractors, such as Solomon and Moses Medina, Mynheer Hecop, Vanderkaa and Machado, were for the most part Spanish or Dutch Jews of varying reliability and venality. If they sometimes gave short-weight or added sand to the corn-sacks it should be remembered that they were often owed huge sums by the governments that required their services. It was, (of course) the poor soldier who suffered most: all too often neither his rations* nor his pay materialised on time, whilst the effects of wartime inflation on prices of such staples as bread could be a further detrimental factor. Nevertheless, under

* Each soldier was entitled to 1½ lb loaf of bread a day, at an average price of 1¾d (or the equivalent) in the Cockpit.

Marlborough, the situation was somewhat improved, and he could justly claim that, '. . . everything has been so organised, and there has been so little cause for complaint, that all know our army in Flanders has been regularly supplied with bread during the war. . . .'[15] Paradoxically, the Duke would be brought down by his enemies on false charges of malversation in connection with the 'bread money' in 1712. Certain it is that the men in the Cockpit of Europe never suffered to the extent of their less fortunate comrades in Spain, where both geography and inept administration conspired to cheat them of their due.

Behind the trains came hundreds of 'grand' and 'petty' sutlers and vivandières supplying meat and brandy and other 'luxuries', ministring to the troops needs, in a rough and haphazard way, and looting whenever possible, stripping the still warm corpses on the battlefield. These human scavengers—typified by Mother Ross—did a little to supplement the wholly inadequate ambulance and hospital services.

The medical authorities were headed by a Physician, Surgeon and Apothecary to the Forces, but these officials had scant resources or influence. There was no monetary vote for hospitals or medical services as such, charges being levied against 'contingencies' or 'extraordinaries of war' funds. The regimental surgeons and their mates were rarely the luminaries of their profession, and were in any case hopelessly inadequate in numbers. Although William III had made provision for one cart per regiment 'for the surgeon's chest' there were no ambulances; empty bread carts were habitually pressed for this service. Field hospitals were not organised according to a proper establishment (except in Dutch armies), but were set up haphazardly in towns or villages to the rear. Treatment within them was all too often 'a combination of magic and carpentry'[16] and it has been estimated that a casualty had a one in three chance of surviving a serious wound. Nevertheless some slight steps were tentatively taken to improve medical administration, and from 1705 a Commissioner for Sick and Wounded was attached to headquarters.

Marlborough's manifest sympathy for his men will emerge many times in the chapters that follow, but even the Duke could do little to ameliorate the harsh conditions. A few of the seriously wounded or aged might be sent to Chelsea or one of the other hospitals as a Pensioner; the great majority were turned off without recompense to look after themselves as best they might or be sustained by the notorious Poor Law. Widow's and dependants received little assistance, although every regiment was by custom allowed to claim 'dead-men's-pays' on a number of vacancies in the establishment, and from 1708 this practice was recognised in the Mutiny Act. Dead officers' effects were auctioned off for the benefit of their families, who might also receive a levy or even the asking-price for the vacancy from the next incumbent.

Small wonder that the rank and file had grievances, most particularly over pay, food and booty. Marlborough had some success in improving the situation as regards the first two, and issued strict regulations to control the last. The ever-present dangers of desertion, drunkeness, plundering and straggling called for harsh discipline, or so most contemporaries believed, and the whipping triangles, the noose or the firing squad were often in evidence. Yet Marlborough, in the words of Thomas Lediard, 'secured the affection of his soldiers by his good nature, care for their provisions and vigilance not to expose them to unnecessary dangers,* and gained those of his officers by his affability; . . . the poor soldiers who were (too many of them) the refuse and dregs of the nation, became tractable, civil, orderly, and clean, and had an air and spirit above the vulgar.'[17]

Their officers posed different problems. In an age when almost all promotion went to those who could pay or exert influence, there were many anomalies and injustices. To some wealthy socialities, a commission was little more than a financial investment, and they bought, exchanged or intrigued their ways to the command of regiments with scant interest in the men they commanded. Many better but poorer men saw deserved places go to less worthy subordinates or outsiders, and the practice of commissioning children became such a scandal that in the end the abuse had to be tackled by authority and was restricted, an age limit of 14 being imposed.

An associated problem was officer-absenteeism. Large numbers malingered in England, putting off joining their regiments for as long as possible, and at times even the Captain-General had to intercede with individuals personally. He also made occasional examples, but the evil went on virtually unchecked. So did the practices of duelling and brawling. Standards of personal conduct amongst officers were often coarse and undesirable by modern standards, but it was a rough age. There were no officer-training establishments to weed out the unsuitable or undesirable: The officer, like the private, learnt his profession 'at the cannon's mouth' although a few of the most favoured might undergo a period of apprenticeship on the staff of a great commander.

Of course there was considerable gold amongst the dross; many officers were both conscientious and able—typified perhaps by Captain Robert Parker—and deeds of conspicuous gallantry were never lacking on days of action. Many colonels and captains almost bankrupted themselves raising credit to enable their men to buy food when the paymasters failed to produce money on the dates due. To his credit, Marlborough did what he could to encourage higher standards. He tried to secure rewards or promotions for the deserving, and often intervened to see fair play, using his right to approve purchases of commissions as an instrument. While he was in high favour with Queen Anne, his recommendations were invariably accepted, but in later years as his influence waned the reverse became the case. Even his stand against the making of political appointments within the army began to be undermined as his enemies became more vocal and

* See p. 294 below.

predominant. But from first to last his subordinates could count on his undivided, courteous attention to their pleas and problems, and the high morale his genuine care for both officers and men engendered even survived his fall, and has been immortalised in the writings of such soldiers as Sergeant Milner, Corporal Bishop or Private Deane—one and all self-appointed chroniclers of the British Army.

Operations of War

To conclude this chapter, it is proposed to describe the main features of military operations at this period. Eighteenth-century wars have a particular atmosphere of their own—a blend of deadening methodicism and an apparently leisurely approach to warfare, but appearances could be deceptive, and under the guidance of a few skilled commanders the conduct of campaigns could become both dynamic and decisive.

At the onset of spring, the troops would be summoned from their winter quarters to rendezvous at a chosen fortress where materials of war would already have been massed over the preceding months. There the formal musters would be held, determining the official strength of every regiment, the new drafts of raw recruits being hastily pushed into line. Many soldiers would still be sick after the long months in insanitary billets and morale was often low, justifying the ancient adage 'the army passed over into Flanders and swore horribly.'

Once the preliminaries were completed—and the last formations had arrived (mercenary contingents were proverbial for tardy appearance)—the army would set out for the scene of war. Eighteenth-century armies almost always moved as a single mass, occupying much road-space. There was no thought of marching in a series of formations over a broad area—although corps were quite often detached to perform secondary tasks whilst garrisons would be told off for the fortresses. Field armies marched in a series of columns, either by 'wings' or by 'lines' according to the assumed position of the foe (see diagram on p. 85), the cumbersome guns and pontoon-waggons being allocated the best available road in the centre, the myriad supply vehicles being kept to the rear. The Lieutenant-General-of-the-Day (appointed from a roster) was responsible for keeping good order in the columns, being assisted by the Provost-Marshal and his assistants (sometimes called 'archers'), further general officers and the Waggonmaster-General.

The cardinal sin was for a subsidiary column to block the progress of the artillery train; in 1705 the Dutch General of the Foot, Slangenberg, was dismissed the army for holding up the guns to allow his personal baggage to pass at a critical moment, and so much importance did Marlborough lay on this form of march-discipline that he later ordered any sutler's waggon attempting to creep up from the rear to be plundered on the spot. Other ordinances severely restricted the amount of private transport allowed to accompany the army, Generals-of-Foot being confined in 1708 to one coach and three waggons apiece, brigadiers to one of each. Regiments were strictly forbidden to send back a detachment to 'hasten by force' the progress of their own baggage.[18]

Although parties of engineers and pioneers laboured ahead to improve the way, and the columns were at all times protected against surprise by a screen of dragoons, it was rare for any army to average more than ten miles a day. Many were frequently slower; the French (despite edicts to the contrary) allowed far more baggage to accompany their forces. St. Simon, an ordinary though aristocratic trooper in the *Mousquetaires du Roi*, boasted of his numerous valets, the private field-kitchen and service of silver plate 'at least as good as that of a general officer', and he was only one of many.[19]

Such slow and stately progresses, usually beginning at dawn and halting at dusk, were hard to disguise from the enemy's patrols or spies, making surprise difficult to achieve. Marlborough, however, had his own methods of overcoming this difficulty. His military chest was often rich enough to permit the duplication of sets of prestocked depots as in 1704 when both Coblenz and Philippsburg were provisioned to confuse Villeroi and Tallard.* The Duke also practised marching his men by night—both strategically, as during the march to the Danube, and grand tactically, as before the battles of Blenheim and Oudenarde, or the forcing of fixed lines (as in 1705 and 1711). By thus literally 'stealing a march' he proved able both to delude his opponents and force major actions on a number of occasions. One prerequisite of success was a high standard of morale, and this he was invariably capable of inspiring. *Esprit de corps* alone made possible such feats as the covering of 40 miles in 18 hours during the night of 4/5 August to storm the lines of *Non Plus Ultra* in 1711.†

Some way ahead of the main body moved the Quartermaster-General's reconnaissance party seeking out the best camp-site for the next night's halt. On occasion this party encountered the enemy, as before Ramillies, when Cadogan and the French both selected the same camp area for 23 April. Under normal circumstances, this party's main duty was to mark out the limits of a suitable area, having regard to its general security against surprise, its proximity to a source of fresh water, and its accessibility for the artillery.

Encampments were laid out to reproduce the line of battle. The horse lines were generally massed on the flanks, the infantry bivouacs placed in the centre, and the guns and munition waggons placed some way apart in a separate encampment under special guard to reduce the danger of camp-fire sparks lighting the powder. Regimental representatives marked out their unit lines, horse formations being generally allocated a 50 yard space with intervals of the same order, the foot receiving 100 yard frontages and similar spaces so as to enable the men to form up in battle array in case of an alarm. The colours or standards were prominently displayed at the head of each encampment as a rallying point, and

* See below, p. 129.
† These incidents will be found at pp. 214 and 289 below. See map p. 290.

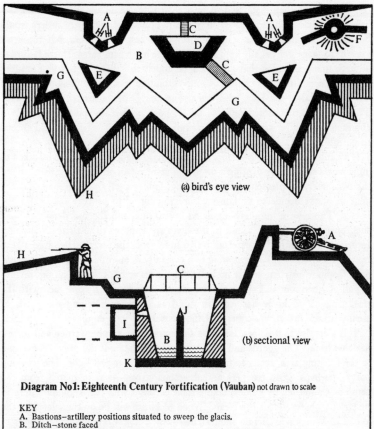

(a) bird's eye view

(b) sectional view

Diagram No 1: Eighteenth Century Fortification (Vauban) not drawn to scale

KEY
A. Bastions–artillery positions situated to sweep the glacis.
B. Ditch–stone faced
C. Sally-port Bridges (temporary)
D. Démi-Lune–designed to cover the wall connecting two bastions (or curtain)
E. Ravelin–designed to cover the vulnerable angle of a bastion
F. Tenaille–walls constructed to protect the face of a curtain-wall
G. Covered Way and Traverse–used to protect the ditch and enfilade the glacis.
H. Glacis–an area of levelled, sloping ground, affording a clear field of fire
I. Counterscarp Gallery–designed to cover the ditch for the opening of mining galleries
J. Palisade–of sharpened stakes; used when the ditch was unflooded
K. Scarp

the troops were then dismissed to raise their ridge-tents, water the horses, and light camp-fires ready for the evening meal. The grand and petty sutlers would be allowed to situate their waggons near their respective units, but the great mass of baggage was usually kept away from the main camp area. It was failure to observe this precaution that put the final touch to Villeroi's rout at Ramillies as will be seen in a later chapter. Camp discipline was the responsibility of the Major-General-of-the-Day, who was also in charge of the security precautions. These comprised mounted vedettes, sentry posts, and main and grand guards of 100 men kept under arms within the camp area. Fusilier regiments had special responsibility for the security of the artillery encampment.

If a camp was occupied for more than a single night, steps would be taken to improve its security by digging a ditch and creating an earthern rampart around the perimeter, supplemented by palisading. Under such static circumstances, a general might decide to organise a 'foraging foray' to procure fodder for the horses. These were minutely-regulated operations, and the full details for one such operation are to be found in the Tyrawly Papers in the British Museum. Issued at the 'Camp of Rousselaar' on 30 June 1706, the foraging involved all the cavalry regiments of the right wing in a carefully demarcated area near Wynen-dael. Copious instructions are included for the security of the operation, involving all of 1,000 foot and 160 horse, whose orders were clearly designed with the thwarting of would-be deserters in mind as much as avoiding the perils of enemy attack (as at Walcourt).* Officers were strictly enjoined to keep their patrols alert, 'so that if foragers leave the escort they can be warned and forced to come back.' The guards and vedettes were marched out the previous evening to the foraging area, ready to take up their positions at first light. The foraging party—perhaps 4,000 troopers and dragoons strong—was to march from the camp at 5 a.m , led by guides, taking their carbines with them. Bounds were to be strictly observed 'for the Grand Wood of Hulst will be on their left and the Wood of Winendale (sic) on their right'—which might tempt some troopers to make a dash for freedom—and the participants were to be severely warned not to pillage, being 'forbidden to enter into any house or village.'[20]

Armies manœuvred, marched and counter-marched attempting to threaten the foe's communications or pass through his permanent lines with a view to inducing him to abandon a particular area, which could then be 'put under contribution'—the inhabitants being required to furnish quantities of supplies, horses or waggons—and sometimes a labour force as well—against payment (or more often the vague promise of it). Such manoeuvrings were particularly common towards the end of a campaign, as each side sought to occupy the most favourable areas for winter quarters, but they might occupy a complete campaign in this way. As Defoe remarked, 'Now it is frequent to have armies of 50,000

* See p. 32 above.

men of a side standing at bay within sight of one another, and spend a whole campaign in dodging—or, as it is genteely termed—observing one another, and then march off into winter quarters.'[21]

Second, armies manœuvred in connection with siege operations—either to cover the troops in the trenches or in attempts to interfere with their work and relieve the beleagured garrisons (see below). Thirdly—and less frequently in this period—armies moved to court or to force a major engagement on their opponent. But as the Earl of Orrery had been moved to observe in 1677, 'we make war more like Foxes than Lyons (sic) and you have twenty sieges for one battel,'[22] and the trend was even more observable at the close of the century.

Sieges were undertaken for a number of reasons. First the capture or recovery of a major town was a measurable achievement, carrying with it control over the neighbouring hamlets and countryside, and might provide a useful pawn in peace negotiations. Secondly, many governments believed them to be less expensive in human life—often erroneously,* for insanitary trenches and the hot European summers caused many casualties. Thirdly, sieges had become so formalised and predictable that less-inspired commanders welcomed the excuse to indulge in static warfare. Finally, the Cockpit and its adjacent areas contained so many fortresses that no general—not even Marlborough or Eugene—could ignore or byepass them. The safety of every army's lines of communication was of paramount concern for logistical reasons, and the risk of raiding parties from enemy garrisons interfering with supply or munition convoys could not be lightly entertained.†

Over the preceding generation the science of defensive engineering had made great progress compared to the relative stagnation of the artillery arm. As a consequence, properly fortified towns could rarely be taken by a *coup de main* unless treachery or demoralisation had paved the way, and besiegers had to resort to lengthy and elaborate procedures to achieve success. The great French engineer, Sebastien le Prestre, Seigneur de Vauban (1633–1707), working from earlier models, had virtually imposed a series of standards on both defence and attack.[23] 'A town invested by Vauban is a town taken,' ran a contemporary adage; 'a town defended by Vauban is a town held.' His defences centred around a bastion trace,‡ each bastion providing a gun platform. In the simplest of terms, his concepts were four: to suit the defences to the configuration of the ground; to design defences that would offer the smallest target to the enemy and yet produce a deadly output of enfilade fire (both musketry and cannon) to sweep all approaches; to organise these defences in depth; and finally, to make provision for the conduct of an active defence by the garrison. The defending commander was

* See p. 237 above.
† But see below p. 226 for one attempt by Marlborough to solve this problem.
‡ Towards the end of his career Vauban preferred '*tours bastionées*'—his 'third order' of military architecture.

enjoined to make sorties against the enemy's works to cause maximum damage, to dig mines beneath his trenches and battery positions, and to use every wile to delay the development of the siege and thus increase the prospect of relief. Vauban also established the convention that a defender was entitled to 'beat the *chamade*' and negotiate for the best available terms after withstanding 48 days of formal siege, or when the enemy had overcome the outworks and created a 'practicable' breach in the main *enceinte*. Expensive stormings and associated atrocities of rape, arson and uncontrolled looting, were discouraged. Vauban preferred the shovel to the sword as the main determinant in a siege's outcome, but Louis XIV was insistent that his garrison commanders should also repel at least one major assault before treating.

Vauban also improved and regularised the forms of attack, and in his long career personally conducted no less than 53 sieges. His most original concept was to base the attack on a succession of parallel trenches, linked by indirect approaches, which crept forward to the very edge of the *glacis* or the ditch. Thereafter mine galleries were driven beneath the foe's bastions and breaching batteries of heavy siege guns established on the glacis, both measures being designed to create a breach in the bastion trace beyond.

The sequence of a major siege was as follows. After the target had been selected, 'an affair of cabinets' in Vauban's opinion, several months were often taken up in making preparations—collecting timber, tools, munitions, horses, transport and the myriad other items required. Then the army marched on its objective, and as it drew within range it would often split into two parts; one detachment continuing towards the town, the other drawing apart to serve as a covering force in the hope of obviating the possibility of a relief force fighting its way through to the garrison.

Once the besieging detachment was close to the town, cavalry were sent off to close all roads. The town was now blockaded, and it was the custom to summon the defender to surrender with no more ado—but it was equally expected for him to return a courteous but defiant reply. The besieger next set about creating lines of contra- and circumvallation around the town (see diagram) out of cannon range, employing large numbers of pressed local peasantry or an imported workforce for the task. These lines were intended to complete the physical isolation of the foe and to create a safe camp area for the besiegers and their stores, secure from sudden attack from both within and without. Vauban's timetable[24] allowed nine days as an average period for this, but it was often longer. Once completed, a town was deemed to be properly invested.

In the meantime the attacking commander would have conducted careful surveys of his target, and decided upon the best sectors for the mounting of 'attacks'. It was the practice to begin several to keep the defender guessing for as long as possible. Now the time had come for the third important moment in the siege— 'the opening of the trenches', or construction of the third parallel some 600 yards

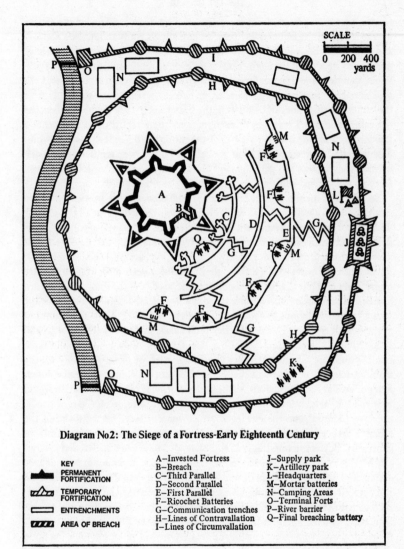

Diagram No 2: The Siege of a Fortress–Early Eighteenth Century

KEY

PERMANENT
FORTIFICATION

TEMPORARY
FORTIFICATION

ENTRENCHMENTS

AREA OF BREACH

A–Invested Fortress
B–Breach
C–Third Parallel
D–Second Parallel
E–First Parallel
F–Ricochet Batteries
G–Communication trenches
H–Lines of Contravallation
I–Lines of Circumvallation

J–Supply park
K–Artillery park
L–Headquarters
M–Mortar batteries
N–Camping Areas
O–Terminal Forts
P–River barrier
Q–Final breaching battery

(maximum cannon range) from the defences. This done, it provided the station for the 'guard of the trenches'—a force of foot always ready to repulse a sortie—and formed the basis for further activity. Next, parties of pioneers and peasants, under the direction of the engineers, would commence to sap forward using gabbions, mantlets and fascines* to drive a zig-zag approach trench towards the designated site for the second parallel, or lateral, trench, some 400 yards from the target. By this time, all being well, the heavy siege train would have reached the camp, and small batteries of cannon would be established to commence a ricochet bombardment with a view to dismounting the defender's cannon, whilst howitzers and mortars began to drop shells or bombs over the defences to discourage the gunners and garrison, and also to terrorise the townsfolk. At Venlo, in 1702, this proved sufficient to bring about a capitulation.[25]

So matters proceeded until the second, and then a third parallel had been established and garrisoned. Vauban laid down nine more days for all this digging under favourable conditions, but rock outcrops or rain could obviously cause delays—and enemy sorties were to be expected at this time. Ten days were next allowed for the capture of the enemy's 'covered way' and of a '*demi-lune*' in the ditch. Then the heavy guns (six or eight in number) were brought right forward under cover of night to a prepared position on the edge of the ditch. This opened a ceaseless bombardment at a range of 200 yards or less, designed to crumble the facing bastion-wall, foot by foot, causing a slope of falling rubble to accumulate at the base of the ditch. Mining parties would also be hard at work underground conducting their perilous calling. Four to eight days might be devoted to these tasks. Two more saw the attackers in possession of, or close proximity to, the main breach, and at this point the foe would again be summoned to surrender. After a few days of negotiation, in the vast majority of cases a convention would be signed, by which the defender agreed to submit in return for agreed conditions—withdrawal into the citadel in return for surrendering the town, or the right to free evacuation for instance. Terms granted varied enormously in generosity, but as the war dragged on they tended to become stiffer, and eventually Marlborough would be satisfied with nothing but surrender of both officers and men to become prisoners of war.† On the agreed date the gates would open and the erstwhile defenders would march out to pile arms and accept their fate.

Of course many complications were often encountered before this outcome was reached. The covering force might have had to counter a whole series of enemy thrusts and diversions from outside the area.‡ Convoys of supplies moving up to the siege lines might be ambushed and captured, or attempts be made to force supplies or gunpowder through the lines to the garrison beyond. Sieges were rarely straightforward. On the other hand the vast majority ultimately ended in

* Hollow baskets filled with earth, timber shields, bundles of branches.
† See p. 297.
‡ See pp. 297 and 333.

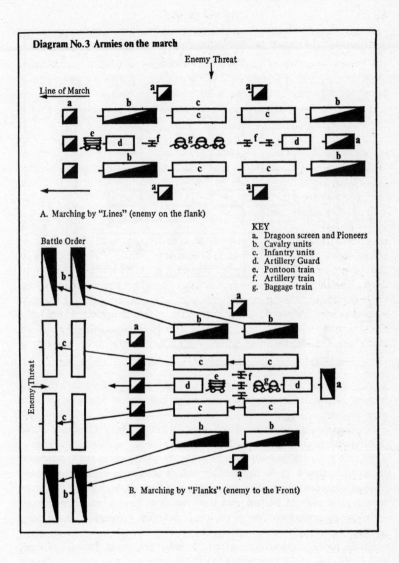

Diagram No.3 Armies on the march

Enemy Threat

Line of March

A. Marching by "Lines" (enemy on the flank)

Battle Order

KEY
a. Dragoon screen and Pioneers
b. Cavalry units
c. Infantry units
d. Artillery Guard
e. Pontoon train
f. Artillery train
g. Baggage train

Enemy Threat

B. Marching by "Flanks" (enemy to the Front)

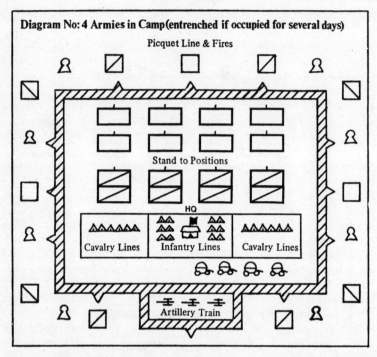

Diagram No: 4 Armies in Camp (entrenched if occupied for several days)

Picquet Line & Fires

Stand to Positions

HQ

Cavalry Lines   Infantry Lines   Cavalry Lines

Artillery Train

success for the attacker, other things being equal, for in the long term the odds were on his side, relieving armies often being unwilling to fight a major battle over the issue.

Sieges were as a rule extremely expensive in terms of both material and time. Their length varied enormously: Marlborough's longest was the 122 day siege of Lüttich in 1702; his shortest, that of Cork in 1691—all over in 128 hours. Many however, fit into a 40–60 day bracket, which accords in general terms with Vauban's standard. Casualties, too, could be severe on both sides, but active commanders most of all lamented the amount of time taken up with these elaborate operations. A few sieges could take up a complete campaigning season.

Lastly, we must examine the nature of land engagements. In size and scope these obviously varied enormously from skirmishes involving a few dozen men apiece, and actions undertaken by hundreds, to major battles involving tens of thousands.

Troops advanced to close contact in a number of columns; Marlborough and Eugene marched on the Nebel with nine during the early morning of 13 August 1704. The rival armies then deployed into battle order, some 600 yards apart.

An army habitually formed two main lines of battle, each comprising a left and a right wing, leaving an interval of between 300 and 600 yards. There was a growing practice of forming a third, shorter, line of reserves—often dragoons or light cavalry. As the brigades of horse and foot moved to their appointed stations and the guns were heaved into place, the general officers rode to their command posts. These were determined in accordance with strict seniority, the post of honour (the right wing of the first line) being the perquisite of the senior lieutenant-general present, the left of the second line being reserved for the most junior.

The actual formations adopted varied in detail according to the configuration of the ground, the tactical plan and certain national preferences. The French tended to favour massing cavalry on the flanks with infantry in the centre—a conventional distribution. Marlborough usually (as at Blenheim and Malplaquet) held much of his horse in central reserve ready for the *coup de grâce*, supporting his flanks with smaller mounted detachments. Imperial commanders often alternated cavalry and infantry brigades down both battle-lines, and when fighting the Turkish hordes, enclosed the whole within barricades of *chevaux de frise*. These were tendencies rather than hard and fast rules—at Malplaquet, for example, Marshal Villars, like the Allies, massed his cavalry to the rear. Contemporaries placed great significance on this formal ordering of the lines. 'Battles are won not by numbers,' observed Turpin de Crissé, 'but by the manner of forming your troops together and their order and discipline.'[26]

Such preparations could be very time-consuming—the Allies needed nine hours before Blenheim and a leisurely 20 before Malplaquet (to include the initial bombardment)—and this might mean that the opponent, if he wished to avoid action, was on occasion afforded sufficient time to break contact and march off to some impregnable position. The Duke, however, was skilled at getting so close to his enemy before revealing his presence or intention (by use of night marches and other forms of deception) that the foe had no option but to accept action. On one occasion in 1708, however, Marshal Vendôme fooled the Allies by leaving colours displayed in hedges and bushes whilst the French beat a hasty retreat.

Once the (Sergeant)-Major-Generals were satisfied with the alignments, the battle would open. The great guns spoke, the cavalry wheeled, the infantry battalions, in their strict linear formations, prepared to advance or stand firm. Advance into action was a leisurely affair, frequent halts being ordered to check the alignments after the negotiation of obstacles, the least of which could throw a battalion into great disorder. If streams or marshy ground were to be encountered, dragoons would ride ahead of the lines bearing fascines of brushwood or trusses of straw, throwing them down to form rough causeways.

The format of major battles was reasonably stereotyped. They were essentially attritional in nature, each side pounding relentlessly away on a number of sectors until they gained an advantage. It was rare—but not unknown—for the complete

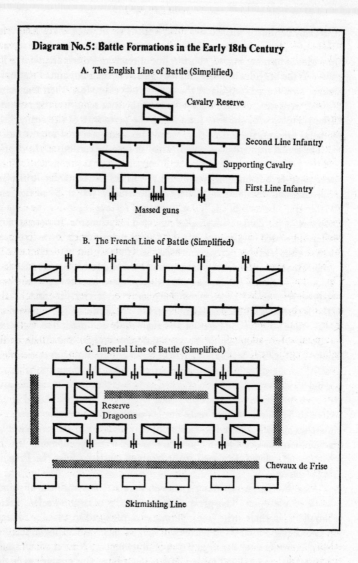

Diagram No.5: Battle Formations in the Early 18th Century

A. The English Line of Battle (Simplified)

Cavalry Reserve

Second Line Infantry

Supporting Cavalry

First Line Infantry

Massed guns

B. The French Line of Battle (Simplified)

C. Imperial Line of Battle (Simplified)

Reserve Dragoons

Chevaux de Frise

Skirmishing Line

battle-line to be in action at once; this was the case during the afternoon engagements at Blenheim. As far as grand tactics were concerned, the French generally tried to turn one or both flanks of their opponent's line with their wings of cavalry. Marlborough preferred to pin down the enemy's flanks with his initial attacks, draw in and neutralise the foe's reserves by the ferocity of these secondary onslaughts, and then mass a superior force in the centre (mostly cavalry, but with a number of battalions in support) for a large-scale breakthrough. Although Oudenarde was an exception to the general scheme, this was the basic grand tactical pattern at Blenheim, Ramillies and Malplaquet. It is noteworthy that by 1709 the French were aware of what the Duke and Eugene might attempt; they were becoming a trifle predictable, and this in part accounts for Villars' ability to hold the superior Allied army to only a technical victory. It is also of interest that in this war, whether in Flanders, near the Danube or in Spain, the Allies invariably seized the initiative and inaugurated the attacks against basically passive opponents. A century later these roles would largely be reversed during the long Napoleonic wars—the French usually making the initial attacks.[27]

Victories were rarely as clear-cut as Marlborough's great trio of successes. The pounding-match continued until one side or the other deemed the game not worth the candle, and conceded the honours of the day. The victor was often far too exhausted from his exertions—as at Malplaquet—to be able either to force a continuation of the action or to inaugurate a pursuit. The fact that west European armies adopted different formations for marching and fighting further militated against effective exploitation of success: it took too long to reorder their confused formations. Marlborough's relentless pursuit after Ramillies, which resulted in the capture of over half the Spanish Netherlands, was unique at this time; the Allies were in no position to mount similar pursuits à l'outrance after their other victories, least of all after Malplaquet. In most instances, therefore, the victor remained satisfied with the physical possession of the battlefield, and spent some time reordering his army, caring for the wounded, and (in the case of the French) singing a Te Deum, before resuming active operations.

Battlefield success therefore went to the side capable of standing the strain of combat longest; victory was a composite achievement made up of a large number of small, local successes at brigade or even regimental level. In such circumstances, given the general similarity in weapons, equipment and organisation, two factors were of paramount importance: the respective degree of martial talent displayed by the rival commanders-in-chief, still very much in personal charge of the battle; and details of tactical doctrine and employment which alone differentiated the opposing formations.*

* Even uniforms were not sufficiently distinctive. The wear and tear of campaign often caused the badly-fixed colours to run or fade, and much use was made by the Allies of green branches or bundles of straw worn in the hat for recognition. The French similarly used white rosettes.

Diagram No:6 Infantry & Cavalry Tactics Early Eighteenth Century

KEY

☐ Platoons of the "First Firing" (three ranks deep)

■ Platoons of the "Second Firing"

▨ Platoons of the "Third Firing"

⚓ 1½ Pdr field pieces

z Numbers relate to order of Platoon discharge within the "Firings"

A. 17th Century Pike/Matchlock Combination

Musketeers   Pikemen   Musketeers

☐   ☐   ☐

Grenadiers form 4 detachments to guard corners

B. Formation of Square by Divisions

I   II   III

C. Fire by Platoons organised into the "Three Firings"

Grenadiers	I Div.					III Div.				Colonel		IV Div.					II Div.				Grenadiers
z 15	1	7	3	11	5	9	13	17	18		14	10	6	12	4	8	2	16 z

60 Paces

D. French Battalion firing by Company Volley or Battalion Lines one rank at a time (five ranks deep)

Support Sqn.   First Sqn.

200 paces

E. English Two Squadron Charge (cold steel) 2 ranks deep 3 troops to a squadron

Half-troops retiring to reload

50 paces

F. French Cavalry Fire-action (pistols) —prior to mêlée (swords)

Underlying all Marlborough's successes in the field were certain fundamental tactical advantages. The French and Spaniards, with half a century of success behind them, proved less capable or willing to adjust their methods to make the most of the improved firepower of the infantry arm. The Allies—properly inspired by their leader—proved more adaptable to new concepts of fighting.

In the case of *l'arme blanche*, the French tended to regard their cavalry as an instrument of mobile firepower rather than as one of shock action. Their *compagnies* were trained to ride forward at the trot, troop behind troop, to rein in some 30 paces from their opponents in order to discharge their pistols or carbines. This done, the formation broke and rode to the rear to reload whilst the second troop advanced to repeat the operation. Such elaborate drills looked superb on the paradeground, but were impractical in battle unless the opponent operated along similar lines. The French used the sword for the *mêlée*; once the fire-cycle was complete, their troopers would spur forward, fling their pistols at their opponents heads, and close for a series of individual combats.

This was not the practice of Marlborough's troopers. He was insistent that shock must be the order of the day for his cavalry, and to this end '. . . would allow the Horse but three charges of powder and ball to each man for a campaign, and that only for guarding their horses at grass, and not to be made use of in action.'[28] Twin squadron charges, the troopers riding knee by knee in two pairs of ranks, one and all wielding cold steel, was the sole approved mode of mounted action. Such 'charges', however, were only delivered at a fast trot at this period (save in Sweden) for fear of disordering the formation's alignment if a gallop was authorised. This notwithstanding, English and Dutch cavalry usually won the honours of engagements against their less mobile opponents—Palmes' success over the *Gendarmerie* at Blenheim being a fitting example.* Massed cavalry, indeed, were used by Marlborough to complete three of his four victories.

The infantry were expected to play an important role in the Duke's cavalry attacks: from first to last he was the proponent of combined action, whether offensive or defensive. Thus at Blenheim the solid support provided by the 27 battalions of foot in the centre, moving up close behind the horse, enabled the Allied cavalry to reform after their initial repulse. Similarly at Malplaquet, General Orkney's eleven battalions proved of vital assistance to the massed formations of Allied horse. So fierce were the French counterattacks that 'I really believe, had not ye foot been here, that the enemy would have driven our Horse from the field.'[29] Such cooperation was far from coincidental.

The French similarly clung to outdated concepts where the employment of infantry was concerned. In days of pike and matchlock, battalions had formed islands of resistance on the battlefield and were rarely used with much flexibility or imagination in any but basically defensive roles. Despite the changeover to superior weapons by 1703 already noted, the French still formed up four to five

* See p. 146 below.

lines deep, each man in a file immediately behind his neighbour, which meant
that only the front three ranks at the most could fire at any one time, the front
rank kneeling, the second crouching, the third standing upright. This predeliction for line, company and even battalion volleys made effective control and
accurate fire hard to achieve and maintain which meant that much firepower was
wasted.

The British and the Dutch, on the other hand, employed far more developed
infantry tactics designed to produce the maximum output of effective fire from
the linear formations. The practice of drawing up only three ranks deep gave a
battalion a broader overall frontage, and that of 'staggering' the men in each file to
enable each to fire unhindered by his colleagues was another minor, but cumulat-
ively important modification. The real secret of success, however, lay in the
adoption and development of the platoon firing system (see diagram, p. 90). By
this, after the battalion had formed up, the line was sub-divided into 18 equal
platoons of 30–40 men, half the *élite* grenadier company taking post at each extremity of the line. The platoons were then told off into 'firings' of six platoons
apiece, not contiguous groups, but scattered proportionately down the line.
Sometimes the fire of the entire front rank would also be reserved as a fourth
'firing'. The colonel (or his deputy) and his pair of drummers took post to the
fore of the centre, the second in-command and the colour party drew up to the
rear, whilst the major and adjutant hovered on horseback on the extreme flanks,
ordering the lines. A subaltern and a sergeant were told off to supervise each
platoon, any spare officers taking up positions in the rear of the battalion line.

After advancing towards the enemy, the battalion would halt at 60 yards
range. On the order 'First Firing, take care!' the platoons of the first six platoons
would prepare to discharge, giving fire either together or in a patterned sequence.
Next, as these platoons opened order to reload, the platoons of the second firing
would come to the present and fire in turn. The remainder, which included the
grenadiers, then gave the third fire. By this time (approximately 30 seconds), the
first sub-units would have finished reloading and would be ready to fire a second
time, and the whole process would be repeated. A second form of this manœuvre
—firing by groups during a continuing advance—was well exemplified during
the battle of Malplaquet.* As Captain Robert Parker described it, 'this is

---

* '. . . When the army advanced to attack the enemy, we also advanced into that part of
the wood, which was in our front. We continued marching slowly on, til we came to an
open in the wood. It was a small plain, on the opposite side of which we perceived
a battalion of the enemy drawn up, a skirt of the wood being in the rear of them. Upon
this Colonel Kane, who was then at the head of the Regiment, having drawn us up, and
formed our platoons, advanced gently towards them, with the six platoons of our first
fire made ready. When we had advanced within a hundred paces of them, they gave us
the fire of one of their ranks: whereupon we halted, and returned them the fire of our six
platoons at once; and immediately made ready the six platoons of our second fire, and

undoubtedly the best method that has yet been discovered for fighting a battalion.'[30] The advantages it conferred were threefold: first, the enemy was exposed to continuous fire against every part of his line—he was afforded no respite whilst the hostile battalion reloaded, but was psychologically under continuous pressure; second, the system called for precise control by the subordinate officers and sergeants who could thus influence the general effectiveness and accuracy of their platoons; and thirdly, at any time one third of a battalion would be reloaded and capable of dealing with an unexpected development.

This system, originating from Swedish practice under Gustavus Adolphus, had grown up in the English and Republican forces over the years from 1688. Marlborough did not institute it, but he insisted on frequent drills and practices with live ammunition, both in season and out, and thus helped create the most devastating infantry in Europe. Two or three minutes of the kind of pressure described above was enough to shake the morale and cohesion of most opponents, and when followed by a cheering bayonet-charge, it usually proved decisive at unit level. Here lay one secret of the Duke's success on the battlefield.

Tactically, the artillery were grouped in batteries of six or eight pieces. There was little to distinguish the hostile batteries one from another, but it is notable that Marlborough and Villars took unusual care (for the time) in siting their guns. The English also specialised in moving guns forward to new positions after the opening of the engagement—a rare development. Of great tactical importance was the Allied practice of adding two light, one-and-a-half or three-pounder guns to each battalion for close fire support. Discharging bursts of grapeshot or 'partridge' at the enemy from close range, these pieces substantially aided the winning of the battalion firefights which as we have seen made up the core of a major engagement.

After describing some aspects of the organisation and handling of armies, let us now turn to see Marlborough and his Allies putting them to use.

---

advanced upon them again. They then gave us the fire of another rank, and we returned them a second fire, which made them shrink; however, they gave us the fire of a third rank after a scattering manner, and then retired into the wood in great disorder: on which we sent our third fire after them, and saw them no more. We advanced cautiously up to the ground which they had quitted, and found several of them killed and wounded; among the latter was one Lieutenant O'Sullivan, who told us the battalion we had engaged was the Royal Regiment of Ireland. Here, therefore, there was a fair trial of skill between the two Royal Regiments of Ireland, one in the British, the other in the French service; for we met each other upon equal terms, and there was none else to interpose. We had but four men killed and six wounded: and found near forty of them on the spot killed and wounded.' (*Parker* (1968 edition) p. 88-9).

Clearing the River Lines, 1702-1703

'The Duke led to the field the Army of the Allies. He took with surprising rapidity Venlo, Ruremonde, Stevenswaert, Liege. He extended and secured the frontiers of the Dutch. The enemies, whom he found insulting at the gates of Nimweghen were driven back to seek for shelter behind their lines. He forced Bonne, Huy, Limbourg in another campaign. He opened the communication of the Rhine, as well as the Maes. He added all the country between these rivers to his former conquests. . . .'

From the inscription on the Column of Victory,
Blenheim Palace (continued).

By the end of March 1702, Marlborough was ready to cross the Channel to tackle a veritable multitude of daunting problems affecting the none-too-strong Grand Alliance. He visited the Hague for a ten days mission to settle matters with Heinsius and Goes (the Imperial ambassador) and to rally the States-General. With great pertinacity he tried to persuade the Dutch to appoint Prince George of Denmark 'the Generalissimo' of all their forces in the interest of unity of direction, but this in fact was never to be. Nor, as we shall see a little later, would Marlborough ever hold any official position of supremacy over the Dutch armies except under special circumstances. Instead they appointed the old Prince of Nassau-Saarbrücken as temporary Field Marshal. Thus the problems of coalition warfare, which William III had handled so adeptly on the whole, soon began to plague his military successor with a vengeance. However, he was able to rally Dutch confidence in the serious intent of the new English monarch and government to prosecute William's plans to the letter, and in return he allowed the supreme command issue to be shelved, and agreed to Dutch plans to invest Kaiserswerth on the Rhine. Even more important, he induced Goes to accept the *praetensus* eighth clause (conceded on 4 April) and induced all the signatories to settle a firm date for a joint declaration of hostilties.

Although war had still to be formally declared (the Allied Manifesto, signed by England, the United Provinces and Austria would only be made public on 15 May)* and Louis XIV would make the most of the propaganda opportunity to represent himself as the aggrieved party, there was no disguising the extent of French preparations over the winter months. Royal orders were issued raising 100 new regiments; 17 senior officers were promoted Lieutenant-Generals, 49 more became Major-Generals, and no less than 81 received brevets as Brigadier-Generals. Apart from in North Italy, where a second campaign was about to open, the French began to mass forces on the Upper Rhine and in Flanders. In this last region two armies were designated, both under the overall command of another royal grandson, the Duke of Burgundy, newly appointed Vicar-General for the Low Countries. One, commanded by the veteran Marshal Boufflers, would comprise the French troops, and operate along the Lower Rhine; the other, under the Marquis de Bedmar, mainly Spanish troops, would link Boufflers with the Channel.

The situation facing the United Provinces strategically was as serious as anything since 1672. Not only did the loss of the Belgian fortresses pose a major frontal threat to the river barrier, but the accession of Liége and Cologne to the French cause implied a menacing outflanking danger from the south. Could the Dutch and their Allies successfully meet both threats? Fortunately for them, all available French resources were stretched to the utmost along the three main fronts, which made it impossible for Louis' generals to build up a complete superiority against the United Provinces. Furthermore, Dutch retention of Maastricht comprised a serious interruption of French communications on the Meuse river line.

The French monarch was determined to maintain the pretence of injured innocence for as long as possible. After the first brush with Imperial troops near Bonn on 7 April, Marshal Boufflers (who, in Burgundy's absence at Versailles, was *de facto* commander-in-chief) asked his master for definitive orders. 'The Emperor's interest . . . is being served by the Elector Palatine,' replied the monarch, 'who is seeking by all sorts of evil ways to start the war. You are in a condition to make him regret it.'[1] Boufflers was empowered to invade enemy soil when it became advisable, and was authorised to retain 11 battalions earmarked for the German front until 1 June as a ruse. At this time Boufflers could dispose of some 115 battalions and 73 squadrons in all, divided between three commanders; Bedmar was holding the sector from Namur to the Channel, General T'Serclaes commanded on the Meuse, whilst Count Tallard, the erstwhile ambassador to London, held the Cologne area. Additionally, there were strong garrisons in Antwerp, Bonn and Liége, and detachments in Guelderland and Ruremonde.

* The aims of the Alliance as given in this declaration made no mention of removing Philip V from the Spanish throne, but stressed the need for Dutch and German security, compensation for the Emperor in Italy, and trade concessions for the Maritime Powers.

Facing them, in mid-April, were an array of Allied generals of varying capability. The largest force was that of the Prince of Nassau-Saarbrücken, (22,000), about to march off to besiege Kaiserswerth on the Rhine (from 18 April) in the hope of strengthening the lamentably weak Dutch defences leading towards Nimwegen, the 'gateway to Holland'. Godert de Ginkel, Earl of Athlone, held 18,000 men (including most of the British forces) in a camp being established at Rosendal. The Comte de Tilly had 16,000 near Xanten; the aging General Menno van Coehoorn, expert-engineer, was at the head of 15,000 in Dutch Flanders near the coast. The remainder, except for 6,000 serving aboard the Dutch fleet, were split amongst garrisons, including no less than 17,000 at Maastricht. In all, this comprised on paper an Allied force of perhaps 150,000 men, although many mercenary or 'treaty' units had still to join their respective commanders and the state of readiness of most formations was lamentably behind schedule. Nor, of course, had Marlborough himself yet appeared in the field: diplomatic and political considerations were taking up all his time at London and the Hague.

Somewhat puzzled by the slight vagueness of Louis XIV's instructions, and still short of munitions and men (he could only muster 51 battalions and 100 squadrons for a field force out of a total army which now numbered 129 battalions and 133 squadrons at this juncture) and transport, Boufflers adopted a defensive posture for the time being. His original intent of advancing his field army to Ruremonde, whence it might operate towards Juliers or Cologne as circumstances might dictate, was at once put into operation on 18 April when he first learnt that General Blainville and 5 battalions had been blockaded in Kaiserswerth. 'All this,' he informed Versailles, 'makes it very important to advance into Gelders (Guelderland) and try to oppose this enterprise.'[2] By this time, instructions from Louis were on their way authorising the Marshal to take all necessary steps to foil Allied intentions. However, Boufflers was delayed somewhat by the late-arrival of the *Maison du Roi*, the élite force of the Bourbon monarchy.

Yet Boufflers was no ninny. Crossing the Meuse on the 21st, he occupied the camp at Ruremonde, and then pounced forward to frighten Tilly into abandoning the strong position of Xanten a week later. The discomfited commander fell back on Cleves, and was joined thereabouts by Athlone with 28 squadrons and 11 English battalions the next day, making a total strength of about 35,000 men. The French promptly camped around Xanten; the first move in chess-board warfare had gone in their favour, but they held an exposed position. A party of 700 reinforcements were sent off to Kaiserswerth and joined the garrison. On 3 May the Duke of Burgundy and his entourage joined the Xanten encampment.

Before they could contemplate further large-scale operations, the French needed to bring up a huge convoy of artillery, munitions and baggage from Brussels. The large garrison of Maastricht posed a possible danger to this manœuvre, and Boufflers was hard at work arranging security measures when a thunderclap was heard from the Channel. It transpired that Coehoorn had suddenly seized Middelburg, passed the Spanish lines, and was now in a position to threaten Bruges. This particularly alarmed Louis. 'I even feel that their moves must be the real, long-awaited Anglo-Dutch design: they besieged Kaiserswerth and advanced the Comte de Tilly to Xanten so as to oblige you to move all my forces towards the Rhine, whilst all the time they were preparing to launch their major effort near Ghent, Bruges and Ostend. This situation strikes me as being highly embarrassing. . . .'[3] In some alarm the King ordered Boufflers to readjust his dispositions so as to reinforce the shaky northernmost sector to 33 battalions and 29 squadrons (from 21 to 25 respectively). This order he had no resort but to obey.

How far Coehoorn's stroke was the result of a deep-laid plan and how far it was a fortuitous coup is still unknown, but there is no doubt that it regained the initiative for the Allies for a brief period. Bedmar thought of fighting the Dutch on the 13 May, but deemed them too well positioned, and next day Fort St. Donas fell to the Allies. However, during this time a secret enterprise to seize Namur by a *coup de main* failed when a disaffected officer betrayed the plan, and the 14 battalions and 17 squadrons sent on this service were diverted towards Huy, only again to be disappointed (10th) when T'Serclaes reinforced the garrison in the nick of time. Thus the Allied raids—they do not really deserve the appellation of an offensive—petered out.

This enabled Boufflers to redirect his resources to the task of bringing up the vital convoy. Leaving Brussels on 20 May, the long waggon-train reached Xanten safely six days later, to the great relief of the French high command, for all their personal baggage and comforts were with it. All this while the siege of Kaiserswerth dragged inconclusively on, but the garrison was running perilously short of ammunition. Boufflers therefore resumed his earlier plans to interfere in the siege. In early June he felt strong enough to summon 10 battalions and 20 squadrons from Bedmar and to mobilise Tallard's forces as well for a sudden concentration. This, he calculated, would enable him to launch 44 battalions and 104 squadrons against a drowsy Athlone (40 battalions and 60 squadrons), presently comfortably encamped at Cranensburg near Cleves. As reconnaissances revealed that the position was strong, Boufflers set himself to outflank Athlone and if possible surround him after he had abandoned Cleves. This was all timed so as to forestall any possible transfer of Allied troops from before Kaiserswerth, should that town fall.

Early on 10 June the French forces set out in a number of columns, and began to converge on the camp. Only at 6 p.m. did Athlone become aware of the trap closing about him; two hours later every Allied soldier was on the road, abandoning much equipment, as Athlone began a desperate race to reach the safety of the walls of Nimwegen. Robert Parker took part in these anxious hours: 'Many of us had sent our horses to Nimwegen for forage, and for the want of them were

obliged to leave our tents and baggage behind us. . . . By daylight the enemy's
horse began to appear on both sides of us. This made us mend our pace . . .
(but) . . . at length we arrived safe within the outworks of Nimwegen.'[4]

The upshot was a narrow escape for the forces under Athlone's command.
After a brief engagement along the glacis of Nimwegen, the Earl conducted a
further withdrawal beyond the city, covered by its guns. The cost of this *débâcle*
(which might have been worse) was 1,000 Allied killed, wounded and captured,
besides the loss of 400 artillery horses and 1,500 more belonging to the food
convoys, besides many head of cattle and tons of supplies both *de guerre* and *de
bouche*. For their part, the French lost only 50 killed and 80 wounded. The Duke
of Burgundy was much commended for his good behaviour at this, his first
major action.

Following this incomplete success, Burgundy and Boufflers moved off to
Cleves, and placed the area under contribution. There, on the 14 June, he
received a convoy of provisions from Venlo which made it feasible to consider
further action; news also arrived that on the 11th part of Bedmar's forces had
successfully recovered Middelburg from the Dutch, and that Coehoorn, greatly
outnumbered, had been forced to fall back whence he had come. These good
tidings freed Burgundy's hands to revert to the old plan to succour Kaiserswerth.
As a preliminary, Tallard was sent off with a corps to Rheinberg, but this effort
was too late. On 15 June, after a stalwart defence, de Blainville agreed to surrender the town in 48 hours. In return he received the full honours of war, he and
his garrison being permitted to march out to Venlo. Thus, Allied failure on the
northern flank was balanced by a real, if long-delayed success on the Rhine.

The display of Allied ineptitude before Nimwegen made it clear that it was
high time their affairs were taken in hand by a competent commander. Many
Hanoverian and Danish detachments, forthcoming by the recent treaties, were
still absent from their places of duty, and it would not be until July that all were
present and ready for action. Moreover there were already distressing signs of
English indiscipline of the sort that had marked the start of the previous war.
On the 8 May, Marlborough wrote (most severely for him) to Heinsius concerning an undisclosed incident: 'I am extremely concerned that the English have
behaved themselves so ill: I have not yet heard from Brigadier Ingoldsby who
commanded them, but you may be assured that all imaginable care shall be
taken to prevent the like for the ᶜ·ᵗture as well also all the reparation that can be
desired for this insolence committed.'[5] Perhaps we may hazard that the old
temptations of bottle and wenches had proved too much for the newly-recruited
soldiery, abroad for the first time in their lives and homesick into the bargain.

This was a fitting moment for both sides to reconsider their strategy. Arriving
once more at the Hague in early June, Marlborough first had to settle two
outstanding matters. As the Dutch absolutely refused to appoint the Prince of
Denmark as their *generalissimo* (probably not to Marlborough's secret displeasure),

the command question needed urgent attention. The Regents of the United Provinces had no desire to saddle themselves with an overlord—since William's death there had been a notable recrudescence of strong republican feeling in many areas. On the other hand, for the sake of efficient command function, some arrangement would have to be worked out. Few championed the questionable claim of the ambitious King of Prussia that he deserved the senior overall command; most preferred Marlborough, who was well known and even better liked as a diplomat although still very much an unknown quantity as a soldier. In the end, in early July, it was decided that on those occasions when Dutch and German troops served alongside English forces in the same army, the joint-command should be vested in the Earl, but at no other time. There was no question of appointing Marlborough their Deputy-Captain-General, as many historians claim was the case; his position remained obscure and unofficial as regards legal status throughout the war, and the fact that in 1712, upon his fall, there was no need to remove him formally from authority over Dutch forces, would seem to strengthen this assertion.[6] Under all other circumstances, there-fore, except those cited above, Dutch troops were answerable only to Dutch generals. Marlborough's moral predominance, however, would give him im-mense influence at all times, but it is important to grasp his status to explain those occasions when he failed to gain his way with the United Provinces. Further-more, the States General insisted that the Earl should be accompanied by five Field Deputies, veritable political commissars, who were empowered to exercise a veto over proposed operations insofar as they involved Dutch troops.

The second matter was even more contentious. To the great annoyance of their English and German allies, there were positive indications that the Dutch were continuing to trade with France and Spain, pursuant to their century-old status as the 'carriers of Europe', and that Amsterdam was still sending remit-tances to France by bills of exchange. The English government therefore charged Marlborough to remonstrate strongly against this practice. 'If it be possible I should be glad to have an answer to my memorial for the forbidding (of) the commerce by letters . . .' he wrote to Heinsius on 29 June.[7] The Dutch, however, proved elusive, and the matter would continue to add a strain to Allied relations.

He also faced difficulties when strategy was discussed. Avid to seize the initiative without delay, Marlborough championed a major attack into Brabant, but the more cautious Dutch favoured safer operations along Rhine and Meuse. This rankled a great deal. Had his concept been adopted, the French '. . . must then have had the disadvantage of governing themselves by our motions, whereas we are now obliged to mind them.'[8] Once he had joined the Allied army in camp near Duckenburgh (early July), matters still being unresolved, he was still more impatient at the inactivity this forced upon him as week followed week in useless correspondence. Aware of the inherent weakness of the current French position near Cleves, Marlborough pleaded for a three-part offensive to capitalise the situation. If strong demonstrations could be mounted from Graves and Nimwegen to distract the foe, it might be possible to advance the main army along the left bank of the Meuse and thereby sever the French communications with their bases providing, thirdly, that a substantial force could also be found for the Lower Rhine sector so as to contain the French right. Any other course of action would rule out the chance of battle which Marlborough, untypical of his day, was already obviously keen to force, or 'it will not (otherwise) be in our power to engage the French army or to oblige them to repass the Meuse . . . I beg the favour of a speedy resolution for nothing is so bad as to stay here.' But four days later (9 July) he was still remonstrating that 'if this humour can't be overcome, we shall never do anything considerable.'[9] But still the Dutch experts temporised.

Louis XIV and Boufflers proved more decisive, as was typical of the highly centralised (if often misguided and mistaken) French higher command system. Writing on the 18th, Louis XIV instructed Boufflers to retain Tallard on the Rhine and send him towards Bonn so as to mount a distraction towards the United Provinces whilst Burgundy and the main army moved off to besiege Julich (or Juliers) on the Roer as a preliminary to an eventual onslaught against Maastricht. A force of 55 battalions and 104 squadrons should, Louis XIV considered, suffice for the task. Boufflers, in his reply dated 22 June, was not so confident about the plan's feasibility. 'It is not without difficulty,' he asserted, on account of the lack of canals or waterways in the target's vicinity, the need to support Tallard's detached corps if it encountered trouble, and general problems of supply in the area.[10] Nevertheless, the Marshal began to collect material and artillery, and hoped to be able to start on the new venture by 10 July.

Events on the Rhine, however, caused the abrupt cancellation of this offensive plan. 'Landau is besieged,' wrote the King obviously in some perturbation, on the 20th, revealing that the Margrave Louis of Baden and an Imperial army of 25,000 had blockaded the town on 16 June. 'The feebleness of (Catinat's) army has always worried me; this increases daily as Baden's army grows. . . . You know the importance of this place which equally guards the entry to Alsace and the approaches to the Saar. . . .'[11] In sum, Boufflers was forthwith to detach 12 battalions and 16 squadrons from Tallard and T'Serclaes to form a special force. 'You will still be able to conduct a glorious campaign,' the monarch hopefully concluded. Boufflers again indicated his compliance, and resumed the defensive.

There were already signs that the Allies were at last on the move; the Prince of Nassau-Saarbrücken had reinforced Athlone and the Breda garrison had also taken the field, and together they crossed the River Waal on 6 July and headed for Graves. For the time the French remained watchful but inactive, save for preparing and sending off the Landau detachment (which marched on the 15 July), and taking measures to ensure the safe arrival of a bread convoy from Malines (which arrived at Ruremonde on the 14th).

When Marlborough heard of the detachment from Cleves, he expressed himself forcibly in a further letter to Heinsius on 18 July. 'I am afraid M. Boufflers has made his detachment for the Upper Rhine, so that I beg there may be no time lost in sending all things necessary to Nimwegen, for should we remain long idle it would be scandalous.'[12] At length, on the 23rd, he could report that 'the Council of War has unanimously resolved to pass the Meuse.' At last, the main Allied campaign could open. Soon 60,000 men were in motion towards Graves as Marlborough manœuvred to draw Burgundy's main forces away from Cleves and Gelderland.

The Prince, meantime, had assimilated the 12 battalions of the former garrison of Kaiserswerth into his army (on double-rations as a mark of favour for their stout defence) and continued to watch Marlborough's moves with the greatest care. On 26 July the Allies passed the Meuse on three bridges of boats and proceeded south towards Lille St. Hubert via Eindhoven. Burgundy, still unsure of the nature of the threat, moved back to Venlo the next day, and thence moved to Ruremonde (28th) where the French recrossed the Meuse. His further march towards Bray was delayed several hours by supply difficulties, but by this time the French high command was fully alarmed, so the day's march was pushed until 11 p.m. With only 53 battalions and 92 squadrons (including Tallard's force marching up from the Rhine after urgent recall), Burgundy was both overstretched and outnumbered, facing as he did an Allied army encamped at Lille St. Hubert and Little Breugel computed at fully 70 battalions and 150 squadrons. He had no option, however, but to press his march, and so at dawn on 2 August the French set out in three lines of battle,* massing their baggage in the centre.

Thus Marlborough, to quote Robert Parker, had forced the foe 'to quit their camp and dance after him'; now, on the 2nd, 'we were just between them and home and they had no way homeward but by marching over a heath which was within half a league of our camp.'[13]

It would seem that an ideal battle situation existed: the French were committed to a perilous march straight across the front of the stronger Allied army, which was drawn up and only awaiting the word. But the order never came. The Field Deputies on Marlborough's staff waited upon the Captain-General and expressed their unwillingness to see Dutch troops fight in an action, which, in their view, was rendered unnecessary as the foe was clearly in retreat. The Earl must have been sorely tempted to override these protests—and he had it in his power to do so. However, he was also cognisant of the need to gain the confidence of the Dutch in his judgement, and so, rather than cause an immediate crisis in Anglo-Dutch relations at the start of the first campaign, he chose to throw away the chance of a near-certain victory. Here we see the conflict between military and political priorities—an aspect of these ten campaigns which will all too often recur. As a soldier Marlborough was wrong to throw up the opportunity;

* See p. 85 above.

as a statesman, he chose the right course. 'This was very fortunate for us,' recorded the Duke of Berwick who was with Boufflers; 'for we were posted in such a manner that we should have been beaten without being able to stir. . . .'[14] What emotions raged beneath the Earl's calm exterior we can only imagine, but by way of a little revenge he had the Deputies accompany him forward to observe the passage of the French army, and 'upon this they all acknowledged that they had lost a fair opportunity of giving the enemy a fatal blow.'[15]

A chance for battle recurred the next day, but once again it was let slip for the same reason. A recent historian has suggested that Marlborough's intention was to 'harrass, not destroy' the enemy at this juncture, citing his letter to Godolphin on 30 July which states that 'we shall endeavour to make their march uneasy' in support.[16] This is to read too much into the phrase; on the 30th Marlborough still was some way from his objective at Hamont, and could still not know exactly how matters would develop. As to his intention to engage the enemy, we have already cited his letter to Heinsius of 9 July.

So the Allies lingered around Hamont and Peer preparing to besiege Venlo, whilst the French, relieved at their narrow escape, resorted to a period of complex chess-board manœuvring for a matter of several weeks, the full details of which cannot be given here. Suffice it to say that Marlborough was still seeking a new, favourable battle situation. When an Allied supply convoy hove in sight on the 16 August, Marlborough sent off General Opdam with 4,000 men to escort it to safety. This was, in Sir Winston's phrase a 'glittering bait' designed to lure the French into accepting action, but Boufflers realised the trap at the last moment and veered away. Marlborough continued to play his opponent southward, apparently retiring ahead of the French as they continued southwards. A good position on the Plain of Helchteren suddenly presented itself, and on 23 August the Allies were once again drawn up for battle. Once again—for the third time in a month—the opportunity was wasted. For two days there was desultory cannonading; the best chance of engaging the foe not fully deployed was late on the 23rd, but General Opdam failed to launch his attack against Boufflers' left, as ordered, and night intervened. Next day, with both sides fully arrayed, it was the Deputies who again stepped in. . . . 'We had all the advantage a tired, disorderly and inferior army could give to good troops,' wrote a Scots Fusilier, 'but the States were against fighting. . . .'[17] By dusk, the enemy had beat a successful retreat towards the Hechtel Defile. Two days later and he was safely at Deringen, and all was quiet once more.

So distressed was Marlborough with this puny Allied display that he forthwith sent a trumpeter under flag of truce to proffer his apologies to Boufflers and Berwick for failing to engage them. There were still traces of chivalrous conduct and gentlemanly manners amidst the dust and stink of war in the early eighteenth century, or so it would appear.

Cheated of the chance of a victory that 'we should have celebrated (upon)

St. Lewis's Day' (25 August) by his own confederates, there were still strategic gains to be acquired out of the precipitate retreat of the French. General Opdam was sent off to redeem his reputation by besieging Venlo on the Meuse, under the supervision of Nassau-Saarbrücken and the Dutch master-engineer, Coehoorn. The investment opened on the 29th, the Allies employing 34 battalions, 26 squadrons and 10,000 peasantry from Munster. Burgundy's reaction to the news was to plan a march on Werth, but his generals dissuaded him on the grounds of the good position the Allies were holding, the poverty of the already ravaged countryside, and the danger of running their heads a third time into a trap of Marlborough's making. Instead, Boufflers argued in favour of reinforcing Bedmar's attempt to capture Hulst on the Channel coast (an operation already ordered on the 24 August), hoping thereby to divert the Allies from Venlo on the inner flank. The King agreed, and six battalions and as many squadrons were sent off to the coast, but the concept was misconceived, for the defenders had easy access to reinforcement by water, and on 2 September the enterprise was abandoned, after 'M. de Vauban had recognised the thing to be impossible.'[18] As Boufflers accurately described it, the French in Flanders were feeling the severe effects of strategic consumption (he did not, however, employ the term), whilst the far superior Allied army was admirably placed in a central position from which it might undertake any number of offensive and hurtful operations. By its geographical location, the siege of Venlo spelt peril for Ruremonde and Stevenswaert, but Boufflers was also anxious for both Liége and Brabant. There are many signs that Boufflers had by this time lost his nerve; perhaps for that reason, the Duke of Burgundy set off for Versailles on 6 September, leaving the French army encamped at Berlingen.

The siege was pressed with all vigour, for Marlborough now had plans beyond Venlo itself. As early as 2 August he had described to Heinsius the opportunities the capture of Ruremonde would present – 'which will be of great use to (for) the winterquarters and a certainty of beginning the next campaign in the enemy's country.'[19] Now his strategic vision was ranging still farther afield, as we shall see in a short space.

Before Venlo, both the town and Fort St. Michel were under full-scale attack* by 12 September. A sudden assault on the former resulted in its capture (18th), many of the garrison being put to the sword, and by the 23rd 67 24-pdr. cannon and 140 mortars were pouring shot and shell into the town. M. de Varo, the Governor, capitulated on 25 September and was allowed to march out with his surviving garrison and head for Antwerp. Stevenswaert's turn was next; invested that same day, it fell on 2 October, M. de Castellas evacuating to Namur. A similar fate was meted out to Ruremonde. Already invested by cavalry on the 26 September, the Comte de Hornes offered a hopeless defence under a hail of fire from 60 24-pdrs,

---

* Hitherto operations had been restricted to a blockade.

50 large and 100 small (coehoorn) mortars. A practicable breach having been made in the main defences, he too, capitulated on 6 October, and marched away for Louvain. The sun was at last shining on Allied arms, and although some wet weather had been experienced in September which Marlborough declared 'has given me the spleen', the season was still possible for further operations. 'We have had a good deal of rain and the weather looks as if we shall have more; how-ever I think we can't miss of clearing the Meuse as also forcing Marshal Boufflers to abandon Toneres.'[20]

This optimism was not misplaced, for by this time Marshal Boufflers was even deeper in the strategic mire. His only concept for attempting to save Venlo and Ruremonde had been to mount yet another of his beloved 'diversionary attempts', this time by sending Tallard with 16 battalions, 25 squadrons and 12 guns to the Rhine sector, there to look to the defences of Bonn, besiege and take the Abbey of Sieberg, and (hopefully) put the wind up the Dutch in that quarter. The Count had marched by a devious route (designed to put the Allied sleuths off the scent) on 18 September, but in fact his operations were to prove strategically useless. Boufflers' only other contribution was to send off detach-ment after detachment to strengthen garrisons here, there and everywhere throughout Flanders, thus still further weakening his field army, which, by early October, had shrunk to little more than 25,000 men. As for the diversion, the Allies were so strong—with two armies in the field—that they could afford to observe Tallard's peregrinations with equanimity, and complete their current batch of sieges before sending a force of Hanoverians and Prussians to reinforce the southern region to a strength of 15 battalions and 25 squadrons.

Boufflers, out-generalled and out-numbered, was by now completely domin-ated by his opponent. After sending yet another four battalions into Liége, he suggested to Versailles that his best course of action would be to retire the rest of his forces behind the River Mehaigne, well to the westward, so as to protect Brabant at least from Allied attack. This suggestion loosed a storm of invective at the Marshal's head. The Minister of War, Chamillart, demanded that the safe-ty of Liége should be given the uttermost priority, if only for the political reason of keeping the newly recruited House of Wittelsbach faithful to the cause. Louis agreed, and issued a strict order on 28 September to this effect. Boufflers riposted by sending the opinion of General Puységur in support of his concepts, and the King was pleased to give the Marshal his head once more, providing the defences of both the citadel of Liége and neighbouring Fort Chartreuse were fully manned. By this time Tallard had reached Bonn, but had failed to make any further progress, so Boufflers busied himself sending two further battalions into Liége and a similar force into Limburg. Thus the French field army continued to move towards voluntary liquidation.

At length Marlborough revealed his hand. Despite the late season, the deterior-ating weather, and the serious sickness in his army's ranks, he was determined to take Liége. On 13 October a force of 50 squadrons suddenly invested the city, whilst troops from Ruremonde similarly isolated the Chartreuse. The citadel only just had time to close its gates before the Allies were within the city, so sudden had been the onslaught. The Earl agreed to the citizens' entreaties not to attack the French-held forts from the city-side, and on 20 October opened two sets of trenches against the citadel. Next day 65 large pieces of artillery opened fire, and two days later a practicable breach had been battered. At 4 p.m. a picked force of 1,000 grenadiers supported by ten battalions stormed forward. Their attack was successful, and even better exploited. Captain Parker accompanied Lord Cutts on this hair-raising exploit: 'We rushed up to the covert-way (*sic*) the enemy gave us one scattering fire only, and away they ran. We jumped onto the covert-way, and ran after them. . . . We seeing them get into the ravelin pursued them, got in with them, and soon put most of them to the sword. They that escaped us, fled over a small wooden bridge; and . . . we pursued them . . . exposed to the fire of the great and small shot of the body of the fort. However we got over the fausse-braye where we had nothing for it, but to take the fort or die. They that fled before us, climbed up by the long grass, that grew out of the fort, so we climbed after them. Here we were hard put to it, to pull out the palisades, which pointed down upon us from the prospect . . . But as soon as they (the garrison) saw us at this work, they quitted the rampart, and retired down to the parade (ground) . . . where they laid down their arms, and cried for quarter, which was readily granted them.'[21] The Governor, M. de Violaine and 1,700 men were made prisoners of war.

News of these developments threw Boufflers into even greater confusion. He decided to evacuate Tongres and fall back to the Demer line, sent messengers to warn Tallard to prepare to return to the Meuse forthwith, but before leaving he considered it advisable to raze the defences of nearby Huy. Advised that this task would take all of three months to complete, the Marshal changed his mind and instead reinforced its garrison with 500 men. Unbeknown to either Boufflers or Versailles at this time, Villars had on 14 October won a substantial victory over the Margrave of Baden at Friedlingen on the Upper Rhine. This success substantially meant that the French would be able to link up with the Elector of Bavaria, who had recently seized the imperial city of Ulm on the Danube, but this event had little or no immediate effect on the situation in Flanders, although the longer term implications would in due course throw the very existence of the Grand Alliance into question.* Another late success for French arms was Tallard's occupation of Trèves and Trarbach on the River Moselle, (25 and 27 October) which opened a new route to the Rhine.

Meanwhile, back at Liége, the Prince of Hesse-Cassel was making slower progress—largely owing to heavy rain—in his efforts to take the Chartreuse fort, which was being held by M. de Millon and five battalions. This officer, however,

* See chapter 7.

had just received an amazing smuggled message from Boufflers, directing him on
no account to face a storming but to surrender on discretion. (Similar messages
had been sent to the governors of Limburg and Huy). His resolve weakened by
this instruction, which clearly revealed that no relief attempt whatsoever was
envisaged, de Millon beat the *chamade* on 29 October after sustaining a furious
Allied bombardment, and marched away with his men for Antwerp two days
later. Thus a further significant success was gained by Marlborough's arms; the
capture of Liége was a fitting climax to a brilliant, if on the whole conventional,
first campaign. The threat to the United Provinces along the Meuse had been
largely removed, an ally of France (although admittedly a minor one) had been
all but eliminated (the Bishop of Liége would soon be a mere pensioner of
Louis XIV), and the Allies were left in an excellent position for the beginning of the
next campaign.

Marlborough had already been considering plans for 1703 for some time. On
14 October he revealed part of his intentions in a secret letter to the Grand
Pensionary. 'The taking of this place (Liége) will very much enlarge your winterquarters (*sic*) so that you need not have so many troops in your Provinces. I
dare not let your officers . . . know my thoughts as to what ought to be done next
Summer, for they can't keep anything secret; but that which I wish might govern
the winterquarters is, that as many troops as the places upon the Meuse are
capable of receiving should be lodged there, as also between the Meuse and the
Rhine, so that when it might be proper they might be able in one week's time
(notice) to form an army of 50,000 men; the other consideration should be to
quarter so many men on the Brabant side as might be able to form an army at the
same time.'[22] Herein, as we shall see, lay the genesis of the campaign of 1703.

The year 1702 still held two important happenings for Marlborough in person.
As he travelled with a few colleagues by boat down the Meuse on his way to the
Hague on 6 November, the party was intercepted by a French patrol from the
garrison of Gelder. Most of the boat's occupants were in possession of valid
laissez-passer documents as were habitually issued by all headquarters and governments to enemy nationals of importance, but not Marlborough. Fortunately,
thanks to the quick thinking of Gill, one of his clerks, the situation was saved.
This man found an old pass originally issued in the name of *Charles* Churchill,
the Earl's brother, and managed to slip it to the Captain-General. This intelligent
act earned Marlborough his freedom and the clerk a pension for life. We may
also guess that a little more than mere passes changed hands at the same time,
for the French lieutenant commanding the patrol soon after deserted to the
Allied side, and was promoted a captain in the Dutch service. News of this
escapade, so similar to the one that had been survived in 1689*, brought the
population of the Hague out in force to see their English hero's safe return on
7 November. 'Till they saw me,' recorded Marlborough, 'they thought me a

* See p. 31 above.

prisoner in France, so that I was not ashore one minute before I had great crowds of the common people, some endeavouring to take me by the hands, and all crying out welcome. But that which moved me most was, to see a great many of both sexes crying for joy.'[23] Clearly he found this demonstration of popular affection—so recently earned—most touching.

The second event took place shortly after his return to London. Queen Anne, delighted at the outcome of her protégé's first essay at independent command, hastened to confer a dukedom upon him. Privately Marlborough was delighted by this further advancement, which the Queen, in place of an *appanage*, declared would be accompanied by a grant of £5,000 for life from the Post Office funds. Parliament was in a less generous mood, however, and to save the Queen embarrassment, the Duke formally declined the monetary settlement. Sarah, predictably, was full of indignation at this 'ingratitude,'* and even counselled refusal of the title. But her husband thought otherwise. Apart from the gratification of personal pride, he was aware that his future dealings with European Emperors, Kings and Princes might well be aided by the noble title of Duke. Certainly Heinsius, who was consulted on the matter, pressed this point. 'You will know by the news you have from England,' wrote Marlborough somewhat coyly on 4/15 December, 'that the Queen has done me the honour of making me a Duke, which if it should prove other than well, you as a friend will be much concerned in it, *I having given way to it* (this author's italics) more upon your judgement than my own....'[24] We may possibly question the modesty expressed in this letter, but it was indubitably a deserved honour.

So ended the first full year of the war of the Second Grand Alliance. On balance neither side had drawn notably ahead of the other at this juncture. If Flanders had proved an Allied triumph, the Court of Versailles could console themselves with memories of successes over the Emperor in North Italy (Santa Vittoria and Luzzara) and above all on the Upper Rhine. Moreover, an Anglo-Dutch descent commanded by the Duke of Ormonde with 16,000 men on Cadiz in September (designed to acquire a base which would enable the Allied joint-fleet full access to the Mediterranean) had proved as great a fiasco and an even greater disgrace owing to the looting of Port St. Mary, as the Camaret Bay affair of six years earlier. A considerable facesaver had been Admiral Rooke's fortuitous capture of much of the Spanish *flota* (or treasure fleet) in Vigo Bay on 12 October during the homeward journey; booty to the value of three million pounds was the very welcome outcome of this exploit.

* * *

There can be no denying that Allied morale, despite the varied turns of Fortune on the various fronts, was higher at the end of the year 1702 than at its start.

* See p. 9 above.

FRANCE, FLANDERS AND
THE LOWER RHINE

The Hague

Rotterdam

Breda

Bergen-op-Zoom

Middleburg

Santoliet

Lillo

Eckeren

St. Job

Sluys

St. Nicolas

Antwerp

Ostend

Bruges

Lierre

Little Nett

Leffinghe

Oudenburg

F L A N D E R S

Nieuport

Furnes

Canal de Moulinet

Wynendael

Ghent

PAYS DE WAES

Malines

Great

Dunkirk

Dixmude

Thourout

Bruges-Ghent Canal

Dendermonde

Vilvorde

Louvain

Parc

to CALAIS ←

Yser

Rousselaer

Lys

Gavre

Alost

Asche

Senne

Brussels

Aa

Ypres

Courtrai

Oudenarde

Ninove

Anderlecht

FOREST OF SOIGNIES

Corbec

St. Omer

Cassel

Warneton

Menin

Scheldt

Kerkhoff

Grammont

Hal

Yssche

Neérysche

Messines

Comines

Hauterive

Herfelingen

Ysse

Waterloo

Lasn

Armentières

Le Quesnoy

Helchin

Lessines

Enghien

Braine l'Alleud

Génappes

Marque

Pottes

Leuze

Steinkirk

Nivelles

Dyle

Aire

Lys

Lille

Ath

Soignies

Gembloux

St. Venant

Deule

Tournai

Lillers

Béthune

Pont-à-Vendin

Mortagne

Jemappes

Laue

La Bassée

Condé

Haine

Sirault

Fleurus

Lens

Courrières

Orchies

Mons

to MONTREUIL ←

A R T O I S

VIMY RIDGE

Saut

Scarpe

St. Amand

Quiévrain

St. Ghislain

Seneffe

Trouille

Sambre

Charleroi

Pont-Auby

Vimy

Ft. Scarpe

Marchiennes

Valenciennes

Blaregnies

Vitry

Douai

Neuville

Denain

Malplaquet

Avesnes-le-Comte

Gy

Mont St.Eloy

Bavai

Maubeuge

Frevent

Arras

Villers Brulin

Goeulzin

Mordaing

H A I N A U L T

Quesnoy

Canche

Arleux

Aubencheul-au-Bac

Eirun

Selle

Landrecies

to ABBEVILLE

Sensée

Wavrechin

Cambrai

Bouchain

Le Cateau

Bapaume

Schelt

Ancre

Albert

Meuse

Charleville

Péronne

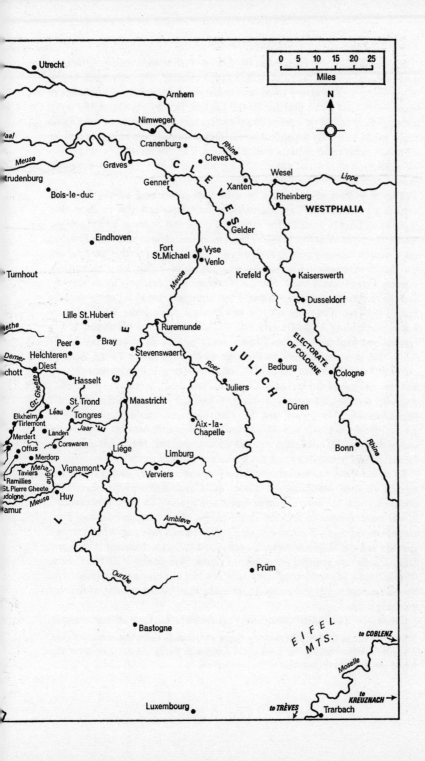

The general mood was reflected in the English Parliament's voting of the complete service estimates, together with a supplementary, without serious demur. The Commons also agreed to an 'augmentation' for the forces in Flanders of 20,000 men (half to be paid for by the English, half by the Dutch) for 1703, although they tacked on a proviso to the effect that the provision of the English share would be wholly dependent on the Dutch formally agreeing once and for all to halt commercial contacts with the enemy. This the States-General eventually undertook to do (most unwillingly) for one year from 1 June—but the agreement would soon become a dead-letter.

The New Year of 1703 also brought further evidence of the Alliance's relatively good repute. Two not unimportant countries began to show clear signs of wishing to abandon the cause of France and Spain to join the Allies. Victor Amadeus of Savoy, despite close family connections with both Bourbon royal houses, took umbrage at their unwillingness to grant further financial aid, and began to negotiate with the Emperor, at no little risk, let it be said, for sizeable French forces under Marshal Vendôme were currently in his country, and the secret was soon an open one. Final agreement would not come until the end of the year. The other country was Portugal. King Pedro was anxious to have the crippling Anglo–Dutch naval blockade lifted from his shores, and in return for complex guarantees (which would include an undertaking by the Allies that they would work to dethrone Philip V in favour of the Austrian claimant,* an expeditionary force of 20,000 men (he eventually settled for 12,000), and the presence of the Archduke Charles at their head), he, too was prepared to forgo his Bourbon alliances, and change sides. A first treaty to this effect was promulgated in May, 1703, and Sir Paul Methuen, English ambassador to Lisbon, would negotiate the two important treaties that bear his name by the end of the year. This defection was welcomed at the time, but as will be seen its ultimate effect would be to ruin the whole war effort of the Allies.

Of course there was enough work of a preparatory nature during the winter months to keep Marlborough's fertile mind and diplomatic manners fully occupied. It was one thing to gain parliamentary approval for the 'augmentation'; it was quite another to find the actual troops, three-quarters of whom must come from Germany. So time-consuming negotiations were put in hand at both London and the Hague to persuade, cajole and bribe the Kings of Prussia and Denmark, and the assorted princelings of Hesse, Saxe-Gotha, Holstein, Zwerin, Wolffenbüttel, Munster, Osnabruck and Oostfrise to provide new regiments on agreed establishments and acceptable terms in time for the opening of the next year's fighting.

There were also innumerable Allied squabbles to solve, or at least mitigate.

---

* This was almost the first time that this clause was formally embodied in the war aims. A similar proviso would be included in the treaty with Savoy. In the long term, this would prove a fatal enlargement of the *causae belli*.

Besides the difference over the trading with the enemy question, Anglo-Dutch relations were further tried by Queen Anne's threat to go to law to recover some jewels in the possession of the Princess of Nassau (April), and her government's insistence that the Dutch must float a loan of £200,000 'for the better securing a regular payment to her troops in your service'. It would seem that the maintenance of large numbers of troops abroad incurred as large a problem in regard to convertible currency as the stationing of British soldiers in West Germany as part of the NATO shield in the 1960s. More serious still, in English eyes, was the failure of the Dutch to meet their naval obligations. First they were late in providing three battalions and a squadron for an expedition to the West Indies, which had already sailed without them; in the end, the Queen agreed to release the Dutch from this obligation in January and put them 'at liberty for any other service' in connection with the Portuguese negotiation. But when the Dutch were similarly remiss in regard to the Allied fleets in the Channel and North Sea later in the year, Marlborough had to warn Heinsius (21 May) that 'your ships not being ready has made a great noise in England.'

Nor were these the only strains. The Emperor was seriously at odds with the Republic over the exacting of an oath of allegiance to the United Provinces from the cities of Venlo and Ruremonde the previous year (he considered them private Austrian preserves), and as the campaigning season approached there would be the habitual difficulties with such princes as the Elector Palatine and the Hessians over non-payment of raising-money and march fees for their new regiments. These stresses notwithstanding, the Alliance held together.

Home politics were also exacting. The religious strife occasioned by the Tory Occasional Conformity Bill of the previous Autumn (the brainchild of Robert Harley and his able but scheming protégé, Henry St. John, M.P. for Wootten Bassett) threatened a political trap for the 'Moderates', Marlborough and Godolphin, but they avoided Lord Rochester's machinations by appearing to support the Bill whilst in secret opposing it, and in the end it was shelved in February. Soon thereafter, the 'Cockpit' group engineered the resignation of the difficult Rochester.

These months also held two important family events for the Marlboroughs. The first, and happier one, was the marriage of their third daughter, Elizabeth, to the Earl of Bridgewater on 9/10 February, '. . . my daughter being to be married this evening I have no more time than to assure you of my being . . . etc.' as ended one letter to the Grand Pensionary. The second, infinitely sad, event, was the sudden death of their only son, the 17-year-old Marquis of Blandford at Cambridge, from small-pox, on the 23rd, which plunged the Duke into 'the greatest sorrow in the world' and necessitated a five-day rest at St. Albans to get over the first shock at a time when he was expected in Holland. Soon after he confided to Lord Ailesbury that the boy had been 'the finest young man that could be seen. . . . I have lost what is so dear to me, it is fit for me to retire and not toil and labour for I know not who: my daughters are all married.'[25] Mercifully, perhaps, military preoccupations would soon take up all the grieving father's attention.

Louis XIV had not been inactive over the winter. The loss of Rheinberg in February (the siege had dragged on since the previous autuumn) was balanced by the failure of an Allied winter-stroke against Trarbach, relieved by Tallard the previous month. The King was now determined to mount a major effort on the German and Italian fronts in 1703, relegating the 'cockpit' to a secondary role in his strategy for the present. For once Marlborough was somewhat in error* when he asserted (23 January) that 'whatever shoe (i.e. show) the French may make of sending troops to Germany, I am very confident they will open this campaign by making the siege of Liége if they can be in the field before us.'[26] As the French saw it, any efforts against Liége or Dutch Flanders could only be undertaken if this would afford diversionary aid to Marshal Villars' campaign on the Upper Rhine or Marshal Vendôme's in the Milanese. More formations were being raised for these various fronts, and in a burst of enthusiasm Louis XIV created ten new marshals, 23 lieutenant-generals, 80 major-generals and 31 brigadiers. Boufflers' rather pathetic showing in Flanders the previous year resulted in his being appointed as merely second-in-command to the court favourite Marshal Villeroi, the new front commander. But Louis also had his problems; his fronts were as extensive as ever; his Allies (save only Max Emmanuel of Bavaria) were wavering in their loyalty (to say the least); and to cap it all the late months of 1702 had seen the start of a Protestant armed revolt in the Cevennes, where the *camisards* (so called on account of the white shirts that identified them) soon required the attentions of a complete French army under Marshal de Montrevel. This particular difficulty the Allies were to do all in their power to exacerbate; in May Queen Anne would secretly convey her decision to supply arms and money to the Huguenots if they would accept a number of Allied officers to supervise their use.[27] Thus the concept of military 'advisers' and the incitement of guerrilla wars were not wholly unknown in the early eighteenth century. Nor was this type of subversive activity to prove an Allied prerogative; far more serious than the Camisard Revolt would be the Hungarian popular rising under the patriot Racoczi, which, liberally aided by French gold and munitions, would place Vienna itself in peril in 1704 and drag on for seven mortal years. It was, therefore, a case of 'tit for tat'.

The Allied generals (less Marlborough, who was represented by Lord Cutts), met at Wesel in mid-February. An early complication was the death of the Earl of Athlone from apoplexy (on 13 February); even graver was the arrival a little later of grave tidings from the Rhine front. It seemed that the French had won the annual mobilisation race with a vengeance, at least on that sector, for on 24 February Marshal Villars abruptly appeared before Kehl on the east bank of the

* But see p. 114 below.

Rhine; the key to the Black Forest passes and thence to the distant Danube, and had it in his possession by 10 March. The same date, the Elector of Bavaria won a battle at Scharding over the imperial general Count Schlick, and soon thereafter Court Styrum's army was on the defensive. The road to Bavaria and beyond thus lay invitingly open. Small wonder that Lewis of Baden sent urgent entreaties for help to London and the Hague. Even before these twin setbacks, the Wesel conference decided (8 February) to form a corps to operate on the Meuse (initially of ten Dutch battalions, ultimately of twice that number besides eight squadrons, or near 20,000 men) in the hope of bolstering the Austrian position. This decision caused Marlborough some unease; detachments on this scale could only have a grave effect on the operational power of the two armies the Allies were to form in the Low Countries. 'I wish we could hear any good news from the Upper Rhine,' he noted lugubriously, for as always he was preyed upon by the most pessimistic moods prior to entering upon a campaign, 'but our letters from Vienna give us but a very melancholy prospect.'[28] Still anxious for Baden, the Allies further decided to give the highest priority to the siege of Bonn on the Rhine, expensive though that would inevitably be in terms of troops committed owing to its position. Still the cries for help from Vienna persisted. Marlborough, for one, was not over-impressed. He privately accused the Emperor and the German princes of being deliberately backward in fielding their military contingents in the hope of squeezing thereby even greater money grants out of England and the Republic. They were also too prone, in his view, to 'flatter themselves that you (the Dutch) must help them.'[29] At last, on 17 March, the Captain General arrived in person at the Hague.

The Allied plan for the Low Countries was based upon the formation of two equal armies, one on the Meuse, the second on the Rhine, based upon Maastricht and Coblenz respectively. The use of these forces would fall into two phases; first, Marlborough and the Rhine army would move to capture Bonn; then, the two armies would either reunite to prosecute the major attack of the year—an advance on Lierre and Antwerp to capture those towns and raze the French lines guarding Brabant—or act apart if this seemed more convenient, that is to say Marlborough on the inner flank would engage the attention of the French field army whilst the Dutch pushed through to take the great *entrepôt* of Antwerp. It is not clear how far this 'Great Design' (Antwerp) was Marlborough's own conception, although as we have seen he had taken preliminary steps the previous year.* What is certain, however, is that he threw all his energy into the scheme's implementation, and he was certainly aware that success or failure would rest to a large measure on two factors: the speed with which the Allied forces in the Low Countries could take the field, and the concomitant situation upon the Upper Rhine, where, it will be remembered, the French had already built up a commanding superiority.

* See p. 106 above.

A lightning tour of the fortresses of the Meuse in early April revealed that little had been done to repair and improve their defences over the winter. Even worse was the apparent unwillingness of the Allies to enter the field despite (or possibly because of) the rumble of distant disasters befalling the Emperor's forces higher up the Rhine. However, news that the Duke was in Flanders caused Louis XIV to send Marshal Villeroi hastening from France to assume his command with orders to attempt a distraction towards Liége. Preparations had barely begun when the King countermanded this instruction. Two days after he had begun the investment of Bonn (25 April), Marlborough noted that 'I have seen a letter from Paris that the siege of Bonn is but a feint, but that the real design was upon Antwerp.'[30] This, of course, was substantially correct, and fearful lest his sole army should be drawn away from the north towards the Meuse, and then become involved in a static siege, Louis XIV ordered his marshals to abandon all thought of such an offensive. At this juncture, the French and Spaniards had only 60 battalions and 103 squadrons for their field army (camped in two parts around Diest and Namur) besides a further 19 battalions and 12 squadrons under Bedmar holding the defensive lines in Brabant, and a further 22 in garrisons. All were at their initial posts by 4 May; the same was not the case with all the Allied contingents, many of which were still clamouring for money before they would move. Only 20,000 had so far assembled at Maastricht, or rather less than half the intended force. Fortunately Marlborough was able to speed initial sums from England to satisfy the loudest clamourers, but the English contingents were still assembling around Eindhoven at the end of the month. On the 27th, Marlborough interviewed the Elector Palatine about possible operations on the Moselle, 'and you will depend upon it that they will not keep it a secret'. In this way he hoped to confuse the foe with false intelligence, a standard practice of the Duke.

The 4 May saw the Allies breaking ground before Bonn, three attacks being prepared. Despite the expressed resolve of the Governor, M. d'Alègre, to offer a staunch defence with his ten battalions, it only took 11 more days to induce him to capitulate. He was allowed good terms, and marched out with 3,600 men towards Luxembourg. This was an auspicious opening to the campaign in the south, but it was just as well for on the 9th Villeroi had launched a surprise attack on the drowsy Allied formations on the Maastricht sector, seized the outlying post of Tongres (capturing intact two battalions and much gear), and set many Allied detachments, still in winter quarters, scurrying for Maastricht, where they were joined in the nick of time by the 10,000 English troops from Eindhoven and six battalions and 25 squadrons from before Bonn, a reinforcement which checked the rout. The French deemed the Allies too strongly positioned, and fell back, razing Tongres, but the morale of their troops was raised by this successful raid.

On 19 May Marlborough was personally back in Maastricht. He was still resisting Dutch pressures to send a substantial force to aid Baden, arguing that too little aid would not do the business whilst enough would ruin all chances of a success in Flanders that year, which was already threatened by the need to find troops for Portugal. 'I beg you will not omit any of the preparations for the *Great Design*,' he entreated Heinsius. Soon 70 battalions and 120 squadrons were around Maastricht, the balance of the Bonn army being sent by boat to Bergen-op-Zoom ready for part two of the year's offensive. Marlborough was convinced that preliminary steps should be the sieges of Huy on the Meuse and Ostend on the coast, to keep the enemy in doubt whilst the Design's final preparations were completed (the target date for this being 10 June), but both schemes were vetoed by Coehoorn, who was the United Provinces' master-strategist as well as their master of siegecraft. Marlborough absorbed this double-rebuff with his habitual grace, but he would later regret doing so.

Marshals Villeroi and Boufflers, meantime, were preparing to receive the Allied blow, wherever and whenever it might come. The Marquis de Bedmar was reinforced on the western sector to 53 battalions and 12 squadrons to face Coehoorn's 40 or so battalions massing around Sluys. In the centre, five battalions and 11 squadrons watched the superior forces of General Opdam (encamped near Lillo), whilst further east the two marshals with 61 battalions and 101 squadrons of the main army carefully observed Marlborough's movements. Their remaining 65 battalions comprised garrisons. At last on the 28th the Allied field army advanced to within two leagues of the French position west of Tongres, and a battle seemed possible, but the Allies veered away towards Russon in the direction of Huy. A ten day pause ensued.

On the coast, however, all was activity. New battalions were arriving by sea and river, and Generals Coehoorn, Spaar, Opdam and Tilly with their five corps kept Bedmar off-balance and in a lather of anticipation. The two first-named generals had 8 battalions besides dragoons at Sluys, 5 battalions and two regiments of mounted troops near Sas-de-Gand and as many more at Biervliet; Opdam was commanding 9 battalions at Lillo; and Tilly held four more and five mounted regiments at Breda. Yet the Dutch seemed unwilling to move off, and week followed week with little to report.

This tried Marlborough's patience to the limit. On 5 June he was remonstrating with Heinsius that it was 'inexcusable to the Emperor, and the Empire, if we amuse ourselves with little projects at a time when they think we should put ourselves upon the defensive and send all the rest of the troops to their aid.' Seventeen days later he was again expressing his frustration about the conduct of the campaign, 'which I think will be the last I shall be able to serve you in. . . .' These barely concealed threats of resignation also reached Queen Anne's ears. 'The thoughts that both my dear Mrs. Freeman and Mr. Freeman seem to have of retiring gives me no small uneasiness,' she would write in October; 'Give me leave to say you should a little consider your faithful friends and poor country, which must be ruined if ever you should put your melancholy thoughts into execution. As for your poor, unfortunate, faithful Morley, she could never bear it ... I never will forsake your dear self Mr. Freeman nor Mr. Montgomery, but always be your constant, faithful servant; and we four must never part.'[31] She would one day be in a very different mood.

On 9 June, Marlborough feinted towards Huy; the marshals obligingly followed his move, and several weeks of what Defoe would dub 'dodging, or as it is more genteely called, observing one another' ensued. No major engagement followed, although one seemed close on the 22nd, but at least the Duke was carrying out his strategic role of keeping the marshals fully occupied and away from the central and coastal sectors. But little but reconnoitring and a little mutual manœuvring was reported from the coast until at 3 a.m. on 27 June, at long last, the Dutch attacked a weak sector of Bedmar's lines at Calishoek and Steckene, routed M. de Hessy and five raw battalions of recruits, and drove a wedge through the lines. Unfortunately at this juncture their resolve ran out, and the Dutch had no thought of exploiting their success beyond pillaging Steckene and taking the Fort de Perle. Thereafter, General Opdam lost no time in taking himself to Eckeren, where he set about constructing an entrenched camp. Thus an auspicious, if sadly delayed, opening was allowed to peter away into inactivity, returning the initiative to the enemy.

This time the French did not blunder. Marshal Boufflers spirited away from the main army at Diest some 30 companies of grenadiers, 15 squadrons of cavalry and as many of dragoons, and forced-marched these troops northwards to join Bedmar. By dint of fine marching, which almost equalled Marlborough's later achievements in this field, eleven leagues were covered on the 29 May, the tired troops reaching Bedmar's lines at midnight. Marlborough had no immediate news of this move, which was intended to make it possible for Bedmar and Boufflers to launch an attack on Opdam's position. Early on the 30th, the French and Spaniards, 28 battalions and 49 squadrons strong, advanced in four columns. The outcome is best left to Marshal Boufflers' report to Versailles.

'Yesterday, Sire, there took place a very hard-fought and determined combat ... in which your Majesty's army brought off the advantage and all the marks of victory, chasing the enemy from their camp, remaining the complete masters of the field of battle, taking four cannon [in fact six] and two mortars, all their munitions of war and several standards, together with more than 300 waggons and numbers of pieces.'[32]

The battle of Eckeren was a humiliating check for the Allies, their strategy of the Great Design, and above all for General Opdam. That general fled the field and ran for Breda, convinced that all was lost, leaving several colleagues, Generals Slangenberg, Hompesch and Hop, to fight the action through before retreating to Lillo in good order. For a cost of 132 officers casualties and 1,067 rank and file, the French and Spaniards inflicted 4,000 losses on their adversaries, took 800 prisoners, besides artillery (already mentioned), 40 coehoorn mortars, six colours, two cavalry standards and 300 munition waggons. This was a substantial success, which rebounded to the credit of the previously criticised Marshal Boufflers who rejoined the main army in high spirits with his jubilant men on 3 July. Among the officers cited for gallantry was one 'M. de Mérode-Westerloo, Brigadier', whose future exploits in this war we shall have occasion to cite on later pages. As Boufflers somewhat sceptically remarked, 'I do not doubt that M. de Marlborough and the States General will be much mortified by this set-back at the very time they are planning to invade the whole of Flanders.'

The Captain-General was not wholly surprised by this setback, disappointing though it obviously was. Opdam 'is very capable of having it (defeat) happen to him',[33] he remarked. He had tried to warn the Dutch of what seemed to be afoot, but not in time, and had been most anxious: 'I have not sleep (sic) two hours these last three nights' he had written on the fatal 30 June. To the Grand Pensioner's formal commiserating message he positively snapped back on 4 July that 'If you have a mind to Antwerp and a speedy end to the war you must venture something for it.'[34] But he recovered his composure, and was soon trying to smooth the ruffled feathers of Coehoorn who had resigned his post as Senior Engineer of the Dutch forces in a tiff over seniority and precedence vis-à-vis regular officers.

But the Eckeren fiasco had without a doubt compromised the Great Design. Although as late as 26 August Marlborough would be wistfully writing 'I can't but persuade myself if all would but act heartily (sic), we might yet make the siege of Antwerp,'[35] it was not to be. As Villeroi and the Allies continued to march and counter-march, a discordant Allied council-of-war at Bergen-op-Zoom heard Coehoorn veto the project once and for all.

The disagreements would become increasingly vocal and bitter in succeeding weeks. Eckeren started a veritable train of ill fortune for the Allies. The Dutch wanted to replan the campaign to include the bombardment of Namur; Marlborough was at his most persuasive in trying to gain agreement to a major onslaught on the French lines between Deurne and Oleghem, where he knew them to be both weak and ill-supported. Matters came to a head on 24 July, when Marlborough stood ready to attack at the head of 85 battalions and 150 squadrons; the French army, far weaker, drew up in a line of battle after entering the lines from their camp at St. Job. Once again nothing happened. This time it was not the Dutch Field Deputies but the Dutch generals who sulkily vetoed Marlborough's plan. 'Your Deputies are so well inclined to do everything that is right that I could wish with all my heart they had been in the army two months ago,' he wrote to the Hague on 2 August. 'We ought to have taken Huy as soon as I came from Bonn, but you know that was overruled by M. Coehoorn.'[36]

The French, meanwhile, were caught on the horns of their usual dilemma. However successful their measures to blunt the design on Antwerp in late June, they could still not be certain what the Allies would attempt next. Antwerp might still be attacked, as might Brabant, or Huy. 'As regards the siege of Huy,' wrote Louis XIV on 6 August, nine days before it became clear the foe had indeed selected this course of action, 'you know its importance and the unfortunate effects its loss would entail; but I cannot believe the enemy will attempt it so long as the army you command is so close to them. . . .'[37] He went on to stress how important it would also be to reinforce the Meuse-Moselle area, as it would be desirable to be in safe occupation of Trèves before quartering the troops that Winter. The marshals, however, decided that Brabant must continue to be the focal point of their attentions, and accordingly the Governor of Huy, M. Millon, was helpfully instructed that he should expect no substantial relief in the event of a siege, but that he must hold out for four to five months.

At last, on 13 August, Marlborough's movement began. Leaving Borckloom, his army headed for Huy. The French riposted by sending M. de Noyelles to the heights near the town to observe and if possible hinder the Allied deployment. He was followed by M. Pracontal and a further corps. Although Huy was invested on the 15th and the town was occupied two days later, the Allied siege of the castle was slow in its early stages, and not until M. Pracontal's corps was withdrawn on the 24th was real progress obtained. The next day Forts Joseph and Picard fell to the Allies, and M. Millon and his 1,000 men in the castle were exposed to the full fire of 70 guns and 46 mortars. On the 25th a large breach gaped invitingly in the castle wall, and after beating off two assault attempts, causing and sustaining heavy losses, Millon offered to capitulate on terms. This was refused, and next day the unfortunate governor, knowing his garrison must collapse under a further attack, surrendered himself and his survivors as prisoners of war. In due course Lord Cutts would arrange a cartel with the French high command whereby these troops were exchanged for the two Allied battalions lost at Tongres earlier in the season.

This was satisfactory for the Allies, but Marlborough, who had been covering the siege from near the lines, was far from content. Another excellent opportunity had presented itself for attacking the neighbouring lines, but once again a council-of-war had refused to give unstinted approval—the Dutch generals again being the trouble. 'You will see by the letter . . . that my opinion is for attacking the lines, as well as those generals which have signed the paper' [whose number included the mercenary generals commanding the Danes, Hessians, Brunswickers and Luneburghers] he wrote to Heinsius on the 26th. 'The other paper, signed by the generals of the left (the Dutch) is taking a great deal of pains to avoid giving an opinion. . . . For God's sake take a vigorous resolution, for the enemy is frightened and we shall beat them wherever we see them.' A fortnight later he was still complaining stridently: 'I do call God to witness that after I had seen them (the lines) upon Wednesday and Thursday I was confirmed in my opinion that we should have forced them with the loss of very few men. . . .'[38]

Yet amidst all the manifold strains of coalition warfare, which caused his old migraines to afflict him once more, he could find time to request the Dutch Government to grant a permit for his kinsman, the Duke of Berwick, to purchase and export eight coach-horses from Holland! Eighteenth-century warfare contained many contrasts.

The French were busy watching Coehoorn on the coast, and soon Bedmar was causing a new, improved series of lines to be constructed in the Pays de Waes district facing Antwerp; other preparations of a similar kind were being made to secure Namur at the other extremity of the French lines. But following the unanticipatedly rapid loss of Huy, which had been reputed a nigh-impregnable position, there were strong fears for Léau, Diest and Limburg. The last-named town was already deemed as good as lost, and its Governor, M. de Reignac, was instructed to accept a good capitulation if he was besieged. For some days, however, Allied dissensions caused a virtual paralysis in operations. After his abortive reconnaissances of the Lines on two successive days already referred to (5 and 6 September), Marlborough fell back from the Hannut area, and three days later invested Limburg whilst the main army encamped at St. Trun. This operation, probably because of Allied disunity, was very slowly pressed. The trenches were only opened on 14 September, and it was not until the 23rd that enough guns had appeared to make the siege a reality. When de Reignac, pursuant to his instructions, asked for terms, he was curtly rebuffed. This so stung him that he forthwith launched two telling sorties against the Allied siege-works which did much damage. But on the 26th the massed batteries blazed into life, and the following day the Governor was compelled to surrender as prisoner-of-war. It is evident from these harder Allied conditions that the struggle was becoming more bitter as the months dragged by, and Marlborough was in any case incensed by the recent need to detach some of his precious battalions for service in Portugal from early September (although he had whittled down the original demand to comprise but three regiments of foot, Portmore's, Stanhope's and Blood's, and Lord Raby's Regiment of Dragoons).[39]

So October opened, and the autumn tints began to colour the trees of the Low Countries. A serious setback was now reported from the Danube front, where Marshal Villars and the Elector of Bavaria, after overplaying their hand earlier in the summer by advancing as far as Innsbruck, from which they had to beat a hasty retreat for reasons of strategic consumption, had rounded upon the Imperial commander Styrum and thrashed him at the battle of Höchstädt on 20 September, inflicting 4,500 casualties for only 1,500 sustained, also taking 37 guns and throwing the whole system of imperial defence in the Danube theatre into complete confusion. 'I am afraid the ill news of Count Styrum being beaten will make the Moselle project very difficult,' commented the Captain-General, who had until now been contemplating a finale for the year against Marche and La Roche in the Moselle valley. The most serious and immediate consequence of this defeat was that it allowed Marshal Tallard to undertake the siege of Landau with impunity. Both sides rushed to send aid to the imperial fortress. The Allies detached the Prince of Hesse-Cassel and 22 battalions for the duty of relieving the city; the French sent off (10 October), M. de Pracontal, whilst the Marshals moved their army to Namur as if presaging an advance on Huy and Liége in order to keep Marlborough fully occupied. The result of these moves was seen on 15 November, when Pracontal reinforced Tallard extremely opportunely as he was moving to attack the Hessian camp at Spire. The result was another French victory, and the consequent fall of Landau (12 November). This implied that the French could expect a virtually free path over the Rhine from Strasburg towards Bavaria the next year, for Baden's laboriously-constructed Lines of Stollhoffen were now virtually outflanked and rendered useless except as an observation position. The Allies reacted to this new disaster by sending a further corps to the Meuse to avert the danger of Tallard pressing northwards once again.

Morale amongst the French forces on both the Rhine and in the Low Countries was accordingly raised by these developments; that of the Allies correspondingly lowered. Marlborough had great difficulty in keeping the Dutch in the field until the end of October, and in the end had to turn to his former opponents, the States-General's watchdogs, to get compliance with his wishes. 'The Deputies have promised me that they will tell their generals very plainly that the army must continue in the field all the month . . .', he wrote on the 11th. The French marshals, on the other hand, were all for a new attack towards Lillo, but Louis XIV had too many problems on his hands by this juncture to permit this. Savoy had now at last come openly out on the Allied side (on 8 November) following Marshal Vendôme's high-handed arrest of several Piedmontese generals on 29 September. Portugal's intentions were no longer a secret, and despite the delay of the Archduke Charles (or Charles III of Spain as he was now known to his supporters) in storm-bound Dutch ports, the impending Allied invasion of Spain necessitated the finding of a new French army, including ten battalions from the Low Countries, for Marshal Berwick to land into the Iberian Peninsula. Furthermore, the Cevennes rising was still at its height. Nevertheless, Louis and his ministers and marshals could draw some comfort from the overall war situation. The promise of the year had been more than fulfilled in Germany, the French still had the upper hand in Italy, and the developments in the Cockpit of Europe had proved far less menacing than had once been feared.

In the Low Countries, both sides were now disbanding their armies into winter quarters. There was still some unfinished business to conclude: on 15 December, the town of Guelder at last capitulated to the Allies, and a strong force, made up of all their garrison forces brought out for an 'airing' before the winter set in, razed part of the lines through Brabant near Merdorp between 27 and 28 December. In a final fling, the aged and very ailing Coehoorn led

1,000 men in what was to be his final raid into the Pays de Waes against Fort Bedmar, only to be driven back by its guns with severe effects for his state of health. Long before this Marlborough had left for London (5 November), not wholly satisfied with the events of the year. But for some time he had been planning the next year's campaign; as early as 11 August he had requested that 'somebody may be authorised by the Emperor to come to the Hague and that he may be fully instructed by Prince Eugene [who by the end of the year would have been recalled from Italy to head the Austrian War Ministry in the crisis that followed the battle of Höchstädt], how the next campaign might be managed, so as that the whole Confederate army might be helping to each other; for it is my opinion if some such resolutions are not taken, Prince Lewis of Baden is capable of forming such projects as may ruin all we design'. Clearly his thoughts had long been turning towards the German theatre of war, despite his earlier unwillingness to send large detachments thither at the expense of the forces in the Low Countries. 'If the French be not some way or other checked there (Germany)' he had written as early as 8 June, 'we shall run great risk of losing the Empire.'[40] By the end of the year this fear was far, far closer to being realised, and it had been amply demonstrated that the efforts of a discordant Alliance in the Low Countries had been patently insufficient to afford indirect support to the Emperor by creating a diversion. Perhaps we may surmise that the Duke's thoughts were already playing with the idea of a personal intervention in Germany without the dead-weight of Dutch doubts and obstruction about his neck. We do not know, but over the succeeding months, fed by the urgings of Prince Eugene championed strongly by Count Wratislaw, the Austrian am- bassador to the Court of St. James, a great project would gradually begin to form in Marlborough's mind which in the fullness of time would establish his right to be considered as one of the great captains of history.

So ended Marlborough's first two campaigns as Captain-General. They are notable for the skill in which a virtually unknown commander took hold of a very discordant Grand Alliance and achieved a great deal along the river lines of the Rhine and the Meuse. They are also notable as demonstrating his skill in waging 'conventional' warfare of the manœuvre type, as understood by his contemporaries. Despite the continual thwarting of his desire to meet the foe in decisive battle, Churchill had shown great ability as a conductor of sieges and associated operations, and had continually frustrated and confused French commanders of far greater experience than himself. He had ridden a very difficult team of subordinates and enforced, despite repeated disappointments, a greater measure of cooperation leading to greater positive progress than his dead master, William III, had ever achieved. Despite rampant jealousy amongst the Dutch generals, he had radically altered the face of events in the Low Countries over two campaigns. Whatever else might still be far from finished, the security of the United Provinces, so doubtful in 1702, had been finally assured. No less than ten major and minor fortresses had been regained, and the fact that the French considered themselves fortunate to have come off so relatively lightly in 1703 should not disguise the extent of the Captain-General's martial achievements that year, dogged by disappointments and setbacks though the summer months had been. As Godart de Ginkel, Earl of Athlone, had described the campaign of 1702 with grudging and ever penitent admiration, 'the success of this campaign is solely due to this *incomparable chief*, since I confess that I, serving as second-in-command, opposed in all circumstances his opinions and proposals.'[40] There could hardly be more impressive testimony than that frank statement from one of Marlborough's Dutch rivals. Of course he had been aided as much by the bungling of his opponents, particularly Marshal Boufflers in 1702—whose reaction to any crisis had been in direct contravention, as we have seen, of General Robert E. Lee's reputed dying words many genera-tions later, 'Don't divide the army'—as he had been thwarted of even greater successes (in all probability) by Allied divisiveness and Dutch caution and obstruction. Still, he had emerged triumphant from a period of apprenticeship on the great stage of European history. He was now a general of international repute in his own right. Future years would see the fulfilment of the promise of his genius, none more so than the stirring events of 1704 to which we must now turn our attention.

Crisis on the Danube, 1704

'The arms of France, favoured by the defection of the Elector of
Bavaria had penetrated into the heart of the Empire. This mighty
body lay exposed to immediate ruin. In that memorable crisis the
Duke of Marlborough led his troops with unexampled celerity,
secrecy, order, from the ocean to the Danube. He saw, he attacked,
nor stopped but to conquer the enemy. He forced the Bavarians
sustained by the French in their strong entrenchments at Schellen
Berg. He passed the Danube. A second royal army, composed of
the best troops of France was sent to reinforce the first. That of the
Confederates was divided. With one part of it the siege of
Ingolstadt was carried on. With the other the Duke gave battle to
the united strength of France and Bavaria. On the second day of
August [O.S.], one thousand seven hundred and four, he gained a
more glorious victory than the histories of any age can boast. The
heaps of slain were dreadful proofs of his valour. A Marshal of
France, whole legions of French, his prisoners, proclaimed his
mercy. Bavaria was subdued, Ratisbon, Augsburg, Ulm,
Meminghem, all the surpations of his enemy, were recovered. The
liberty of the Diet, the peace of the Empire, were restored. From
the Danube the Duke turned his victorious army towards the
Rhine and the Moselle. Landau, Treves, Traerback were taken.
In the course of one campaign the very nature of war was changed.
The invaders of other states were reduced to defend their own. The
frontier of France was exposed in its weakest part to the efforts of
the Allies. . . .'

From the inscription on the Column of Victory,
Blenheim Palace (continued).

'My Lord, I never saw better horses, better clothes, finer belts and accoutre-
ments', declared Prince Eugene, as he completed his inspection of part of Marlborough's cavalry on 11 June 1704; 'but money, which you don't want (lack)
in England, will buy fine clothes and fine horses, but it can't buy that lively air I

see in every one of these troopers' faces.' Never to be outdone in paying compliments the Duke replied: 'Sir, that must be attributed to their heartiness for the public cause and the particular pleasure and satisfaction they have in seeing your Highness'.[1] The rule-defying march to the Danube was practically completed when the two great leaders of the Grand Alliance first met near Gross Heppach not far from the River Neckar. In an hour of deep crisis on the Danube front, the Duke of Marlborough had led a force of Allied troops from the Netherlands over a distance of more than 250 miles to assist the out-numbered and hard-pressed armies of the Holy Roman Empire. This, in itself, was an operation of major military importance—but in the weeks that followed even more stirring news was to be borne by spurring messengers to the capitals of Europe, whose destiny lay in the hands of the English general and his meagre force of travel-stained red-coats.

The year of 1704 had opened with singularly threatening prospects for the Grand Alliance. For the 'Party of the Two Crowns' 1703 had been a year of victory in North Italy and most particularly on the Danube, where the joint achievements of Marshal Villars and the Elector of Bavaria had created a direct threat to Vienna, the capital of the Holy Roman Empire and the 'Achilles' Heel' of the Grand Alliance. The city had only been saved from immediate capture by dissensions between the two commanders, resulting in the recall of the brilliant Villars and his replacement by the less dynamic Marsin, but in the opening months of the following year the initiative remained with the French, and Vienna's fall was confidently anticipated at the Courts of Versailles and Madrid. Racoczi's Hungarian revolt was already threatening the eastern approaches, and on the Rhine Marshal Tallard was preparing to march through the Black Forest with 36,000 men to reinforce the similar number of troops in the vicinity of Ulm under the command of Marsin and the Elector. As soon as the Spring floods receded and the rivers and mud roads of Europe became passable for marching armies, the union of forces would be effected and the march on Vienna resumed. The meagre Imperial forces blocking the road to the capital would soon be brushed aside, their attention distracted by the threat of a possible offensive through the Brenner Pass by Marshal Vendôme's 100,000 strong army, at present in North Italy. To isolate the Danube front from any intervention by the Allied forces stationed in the Netherlands, Marshal Villeroi's 46,000 men were expected to pin the 70,000 Dutch and English troops around Maastricht whilst de Coignies protected Alsace against surprise with a further corps.[2]

The only forces that were readily available for the immediate defence of Vienna in the early Spring of 1704 were the 36,000 Imperialists under the uninspired command of Prince Lewis of Baden, stationed in the Lines of Stoll-hofen to watch Tallard at Strasbourg, and a weak force of 10,000 soldiers under Count Styrum observing Ulm. Austria's peril was fully appreciated at the Schönbrunn—throughout the winter Count Wratislaw and other Imperial envoys had pleaded with the English and Dutch governments for material assistance, but to most appearances with scant success. Although the loss of Vienna would almost certainly entail the collapse of the Grand Alliance, the crises of southern Europe seemed comfortably remote from Whitehall and the Court of St. James, where colonial and commercial considerations were more to the fore in men's minds, whilst the cautious and dyke-minded Dutch Deputies of the States-General were as always principally concerned with the problem of their own national security behind the fortresses of Flanders and the River Barrier.

In the case of England, there were also political problems to resolve. The polarisation of factional attitudes to the waging of the war was increasing. The High Tories advocated a strategy based upon minimum involvement of national forces in Europe and the full employment of an enlarged Royal Navy overseas in pursuit of trade advantages and the capture of enemy colonies. The Whigs, on the other hand, traditionally demanded a large military presence on the Continent. The moderate Tory ministry of Marlborough and Godolphin found itself under heavy fire from both extremities of the political firmament during the winter of 1703/04, as the Whigs dropped all pretence at supporting the conduct of the war. Caught between two fires, they found themselves under heavy Parliamentary attack, which centred upon the issues of Dutch failures, real and imagined, to honour their treaty obligations, problems of recruitment, the intransigence of the Scottish Parliament, and the recent campaign's indecisive character.

In Marlborough's initial absence, Godolphin had to bear the brunt of the furore, and so depressed did he become that he several times sought to tender his resignation. The Duke, aware of the impending crisis in the war which must occur during 1704, was also in a considerable dilemma. On the one hand he had to encourage the Lord Treasurer to remain in office; on the other, he was still far from certain whether he could continue as Captain-General unless his authority over the Allied contingents, and most particularly the Dutch, was made more real. At one point he, too, had talked of retirement from public life—possibly as a measure designed to test the Queen's attitude now that the Parliamentary hounds were baying for blood. As we have seen, the Queen reacted strongly against this suggestion,* and in the name of the nation bade him soldier on.

After his arrival in London on 10 November, Marlborough carefully surveyed the scene whilst continuing crucial conversations with the imperial envoys. The Whigs, he found, were clamouring for his replacement at the head of the armies by the heir-once-removed to the throne, George, Elector of Hanover. With his usual urbanity, Marlborough expressed his willingness to accept such a supercession—but the Queen was never prepared to entertain the concept (her

* See p. 115 above.

attitude to the House of Hanover had always been ambivalent since her youth when she had with difficulty fended off Elector George as a suitor for her hand) and so the proposal lapsed. Next the most virulent Tory critics, led by none other than Nottingham and his clique on the Council (there was as yet scant belief in Ministerial solidarity), resorted to an old idea for embarrassing the leadership by reintroducing the prickly Occasional Conformity Bill in the Commons. As before, Marlborough and Godolphin swam with the Tory tide, voting for the Bill but covertly plotting against it. Once again the Tories passed the measure through both Houses despite the renewed clamour against so partisan a measure in the country at large. This time, however, it was the Queen who refused the Royal Assent, pointing out that the time was not right for such a measure, however deserving. Thus, in Sir Winston's words, 'malice was met by guile and faction baffled by deceit.'

The Tories were furious at this set-back, and it soon became evident to Marlborough and Godolphin that the Ministry must be reconstructed. Nottingham was eventually manœuvred into demanding the dismissal of the Whig Lords, Somerset and Devonshire, from the Council. The Queen's reply was to remove Nottingham's supporters, Seymour and Jersey. Nottingham could but resign, and on 18 May Robert Harley became Secretary of State as well as Speaker, and St. John was appointed Secretary at War. Thus a new Ministry of the centre was fashioned.

To return from the domestic to the international scene, only a handful of enlightened statesmen on each side of the English Channel realised the full and crucial implications of the situation on the Danube. Foremost amongst these was Marlborough. 'For this campaign I see so very ill a prospect that I am extremely out of heart': he wrote on 20 February to his wife Sarah.

It is not known when the Duke first decided to undertake a march to the Danube with part of the Netherlands army, for in an age of lax security and conflicting loyalties he was wise to keep his counsel to himself. All that *is* known is that he was considering such a possibility during the previous Autumn, and that he held long talks with the Austrian ambassador, Count Wratislaw, in London early in 1704—and the topic may have been discussed on previous occasions as well.* After crossing the Channel he reached the United Provinces on 21 April. Further days of discussions followed with Wratislaw (who had accompanied him from England) and Grand Pensionary Heinsius. During his short visit to the Hague in February he had already consulted the ailing veteran Coehoorn on his sickbed 'where', according to the latter's biographer, 'were made all the dispositions for that subsequent campaign which had such glorious and happy consequences'.[4] It is doubtful, however, whether the Duke trusted

---

* For a useful discussion of the part played by Wratislaw, see David Francis's article in the summer 1972 issue of the *S.A H.R. Journal*, pp. 78–100.

Coehoorn with his fullest confidence: probably he restricted their discussions to consideration of the alternative courses of action—namely the prospects of a campaign on the Moselle or a strike over the Middle Rhine towards Landau. Be this as it may, it was only three weeks before his departure for the Danube that he first committed his plan to paper, writing on 29 April to his governmental colleague and confidant, Godolphin, the Lord Treasurer, in the following terms: 'My intentions are to march with all the English to Coblenz and to declare that I intend to campaign on the Moselle. But, when I come there, to write to the Dutch States that I think it absolutely necessary for the saving of the Empire to march with the troops under my command and to join with those that are in Germany that are in Her Majesty's and the Dutch pay, in order to take measures with Prince Lewis of Baden for the speedy reduction of the Elector of Bavaria. What I now write, I beg may only be known to nobody but Her Majesty and the Prince.'[5] His purpose was to reinforce the Imperial forces and destroy the Franco-Bavarian army before Tallard could bring his army to its assistance.

This scheme of seizing the initiative from the foe and thereafter defeating him in detail was extremely bold in the light of early eighteenth-century military experience. The theoretical possibility of such a transfer was doubtless considered in many quarters during the preceding winter—but the political and military problems that stood in the way of success were daunting in the extreme. In the first place it was abundantly evident that the Dutch States-General would never willingly permit any major weakening of the Netherlands' forces—faced as they were by the threat posed by Marshal Villeroi's army. Nor could the Duke ride rough-shod over such opposition; for all his influence Marlborough was never in any real sense a 'supreme commander'—but was precariously dependent on the support of the politicians of the Hague and Westminster.

The States-General posed the greater problem. Even the question of 'the regulating of the command for the next year' was beset with uncertainties, for Cadogan confided to Lord Raby, Ambassador to the Court of Brandenburg, in a letter dated 17 February 1703/4 from the Hague, that unless a satisfactory centralisation was achieved, 'I am afraid our next campaign will be as inactive as the last; nobody can better judge than your Lordship of the necessity of putting the command into a single hand and the impossibility of doing anything without it. One might think the misfortune of Speyerbach might convince these herring-sellers of the inconvenience which unavoidably attends a distinct left and right wing, which is in effect the making a great body of men useless at the best.'[6] The Duke's first problem, therefore, was to overcome or by-pass Dutch obstruction and the only way this could be done was by reticence and guile. Only Anthonie Heinsius could be trusted with his real plans.

Besides such politico-military difficulties at the Hague, a large part of the Allied army was as usual made up of mercenary elements hired from the rulers of the smaller states of the Empire. These princelings were very sensitive to the trend of events, and the apparent prospect of impending Allied defeat entailed failure to honour agreements to supply men and munitions. Marlborough had as usual to cajole, flatter and charm each ruler in turn to secure their unwilling or cautious co-operation in his projects, and they were less than usually forthcoming in the spring of 1704.

To contemporary observers, versed in the recognised principles of warfare, the military dangers inherent in a scheme of the type Marlborough was now secretly preparing would also have appeared prohibitive. His line of march down the Rhine would necessarily pass across the fronts of two large French field armies which were well placed to take Marlborough's army in flank. To add to this peril, from the moment the Duke left the region dominated by the Dutch General Overkirk north of Coblenz until the time he reached the Margrave of Baden in the area of the Lines of Stollhofen, his march would be completely unsupported by friendly covering forces. Even if he was allowed to pass unhindered, his lines of communication along the Rhine would be hopelessly exposed to French interference, for Louis' generals controlled the west bank of the river in its central reaches. This risk accentuated another military problem— that of supply. Burdened by heavy guns and bulky wagons, eighteenth-century armies habitually crawled along the earth roads of Europe at a rate of not more than ten miles a day—and to execute the 250-mile march to the Danube would almost certainly involve a high wastage of men and horses through exhaustion and disease, for adequate food and fodder would be extremely hard to procure for much of the way.

Faced by the combination of these problems, it seemed highly improbable that Marlborough could reach the Danube with an intact army fit enough to fight and win an immediate major battle to secure control of the region—yet only such an outcome would alleviate the peril to Vienna. However, the urgency of the hour demanded radical measures and, as Marlborough wrote to Godolphin on 1 May: 'I am very sensible that I take a great deal upon me. But should I act otherwise, the Empire would be undone, and consequently the Confederacy.'[7] This letter went on to mention 'marching to the Danube' for the first time. Vienna was secretly informed of this on 11 May.

There was need to hasten; on 14 May, Marshal Tallard completed the operation of manœuvring 10,000 reinforcements (including 2,400 cavalry and 200 cannon) through the Black Forest to Ulm, neatly parrying Baden's clumsy attempts to intercept his convoy. The Franco-Bavarian offensive was clearly imminent. Five days later, Marlborough's movement began.

A combination of strategic deception and brilliant administration enabled Marlborough to achieve his purpose. His departure from Bedburg on 19 May at the head of 21,000 men (31 battalions and 66 squadrons) excited little immediate comment, for his declared purpose of campaigning along the Moselle was the logical sequel to the previous year's operations on the Meuse and Rhine and had received the grudging approval of the States-General on 2 May. It was only when he reached Coblenz on the 26th and ordered his troops to cross over to the right bank of the Rhine the next day, pausing but to add 5,000 waiting Hanoverians and Prussians to his strength, that anyone suspected a hidden intention. 'When we expected to march up the Moselle to our surprise we passed over that river by a stone bridge and then the Rhine over two bridges of boats', wrote Captain Parker in his 'Memoirs'.[8]

The first bluff was now over—but Marlborough continued to dominate the situation and keep the enemy guessing. Marshal Villeroi meanwhile was shadowing Marlborough with 30,000 men and had taken up a defensive position on the Moselle; the French general was now forced to report to Versailles: 'There will be no campaign on the Moselle—the English have all gone higher up into Germany.' Dutch anticipation of an immediate French counter-offensive against their weakened forces in the Netherlands thus proved illusory—for Villeroi deemed it his duty to continue to observe Marlborough's movements with 42 battalions and 60 squadrons: 'My forces will continue to cover the advance from the left bank of the Rhine.'[9] This left the Dutch perfectly secure; in any case Marlborough was able to quieten any lingering anxieties by promising that he would return at once to the Netherlands if a French attack developed there, transferring his army in barges down the Rhine at a rate of 80 miles a day. Heartened by this assurance, the States-General promptly voted him their full support and agreed to release the Danish contingent (7 battalions and 22 squadrons) as a reinforcement (10 June).

The march continued, the French still conforming without making any serious attempt to interfere with its progress and Marlborough, thanks to his excellent spies, aware of every contemplated enemy movement well in advance. Now a second possible objective appeared on the horizon: an incursion into Alsace towards the great city of Strasbourg. This great city had only passed into French hands in 1681, and Louis XIV was particularly sensitive about its safety. Marlborough was careful to heighten his new threat by ordering the Governor of Phillipsburg to build bridges of boats across the river and by massing supplies in the fortress as if a major crossing was intended. Although both were by now fairly certain that Marlborough's ultimate destination was the Danube, not only Villeroi but also Marshal Tallard was partially deceived by these preparations, and the latter cautiously postponed his main army's march to Ulm whilst he referred to Versailles for new orders in the light of the new situation. This pause in French operations gave Marlborough and the cavalry time to cross two further major obstacles across his path—the River Main on 3 June and the Neckar four days later, and shortly thereafter the 'scarlet caterpillar' (as the Duke's distinguished descendant has termed it) swung away from the Rhine towards the hills of the Swabian Jura and the Danube beyond—and at last his destination was established without doubt. On 6 June the Duke at last informed the Dutch of his full intentions.

At the beginning of the month, Tallard had ordered his garrison at Tour-le-Seine to interrupt the Rhine traffic[10]—but it was now too late for the Marshal to prevent or forestall the Duke's arrival in the critical theatre. 'This march has hardly left me time to eat or sleep', wrote William Cadogan to Lord Raby, 'We continue it with all imaginable diligence towards the Lines of Stollhofen, where the Luneburghers, Hessians and Dutch already are....'[11] The most dangerous part of the march was safely over, for the Lines of Stollhofen and Baden's army were now close at hand and began to exert a protective influence, whilst a new series of communications, running from the expedition's financial base at Frankfurt down the River Main to the friendly areas around Nuremburg and Nordlingen, replaced the previously exposed system based on the Rhine. Moreover, during the latter stages of the march, Marlborough's army was steadily rising to a total of 40,000 men (47 battalions and 88 squadrons) by the actual or imminent arrival of Danish and Prussian contingents. On 22 June, these forces linked up with elements of Baden's Imperialists at Launsheim. A distance of more than 250 miles had been covered in just over five weeks and Europe applauded a major military feat. Even more amazing, the transferred army was evidently in a fit state to fight immediately: the effects of 'wear and tear' had been kept to a minimum. Some 1200 sick had been left behind *en route*, but the desertion rate had never been lighter.

The secret of the fine morale and first-class condition of the bulk of Marlborough's army lay in the care the Captain-General had lavished on every detail of administration. Aided by his usual handful of assistants—William Cadogan, Adam Cardonnel, and Henry Davenant, his financial agent—a comprehensive scheme of supply arrangements had been planned and implemented. To speed the march, all heavy impedimenta—including the larger guns—had been left in the Netherlands, Marlborough calculating (somewhat hopefully as it proved) that the Imperialists would have enough and to spare. The vital stores and lighter cannon were conveyed by river barges as far as possible, and then carried in specially-designed two-wheel and sprung carts. Initially Marlborough's 21,000 men were accompanied by 1,700 supply carts carrying 1,200 lbs of stores apiece, drawn by 5,000 draught-horses. The artillery needed as many more. At Heidelberg a new pair of shoes awaited every man, and ample gold was carried in the Military Chest for the purchase of supplies which ensured a maximum of local co-operation from burghers and peasants alike.

These measures were supplemented by a carefully-planned march time-table designed to confuse the enemy scouting parties and save the men from undue wear and tear. The main body of the cavalry moved a day or two's march ahead of 'the poor foot'. Captain Parker described the march discipline as follows: 'We frequently marched three, sometimes four days successively and halted one day.

We generally began our march about three in the morning, proceeded about four leagues or four and a half by day, and reached our camping ground by nine. As we marched through the country of our Allies, commissars were appointed to furnish us with all manner of necessaries for man and horse; these were brought to the ground before we arrived, and the soldiers had nothing to do but pitch their tents, boil their kettles and lie down to rest. Surely never was such a march carried on with more order and regularity and with less fatigue to man and horse.'[12] The use of early-morning marches and day-time rests confused the shadowing French cavalry, who could often see no tell-tale dust clouds on the horizon to indicate the Allied position, whilst the men were not called upon to march in the full heat of the day. In recognition for this genuine care for their well-being, the rank and file dubbed their leader 'the old Corporal'*, and the high morale engendered by his fine administration enabled Marlborough to make calls on their endurance that few other generals would contemplate. According to the *cantinière*, Mother Ross, on at least one occasion the Duke '. . . seeing some of our Foot drop through the fatigue of the march, took them into his own coach.'[15]

This feature of Marlborough's generalship contrasts strongly with Marshal Tallard's record during the same campaign: the French march to Ulm in May was carried through at a cost of one third of his army's effective strength through desertion and straggling, mostly during the return march; on his second sortie in July, a large proportion of the cavalry-horses died and according to Mérode-Westerloo, 'the enraged peasantry killed several thousand of our men before the army was clear of the Black Forest.'[14] But the Allied journey had not been without its difficulties—especially for the infantry and guns which travelled two or three days' march behind the cavalry. Owing to torrential rain, several delays were experienced, and French spies reported that 900 sick had been left at Cassel. Nevertheless such losses by the wayside were kept to a minimum, and Captain Blackadder's gloomy prophecy at the outset of the march that 'this is like to be a campaign of great fatigue and trouble' proved over pessimistic.

Whilst the last stages of the main march were being completed, Marlborough rode ahead to meet the Margrave of Baden and Prince Eugene of Savoy at Gross Heppach (10–15 June) to concert plans for the destruction of the Elector of Bavaria's army. At the age of 50, Prince Lewis of Baden was the senior commander in rank and experience if not in years. A long record of distinguished service against the Turk had established his reputation as a fine soldier, but his outlook on warfare had degenerated into wholly 'conventional' attitudes and consequently in 1704 he was cautious to a fault and a stickler for the observance of the proper formalties. The ugly fiery genius of a soldier, Prince Eugene, on the other hand, was not yet 41, but had enjoyed a meteoric career in the Imperial service, being promoted general of cavalry at 26 and a commander-in-chief ten

* The eighteenth-century corporal often carried out the functions of the modern Company Quartermaster Sergeant.

years later.* In most ways he shared Marlborough's disregard for the accepted conventions which favoured the siege at the expense of the battle, but was understandably unpopular with the crusty Baden. This created a delicate command problem—but as usual Marlborough's tact found a solution. To save the Margrave's face, it was agreed that the daily orders should be issued on alternate days by Baden and Marlborough—giving the fallacious impression of a joint command—although in fact it was clearly understood at Vienna that the Duke was senior director and secret arrangements may have been made for the Margrave's removal from command had he proved fatally obstructive.[15]

The three generals between them now commanded a force approaching 110,000 men, which was more than enough to ensure them the advantages of the local initiative. A plan was rapidly confirmed. Prince Eugene was to return to the Lines of Stollhofen to direct a force of 28,000 men with instructions to keep a close watch on Villeroi and Tallard, and to shadow and report on their movements. This was to be a crucial duty, and although Marlborough would have dearly liked to have kept such a kindred spirit at his side, he was aware that it would be safer to retain the troublesome Baden under his own eye. So Marlborough's men marched on through the Swabian Jura to join Baden's Imperialists at Launsheim (22 June), and from there the two generals set out together with a joint 80,000 men to seek out the Elector of Bavaria and Marsin and clinch the success of the campaign. Baden's promise of 40 large cannon, however, was never honoured, and there was also a deficiency of 100 bread wagons to be overcome.

Cadogan had already (30 May) set down Marlborough's original intentions in a remarkable document that seems to have been missed by previous biographers. 'The French having already passed 9,000 recruits (to Marsin), 'tis absolutely necessary to hasten putting in execution the project of reducing the Elector of Bavaria before he can receive a greater succour. In order to (do) it there will be an army left in the Lines of Stollhofen sufficient to prevent the French forcing them or passing the Rhine below Phillipsburg. With the rest of our troops they design forming two armies, each of above 40,000, and *to enter by two ways into Bavaria, one by Donauwörth, the other between Ulm and (the) Lake of Constance* (this author's italics), which will oblige the Elector either to divide his force or else to keep his force entire and act against one, and

---

* Prince Eugene of Savoy (1663-1736), the son of the Count of Soissons and Olympia Mancini (a niece of Cardinal Mazarin), was judged by Louis XIV to be entirely lacking in officer qualities. Consequently, in 1683 he transferred his services to the Emperor. In spite of a feeble physique and an unprepossessing appearance, he soon became a tough and dedicated soldier of phenomenal skill and courage. He made his reputation, and earned rapid promotions, whilst fighting the Turk. He was also a notable diplomat. He had little time for women, and was notorious for his lack of tact and hot temper, but his collaboration with Marlborough (1704-10) was a complete success. Eugene was also noted as an art connoisseur and collector.

so leave the other a free passage to Munich and Ingolstadt: this must necessarily bring him to reason unless he will hazard inevitable ruin by being shut up between two armies, each stronger than his own, that must certainly happen after the taking (of) the two aforementioned places. The whole success of this expedition depends on preventing the French either to force the Lines of Stollhofen or to pass the Rhine below Phillipsburg, which they will probably attempt when their great detachment from the Meuse (Villeroi) has joined their army on the Rhine (Tallard), as their only way left to succour the Elector, we having got (so) far before them as to make their sending any further succour by the Black Forest too late.'[16] This testimony by an officer who served as Marlborough's virtual chief-of-staff reveals that the broad outline of the Allied plan was in existence some time *prior* to the meeting at Gross Heppach, and is of great interest in showing the original proposed solution for bringing the Elector to terms—although in the event, as we shall see, this scheme had to be substantially modified in the light of subsequent events which proved some of its assumptions erroneous—particularly the last. Nevertheless, it provides evidence of Marlborough's capacity for strategic planning, and also proves that Cadogan as well as Cardonnel was fully in the Duke's confidence by this stage, despite Sir Winston Churchill's assertion to the contrary.*

Meanwhile, feverish though indecisive counsels were taking place at Tallard's headquarters in the city of Strasbourg. The Marshal met Villeroi at Landau on 13 June, as Marlborough's staff knew by the 19th, so good was the Allied intelligence system, '. . . but we do not hear they have undertaken anything as yet.'[17] It was imperative that rapid action should be implemented to save Bavaria—but the rigidity of the French command system laid it down that any variations from the original plan of campaign had to be sanctioned by Versailles. As a result Tallard was delayed for almost three weeks awaiting Louis XIV's approval of his scheme to march through the Glotterthal Pass into Bavaria. The Count of Mérode-Westerloo, commander of the Flemish troops in Tallard's army, was openly critical of this delay. In his interesting 'Memoirs', which provide an invaluable account of the campaign as seen from the French side, he wrote: 'One thing is certain: we delayed our march from Alsace far too long and quite inexplicably, for it was contrary to the usual diligence, promptness and vivacity of the French'.[18] Louis' orders (dated 23 June) at last reached Tallard and Villeroi on 27 June: the former was to advance with a force of 40 battalions and 50 squadrons through the Kintzig Valley into the Black Forest to relieve the Elector, covered by Villeroi's slightly stronger army (40 battalions and 68 squadrons) which was to 'advance on Offenburg, observe the enemy, retain them in the Lines of Stollhofen, follow them into Alsace, or join Marshal Tallard if they move all their forces towards the Danube.'[19] Meanwhile de Coignies' corps (10–12 battalions and as many squadrons) would safeguard

* See Churchill, *Marlborough his life and Times*, (1967 paperback edn.) vol. II, p. 277.

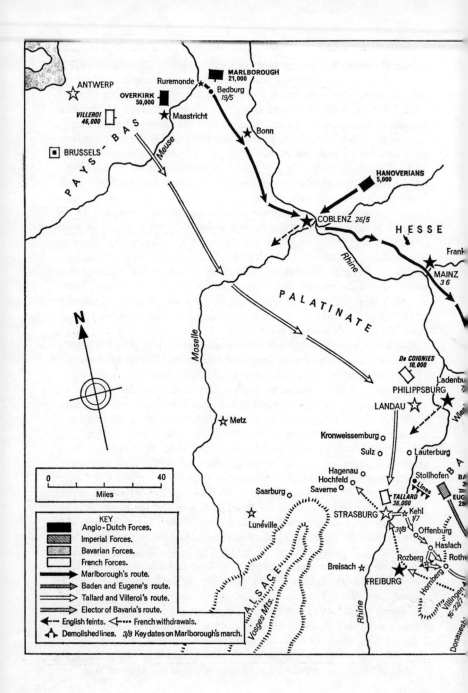

ANTWERP

Ruremonde

MARLBOROUGH
21,000
Bedburg
19/5

OVERKIRK
50,000

VILLEROI
46,000

Maastricht

Bonn

■ BRUSSELS

PAYS - BAS

Meuse

HANOVERIANS
5,000

COBLENZ *26/5*

HESSE

Rhine

Frank

MAINZ
3 6

Moselle

PALATINATE

De COIGNIES
10,000

Ladenbu

PHILIPPSBURG

LANDAU

☆ Metz

Kronweissemburg ○

Sulz ○

○ Lauterburg

Wie

B A

Stollhofen

Hagenau ○

Saarburg ○

Hochfeld
Saverne ○

Lines

TALLARD
36,000

BA
3

EUG
28

0 _____ 40

Miles

Luneville ☆

STRASBURG

Kehl
1/7

31/8

Offenburg ○

Haslach ○

KEY
■ Anglo-Dutch Forces.
▨ Imperial Forces.
▨ Bavarian Forces.
□ French Forces.
➡ Marlborough's route.
⇒ Baden and Eugene's route.
⇒ Tallard and Villeroi's route.
⇒ Elector of Bavaria's route.
◄--- English feints. ◄••• French withdrawals.
Demolished lines. *3/8* Key dates on Marlborough's march.

Breisach ☆

FREIBURG

Rozberg

Roth

Homberg

Villingen.
16-22/7

Rhine

Donauesc

A L S A C E

Vosges Mts.

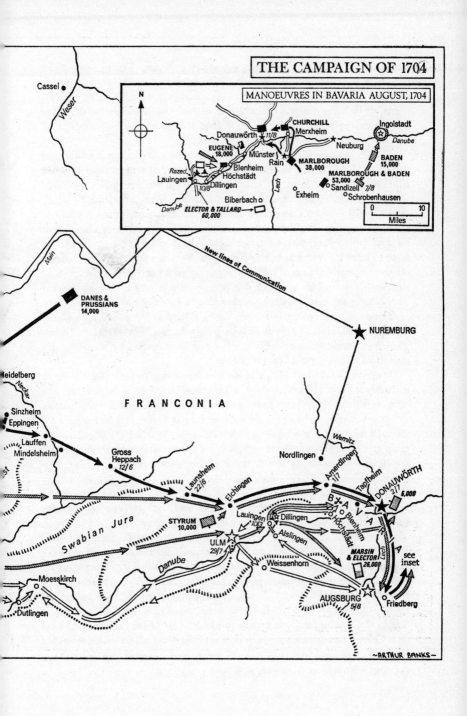

THE CAMPAIGN OF 1704

MANOEUVRES IN BAVARIA AUGUST, 1704

N

Cassel

Weser

CHURCHILL
Merxheim

Donauwörth 11/8
EUGENE
18,000
Münster
Blenheim
Rain
Höchstädt
Dillingen
10/8
MARLBOROUGH
38,000

Ingolstadt
Danube
Neuburg
BADEN
15,000
MARLBOROUGH & BADEN
53,000
Sandizell 7/8
Schrobenhausen

Razed
Lauingen
Danube
Biberbach
Exheim
Lech

ELECTOR & TALLARD
60,000

0   10
Miles

Main

New lines of Communication

DANES &
PRUSSIANS
14,000

NUREMBURG

Heidelberg
Neckar
Sinzheim
Eppingen

FRANCONIA

Lauffen
Mindelsheim

Gross
Heppach
12/6

Launsheim
22/6

Elchingen

Wernitz
Nordlingen
Amerdingen
1/7
Tapfheim
DONAUWÖRTH
2/7
5,000

STYRUM
10,000

Lauingen
10/3
Dillingen
B + A V
Blenheim
Höchstädt
A
R
I
A
see
inset

Swabian Jura

Danube

ULM
29/7

Aislingen

Weissenhorn

MARSIN
& ELECTOR
26,000

Lech

Moesskirch

AUGSBURG
5/8

Friedberg

Dutlingen

~ARTHUR BANKS~

Alsace. On 1 July—at long last—the advance began, Tallard successfully deflecting Eugene's vigilance by using Villeroi to mount diversionary attacks. Mérode-Westerloo records: 'After making a feint-attack on the Lines of Stollhofen, we left the fortress of Kehl and entered the Black Forest down the Kintzig valley. Before we did so, M. Tallard formed us into battle-order. . . .' Villeroi left Kehl for Offenburg eight days later.

Tallard's progress was almost pitifully slow: this was partly due to the poor condition of the cavalry, suffering from an epidemic of a mysterious 'German sickness' (probably a form of glanders), partly to the lumbering convoy—'made up of more than eight thousand waggons of bread, flour and biscuit'*—which the army had to escort through the difficult mountain passes—and not a little to the commander-in-chief's insistence on besieging the little town of Villingen for six days (16–22 July) with his entire army instead of leaving a small covering force to mask its defences. In due course, the French were compelled to break off the siege when Eugene's shadowing army of 18,000 men appeared near Rothweil—for Tallard was misled concerning the strength of this Imperial force, and in any case was determined to avoid a battle before joining his allies.

After seeing the convoy safely into Ulm, Tallard at last joined up with the Elector and Marshal Marsin at Augsburg on 5 August. The French had taken 36 days to complete a march of only half the distance covered by Marlborough's men in an almost identical period of time.

Meanwhile, Duke and Margrave were endeavouring to force the Elector to make peace. The Allies were short of heavy artillery, for the Imperialist siege train on which Marlborough had depended had in fact fallen into enemy hands the previous year, and more guns were held up at Mainz and Nuremburg for several weeks, and in consequence they were unable to attack the large Bavarian camp at Ulm. This was a grave setback as this city constituted a major strategic target, and it forced the abandonment of the 'double-invasion' scheme described by Cadogan. Marlborough and Baden continued on together. Proceeding along the north bank of the Danube, they skirted the even stronger position of Lauingen (Baden obstructing a chance to attack the foe at Giengen without delay.) and unexpectedly appeared outside the fortress of Donauwörth on the afternoon of 2 July—to the considerable surprise of the local Bavarian commander, Comte d'Arco, and his garrison of 10,000 men, who were hard at work modernising the ancient defences. Marlborough hustled the doubtful Baden into sanctioning an immediate assault, to be attempted in the first instance by a picked corps of grenadiers and volunteers totalling 6,000 men, who were to be launched against the strongest sector to draw off d'Arco's reserves. The struggle commenced at 6.15 in the evening, and was extremely bloody. One of the defenders, Colonel de la Colonie, has left a graphic description of the desperate action for control of

---

* Other sources, probably more realistically, put the convoy at 2,000 vehicles and 4 large guns (see Pelet & le Vault, vol. IV, p. 510).

the Schellenberg Heights—the key to the position. 'The enemy broke into the charge, and rushed at full speed shouting at the top of their voices, to throw themselves into our entrenchments, the rapidity of their movements together with their loud noise was truly alarming; and as soon as I heard them I ordered our drums to beat the charge so as to drown them with our noise lest they should have a bad effect on our people. The English infantry led the attack with the greatest intrepidity right up to our parapet . . . (which) became the scene of the bloodiest struggle that could be conceived. During this first attack we were all fighting hand to hand, hurling them back as they clutched at the parapet. . . . At last the enemy, after huge losses, were obliged to relax their hold, and fell back for shelter to the dip of the slope where we could not harm them. A sudden calm now reigned amongst us.'[20]

This apparent Allied repulse was deceptive: to hold the Heights against the onslaught, d'Arco had drawn more and more men from the central portion of his defences, which linked the Schellenberg with the town of Donauwörth. It was against this weakened sector that the Margrave now unleashed the Imperial cavalry backed by supporting infantry—and in no time these troops interposed themselves between d'Arco and the town. De la Colonie resumes the tale: 'At about 7.30 I noticed all at once an extraordinary movement on the part of our infantry, who were rising up and ceasing fire withal. I glanced around to determine what had caused this behaviour, and then became aware of several lines of infantry in greyish-white uniforms on our left flank. I verily believed reinforcement had reached us; no information whatever had reached us of the enemy's success to the left. So in the error I laboured under I shouted to my men that they were Frenchmen and friends.' He was speedily disillusioned, and by 8.30 the remnants of D'Arco's garrison were in full flight for the Danube, where many were drowned when a bridge collapsed. The town of Donauwörth soon afterwards surrendered.

This important success provided the Allies with a crossing-place over the River Danube into the southern regions of Bavaria, and at the same time gave them a terminal and forward depot for their lines of communication running south from Nordlingen.

The victory had been dearly bought. The Allies lost 1,342 men killed and 3,699 wounded. Included in these numbers were no less than 16 general officers (four, including Count Styrum and the gallant Goor, being killed) and 375 officers (including 79 dead); these very high officer casualties give some indication of the type and ferocity of the engagement. The worst hit unit would seem to have been the Regiment of Baden which lost 320 officers and men. English losses totalled 88 officers and 1,199 other ranks.[21]

For their part the Bavarians and French lost 5,000 men or half their strength. Had Marlborough listened to Baden and postponed the attack, the Allied blood-list might have been far longer—for without siege artillery a direct assault was

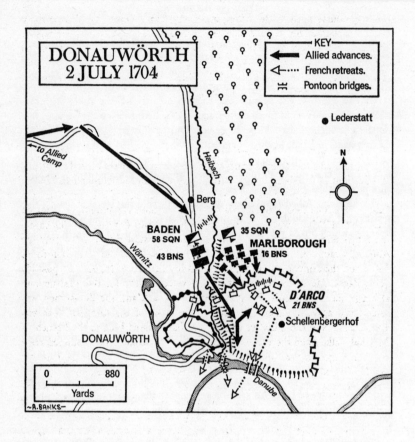

KEY
Allied advances.
French retreats.
Pontoon bridges.

DONAUWÖRTH
2 JULY 1704

Lederstatt

N

to Allied Camp

Haibach

Berg

Wörnitz

BADEN
58 SQN

35 SQN

MARLBOROUGH
16 BNS

43 BNS

D'ARCO
21 BNS

Schellenbergerhof

DONAUWÖRTH

0   880
Yards

Danube

~A.BANKS~

the only course open to the Allies, and every hour's delay gave d'Arco more time to strengthen his defences and summon assistance. But as yet there was no sign of the Elector's main army. The decisive victory that was required to complete the campaign had still to be sought and won, and at this juncture 'Dame Fortune' temporarily transferred her aid to Marlborough's foes and placed his whole achievement in jeopardy.

*   *   *

After the capture of Donauwörth, success began to elude the Allies. The Elector refused either to fight or negotiate—but kept his forces behind the strong fortifications of Augsburg, which were impregnable to Marlborough and Baden without the assistance of a siege train. Similarly the city of Munich defied the Allied army. The Elector of Bavaria was soon informed (14 July) by a smuggled message that Tallard was on his way through the Black Forest—and this cheering intelligence reinforced his policy of inaction whilst for much of July the Allies (73 battalions and 173 squadrons strong) besieged and took Rain (9–16 July), and then impotently ravaged the Bavarian countryside, burning possibly 400 villages. Marlborough must bear full responsibility for this destruction* although he undoubtedly found it hard to stomach and the devastation was undertaken against Baden's protests.[22] The crisis of the campaign was fast approaching, and the initiative appeared to have passed back to the French; if Marshal Tallard and the Elector succeeded in interposing their combined army between Eugene's small force (retreating along the north bank of the Danube) and Marlborough and Baden south of the river, the latter's communications with Franconia would eventually be severed and all the Allied forces placed in a very critical position. Under such disturbing circumstances, Marlborough's brilliant march to the Danube and forceful capture of Donauwörth might only result in a crushing disaster for the isolated and separated armies of the Grand Alliance.

This opportunity of total triumph, however, was to prove too much for the restricted abilities and imaginations of the Franco-Bavarian generals, faced as they were by the genius of Duke John and the fine quality of the men he led. Marshal Tallard was a soldier of great experience and considerable achievement, who, apart from his military career had earned a notable reputation as a diplomat —serving at one time as French ambassador to the Court of St. James and as such, we may surmise, had been known to Marlborough. He was famed for his courtly manners and ostentatious hospitality; 'he would, on occasion, entertain anything up to a hundred officers during the first or second halt of a day's

* As he wrote to Heinsius on 16 July, '. . . we are now advancing into the heart of Bavaria to destroy the country and oblige the Elector on [e] way or other to a complyance.' The Duke underlined this passage in the original document. See also p. 314 below.

march', wrote Mérode-Westerloo, 'keeping two mule trains laden with good
things to eat—and wines too—at the head of the army for this very purpose.'[23]
This generosity contrasts strangely with Marlborough's parsimony: the Duke
rarely entertained his subordinates on a lavish scale—and made a point of dining
at their tables whenever this was possible. This strange streak in an otherwise
extremely liberal character was doubtless due to the financial difficulties experienced in Churchill's youth, but he made up for his deficiencies as a host
with unquestionable military genius. Little need be said here of Tallard's
military colleagues: Marshal Marsin was a competent mediocrity; Max Emmanuel, Elector of Bavaria, was a colourful figure of considerable dash and
ability—but a totally unscrupulous opportunist who had deserted the Emperor
and adopted the Franco-Spanish cause through motives of purely selfish aggrandisement. The Bavarian field forces were considerably weakened by detachments sent to protect the electoral estates—and the Elector's relationship with
his French colleagues was frequently acrimonious for he refused to recall the
majority: this was one positive result of the Allied ravaging of Bavaria.[24] Marlborough's cordial relations with Prince Eugene and his tactful handling of the
Margrave compare very favourably with the strained relations experienced in the
enemy camp.

Following their union at Augsburg, the Franco-Bavarian army set off for the
Danube, intent on isolating Marlborough to the south of the river and intending
to avenge the ravaging of Bavaria by meting out similar treatment to the population of Franconia. Fortunately Marlborough's flexible military mind was equal
to the new challenge. The crisis of the campaign had arrived. It was clearly
desirable to secure an alternative crossing place over the Danube—in case
Donauwörth fell to the French. It was equally clear that the best man for the
task was the Margrave, leaving the Duke and Prince to cover the operation.
Consequently at a conference with Eugene on 7 August, Baden was persuaded to
take 15,000 (24 battalions, 31 squadrons and 30 guns) men to besiege the town of
Ingolstadt 20 miles further down the Danube—a project that had been in the
Duke's mind for some time. Neuburg and its bridge had already fallen to
the Allies, but it was too close to Donauwörth to be safe. Prince Eugene returned
to Hochstädt to note every enemy move. On 10 August he sent an urgent dispatch to Marlborough from Munster reporting that he was falling back towards
Donauwörth. 'The enemy have marched. It is almost certain that the whole army
is crossing the Danube at Lauingen. They have pushed a Lieutenant-Colonel
whom I sent to reconnoitre back to Höchstädt. The plain of Dillingen is crowded
with troops. I have held on all day here; but with 18 battalions I dare not risk
staying the night. . . . Everything, milord, consists in speed and that you put
yourself forthwith in movement to join me tomorrow, without which I fear it
will be too late. In short, all the enemy is there. . . .' 'I am very confident they
will not venture a battaile (sic)', wrote Marlborough to Heinsius, 'but if wee find a

fair occasion, wee shal be glad to venture itt, being persuaded the ill condition of affairs in most partes requires it.'[25]

Marlborough needed no urging; by a series of brilliant marches he concentrated his army and converged his forces on Donauwörth, part crossing the Danube at Merxheim, the rest taking the direct road from Rain over the River Lech. During the 11th, the link-up with Eugene was completed—but no effort was made to recall Baden. There is some evidence that his political reliability was still suspect, and besides the continuing siege of Ingolstadt would help lull Tallard into a sense of false security. Meantime, the Franco-Bavarian army advanced methodically eastwards from Lauingen, not for one moment expecting to be soon concerned in a major battle, and on 12 August Tallard pitched camp behind the small River Nebel near the village of Blenheim (or Blindheim). The same day Marlborough and Eugene carried out a reconnaissance of the French position from the church-spire of Tapfheim, from which they could observe the lay-out of the enemy camp, and thus gain some idea of Tallard's probable battle order, and moved their army forward to Munster—a mere five miles from the French camp. The 'Two Princes'—in direct contravention of the rules of conventional war—had made up their minds to risk everything in an attack timed for the next day. The night was spent in final preparations for the coming conflict, while a dense mist shrouded the Danube valley.

Early the next morning the Allied army was roused from its tents and put in motion towards the Nebel, marching in nine great columns. At six o'clock the first troops came within sight of the French cantonments. Mérode-Westerloo, who had been put in command of the cavalry on the right of the second line, had spent the night in a barn on the outskirts of Blenheim. 'I slept deeply until six in the morning when I was abruptly awoken by one of my old retainers—the head-groom in fact—who rushed into the barn all out of breath. He had just returned from taking my horses out to grass at four in the morning (as he had been instructed). This fellow, Lefranc, shook me awake and blurted out that the enemy were "there". Thinking to mock him, I asked: 'Where? There?' and he at once replied "Yes, there! there!" flinging wide as he spoke the door of the barn and drawing my bed-curtains. The building looked straight onto the fine, sunlit plain beyond—and the whole area appeared to be covered by enemy squadrons. I rubbed my eyes in disbelief.'[26] The Count soon recovered his composure however, coolly ordered a cup of chocolate, and wisely instructed his servants 'to pack my kit with all speed, and to watch Marshal Tallard's retainers and do with my belongings exactly what they did with his.' Shortly afterwards, Mérode-Westerloo rode off to the camp, accompanied by his two aides-de-camp and no less than 13 spare horses. He found everything quiet. 'There was not a single soul stirring as I clattered out of the village: nothing might have been happening. The same sight met me when I reached the camp—everyone still snug in their tents, although the enemy ... were already pushing back our pickets.' The

Count ordered his cavalry to mount—but was careful not to sound the general alarm. 'Soon everyone was on his horse, and I kept them all drawn up at the head of their tents—and then—and only then—did I see the first signs of movement in Blenheim village.'[27]

Marshal Tallard was still in no way worried by these warlike demonstrations to his front. As late as seven o'clock he penned a postscript on to his report of the previous day, and sent the messenger on his way to Versailles. 'This morning (13th) before daybreak the enemy beat the *générale* at two o'clock and at three the *assemblé*. They are now drawn up at the head of their camp and it looks as if they will march this day. Rumour in the countryside expects them to move on Nordlingen. If that be true, they will leave us between the Danube and themselves, and in consequence they will have difficulty in sustaining the depots which they have taken in Bavaria.'[28] The events of the next 12 hours were to prove this forecast singularly unfortunate. An hour later Tallard decided he had better rouse his men, but it was only at ten in the morning, when Colonel Blood's batteries opened fire, that he fully realised he had a major battle on his hands.

The reasons for this miscalculation and lack of awareness on the part of the French commander are not far to seek. By the rules of eighteenth-century chess-board warfare, Marlborough and Eugene had been out-generalled, and the prescribed course for them to follow was a retreat along their lines of communication. In any case Allied 'deserters' had confirmed this assessment of the Allied intentions—for Marlborough had been careful to plant corroborative evidence on the gullible Tallard. The latter further reasoned that his army was in possession of a strong natural position which would be costly to attack—and this made a battle even less likely in an age when economy-minded governments deplored heavy expenditure of virtually irreplaceable man-power and material. 'Our right wing was on the left bank of the River Danube', wrote Mérode-Westerloo, 'with the village of Blenheim some two hundred yards to its front. . . . In front of this village ran a small stream running from its swampy source a mile or so away to the left. . . . The Elector and his men held a position reaching away as far as the village of Lutzingen where his headquarters were situated— with the woods stretching away towards Nordlingen to his front. Before this position was an area of marshy-ground, a few hamlets and one or two mills along the little stream. Blenheim village itself was surrounded by hedges, and fences and other obstacles, enclosed gardens and meadows. All in all, this position was pretty fair. . . .' However, the Nebel made an awkward angle with the Danube.[8] Another advantage of the position was the slight rise set back at a distance of some 800 yards from the Nebel, connecting Blenheim with the village of Oberglau and then on towards Lutzingen. With both flanks secured, and with his army holding a position set behind an area of marsh and stream, Tallard felt he had reason for confidence.

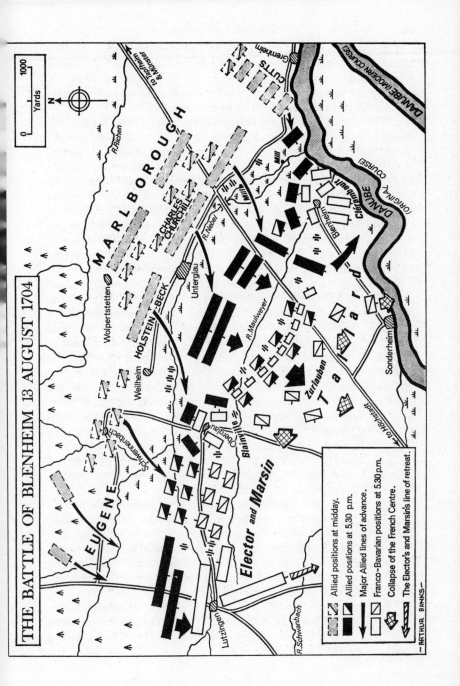

THE BATTLE OF BLENHEIM 13 AUGUST 1704

MARLBOROUGH

CHARLES CHURCHILL

HOLSTEIN-BECK

EUGENE

Elector and Marsin

R.Richen

R.Niebel

Wolpertstetten

Wellheim

Weilheim

Unterglau

R.Maulweyer

Schwennenbach

Oberglau

Blainville

Lutzingen

R.Schwanbach

Zurlauben

T a l l a r d

CUTTS

Oberglau

Mill

Mill

Blenheim

Clérambault

Sonderheim

DANUBE (ORIGINAL) COURSE

DANUBE MODERN COURSE

to Hochstedt

to Tapfheim & Munster

N

0   1000
        Yards

Allied positions at midday.
Allied positions at 5.30 p.m.
Major Allied lines of advance.
Franco-Bavarian positions at 5.30 p.m.
Collapse of the French Centre.
The Elector's and Marsin's line of retreat.

~ ARTHUR BANKS ~

In addition to these natural advantages, Tallard possessed a slight superiority in overall numbers—56,000 French and Bavarians facing 52,000 Allies—and a definite advantage in artillery—90 cannon against 66. His force consisted of 70 battalions and 143 squadrons, whilst Marlborough and Eugene deployed rather more cavalry (178 squadrons) but only 66 infantry battalions.

In spite of being surprised and forced to accept battle, Tallard was fortunate enough to be given ample time to draw up his battle formation—for although Marlborough's left and centre were ready by ten o'clock, Eugene was delayed on the right by hills and wooded country and was only in position after midday. The French commander used this respite to bombard the Allied bridging parties and to deploy his troops along the three-mile front. A strong garrison of infantry (initially nine battalions) was placed in the village of Blenheim, with 12 squadrons of dismounted dragoons (whose mounts had died of 'German sickness') holding the interval between the village and the Danube. Slightly to the left and rear of Blenheim he drew up 18 battalions in two bodies to constitute his infantry reserve. All the forces in the immediate vicinity of Blenheim were put under the command of the Marquis de Clérambault. In the open space between Blenheim and Oberglau, Tallard placed 64 squadrons of cavalry (16 squadrons being drawn from Marsin) under General Zurlauben; these units were drawn up in a double line, supported by three brigades of infantry (nine battalions) and several batteries of artillery. Marshal Marsin drew up 14 battalions under General de Blainville in and around the village of Oberglau, and beyond this strongpoint were arrayed the remaining 67 squadrons of horse supported by a dozen battalions whilst the left flank was held by 16 battalions of Marsin's and the Elector's infantry in the vicinity of Lutzingen. Cannon were stationed at various points along the whole front, the largest concentration being in and around Blenheim and south of Oberglau.

These dispositions reveal Tallard's probable plan of battle. To first appearances, the weakest section of his position was the area between Blenheim and Oberglau, held by virtually unsupported cavalry—drawn up at a considerable distance from the Nebel. Tallard may have hoped to lure Marlborough to cross the Nebel against this sector, and whilst the Allies were struggling through the marshes, they would be caught in cross-fire from Blenheim and Oberglau. The moment the survivors reached the firm ground beyond the Nebel, they would be attacked on each flank by the village garrisons and the infantry reserve; the *coup-de-grâce* would then be administered by the massed French cavalry, charging downhill into the already disordered ranks of the Allied centre who would be flung back in red ruin upon the marshes and streams.

This plan held a fair prospect of success if all its parts were implemented— but the spy-glass of the Duke of Marlborough had not failed to notice several grave errors in the French dispositions. Owing to the strained relations existing between the respective commanders, the Franco-Bavarian army had in fact

Illustrations

1 John, First Duke of Marlborough, and Colonel John Armstrong his Chief Engineer, by Seeman, *c.* 1711. 'As like him as ever I saw,' was Duchess Sarah's comment on this portrait, painted in the Duke's middle age

2 Burning of the *Royal James*, 1672, during the Battle of Solebay, where John Churchill earned a captaincy in the Admiralty Regiment

3 John, First Duke of Marlborough by Sir Godfrey Kneller. 'This was once a man' Marlborough remarked in old age

4 Sarah, Duchess of Marlborough by Kneller

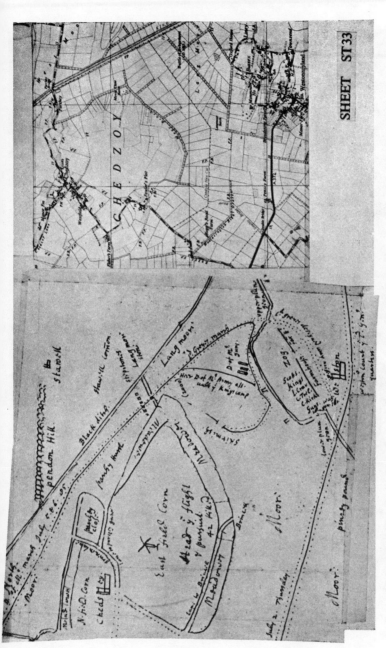

SHEET ST 33

5   Battle of Sedgemoor, 6 July 1685. A contemporary sketch (left) by the Rector of Chedzoy (Courtesy of Hoare's Bank) and the modern 1/25,000 map. The countryside has not changed greatly. (Crown copyright reserved)

6 A wax portrait of Louis XIV, King of France 1661–1715, whose ambitions led to 50 years of European conflict

7 William III, King of England 1689–1702 from a contemporary medal

8 Anne, Queen of England 1702–14 from a medal struck to commemorate Rooke's naval victory in 1702

9 Anne Stuart

10 William of Orange by Faithorne

11 Queen Anne playing-cards designed by J. Spofforth, depicting important military and naval events of the War of Spanish Succession

12 Marlborough in the years of his prime, after Kneller

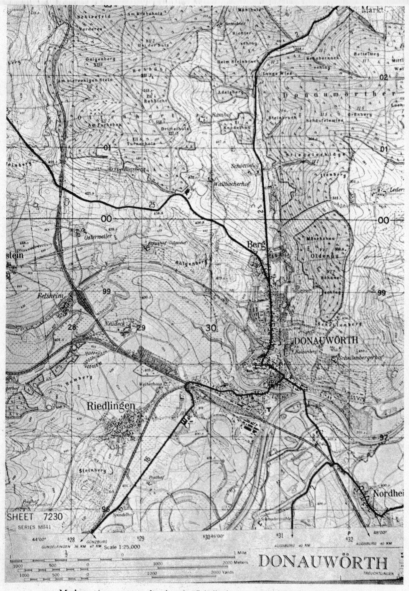

13 Modern 1/25,000 map showing the Schellenberg, scene of the famous action of 2 July 1704. (Courtesy of the Bavarian *Landesvermessungsamt*)

14 Battle of Blenheim, 13 August 1704. Blenheim village surrounded on left; French cavalry routed in centre; the Elector and Marsin in retreat on right

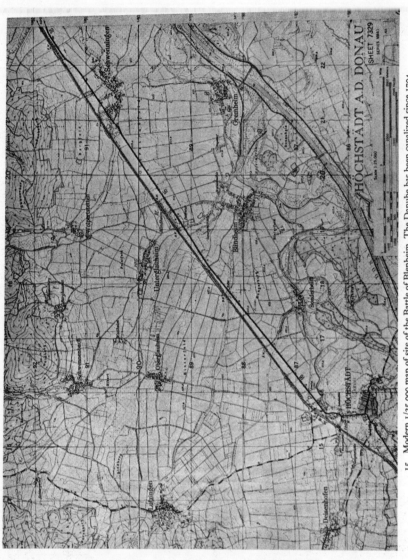

15 Modern 1/25,000 map of site of the Battle of Blenheim. The Danube has been canalized since 1704.
(Courtesy of the Bavarian *Landesvermessungsamt*)

16 Sidney, 1st Earl Godolphin, after Kneller

17 William, 1st Earl Cadogan, attributed to Laguerre

18 Henry of Nassau, Count Overkirk, by an unknown hand

19 François-Eugène, Prince of Savoy, by Jacob van Schuppen

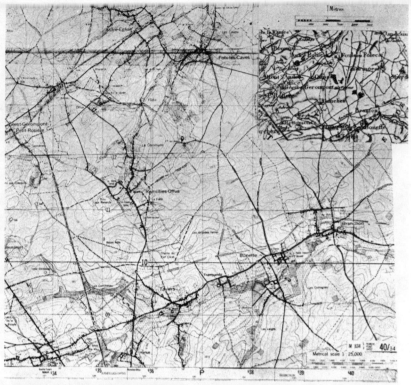

20 Modern 1/25,000 map of the Ramillies battlefield, May 1706; inset shows eighteenth-century map of the same area. (Courtesy of the Belgian *Institut Géographique Militaire*)

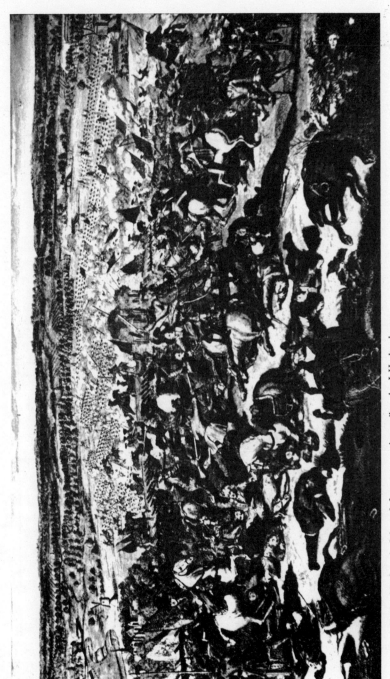

21 Battle of Oudenarde, July 1708, from an engraving attributed to J. Huchtenburg

22   Modern 1/25,000 map of the Oudenarde battle area; the inset shows part of a near-contemporary map. (Courtesy of the Belgian *Institut Géographique Militaire*)

23 Battle of Wynendael, September 1708, depicted on a tapestry at Blenheim
Palace. Note the weaponry and light munitions wagons in the foreground

24 Wynendael, September 1708: modern 1/25,000 map with eighteenth-century inset. (Courtesy of the Belgian *Institut Géographique Militaire*)

Triomphe des Alliez

LE SIEGE DE TOURNAY Par les Hauts ALLIEZ. DE BELEGERING van DOORNIK Door de Hoog GEALLIEERDEN

25 Siege of Tournai, 1709, engraved by P. Mortier. Note the approach trenches, the fascine-protected batteries (left and right) and the mortar detachments in action

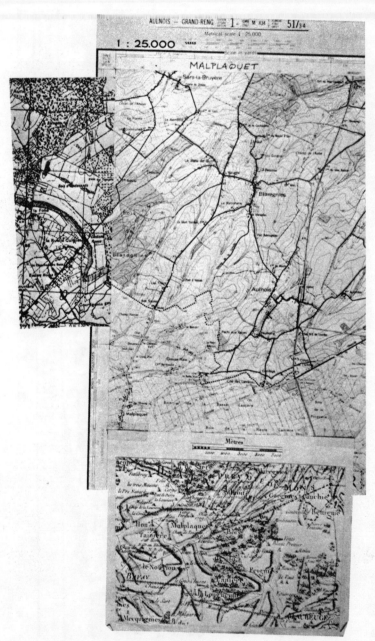

26 The battlefield of Malplaquet: modern 1/25,000 map and near-contemporary
inset. (Courtesy of the Belgian *Institut Géographique Militaire*)

27 Marshal François de Neufille, Duc
de Villeroi

28 Marshal Louis-François, Duc de
Boufflers

29 Marshal-General Claude-Louis-Hector,
Duc de Villars

30 Marshal Louis-Joseph, Duc de
Vendôme

THE
SIEGE of DOWAY
Aprile 1710

31 Contemporary print of the Siege of Douai, 1710. Note the approach trenches and parallels

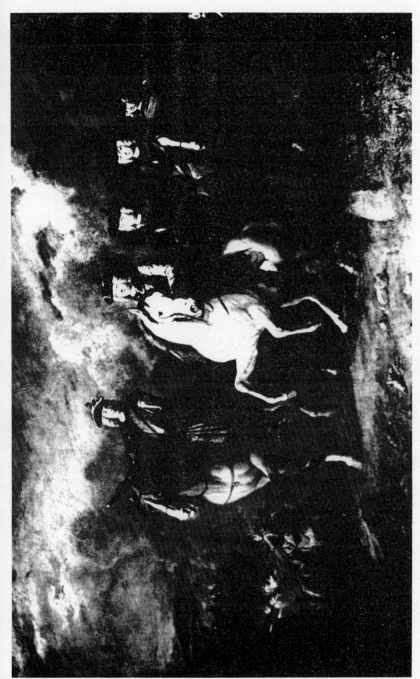

32 Marlborough and his Staff by Van Bloeman and Bossche. Painting at Culford Hall School

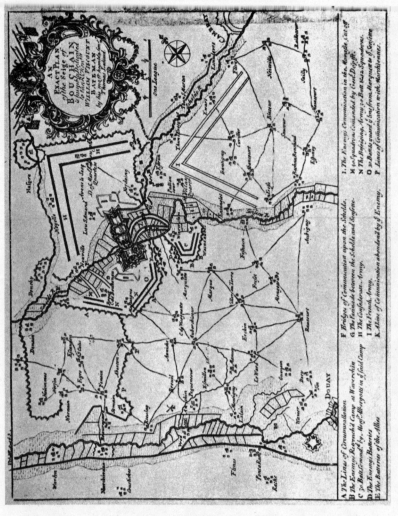

A The Lines of Circumvallation.
B The Enemys Reynol'd Camp at Wavrechin.
C 3d Batt Ground 4 by. Maj.lle Margate in ye field Camp.
D The Enemy Batteries
E The Batteries of the Allies.

F Bridges of Communication upon the Schelde.
G The Cascade between the Schelde and Sensee.
H The Confederate Army.
I The French Army.
K Lines of Communication abandon'd by ye Enemy.

1. The Enemys Communication in the Mangle. Oct 18th.
M 10 Squadrons Commanded by Genl. Dopff.
N The Beseiging Army; But Sit 2 Squadrons.
O 2 Battaly: quard & long from Harrycourt & Seniam.
P Lines of Communication with Marlbricents.

33 Contemporary diagram illustrating the operations around Bouchain, 1711—Marlborough's last achievement in the field.
Note the lines of circumvallation and communication

been drawn up in two practically independent wings, and not in a single, integrated battle-line. This would make it difficult for Tallard to support one flank with troops from the other. Marlborough also noted the perils and possibilities of Tallard's chosen 'killing-ground' in the centre—but realised that if the garrisons of Blenheim and Oberglau could be firmly contained within their defences, the French centre would be dangerously exposed without hope of reinforcement. It would probably be fallacious to assert that Marlborough worked out a detailed plan before the opening of the battle, but no doubt his trained eye appreciated the flaws in the French position.

During the time the two generals were making their preparations, the rival forces stood in plain view of one another. 'The two armies in full battle-array were so close to one another that they exchanged fanfares of trumpet-calls and rolls of kettle-drums', recorded our Flemish cavalry commander, but very soon the batteries on both sides opened fire, 'whilst the French, following their usual deplorable custom, set fire to all the villages, mills and hamlets to our front, and flames and smoke billowed up to the clouds'. To minimise the effect of the cannonade, Marlborough ordered his infantry to lie down in their ranks, whilst he in person rode from point to point on his white horse checking the siting of the artillery. Divine service was also celebrated at the head of each regiment.

A little after 12.30 a galloper from Prince Eugene informed Marlborough that all was ready on the right, and Lord Cutts at once advanced with the 20 battalions and 14 squadrons of the Allied left wing against the village of Blenheim. His leading brigade held its fire until within sword's distance of the French palisades, but the French garrison repulsed the attack and killed the brigade commander, Lord Rowe. The second brigade, however—ably assisted by five squadrons of cavalry—scattered the counter-attack launched by eight squadrons of the crack French Gendarmerie cavalry, and after pausing to lengthen his line, Lord Cutts launched a second assault. This, too, was driven back with heavy loss, but the Blenheim commander, the Marquis de Clérambault, was so impressed by the fury of these onslaughts that he promptly ordered all 18 battalions of Tallard's infantry reserve to enter the defences of the village. This was done without any reference to the commander-in-chief—and constituted the worst French error of the day. 'The men were so crowded in upon one another that they couldn't even fire—let alone receive or carry out any orders. Not a single shot of the enemy missed its mark, whilst only those few of our men at the front could return the fire . . .', wrote Mérode-Westerloo, an observer of the scene from the cavalry lines, '. . . to make things even worse, the village had been set on fire by the French troops and our poor fellows were grilled.' By two o'clock, 16 Allied units were containing 27 French battalions and 12 dismounted squadrons within the village, and Marlborough had secured his left flank.

Tallard, meanwhile, had been visiting Marsin, and was not therefore available to countermand his subordinate's rash and unauthorised squandering of the infantry reserve. The Marshal's attention was in any case fully occupied watching the almost unbelievable rout of eight squadrons of the *Gendarmerie* at the hands of only five English squadrons under Colonel Palmes. This reverse—though slight in itself—shook the French commander-in-chief's faith in the ultimate victory of his army and some time after the battle he ascribed his defeat to 'first, because the Gendarmerie failed to overwhelm the five English squadrons'.[30] Elsewhere the situation was favourable; away on the left, Prince Eugene's 92 squadrons and 18 battalions were receiving a rough time from the numerically-superior Bavarians, whilst the village of Oberglau in the centre was holding its own with ease.

Once Blenheim was safely masked, Marlborough was free to turn his attention to the Prince of Holstein-Beck's initial assault with ten battalions on de Blainville's defences. The garrison of Oberglau severely checked the leading battalions, issuing forth from their positions to rout them with the bayonet. Foremost amongst the units engaged in this task were the 'Wild Geese'—the regiment of Irish Catholic exiles serving in the French pay. The arrival of part of Tallard's first line of cavalry almost turned this defeat into a disaster for the Allies, but the exploitation of their initial success was badly handled, and this gave Marlborough just sufficient time to lead up three reserve Hanoverian battalions and several batteries to rally the wavering line.

While these stirring events were taking place before Blenheim and Oberglau, the first and second lines of the Allied centre were steadily crossing the Nebel and taking up new positions on the French side. Marlborough's centre was drawn up in a unique formation—four lines deep. The front line consisted of seven battalions (not including the ten already in action under Holstein-Beck); this formation was intended to cover the cavalry squadrons, formed up in two lines totalling 72 squadrons to the infantry's immediate rear. In reserve behind these mounted troops stood a further 11 battalions of infantry—and command of the whole of the centre was entrusted to General Charles Churchill, the Duke's able brother.

The crisis of the day took place about 2.15 p.m., when a French cavalry attack practically penetrated the right flank of Marlborough's centre. In some anxiety, Marlborough sent an urgent appeal for assistance to his comrade-in-arms, Prince Eugene, who was desperately engaged on the farther side of Oberglau. Nevertheless, so great was Eugene's trust in Marlborough's judgement that he at once detached a brigade of Imperial cuirassiers under General Fugger to the centre's assistance. These cuirassiers fell like a whirlwind on the flank of Marsin's second cavalry attack, and scattered it in confusion. Although the Prince of Holstein-Beck had been mortally wounded in the first assault, his men were heartened by this improvement in their fortunes, and once more returned to the attack against Oberglau, and by three o'clock de Blainville's garrison had been forced back into the village's defences where they were firmly contained.

Tallard had now missed his best opportunity of victory and Marlborough had surmounted the crisis of the battle.

The deployment of the centre continued with both its flanks secure, and for the space of an hour a comparative lull descended on the battlefield. There is little cause to wonder at this, for the entire line of both armies had been heavily engaged for more than two and a half hours. By four o'clock Marlborough's centre was firmly planted in the midst of the French line—its 81 fresh squadrons (nine had been transferred from Lord Cutts' wing) supported by 18 battalions and several batteries of guns. All Tallard could produce to face this imposing array were the blown and dishevelled remnants of his original 64 squadrons— most of which had already been in action. In desperation before the impending storm, the French commander called for infantry reinforcements to sustain his horsemen, but thanks to Clérambault's earlier folly the only units available were nine battalions of raw recruits. In spite of their local superiority, Marsin and the Elector declined to send assistance from the left on the grounds that they were too busily engaged trying to check Eugene's infantry, who were working their way round the Lutzingen flank in their third major onslaught of the day.

The outcome of the battle in the centre was now practically a foregone conclusion. Mérode-Westerloo had done his best to retrieve the situation: 'I rode over to Blenheim, wanting to bring out a dozen battalions (which they certainly did not need there) to form a line on the edge of the stream supported by the cannons and the debris of my squadrons. The brigades of Saint-Ségond and Monfort were setting out to follow when M. de Clérambault in person counter-manded the move, and shouting and swearing drove them back into the village.'[31] Clearly that officer had lost his nerve during the excitements of the day, and would not admit his earlier error even at the eleventh hour. To gain a temporary respite, Tallard ordered his remaining cavalry to charge, and the Allied advance was checked for a short while. Major-General Lord Orkney, however, was at hand to remedy the damage: 'I marched with my battalions to sustain the horse, and found them repulsed, crying out for foot, being pressed by the Gendarmerie. I went to the head of several squadrons and got 'em to rally on my right and left, and brought up four pieces of cannon and then charged.'[32] Marlborough's wisdom in placing infantry battalions in close support of his cavalry in the centre was now fully proved. By 5.30 the advance was again under way; the nine French battalions were overwhelmed by close-range artillery and platoon fire, and the remnants of Tallard's squadrons vainly tried to check the tide with their pistols and carbines. It was soon over: the French recruits were decimated by Colonel Blood's nine guns loaded with 'partridge shot', overrun and died where they stood, 'in battalion square in the best order I ever saw till they were cut to pieces almost in rank and file'.[33] The French cavalry was borne back by weight of numbers and completely broken, Mérode-Westerloo's horse being carried along 'some three hundred paces without putting hoof to ground' so tight was the press, until both mount and rider were hurled 20 feet down a ravine near the village of Sonderheim. Upwards of 3,000 French horsemen were drowned trying to swim the Danube. The crowning disaster for the French cause was the capture of Marshal Tallard by some Hessian cavalry as he tried to reach Blenheim—and deprived of its leader, French resistance rapidly deteriorated. Away on the left Marsin and the Elector decided the day was lost, and at once set about extricating their own units for a retreat towards Höchstädt, leaving the Blenheim garrison to its fate. Marlborough's attempt to organise a force to prevent Marsin's withdrawal failed owing to growing confusion in the field.

By six in the evening, General Charles Churchill had completed the encirclement of the village. But his men were understandably weary, whilst the majority of the French garrison had hardly discharged a shot all day, and the 27 battalions might well have fought their way out had not their commander slipped away unnoticed in the confusion and drowned himself in the Danube. Leaderless, the French hesitated, affording Orkney enough time to bluff them into surrender. The firing of the cottages 'we could easily perceive annoyed them very much, and seeing two brigades appear as if they intended to push their way through our troops, who were very much fatigued, it came into my head to beat a parley, which they accepted of and immediately their Brigadier de Nouville capitulated with me to be prisoner at discretion and lay down their arms.'[34] Threatened by massed Allied guns, unit after unit followed their example, but it was not until nine in the evening that the last regiments—among them the cream of the French army—accepted terms. The Regiment of Navarre ceremonially burnt its colours to prevent them falling into enemy hands, and with this last act of symbolic defiance, the hard-fought battle of Blenheim came to an end.

It had been a glorious victory, at one stroke saving Vienna, reversing the tide of the war and establishing the reputation of John Churchill, first Duke of Marlborough, as the champion of the Grand Alliance and one of the great captains of history. The details of the French losses are hard to determine with any accuracy. It would seem, however, that the prisoners included some 40 generals and up to 1,150 more junior officers, besides the 11,000 rank-and-file who surrendered in Blenheim village alone; 2,000 more were made captive on other sectors. As for the Allies, various sources indicate that the troops in Anglo-Dutch pay lost 654 officers (190 killed) and 8,029 rank and file (including 3,102 dead). Losses amongst the Imperialists were in the region of 4,200.[35] The events of 13 August, 1704—which had culminated in the capture of the French commander-in-chief and the destruction of two-thirds of his army, were to have immense repercussions throughout Europe. At a cost of 13,000 Allied casualties, Marlborough and Eugene had inflicted a loss of 20,000 killed and wounded on the foe, and taken a further 14,000 prisoners of war along with 60 cannon, 300 colours and standards, and the entire contents of the French camp. For the first time in over 40 years the forces of Louis XIV had sustained a major defeat, and thereby forfeited their claim to military predominance. 'The true account of this battle was concealed from Old Lewis for some time', claimed Captain Parker, 'but when he came to know the truth of it, he was much cast down; it being the first blow of any fatal consequence, his arms had received, during his long reign. And he said in a passion, he had often heard of armies being beaten, but never of one taken'.[36] Mérode-Westerloo summed up the case against Tallard's army when he wrote: 'The French lost this battle for a wide variety of reasons. For one thing, they had too good an opinion of their own ability—and were excessively scornful of their adversaries. Another point was their faulty field dispositions, and in addition there was rampant indiscipline and inexperience displayed in Marshal Tallard's army. It took all these faults to lose so celebrated a battle.'[37] Above all, however, the victory was due to the generalship of Marl-borough: the bold night advance, his firm, flexible control of the battle at its different stages, his personal intervention at the places of crisis, and his proven ability to weld a multi-national army into an integrated weapon of high morale and single-minded purpose, contrasted most markedly with Tallard's muddled leadership and weak authority. In Prince Eugene, the Duke was fortunate to find a kindred spirit willing to co-operate to the full in accepting Marlborough's overall direction of the struggle. He was equally fortunate in his subordinate generals and in the calibre of the men they led. As Orkney, with true insular under-statement, wrote after the battle: 'Without vanity, I think we did our parts',[38] and that has also been the opinion of succeeding generations.

The fruits of victory were impressive: the remnants of the Elector's and Marsin's forces limped away, passing over the Danube at Dillingen and Ulm, and eventually found their way back to Strasbourg—but only after losing a further 7,000 men through desertion by the wayside. The 'German sickness' continued to ravage the horses; from his personal equipage, Mérode-Westerloo lost no less than 97 horses during this period through sickness 'besides the thirteen that were killed or injured on the battlefield.'

The Allies followed up their advantage, although the French captives proved a complication. 'We cannot march from hence.' wrote the Duke from Steinheim near Blenheim on the 17th, 'til we can find some way of disposing all the prisoners which gives us great trouble, for we have no garrisons to send them to.'[39]

The victory and its exploitation would rally the morale of the Grand Alliance. Ulm and Ingolstadt soon fell, and with them all of Bavaria, and many German princelings were won over to support the cause more effectively as the victors marched behind the fleeing French to recross the Rhine.

All this, however, still lay in the future as the evening shades of 13 August deepened into night and the sounds of battle and pursuit receded into the distance towards Höchstädt. A weary but triumphant Marlborough at last found time to scrawl the famous Blenheim message to Sarah on the back of a tavern bill: 'I have no time to say more but to beg you will give my duty to the Queen and let her know her army has had a glorious victory. Monsieur Tallard and two other generals are in my coach and I am following the rest. The bearer, my Aide-de-Camp Colonel Parke, will give her an account of what has passed. I shall do it in a day or two by another more at large.'[40] Five years were to pass before the French armies redeemed their reputation, and for the first time for centuries England had assumed the military leadership of Europe.

The Illusion of Success, 1705

'That he might improve this advantage, that he might push the sum of things to a speedy decision, the Duke of Marlborough led his troops early in the following year once more to the Moselle. They whom he had saved a few months before, neglected to second him now. They who might have been his companions in conquest refused to join him. When he saw the generous designs he had formed frustrated by private interest, by pique, by jealousy, he returned with speed to the Maes. He returned, and fortune and victory returned with him. Liege was relieved, Huy retaken. The French, who had pressed the Army of the States-General with superior numbers, retired behind entrenchments which they deemed impregnable. The Duke forced these entrenchments, with inconsiderable loss, on the seventh day of July [O.S.], one thousand seven hundred and five. He defeated a great part of the army that defended them. The rest escaped by a precipitate retreat. If advantages proportional to this success were not immediately obtained, let the failure be ascribed to that misfortune that attends most confederacies, a division of opinions where one alone should judge, a division of powers where one alone should command. The disappointment itself did honour to the Duke. It became a wonder to mankind how he could do so much under those restraints which had hindered him from doing more. . . .'

From the inscription on the Column of Victory,
Blenheim Palace (continued).

The campaign of 1704 lasted considerably longer than was usual, as the Allies sought to wring the maximum advantage from the situation created by their great success at Blenheim. Their objects were to achieve favourable positions both on the Upper Rhine and along the Moselle from which to launch new major blows the following spring. Leaving the Imperial forces to besiege Landau, Marlborough transferred his attention to the Moselle sector. On 26 October, Trèves was surprised and taken. Neighbouring Trarbach proved more obstinate, and a formal siege had to be opened on 4 November which would only be brought to a successful conclusion on 20 December. But the Duke could leave such matters to his subordinates; more pressing concerns demanded his careful consideration before he could contemplate a return to England.

Dramatic success on the Danube had to be balanced against dangerous developments in North Italy, and if Savoy was to be saved to the Grand Alliance, considerable aid would have to be despatched thither in time for the next campaign. It therefore behoved Marlborough to pay visits to the courts of Berlin and Hanover, there to try and resolve inter-Allied difficulties and at the same time gain firm undertakings of future help. Great success blessed his mission. From Frederick I of Prussia the Duke extracted promises, amidst great feasting, that Prussia would not intervene in the struggle between Saxony and Sweden focussing upon the throne of Poland (a development that could have fatally distracted the attention of many a German prince away from the war with France and Spain). Further, the monarch promised a contingent of 8,000 men for service in Italy in return for a subsidy of 300,000 crowns. The Electress Sophia of Hanover equally proved no match for the victor's urbane charm. Wherever he travelled, Marlborough was hailed as the saviour of Europe, and his triumphal progress at length brought him to a series of policy meetings at the Hague. At last he could sail for England, arriving at Greenwich on 14 December (O.S.).

In England, predictably, a further tumultuous welcome awaited him, only slightly tarnished by the contemporaneous political strife over the renewed Occasional Conformity Bill and the unscrupulous (though unsuccessful) tactics adopted by the extreme Tories in the hope of forcing it through Parliament. Both Houses, however, hastened to present Addresses, and the Tories gave further evidence of their approval of martial developments by passing the military estimates almost without demur, besides voting a sizeable augmentation for the army (and a smaller one for the Royal Navy) and agreeing to the costly subsidy treaties. As for the Queen, she hastened to lavish upon her favourite the royal manor of Woodstock, the promise of a fine palace to be built at the nation's expense, the colonelcy of the First Guards, and a grant of £5,000 p.a. from the Civil List for Anne's lifetime.

Politically, however, the scene remained somewhat clouded. The Queen eventually decided to dissolve Parliament, and the future of the Ministry remained in doubt as the new *cause célèbre* of the Aylesbury Electors became the focal point for intrigue and recrimination. Many moderate Tories followed their extreme brethren into the wilderness, as the Whigs made much ground in the new House of Commons. Under the prevailing circumstances, it proved desirable for both Godolphin and Marlborough to shift some little way towards the Whigs. There were also a few signs that the Queen was cooling towards Sarah, who was too blatantly playing the part of Whig agent. On the family front,

however, March 1705 saw the marriage of the Duke's daughter Mary to John
Montagu.

At Versailles, meantime, Louis XIV reassessed the war situation and laid his
plans. Local successes in North Italy, in the Cevennes, and along the Portuguese
frontier only slightly offset the disasters that had been suffered along the Danube
and Upper Rhine. Defensive concepts were therefore to the fore, as it was clear
that the arms of the Grand Alliance would enjoy much of the initiative once the
campaigning season opened. The greatest peril seemed to lie either on the
Scheldt, or on the Meuse. The King therefore prepared three armies, notifying
their commanders that they were to act in close co-ordination once the Allied
line of attack had been revealed. In Flanders, the command of an army of 80
battalions and 100 squadrons was to be shared by the now landless Elector of
Bavaria and Marshal Villeroi; this force was to base its operations on Namur
and Antwerp. On the Meuse, Marshal Villars was to head 70 battalions and 100
squadrons based upon Metz, with orders to take special care for the safety of
Luxembourg, Longwy, Thionville and Saar-Louis—comprising the gateway to
Lorraine. In Alsace, Marshal Marsin was to build lines along the River Moder
and protect the Saverne Gap, with a force numbering 50 battalions and 60
squadrons: it was hoped that this army would be sufficient to contain any further
Allied attempts to gain ground in that quarter.

It was also planned to provide Marshal Tessé with 100 battalions and as
many squadrons for North Italy, and aid in arms and money was to be sent to
the Hungarian rebels as in the previous year. No effort was to be spared in filling
the gaps in the regiments from the militia, and special missions were sent to
Switzerland's studs to purchase sufficient horses to make good the losses sustained to battle and disease. The results of these orders and associated efforts
were impressive, and it appears that France proved capable of putting some
250,000 men into the field in 1705. But the King made it clear at conferences in
both February and April that the initiative—at least on the eastern frontiers—
was to be left to the foe in the first instance. Special attention was to be paid to
the movements of the English battalions and squadrons, 'the best troops of the
Allies',[1] when they quitted their winter quarters.

Allied plans for 1705 had been under active consideration since the previous
autumn. The original scheme envisaged a co-ordinated double-thrust into
Lorraine, Marlborough up the Moselle, Baden striking from Landau. The major
objective was to be the fortress of Saar-Louis, whose capture might be expected
to bring over the Duke of Lorraine and thus lay bare a lengthy stretch of the
French frontier—an eventuality which would leave Louis XIV with scant recourse
save the acceptance of a dictated peace. Meanwhile in Italy, Prince Eugene—
suitably reinforced by German contingents—was to bolster faltering Savoy,
whilst in the Netherlands, General Overkirk neutralised the neighbouring
Franco-Spanish forces. Subsidiary efforts would include a new Austrian drive

against the Hungarian rebels, and new (if minor) initiatives by Lord Galway in
Portugal where matters had gone badly in 1704.

From the time of his arrival at the Hague on 14 April 1705, however, it
became clear to Marlborough that any hopes for an early start to the campaign
were over-sanguine. The problems of coalition warfare crowded in upon him.
First it was the Dutch who refused to unify the command of all their forces under
his baton (a point the Duke conceded with his usual grace and tact) and then
queried the dates for the massing of the Anglo-Dutch forces at Maastricht and
Trèves. By early May these difficulties had been smoothed over, but they proved
but the harbingers of further troubles. The Prussian and Palatine contingents
were seriously behind schedule in taking the field, but of far graver importance
was the Margrave of Baden's pronouncement (made to the Duke at Rastadt
on 20 May after a number of postponements of the interview) that there was no
prospect whatsoever of his producing the envisaged 50 battalions and 60 squadrons of imperial troops, and that in consequence the offensive from Landau could
not be implemented. A series of circumstances had led to this *démarche*, including
a winter of administrative neglect, the sudden switching of troops from the
Rhine to Italy (where Eugene's forces were barely in better shape than Baden's),
and a deterioration in the Margrave's health occasioned by the reopening and
subsequent mortification of a foot wound received at Schellenberg in July
1704. It has also been suggested that another reason for the generally unco-
operative attitude of Baden in 1705 was his desire to avenge the slights (as he
probably saw them) of the previous August*, but the validity of this claim has
never been fully tested. This all amounted to a bitter disappointment for
Marlborough. 'I find soe little zeal for the common cause that it is enough to
break a better heart than mine,' he confided to Heinsius on 11 May. 'According
to the promises I have had all this Winter from Vienna,' he later wrote to Harley
from Trèves, 'I was in good hopes the Prince of Baden would have been enabled
to have seconded me in these parts with considerable force, so that we might have
acted with two separate armies; but you will be surprised to hear that all he can
bring at present does not exceed 11 or 12 battalions and 28 squadrons. . . . The
Prussians and several others cannot be here sooner, so that it will be about the
10th of the next month before we shall be able to move.'[2]

Relations with Vienna were further complicated by the death of the Emperor
Leopold I (5 May) and the accession of Joseph I. Although the new Emperor
was a fervent admirer of Marlborough, the Schönbrunn had long harboured
grave doubts about the British ambassador, Stepney, who persistently meddled
in the Hungarian troubles. Unless he could soon be replaced, without loss of
national prestige, there might well be a crisis in Anglo-Austrian relations—
even the vital ally, Count Wratislaw, was badly aggrieved. Much diplomatic oil,
therefore, had to be poured on these troubled waters, absorbing still more of

* See p. 140 above.

Marlborough's precious attention. His son-in-law, Sunderland, was sent to Vienna to mediate in these disputes.

To cap all, on his arrival at Trèves, the launching-point for the major Allied offensive, the Duke learnt that a major supply contractor, M. Centery, appointed by the Dutch, had deserted to the enemy after failing to provide the stipulated stores of flour, corn and forage. This grave logistical problem—added to the detrimental effects of recent bitter weather, 'which had destroyed all the grasse and oates'[3]—meant that Marlborough would be compelled to move by early June to find fresh pasture for his cavalry, whether Baden had appeared or not. This would entail entering the campaign without a marked preponderance of men, for Villars was in the process of receiving reinforcements from Villeroi and Marsin which would increase his strength to 73 battalions and 125 squadrons— perhaps 52,000 men—as against the Duke's 79 battalions and 94 squadrons. Under the circumstances, there was scant chance of the Allies being able to besiege Saar-Louis for the Duke was faced by 'another difficulty, which gives me much pain, which is the 3,000 horses that the local Princes should have furnished me with for bringing up the artillery and munitions for the siege, but of which I still have no news . . .',[4] as he wrote to Overkirk on 7 June.

On every side frustrations abounded, but move the army must whether or no its strength was barely 60,000 men. Marlborough was nevertheless still sanguine about Allied prospects; '. . . if Marshal Villars has power to venture a battle, he may have it. Though I want one-third of the troops that are to comprise this army, I depend so much upon the goodness of these I have here that, with the blessing of God, I do not doubt of a good success,'[5] as he confided to Godolphin on 2 June.

The army set forth from Trèves that very day, marching to Consaarbruck and crossing both the Moselle and the Saar in its vicinity. Two columns then headed for Sierck, the countryside proving broken and difficult. It soon became evident that for all Villars' bravado he was not prepared to leave his strong position. The infantry of his right wing were holding the Heights of Kerling, with dense wood-land protecting their flank. The centre was placed on the Heights of Früching, which had been entrenched. The French left ran from the hamlet of Königsberg down to the Moselle, with cavalry deployed to the fore. All in all this comprised a strong position. Marlborough's artillery reached Elst on the 4th, but the ground to the fore of the Allied encampment was so difficult—particularly in the centre around the Ravine of Mensberg—that it offered scant hope of enabling the Duke to close with his opponent. Yet his present position, if it could be maintained, might serve to cover a siege of Saar-Louis, if and when that could be undertaken with Baden's tardy co-operation. So a period of two weeks' inaction settled over the scene—a pause that further favoured Villars as a further 35 battalions were hastening to his aid from Flanders and the Rhine.

The generals exchanged civilities under flag of truce. 'M. de Marlborough has sent me a quantity of English liquors, palm wine and cider,' reported Villars; 'I could not receive more courtesies. I am responding as best I can.'[6] Both commanders, however, were riled by the present inactivity. Villars bombarded Versailles with requests for leave to attack the Allies—in vain. Marlborough chafed at the continued delay in the arrival of the imperialists, who were slowly marching up by an unnecessarily circuitous route through Kreuznach under command of the Comte de Frise (Baden's wound having taken a turn for the worse). The Duke sent Cadogan to hasten their march, it seeming impossible that the main body could reach Trèves before 18 June at the present rate, and for a time Marlborough assumed personal responsibility for the supply of the army— an aspect which was now causing grave disquiet. 'Our general's chief care at present is to subsist his Army, and second to press the German Princes to be punctual to their promises,' wrote Michael Richards in his diary. 'To ye first, ye Qr. Mrs. have been sent out to look for forage and to occupy the proper posts for security of fetching it.'

Suddenly, important tidings reached Allied headquarters from Flanders.[7] It seemed that Villeroi had pounced on Huy and taken the place on 10 June, before pressing on towards Liége. In manifest alarm, the States-General were demanding Marlborough's immediate return, and he could not afford to ignore the call. This would involve the abandonment of all schemes against Saar-Louis, but it also afforded a justifiable reason for breaking away from the present unpromising situation. For, like Marshal Massena facing the Lines of Torres Vedras in 1810, Marlborough was in an unenviable position before Sierck. As Richards summarised his position: 'In fine, their (sic) appearing nothing but disappointment on (the) one hand and on ye other hand the French proceedings too much apprehended in Holland ... made the Duke of Marlborough resolve of quitting these parts to succour them on the Meuse.'[8] This course of action was already under consideration before the news of developments further north arrived.

The disengagement was achieved with all of Marlborough's habitual skill and resource. Arrangements were made for a force of Westphalians and Palatine troops to garrison Trèves, whilst Baden was to absorb the tardy Prussian and Württemberg contingents to build up his strength to near 60 battalions and 95 squadrons—a sufficient force, it was deemed, to hold Villars in check and even to permit a local offensive on the Rhine if Villars split his army after discovering Marlborough's departure. Then, on the afternoon of 17 June the 'great baggage' was sent away, and at ten o'clock that night the main army struck its tents and marched off at midnight 'without drum or trumpet until daylight' covered by a rearguard of 20 squadrons and 1,000 grenadiers.

The operation was successfully carried through; after safely passing the difficult Taverne Defile, Marlborough allowed his men some rest near Trèves before dividing them into three columns for the return to the Meuse. A careful march time-table was drawn up, which allowed a halt every fifth day. The march over the Eifel was pressed with all dispatch 'insomuch that we were but half the time in returning that we took in going up' (Parker).[9] The heavy guns and baggage were sent off in barges towards Coblenz. Thus the emergency measures conceived the previous year were implemented in 1705 with great efficiency.

News that the city of Liége had opened its gates on the 18th, and that the citadel was in dire peril, caused Marlborough to leave the army on the 20th and ride ahead with a picked force of cavalry and dragoons (carrying a party of grenadiers) to join Overkirk. By the 27th the Duke had reached Maastricht, whilst the army, after reconcentrating at Duren, was approaching Aix-la-Chapelle. By this date it was already known that this prompt movement had saved Liége, for on 24 June Villeroi had struck his camp and retired to Tongres and thence to Landen. On 2 July, Marlborough crossed the Meuse to camp at Haneffe, where he was joined by Overkirk's field army. This meant that the Allies had a fair superiority of force in Flanders at this juncture—possibly 117 battalions and 114 squadrons in all, to Villeroi's estimated strength of 80 battalions and 130 squadrons.

So ended the first phase of the campaign of 1705. In sum, the Allies had little reason for contentment: their offensive plans had been ruined, and they had ultimately been compelled to dance to the enemy's tune. The weaknesses of coalition warfare had again been only too convincingly demonstrated; Marlborough's bitterness at the endless delays and evasions is evidenced by the extraordinary message he sent to Villars on leaving the Moselle, apologising for providing him with such poor sport. The French were understandably cock-a-hoop. 'What a disgrace for Marlborough to have made false movements without any result!' exulted Villeroi. 'What divisions there must be amongst his generals.'[10] The French strategists were far happier to have drawn the Duke to the Flanders front, 'where the country was covered by a chain of fortified towns suitable for warding off reverses, an advantage wanting on the Moselle.'[11] Versailles at once issued orders for bringing Villeroi's strength up to 100 battalions and 150 squadrons (Villars' command being reduced to 60 battalions and 90 squadrons in the process), although it would be some time before this redeployment could be carried out.

Marlborough's first reaction was to consider a return to the Moselle—he still hankered after Saar-Louis as the best gateway in France—but this was not to be. On 27 June the commander of the Trèves garrison—Count d'Aubach—cravenly abandoned the town, burning the ammassed stores, and retired to Trarbach, at the first sign of French activity. This unanticipated disaster, together with the Emperor's transfer of more troops from the Rhine to Italy, ruled out any possibility of an allied offensive on the Moselle in 1705. Indeed, Marlborough would never again campaign outside Flanders.

The Captain-General was determined to make the best of the situation. The first task was to regain Huy, and on 6 July Overkirk was entrusted with the overall supervision of the operation from his camp at Vignamont. The main army, meanwhile, moved to Lense-les-Béguines, but as Villeroi (his head-quarters at Merdorp) did not deem the isolated post worth the risk of a major engagement, the French garrison was induced to surrender on 11 July.

Marlborough was now working on a bolder plan, involving the passage of the Lines of Brabant as a preliminary to forcing a battle situation upon the cautious Villeroi before he could receive reinforcements and before Marsin might move to join Villars in a joint-venture against the Margrave on the Rhine. The Lines of Brabant extended northwards from Namur to Antwerp—a distance of some 70 miles—describing a large, convex arc, and thence to the sea. Much hard work had been employed in their development over recent years, and whenever possible waterways—the Mehaigne, the Gheetes (Greater and Lesser) and Demer —supplemented by judicious flooding, had been incorporated to link and support a network of fortresses, which included Léau, Diest, Aerschot and Malines. Extensive use had also been made of earthworks, barricades and entrenchments. The purpose of these works was not so much to prevent as to delay a hostile incursion and thus provide the defending forces with time to concentrate behind the threatened sector and make its passage inordinately expensive to the attacker. The lines had been probed a number of times in 1703 and 1704 by small Allied forces, but nothing on the scale now envisaged by Marlborough had to date been seriously contemplated. Of course, Dutch objections to such a scheme—led by General Slangenberg, a particularly virulent critic and opponent—had first to be circumvented, Marlborough giving an undertaking that he would not press the crossing if it proved strongly held. The selection of the best place to attack required much careful consideration. The easiest sector, in terms of obstacles, lay to the south of the Mehaigne; on the other hand, the foe was equally aware of this factor. The sector near Léau was far more formidable to all appearances, but a 'gentleman of the country' revealed that it was but sparsely garrisoned. The Duke therefore determined to attack in the vicinity of Heylissem, Elixhem, Wanghé and Orsmael, at the same time creating the appearance of a drive towards the southern sector, using Overkirk's Dutch for the purpose. As that general wrote to the States-General, describing the plan in a letter dated 18 July, '. . . I was to march from Vinamont (*sic*) during the morning (of the 17th) with the States Army, and post myself before their lines on the other bank of the Mehaigne near Maffle, so as to alarm them and see if they would give way there, while M. the Duke of Marlborough would march in the evening, after retreat, with his army towards Heylissem to execute our true design, whilst I, on my side, would repass the Mehaigne, also after retreat, to sustain the Duke.'[12]

The scheme was put into execution on 17 July. As Overkirk advanced west-wards in leisurely and ostentatious style, Marlborough's engineers and

'tin-boat-men' built a total of 20 pontoon bridges over the Mehaigne as if presaging the Duke's imminent movement southwards in support of the Dutch. The
Elector of Bavaria and Villeroi were impressed by these developments, and
ordered a general alert along the whole Lines area. They became increasingly
convinced that the Allied attack would come well south of Merdorp, and
massed most of their men near the Mehaigne.

As soon as dusk had fallen, the dust-stained Dutch column, to its surprise
and considerable chagrin, received orders to swing northwards over the Mehaigne
Landen and the target area beyond: By this time Marlborough's men were also
moving north. 'Thus we marched all night,' recalled Parker. Count Noyelles
and General Ingoldsby led the advance with 38 squadrons and 20 battalions,
accompanied by 600 pioneers, the cavalry carrying trusses of hay to serve as
extemporised fascines once the innundations and rivulets were encountered.

Some little difficulty was experienced in finding suitable crossing points over
the streams, and two vital hours were wasted, but the assault forces, 'by peep of
day, came near to Orsmael, where the Gheete runs before their line ...', as
Orkney recalled. 'Though the passages were very bad, people scrambled over
them strangely.'[13] It was a notable achievement. 'The lines here were extremely
strong,' noted one anonymous commentator, '... and yet thus were we, without
much trouble or any loss, made Masters of a passage thorow (sic) them by means
of this conduct; ... for had not the enemy by this strategem been diverted
from their guard here, 10,000 men might with much ease have defended ye place
against 100,000.'[14] In fact the local guards offered scant resistance, and, being
'much surprised, gave us only one fire and made off.' (Parker). Soon the pioneers
were breaking down the barriers and improving the bridges, and Allied troops
began to pour over the lines at the selected points. Three regiments of French
dragoons billeted in Orsmael badly disgraced themselves. 'These dragoons,
instead of defending the two crossings and giving warning to our left wing of the
enemy's arrival', wrote Villeroi subsequently, '... headed for Léau without
giving the alarm. When the news reached the left ... two hours had already
passed since they began to enter.'[15] Thus Marlborough had once again proved
capable of surprising the enemy.

By the time the first alerted defenders from the south began to appear (about
7 a.m.) Marlborough had 16 squadrons of British cavalry as well as the Hanoverian and Hessian horsemen of the advance guard, together with some infantry,
drawn up in two lines near Elixhem, with more troops approaching every minute.
His approaching opponents comprised 33 squadrons of understrength Spanish
and Bavarian horse commanded by Generals d'Alègre and Hornes, and 11
battalions of Bavarian foot commanded by Count Caraman, besides ten triple-
barrelled cannon. Seeing themselves already outnumbered, the generals boldly
resolved to attack at once, and both forces flung themselves forward into combat.

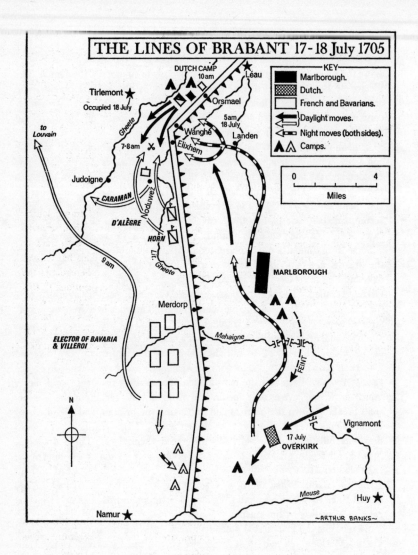

THE LINES OF BRABANT 17-18 July 1705

DUTCH CAMP
10am

Léau

Tirlemont
Occupied 18 July

Orsmael

5am
18 July

Wanghé

Landen

Elixhem

to
Louvain

7-8 am

Judoigne

CARAMAN

D'ALÈGRE

HORN

MARLBOROUGH

9 am

Merdorp

FEINT

ELECTOR OF BAVARIA
& VILLEROI

Mehaigne

Vignamont

17 July
OVERKIRK

N

Meuse

Huy

Namur

~ARTHUR BANKS~

KEY

■ Marlborough.
▨ Dutch.
□ French and Bavarians.
◀━ Daylight moves.
◁┅ Night moves (both sides).
▲ △ Camps.

0   4

Miles

A sharp cavalry engagement developed. In the first brush, the Duke himself led a charge, and routed the first Bavarian line, the Scots Greys taking several cannon. Both d'Alègre and Horn became casualties at this time. A renewed Allied charge routed the second line of hostile squadrons, Marlborough once again being in the thick of the *mêlée*. Indeed, he came close to serious mis-adventure, for, as Orkney recorded, 'a fellow came to him and thought to have sabred him to the ground, and struck at him with that force, and, missing his stroke, he fell off his horse,'[16]—to be despatched by Marlborough's trumpeter.

By 8 a.m. the enemy horse was everywhere routed, and Marlborough's army was almost over the Lines, although the Dutch had still to cross. Only Caraman's infantry stood firm before him. That officer, with exemplary coolness, formed his battalion into a large square and began to conduct an orderly withdrawal south-wards, 'breaking down ye bridge at Nodway (*sic*: Noduez) to secure their retreat.' Marlborough's superiority was massive—but for once he hesitated to unleash an all-out attack that must have destroyed the Bavarian foot. This has earned some justifiable criticism; without accurate news of Villeroi's whereabouts the Duke settled for caution and called a halt. In fact he was over-cautious in this instance, for Villeroi's sole thought at this juncture was to escape over the Greater Gheete into Louvain, and in any case the French army was only on the road from Merdorp by 9 a.m., so tardily had they received news of what was afoot. As a result, Count Caraman succeeded in covering his superior's cross-country withdrawal—perhaps rout would be a more appropriate term—and Marlborough contented himself with taking possession of Tirlemont, whilst the weary Dutch (who had covered 27 miles of road in the past 30 hours) thankfully set up their tents and went to disgruntled rest at 10 a.m.

These successes had cost the Allies barely 50 casualties (some sources say 200)—to a French loss of perhaps 3,000 (although Villeroi was at pains to represent his losses at under 300). A great deal more might possibly have been achieved. The boldness of the hours of darkness had given way to unusual prudence in the morning light. Yet the achievement was considerable—a major incursion had been made through vaunted enemy positions, and the fortress of Louvain was now in peril. Within a few days a 50 mile stretch of the Lines of Brabant would be in Allied hands, including the towns of Aerschot, Diest and Léau. Yet, as Sir Winston Churchill was prepared to admit, 'it certainly seems that Marlborough flagged.'[17] However there is no doubt that Marlborough was personally delighted with the outcome, as his letters clearly reveal. The warm ovation he received from the English troops particularly moved him.

The 19th saw a return of all his old energy and determination. The army marched on the French, now drawn up behind the River Dyle, and routed part of their baggage trains and escort, taking another thousand prisoners. Bad weather occasioned several days of delay amidst growing dissension, for the Dutch generals were now hesitant to authorise a major engagement, and refused to agree as to the best point at which to attempt the river crossing. Marlborough, only too aware that the opportunity was hourly passing, for French reinforcements were already known to be on their way, was in near despair as day followed day without action. At last, on 30 July, the council-of-war agreed to a move over the Dyle at Corbeck and Neergsche to the south of Louvain, supported by a diversion to the north. But this time Villeroi was not completely fooled, and moved in time to block the first crossing—an event that occasioned much unproven speculation regarding treachery or indiscretion on the part of members of the Allied staff. The lower crossing was safely secured, however; part of the army passed over—and again it seemed that battle was close. But Dutch nerves—or obstruction—prevailed once more, and the now almost customary veto was pronounced by Slangenberg, leaving Marlborough with no option but to call off the operation and march off to camp at Meldert.

The second phase of the campaign had reached its conclusion. Much had been achieved in the terms of early eighteenth-century warfare, yet so much more might have been gained had circumstances proved more favourable. Allied indecision and jealous bickering—and an unusual manifestation of personal hesitation—had robbed Marlborough of another opportunity.

A general less devoted to his cause might at this point have abandoned all further attempts to promote a decisive success in Flanders that year, but the Duke was still determined to exploit what remained of his initiative. First, he collected five days' rations of bread for the army, and called up a convoy with six days' biscuit from Liége, thus securing a period of independence from his supply depots and field bakeries.* Simultaneously, he summoned a small siege train to Meldert—again with a view to securing operational flexibility. On 13 August he informed Count Sinzendorff that 'we are going to march next Saturday to the source of the Dyle, in an attempt to lure the enemy into an action before their reinforcements can arrive from the Upper Rhine. It is too much to hope that things should be so arranged there as to prevent them from detaching (forces) towards both here and Italy, and it is very necessary that we should seriously consider sending some aid as soon as possible to Prince Eugene.'[18] The breadth and scope of Marlborough's strategic awareness is again in evidence, and we shall return to events in Italy on a later page.

On 15 August the new advance began, covered by General Spaar's diversionary attack on the distant coastal sector. Overkirk's army marched a little to the left of Marlborough's columns, and between them they commanded all of 100 battalions and 160 squadrons. By nightfall they had reached Corbaix and Sombreffe. Villeroi had been awaiting a move for several days, but still could only guess at the ultimate intention. For Marlborough had so positioned himself that he could threaten Hal, Brussels, Louvain, Mons, Charleroi and even Dendermonde. Where would the blow fall? In great trepidation the outclassed and bemused

* Armies normally baked for four days at a time.

Villeroi set out to strengthen every threatened sector, inevitably weakening his field force in the process until it numbered barely 70 battalions and 120 squadrons.

In blazing heat, the Allies now crossed the Dyle at Genappes, and then abruptly swung north as if to threaten Brussels. Since the 15th they had already covered 33 miles of road. Villeroi, believing he had at last penetrated Marlborough's design, hastened to call up Grimaldi from Brussels to block the high road running through Waterloo, and began to concentrate his army behind the River Yssche. But all at once the Allied columns swung away from the high road and headed towards the main French army, whilst General Churchill, at the head of 20 battalions and as many squadrons, clandestinely made his way through the Forest of Soignies to take up a concealed position threatening the French flank and rear. Meantime, all French attention was concentrated on Marlborough himself as the realisation spread that he was seeking nothing less than a major battle. With frantic haste the French threw up earthworks to strengthen the line of the Yssche, acknowledging that it was now too late to refuse action if the Allies pressed on.

By 10 a.m. on 18 August both Marlborough and Churchill were in their chosen positions. The Duke consulted Overkirk and received his full agreement to an immediate battle. Then a snag occured, owing to the late arrival of the artillery without which the battle could not be joined. 'We were now drawing near the enemy,' recorded Parker, 'and his Grace had sent orders that the English train of artillery should make all possible haste up to him; but as they were just upon entering a narrow defile, Slangenberg came up to the head of them, and stopped them for some hours, until his baggage had passed on before them, a thing never known before. . . .'[19] This insolent act would not go either unnoticed or unpunished.

Vital time was passing, but by midday all was at length prepared. At that very moment however, the subordinate Dutch generals, despite their leader's openly expressed opinion, suddenly developed serious doubts about the wisdom of the impending battle. Slangenberg inspiring them, they insisted on a new delay for further reconnaissance of the proposed crossing points—and neither Overkirk nor the Dutch Deputies saw fit to persuade them of the error of their ways although every hour that passed was enabling the foe to improve their positions. Soon it was 4 p.m., and evidently it was impracticable to order the attack that day. In silent rage Marlborough ordered the abandonment of the whole operation, and began to withdraw his forces towards Meldert. A vastly relieved Villeroi was not slow to claim a victory. Louis XIV agreed. 'You need not doubt the joy your letter of the 20th instant afforded me,' wrote the King, 'and the satisfaction I had to learn that the great din that accompanied the Duke of Marlborough's march has all been ended in a shameful retreat.'[20] The French spoke at length of the 'mortified adventurer', and their self-confidence perceptibly rose. Perhaps Blenheim could be put down to a fluke? Was the vaunted

'*Malbrouck*', after all, in modern parlance, 'a paper tiger'? Nevertheless, Louis XIV used the favourable atmosphere of the moment to launch a new peace offensive, but his terms were still wholly unacceptable to the Allies.

Many authorities agree that these mischances robbed Marlborough of potentially his greatest victory. As an obstacle, the Yssche was less daunting than the Nebel in 1704, whilst he had Villeroi at a huge numerical disadvantage, and his brother's hidden position* was well chosen to achieve a decisive result—in many ways providing an interesting forecast of Napoleon's battle-system of a century later.[21] Such a success would almost certainly have cleared the French out of the Spanish Netherlands, and might even have ended the war.

This glittering prospect having eluded him through no fault of his own, Marlborough made it clear that he would be responsible for no more major operations in 1705. It is true that General Dedem was sent off to besiege Léau (captured on 6 September), whilst other parties razed the captured lines from Tirlemont to the Mehaigne. A demonstration was also pushed over the Demer on 19 September in the hope of dissuading the French from transferring troops from Flanders to the Rhine, but these were merely routine moves. Marlborough also allowed himself to be persuaded by the urgent entreaties of the States-General into undertaking the capture and destruction of Santoliet (which fell on 29 October), but this permitted the emboldened French to repossess Diest (on the 25th). 'And so this campaign ended almost where it had begun,' acidly commented the critical Mérode-Westerloo who had newly transferred his sword to the side of the Grand Alliance.[22] By late November, both armies had entered winter quarters.

Marlborough for once made no attempt to disguise his deepest feelings. On 18 August he had written to the States-General that, 'I feel so strongly that I cannot prevent myself from repeating, on this occasion ... that I find myself here with far less authority than when I had the honour to command your troops last year in Germany.'[23] One result of his strong remonstrations was the dismissal of the obnoxious Slangenberg, the States being prevailed upon to send him 'a dismiss' which was no more than he deserved.

The military disappointments of 1705 were partly compensated for by Marlborough's successes on the diplomatic front; a further lengthy tour of Allied courts and headquarters proved worthwhile. At Dusseldorf the Elector Palatine was persuaded to find troops for Italy in 1706; at Frankfort the recalcitrant Baden was able to reveal that he had, after all, managed to make himself master of Hagenau, thus securing good winter quarters to the west of the Rhine; at Vienna, ruffled feathers were smoothed down, and the Emperor reconciled with Prussia and the United Provinces, and his grant of the principality of Mindelsheim to the victor of Blenheim was confirmed and conferred. The homewards journey took Marlborough through Berlin and Hanover, where

* See p. 257 below for a similar plan put into effect at Malplaquet, 1709.

fair-sounding promises of prompter assistance for 1706 were extracted. The Duke's mind was now full of plans for the coming year; his concern for the fortunes of the House of Savoy and the Imperialists was deepening. 'It seems to me,' he wrote to Wratislaw on 5 October, 'that it is high time to think seriously about this war in Italy, which employs so great a number of enemy troops who would fall upon our backs everywhere if we were driven out of it.' The grandiose idea of a march to Italy was burgeoning in his fertile mind.

At last he was able to head for the Hague and thence for home. At least he could congratulate himself on a reasonably satisfactory diplomatic achievement. As C. T. Atkinson has written, '. . . if the Duke returned home dissatisfied with the results of the year's operations, he had no reason for dissatisfaction with those of his subsequent diplomatic labours. If 1705 had been a disappointment, 1706 promised ample compensation.'[25]

9

'Annus Mirabilis', 1706

'Powers more absolute were given him afterwards. The increase of his powers multiplied his victories at the opening of the next campaign. When all his army was not yet assembled, when it was hardly known that he had taken the field, the noise of his triumphs was heard over Europe. On the twelfth day of May [O.S.], one thousand seven hundred and six, he attacked the French at Ramillies. In the space of two hours their whole army was put to flight. The vigour and conduct with which he pursued his successes were equal to those with which he gained it. Louvaine, Brussels, Malines, Liere, Ghent, Oudenarde, Antwerp, Damme, Bruges, Courtray, surrendered. Ostende, Menin, Dendermonde, Ath, were taken. Brabant and Flanders were recovered. Places which had resisted the greatest generals for months, for years, provinces disputed for ages, were the conquests of a summer.

Nor was the Duke content to triumph alone. Solicitous for the general interest his care extended to the remotest scenes of the war. He chose to lessen his own army that he might enable the leaders of other armies to conquer. To this it must be ascribed that Turin was relieved, the Duke of Savoy reinstated, the French driven with confusion out of Italy. . . .'

From the inscription on the Column of Victory,
Blenheim Palace (continued).

The war was still a very long way from being won that winter, but it is clear that Marlborough considered that the most important events of 1706 would take place away from Flanders. Both Italy and Spain figured prominently in his thoughts, and it is necessary to summarise developments there during recent years if the *annus mirabilis* of 1706 is to be examined in its true setting.

In North Italy, scene of the very first operations of the war, dispute had centred around the Duchy of Milan. An original war aim of the Grand Alliance had stipulated the region's clearing of the French. Although the fortunes of war had swung to and fro from year to year, by 1704 the balance was shifting in the French favour. Even the defection of Savoy to the Grand Alliance in 1703 had proved as much of a bane as a blessing, for the practical implications for its support in terms of both men and money were immense. However, it did ensure that the greater part of Vendôme's attention was concentrated against Victor Amadeus, for the French Marshal's first preoccupation had to be with the safety of his communications with France. By late 1704, much of Savoy had been overrun, and but for Marlborough's timely transfer of contingents from Prussia and the Palatinate, and the Emperor's dispatch of Prince Eugene to command in the theatre, the Court of Turin must have succumbed to French pressure. In the event the year 1705 proved indecisive; the gory battle of Cassano in August led to the withdrawal of Eugene towards the Adige but at the same time made the siege of Turin unfeasible that season for the French. Vendôme, however, was determined to encompass its fall in 1706. The question, therefore, was whether the Allies would prove capable of reinforcing the area again before this blow fell. Here, therefore, lay one area of anticipated crisis.

Very different, at this juncture, was the situation prevalent in Spain. If we except the abortive Cadiz fiasco of 1702 and the windfall won at Vigo Bay,* it had not been until Portugal's adherence to the Grand Alliance in 1703 that Allied attention had been seriously attracted to the Peninsula. The advantages to be earned from a superior naval presence in the western Mediterranean had long been fully appreciated by Marlborough, but it had been Portugal's concern for her national security *vis-à-vis* Spain, together with Anglo-Dutch awareness of the need of Lisbon for a truly secure naval base where the combined fleet could winter within striking distance of the Mediterranean, that had little by little led to the adoption of a new major war aim—namely the removal of Philip V from the Spanish throne and his replacement by the Habsburg claimant, the Archduke Charles. This had long been an Austrian ambition, but no such clause had figured in the original treaties of the Second Grand Alliance.

The earliest campaigns along the Hispano-Portuguese frontier in 1704 had been fiascos, only slightly redeemed by the fortuitous capture of Gibraltar and the subsequent naval success of Malaga. The year 1705, however, had proved very different. Gibraltar's garrison had successfully sustained a major siege (February to April), considerable ground had been made along the Portuguese frontier, and, most important of all, an Allied force under the command of the mercurial Charles Mordaunt, Earl of Peterborough, had successfully invaded Catalonia and ultimately captured Barcelona (9 October), with the result that by the year's end two Spanish provinces (Catalonia and Valencia) had largely passed into Allied hands. Consequent on these successes, there was now much talk of an advance on Madrid in 1706. The English government promised more men and money, and also planned a Huguenot descent against the western coasts of France as a diversion which should benefit the Allied efforts in both

* See p. 107.

Spain and North Italy. Thus in Spain at least, the tide was deemed to be running strongly in the Allied favour, and there is no indication that Marlborough thought differently, as some historians have asserted.

Indeed, as Dr. Burton has recently pointed out, there is much evidence that in early 1706 the Duke saw strong prospects of final victory being won in Spain and North Italy in conjunction. Advised in January that the whole east coast of Spain might very shortly declare for Charles III, he wrote to Heinsius, 'I pray God this may prove true, for we are here very much persuaded that good success in those countries might make us hope for a good peace.'[1] In the fullness of time, the Spanish involvement would come to be bitterly repented, but in 1706 the omens appeared bright enough. At the outset of the struggle the Spanish Bourbons appear to have had the services of barely 18,000 regular troops and some 48 ships and galleys in Spain and its surrounding waters. As one grandee had admitted in 1701, there were 'insufficient ships and soldiers for our defence . . . in most towns one can hardly find a musket, arquebus or pike.'[2] Such troops as there were left much to be desired in terms of equipment or efficiency, and Louis XIV soon found himself committed to a massive programme of economic and military aid in support of his grandson. Senior officers, troops, training missions and economic advisers crossed the Pyrenees in a steady stream.

*   *   *

During a winter of relative political accord in England, Marlborough laid plans for his bold march to Italy with his wonted care. But once again, after crossing to the Hague (25 April), he found disappointments and complications on every hand. The Dutch, despite at first seeming receptive to the idea of reinforcing Italy from the north, became suddenly alarmed when they learnt that Marlborough was considering going thither in person, and began to demand guarantees. The Danes, Hessians, Hanovarians, and above all the Prussians, despite earlier undertakings, found, or invented, pressing reasons for witholding their support. So preparations were again everywhere behind hand, nowhere more so than on the Upper Rhine where the ailing and crusty Baden could field barely 7,000 badly-equipped troops and refused to discuss his plans, if any. Marlborough set out to tackle this mountain of obstruction with all his old verve, but suddenly everything was vitiated by the arrival of grave tidings from Rastadt early in May.

It transpired that the Court of Versailles had been at pains to spring a double-surprise on their opponents in both Alsace and northern Italy. On the former front, with great secrecy, Marshals Villars and Marsin prepared an early offensive against Baden's unwary forces. On 1 May they struck, and at once bundled the Imperialists out of their positions behind the Moder Line, recaptured Hagenau, and drove the Margrave's discomforted troops to the east bank of the Rhine, thus creating a threat to Landau. This setback was in itself enough to rule out any prospect of transferring a sizeable part of the Flanders' armies to Italy. Yet the news from that quarter was equally discouraging. As the second part of Louis XIV's strategy, Vendôme had launched an unseasonably early offensive against the Imperialist troops who were still in winter quarters along the River Chiese and near Lake Garda. On 19 April the battle of Calcinato had been fought, the Imperialists being pushed back in dire confusion beyond Salo where they were rallied by Prince Eugene in the nick of time. Thereafter Vendôme set himself the task of blocking any attempt by Eugene to march to the aid of Savoy, where the Duc de la Feuillade was actively preparing to undertake the long-anticipated siege of Turin. Thus, the first military events of 1706 were decidely in the French favour, both on the Rhine and in the Po valley.

The reaction of the States-General to these tidings was to withdraw still more of their previous concessions concerning a transfer of troops. However, the extent to which Marlborough was in fact committed to the concept of such a staggering march to Italy is debatable, at least in so far as it may be said to have represented his main concept for 1706. There can be no questioning the amount of diplomatic and other preparation the Duke undertook to prepare the way for such a scheme. The Commons were persuaded to vote £334,000 in subsidies for the furtherance of the cause in North Italy, and on 25 April 1706, the Queen had secretly granted her general specific permission, 'to march forthwith to Italy', with or without Dutch consent.[3] At a lowlier level, Parker noted that in May the Duke had ordered, 'six handmills for grinding corn to be delivered to every British regiment, as well horse as foot. This occasioned a report that he designed to march us to Italy . . . which had been a fine jaunt indeed.'[4]

Against this evidence, however, must be set a letter Marlborough wrote to the Emperor on 9 May 1706, shortly after he had learnt of Baden's disaster on the Rhine. In this he strongly deplored his failure 'since my arrival here' to procure the States-General's agreement 'to *the project of the Saar*, this being the place where it seems to me that we could attack the enemy the most effectively.' Having failed in this, he goes on, he had 'pressed them to provide a reinforcement of 20,000 men for Italy, which is the project which I wrote to Count Wratislaw that I had in mind *in case the other scheme fell through* (this author's italics) so as to give the Prince of Savoy the superiority, expressing the intention, if I could succeed, of joining them myself before this corps arrived in Lombardy.'[5] The best he could now extract from the Dutch was a force of 10,000 men for Italy, providing, 'I remain here personally.' This document would seem to reveal that the Duke's favourite scheme for 1706 was, from the first, a return to the Moselle-Saar region, with the 'fine jaunt' to Italy being his second proposal. The point is largely academic, however, as Baden's misfortunes and Dutch timidity effectively compelled him to undertake another campaign in Flanders however much this might be against his declared wishes.

For he could conceive of no real possibilities of success there. The French would never be so foolhardy, to his way of thinking, as to leave their strong positions and attack his army, even if Villeroi was first reinforced by substantial transfers from Marsin's command. The best French strategy would be to remain on the defensive in the Netherlands and thus increase their power to attack in Italy and, possibly, in Spain.

In fact, however, Louis XIV had already enjoined otherwise. News of the successes in Italy and along the Rhine had encouraged him to expect positive achievements in Flanders as well. Villeroi, at the head of some 60,000 men near Louvain, was accordingly ordered to undertake the recapture of Léau as a preliminary move whilst Marsin moved north to Metz ready to reinforce him; indeed, his cavalry was to ride ahead to effect a junction as soon as possible. Thereafter, if all remained quiescent on the Moselle, both armies would take the field in Flanders. Behind all this demand for activity lay Louis' desire to conceal his country's growing economic exhaustion behind a military facade of meaningful activity. He thus hoped to secure a 'fair' peace. 'I can think of nothing which can better induce them to come to an agreement which has become necessary now', the King had written, 'than to let them see that I have sufficient forces to attack them everywhere.'[6] Such was the keynote of French strategy for early 1706; with no less than eight armies in the field Louis was playing for high stakes. The disasters that awaited his arms that year would therefore be that much the more telling.

Marlborough had some knowledge from his own secret sources of the broad intent, if not the detail, of the French plan to move Marsin towards Flanders. Once such a move had been completed, the French strength in the theatre would be such as to make any effective Allied operations very difficult to undertake; meantime, the possibility of a French onslaught on the Moselle had also to be considered. Accordingly he took the field on 13 May and moved to the Camp of Tongres despite the continued absence of the Danish and Prussian contingents. 'God knows I go with a heavy heart,' he confided to Godolphin, 'for I have no prospect of doing anything considerable unless the French would do what I am very confident they will not . . .'[32]—in other words, court battle. Advancing along the general line of the River Mehaigne, the army crossed the area of the razed lines with the general intention of making at least a demonstration towards Namur in the none-too-sanguine hope that this might draw the French out.

However, the whole Allied army, from Captain-General to last-joined recruit, was soon to be surprised. Villeroi was, in fact, already on the move southwards at the head of 74 battalions and 128 squadrons. His new boldness was the product of two influences: a growing confidence in his ability to out-general Marlborough, and an increasing impatience with the repeated urgings of Versailles to avenge Blenheim: this combination made him 'resolved to put all at stake' (St. Simon), and accordingly the Franco-Bavarian army crossed the Dyle and marched boldly on Tirlemont, deliberately seeking out the Allies.

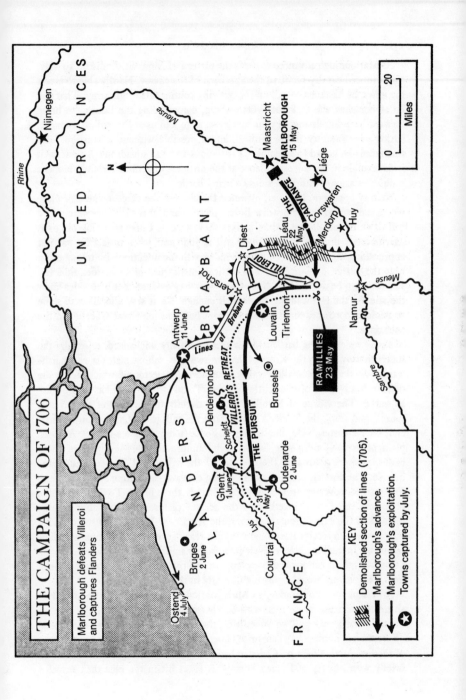

THE CAMPAIGN OF 1706

Marlborough defeats Villeroi and captures Flanders

UNITED PROVINCES

Nijmegen

Rhine

Meuse

Maastricht

MARLBOROUGH 15 May

Liége

Corswaren

THE ADVANCE

Huy

Merdorp

Diest

Léau 22 May

VILLEROI

Meuse

Aerschot

Namur

B R A B A N T

Antwerp 11 June

Louvain

Tirlemont

RAMILLIES 23 May

Lines

Dendermonde

VILLEROI'S RETREAT OF BRABANT

Brussels

Scheldt

Ghent 1 June

31 May

THE PURSUIT

Oudenarde 2 June

F L A N D E R S

Lys

Courtrai

F R A N C E

Bruges 2 June

Ostend 4 July

Sambre

KEY

Demolished section of lines (1705).

Marlborough's advance.

Marlborough's exploitation.

Towns captured by July.

0   20
Miles

As Marlborough advanced towards the plateau of Mont St. André on 19 May, his advanced cavalry reported the approach of the enemy. Hardly able to credit the news, he hastened to call up the outlying contingents of his army. That day he admonished the Duke of Württemberg, commanding the Danes, 'to bring forward by a double-march your cavalry so as to join us at the earliest moment, letting your infantry follow with all speed possible without exhaustion.'[7] By this means he hoped to assemble 74 battalions and 122 squadrons. A new spirit is discernible in his correspondence at the prospect of action: certainly it was a unique occasion—with both sides courting battle.

Neither opponent, however, expected the clash at the exact moment or place where it occurred. Villeroi still believed (on the 22nd) that the Allies were over a full day's march distant, when in fact they were at Corswaren; for his part, Marlborough deemed Villeroi to be still at Judoigne, when in fact he was fast approaching the plateau of Mont St. André with the intention of pitching camp near the village of Ramillies. The tactical intelligence of both sides thus left something to be desired; the 'fog of war' was very evident. Yet both sides knew the site for the forthcoming battle well enough, for it was a location of some strategic importance, commanding the area between the Great Gheete and the Mehaigne.

Today much of the battlefield remains essentially unchanged, especially the southern area. From the River Mehaigne two low, rolling plateaux run north-wards, divided by a shallow valley, the northern sector of which holds the marshy headwaters of the Little Gheete. Today, this stream has all but dis-appeared. The village of Ramillies stands slightly to the west of the original source, and along the former's banks stand the villages of Offus, Autre-Église, and, on the eastern side, the hamlet of Foulz (today Foix-les-Caves). A broad plain, perhaps, 1½ miles wide, lies between Ramillies and the Mehaigne, on whose banks, projecting towards the east, stand the villages of Taviers and Fran-quenée. The French position ran in a long concave curve from Autre-Église to Franquenée, covering an area of approximately three miles. To the East of the plain and the Little Gheete rises the second plateau, that of Jandrenouille, divided by the small tributary stream, the Jeuche (or Jauce). This second ridge was destined to receive the Allied army. In rear of the crest there runs a shallow re-entrant, invisible to the French even from Ramillies church-tower, following a north-south direction, and lying opposite to the northern half of the French line. This feature would figure significantly in the coming struggle.

At 1 a.m. on Whitsunday, 23 May, Marlborough ordered Cadogan to ride ahead through the dense mist with 600 horse to reconnoitre a suitable site for the army's next camp. Two hours later, the main body broke camp and moved off westwards in three large columns. There was still no idea about the proximity of the foe. At about 8 a.m. Cadogan had just passed Merdorp when he brushed briefly with a party of French hussars. A short lift in the mist then revealed dense columns of horsemen massing beyond; the news was galloped back to the Duke's headquarters.

Within two hours Marlborough, accompanied by Overkirk, the Dutch Deputies and the Allied staff, had joined the Quartermaster-General. As it was still uncertain whether the mist shielded the whole of Villeroi's army or only a strong force of horse told off to cover some other move, Marlborough's first order was to hasten his own cavalry to the fore. Then, suddenly, the mists rolled aside, and the distant skyline stood at last revealed, packed with Villeroi's army. It made a splendid sight, for the campaign had only just begun, and time and weather had not 'dimmed its brilliancy'. More Allied aides dashed off to hasten the approach of the infantry and guns, and the army fanned out into eight columns as they passed over the razed lines.

Marlborough, meantime, was conducting a careful reconnaissance of the area. His keen eye for ground had already sized up the problems posed by the marshy Little Gheete running away to the right, and the equally problematical ground bordering the Mehaigne to the left. He had also noticed, we may be sure, the vital re-entrant. The significance of Ramillies set slightly to the fore of the main French lines as the key to the French position, was also appreciated, and with it the importance of the broad cavalry plain immediately to the southwards. This area was too broad to be dominated by enemy fire from Taviers and Ramillies. Finally, the advantages that would be conferred by occupying the chord to the French arc were carefully analysed. It would probably be erroneous to attribute a set-plan to the Duke at this time, but he doubtless was aware of the broad opportunities the ground ahead could offer or deny him.

The army was ordered to take up a standard battle formation. On the far right, towards Foulz, the British battalions and squadrons took up their posts in a double line near the Jeuche stream. The centre was formed by the mass of the Allied infantry, perhaps 30,000 troops, facing towards Offus and Ramillies. On their left General Overkirk drew up the Dutch and Danish horse, some 69 squadrons strong, whilst battalions of Dutch Guards took post on the extreme left. As was his wont, Marlborough carefully supervised the siting of his 100 cannon and 20 howitzers. Thirty 24-pounders were massed facing Ramillies; further batteries overlooked the Little Gheete, and two pieces were attached to the Dutch Guards on the left.

The French dispositions along their concave line were as follows: to the fore, on Villeroi's extreme right, five battalions had been placed in Taviers and Franquenée, but no troops had been told off to hold the Mehaigne marshes on their flank, an important oversight. The main right wing comprised 82 squadrons, including the *Maison du Roi*, with several interleaved brigades of infantry in support, the whole facing the open plain. In the centre, 20 battalions and a dozen triple-barrelled cannon were placed around Ramillies, with further foot to its rear. Further north, overlooking the Little Gheete, were more

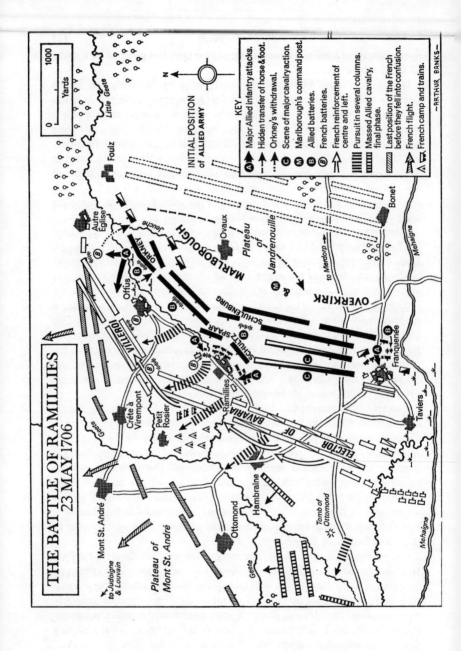

THE BATTLE OF RAMILLIES
23 MAY 1706

1000
0
Yards

N

INITIAL POSITION
of ALLIED ARMY

KEY

A — Major Allied infantry attacks.
→ Hidden transfer of horse & foot.
⋯ Orkney's withdrawal.
G — Scene of major cavalry action.
M — Marlborough's command post.
B — Allied batteries.
B — French batteries.
B — French reinforcement of centre and left.
‖‖ Massed Allied cavalry.
‖‖ Pursuit in several columns.
▨ Last position of the French before they fell into confusion.
⇨ French flight.
⚑ French camp and trains.

Little Geete

Foulz

Autre Eglise

Jauche

ORKNEY

MARLBOROUGH

Plateau of
Jandrenouille

Ovaux

Offus

to Merdorp

Bonet

OVERKIRK

Mehaigne

VILLEROI

SCHULTZ

SPAAR

SCHULENBURG

Franquenee

M &

G

Crête à
Viremont

Petit
Rosier

Ramillies

BAVARIA

Taviers

Geete

ELECTOR OF

Mont St. André

Plateau of
Mont St. André

to Judoigne & Louvain

Ottomond

Hambraine

Tomb of
Ottomond

Mehaigne

~ARTHUR BANKS~

battalions and guns, and, finally, 50 squadrons of horse were taking post around Autre-Église.

Of the two armies, Marlborough's was the more compactly deployed, for although in numerical terms there was not a great deal to choose between them, the French occupied a longer line. The Allies, moreover, enjoyed a considerable advantage in artillery, and Marlborough was aware that by cunning use of the concealed re-entrant he could transfer troops from his right to the centre or left far more easily than the foe.

At about 1 p.m. the guns spoke. A little later, two columns set out from the extremities of the Allied line as Marlborough took the initiative as usual and set out to probe the enemy positions and the ground on the flanks. In the south, the Dutch Guards, using their two cannon to blast a way through houses and walls, made short work of Franquenée and Taviers. By 3.15 p.m. both villages had been overrun. This development caused concern to the French sector commanders, and a force of 14 squadrons of dragoons and two battalions of Swiss troops, supported by a Bavarian brigade, were sent out from the right wing in an extemporised counter-attack. Disaster ensued. The dragoons, after dismounting amidst the marshes, were caught by the advancing Danish cavalry and decimated, and soon the Swiss had also taken to their heels, sweeping away the greater part of de la Colonie's supporting Bavarians in their flight. The loss of the villages, and the dispersal of much of the available French and Bavarian infantry in the sector, implied a serious threat to the flank of the French right wing.

Meantime, on the opposite flank, General Lord Orkney's bold advance at the head of the massed British battalions (12 in all) was taking up all of the Elector's and Villeroi's attention. Their command post had been established near the village of Offus. With growing fascination the commanders watched the red-coated battalions negotiate the difficult Gheete marshes and then press on towards the French line. This brought to Villeroi's mind a special instruction from Versailles—'to pay special attention to the sector which will receive the first shock of the English troops.'[8] Accordingly, anxious for the safety of his left wing, beyond which ran his main communications to Louvain, Villeroi began to transfer battalions from his centre to reinforce the left, drawing more foot from the already weakened right to replace them.

How far Orkney's advance was planned as a feint is still a subject of debate. It is probably more accurate to surmise that Marlborough launched Orkney in a serious probe with a view to sounding out the possibilities of the sector. The issue of cavalry support was the deciding factor. Although a few English squadrons were able to traverse the marshes and streams, it was soon evident that proper co-operation would not be practicable, and it was always a cardinal tenet of Marlborough's battlecraft to place horse, foot and guns in mutual-support, both in attack and defence. By 3.30 p.m. it was fairly clear to him that the battle could not be won on the Allied right: as at Blenheim, two years before, the road to victory would lie through the enemy centre, once it had been properly prepared.

In the centre, meantime, General Schulenburg was making steady progress towards Ramillies. It accordingly behoved Overkirk to advance his massed squadrons 'in four dense lines like solid walls,'[9] in support of the infantry. This movement constituted a challenge to the remaining 68 squadrons of the French right which they were glad to accept. The first clash favoured the Allies, but the remaining French battalions proved capable of preventing any exploitation. Battle royal was then engaged. The *Maison du Roi's* counter-attack broke through two successive lines of Dutch horse, but then the platoon firing of four Allied battalions earned a respite for their harrassed horsemen. Nevertheless, Overkirk's cavalry had been forced to give ground, and this left Schulenburg's left flank dangerously exposed.

From his vantage point slightly in rear of the main battleline, Marlborough was at once aware of the danger. He made several hard and fateful decisions. The first was to order the recall of Orkney's attack on the far right: in the first place the Duke was now persuaded that the Gheete marshes precluded any real chance of supporting the foot with horse and guns; then again, he had more urgent work for the cavalry of his right wing in support of his left. Orkney's recall proved easier to order than to have implemented. The fiery Scotsman was making famous progress at the head of the red-coats, cavalry or no cavalry. 'The village of Autre-Église was in our grip, but as I was going to take possession I had ten aides-de-camp to me to come off, the last being the Adjutant-General himself.'[10] Grudgingly, the battalions began to withdraw, but made short work of an attempt by some French formations to follow them up.

Marlborough's second decision was to summon the cavalry of the right to the aid of his threatened left centre. As Orkney fell back under Cadogan's watchful eye towards Foulz, first 18 squadrons, and then a further 21, received orders to fall back into dead ground and set off to their left down the concealing re-entrant. This would only leave the English squadrons to support Orkney, but there was little danger of serious French attack in that quarter. The transfer went unnoticed by the French, thanks to the combination of the battlesmoke and the favourable terrain, and Villeroi made no attempt to transfer any of his 50 squadrons from his left, where of course the obstacle of the Gheete marshes was every bit as intractable to the French as to the English.

At this juncture Marlborough flung himself into the cavalry action sword in hand. He took part in two charges at the most critical point at the head of his squadrons, and this (as at Elixhem in 1705) almost proved his undoing. Thrown from his horse in one *mêlée* he, '. . . was rid over, but got other squadrons to his aid which he led up,' recounted Orkney. The Duke's staff came rushing to his aid, and General Murray brought up two battalions of Swiss in the Dutch pay to cover the Captain-General. An aide led up a spare horse. 'Major Bingfield (Bingham), holding his stirrup to give him assistance onto his horse, was shot by a cannon ball that passed through Marlborough's legs.'[11] Thereafter, the danger passed, but it had been a critical scrape. Some commentators assert that Marlborough was wrong to expose himself so rashly—as he had also done in August the previous year. But the Duke was a skilled assessor of a difficult situation, and was probably aware that his personal intervention would play an important role in rallying the horse.

So at any rate it proved. Time was won for the arrival of the transferring squadrons, which in due course gave the Allies a 5–3 advantage on the sector. Soon 25,000 French and Allied cavalry were heavily engaged, and little by little weight of numbers began to tell, and the French had to give ground. The climateric blow was delivered by the Danish horse, which wheeled to penetrate the *Maison du Roi's* flank. The Danes, 'profiting by their superiority of numbers, surged through the gaps between our squadrons,' recalled de la Colonie, a spectator of these events, 'and fell upon their rear, while their four lines attacked in front.'[12] Abruptly, the French right gave way, the discomfited squadrons attempting to reform a new line at right-angles to their original front. But the Danes offered them no respite. Sweeping forward and reforming so as to face north, they were soon in possession of the tumulus known as the Tomb of Ottomond (d'Hottomont). At that point the exploitation was suspended for the time being to reorder the army.

The attack on Ramillies village—now forming the hinge of the French hairpin-shaped line—rose to a new intensity as Schulenburg's battalions, accompanied by the Scots Brigade and two British battalions, stormed the outer defences. It proved hot work. As Brigadier John Campbell led the second assault, he received three slight wounds from spent musket-balls.

Between five and six o'clock a pause settled over the field, but on the right a new transfer of troops was taking place. When Orkney's double line of battalions had reached the crest of their original position, the first line to arrive was ordered to march over the summit into dead-ground before halting. The second line halted just short of the crest. Aides-de-camp then ordered the six concealed battalions, less their colour-parties which remained behind the ridge to preserve the appearances of a second line, to turn left and march off towards the centre, there to form the reserve. Once again Villeroi was fooled—and he still seemed to have had no real idea of the gravity of the situation developing beyond Ramillies. All the troops of his left centre and left therefore—perhaps 30 per cent of the army—remained mesmerised by the very thin line of Orkney's troops holding the opposite crest beyond the valley and the regimental colours they could see beyond.

At 6 p.m. Marlborough ordered the general attack. Allied superiority on the left could not be long denied, and within half-an-hour the French line was again beginning to crumble. Now, far too late, Villeroi tried to redeploy his 50 unused squadrons, but a desperate attempt to form some sort of line behind Ramillies foundered amongst the tents and baggage wagons of the French camp. Growing chaos led to retreat; retreat soon became flight. 'We had not got 40 yards on our retreat', noted the Irish renegade Peter Drake, 'when the words *sauve qui peut* went through the great part, if not the whole army, and put all to confusion. Then might be seen whole brigades running in disorder.'[13]

Soon the French army had disintegrated into a horde of fugitives. Fifty cannon and 80 standards and colours were abandoned to the triumphant allies, who also took possession of the entire French camp and trains. Surrenders mounted: Mordaunt's and Churchill's regiments of foot drove three enemy battalions into the marshes at the source of the Gheete, whilst the Scottish Brigade routed the proud *Régiment de Picardie*. Obstacle or no, the Little Gheete was soon passed by Lumley's cavalry on the right, and the Scots Greys and King's Dragoon Guards thundered forward at the gallop (a rarity at this period) to round up the *Régiment du Roi* as the French fled for Judoigne. To Lumley's right, General Wood almost captured Villeroi and the Elector at a cross-road near St. Pierre Gheete, but unaware of their identity contented himself with making prisoner two Bavarian Lieutenant-Generals. Far to the south, the remnants of de la Colonie's brigade headed away in the opposite direction for Namur. The pursuit was pressed without respite. 'The Danish horse were a great weight to incline the victory on the side of the Confederates,' comments Lediard, 'and the English had the honour to complete it, they having the greatest share in the pursuit.'[14] By midnight Marlborough and his staff were at Meldert, all of 12 miles from the field. There, after almost 20 hours in the saddle, the 56-year-old Duke stiffly dismounted to snatch a few hours rest, thoughtfully inviting the critical Dutch Colonel Goslinga to share his cloak on the ground. Meanwhile, Colonel Richards was already riding for London with official news of the victory.

So ended 'the great and glorious day of Ramillies' (Blackader). For a loss of 1,066 killed and some 2,560 wounded—far less than at Blenheim—the Allies had inflicted at least 13,000 casualties on the French, and if subsequent deserters and stragglers are added, several authorities avow that less than half of Villeroi's original army were under any semblance of order on the morning of the 24th.

Marlborough's gift for sizing up a position, his skill at controlling the form and detail of a major conflict, had been once again amply demonstrated. The effects of his success were to be momentous. As Marlborough's first major biographer wrote, 'this victory decided the destiny of the Low Countries . . . after the battle a general revolution followed . . . and the Allies were blessed with a continued chain of conquests.'[15]

It was not until the 26th that full news of the disaster reached Versailles. The tidings arrived hard on the heels of others announcing the failure of the Spanish Bourbons to retake Barcelona from the Allies after a long siege. After considering the various reports that came to hand, King and Minister levelled five main criticisms at the discredited Villeroi. First, that he had courted battle without ascertaining his foe's strength. Second, that he had fought without awaiting Marsin's arrival. Third, that he had failed to reinforce his right wing. Fourth, that the Marshal had placed insufficient infantry to hold the marshes near Taviers, and had thus compromised the safety of the right. And lastly, that he had erroneously deployed that wing on the battlefield, with the result that only the first line of infantry and the first of horse, supported by only a few squadrons from the second, had been able to fight to their best advantage.[16]

In reply the hapless Villeroi vainly pleaded the royal orders of 6 May in defence of his decision to fight. He could not disguise the outcome. 'I cannot foresee a happy day in my life save only that of my death,' wrote the disconsolate commander. The King lost little time in sending Chamillart on a mission to his headquarters to supervise Villeroi's further actions, pending arrangements for his supercession.

The consequences of Ramillies were to prove dramatic. 'We now have the whole summer before us,' wrote the victor, 'and with the blessing of God I shall make the best use of it.'[17] As the demoralised French reeled back in disarray, fortress after fortress fell to the triumphant Allies. 'Towns that we thought would have endured a long siege are yielding without a stroke,' wondered Colonel Blackader.[18] The French made no attempt to hold the River Dyle, and on the 25th Marlborough occupied Louvain. The following day his troops were in Vilvorde, and the 28th saw the Allies entering Brussels, capital of the Spanish Netherlands.

Marlborough was quick to exploit the welcome the local inhabitants—adept at hailing successive conquerors—hastened to offer him. On the 27th his headquarters promulgated a severe warning against marauding, 'it being our intention to protect the said country and all the inhabitants thereof as good subjects of his said Majesty (Charles III) in the full and perfect enjoyment of all their estates, goods and effects. We do hereby strictly forbid all the officers and soldiers of our army to offer the least injury to ye said inhabitants, and on the contrary (enjoin) they do give them all necessary aid and assistance....'[19] Strict penalities for non-compliance were announced, and compensation for civil injury promised.

The French high command was now hoping to rally behind the line of the Scheldt in the vicinity of Ghent. Marsin meanwhile, swung towards Maubeuge and Mons at the head of 14 battalions and 11 squadrons, pausing only to garrison Ath and Charleroi, with the intention of creating a relatively secure southern flank.

Marlborough, however, would afford his foe no respite. As Villeroi hastily continued to split up his army into garrisons, the Allies marched on Alost, and then headed for Gavre. By-passing Dendermonde, the Duke advanced on Courtrai. This move posed a threat to Villeroi's communications with France, and immediately the Marshal ordered the abandonment of Ghent, Bruges and Damme, and on 31 May retired over the Lys. At Courtrai he was met by Chamillart, who unexpectedly approved Villeroi's abandonment of the Scheldt line despite the horror of the court when this further cession of terrain was communicated.

Early June found the Minister of War in serious conclave with the Elector and Villeroi at Lille, taking measures for the defence of the frontiers of France—now their sole preoccupation. On the 3rd Chamillart departed for Versailles; the same day saw Bruges open its gates whilst Marlborough led part of his army towards Antwerp. There the Spanish Governor, the Marquis of Terracena, was in no mood to offer even a token resistance, and constrained the French part of the garrison to join him in surrendering the town on the 6th. Only Dendermonde remained untaken, the garrison using extensive inundations to fend off the Allies.

The time had come for a careful consideration of future strategy. Marlborough argued for a drive to the coast against Ostend and possibily Dunkirk—that perennial nest of privateers which wrought much havoc on English merchant shipping in the Channel. But at the council of war, Overkirk was less than enthusiastic, demanding a march against Namur, and it behoved the Duke to pay a visit to the Hague (8–13 June) to persuade the States-General of the value of his plans. Villeroi meantime could but guess at the direction of the next Allied blow, but he was only too aware that reinforcements (recalcitrant Prussians and Dutch garrison troops) were pouring into Marlborough's camps, bringing his strength to the neighbourhood of 100,000 men. The responsibility for meeting this imposing armament would not much longer remain his, for Louis XIV had decided to recall the successful Duc de Vendôme from Italy to replace the erstwhile favourite. At the same time Versailles was making vast efforts to build a total field force in Flanders of 90 battalions and 150 squadrons by 1 August, transferring a total of 30 battalions and 26 squadrons from the Rhine in two detachments. Even so the King was not envisaging any bold French initiatives. 'If you were obliged to fight, I would not consider you strong enough,' the King wrote, 'but it seems to me you should have a sufficient force to prevent him (the enemy) undertaking anything.'[20] In any case, by mid-June Villeroi's field army had virtually ceased to exist—no less than 110 battalions having been scattered between eleven fortresses.

At the Hague, Marlborough won his way, and soon the Allies were marching for Ostend. A naval squadron bombarded the town, and on 16 June a strong force set out from Bruges; these inescapable signals caused the French to rush more troops to the coastal sector, where the aged Vauban was appointed to command. At the same time another Allied corps headed for Dendermonde to reinforce the blockade, covered by the Hanovarian and Prussian contingents from their camp near Vise on the Meuse.

Overkirk was entrusted with the siege of Ostend, at the head of 25 battalions and 30 squadrons, whilst Marlborough (56 battalions and 132 squadrons) took up a covering position at the Camp of Rousselaer. The trenches were opened before Ostend on the 24th, and a second naval bombardment followed two days later. Villeroi had neither the means nor the mind to intervene. On 4 July, Marlborough visited the siege works, and witnessed the storm of the counter-scarp on the 5th. This enabled the breaching batteries to be mounted on the covered way, and under this threat Count de la Motte beat the *chamade* and surrendered the celebrated fortress after a bare three weeks. In the early seven-teenth century, a stauncher garrison had defied a Spanish army for as many years.

Before Dendermonde, meantime, the Allies were making scant progress. Even an eight-day bombardment in late June failed to shake the resolve of the garrison, and by 5 July matters had returned to a mere blockade. By this juncture Marlborough had decided to march on Menin instead of Dunkirk, the capture of which might well have led to serious political complications with the touchy Dutch. Through Menin ran a surer route to the frontiers of France, and the Duke was hopeful of a supporting Allied descent against the French coastline to distract his enemy.

Menin was one of Vauban's masterpieces. It was held by 12 battalions and 3 squadrons of dragoons under Count Caraman, hero of Elixhem. Its magazines and storehouses were full, and judicious flooding had improved its defensive capacity. By 23 July, General Salisch had arrived under the walls with 22 battalions and 40 squadrons. By 5 August, the Allied lines were complete, and the trenches were opened the next day.

Meantime, Marshal Vendôme had arrived from Italy. After a brief visit to Versailles he reached Namur, where on 4 August he formally took over command from Villeroi. His first impressions of his Spanish and Bavarian colleagues were not notably favourable. After a visit to Valenciennes he reported to the King that 'everybody here is only too ready to raise their hats at the mention of Marl-borough's name.'[21] Nevertheless he at once began to plan the assembly of 75 battalions and 150 squadrons around Lille with the intention of making an attempt to support the newly-besieged garrison of Menin.

By 9 August, 40 cannon and as many mortars were in action against Menin's defences, and yet more artillery was on its way to the siege. Vendôme's declared intention of moving his army forward to the Lower Deule so as to threaten interference with the Allied operations about Menin was made more difficult to implement by the need to detach 15 battalions to watch the coast, where an Allied landing from the sea could not be ruled out. This requirement effectively reduced Vendôme's ability to undertake any ambitious project, but on 15 August he sent out strong French columns from Lille and Tournai to attack part of Marl-borough's covering army as it was foraging. The French achieved surprise, and drove in the outlying detachments with some loss. Worse was to follow: a

French raiding party captured the indispensable Cadogan. 'I was thrust by the crowd ... into a ditch,' he wrote to Lord Raby on 17 August. 'With great difficulty I got out of it and with greater good fortune escaped falling into the Hussars' hands who first came up with me.' He was made prisoner by French carabiniers, 'from whom we met with quarter and civility, saving their taking my watch and money.'[22] His captivity did not prove of long duration, however. Marlborough, understandably anxious to recover his invaluable lieutenant, brought every pressure to bear to secure his exchange, and eventually he was released in return for Lieutenant-General Pallavicini.

Despite these alarums, the siege of Menin itself proceeded remorselessly, 'the briskest and regularest carried on in the whole war' in the opinion of Sgt. Millner.[23] The 15th saw the costly but successful storming of the covered way— 1,400 casualties being sustained by the assault force. This event proved the turning-point of the siege, and by the 21st a large breach had been battered in the main defences. Next day Count Caraman capitulated on terms, and was allowed to march out with full honours and evacuate his garrison to Douai.

Where would Marlborough direct the lightning to strike next? Vendôme hastily worked to improve the Lines of Commines in the belief that Ypres would prove the next target, although Versailles feared for Lille. But the Duke—who was far from well at this period—proved in no hurry to reveal his hand. His brother Charles was sent off with six battalions and all of 60 guns to strengthen the forces before Dendermonde, whilst the main army remained in camp at Helchin until the end of the month.

The days of Dendermonde were now numbered. The Allied trenches were re-opened on 1 September, and on the 6th M. de Vallé and his staunch garrison marched out just before the autumn rains began to fall.

Marlborough was meanwhile marching his main army towards Ath, whose capture was deemed important if the security of Brussels was to be assured over the winter. Some 10,000 troops moved up by way of Alost and Grammont, whilst Vendôme crossed the River Marque to the vicinity of Valenciennes with the plan of delaying the investment. It proved a vain hope. On the night of 20/21 September Overkirk opened the trenches, covered by the main army from near Leuze. The garrison made a fight of it, however, conducting two sorties on the 27th, but the loss of three sectors of the covered way on the 28th induced the town's commander to sue for terms on 1 October. The negotiations broke down once, but the outcome was not long delayed, and on 2 October the garrison agreed to surrender as prisoners of war.

The capture of Ath was to prove the last conquest of 1706. On the 11th Marlborough ordered a probe towards Mons and Charleroi, but as he had already written to Harley on the 4th, 'the continued rains we have had for several days past have made it almost impracticable to undertake another siege.'[24] Finally, the Duke held a review of the army on the 25th and next day quitted the camp, leaving Overkirk in charge of the dispersal of the troops into winter quarters; no less than 50,000 men would be left to garrison the conquests of the year.

So ended the *annus mirabilis* of 1706 in the Netherlands. If much had been achieved there, no less a success had blessed Allied arms in North Italy. On 7 September, Prince Eugene had routed the French army of the Duc d'Orléans and Marshal Marsin hard by Turin, thus at one stroke raising the siege of the Piedmontese capital and rendering a continued French presence in the Lombard Plain virtually impossible. News of Eugene's victory at Turin reached Marlborough during the siege of Ath. 'It is impossible,' he wrote to Duchess Sarah, 'for me to express the joy it has given me; for I not only esteem, but really love that Prince.'[25]

On the Upper Rhine, Villars had been compelled to resume the defensive after the initially auspicious opening to his campaign, as battalion after battalion was drafted away to reinforce the collapsing Flanders front: ultimately he lost 40 battalions and 68 squadrons in that direction. There was thus no possibility of his undertaking the re-capture of Landau.

Only from Spain was there reasonably satisfactory news for the French King. True, the failure of Franco-Spanish arms to retake Barcelona in May had been an early setback, and subsequently, Lord Galway's army had marched from Portugal to occupy Madrid. But dissensions, poor cooperation between the various Allied commanders and growing supply problems in the inhospitable theatre, had eventually led to the evacuation of the Spanish capital and a difficult retreat towards Valencia. This was a disappointment for Marlborough. Similarly, the hopes that had been placed in an amphibious force under Lord Rivers achieving some notable coup in association with the French Huguenots, or possibily against Cadiz, had been dashed, largely through bad luck and even worse weather. So the year ended without any decision being reached in the Iberian Peninsula.

All in all, however, the war situation had changed beyond all recognition since April. French hopes had almost everywhere been dashed. But one area of growing crisis remained to worry the Allies. In North Germany, the scale of Swedish involvement in Saxony was steadily increasing, and any further expansion of the Great Northern War into that region would inevitably have a detrimental effect on the war effort of the Holy Roman Empire. If only this peril could be circumvented in good time, then the Allied prospects for 1707 seemed most alluring. The French court was already tentatively seeking terms of peace. The next twelve months might well see the final collapse of the Bourbon cause; at the very least, the omens seemed propitious.

Frustration in Flanders, 1707

'These victories gave the Confederates an opportunity of carrying
the war on every side into the dominions of France, but she continued to enjoy a kind of peaceful neutrality in Germany. From
Italy she was once alarmed and had no more to fear. The entire
reduction of this power, whose ambition had caused, whose
strength supported the war, seemed reserved to him alone who had
so triumphantly begun the glorious work. The barrier of France on
the side of the Low Countries had been forming for more than
half a century. What art, power, expense could do had been done
to render it impenetrable, yet here she was most exposed, for here
the Duke of Marlborough threatened to attack her. . . .'

> From the inscription on the Column of Victory,
> Blenheim Palace (continued).

Following the major Allied successes of 1706, it seemed to most contemporary
observers that the Bourbon cause was doomed once and for all. That the end of
the war was not, in point of fact, even on the horizon, was largely due to those
perennial scourges of great coalitions at war—doubt and discord. The major
weakness of the Alliance, that of Grand Strategy, was again to reveal itself in an
aggravated form now that Allied prospects seemed so promising. In the words of
Sir Winston Churchill, 'at the end of 1706 the Grand Alliance was once again
found incapable of enduring success'.[1]

Indeed, ominous cracks in the facade of Allied unity had appeared shortly
after that 'great and glorious day of Ramillies'. As the Allied army marched from
triumph to triumph through the welcoming Flemish-speaking provinces of the
Spanish Netherlands, conducting more of a liberation than a formal conquest,
the political atmosphere took a turn for the worse. The vague stipulations of 1701
concerning the future government of the region at once became manifest. The
Dutch—seeking a secure fortress barrier against the possibility of future French
aggression—clashed with the Austrian government over the issue of garrisoning,
and the financial support for those towns the States-General deemed essential

for their national security. The quarrel centred around the question of the Regency. The Dutch would not countenance the Emperor's claim to exercise the chief authority in the name of the absent Charles III, presently in Spain. At first England favoured the Dutch case, although the government was never willing to relinquish control over Ostend and Dendermonde (once these came into our possession), for these two places were of great commercial as well as strategic importance. Scenting an opportunity to sow discord between the Maritime Powers, the Emperor Joseph then offered, on his brother's behalf, the Governor-Generalship of the Spanish Netherlands to Marlborough.

The Duke was sorely tempted. He was not yet so sated with honours and riches as not to be attracted by the prospect of a further £60,000 per annum. But he was even more keenly aware of Dutch hostility to the proposal, and so, in the interests of the common cause, he regretfully declined the honour. 'I infinitely prefer their (the States-General's) friendship before any particular interest to myself,'[2] he informed Heinsius. In the view of Dr. A. L. Rowse, this act of self-denial brought Marlborough to his 'personal summit'[3] but unfortunately the episode left a lingering suspicion in Dutch minds that would never fully disappear. In the end a compromise was reached, whereby, from July 1706, a Flemish Council of State ruled the Spanish Netherlands on behalf of Charles III, under the joint-Regency of England and Holland, represented by Marlborough (later aided by Cadogan) and Johan van den Bergh respectively. Owing to the Duke's many other preoccupations, Dutch influence tended to predominate, but the arrangement worked reasonably well for almost a decade although the Marlborough correspondence was considerably increased, and the issue of the Dutch Barrier dogged Allied relationships for the remainder of the war.

Partially thwarted in one direction, the Schönbrunn turned its attention to another, namely Italy. Using a minor setback sustained by the Prince of Hesse at the action of Castiglione (9 September 1706) as a pretext, Austrian plenipotentiaries negotiated with the French forces still in North Italy, and on 13 March 1707 signed a convention which permitted the isolated troops—perhaps 20,000 in all—unconditional repatriation. This windfall of experienced soldiery proved very much to the Bourbon advantage. Next, eager to consolidate the Austrian hold on Italy as a whole, the Emperor began to press for an early expedition against Naples, making it clear that he anticipated the support of the Anglo-Dutch fleet and 5,000 of their troops. This selfish proposal, as we shall see, ran wholly counter to Marlborough's concepts of strategy for 1707, and was destined to have an adverse, even a fatal effect, on the major scheme. When we add to these difficulties the increasingly vociferous demands of Hesse and Prussia for the return of their forces from Italy, the deteriorating situation in Spain and above all the growing crisis in northern Europe occasioned by the successes of Sweden at the expense of Augustus of Saxony, which threatened a major involvement of the Empire in the Great Northern War (subjects to which we shall return on a later page), it can be appreciated that the Second Grand Alliance was facing a period of rough weather, and all Marlborough's skills as arbitrator and conciliator were once again to be in great demand on the international scene.

Threatening clouds also hung over domestic politics. Godolphin, now sundered from the Tories and increasingly dependent upon Whig support, found himself facing a major crisis over the proposed appointment of the free-thinking Earl of Sunderland, Marlborough's Whig son-in-law, to the post of Secretary-of-State in place of the present incumbent, Sir Charles Hedges. The intensely religious Queen was bitterly opposed to the proposal, but the Whigs—who had secured a majority in the Commons at the election of 1705—would settle for nothing less, and with the critical stages of the legislation designed to create the United Kingdom of Great Britain pending, Godolphin had no room for manœuvre. Duchess Sarah, of course, was deeply implicated in the plots to foist Sunderland on the Queen—another aspect that Anne could not but bitterly resent—and the Duke was inevitably drawn into the *imbroglio*, largely unwillingly. In the end, Marlborough had to force the Queen's hand. 'By this, do not mistake me,' he wrote to his wife, who showed the letter to the Queen, 'for I am very sensible that if my Lord Treasurer be obliged to retire, I cannot serve in the Ministry.'[4]

In despair the Queen gave way, and on 3 December Sunderland received the seals as Secretary of State. The Whigs were jubilant, and made no further difficulties over the votes of supply for the war, or the Union with Scotland. But it was another nail in the coffin of the 'special relationship' which had linked 'Mrs. Morley', 'Mr. and Mrs. Freeman' and 'Mr. Montgomery' for so many years. The Queen began to turn increasingly to the sympathetic blandishments of Abigail Hill,* whose secret marriage to Colonel Masham she attended in early 1707 to Sarah's wrath (she had not been privy to her kinswoman's match). Anne was also coming to rely more and more on the advice of Robert Harley,* the

---

* From humble and impecunious origins, Abigail Hill (later Mrs. Masham) owed her first humble appointment at court to her distant relative, Sarah. From being the menial servant of the Queen, she moved steadily forward to become her main confidant and friend, supplanting her original benefactress. Her motherly and comforting nature contrasted markedly with Duchess Sarah's waspishness, and as she became increasingly ill Anne turned ever more to her Bedchamber woman. Abigail became 'the creature of Robert Harley', another distant relative, and made use of her influence to secure his advancement, together with that of her n'eer-do-well brother, General 'Jack Hill'. Her influence reached its peak between 1710 and 1714, and vanished abruptly on the Queen's death. Nicknamed 'Carbuncles' by her enemies on account of her unprepossessing appearance, she was implicated in Bolingbroke's shady financial dealings in the South Sea Company.

senior Secretary-of-State, at Godolphin's expense—another development that promised future trouble.

Such was the ominous London background to which Marlborough returned on 26 November. He might be greeted by cheering crowds, have honours and addresses showered upon him as the hero of Ramillies, have his Dukedom made hereditable by his daughters, and receive his financial grant from the Post Office in perpetuity as rewards from a grateful Parliament, 'but underneath all was insecure.'[5]

The war had still to be won—or a genuine peace negotiated—all these distractions notwithstanding. For a time, there were hopes that the war could be brought to a rapid conclusion. By late 1706, Louis XIV was prepared to accept terms† which would to all intents have satisfied the declared aims of the Grand Alliance. Marlborough, we know, was offered a substantial bribe to secure his support. But the Allies, emboldened by success and subject to many varied pressures, were now committed to enforcing a 'no peace without Spain' formula. By this, Charles III was to receive the *entire* Spanish inheritance, nothing more, nothing less. From this position neither the Austrian government nor the Whig Party would budge, and the Dutch, though at first more flexible in attitude and tempted by the offer of the long-sought Barrier, were not prepared to endanger the Alliance over the issue. Of course there were many shifts of policy and shades of opinion over the months, but by early 1707 the Whigs, becoming ever more powerful and vociferous in Parliament, were adamant that Philip v must be replaced by Charles III. Insular trade interests in the Mediterranean and Levant were as strongly opposed to any suggestion that Philip might receive the Two Sicilies in compensation as were the Austrian Habsburgs, and this effectively closed another means of achieving compromise. And so the tentative negotiations, together with Louis XIV's call for a peace congress, came to naught. French authorities and other hostile critics assert that Marlborough and Heinsius were determined to prolong the war for the preservation of their own influence and, in the case of the Duke, for the lining of his pocket,[6] but there

* Originally a Welsh attorney, Robert Harley became a master at managing the House of Commons in the Tory interest. Artifice and intrigue were 'Tricky Dicky's' second nature, but he generally subscribed to a Moderate Tory line. He was also known as 'the Dragon', being opposed to corruption, at least in others. A distant relation (like Duchess Sarah) of Abigail Masham (*née* Hill), he used her influence with the Queen to undermine the Marlborough-Godolphin ministry and to secure his own preferment. For some years he served as Speaker of the Commons and later became senior Secretary-of-State, but in 1710 became Lord Treasurer. His ministry fell in 1714 when he quarrelled with both Bolingbroke and Mrs. Masham.

† Louis XIV offered to recognise Charles as King of Spain, the Indies and the Spanish Netherlands to award the Barrier fortresses to the United Provinces, and recognise the Protestant succession in England, in return for the award of Naples, Sicily and the Milanese to his grandson in compensation.

is little concrete evidence to support these charges. Indeed there are many
indications that Marlborough was becoming increasingly tired of the heavy-
weight of responsibility he bore campaign after campaign, and longed for the
time when he could take a less active part in public affairs. At the present
juncture, however, he was not convinced of the genuineness of the French
peace protestations, so the war had to continue for at least another year. The
French military performance in 1707 would indeed show that her powers of
resistance were far from exhausted.

Marlborough, therefore, had no alternative but to plan a further campaign.
The scheme that emerged proved one of the most grandiose of the war—a fact
that made its total failure even more salutary. But it would be erroneous to
believe, as is sometimes asserted, that Marlborough planned from a position of
overwhelming strength. We have already examined some of the contentions and
disputes dividing his Allies. There were also military reasons for concern. In the
first place, the Duke was far from content about the situation on the Rhine where
the ailing Baden was an increasing liability. On 28 October 1706 the Duke had
sought Eugene's views 'particularly as regards the Upper Rhine where it is highly
desirable that matters should be placed on a better footing than in the past, so as
to keep the enemy busy there as well as elsewhere. However, as I do not have a
code for communicating with Your Highness, I cannot express myself as openly
as I might, for fear of accident. . . .' Throughout the winter[7] French raiding
parties were probing far beyond the Rhine into Franconia and Swabia, and the
unfavourable impression left by these pin-prick depredations was not really
counteracted by the more dramatic but isolated incident when a Dutch party
penetrated to within a few miles of Versailles itself, and captured the Dauphin's
Equerry on Sèvres bridge. However, on 4 January the Margrave of Baden died of
blood-poisoning, causing the Duke to write that now was the time to appoint 'a
general of reputation and authority . . . to put affairs on the Rhine in order . . .',[8]
at the head, he hoped, of an army at least 45,000 strong. Vienna's announcement
that the Margrave of Bayreuth was to succeed to the command did not wholly
reassure the Captain-General, and subsequent events were to more than bear out
his courteously-concealed hesitation.

Marlborough's major anxiety was directed towards Spain. His high hopes of
decisive success in that theatre during 1706 had been largely dashed. A lethal
combination of dissenting commanders (with Peterborough well to the fore until
his recall in March 1707), inadequate military resources, general lethargy in an
inhospitable theatre, and an increasingly hostile Castilian population, had
rendered the occupation of Madrid merely transitory, and by the year's close the
Bourbon commanders had regained Castile, Murcia and southern Valencia. The
Duke's spies were soon informing him that the French were planning a large-
scale offensive for the next year, and he doubted the ability of Charles III to withstand the onslaught even if the promised reinforcement of 10,000 troops reached

the theatre in time. The unpromising aspect of Spanish affairs forms the essential background for understanding Marlborough's grand design for the year.

His plan, in the simplest terms, was to launch two telling offensives against France. One would be under his own command, based upon Flanders. The second, and by far the more important of the two, would take the form of an allied drive from North Italy along the Ligurian coast into Provence, with the capture of Toulon as its immediate objective. This enterprise, first suggested by the Duke of Savoy soon after the victory of Turin, and agreed to by the Court of St. James by February 1707, would be commanded by Prince Eugene, and supported by the Anglo-Dutch fleets.

The capture of the great French Mediterranean naval base was the pivot of Marlborough's whole strategy for the year. He was convinced that once the threat became apparent, Versailles would have no recourse but to rush forces from Flanders, and even more significantly, from Spain, in an attempt to prevent Toulon's fall. Such a development would relieve the incipient crisis in Catalonia and Valencia, and enable Marlborough to bring heavy pressure to bear against a weakened Vendôme in Hainault and French Flanders. The duty of the light-weight Margrave of Bayreuth would be merely to keep safe the Lines of Stollhofen whilst the great events of the year developed at the opposite extremities of the French frontiers. As much aid as possible would be sent to Charles III in eastern Spain. To the Captain-General's way of thinking, the French could not be strong on all sectors at once, and that therefore a major Allied incursion deep into France must result from at least one point of the compass. Once Toulon had been captured, it could become the forward base for a general Allied advance deep into the heartland of France, a development that must surely bring Louis XIV to sue for peace on any terms.

The plan appeared masterly; England and the United Provinces agreed to raise and pay a further 28,000 troops, half of them from German sources; each infantry company was to receive ten more men, and every cavalry troop eight. The Admiralties were in full accord. Money was made available to assist Savoy and, if necessary, Austria. But in the attitude of the last-named power lay the fatal rub. Vienna would not be persuaded that the Toulon venture must receive the first priority. Not even Marlborough's promise (7 March) that the fleet of the Maritime Powers would be made available *after* the success of the Toulon venture would deflect the Emperor from his obsession with the need to occupy Naples early in the year. Even Prince Eugene, the close comrade-at-arms of the Captain-General, was decidedly lukewarm over the Toulon project, being aware of the Schönbrunn's half-heartedness, and distrustful, as a continental commander, of the role to be played in the scheme by sea-power.

Marlborough pleaded his case with all his skill in letter after letter. One, dated 27 December 1706, is worth citing at some length. 'Here,' wrote the Duke to

Eugene from St. James, 'we are counting on the project of *Provence* and *Toulon*' (italicised words being in cipher). 'And as it is arranged that Your Highness will command the army of Italy, so as to afford the army the best possible chance of success in its enterprises we are making the strongest representations to the court of Vienna, and to the other princes who have troops in Italy, to put in hand everything necessary to recruit them and have them ready in good time; in the case of necessity, we are even prepared to advance (further) money to His Royal Highness (the Duke of Savoy), so that nothing shall be lacking for this affair which is of the greatest consequence to the common cause.

'We are becoming increasingly aware that the enemy will turn their greatest attentions towards Spain, to such a degree that, to avert the setbacks that could befall us in that country, it is vital to provide a powerful diversion from all sides at the outset of the campaign, although I hope that the reinforcement that my Lord Rivers is taking to the King, consisting of at least 10,000 men' (in fact a little over 3,000 actually materialised) 'will enable His Majesty not only to protect himself against insult, but also put him into a condition to take the offensive.

'As for the Low Countries, where my fate will summon me, as Holland refuses to lend a friendly ear to the *Moselle* project, on the grounds of the expense it would entail, it seems to me that the enemy will adopt the defensive; and as they are working to build lines and taking other precautions, I can reveal to Your Highness that my hopes for that area are not too high. Perhaps we shall be able to take some town, an event of no great consequence, but if the occasion for a fight offers you can rest assured that I shall not neglect it.'[9]

This document, not cited by Sir Winston Churchill, reveals a great deal of Marlborough's thinking at this juncture—his continuing anxiety for Spain, the central significance of the Toulon venture in eventually securing its final conquest for the Habsburg claimant, his willingness to take the second place in the year's affairs in the interest of the cause. But his pleadings were not to be heeded. The Emperor pressed ahead with his scheme to send 8,000 men under General Daun towards Naples, diverting desperately-needed men, money and supplies from both Charles III in Spain and from Victor Amadeus and Prince Eugene in north-west Italy. The effects of this selfish stubbornness will become clear on a later page.

Meanwhile, what of King Louis? Typically, the rejection of his peace offer induced a new determination to defend the interests of France and Spain. Between January and March vast preparations were put in hand. Some 21,000 militia were mobilised, and new drafts sent to the five main armies. Recruiting parties scoured France, and commissaries procured supplies for the arsenals by hook or by crook. The marshals were summoned to Versailles to discuss plans and receive their orders. In Flanders, the Elector of Bavaria (who had re-established his viceregal household at Mons) and Marshal Vendôme, at the head of 100,000 men, were to proceed with caution to recover Huy and Liége, but without risking a major engagement. As Marlborough's spies had informed him, vast efforts were put in hand to prepare two new lines of defence to guard the north-eastern frontiers. The first running from the Meuse to the Sambre, and thence by way of Mons and Tournai to Ypres, and finally to the coast at Nieuport; the second, lying further to the rear, was based upon the Canal de Moulinet and the rivers Sensée, Upper Deule and Lys, incorporating the fortresses of Aire and Neuf-Fossé.

In the south of France, meantime, Marshal Tessé at the head of 8,000 men was made responsible for preventing any Allied attempt to invade Dauphiné or Provence, should they so design (although Versailles had no hint of the Toulon project before June). The security of central France, where further risings were feared, was entrusted to M. de Roquelaure. Clearly, from the proportionate deployment of his troops, Louis XIV was far more anxious for the safety of his northern frontiers than for the security of the south.

Such were the defensive arrangements. As far as offensive projects were concerned, these were two in number. On the Rhine front, Marshal Villars and 40,000 men were to mount a surprise attack on the Imperial troops holding the Lines of Stollhofen, and in the event of success, were to drive deep into Germany as a means of distracting the Allies from their own schemes. The highest priority however was to be given, as Marlborough already knew, to the Spanish theatre. There the Duc d'Orléans and Marshal Berwick, at the head of the 48 battalions and 131 squadrons of the refurbished Spanish army and perhaps as many of French troops, seconded by Marshal de Noailles and the *Armée de Roussillon*, were to undertake the clearance of the Allies from Valencia and Aragon, aiming to besiege Lerida as the climax of their campaign.

Once again, therefore, Louis XIV and his advisers produced a comprehensive plan of campaign. Not even the most optimistic, however, could have foreseen the degree of success that would attend its implementation.

Indeed, as a counterweight to any further deterioration in the French military position, Louis XIV was eager to induce King Charles XII of Sweden to enter the arena, either in the guise of arbitrator in new peace negotiations, or, if that proved impracticable, in a more active capacity in North Germany. Since 1700 the youthful warrior-king had been deeply embroiled in the Great Northern War against Russia and Saxony over the issues of the Polish Succession and the control of the South Baltic shore. The year 1706 had proved most favourable to his arms, and his army had wintered around Altranstadt. Now he had quarrels with Austria over the treatment of the Silesian Protestants and other issues. French embassies were soon hard at work trying to persuade Charles and his advisers to press his quarrel with the Elector of Saxony (who claimed to be the rightful King of Poland) to its logical conclusion, Versailles being aware that any Swedish intrusion into the Emperor Joseph's hereditary dominions would inevitably lead to a full-scale conflagration in the Empire which could be immensely to France's military advantage. In such an event, some authorities even predicted the dissolution of the Empire.

This dire possibility was well to the fore in both Marlborough's and Heinsius's minds. On 10 December 1706, the Duke had written to our prickly friend, Mérode-Westerloo, the Flemish magnate, that if the Allies '. . . are to be in a position to re-establish perfect tranquility in the North, it is far preferable that the King of Sweden should turn his arms against the Tsar, than that he should remain (in Saxony) to give umbrage to the Allies instead.'[10]

No sooner, therefore, had the Duke reached the Hague (only on 18 April after a frustrating period of almost three weeks of unfavourable weather for the crossing) than he announced his intention of making a pre-campaign visit to Altranstadt, there to interview Charles XII in the hope of satisfying, in the words of a distinguished modern biographer of that monarch '. . . some of his objectives in return for a promise of future moral if not military commitment to the Allied side.'[11] If practicable, the Swedes were to be encouraged to march against Russia.

Leaving Overkirk with orders for the assembly of the army, Marlborough entered his coach on 20 April, and travelled to Altranstadt by way of Hanover. He reached his goal late on the 26th, and at once sought an interview with Count Piper, Charles's most influential minister. The opening of the first meeting was not propitious, whether by accident or design on Piper's part is not certain. The story goes that the Count kept Marlborough (sitting in his coach at his gate) a considerable time before coming out to greet him. When at last the minister made an appearance Marlborough descended from his coach and without a word 'went aside as if to make water.'[12] Then, his point made, and feelings generally relieved, he was at once courtesy and affability itself.

Thereafter, the conference proved a great success. Marlborough employed flattery to win his way with Charles XII, and rather surprisingly this approach appears to have impressed the usually austere monarch, who is known, however, to have been a genuine admirer of the Duke's martial gifts. After presenting the Queen's profuse regrets at her inability to be present in person, Marlborough went on: 'I wish I could serve in some campaign under so great a commander that I might learn what I yet want to know in the art of war.'[13] This bland and affably insincere remark was widely appreciated throughout the Swedish Army, and the talks proceeded apace. Marlborough hinted strongly that if Charles decided to invade Russia, England would be prepared to guarantee his back, and even recognise Stanislas as King of Poland in place of Augustus of Saxony. As Lediard comments, 'he knew the character of Charles, and his foible,' and so Marlborough's golden tongue largely had its way. Whether or not the tortuous paths of diplomacy required a little oil of a more tangible sort is still subject to some debate. Some sources mention a *douceur* of 100,000 guineas for Count Piper, but Professor Hatton is convinced that 'Count Piper was not bribed, though his wife received a courtesy present of a pair of diamond ear rings.'[14]

Be that as it may, by the time Marlborough left Altranstadt he felt confident that his mission '. . . had entirely defeated the expectations of the French court from the King of Sweden,' and that Charles XII, 'that ambitious youth' as Parker somewhat presumptuously calls him,[15] was set upon an invasion of Russia, which must be lengthy. The Duke was not overly impressed by what he had seen of the Swedish army's administrative arrangements, and perhaps he felt some premonition of the fate that awaited it at Pultava in 1709. In any case he was satisfied to have secured Charles's agreement to the appointment of an English observer to his staff—the astute Captain Richard Jeffereys. Long months of negotiation still lay ahead before Austria and Sweden would sign the Con-vention of Altranstadt (1 September 1707), but the Duke had at least prepared the ground for a favourable outcome, having, in Lediard's words, 'entirely dis-sipated the jealousies some of the Allies had conceived of His Swedish Majesty's designs.' Brief visits to the Elector of Saxony and the King of Prussia followed, and on 9 May Marlborough, after 'meeting four kings in four days', was back at the Hague.

Versailles had been aware of this mission to Saxony, and on 27 April Louis had ordered Vendôme to exploit Marlborough's absence by moving the French army from Mons towards the Meuse, in the hope thereby of drawing the Allies away from French Flanders. By mid-April the Marshal had available on paper 130 battalions and 206 squadrons, whereas the Allies, with many more garrisons to find than in earlier campaigns, were still hard pressed to field 100 battalions and 150 squadrons in the vicinity of Brussels. However, Vendôme was in no position to enter into operations at this juncture; there was a shortage of grass and fodder, and his formations were much dispersed and would require another 12 days to concentrate. He therefore proposed to send off only part of his army towards the Meuse—a decision that accorded with the Elector of Bavaria's anxiety for the safety of Ypres—and with this adjustment Louis XIV had to be content. The King agreed that Vendôme should select his course of action, providing he regarded the distraction of Allied attention away from Flanders as his paramount aim. Armed with this virtual *carte blanche*, Vendôme assembled his army behind the Estinnes stream near Mons, and advanced towards Nivelles with the intention of creating an apparent threat towards Brussels, not Huy and Liége, as originally envisaged. General Lamotte was left to guard the coastal sector.

Then, unexpected tidings from Spain broke like a thunderclap. The Duc d'Orléans had barely assumed the supreme command, and his troops were still awaited, when General Galway with 15,000 troops suddenly advanced against Marshal Berwick and attacked the 25,000 strong Bourbon army on 25 April at Almanza. The outcome was a disaster for Galway—and, as it proved, for the chances of the Allies in Spain. 'By Almanza, the Marshal Duke of Berwick saved the Bourbon Succession.'[16] The divided and quarrelsome Allies would soon find their influence restricted to Catalonia, as Orléans swept northwards into Aragon and Berwick swung south into Valencia, recapturing town after town. The news of this development reached Flanders several weeks later. 'This ill-success in Spain has flung everything backwards,' lamented Marlborough on 23 May, 'so that the best resolution we can take is to let the French see we are resolved to keep in the war so that we can have a good peace.'[17] The Toulon expedition was now more vital than ever if anything was to be salvaged from the wreck of Allied hopes in Spain; for there was no longer any prospect of a rapid conquest of that country in the names of Charles III. But, very unwisely, the attempt would be continued for five more years. From April 1707 the Iberian Peninsula became a mill-stone around the Grand Alliance's neck, and Marlborough had at once to find nine battalions and six squadrons from his already inferior army in Flanders for immediate transfer to Spain. Even worse, the set-back reinforced the innate Dutch caution, and Marlborough would once again be faced by obstructive Deputies.

As for the Toulon expedition, there seemed no prospect of its getting under way before June owing to Imperial obstruction, the late arrival of the Allied fleet, the illness of the Duke of Savoy, not to forget the mounting of Daun's offensive against Naples and Gaeta. Thus vital time was slipping away.

Vendôme's army was much heartened by news of Almanza. Marlborough, though personally despondent for a number of days, was more eager than ever to take the field. On 21 May he assumed command of the army (now 97 battalions, 164 squadrons and 112 guns strong) near Brussels and ordered an advance towards Hal to counter Vendôme's movements, leaving General Spaar to guard the coast. Earlier ideas of marching against Mons or Tournai were now out of the question; instead, he hoped to cover Brabant, and seek an opportunity of snatching a battle on favourable terms if Vendôme could be induced to accept action. As the French marched towards Gosselies (26th), the Allies made corresponding moves, camping at Soignies. Vendôme had now found a promising position for a camp at Gembloux, and expected the Allies to move to Nivelles so as to interpose their army between the French and Brussels, or alternatively to take the bait and march off to besiege Mons, thereby uncovering Brussels and Louvain. Marlborough's desire at this moment was to stay at Soignies, making demonstrations towards Mons as if presaging an intention to besiege it, but a cautious Allied Council of war recommended an advance over the River Senne towards Nivelles. The Dutch deputies, however, were adamant that no major action should be undertaken. The Duke pretended to adopt their advice, but on receipt of news from Cadogan that the Senne crossings were ill-suited for this purpose, he ordered a withdrawal towards Brussels instead, to the annoyance of Colonel Goslinga and the other Dutch representatives. The army was back near the capital by the 29th. The object of these somewhat pointless manœuvres was Marlborough's attempt to convince Heinsius that he must be given a free hand; the Duke also hoped that his seeming indecision would induce the foe into boldness and error. But Vendôme was not to be drawn, so the Allies entered a strong camp at Meldert, south-east of Louvain (1 June), where they were destined to remain, largely inactive, for almost two and a half months.

One reason for this inaction was the arrival on 30 May of tidings revealing another serious setback for the Allied cause, this time on the Rhine. Although Marlborough (alerted by his spies that something was in the wind) had tried to warn the Margrave of Bayreuth to be on his guard, Marshal Villars pulled off a masterly surprise against the Lines of Stollhofen on the night of 22/23 May. Disguising his intentions by ostentatiously attending a ball at Strasbourg, the Marshal slipped away to lead a strong column through the foggy night to outflank the drowsy Imperialists, and aided by a 6 a.m. diversionary attack against the Isle of Alexander, shortly after first light, had made himself master of the strong lines. The Imperial forces melted away before the jubilant French, and on the 24th Rastadt fell without any attempt at a defence. By 8 June the French were in Stuttgart. This French triumph meant that south-central Germany, and even the Danube, were once again threatened by the French, who by the 22nd of the month were deep into Swabia levying contributions.

The new disaster, barely a month after Almanza, caused Marlborough great anxiety and made the Dutch even less cooperative. Far from Allied operations being successful in distracting French forces, it was Allied battalions and squadrons that were having to be redeployed post-haste—some to Spain, now others to the Upper Rhine—Marlborough at once detached three battalions of Palatine troops, and a regiment of both horse and dragoons. He also diverted the march of newly-engaged Saxon reinforcements to the region—to bolster crumbling resistance and stave off the threat of lasting disaster. 'You may judge the surprise and disquiet we feel about the setback on the Rhine . . .' the Duke wrote to Count Wratislaw on 6 June. 'In God's name lose no time in retiring the Margrave, and send there a general from the active list; and if it is possible, reinforce him with the Danes, and other troops besides . . . I will finish by informing you that England and Holland base all hopes on the projects concerting in Italy, being persuaded that the fortune of the campaign, and indeed of the whole war, depends on them.'[18] He was not encouraged, however, by news that the advance on Naples despite all his pleadings had been commenced the preceding month, and Prince Eugene was still reporting delay after delay in launching the Toulon project.

Marshal Vendôme, meantime, was bombarding Versailles for leave to undertake the siege of Huy. Recent Allied setbacks, he argued, together with French superiority in cavalry and the suitability of the open plains around Gembloux for mounted action, made an Allied attempt to force a decisive battle extremely improbable, especially as any move towards the Meuse could be countered by the French crossing the Mehaigne, thus opening a line of attack towards Louvain and Brussels. Versailles, although it had originally suggested the recapture of Huy, was not convinced. 'Such a conquest (of Huy)' the King had responded to an earlier request from Vendôme, 'would in no way affect their (the enemy's) projects, and if they saw you engaged near the Meuse, they could adopt the course of an advance into Flanders to take one of my towns, so that you would have to abandon your enterprise to head them off.'[19] Now, in early June, the situation was different, riposted the Marshal. He had discovered that the Allies were detaching substantial forces for Spain, that a second force was under orders for the Rhine, and that Marlborough had been persuaded to send a further 6,000 men to strengthen his garrisons. Such diminution of strength would rule out any bold Allied initiatives. Versailles remained adamant, enjoining no action against Huy until the receipt of further orders. This hesitation partly stemmed from a general satisfaction with the way in which Vendôme's army was carrying out its main mission (namely the distraction of the Allies from French Flanders) and partly from a growing anxiety about impending developments in the south of France, where disturbing Allied moves were being reported by Tessé.

Eugene and the Duke of Savoy were at last about to move. Not a hint of what was in the wind had reached Versailles until 10 June, so effective had been the feigned Allied preparations for sending massive support to Spain, and their genuine operations against Naples, in lulling French suspicions. Even now, the French strategists considered Dauphiné, and not Provence and Toulon, as the Allied objective; an Imperialist feint towards Susa continued to fool them. With barely concealed impatience, Marlborough bided his time at Meldert, keeping a wary eye on Vendôme's movements, and anxiously awaiting the arrival of every courier and mail-bag from the Mediterranean. The weather was hot that year in Flanders. 'It is most certain that when I was in Spain in the month of August (this probably refers to the period he spent at Tangier*) I was not more sensible of the heat than I am at this minute,'[20] he wrote to Sarah on 26 June.

On 30 June, Eugene set out at the head of 35,000 men towards Toulon. At this juncture Tessé commanded only 8,000 men, and the defences of Toulon were decrepit. Some 90 miles lay between the Allied army and their goal, and Admirals Sir Cloudisley Shovell and Norris with 70 warships were at hand to offer every support. It is true that the army (only 15 per cent of which was provided by Austria) was in many respects too weak and shockingly under-equipped thanks to Viennese parsimony and neglect, but this alone cannot explain, or excuse, the slow rate of advance. It took Eugene all of eleven days to close up from Pignerol to the River Var; only on the 16 July, after a further five days march, did he reach Cannes, a mere 18 miles beyond the river. The crawling column passed Fréjus on 19 July and at last appeared beyond the eastern defences of Toulon a week later. True, some resistance had been encountered from Tessé's

* See above, p. 5.

retiring cavalry and the local populace, but the real reason behind the slow advance lay in the attitude of the commander-in-chief. In short, Eugene's heart was not in the project; he had no previous experience of combined operations, and distrusted and resented the entreaties of the English admirals who appreciated only too well how fast time was slipping away from them. There are also indications that Charles XII of Sweden was in close touch with the Duke of Savoy, possibly persuading him to *festina lente*, for too overwhelming an Allied success in the south might lead to the total collapse of French resistance—a development that would not be to Sweden's advantage if it released Saxon troops for service in northern and eastern Europe. What is certain is that Charles postponed his definitive decision to march against Russia, and delayed the signature of the Convention of Altranstadt with Austria, until he knew that the Toulon project was doomed beyond repair.

No charges of lethargy can be levelled against Versailles at this juncture. Reinforcements were soon marching towards Toulon from every point of the compass. As early as 18 June, a force of four battalions was ordered to leave Vendôme's army and set off for Dauphiné. Similar detachments were soon on their way from the Rhine, and on 1 August, Louis XIV ordered a further 13 battalions and six squadrons to leave Flanders. 'This considerable diminution of forces will no doubt produce a bad effect in the countryside', wrote the King to Vendôme, 'and may reanimate the courage of the Duke of Marlborough, but it is not possible to avoid this without running great risks in Provence.'[21] On 18 August, Marshal Berwick and the greater part of his army were recalled from Spain. Exactly as Marlborough had foreseen, the Toulon attack was disrupting the entire French war effort; unfortunately, the means to exploit this development no longer existed in Spain, in Flanders or on the Rhine. Everything depended therefore on what Eugene could achieve before Toulon (where Tessé now had all of 20,000 men).

Marlborough's anxiety for Eugene's fortunes caused a return of his migraine. 'I have been uneasy in my head . . .' he wrote on 4 August, 'but if the siege of Toulon goes properly, I shall be cured of all diseases except old age.'[22] He was ever demanding permission to attack Vendôme, now that his opponent was being substantially weakened by drafts for Tessé, but the Dutch veto remained in force. 'Our friends will not venture,' the Duke confided to Harley, 'unless we have an advantage, which our enemies will be careful not to give.'[23] His critic, the Dutch Colonel Goslinga, who on the one hand accused Marlbrough of avoiding action to fill his pocket, on the other somewhat inconsistently records that 'we received in this camp (Meldert) positive order from our masters to risk nothing. The reasons for these fine orders were the uncertain outcome of the Toulon expedition and the superior strength of the enemy.'[24]

Marlborough was nevertheless determined to shift the French from the fertile plain of Gembloux. After ostentatiously feinting towards the main enemy position, the Allies broke camp at dusk on 10 August and headed for Genappes to turn the French left flank. The foe realised what was afoot, and at once retired 'with all imaginable precipitation' (Lediard) in seven columns towards Seneffe, Marlborough close on their heels. Torrential rainfall forced the Duke to pause for part of the 12th, and the wary Vendôme, like Marlborough barred from accepting battle, always kept slightly ahead. There was a chance on the 12th that a bold dash might catch the French rearguard of General Albergotti, and to this end Marlborough ordered Count Tilly to take 40 squadrons and 5,000 grenadiers and surprise the enemy. Unfortunately, Tilly proved incapable —thanks to the darkness, the rain and lack of maps—of executing the letter of his instructions, and by dawn on the 13th the enemy had again taken to the road and was not to be caught. The Duke has earned some criticism from both Goslinga and Colonel Cranstoun for selecting the aged Tilly for the task, and for not properly briefing him in person on his mission, relying instead on written instructions. Still the rain poured down, and both armies were soon exhausted, the French near Ath, the Allies at Soignies. The brief spurt of activity died away amidst the inclement weather late on the 14th, very close to where the first operations of the year had opened. Vendôme proceeded to occupy a camp near Tongres.

So matters rested, with nothing but demonstrations on both sides, until the 25 August when the French camp learnt of Eugene's retreat from before Toulon. These tidings soon spread over no-man's land. 'We have learned from France' wrote the Duke on 7 September to a Palatine General, 'that the Duke of Savoy has quitted the siege of Toulon and retreated, which as you may well believe has caused much chagrin after the hopes we had founded on the capture of this place.'[25] Confirmation arrived some time later in despatches from Brigadier-General Palmes, Marlborough's personal emissary on Eugene's staff. The crowning disaster of a bad year had indeed taken place.

In Marlborough's opinion, Prince Eugene had reached Toulon's outer defences a full five days later than might reasonably have been expected. Marshal Tessé had made good use of this respite to throw up new defences, on the hills overlooking the town, but they were still relatively incomplete. The English admirals besought the Prince to assault them without delay, but Eugene was not prepared to heed their advice, insisting upon the opening of formal trenches, and similarly rebuffed their offer to supply and if need be, evacuate, his army when it became clear that his greatest anxiety was for his tenuous line of communication with Nice. For over a month the Allies remained outside Toulon, with sickness rampant in their ranks. 'Although the Admirals do not comprehend land warfare,' wrote Eugene to Vienna on 14 August, 'they adhere obstinately to their original point of view without even heeding any contradictory arguments. They insist on staking everything on the siege of Toulon, although the impossibility of success is as clear as daylight to them . . . I must repeat once again that this siege of Toulon is wholly impracticable.'[26] Despite this manifest pessimism, some progress had been made. Mont Ste. Catherine had been taken in early July, and trench lines opened to the east of the city, but it had never become a regular siege as French access from north and west was never interrupted. The operation was therefore more of a partial blockade and, of course, the defending forces were growing stronger almost daily. Nevertheless, a French admiral had ordered the naval vessels within *la grande rade* to be half-sunk when the Allies first appeared before Toulon, ostensibly to protect them from the attentions of Allied gunfire, and particularly from that of bomb-ketches. This measure was not as extreme as has sometimes been suggested, and did not imply that Toulon was on the point of falling, for the French intention was to refloat their men-of-war from the shallow waters after all fire-peril had passed. Unfortunately, the task had been bungled and they left the vessels on the bottom too long, and a number were totally lost.

The evening of 21 August, after firing off as much ammunition as possible, Eugene's army struck its tents and retired to the east in five columns, the fleet taking off the guns, the sick and the wounded. They were not pursued. Ten days later the army recrossed the Var. The subsequent capture of Susa did nothing to conceal the total collapse of the Toulon venture, and with it of Marlborough's lingering hopes of dealing a war-winning blow in 1707.

Not unnaturally, new life and confidence again surged through the French armies. Marlborough somewhat half-heartedly made threatening moves up the left bank of the Scheldt towards Helchin (where a major camp was established in early September) as if considering an attack on Tournai, but Vendôme was not to be drawn, spending his time in strengthening the Lines of Commines. French partisans raided Ghent and set fire to a number of magazines. By mid-September both armies were splitting up to enter winter quarters. 'So ended the campaign,' runs the French official history, 'during which, without a major action and without the spilling of blood, M. le Duc de Vendôme succeeded in disconcerting the vast projects of the enemy, and also in fulfilling all the objects that the King prescribed for him. . . .'[27]

For the Allies, 1707 had been a grim year. On the major war fronts, everything had gone wrong. In Flanders a state of stalemate continued. In Germany, Villars' raiders had reached the Danube, and his army exacted costly contributions (totalling 2,545,000 gold livres) from an area extending over 50 leagues beyond the Rhine before falling back into French territory at Versailles' insistence, covering 150 miles to Phillipsburg in only six days. In the south, both Toulon and Provence had survived the invasion; the soil of France was once more clear of the enemy. In Spain, the provinces of Valencia and Aragon had been largely returned to their Bourbon allegiance, and the military power of the Allies severely shaken, if not broken. A final disaster was the death of the gifted Shovell, wrecked off the Scilly Isles on his way home in October. To set against this tale of Allied disappointment could only be set the dissuasion of the Swedes from intervening in the struggle with France (finally confirmed on 1 September), the Habsburg conquest of Naples, the consolation prize of Susa, and the turning point in the long-seated Hungarian revolt, where Racoczi had at last over-played his hand and lost much of his popular support (although the struggle would smoulder on until 1711).

In the words of a recent biographer of Prince Eugene: 'In 1707, Fortune had once more favoured the centre against the circumference.'[28] Allied disunity in aim and lack of co-ordination in action had led to the reaping of a bitter harvest. The crowning failure before Toulon had been due to the unwillingness of Vienna and the untypical irresolution of Prince Eugene; perhaps, as N. P. Henderson has suggested, his greatest failing was not to hold out against the idea of the Toulon enterprise which he never really favoured; but loyalty to the cause, and to his comrade and friend Marlborough, caused him to give way against his own instincts.

Small wonder that the Whigs were baying for Godolphin's blood in Parliament, or that the Tories were fast crystallising into a near-formal opposition in their criticism of the conduct of the war. When a weary and despondent Marlborough returned to his native shores in mid-November, after lengthy consultations at the Hague and a rapid visit to Frankfurt to secure further men for the next campaign, he found waiting a whole series of interrelated problems: scheming colleagues, a hard-pressed Godolphin, a wife fast losing the royal favour, a brother standing charged with maladministration, and a restive parliament which would have to supply more men and money than ever before if the year's setbacks were to be repaired. In late 1707 it indeed seemed as if fortune might have turned away its face, and that Marlborough could soon be buried in the ruins of the war. Small wonder he was described by Colonel Cranstoun as being 'much out of humour and peevish;'[29] he had all too much reason.

The Full Panoply of War, 1708

'To cover Ghent and Bruges that they had gained by surprise, or had been yielded to them by treachery, the French marched to the banks of the Scheldt. At their head were the Princes of the Blood, and their most fortunate General, the Duke of Vendôme. Thus commanded, thus posted, they hoped to check the victor in his course. Vain were their hopes. The Duke of Marlborough passed the river on their right, he defeated their whole army. The approaching night concealed, the proximity of Ghent favoured their flight. They neglected nothing to repair their loss, to defend their frontier; new Generals, new armies, appeared in the Netherlands; all contributed to enhance the glory. None were able to retard the progress of the Confederate armies. . . .'

From the inscription on the Column of Victory,
Blenheim Palace (continued).

The parliamentary winter session of 1707–8 proved a dramatic, wearing and intrigue-dominated period which gravely affected Marlborough's future. Only the briefest summary of the complex political events can be included here, but they cannot be passed over without some mention.

The Duke's future was bound up, as always, with the fortunes of Sidney Godolphin. Since the Autumn, the Lord Treasurer, politically largely isolated as we have seen, had been involved in a storm with the Whigs over the Queen's appointment of two High Tory bishops to vacant sees. The Whig junto unjustly accused both Godolphin and Marlborough of being privy to these preferments, when in fact the Queen had not consulted them at all. The Whig threat to withdraw their support from the Ministry could not be ignored, and by the New Year a compromise had been reached whereby two divines acceptable to the disgruntled Whigs were also offered prestigious ecclesiastical vacancies. The lesson to be drawn from this episode was that the Queen was now seeking advice outside the original charmed circle.

The Toulon fiasco also had its parliamentary repercussions. The Lords had long shown a keen and censorious interest in the Admiralty Board (and in 1705 had conducted a full-scale investigation into its affairs), but now the charge was made that the naval requirements of the Toulon expedition had resulted in further serious losses to the merchant shipping of the realm at the hands of the French privateers operating out of Dunkirk and St. Malo. Since 1702, at least 1,150 vessels of the trades operating out of London alone had fallen prey to this perennial menace, and now the strong mercantile interests in Parliament were demanding the head of Admiral George Churchill, who stood charged with maladministration and corruption. The critics could point to the loss of 11 vessels from the autumn convoy destined for Lisbon as evidence of Admiralty incompetence, whilst the sad loss of the popular Sir Cloudisley Shovell and three ships of war in the Scillies could also be represented as being largely due to Admiralty bungling of movement orders. In fact the charges miscarried, and Marlborough was not compelled, as some had hoped, to intercede with the Whigs on his brother's behalf. In the first place, Admiral Churchill was staunchly supported by Prince George of Denmark, the semi-retired Lord High Admiral, and the Queen would not countenance any criticism that might, at one remove, be laid at the door of her rather ineffectual, and now ailing, spouse. Then again, the Admiralty, through its brilliant spokesman Robert Walpole, was able to demonstrate in debate that the overall naval record had been more than reasonable. Since 1702, over 70 French warships (without counting their losses at Toulon), 175 privateers and 1,346 sail of enemy merchant-shipping had been taken or destroyed for a loss of only 35 warships, whilst over 300 merchant ships had been recovered from the enemy. Considering the extent of the Royal Navy's commitments, and the repeated failure of the Dutch to supply their treaty quotas of naval shipping, this did not amount to a bad showing. So the furore died away as the session proceeded, the critics being appeased by undertakings to increase the scale of naval protection for the trade fleets.

So far so good, but the Ministry's critics had also turned to attack the overall conduct of the war. Inspired by Peterborough's incessant complaints, and supported by the advocacy of the brilliant General Stanhope, soon to be appointed to replace Galway, a demand was put forward for the transfer of 20,000 troops, and possibly even Marlborough himself, from Flanders to Spain. This political intrusion into matters of strategy—and factions of both parties were involved—amounted to poaching upon what Marlborough considered as his just preserves. When the proposal was debated in the Lords on 30 December (N.S.) in the presence of the Queen, Marlborough spoke with great heat and even ill-temper in opposition. Such a transfer would prepare the way for a run of disasters in the Low Countries, he asserted with remarkable prescience, and. with customary adroitness he spiked the critics' guns by declaring that Prince Eugene at the head of 11,000 Imperial troops might soon be sent to the Spanish theatre. He already knew that this was very unlikely to transpire, and Vienna's rejection of the proposal came as no great surprise to him in January, but, as he confided to the Imperial Ambassador's secretary, he 'did not intend to send troops (from Flanders) into Catalonia for the new campaign.'[1] The Lords were induced to adopt a more compliant attitude by this half-revelation, and joined the Commons in passing a resolution that there should be no peace whilst the House of Bourbon retained power over Spain or the Spanish Indies.

Thus another storm had been weathered, but the Ministry's barque was still far from reaching calm water—indeed the worst of the weather was still to come. Godolphin's rivals, in particular Harley, were determined to occasion his fall. The full crisis burst in January 1708. Robert Harley, the Queen's moderate-Tory favourite, had recently encountered difficulties when one of his confidential clerks, William Gregg, was charged with passing secret documents to France and convicted of high treason. The Whigs tried to ruin Harley, but in vain as Gregg staunchly refused to implicate his master. However, the Secretary-of-State felt that he had received scant support from Godolphin, (who may have invited him to broaden the Ministry's support by cultivating sections of the Tories, before denouncing these activities) and decided that the time had come for the show-down. The occasion was the Ministry's Conscription Bill. A military career had never been popular with the British population at large, least of all following years of defeat, but 20,000 recruits had now to be found for Flanders and Spain. In 1707, the bounty-rate had needed to be doubled from 40/- to 80/- per recruit, and this inflationary figure had again to be offered in 1708.[2] But any prospects of compulsory service (although long accepted for the Navy) caused much opposition, and by adroit but concealed management Harley procured a defeat of the proposal by 185 votes to 177 on 27 January. Worse was to follow. Harley's confederate, Henry St. John,* prompted by a carefully timed question in the House, suddenly revealed that only slightly over one quarter of the troops Parliament had voted for service in Spain had been physically present at the battle of Almanza. This sensational revelation resulted in a second telling defeat for the Ministry, without even the formality of a division.

The Queen now indicated that she expected Godolphin to resign forthwith. On 20 February she received the Lord Treasurer's resignation, and also that of the Captain-General (despite a royal plea that he should reconsider). With the

---

* Henry St. John, later Viscount Bolingbroke, was 'a brilliant, fugitive rascal, prone to bully or grovel' (W. S. Churchill). A fine orator and scholar, he successively wooed the extreme Tories, then Robert Harley, and ultimately Marlborough. He made an excellent Secretary-at-War from 1703, but his unscrupulous ambition (and Jacobite sympathies) earned him the nickname of 'the Sneaker', and he was instrumental in plotting against Marlborough and Godolphin in 1708, and did much to secure his fall in 1711. Much of the negotiation of the Peace of Utrecht fell to his lot, but his nerve broke during his brief days of power after Harley's fall. He was a notorious rake of dubious financial integrity.

Queen firmly behind him, Harley now believed he had won, and prepared to form a ministry of the centre, but his erstwhile colleagues knew what they were about, although the stakes were indeed high. At the first cabinet meeting after the resignations, the Duke of Somerset in a dramatic scene declared that 'he could not imagine what business could be done as neither the General nor the Treasurer were there.'[3] In other words the moderate Whigs would not accept Harley's leadership.

Within two days Harley's bubble had burst. Despite the Queen's entreaties, he insisted on surrendering the seals of office, and was followed into the political wilderness by St. John and several more. The Queen had no recourse but to reappoint Godolphin and Marlborough, and to make Henry Boyle, a moderate Whig, Secretary in Harley's place, whilst Walpole succeeded St. John as Secretary-at-War. The Whig triumph was now complete. For the first time since 1704, the so-called 'Godolphin Ministry' had adopted a single-party hue, and one that was contrary to the Queen's wishes to boot. An important constitutional principle was emerging—that a ministry depended more on the political configuration of Parliament than on the personal wishes of the sovereign.

Thus the kaleidoscope of British politics (for such we must now term them since the Act of Union) had settled into a new pattern. The change was fraught with the utmost significance for both Marlborough and Godolphin. Contrary to their wishes, they had been forced into the arms of the Whigs. Marlborough had always refused to become a 'party-man' one way or the other, but now, in the words of Dr. Rowse, he would 'become the military executant of Whig policy,'[4] —which was committed to winning the war, cost what it might. His overall control over the top-level political direction of the struggle was about to lapse, and with it his ability to procure a reasonable peace. Equally significant, the Queen was now the enemy of her own ministry. The 'special relationship' was once and for all a thing of the past, and obviously there was absolutely no chance of Duchess Sarah regaining lost ground in the Queen's affections, now that her Whig friends had triumphed so positively. Thirdly, Harley and St. John could not but harbour a lasting grudge against the men who had bettered them in 1708. Moreover, the opposition to the war policy had now become solidly Tory, so that the effort was no longer truly national. Their revenge would come within three short years. Thus Marlborough and Godolphin might feel relieved that they had survived a perilous period and gained the necessary votes of supply for the continuation of the war, but the reality of their respective positions had altered beyond all recognition—and altered for the worse.

We must now return to the consideration of the war as a whole. Marlborough the politician might have weathered a severe domestic crisis; Marlborough the statesman now had to induce the Grand Alliance, benumbed or scandalised by the setbacks of 1707, to adopt an effective strategy for the continuance of the war towards a favourable conclusion.

The French court had once again put forward tentative peace feelers during the winter months, but in January the mission of M. Ménager to the Hague had come to an abrupt conclusion when the United Provinces indicated that minimum terms would include the removal of Philip V from the Spanish throne and the cession of Ypres, Menin, Condé and Maubeuge to form part of the Barrier. These stipulations outraged Louis XIV, who regarded them as wholly unrealistic following the French recovery of 1707.

The undoubted Allied setbacks of that year had led to a long exchange of views between Marlborough and Heinsius during meetings at the Hague in October and November 1707, and thereafter in correspondence. First the possibility of remounting the double-invasion of France through Flanders and Dauphiné was mooted, but it was soon evident that there was little to be hoped for from the Italian front, for the King of Prussia and Landgrave of Hesse were now insisting on the recall of their forces, and it would soon be necessary to transfer the Palatine formations to Spain. There were no signs that Vienna was prepared to be more co-operative in the region than formerly, and the Duke of Savoy could undertake nothing on his own. Next the idea of sending Prince Eugene to Spain at the head of the Palatine troops and a sizeable Imperial contingent was considered but, as already recounted, this neither suited the Emperor nor Eugene himself, although it was agreed that the Palatine troops should be transferred there. Heinsius was of the opinion that Spain should be the scene of a further major Allied effort, but Marlborough was in favour of staking everything in Flanders. 'My fears for Spain are as great as yours . . .' the Duke wrote to the Grand Pensionary, 'but if you could order it so that we might have success in Flanders, I should hope to gain Spain by (way of) France.'[5] Heinsius agreed, but was unwilling to increase the size of the Dutch forces—an issue that caused no little recrimination. So the debate dragged on inconclusively, and all parties were relieved when the Emperor suggested that a formal conference of the major powers should meet in April at the Hague, which Prince Eugene would attend in person as Austria's chief delegate.

Versailles, meantime, unencumbered by any requirement to consult its adherents, had already determined its broad plans for 1708. Stung by the high-handed attitude of the Dutch in the recent negotiations, Louis was determined to mount another major effort to follow up the successes of the previous year—despite the exhaustion of the French economy, and a recent rash of mutinies in pay-starved French formations. Somehow or other five armies were again to take the field, special priority being accorded to those serving in Flanders (as Marlborough had surmised would be the case) and on the Rhine. There was also to be considerable cross-posting of senior commanders, save for Vendôme and the Duc d'Orléans who retained their present appointments. Thus the Elector of Bavaria and the Duke of Berwick were appointed to the Rhine army, and Marshal Villars, protesting volubly, was transferred to Dauphiné, whilst the King's grandson, the Duke of Burgundy, was sent to share the command with Vendôme in Flanders, accompanied by the Chevalier de St. George (Pretender to the British throne) the Duc de Berry and the future Marshal Matignon.

The Flanders armament was to be built up to 131 battalions and 216 squadrons as early as possible that year, and there was a scheme afoot for a sudden descent upon Antwerp with the aid of disaffected citizens (although it proved abortive as the Allies got wind of the plot in good time). The army of the Rhine was to be 79 battalions and 138 squadrons strong, charged with consolidating what was left of Villars' gains and preventing any large-scale Allied transfers of troops from the region to Flanders, should this be attempted. The Army of Dauphiné was given a wholly defensive role. As for Spain, the Duc d'Orléans, joined by Marshal Bezons, and assisted by de Noailles's Army of Catalonia, was to press on with the liberation of the eastern sea-board.

The French court was also preparing a special venture—a sudden descent upon Scotland in March. Jacobite agents and sympathisers were reporting a wave of popular Scottish disillusion with the first effects of the Act of Union— particularly in the Highlands—and the opportunity to create a running sore in the British Isles was clearly not to be ignored. At best, a civil war might be the result. At the very least, it could be hoped the venture would distract British forces from Flanders. Under conditions of supposedly great secrecy, therefore, an expedition was prepared at Dunkirk. The 20-year-old Pretender was to accompany a force of 12 battalions (some 6,000 men) under the command of the Comte de Gacé (soon to be created Marshal Matignon), Louis XIV having rejected the application of Berwick for this appointment. The successful French sailor, the Comte de Forbin, was to convoy the 15 transports and escort the force with five men-of-war and perhaps 15 privateers. The holds would contain 13,000 stand of arms, ready for arming Scottish dissidents who would hopefully flock to join the standard of James III.

The implementation of this plan was dogged by difficulties and delays which inevitably resulted in leaks of information. First the weather was unfavourable; next the Chevalier developed 'an ague' (in fact measles); and by mid-February Marlborough was aware of the broad enemy intention. On the 17th the Duke warned Cadogan, wintering at Bruges, to keep a close watch on what was developing at Dunkirk. Soon a spate of information, reliable and not so reliable, was flooding across the Channel. An all-too-rare glimpse is available of Marlborough's intelligence agencies at work, for the British Museum contains the relevant section of the Dutch State Papers.[6] From early March, Cadogan was receiving information from 'correspondents' at Mons and Lille. Every rumour, delay and movement was reported to the Court of St. James, and the government was thus enabled to take counter-measures. Admiral Byng sailed from Deal with 15 British and three Dutch men-of-war to blockade Dunkirk, supported in due course by a second squadron of 20 warships. Parliament, informed of the peril on 15 March, forgot its bitter divisions and rallied to the throne, passing stringent anti-Jacobite legislation. For a while public confidence waned. A run on the Bank of England was only checked when Godolphin transferred all remaining bullion to the Tower, suspending repayments, but soon after the near-hysteria subsided.

The militias were alerted, but it was clear that regular battalions would have to be recalled from Flanders. The 'ten eldest regiments of foot' were ordered to Ostend under Cadogan and Brigadier Sabine. There they boarded ship on 15 March, and sailed at 10 a.m. on the 17th ('it blowing a fresh gale') under convoy of ten warships. Four storm-tossed days later the ships were off Teignmouth, 'where we lay for further orders, labouring under many inconveniences, having only ye bare deck to lye upon, which hardship caused abundance of our men to bid adieu to ye world,'[7] as Private John Deane of the Foot Guards recorded.

The French at last left Dunkirk on the 17th, when the gale scattered the blockading squadron. After being driven into Nieuport, by a shift in the gale, the expedition again sailed during the night on the 19th, as Mr. King, Aide-de-Camp to Cadogan hastened to report from Brussels.[8] Two days later the French had reached the Firth of Forth, but no landing was attempted as contacts with the shore were discouraging, and Byng's fleet was too close behind. Therefore Forbin sailed on towards Inverness, but it was now accepted that the expedition had scant chance of making a successful landing. In due course, for the loss of one ship, the French regained Dunkirk, their less barnacle-encrusted hulls enabling them to outsail the Allied vessels.* And so, in Lediard's words, '. . . this vast project vanished into Air'. The ten British battalions 'sailed back to Ostend, where we disembarked the 14th of April,'[9] as Captain Parker, another participant, recorded. These alarms being safely past, the nation settled back into near-normalcy, and Marlborough, sickened by home politics and new disagreements with the Queen, could gratefully and safely take ship for the Hague (12 April), where the Allied conference was now imminent.

The discussions proceeded much as Marlborough had hoped. His plan was to divide the available forces in the Netherlands and Germany into three armies; the largest would be under his own control in Flanders—100 battalions and 150 squadrons—seconded by the aged Overkirk, 'who, not withstanding the infirm state of health he laboured under, preserved a vigorous mind, and seemed resolved to dy (sic), like a hero, in the field . . .';[10] a second army, under Prince Eugene, made up of 21,000 Palatine, Würzburg and Baden-Baden troops in the British and Dutch pay, an Imperial contingent and a detachment from Flanders—perhaps 45 battalions and 60 squadrons in all—was to collect on the Moselle; the third, some 37 battalions and 47 squadrons strong (approximately 43,000 men in all) would operate on the Upper Rhine under a new commander, George,

---

* A useful account of this abortive expedition by C. Sinclair-Stevenson was published in *History Today*, April 1971.

Elector of Hanover, (after his mother, heir-presumptive to the British throne).

The Duke hoped to use the relative weakness of his Flanders' army (weak by comparison to the enemy's forces already listed) to lure Vendôme into decisive action. Marlborough conceived of abandoning Brussels if necessary, and of basing his operations upon Antwerp; then, by a rapid strategic transfer, he intended to bring Eugene's army north from the Moselle to join his own, and thus obtain a commanding superiority for the battle his heart was set upon achieving. 'When I left England,' the Duke would write some little time later, 'I was positively resolved to endeavour by all means, a battle, thinking nothing else would make the Queen's business go well. . . .'[11] In his opinion, only a major success in the field would rally the Grand Alliance from its present, somewhat apathetic, attitude.

The switch of Eugene would reduce the Allied strength on the Middle and Upper Rhine regions to the minimum compatible with a cautious defence, and there lay the rub, for the Elector of Hanover was highly suspicious of the proposal to create three armies—being fully aware of the possible implications for his own area of responsibility even though he was not informed of the planned transfer—and it needed the most careful handling by Marlborough in person to secure his grudging acquiescence. It required the promise of 2,000 further horse for the Rhine army (to be provided from Eugene's forces) to gain the Elector's co-operation; '. . . and as for joining the two armies, we thought it best not to acquaint the Elector with it, so that I expect when that is put in execution, he will be very angry . . .',[12] as Marlborough admitted to Godolphin on 3 May. But as had been the case in early August 1704 with the Margrave of Baden, the Captain-General was prepared to hoodwink certain of his colleagues when the cause required it. Considerations of security meant that the full plan was only communicated to Eugene, Heinsius and Godolphin. As it was clearly vital that no obstruction should be encountered, Heinsius promised that the Field Deputies for the year would be given the strictest instructions not to interfere with Marlborough's orders once the campaign had opened.

The Duke was also eager to mount a 'descent' in support of the major operations: he was aware of the value of a force with an amphibious capacity against an enemy with a lengthy coastline—it could cause great dislocation to the foe's balance of forces. Had not the recent French raid demonstrated the point? Accordingly, Lieutenant-General Thomas Erle and 11 British battalions were placed aboard transports off the Isle of Wight, there to await further orders.

For the rest, Generals Stahremberg* and Stanhope were ordered to adopt a strict defensive attitude in Spain, and the Duke of Savoy was given a similar

---

* Stahremberg had been commanding against the Hungarian rebels, but as a sop to Vienna he was now offered the senior command in Spain. London also agreed to pay for the Imperial troops being transferred there, and approved the sending of the 7,000 strong Palatine contingent.

role (with 56 battalions and some 10,000 cavalry) amidst the Ligurian Alps. The crisis of the year would take place in Flanders; much would therefore depend upon getting the armies ready to take the field in good time. As usual, this proved far easier to order than to implement—particularly as regards the army on the Moselle. Furthermore, the need for Marlborough to visit Hanover in early May whilst Eugene undertook a recruiting mission to Mainz increased these delays, and it was only on 21 May that the main army, perhaps 90,000 strong, was assembling at Anderlecht near Brussels, and it was well into June before the Moselle army was ready at Coblenz, some 150 miles away.

The French army of Vendôme and Burgundy was thus in a position to take the initiative. Their basic aim, as in 1707, was to draw the Allies away from French Flanders, but Vendôme had at last secured permission to risk a major battle if this could be procured under favourable conditions. To his way of thinking, this double-purpose could best be achieved by besieging Huy on the Meuse—where the open plains would favour the superior French cavalry in any general engagement. But Burgundy, 26-years-old and decidedly over-confident in the military ability conferred by his royal blood, was in favour of an initial advance towards Brussels to exploit the growing ill-feeling against the Dutch amongst the Flemish population. From their first conference at Val-enciennes on 16 May, therefore, the French commanders-in-chief found them-selves at odds—a story that was to be repeated in the weeks and months ahead. It would not be going too far to describe their relationship as one of mutual antipathy from the outset. The able Vendôme (aged 54) prided himself as a 'soldier's general', and his 'simple' habits were bound to offend the timid, courtly and religious Prince of the Blood, not half his age. Mérode-Westerloo had served under Vendôme in North Italy (1703) where he noted that 'this prince was insolently wont to receive all the *monde* seated on his *chaise-percée* all bespattered with tobacco, and wearing a shirt he would only change once a week.'[13] It is surprising that Louis XIV had chosen so ill-assorted a pair for the key command in 1708.

In the event, Burgundy had his way, and after massing about Mons the French army advanced over the River Haine on 26 May and marched towards Hal, camping at Soignies. The Allies thereupon moved south of Hal, which induced the French to move eastwards over the River Senne to Braine l'Alleud (reached on 2 June) there to mount a threat towards Louvain. Marlborough again moved to block them, switching his army through Brussels late on 2 June to occupy a camp at Terbanck, immediately south of Louvain, which they reached next day—this being a repeat performance of the exact manœuvre employed the previous year. Marlborough was aware that Eugene was still not capable of taking the field, and until the envisaged junction between their armies had taken place he could not afford to surrender control over the Brussels area despite the massed stores already placed at Antwerp in readiness for the onslaught up the

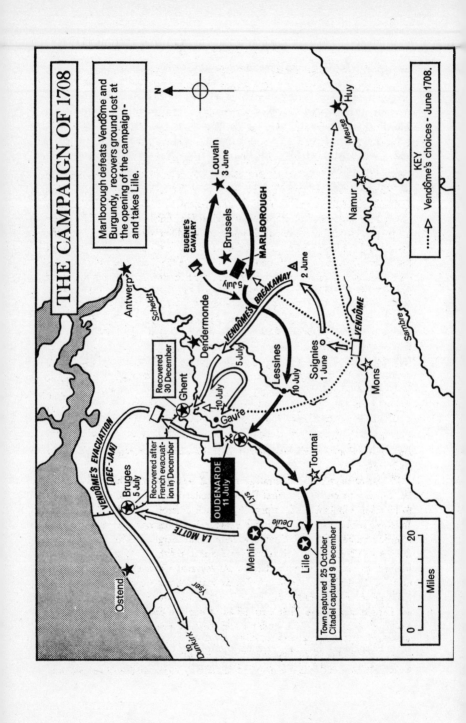

THE CAMPAIGN OF 1708

Marlborough defeats Vendôme and Burgundy, recovers ground lost at the opening of the campaign - and takes Lille.

N

KEY

⇢ Vendôme's choices - June 1708.
⇢ Vendôme's choices - June 1708.

Huy

Meuse

Louvain
3 June

Namur

Brussels

MARLBOROUGH

EUGENE'S
CAVALRY

5 July

VENDÔME'S BREAKAWAY

2 June

VENDÔME

Sambre

Antwerp

Scheldt

Dendermonde

5 July

Mons

Soignies
1 June

Lessines

10 July

5 July

Recovered
30 December

Ghent

10 July

Gavre

Tournai

VENDÔME'S EVACUATION

[DEC-JAN]

Recovered after French evacuation in December

OUDENARDE
11 July

Lys

Deule

LA MOTTE

Bruges
5 July

Menin

Lille

Town captured 25 October
Citadel captured 9 December

Ostend

Yser

Dunkirk

0   20

Miles

Scheldt towards French Flanders. Indeed, it is now clear that Marlborough was prepared to evacuate Brussels and concentrate all Allied resources on the Scheldt section.

A month-long pause now settled over operations in Flanders. The French high command was still at odds concerning the best course to pursue. Versailles was cautious, following news that Prince Eugene had recently arrived at Coblenz and was trying to form his army there. Vendôme was still adamant that the siege of Huy was the best means of solving the present impasse, and on 5 June the King signified his agreement, but Burgundy challenged the order and it was again placed in abeyance. On 11 June, after reconsidering the matter, Versailles ordered the suspension of preparations against Huy until such time as Eugene's purposes were definitely revealed, much to Vendôme's annoyance. Thus the month of June slipped past in hesitation and inactivity in Flanders, although there were signs of movement on the Rhine. There the Elector of Bavaria on his own initiative (or rather at Berwick's entreaty) had already sent a strong corps under M. de St. Frémont to Saarbrücken in late May to observe developments on the Moselle, and on 5 June had placed Marshal Berwick in command of this detachment which eventually numbered 46 battalions and 103 squadrons, with orders to shadow any move by Eugene. However, it was not until 29 June that Eugene was in a position to leave Coblenz at the head of a mere 15,000 men (18 battalions and 43 squadrons); he gained a three day start over Berwick, but by 7 July the Marshal was 'burning the roads' towards Flanders at the head of 34 battalions and 65 squadrons (27,000 men). Marlborough's intelligent kinsman had from the first suspected that Eugene might attempt some such move 'in imitation of the Duke of Marlborough's conduct in 1704 . . .' in order to '. . . make a sudden incursion into Flanders with a suitable force to crush the King's army and invade France upon that side.'[14] Berwick was determined to impede any such move.

If Marlborough's overall strategy for 1708 was thus something of an open book to at least one of the ablest French commanders, the Duke was also about to be taken completely by surprise by French enterprises in the Netherlands. June had seen constant negotiations between Versailles and the camp at Gembloux over a bold suggestion put forward by Count Bergeyck, Minister of War of the Spanish Netherlands. His clandestine contacts with the citizens of the great Flemish towns of Bruges and Ghent had revealed a marked degree of resentment to Anglo-Dutch rule—and also to depredations allegedly committed by Cadogan in the interests of the army. He therefore proposed a sudden advance by French columns to these two places, where the disaffected portion of the populace would cooperate in returning them to French control. Louis XIV approved the venture, and M. de Chémerault was appointed to lead a column of 2,000 horse and as many foot from the main army against Ghent, whilst Count de La Motte would lead a force of 10 battalions, seven squadrons and six guns from the Lines of Commines towards Bruges. The main army, led by Grimaldi's advance guard, would cover and support these flying columns by moving westwards over the Senne and then the Dender, disguising its initial movements under the pretence of conducting a large-scale foraging. The operation was to begin early on 4 July, and reach its climax on the 5th.

For once Marlborough seems to have ignored the omens. He was fully aware of the local feeling, and had recently posted Major-General Murray with two battalions and four squadrons at the gates of Ghent in an attempt to over-awe the dissident elements. He was also warned, by Mérode-Westerloo (if we are to believe his account), who had learnt of the plot from a sure source in Lille, 'but he treated my news as something of no account, telling me that it was impossible.'[15] It is hard to believe that the Duke was deliberately allowing the French their head in the hope of forcing them into a decisive battle thereafter—for the risks were altogether too daunting, especially as he had largely implemented the abandonment of his base at Brussels. We must conclude, therefore, that for once Marlborough was completely fooled, and chose to discount such rumours as reached his ears.

On 4 July, Grimaldi's advance guard left the French camp and moved on Ninove, as if to forage. That evening the main army followed, and away on the coastal sector La Motte set out on his forced march. As the French continued westwards through the 5th, the Allies broke camp and marched to Anderlecht after crossing the Senne near Brussels. Before the day was out the French had occupied Alost, and their main body was crossing the Dender at Ninove, covered by Albergotti's rearguard. By that time, the flying columns had almost fulfilled their tasks. At 3 a.m. on the 5th, by employing the ruse of pretending to be a party of deserters, 60 men of La Motte's force secured a gate at Bruges and took uncontested possession of the city. By the afternoon of the same day, M. de Chémerault had infiltrated Ghent with the aid of the Grand Bailiff, and closed its gates against Murray. The Allied garrison was shut up in the castle (where it surrendered on the afternoon of the 6th). At a stroke, the French had made themselves masters of the middle Scheldt and the canals leading to the coast. By so-doing they had interposed a barrier between Marlborough and Ostend, effectively severing his shortest communications with England, whilst Menin and Courtrai were also isolated. This *coup* returned much of Spanish Flanders into French hands, and constituted a serious blow to Marlborough's prestige and thus to the morale of the Allied army.

With the main French army crossing safely over the Dender, and their pioneers hard at work breaking down the bridges at Alost and Ninove, it was not a time for Allied complacency. 'This little contretemps again caused the Duke of Marlborough to begin marching with a vengeance,' recorded Mérode-Westerloo somewhat acidly. By a superb display of forced marching the Allies had almost caught the French army in two separate columns at the mill of Goyck, mid-way between Tubize and Ninove on the afternoon of the 5th, but the rearguard safely passed the river for the loss of only part of their baggage. This they achieved by resort to a ruse. The French army, according to Sergeant Millner, 'falsified and flourished its colours in the scrub in our front, as if all their army had been there a-posting to give our army battle.'[16] Cadogan was away visiting Eugene—which perhaps accounts for the success of this trick, and Marlborough was suffering severely from his migraine and a fever by this time. With no sign of Eugene's army arriving to assist him he was soon plunged into the deepest depression.

Three issues were now of paramount importance. Which side could first achieve a full junction of its forces? Which force would first occupy the Dender crossings at Lessines? Would the French be able to seize Oudenarde, and thus complete their control of the central Scheldt, before the Allies could reinforce it? If the Allies could move through Lessines to Oudenarde, and there cross the Scheldt, they would be in a position to sever Vendôme's communications with his main bases at Lille and Tournai. Timing would now be of the very essence, but the Duke's state of ill-health was no advantage.

However, the Allies were aided by a return of discord to bedevil the deliberations of the French generals. Vendôme wished to move on Oudenarde at once; Burgundy demurred, favouring a siege of Menin, and appealed to Versailles. The King eventually supported his grandson and authorised only a blockade of Oudenarde, for Louis XIV was still anxious about the position of Eugene's army and its ability to intervene. His generals meantime forecast that Marlborough would now move against Namur or Charleroi, so on 9 July they decided to march on Lessines.

These delays and dissensions enabled Marlborough, despite his 'being much indisposed and feverish' (Lediard) to achieve two vital tasks. The first was to send Brigadier Chandos and 700 reinforcements into Oudenarde post-haste on the night of the 7th. The second was to prepare a dash for Lessines to secure the vital crossings there. After baking eight days bread at Assche, the Duke ordered the army's baggage and transport to be reduced to the bare minimum. Generals of foot were permitted to retain three waggons and a coach; other generals two waggons and a coach; Brigadiers one of each, colonels a pair of waggons. The strictest march discipline was to be observed, as the army marched southwards to camp at Herfelingen on the 9th, where Marlborough's spirits rallied with the arrival of Eugene—but not his army, for the Prince had pressed on four days ahead of his cavalry which was still approaching Brussels, closely watched by Berwick's shadowing forces which were nearing Namur.

Later that day, Cadogan led off a picked body towards Lessines, followed by the main army which broke camp at 2 a.m. the next morning. Throughout the 10th both armies were moving on Lessines from opposite sides of the Dender, but Cadogan was in the town well before dawn and Marlborough had won the race with some hours to spare. The French (Burgundy not desiring to force a battle at this stage—to Vendôme's disgust) forthwith swung away northwards towards Gavre, intent on placing the Scheldt between the Allies and themselves, and called off the blockade of Oudenarde as the Allies began to pour over the Dender. Marlborough was now poised to strike, but the French were barely aware of their peril, calculating that the Allies could hardly reach the Scheldt before the 12th at the earliest. However, it would soon be the turn of the French to be surprised.

By nightfall on the 10th, therefore, the French army was camping on the east bank of the Scheldt near Gavre (about six miles north of Oudenarde), whilst Marlborough's camp-fires blazed along the west bank of the Dender, some 15 miles south-east of Oudenarde. The Captain-General, in consultation with Eugene, had now decided to make a rapid advance to that town, with the intention of passing the Scheldt at the earliest possible moment, if possible before the French could complete their own crossing. It was vital to establish pontoon-bridges over the river in advance of the army's arrival, so at 1 a.m. on the 11 July the trusted Cadogan again set out at the head of 16 battalions, 8 squadrons, 32 regimental guns,* the pioneers and the bridging-train. His orders were to improve the road, establish five pontoon bridges to the north of Oudenarde and thereafter establish a protective bridgehead over the Scheldt. By 9 a.m. Cadogan was in sight of the river, and reported back to Marlborough that the French were still six miles away at Gavre to the east of the Scheldt. By midday the first British battalions were over the great river, and shortly thereafter all the bridges were completed and awaiting the approaching army. The French, meantime, had started to cross at Gavre in leisurely fashion at about 10 a.m.

On receipt of Cadogan's message, Marlborough at once set off at the head of 40 squadrons to join his subordinate, eager to complete the transfer of his army before the French awoke to his intention. By 1 p.m. General Natzmer's Prussian cavalry were thundering over the wooden timbers to join Cadogan's advance guard, 11 battalions of which had advanced to the line of the River Diepenbeck with General Rantzau's squadrons on their left. Marlborough rode forward with his staff to conduct a personal reconnaissance near the village of Eyne, sending back urgent messages to his perspiring infantry on the road from Lessines, desiring them 'to step out.' There were now unmistakable signs that the French were crossing at Gavre in force, but as a precaution in case Vendôme and Burgundy reversed their line of march Marlborough posted part of his cavalry near Eename to the east of the Scheldt to protect his northern flank.

Shortly after one o'clock the first contact was made with French forces. General Biron, at the head of the seven battalions and 20 squadrons of horse forming Burgundy's advance guard, was marching towards Heurne, completely

* 2 three-pounder or lighter pieces were habitually attached to each Allied battalion, See above, p. 73.

oblivious of the Allied presence, when his foraging cavalry brushed Rantzau's squadrons. Reacting commendably swiftly, Biron sent forward his 12 remaining squadrons to check Rantzau's pursuit of the discomfited foragers. Climbing the church tower at Eyne, Biron could clearly see the dustclouds announcing the approach of the main Allied army and by 1.30 p.m. messengers were spurring back to Gavre to alert the generals of Marlborough's presence. 'If they are there, the Devil must have carried them,' expostulated Vendôme on hearing the news, 'such marching is impossible.'[17] In the past 60 hours parts of the Allied army had indeed covered all of 50 miles, an astounding distance in the lights of the time. The two armies were now so close that there was little question of either refusing battle; the celebrated struggle of Oudenarde had in fact already begun.

The ground over which the battle was to be fought falls into three main sections, conveniently demarcated by three streams which run broadly parallel in their western courses. In the north, the River Norken (today the Leedsche-beek) flows eastwards towards Gavre and the Scheldt at the southern foot of a number of ridges known as the Heights of Huysse. More high ground lies to the south and west above the town of Oudenard, where the Boser Couter provided what was to prove the key to the battle-area; a fair road, much of it lying in dead ground runs over this hill to the village of Oycke. South of the River Norken and to the east of Oycke, extends an area of low-lying cultivated countryside, containing a number of small woods, ravines, hedges and hamlets, including Roijgem, Mullem, Herlegem, Diepenbeke, Schaerken, Groenewald, Heurne and Eyne, all of which will figure in our narrative. This area, forming the base of a natural amphitheatre, is bisected by the Marollebeek Stream, which runs parallel to the Norken for half its course before swinging south and west towards its confluence with the slightly larger River Diepenbeek, which in turn flows past Schaerken and Eyne and thence into the Scheldt whose banks are marshy. The Diepenbeek effectively forms the southern boundary of the area of broken ground, for beyond it, stretching towards Oudenarde, lies an area of open plain, well-suited for cavalry action. The main road from Oudenarde to Ghent runs through Eyne in a northerly direction, whilst a smaller road branches off through Heurne towards Gavre (today Gavere). As for Oudenarde itself, it was a fair-sized town with modern fortifications lying on both banks of the Scheldt. Within the town were two stone bridges and two other temporary crossing places.

Given the French superiority of cavalry overall, it would be to their advantage to force the Allies out of the broken ground into the plain, as Marlborough was well aware. Neither side desired to fight on the open ground east of the Gavre road for the area within the sweeping curve of the Scheldt would allow scant room for manoeuvre and the river would threaten disaster to the defeated party. The Duke was determined, therefore, that the main engagement should be fought in the vicinity of the Diepenbeek. He had the advantage over Vendôme and Burgundy of having had a chance to view and assess the ground. The Duke was also well aware—from intercepted correspondence and the gossip of deserters—of the poor relations between the two French commanders, and this knowledge in part persuaded him to press for battle, despite the risks involved, without further delay.

The form of action would be a planned encounter battle, in which the Allies lured the French into unpremeditated action by a display of apparent weakness, and then exploited the local conditions by dint of superior generalship and better use of terrain.[18] For both sides it would be a race against time—and victory would go to the general who could first bring up, and commit, his entire force. In this respect Marlborough was labouring under two serious disadvantages: in the first place, most of his troops had a longer distance to cover to reach the field than their opponents, who might therefore be expected to join the battle earlier and less tired; and secondly, the Allies had to debouch over a large river in close proximity to the foe, and would run the peril of being destroyed in detail. On the other hand the Duke knew his men—their willingness to make major efforts on his behalf and their reliability in battle; he also knew enough of the characters of his opponents to gamble on French confusion and delay providing him with the bare minimum of time he required to assemble his army. But, as we shall see, it was to be a very narrow margin indeed.

It is generally estimated that the Allies fielded some 80,000 men—namely 85 battalions and 150 squadrons—to the 85,000 troops of Vendôme and Burgundy (90 battalions and 170 squadrons). Owing to the nature of the engagement, neither side was in a position to draw up the formal lines of battle so beloved of eighteenth-century generals, but would feed formations into the battle as they arrived. Such an ever-changing situation would test the respective commanders' powers of observation, divination and control to the uttermost. Neither army— owing to the particular circumstances of the day—would make much use of artillery, for most of the heavy pieces were left far behind on the roads with the exception of the 32 light regimental cannon which had accompanied Cadogan and a few more batteries on either side.

Vendôme's first order was to Biron, enjoining him to engage Cadogan's 12 battalions (the remaining four were guarding the bridges) with the seven Swiss battalions of the advance guard, promising him reinforcements. The Marshal at first planned to repulse Cadogan from the Eyne-Heurne vicinity as a pre-liminary to forming some sort of battle-line between the Scheldt near Heurne and the Boser Couter near Mooregem, which would have left Marlborough with no room to deploy let alone manœuvre. But the first delays and confusions of the day now hit the French command, and by the time Biron was ready to advance with four battalions and his 12 squadrons, he found himself facing the whole of Cadogan's foot (the bridges now being held by the debouching Allied cavalry) and a considerable number of squadrons. Nor was there any sign of the promised French reinforcements; Lt. General Puységur, * chief of staff, reported to Marshal

* Author in later life of a remarkable treatise on the Art of War.

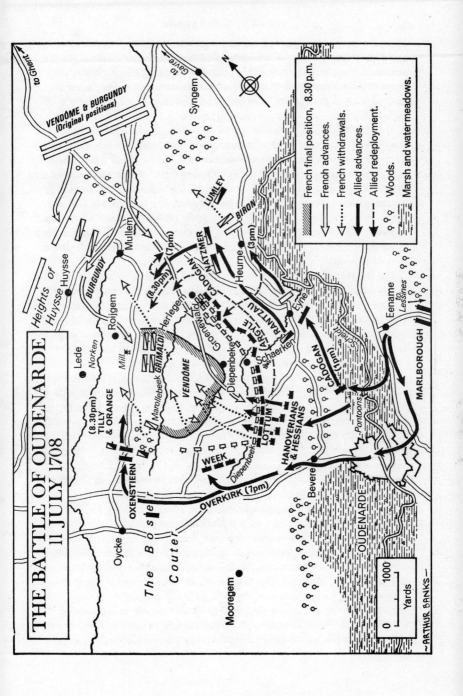

THE BATTLE OF OUDENARDE
11 JULY 1708

VENDÔME & BURGUNDY
(Original positions)

Heights of Huysse Huysse

to Ghent

to Gavre

Syngem

N

French final position, 8.30 p.m.
French advances.
French withdrawals.
Allied advances.
Allied redeployment.
Woods.
Marsh and water meadows.

LUMLEY

BIRON
(3pm)

Heurne

NATZMER

CADOGAN

(8.30pm)

(7pm)

Mullem

BURGUNDY

Rollgem

Lede

Norken

Mill

Herlegem

Groenewald

Diepenbeke

Schaerken

ARGYLE

RANTZAU

Eyne

Scheldt

Eename

to Lessines

MARLBOROUGH

CADOGAN
(1pm)

GRIMALDI

VENDÔME

Marollebeek

(8.30pm)
TILLY
& ORANGE

Orange

LOTTUM

HANOVERIANS & HESSIANS

Pontoons

WEEK

Diepenbeek

OXENSTIERN

Oycke

OVERKIRK (7pm)

Bevere

OUDENARDE

The Bossier Couter

Mooregem

0   1000
Yards

~ARTHUR BANKS~

Matignon that the area around the Diepenbeek was unsuitable for cavalry action, and that officer thereupon countermanded Vendôme's instructions for the advance to Biron's aid. Puységur then informed Vendôme, who decided to adopt a new position below the Heights of Huysse, abandoning his earlier scheme for a bold advance to the Heurne-Mooregem line, and sent a messenger to call-off Biron's attack.

This, however, the aide was too late in delivering. At 3.00 p.m. Cadogan had swept forward in massive strength against the unsupported Biron; three battalions of Swiss near Eyne were soon overwhelmed, and the fourth was butchered by Rantzau's cavalry near Heurne. The surviving three battalions and the horse thereupon retired north of the River Norken, hotly pursued and harried by Rantzau, until he came under fire from a French four-gun battery (the only French guns actually in action on the 11th) newly established near Mullem. The approach of a further 15 enemy squadrons now dictated a withdrawal, and so the triumphant horsemen fell back with ten enemy standards and two kettle-drums in their possession.

The first round had therefore gone decidedly in Marlborough's favour. Cadogan (who had advanced to Heurne) had won time for the arrival of a considerable part of the main army, the cavalry of which was now being routed through Oudenarde to leave the pontoons open for the foot. Burgundy meantime, stung by news of Biron's débâcle, had at 4 p.m. ordered his wing of the army to prepare for battle. The initial skirmish between advance guards was about to develop into an action—the process of escalation was setting in.

Cadogan's success meant that Marlborough could fight amidst the cultivated fields, which would be to the advantage of the superior Allied infantry, and deny the foe the free use of their predominant cavalry. Cadogan now swung his line to face west along the line of the Marollebeek, leaving Rantzau (8 squadrons) and the newly deployed Natzmer with his 20 Prussian squadrons to guard his exposed right flank and rear. The Duke had meantime personally supervised the siting of a battery of six guns near Schaerken, and was by 5 p.m. placing Argyle's newly-arrived 20 battalions (16 of them were German formations) on Cadogan's left to extend the infantry line to the confluence at Schaerken.

While these Allied manœuvres were taking place, Burgundy had ordered General Grimaldi to advance over the Norken at the head of 16 squadrons as the precursor of a general movement by the French right and centre, but that officer reported that the going was too treacherous and fell back, with Burgundy's permission, to Roijgem, where the Prince had established his headquarters near a windmill. Burgundy then ordered six battalions to attack the Prussian troops holding Groenewald—but by 4.30 p.m. this enterprise had also been repulsed. Hearing the sound of firing, Vendôme rode off at the head of 12 battalions to supervise the action, but did not see fit to pause at Roijgem mill to concert any plan of action with Burgundy. Instead he rallied the two brigades repulsed from Groenewald, and led them forward again with his own force in a new series of attacks against the Allies behind the Marollebeek between Herlegem and Groenewald. Cadogan and the Prussians withstood this pressure, and Vendôme ordered up more and more infantry from the French right until 50 battalions were engaged.

Marlborough's anxiety for Cadogan's left flank—should the foe extend their attack to Schaerken—was partly relieved by the arrival of Argyle's troops as already mentioned, but the Duke was well aware that there were still all of 30,000 French of Burgundy's left wing still uncommitted to battle. His own army was still not fully arrived. The stakes were rising alarmingly.

However, French confusions saved the day. It seems that Burgundy misunderstood Vendôme's overall concept for the deployment of the army as a whole, and believed that the Marshal wished to have the army drawn up along the Heights of Huysse, and not in the Norken valley to its front. The Prince gave orders to his left wing accordingly. Then a messenger appeared from the embattled Vendôme who, half-pike in hand, was in the very thick of the fray, asking him to advance over the Norken with the French left wing to defeat Natzmer and Rantzau and then roll up the Allied line. It is hard to see how this manœuvre, properly executed, would not have won the day for the French. In fact, it was never executed at all. Puységur made his second disastrous intervention of the day, and advised Burgundy that the Norken's banks were too swampy to permit the passage of large numbers of cavalry. This was patently untrue, as later events would show, but Burgundy agreed, and countermanded the advance, sending an aide to inform Vendôme of his decision. This officer seems to have been killed for the message never reached Vendôme, who at about 5.30 p.m. launched a major attack on his sector in the belief that Burgundy would be taking complementary action on the left. The struggle for the hedgerows reached a new climax, as the 50 French battalions clawed their way forward, yard by yard, against Marlborough's 36 battalions and six guns. The Allied line began to give ground before the pressure, and it seemed that Vendôme might yet press them onto the open plain beyond the cultivated country; the crack *Maison du Roi*, the *Gendarmerie* (smarting to avenge the slights of Ramillies), and two other brigades of cavalry from the right, were waiting this moment with impatience. But their moment would never come, for in the very nick of time Marlborough received news that Lottum was marching up from the bridges with 20 more battalions. These troops were used to extend the line from Schaerken along the southern bank of the Diepenbeek just in time to meet a new French attack. At this juncture (about 6 p.m.), Marlborough handed over command of the Allied right to Prince Eugene, and himself rode over to supervise the fighting on the Diepenbeke. He was still very worried about the safety of his weak right flank, should the French left wing attack, but now aides rode up announcing the arrival of 18 new battalions of Hanoverians and Hessians in rear of Lottum, whilst General Lumley with a body of horse was reported as having passed through Oudenarde immediately in front of Overkirk's Dutch wing of the army, both horse and foot, which was however being seriously impeded by the breakdown of one of the bridges in the town.

With his unerring eye for ground and tactical possibilities, Marlborough used the latest-comers to bring off a most difficult manœuvre. Ordering the Hanoverians to move forward as if to reinforce Lottum, the Duke ordered the latter's battalions to disengage from the front (less their colour-parties—a repeat of the trick usefully employed at Ramillies), reform in rear, and then march off, together with Lumley's 17 British squadrons, to pass behind Argyle and Cadogan and thus reinforce the right wing. Such a movement at the height of the battle needed a cool mind to conceive and great skill to execute, but Marlborough was equal to the occasion, probably recalling a similar manœuvre he had once executed on a far smaller scale 23 years earlier at the battle of Sedgemoor.*

At least partially reassured for the safety of his right wing (now 56 battalions strong) Marlborough could turn all his attention to preparing the *coup de grâce*. The transfer of Lottum took half-an-hour to complete, and this welcome aid enabled Eugene to retake Herlegem and Groenewald. This event proved to be the passing of the crisis for the Allies.

Prince Eugene prepared to take the initiative and counterattack in order to win a respite for his hard-pressed and near-exhausted battalions. After Lumley had filled his place abreast the Ghent highroad, Natzmer led his cavalry in a splendid charge to the north of Herlegem. The horsemen crashed through the first lines of horse sent to meet them, scattered two battalions of foot, and almost reached the mill of Roijgem (about 7 p.m.) before being tellingly counter-attacked by the *Maison du Roi*. Most sources agree that Natzmer lost almost two-thirds of his men in this attack, but it served to win Cadogan's, Argyle's and Lottum's foot a breathing space and also to increase the growing demoralisation of the French army; perhaps even more importantly, it distracted all attention from what was transpiring at the further extremity of the battlefield, which was now in the form of a concave arc, two miles long.

At 7 p.m., Marlborough had launched the Hanovarians in an attack against Diepenbeke village, adding General Week's eight Dutch battalions to extend their line so as to outflank the French foot—now 68 battalions in all. But this move was also a cover, for Marlborough was anxiously awaiting news that Overkirk had reached his appointed position for the master-stroke. The Duke had ordered the Dutch general to take Count Tilly's 12 Danish squadrons and General Oxenstiern's 16 Dutch battalions—comprising the Allied left—up the partially sunken road onto the Boser Couter, and thence to Oycke. Once there, he was to face east, and at Marlborough's order, sweep down onto the flank and rear of Vendôme's wing of the French army by advancing on Roijgem. But the

* See above Chapter 2, p. 20.

minutes were passing, and the approach of dusk meant that very little time remained if the stroke was to be effective. At last, by 7.30 p.m. all was in readiness. The signal was given.

The youthful Prince of Orange well to the fore, the Dutch thundered down, '. . . having been obliged to make a great round to come at them . . .',[19] as Overkirk reported to the States-General, against their opponents, who were completely taken by surprise. 'The troops on our right gave ground so fast,' wrote St. Simon 'that the valets of the suites of all that accompanied the Princes fell back upon them with an alarm, a rapidity and a confusion which swept them along with extreme speed and much indecency and risk towards the main battle on the left.'[20] Neither the *Gendarmerie* nor the *Maison* could stem the tide, and Vendôme's attempts to transfer troops from left to right came to naught in the prevailing confusion and maelstrom of fire.

By 8.30 p.m. the Dutch were nearing Roijgem, and half-an-hour later the French right wing had disintegrated. At 9 p.m. the two French commanders met (for the first time since 2 p.m.) near Huysse. A growing shortage of ammunition had induced Burgundy to order a general retreat on Ghent. This was furiously opposed by Vendôme, who still talked of reopening the battle next morning—but the die was cast.

The question now was how many of the French right could escape from the closing trap, as Overkirk drove in one flank and Eugene the other. The deepening night and the onset of rain proved the salvation of some considerable number. 'The night now coming on,' wrote Lediard, 'and the fire being directed so many ways at once that it was impossible to distinguish friends from foes, the Confederate Generals gave positive orders to their troops to cease firing, and to let the routed enemy escape, rather than to venture putting themselves into disorder.'[21] As a result, many Frenchmen escaped through the gap, though many more fell for the ruse practiced that night by Huguenot officers of calling out the names of French regiments to rally their scattered members, and make them prisoner. In the prevailing gloom and downpour it proved difficult to mount an immediate pursuit of the remainder, so the army lay on its arms all night and awaited the dawn.

Casualty figures are, as usual, hard to establish with any accuracy. The Allied figures* are generally agreed to have been about 825 killed and 2,150 wounded,[22] but the French claim they lost only about as many killed and wounded and a mere 1,800 prisoners (including 300 officers).[23] Some Allied sources put the French loss as high as 6,000 killed and wounded besides 9,000 prisoners and a

---

* This Dutch source reveals that five generals became casualties, 76 officers were killed and a further 274 wounded, as compared to 749 and 1,871 Allied rank and file in the two categories. Of these casualties only 175 were British (to include the wounded Major-Generals Meredith and Lauder) whilst the Dutch suffered 348 killed and 1,152 wounded. The Danes lost 207 killed and 398 wounded.

further 5,000 deserters.[24] These figures are probably a little exaggerated, but the French would certainly seem to have lost 7,000 captives, including 709 officers.

The French infantry (such as had been engaged) had fought well yet still had been defeated, which was an even more telling blow to their morale. Not unnaturally, their generals tried to minimise their catastrophe. 'So all that took place was a rough infantry combat . . .' wrote M. d'Artagnan, '. . . As we have lost no artillery, no colours, no standards, and no baggage, this should only be called a large-scale infantry combat; but it is true that it was one of the roughest I have ever seen. However it was not as bloody as it could have been, not as others I have seen.'[25] As for Vendôme, he was with some reason highly critical of Burgundy's part in the battle. 'I cannot comprehend how 50 battalions and 180 squadrons could be satisfied with observing us engaged for six hours and merely look on as though watching the opera from a third tier box.'[26] Marlborough had been aware of the risk he had taken, but his awareness of the vital need for a battlefield success to offset earlier setbacks had led him to take a carefully-calculated risk. 'This only made me venture the battle yesterday, otherwise I did give them too much advantage . . . I hope I have given such a blow to their foot that they will not be able to fight any more this year. My head aches so terribly that I must say no more,'[27] he wrote to Godolphin the next day. He regretted that only the onset of night had robbed him of an even greater victory, which might have won the war. As it was, the French were confidentially prepared to admit to Versailles that 'forty of our regiments are reduced to a wretched condition.'

In this great engagement we see Marlborough's talents as a general fully displayed. Despite ill-health, he was able to snatch at a chance of giving battle under circumstances that few other commanders would have judged possible, let alone advisable. His eye for ground, his sense of timing, his ability to extemporise solutions with the aid of limited, though excellent resources, and his keen knowledge of his foes' characters, foibles and clashing personalities—all these attributes were amply demonstrated. Of course he was fortunate to have the experienced and gifted Prince Eugene at his side, and to be blessed with such capable subordinates as Cadogan, Lottum and Overkirk and such a loyal and reliable rank and file, but from first to last Oudenarde had been his personal achievement.

Oudenarde at one stroke completely transformed the situation in the Cockpit once more. The strategic initiative, which the French had so boldly seized on the first days of July, had again been wrested from them. The dissensions and confusions of the French high command in Flanders contrast most markedly with the atmosphere of calm and co-operation habitually pervading Marlborough's field headquarters in good times as well as bad. This would be amply demonstrated during the five more months of eventful campaigning that still lay before the jubilant Allied army before it would return into winter quarters. The wonders and tribulations of the year had not yet been even half revealed.

Vauban's Masterpiece

'Lille, the bulwark of this barrier, was besieged. A numerous garrison and a Marshal of France defended the place. Prince Eugene of Savoy commanded, the Duke of Marlborough covered and sustained the siege. The lines were seized, and the communication with Holland interrupted. The Duke opened new communications with great labour, and greater skill, through countries over-run by the enemy. The necessary convoys arrived in safety. One alone was attacked. The troops that attacked it were beaten. The defence of Lille was animated by assurances of relief. The French assembled all their force. They marched towards the town. The Duke of Marlborough offered them battle, without suspending the siege. They abandoned the enterprise. They came to save the town, they were spectators of its fall.

From this conquest, the Duke hastened to others. The posts taken by the enemy on the Scheldt were surprised. That river was passed the second time and not withstanding the great preparations made to prevent it, without opposition. Brussels, besieged by the Elector of Bavaria, was relieved. Ghent surrendered to the Duke in the middle of a winter remarkably severe. An army, little inferior to his own, marched out of the town. . . .'

From the inscription on the Column of Victory,
Blenheim Palace (continued).

Oudenarde regained the strategic initiative for the Allies. In the words of one French commentator, the battle 'reduced us, the owners of a far stronger army, to a timid and difficult defensive. . . . We were effectively under the orders of M. de Marlborough.'[1] As the demoralised French army headed north for the Bruges-Ghent canal, their opponents took hasty council as to how best to exploit their advantage. To a degree they were unprepared, for the windfall of Oudenarde had abruptly reversed the situation in Flanders.

The victorious army's position was not without its difficulties. There was no siege artillery closer than Sas-van-Ghent, and the continued presence of the

French in Ghent itself precluded the use of the Scheldt for movement or re-supply. Similarly, the proximity of Marshal Berwick's army (marching hot-foot for Mons from Buissière) constituted a threat to the tenuous land communications linking Oudenarde with the military depots of Brussels. The French, with their remaining aggregate of 125 battalions and 230 squadrons, could not be ignored by Marlborough's and Eugene's combined forces, although the low ebb of Gallic morale was further evidenced by their hasty abandonment of Warneton and the Lines of Commines on the approach of the Allied army on 15 July. This move effectively threatened French communication with Artois.

The Duke's first thought was to induce the foe to abandon Ghent and thus ease his logistical problem. As Eugene's army approached Brussels, Marlborough feinted towards Ypres, whose loss would have fatally compromised the French position north of the canal—but the enemy refused the bait. Louis XIV, writing to Burgundy on 16 July, expressed his disappointment 'that the first occasion you found yourself in did not have a happier outcome . . .' and went on to insist that 'Your principal object now must be to keep Ghent well-garrisoned and to sustain it' besides enjoining the strict avoidance of another general action. Marshal Berwick was to assume immediate responsibility for the security of the French frontier area.[2]

At an early consultation Marlborough produced one of his boldest plans. Anxious as always to make the most of the present advantageous situation in the hope of winning the war with the least delay, he advocated a march to the Channel coast and then a south-westerly advance along the coast to the mouth of the River Somme, drawing supplies from the combined Anglo-Dutch fleet. Ahead of the main army, Major-General Thomas Erle, presently embarked off the Isle of Wight with 11 battalions under orders for Spain, would be diverted to seize Abbeville, and thus provide the Allies with a forward base for a subsequent move into the heart of France.

This scheme, which would have effectively by-passed the triple-line of French fortresses guarding the frontier, was too unconventional not only for the Dutch (predictably, perhaps) but also for Prince Eugene. For all his bright genius, Eugene never fully understood the possible interaction of land and sea forces—as the fiasco before Toulon in 1707 had already shown*—and he was particularly dubious of Abbeville's suitability for a winter base. Once again, therefore, Marlborough allowed himself to be overruled in the interests of Allied solidarity, and after a few weeks' consideration the Abbeville project was shelved until the following spring, and General Erle—at sea—was sent new orders to undertake a raid against the Normandy coast. 'It will be impossible, owing to the objections of our Allies, to take our joint measures for seconding General Erle's design upon Abbeville,' wrote the Duke on 3 August, '. . . till we are masters of Lille.'[3]

* See above p. 198.

Marlborough's less imaginative colleagues strongly urged that all attention should be focused against this Vauban masterpiece, 'a large and well-fortified place, with a very strong citadel, the capital of French Flanders, the staple of all the trade between the Netherlands and France, and next to Paris . . . reckon'd the chief place of His Most Christian Majesty's dominions.'[4] Lille's capture, they argued, would provide a superb base for the next campaign and a prestige-victory which would resound throughout Europe. It would also disrupt French trade, taxation and military support in the region, and even affect the pestilential privateers operating out of Dunkirk (for many were financed by the city's rich merchants). Its value as a pawn in the peace negotiations—as 'one of the principal keys of France'—would also be incalculable.

The capture of Lille would not by any means be an easy operation, as Marlborough was well aware. Many contemporaries, indeed, deemed it impregnable. Besides its intrinsic strength, set amongst the unhealthy marshes of the Rivers Deule and Marque, and protected by some of Vauban's defensive works*, Lille was within supporting-distance on three sides out of four, of French-held Ypres, Tournai, Douai and Béthune, any of which could support the operations of one or more relieving forces. The Allies' current shortage of heavy artillery has already been mentioned, as has the complication posed by Ghent, whilst the long land communications were vulnerable to attack from Mons, Charleroi and Namur, as were the Allied territories in Brabant. Moreover the French would never cede Lille without an epic struggle; the proposed siege, therefore, would amount to taking the bull by the horns with a vengeance, for the Allies would be deliberately abandoning much of their hard-won initiative, effectively returning it to their opponents.

Certain critics challenged the choice of target. 'Had the Allies only attacked Tournai and not Lille,' surmised Mérode-Westerloo, 'we could have opened up a safe line of communications with our bases, and at the same time continued to protect our own country, and opened up a sure road towards Lille . . . (but) we felt compelled to attack the strongest sector of the whole region.' As Lediard noted, the Allies 'could not attack the enemy in a more sensible (sensitive) part.'[5]

It was some little time before the enemy divulged the Allied intent. The Duke's present position posed possible threats to Ypres, Tournai and even Mons as well as Lille. In an agony of indecision, Berwick (after massing his forces around Douai, 16–19 July) hastily reinforced these garrisons, and the ageing but stalwart Marshal Boufflers (hero of Namur's defence in 1695) was sent to command at Lille, initially with a force of 11 battalions and a single regiment of dragoons.[6]

Marlborough's first problem was to resupply his forces and procure a siege train. The heavy guns had already been sent by water to Antwerp, and thence by

* First taken by the French in 1667, Vauban had reconstructed the defences and built the arsenal, 1668–74. A plaque commemorates his work.

canal to Brussels to meet further munitions and equipment drawn from Maastricht and Huy. Large convoys were being prepared under Eugene's watchful eye, but all this activity could not be concealed from the enemy, who were well placed to block the roads if they so chose. Even before the final decision about the Abbeville project had been taken, it was decided to send out a convoy to Menin as the army badly needed resupply—and this would serve to test the French reaction. The convoy—drawn by 8,000 horses—left on 22 July and reached its destination without let or hindrance on the 25th. Thus emboldened, the Allies prepared the 'Great Convoy', including 80 siege pieces and 20 siege mortars (each requiring 20 and 16 horses respectively) and 3,000 four-horse munition waggons. This huge organisation took up 30 miles of road space, and was divided into two convoys. Security measures were carefully put in train. The convoys were entrusted to the immediate care of the trusted Cadogan and the Prince of Hesse-Cassel; the journey would be covered first by Eugene's army (50 battalions and 100 squadrons) based near Soignies, but once the Scheldt was reached Marlborough would assume this role from the camp at Helchin.

The convoy was about to set out when news arrived that Burgundy was moving forward from Bruges towards Alost at the head of 30,000 men; further parties of French and Spaniards were reported to be making destructive forays towards Cadsand in Dutch Flanders—conceivably as a distraction. Tension and anxiety are both marked in the Duke's letter to Cadogan dated 3 August, which ends with a revealing postscript in Marlborough's own hand: 'For God's sake be sure you do not risk the cannon.'[7] If the trains were lost or seriously damaged *en route* it would spell the ruin of the Lille project.

Late on the 6th the two precious convoys rumbled over the cobblestones of Brussels and headed for the south and west. Mile by mile the long lines of waggons and guns snaked their ponderous way towards Enghien and Ath. Towards the enemy, squadrons wheeled and watched and battalions stood-to. The Scheldt was reached and safely crossed near Pottes on the 10th with still no sign of the enemy, and at last, on the 12th the convoys reached Menin 'without the least annoyance' to the vast relief of everybody concerned. In fact the danger had been more apparent than real, for Berwick had decided that Mons was the real target, and in the ensuing confusion of order and counterorder the opportunity of intercepting the convoy had been let slip.

By the 11th the foe had realised their error, and Berwick narrowly succeeded in rushing further reinforcements into Lille to bring Boufflers' garrison to a total strength of 16,000 men (20 battalions, 7 squadrons of dragoons, 200 horse besides 2,000 citizen militia).[8] Meantime Allied forces under the Prince of Orange and General Wood were closing in on the city, and on the 12th they were joined by Prince Eugene near Marquette and Potteghem. Before another 24 hours had passed, Lille was blockaded on all sides, and one of the most celebrated sieges of modern history had begun.

It had been agreed that Eugene should undertake the siege with 50 battalions and 90 squadrons (mostly Dutch and Imperial troops but including a brigade of five British regiments*), whilst Marlborough covered the operations from near Helchin at the head of 69 battalions and 140 squadrons. They were hopeful that a quick success against the city might release numbers of troops to rejoin Marlborough, thereby easing the ration problem in the siege lines, and at the same time assist the Duke in his efforts to forestall or head-off any French attempt to relieve the citadel. If Burgundy managed to unite his and Vendôme's forces before making such an effort, the Duke's constant aim would have to be to retire towards the siege lines, always keeping his force between the enemy and their objective, until he could be reinforced by the bulk of Eugene's regiments to a satisfactory fighting power.

In front of Lille, Eugene conducted a careful reconnaissance before deciding to attack the city's northern sector. The ground was firmer in this area, the River Marque offered a measure of rearward protection, and the sector was in closer proximity to the main camp of the covering army than would be the case in the south. On the advice of his two Huguenot chief engineers, Des Roques and Du May, the Gates of Magdalen and St. Andrew were selected as the targets despite the strong hornworks in their vicinity. Meanwhile, in stifling heat, the troops and a myriad requisitioned peasants swung picks and drove shovels to construct the peripheral lines of circumvallation (15–21 August), and on the 17th the heavy guns reached the encampments and were parked near the village of Marque. Five days later the trenches were opened and the first parallel started. One minor sortie by part of the garrison on the 26th had done little damage, and after a tour of inspection on 3 September, Marlborough was hopefully predicting a rapid success to Mr. Secretary Boyle. 'Our siege is so far advanced,' he wrote, 'that the engineers intend tomorrow to attack the counterscarp, wherein if we succeed the town must soon surrender.'[9] Such optimistic forecasts would prove sadly inaccurate however.

Not unnaturally, the French command was taking counsel how best to break up the siege. It was self-evident that it would be advisable to mass forces before making the attempt, but the King (from Versailles) was insistent that the junction should take place near Mons whilst Burgundy stubbornly favoured the area of Grammont on the River Dender. In the end the concentration was scheduled for Lessines. Accordingly, on the 26th Berwick left Mons, whilst Burgundy and Vendôme—leaving a mere seven battalions to guard the Bruges-Ghent canal-line —marched east and south. By the 30th, the French had massed over 110,000 men on the Dender. Allied fears that this impressive force might turn against Brussels proved incorrect, for the joint-army broke camp and marched for Tournai, where they passed the Scheldt on 2 September.

* Namely the 16th, 18th, 21st, 23rd and 24th of Foot. They ultimately sustained some 1,500 casualties.

A relief attempt was clearly in the offing, and Marlborough—whose probes from Helchin had failed to prevent the enemy junction—circled warily, moving his camp successively from Helchin to Templeneuve and Péronne, until he reached Frétain near Seclin on 4 September. The same day the French advanced through Orchies to Mons-en-Pevelle on the Marque. A confrontation was close at hand, and Marlborough and Eugene had carefully looked over a possible battle-ground the previous day, 'in case the enemy should, as they still give out, attempt to succour the town.' The Prince now brought up 72 squadrons and 26 battalions from the siege lines to bring the Allied total force to some 80,000 men (209 squadrons and 102 battalions in all), including a detachment of Dutch troops under General Fagel.

Such disparity of force induced the Duke to decide to fight defensively for almost the only time in his career, between the Deule and the Marque. He placed his right at Noyelles behind Seclin, hard by some marshes and close to the lines of circumvallation. The left took post between Fretain and Peronne near the Marque, the line being partly covered by a convenient ravine. The centre, behind Ennetières, was not naturally covered, being part of the Plain of Lille, and here on the night of 5/6 September the troops began to dig earthworks, striving to build a 12 foot wide bank, some five foot high, surmounted by a four foot parapet, strengthened with occasional redoubts and traverses. Batteries were hauled into position, but such work took time, and there was precious little available as the foe was siting no less than 200 field guns opposite the centre by the 5th.

The Allied commanders expected an attack that same afternoon, but their opponents deemed it 'too late' and postponed it until the morrow. The Allies made full use of every hour thus gained to improve their defences. The 6th dawned with a strong sortie by Boufflers from within Lille against the depleted trenches; this was obviously intended to coincide with the main attack from without, but this never came as the French found one reason after another for further delay, and Boufflers was beaten back within the walls. Marlborough felt sufficiently confident about his moral ascendancy over his opponents to release Eugene and most of his infantry, who returned to the lines on the 7th. That evening 15,000 Allied troops launched themselves against the counterscarp; four mines were exploded, and for a loss of some 3,000 casualties four angles of the covered way were occupied. This was disappointing. 'The trenches have been opened now near three weeks . . .' the Duke reported to the Earl of Galway on the 10th, 'and the siege is still going on, our troops being lodged on part of the counterscarp. I must own when they first began I had hopes that by this time we should at least have been masters of the town. The enemy have assembled all the strength they possibly can, and have been encamped for this week past less than a league of us, with a resolution, as they give out, to attempt the relief of the place. We offered them battle twice, but they declined it, and their design seems now chiefly to be to distress us for want of provisions, being at a great distance from our magazines ... but I hope that with the blessing of God we shall succeed.'[10]

The 8th had seen the completion of Marlborough's entrenchments, and the French high command was in ever more acrimonious dispute. Louis XIV sent Chamillart, Minister of War, to headquarters with a direct order for the Marshals to attack with no more ado (he arrived in the camp on the 9th) but even the royal *firman* failed to stir the French from their positions. On the 11th, however, the French launched a massive bombardment against the Allied positions; this caused Marlborough to resummon Eugene briefly from Lille, but he coolly ordered his troops to collect the enemy shot and had them transported to the siege batteries, which promptly fired them into the city. On the 12th the enemy, hoping to lure the Duke from his entrenchments, made a limited advance against Seclin, which the Allies fired before withdrawing into their main positions beyond. By this time even Chamillart had come to agree that the position was too strong to attack, and secretly the decision was taken to break camp and withdraw east. By the 15th, accordingly, the French had struck their tents, demolished their battery positions after firing off as much ammunition as possible, and repassed the Marque en route for Orchies and the Scheldt. The Allies discussed the advisability of a pursuit, but the Dutch were strongly opposed and so Marlborough once again bowed to pressure. Nevertheless, there was no disguising that the first French attempt to relieve Lille had proved a total failure despite their numerical superiority and their possession of the initiative. But Marlborough was still incensed with the lack of real progress at the siege, which 'goes but slowly.'

In close concert with Versailles, the French now devised a new strategy for preventing the loss of Lille—namely the imposition of an all-out blockade along the Scheldt to sever the Allies' land communications with Brussels. If direct confrontation had failed, then a war of supply might serve their purpose. Spies and deserters had already informed the Marshals how urgently needed had been two small convoys of munitions and supplies which reached the Allied lines on the 9th. Louis XIV approved their scheme, and by the 23rd the French had seized and occupied every crossing over the Scheldt, and dug a strong entrenchment before Oudenarde. A project to renew the threat against Brussels was again shelved, however, when it became clear that the Allies had reinforced its garrison from Holland and Brabant.

The abrupt severance of all links with their bases caused much despondency at the siege. 'I am sorry to tell you our situation is such, through the lateness of the season, the slowness with which the engineers have proceeded in their approaches, and the great difficulty we shall meet with in bringing up a further supply of ammunition,' wrote Marlborough pessimistically to Sunderland on the 24th, 'as to make me doubt of the success of the siege.'[11] An assault by 15,000 men on the 21st had gained a little ground against the *tenaille* on the right, but the 1,000 casualties had included Prince Eugene himself, grazed on the forehead

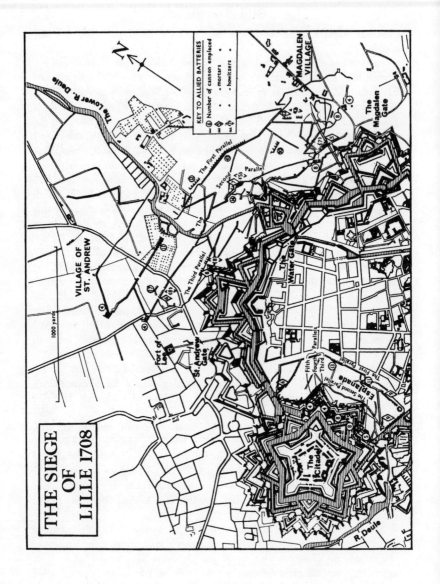

THE SIEGE
OF
LILLE 1708

1000 yards

The Lower R. Deule

VILLAGE OF
ST. ANDREW

Fort of
Lower

St Andrew
Gate

The Third Parallel

The First Parallel

Second Parallel

The

KEY TO ALLIED BATTERIES
Number of cannon emplaced
- mortars
- howitzers

MAGDALEN
VILLAGE

The
Magdalen
Gate

The
Water Gate

Fifth Parallel
Fourth Third

The Second Parallel
The First Parallel

The Esplanade

The Citadel

R. Deule

by a musket ball. For a period, therefore, Marlborough was compelled to shoulder a double-responsibility. Close inspection of the siege works did not reassure him. 'I am so vexed at the misbehaviour of our engineers and others,' he wrote uncharacteristically, 'that I have no patience. . . .' A surprise attack late on the 23rd which resulted in the capture of the left-hand *tenaille* and part of the counterscarp did little to lighten his anxiety and anger. As the Duke complained to Heinsius on the 24th, five weeks' bombardment had failed to take the town. 'I have the spleen and dare say no more,' he ended one letter.[12] As for the troops in camp and trenches, their morale was beginning to suffer as dysentry ravaged their ranks. 'I am in no small pain for you and all my other friends before Lille,' wrote Captain Robert Parker to Colonel Robert Sterne from Dublin. ''Tis a hard case that our poor Regiment must be always pick'd upon (for) all extraordinary commands. May God preserve you and bring you safe off. . . .'[13]

Marlborough was not one to bow before misfortune for long. Very soon his fertile mind was conjuring up an alternative route for his supplies, 'Prince Eugene having declared, that he would be responsible for the success (of the siege) provided he were supported with ammunition.'[14] A possible solution to the current impasse lay in Allied possession of the port of Ostend and their naval command of the Channel. General Erle (newly returned from an abortive raid against La Hogue) was forthwith ordered to land his men at the port and make it and its outskirts secure against possible French attacks from Nieuport or Bruges. Commissaries, meantime, began to prepare a large convoy of munitions ready for the journey to Menin when all was ready. Nevertheless, this was a desperate expedient; not only was the inland route through Wynendael, Thorout and Roulers highly exposed to attack by the Comte de Lamotte from Bruges to the north, but the French garrison at Nieuport controlled sluices which, if opened, could place a barrier of flood-water between Ostend and the interior. This the French immediately attempted, but Erle (after landing on 21 September) proved capable of diverting much of the water, besides occupying the key townships of Leffinghe and Oudenburg (24th) to secure the vital causeway running inland.

Marlborough's original plan had been to use Erle's 6,000 men for a drive towards Bruges once these first tasks had been completed, but it was soon clear that the French were massively reinforcing Lamotte, which ruled out this move. This was in part due to a flash of insight by Louis XIV. Writing to Burgundy about the 18th, he had pressed him 'to close to the enemy not only the passage at Oudenarde but also that at Ostend, from whence they would be able to procure great assistance for the siege.'[15] As a result his generals hastened to reinforce the Bruges area, first sending off M. de Puignon with 25 battalions and 20 squadrons on the 22nd, following this with a further four battalions and as many regiments of dragoons. Another nine battalions would be made available on the 28th, but Lamotte was on the move before they could arrive to swell his veritable army still further.

Some days earlier Marlborough had detached a dozen battalions to assist Erle around Ostend and to form a nucleus for the convoy's escort. Some 700 waggons stood ready, so on the 25th Major-General John Webb was sent off from the camp at Lannoy at the head of 24 battalions (including 4 Scottish formations) and 3 squadrons to cover their movement. At the same time the main army moved forward to the intermediate position of Rousselaar.

On the 27th the convoy and escort (12 battalions and 1,500 horse) left Ostend. The next day, the vigilant Lamotte, after an abortive attack on Oudenburgh, marched at the head of some 23,000 men to intercept the convoy. He came upon it amidst thickly forested country near Wynendael, but barring his way across the most accessible opening he found General Webb and his 6,000 men, drawn up in a triple line. To the fore were the handful of mounted troops backed by ten battalions in three lines. Behind this seemingly inadequate covering force the French could see the waggons moving steadily on their way. About 2.30 p.m. Lamotte's 20 guns (some accounts say 40) opened fire against the 300 Allied cavalry of Count Lottum, whilst the French general crowded his superior forces into no less than 12 lines of units (six of foot to the front, then four of dragoons and two of cavalry) because of the narrowness of the open ground. The resultant action lasted two hours. Webb had concealed part of his forces in the woods on each flank, and when these arose 'out of the earth' the French infantry halted. The Allied volley-firing soon began to reap its grim harvest, and suddenly the French left crumpled and fled towards their right, throwing that, too, into confusion just at the time it was about to overpower two Allied battalions. Lamotte then ordered up his dragoons, but they fared no better. At this juncture there arrived on the scene General Cadogan and a column of cavalry dispatched from Rousselaar by an anxious Marlborough, and this reinforcement induced Lamotte to order the retreat to be sounded. So ended the celebrated action of Wynendael. Webb had lost some 940 casualties. The French admitted to only 450 at the time, but if stragglers and deserters are included the figure must have been nearer 4,000 as the Allies claimed.[16] Some accounts even place them at between 6,000 to 7,000 men.*

The convoy duly reached Menin safely on the 29th, providing 250,000 lbs of powder and several tons of shot—enough for two further weeks of the siege. Marlborough was vastly relieved. 'Our letters should have gone away on Thursday night' he wrote on the 11th, 'but I detained the post because I am willing to give you some account of the success of our convoy with ammunition from Ostend, on which all in a manner depended; and I am now glad to tell you it has come safe to Menin. . . .'[17] In another letter he wrote, 'If they had not succeeded and our convoy had been lost, the consequence must have been the raising of the siege the next day.'[18] One oversight marred the achievement. In his dispatch to

* C. T. Atkinson's account in the *S.A H.R. Journal* for 1956 differs markedly from Lediard, Vol. II, p. 342 *et. seq.* which supposedly gives Webb's own account.

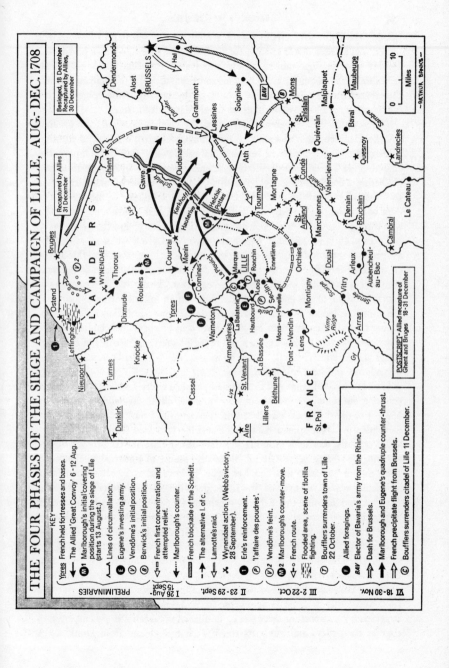

THE FOUR PHASES OF THE SIEGE AND CAMPAIGN OF LILLE, AUG.-DEC. 1708

London the Duke gave credit to *both* Webb and Cadogan, and this oversight earned him an able man's enmity, for the latter had taken no active part in the fighting however important his cavalry's arrival on the scene had been. 'Webb very deservedly acquired great honour and reputation by this gallant action', commented Parker; 'but then he spoiled all by making it the subject of his conversation on all occasions. This he should have left to fame. . . .'[19]

The same 28 September also witnessed the celebrated '*affaire des poudres*' at Lille. Boufflers, too, was short of munitions, and when a smuggled message reached the French command revealing he was down to four days' supply, the Chevalier de Luxembourg undertook a bold operation to ease the situation. Gathering 2,000 horse and 150 grenadiers, he equipped each horseman with a 50 lb bag of gunpowder, ordered them to put Dutch insignia in their hats, and then bold as brass rode for the Allied lines. In the dusk the column bluffed its way through the barriers purporting to be Allied cavalry, and the greater part had passed through the lines before the alarm was given when an officer ill-advisedly shouted to his troop to close up in French. Those that were through at once dashed for Lille, the rest turned and fled for Douai. 'Our men seized their arms and opened fire,' recalled Mérode-Westerloo. 'This made several sparks to set fire to some of the enemy's powder bags; in an instant several hundred of them were hurled into the air.'[20] More shared the same fate as they rode hell-for-leather towards the city; their horse's hooves sent up sparks which ignited more abandoned powder sacks, 'and it was a dreadful spectacle,' wrote the Prince of Hesse to the States-General, 'to see the way strewed with dead carcasses, horses, heads, arms and legs, half burnt.'[21]

It seems probable that 160 Frenchmen perished and a further 25 were made prisoner, but some 40,000 lbs of powder reached Lille in this bold manner. This flouting of danger raised morale within the city, and Louis XIV soon promoted Luxembourg to Lieutenant-General. But Lille remained in pressing danger, and Burgundy was soon ordering the discredited Lamotte (1 October) to re-attempt the sealing off of Ostend 'without exposure to a general combat', and plans were put in train to attack Leffinghe.[22] However, as 43 battalions and 63 squadrons were to be involved, it was decided to entrust the senior command to Marshal Vendôme in the hope of repairing the damage to French prestige sustained at Wynendael.

On learning of Vendôme's arrival near Oudenburg, Marlborough at once crossed the Lys (7 October) and marched for Roulers with 60 battalions and 130 squadrons. This threat was enough for the French who immediately retired on Bruges, but not before opening all the sluices in the area. This action placed the causeway under several feet of water, and Leffinghe became an island. Its garrison, constantly replaced as need arose from Ostend, held off repeated French attacks from Nieuport for three weeks, flotillas of naval boats being employed to counter the galleys and gunboats the French brought up from Dunkirk. 'A struggle of epic greatness flared up in the submerged polders of west Flanders' comments an eminent Dutch historian.[23]

The floods implied yet another challenge to the Allies' ability to continue the siege of Lille. Food, rather than powder, was now at a premium, and Marlborough was obliged to reduce rations to two-thirds the daily rate from 16 October. Nevertheless, extemporisation allied to rationing saw the new storm weathered. Special carts with out-sized wheels ferried supplies from Ostend to barges and fishing boats, which then conveyed them over the floods to dry land, where the empty train-waggons waited. In this way 1,700 barrels of powder were passed over the waters between 7 and 19 October, together with sufficient rations. But strong forces of troops were needed to watch Vendôme at Bruges, both Cadogan and Fagel being employed on this duty, and this led in turn to a dangerous dispersal of Allied forces.

The French overall aim at this juncture was to delay the inevitable fall of the city of Lille until winter set in, which would, it was hoped, postpone the loss of the citadel until the next campaigning season and at the same time keep the besiegers at full stretch. To this end, Louis XIV expressly authorised Boufflers to use half the powder reserved for the defence of the citadel, and the Duke of Burgundy was even given leave to take measures with Berwick with a view to seeking battle if this proved necessary.

These intentions, however, were soon overtaken by events. The limit of Boufflers' ability to defend the city had been reached. By mid-October the Allies had become masters of the covered way, and their mighty siege cannon, repositioned on the counterscarp, had battered a 350 foot breach in the main defences. The garrison's powder supply was already below the recently permitted limit, and everything pointed to a general storm in the near future. Boufflers was aware that this could have nothing but dire repercussions, and so, after consultations with his officers, at 4 p.m. on the 22nd, he 'beat a Parley' and asked for terms. Four days earlier, it should be mentioned, the Dutch veteran Overkirk, had died full of years and honour; in the general excitement his death went almost unnoticed, although Marlborough somewhat unfeelingly commented that thereby '. . . Her Majesty will save the pension.'[24]

Because of his continuing problems of supply, the Allies granted favourable terms. Boufflers and the able-bodied of his garrison were permitted to retire unmolested into the citadel, the sick and wounded were granted free evacuation to Douai, as were Luxembourg's 1,500 cavalry, surplus staff officers and all combatants' families and personal effects. Further, the Allies undertook to exchange all prisoners, give a free pardon to the citizen militia and to guarantee the lives and possessions of the townsfolk. It was also agreed that the citadel should not be attacked from the city-side. In return, Boufflers agreed to evacuate the city on the 25th, permitting the Allies to occupy the Magdalen Gate and the magazines on the 23rd. A three day extension of the cease-fire was subsequently arranged. And so the ten-week siege of the city of Lille came to a conclusion. This delayed success had cost the Allies 3,632 killed and 8,322 wounded—whilst Boufflers had but 4,500 of his original garrison fit for service.

There still remained the citadel to capture, and, to the great indignation of the French, Prince Eugene opened the trenches skirting the Esplanade on the 26th (during the armistice period*) and sited them on the parade facing the town. Boufflers' strident remonstrations were ignored, however, and a new note of grimness had entered the siege. The Allies now lost no time in reducing the besieging forces to the minumum compatible with security so as to ease the ration problem in the lines, and raiding parties were sent deep into Flanders and Artois in search of food and forage. An ultimatum had already been issued to the magistrates of Courtrai ordering them to sell the Allies all remaining grain supplies within ten days, on pain of its being plundered. Brigadier Evans was sent to sweep the countryside around Ypres. 'You must spare no pains nor give ear to the complaints of the peasantry at this juncture,' Marlborough ordered; 'let me know by the return of the courier what we may expect.'[25]

The Allies were incensed to learn of the sudden loss of Leffinghe, stormed on the night of 25 October whilst the garrison were unwisely celebrating the news from Lille, 'the soldiers all drunk and the officers quiet in their beds.' The battle of supply therefore reached a new climax, both ashore and afloat, but the Allies proved capable of maintaining the tenuous link, beating off the French galleys and brigantines. Moreover, the French forces were by now at least as hungry as their adversaries, for their resources were not capable of dealing with a campaign of such extended duration. Boufflers and his stalwart garrison were reduced to two months supplies and but 42,000 lbs of powder, which was being expended at a rate of 1,200 lbs a day.

The strategists of Versailles and Saulchoi had one last card to play. At the suggestion of the Elector of Bavaria, freshly returned to Mons from the Rhine front, the old scheme for an onslaught against Brussels was revived. On 21 November, the Elector reached Hal at the head of 14 battalions and 18 squadrons, and next day found he was before Brussels, confident that he (as a former Governor-General of the Netherlands) would be welcomed by the citizenry. Thanks to the stubbornness of Count Pascale, Military Governor, these hopes proved vain. The Elector thereupon opened a ten-gun bombardment on the 25th against the defences near the Namur Gate, but all to no avail and it was soon evident that he would need to have recourse to a regular siege.

News of this intention had previously reached Marlborough and Eugene. Together they concerted a counter-move. Under cover of a pretence of an advance towards the Bruges-Ghent canal line, numbers of troops were

---

* Each side chose to interpret the agreement in a different light—the Allies claiming that the digging of trenches in no way constituted a breach of the truce as no fire was given. This was really a case of special pleading.

inconspicuously moved from Rousselaar towards the Scheldt, some as if about to enter winter quarters. This served to lull French suspicions. Suddenly bridges of boats appeared over the Scheldt, and early on the 26th four strong columns descended upon Gavre, the lines opposite Oudenarde, Kerkhoff and Hauterive. The local French forces made little attempt to contest the crossing, and lost scant time in retreating for Tournai and Mons. By dusk Marlborough had gained a 30 mile bridgehead. The barrier between Lille and Brussels was now ruptured beyond repair. Furthermore, the Elector of Bavaria was placed in the direst peril of being cut off from Mons. Only a precipitate retreat—made at the cost of his guns and 800 abandoned wounded—enabled him to regain safety. Thus the siege of Brussels and the French policy of logistical interdiction were defeated by the same Allied operation. Above all, Marlborough had won the battle of supply, and regained the initiative once and for all.

The French were at last on the point of acknowledging failure. A final scheme to push a relief force through to Boufflers from La Bassée was frustrated when Marlborough promptly reinforced Eugene with 15,000 men. On 4 December, Versailles ordered the troops into winter quarters. The citadel of Lille was left to its fate, and at 9 p.m. on the 9th, Boufflers signed a capitulation. The garrison was awarded the full honours of war, and on the 11th the Marshal marched out at the head of his garrison and headed for Douai. After a total of three months and 16 days, the Allies had achieved their object at a cost of some 15,000 casualties.

But Marlborough—late season or no—was not yet prepared to abandon the campaign. He was determined to regain Bruges and Ghent.[26] Lamotte still controlled some 67 batallions and 53 squadrons north of the canal, but he had made the error of drawing the great majority into the town for the winter, leaving the canal crossings unwatched. Making full use of this oversight, the Allies had Ghent blockaded on three sides by the 13th, and the arrival of Eugene from Lille on the 18th completed the siege ring. The foe was horrified by the seemingly inexhaustible energy and resource of the Allies, and although Louis XIV hurriedly sent Boufflers to Douai to form an extemporised force of 86 battalions and 130 squadrons with which to attempt the recapture of Lille, this was little more than a gesture of despair. The trenches were opened before Ghent on 23 December, and 90 guns mounted against the town, and Lamotte somewhat tamely surrendered on the 30th.[27] The next day, the troops in Bruges abandoned the town. A sudden violent frost, experienced on the night of 5 January, abruptly brought the long-fought campaign of 1708 to a close, and also inaugurated one of the most extreme winters in European history.

The year of 1708 in Flanders had contained a complete microcosm of early eighteenth century warfare. A large-scale naval enterprise, followed by sudden offensives, surprised towns, a great battle, an even greater siege with every conceivable combination of relief attempt and counter-operation—such had been its turbulent and blood-stained history. Marlborough can be criticised for being taken largely by surprise by the strength and direction of the French spring offensive, and also for abandoning his imaginative scheme against Abbeville after Oudenarde. This plan had many intrinsic merits, not least of them originality, and the Allies held indubitable control of the Channel after the failure of the French naval excursion towards Scotland in April. Perhaps a great opportunity was missed, but the reasons appeared sufficiently compelling at the time. Marlborough's sense of duty as an Allied leader and statesman had again come into conflict with his instincts as a commander, but on balance he was probably correct in his ultimate judgement.

On the other hand there is no faulting the skill with which he regained the initiative in mid-July, albeit at the expense of running into possibly severe danger when he crossed the Scheldt so close to his opponents—but it was a superbly calculated risk, and the outcome of Oudenarde provides the justification. His hold over his troops and his ability to co-operate to the full with Eugene were demonstrated more than a dozen times over these months. He showed impressive flexibility in facing up to the repeated French challenges during the siege of Lille, never being at a loss for a practicable answer. Deteriorating health might make him irritable and even despairing on occasion, but it did nothing to blunt his sense of purpose—that ceaseless search for a favourable peace which, however, he was doomed never to find.

In one other respect too, 1708 held the seeds of future disappointments and setbacks. Marlborough's desire to secure the Captain-Generalcy for life had given his political foes a handle to use against him at Court. Already, Mrs Masham was steadily undermining the position of Duchess Sarah in Queen Anne's affections, and the aftermath of Oudenarde had included the 'affair of the jewels' in connection with the Thanksgiving service at St. Paul's, at the height of which the termagent Mistress of the Robes had hissed at her monarch to be silent before the assembled notables of the realm.[28] In the fullness of time, the Marlborough position at Court would become seriously undermined.

Militarily, however, 1708 had been a successful year for the Grand Alliance. At sea the thwarting of Forbin's raid into the North Sea had been followed by substantial successes in the Mediterranean, including Admiral Leake's capture of Sardinia in August and Stanhope's subsequent capture on 19 September of Port Mahon—a naval base of the first importance. In Spain, it is true, the initiative rested with the Bourbon armies, which continued to make some progress in regaining lost ground, including Tortosa, Denia and (after a very gallant defence), Alicante. In North Italy, the overall situation remained quiescent as did the Upper Rhine front. Flanders, of course, had been the focal point of the year's efforts. As Private Deane of the Foot Guards commented in just summary, the campaign had proved '... very long, tiresome, troublesome mischievous and strange, yet very successful.'[29]

French fortunes had reached almost their lowest ebb; the successes of 1707 and early 1708 had been swept away by the setbacks and disasters of the following months. Although the French had displayed some flexibility of method, and Boufflers' dauntless defence had added further laurels to his reputation, economic ruin and military disaster had been the sole results. These were now to be capped by the destructive rigours of a fearful winter following a failed harvest. There was famine in the land and bread riots in Paris; half the livestock of the country failed to survive the winter; the coinage was 30 per cent depreciated. The possibilities that France would be forced to accept the Allied terms accordingly seemed strong early in 1709. Peace appeared nearer than ever before.

The Bloodiest Day—
Malplaquet, 1709

'As soon as the season of the year permitted him to open another
campaign, the Duke besieged and took Tournai. He invaded Mons.
Near this city, the French Army, covered by thick woods, defended
by treble entrenchments, waited to molest, nor presumed to offer
battle. Even this was not attempted by them with impunity.
On the last day of August [OS], one thousand seven hundred and
nine, the Duke attacked them in their camp. All was employed,
nothing availed against the resolution of such a General, against the
fury of such troops. The battle was bloody: the events decisive. The
woods were pierced: the fortifications trampled down. The enemy
fled. The town was taken. . . .'

From the inscription on the Column of Victory,
Blenheim Palace (continued).

The winter of 1708–9 was one of the bitterest experienced in European history.
From December until early March much of Europe was in the grip of an almost
perpetual frost. Rivers froze over; sea communications were interrupted by
pack-ice in the Channel; cattle and wild-life died in tens of thousands; and,
perhaps worst of all, the seed-corn for the next harvest perished in the ground.
Human beings suffered proportionately, and soldiers on duty faced unusual
hazards. 'During that winter', recalled Méroed-Westerloo, 'you saw men and
horses freeze to death on the march; this actually happened to my regiment
which lost two troopers. . . . They had marched with the regiment on 2 January
1709 wrapped up in their cloaks, but they were nevertheless frozen solid mounted
upon their horses, which also remained upright.'[1]

The general suffering in England and the United Provinces was somewhat
mitigated by the reserves of corn held by both countries, although the Republic's
overall economic position was on the brink of ruin. France was not so fortunate.
The failure of the last harvest added to the general ruin of the economy spelt

famine and death under the prevailing extreme weather. The French Treasury expended its last resources in attempts to buy corn from the Beys of North Africa, but this traffic was effectively halted by squadrons of British and Dutch warships, and the resources diverted to the members of the Grand Alliance. The recently-acquired harbour of Port Mahon (30 September 1708) thus proved its worth, and an almost fatal economic stranglehold was applied to France. The results for France were widespread human misery, growing despair, and internal chaos. The military implication was an inability to collect supplies ready for the next campaign. There were neither pay nor rations, and the inevitable results were mutinies and a flood of desertions. The most informed commentators doubted whether any defence could be mounted along the weakened frontiers the next spring.

Not surprisingly, these conditions induced Louis XIV to place fresh momentum behind his peace offensive. Secret negotiations had, in fact, been proceeding since the previous Autumn. Grand Pensionary Heinsius and Colbert de Torçy, French Minister in charge of foreign affairs, had been privately exploring channels towards agreement through the agency of the go-between, Herman von Petkum. Although he was deliberately excluded from these tentative negotiations, Marlborough, too, was involved in putting out feelers of his own. Signing himself with the monogram 'oo', he exchanged a stream of secret letters with his nephew, the Duke of Berwick. Unfortunately for his reputation, Duke John could not refrain from reminding Versailles of a previously proffered *douceur*, two million gold livres no less, for his good offices in arranging an acceptable peace. 'You may be assured that I shall be wholeheartedly for peace', he wrote his kinsman on 30 October 1708, 'not doubting that I shall find the goodwill which was promised me two years ago by the Marquis d'Alègre. . . .'[2] Winston Churchill suggests that this transparent hint was employed to convince Louis XIV of Marlborough's genuine concern for a pacification, but this is possibly an over-charitable interpretation. In any case the negotiation proved abortive, for the French crown was not at that stage prepared to admit defeat, and the Whig terms of 'no peace without Spain' remained as uncompromising as ever. As for the *duumvirs*, neither Marlborough nor Godolphin could in any way mould grand strategic policy; both were very much on sufferance and subject to the whims of the Whig Junto, dominated by such magnates as Sunderland and Somers.

Given the growing coldness of the Queen, now subjected to almost ceaseless bullying by Sarah, there is small wonder that the Duke was increasingly concerned for his personal position. How could he hope to retain his authority as the *de facto* leader of the Grand Alliance if he was deprived of royal support in London? This anxiety provides one motive behind his request in March 1709 (to be thrice repeated) for appointment as Captain-General for life. His friends and advisers sought to dissuade him from this course on the grounds of lack of precedent and the danger of giving his foes a handle to use against him—the analogy of Cromwell's Major-Generals provided a ready-made and potent weapon—but, 'King John II' (as they later dubbed him) pressed ahead only to receive an evasive reply from Anne, still in mourning for Prince George (who had died in October 1708) and utterly outraged by the tactless Whig pressure for her rapid remarriage. Marlborough, the Queen now classed as an out-and-out Whig. This was both unjust and inaccurate, for the Duke from first to last despised 'party', although his present circumstances had placed him squarely in the hands of the Whigs. He needs must obey the Junto or resign from public life; the latter course had some attractions for him, increasingly weary and ailing as he was, but the incalculable effects such an action might have on the integrity of the Grand Alliance made him stay his hand. Moreover, by the spring of 1709 the prospects of peace seemed alluring. So Marlborough's devotion to the general cause remained predominant. Interested though he was in his own advancement in both status and wealth, he again demonstrated his ability to transcend personal gain when he regretfully turned down a second offer of the Viceroyalty of the Spanish Netherlands from Charles III.

Partly, we may surmise, to avoid too long a contact with English politics, Marlborough spent the months of January and February at the Hague keeping a close eye on his Allies. The price was a measure of the rest at either St. Albans or Woodstock of which he stood in considerable need. When at last he did recross the Channel, Prince Eugene assumed the watching brief. Both generals felt this degree of vigilance was requisite, for there were indications that the French might mount a despairing effort to recover Lille, once the weather improved. Marlborough's excellent spy service brought him regular, if incomplete, reports of what was under discussion behind the supposedly closed doors of Versailles.

In fact, however, Louis XIV was nearer to accepting the Allied terms, severe though these were, than ever before. Faced by what seemed irretrievable and total disaster if the war continued, in March the King despatched President Rouille to reopen talks with the Dutch States-General 'who set themselves up as the arbiters of Europe', instructing him to obtain definite peace proposals. Initially held in secret, these negotiations were later transferred into open session, but two months of talks produced nothing substantial. Louis' hope of securing the crown of the Two Sicilies for his grandson in compensation for the surrender of the Spanish throne proved over-sanguine, as the Allied governments and ruling factions steadily hardened their terms. It is also true that Anglo-Dutch relations were considerably strained when the earlier, secret part of Rouille's mission held at Moerdyk became known. Writing from London, Marlborough warned Heinsius that this '. . . has given here a very great allarum (sic).'[4] In similar fashion, the relations between the United Provinces and Austria were far from cordial, the bone of contention being, as usual, the future of the Spanish Netherlands; but the Schönbrunn also believed that Marlborough had been privy to the secret talks with Rouille, This, it appears, had not in fact been the case, although the Duke's agents, watching his friends as closely as his foes, provided him with a transcript of the negotiations within days of their being held. All this friction and duplicity was somewhat eased by the knowledge, however hardly earned, that Heinsius had resolutely refused to contemplate the conclusion of a separate peace.

So Rouille's mission foundered in its turn; but Louis was still determined to secure peace, cost what it might and must. Accordingly, Torçy in person was sent off to the Hague in April with full powers to both negotiate and bribe. Marlborough's little reward for services (hopefully) to be rendered was raised to a maximum of four million livres, the exact sum depending on the generosity of the terms he might help obtain. The Duke, however, was found to have returned to England. There, before returning to the plenary conference which was now imminent, he demanded that the Junto should appoint a joint-plenipotentiary from their own ranks to share responsibility for any decisions reached. Eventually the choice fell on the young Lord Townshend.

The opening sessions seemed promising enough. Torçy steadily gave ground, and was even brought to agree that Louis XIV, 'as far as in him lay', would concede the forfeiture of his grandson's whole inheritance without compensation. Then, without warning, Marlborough's helpful attitude changed. He had already turned down the privately proffered bribe. He referred at length, to quote Churchill's words, 'to his desire for peace, to his uprightness, to his conscience, to his honour, and frequently to God.'[5] He rejected, once more, the offer of personal reward, and proceeded, together with Townshend, to deliver an abrupt ultimatum. Great Britain would welcome the French King's offer of peace only if France would guarantee, by force of arms if necessary, the unconditional acceptance of the terms by Philip v.

This new, very extreme demand, was inspired by a combination of factors. First, it reflected a growing over-confidence amongst the Allies; they believed they could demand what they chose. Second, it revealed a mounting anxiety amongst the Whigs, following news of Galway's defeat at the hands of de Bay near the River Coa on the Portuguese frontier (7 May), and the earlier cession of the great fortress of Alicante to General d'Asefeld after the heroic but ultimately pointless siege undergone by Major-General John Richards and his stalwart garrison (19 April),[6] that Great Britain might be left ultimately alone with a lengthy and expensive war on its hands if Philip v chose to disregard his Grandfather's agreements—hence the new demands for humiliating military guarantees. Third, Marlborough's detractors, both contemporary and subsequent, have claimed that this slightly discreditable episode reveals that the Duke had a strong desire to keep the war going at any price in order to secure an extension of his increasingly shaky personal authority. Although much of the written evidence on this point is contradictory, it would seem that this is an unjust accusation.

Marlborough, an ageing man nearing his sixtieth birthday, far from enjoying the best of health, longing for the tranquility of retirement, desired peace as much as any man; at this juncture it would have set a seal on his life's work and ended his career on a note of great glory and achievement. Moreover, as we know from a letter subsequently written to Heinsius on 10 July as the summer negotiations approached deadlock, he felt considerable sympathy for Louis XIV. 'I might also own to you', he wrote, 'that if I were in the place of the King of France, I should venture the loss of my country much sooner than be obliged to join my troops for the forcing (of) my grandson.'[7] Once his word would have been law; but now he was little more, politically, than the puppet of his Whig masters, with scant initiative whether for good or ill. Clearly, he was acting under strict instructions—as the presence of Townshend proves. Nevertheless, it was this new issue that effectively doomed Europe to four more years strife.

At Torçy's request, the Allies produced (after much discussion) their definite peace terms in writing, the new contention being incorporated in Articles IV and XXXVII with a further demand that Versailles should signify acceptance by the 1 June. The skilful Torçy sensed that the new conditions, so unreasonably harsh, would enable his master to extricate himself from his previous undertakings, should circumstances and his wishes so permit, and even to denounce the negotiations, possibly gaining a considerable propaganda advantage thereby.

The discussions that ensued at Versailles were long, dramatic and heated. A well-placed spy reported to the Duke that the King had been prepared to accept even the latest humiliation until the Dauphin, in an impassioned speech, had swung the Council of State into a less compliant mood, and induced his Father to reject the terms, part and parcel. The new mood of resistance à l'outrance had another immediate effect in the replacement of the increasingly unpopular Chamillart on 10 June as Minister of War by Daniel Nathaniel Voisin. So the decision for continuing the struggle was taken, but none prophesied anything less than military disaster.

There is evidence that the Allies were not wholly prepared for the resumption of full-scale hostilities. There were three reasons for this. In the first place, the previous campaign had lasted an unprecedentally long time; secondly, the terrible winter had resulted in a critical shortage of forage; and thirdly, all but the most pessimistic soldiers and statesmen had confidently predicted that France would be forced to accept the peace terms. Marlborough had certainly instructed Cadogan to prepare a number of regiments for transfer back to England, and Heinsius had hoped that the intended 'Augmentation' of the forces which Marlborough had requested the previous autumn would not be necessary. Relations between the two Maritime Powers remained somewhat strained over this, and other issues. During the winter a storm of recrimination had blown up in London over the seeming unwillingness of the Dutch to produce their agreed one-third share of the 20,000 men which Marlborough had intimated the previous autumn would be needed, but in fact, the Dutch honoured their part of the bargain, and the British Parliament proved slower than the States-General in voting the necessary supply.[8]

By mid-June, the Allies had assembled 152 battalions and 245 squadrons in Flanders, and a further 42 and 87 respectively were still awaited. Truly there was no shortage of men as the minor powers poured in their contingents, eager to participate in the final defeat of France and thereafter share in the spoils of war, but shortages of rations and fodder dictated a further delay of several weeks duration. It was now patently clear that the war would have to be won in Flanders, for although in Spain the earlier Allied setbacks had given place to a phase of uneasy inaction, there was no question of regaining the initiative.

The French court did its utmost to profit from the short breathing-space. Advised by Torçy, Louis published the humiliating terms he had rejected, and this calculated act released a surprising surge of sympathetic loyalty throughout France. Following the royal example, many nobles and prelates sent in their plate to the Treasury. Unprecedentedly large numbers of the peasantry came forward to volunteer for the army, prompted by genuine patriotic enthusiasm as well as by the rigours of the preceding winter. Unfortunately, there was no easy solution to the dominant problem—that of supply. The Intendants emptied the provincial granaries of the last supplies intended for the civil population, but even so only a trickle of supplies reached the starving armies. Five armies were planned. The Army of Rousillon under Marshal de Noailles, added to the Franco-Spanish forces of de Besons and the Marquis de Bay, under the overall leadership of the Duc d'Orléans, were already in action in the Spanish Peninsula against Charles III and General Galway. Marshal Berwick was appointed to command the army in Dauphiné, opposing Count Daun and the Austro-Savoyard forces in Piedmont. On the Rhine, Marshal d'Harcourt, seconded by the Duke of Burgundy, confronted George, Elector of Hanover. Finally, in Flanders, 'the last army of France' had been ultimately entrusted (from 18 March) to Louis-Hector de Villars following the indisposition of Boufflers. This was obviously the critical command. 'All I have left is my confidence in God and in you, my outspoken friend', ran Louis XIV's message to his Gascon commander.[9]

To face the mounting strength of Marlborough and Eugene, Villars had a paper-strength of 150 battalions and 220 squadrons. 'I find the troops in a deplorable condition—without clothes, arms or bread', he reported to Versailles;[10] he deemed the Spanish and Bavarian troops totally demoralised and defeatist, the French but little better although there were some remaining traces of spirit detectable. For instance, in April the officers of the garrison of St. Venant reported their pressing needs as follows; 'We must ask you for bread as we need it to live. For the rest, we can do without coats and shirts. . . .'[11] Early plans to attempt a coup against Lille (of which Marlborough got wind as we have seen) or to surprise Courtrai had to be abandoned as wholly beyond the present capacity of the famished and under-equipped forces, despite the pressure of Versailles. Instead, Villars suggested that Ypres and Tournai should be strongly garrisoned and then left to their own devices, whilst his available troops set about constructing new lines between Douai and the Upper Lys (to run from La Bassée to Estaires, incorporating the Canal de Crettes and Béthune) behind which his army might in due course assemble. A rapid visit to Versailles secured the requisite permission and the promise of four million livres.

The Intendants, meantime, were making staunch efforts to find supplies. M. de Bernières, Intendant of Flanders, working through Sieur Raffey, his *entrepreneur-des-vivres*, collected barely 4,800 sacks of corn after the most rigorous searching. The Intendants of the Soissonais, Artois, Picardy and Normandy made similar efforts, giving the needs of the army complete priority over those of the local population, but the build-up was critically slow due to the general shortages and the inadequacies of the transportation arrangements.

Villars' forthright self-confidence, added to the arrival of a dribble of supplies, slowly began to put fresh heart into his men. It is true that he was greeted on inspections by ironical chants of 'give us this day our daily bread', and that he was driven almost to distraction by the logistical problems he faced—'. . . my anxieties over our supplies are killing me . . .', he confided to Voisin on 25 June— but little by little morale was rising. He deliberately delayed assembling the army for as long as possible, and sadly put aside all thoughts of a French offensive, but for the rest, adopted as bold a face as possible.

M. Sautai's summary of the character of Marshal Villars, soon destined to emerge as the saviour of France, is of great interest. 'This "child of fortune", as Saint-Simon has called him, possessed an unshakeable faith in his destiny. A braggart with a touch of showmanship about him, he was determined to make everybody appreciate his services and attribute everything to himself; aiming to raise himself to the first rank and firmly establish both his family and his fame, he never neglected any occasion to earn distinction, and on days of battle invariably performed more than his duty. His contemporaries reprimanded him for vanity and shallowness, and for displaying nothing but dash; but at the very least his constant military successes proved that he possessed genuine military qualities, and not simply good fortune. . . . He was one of those generals, rare at the time, who scorned defensive warfare, who did not like to surround himself with lines and entrenchments nor to bury himself in interminable siege warfare. He possessed an understanding of *la grande guerre*, in which the decisive solution could only be obtained through the destruction of the enemy army . . . with this combination of faults and qualities, divining the temper of the nation, as prompt to take hope as to become dismayed, Villars pleased the common soldier.'[13]

As the prospects of peace receded, Marlborough and Eugene prepared for action. On 12 June they joined the army (almost 100,000 men) near Ghent, finding it equipped with '104 cannon, 24 mortars, and 42 pontons (*sic*), with also all other necessaries of War conform', as Sgt. Millner of the 18th Foot recorded,[14] although fodder remained in short supply. Warned of the arrival of the 'Twin Princes' at the front, the next day Marshal Villars alerted his 80,000 strong forces.

The Allies moved forward towards Courtrai. Marlborough's first idea was to march the bulk of his army towards Ypres, covered by an inland feint, with the general intention of piercing the French defences near Dunkirk on the coast as a first move to an advance towards the River Somme in association with a descent from the sea against Picardy—in other words a return to the plan shelved in the previous July.* He fully anticipated that Villars would offer battle, having this on the authority '. . . of the same man that gave me the first notice of the resolutions taken last year for the attacking of Brussels, he being with me this morning and assures me that I may depend upon it. . . .'[15] In fact, Villars' repeated requests to leave to fight a major engagement were at this juncture still being abruptly dismissed by Versailles.

If this plan was to be implemented, the first problem was to pierce the Lines of La Bassée. The trusted Cadogan was sent out disguised as a peasant to conduct a full reconnaissance, but his report was discouraging; even though the lines were still incomplete, Villars' men had carried out their work well. A council-of-war was accordingly summoned. Marlborough spoke of the advantages of attacking Ypres, but the consensus of the Allied generals was in favour of a siege of Tournai on the inner flank. This meant, in effect, that the policy of mobile warfare was abandoned for one of relatively static sieges, as the Duke was well aware, but with his customary grace—reinforced perhaps by a growing weariness of body and spirit—Marlborough bowed to the majority.

Accordingly, the Allied siege train was summoned to Menin as a feint, as if presaging an attack on Ypres or Béthune, whilst the main army advanced boldly on the lines, bearing six days' rations, on 24 June. Villars, who was desperately concerned for Ypres, fell for the bait, and promptly withdrew 3,000 men from the garrison of Tournai whilst his army moved to La Gorgue. Refusing to be deflected from their main purpose, the Allies suddenly swung south and east. Covered by a force under Count Tilly, the Princes executed a rapid march in two columns towards Tournai. Aware—too late—that he had been fooled, Villars attempted to reinforce the recently-depleted garrison, but before he could achieve this, Tilly and the Dutch had invested Tournai on the 27th.

The French command, recovering from their surprise, were vastly relieved that the Allied thunder had been directed in this direction. Ypres was their acknowledged weak point; Tournai, although isolated and undermanned, was a very strong and reasonably-supplied fortress of modern design (particularly the

* See page 224.

citadel), whilst its Governor, the Marquis de Surville-Hautfois, was a highly-experienced officer and still commanded 7,000 men. A defence of two or three months was confidently predicted at Versailles, and that, given the relatively late opening of the campaign, might win France another year's respite. 'We count for much', enthused King Louis on 2 July, 'that by your wise dispositions and the precautions you have taken, all the vast project of the enemy has been reduced to the single enterprise of the siege of Tournai, and you could not at the beginning of the campaign render us more important service than to prevent its fall.'[16] Once again, however, Louis vetoed the forcing of a battle. Villars accordingly busied himself extending the lines from the Scarpe to the Scheldt, biding his time. He also mounted a number of nuisance raids sending d'Artagnan to take Warneton which was razed after the surrender of its 600 strong garrison. He also surveyed the area of the lines, selecting possible battle positions.

For the siege of Tournai, the roles of Lille were reversed, Marlborough commanding the trenches whilst Eugene covered the besiegers from a camp on the Courtrai road. On the night of 7/8 July, the Allies opened the trenches against three sectors of the defences, but the garrison fought back tenaciously, mounting frequent sorties. By the 14th, the Allies had 100 guns and 60 mortars in action, and concentrated their efforts against the Porte de Valenciennes. Three days passed, and the guns began to batter a breach in the main enceinte, but on the 18th the French exploded a large mine which destroyed one of the four main Allied batteries. The garrison followed up this success with a determined sortie on the 20th, which wrecked large areas of the foremost siege works. To date the siege had caused the Allies all of 3,200 casualties besides 600 deserters, and the commanders began to talk darkly of 'another Lille'.

Villars had at last extracted grudging permission to fight if either Valenciennes or Condé were threatened. He promptly moved thither, extending his lines again to include Denain, and maintaining his raiding policy as a measure to improve the morale of his army.

Back at the siege, Marlborough pressed ahead despite the setbacks. Thus between the 25th and 28th a series of localised assaults secured a foothold, then a ravelin, on the right bank of the Scheldt hard by the Gate of Valenciennes. The thundering guns set about pounding three breaches in the walls beyond, and on the 28th de Surville, faced by a general assault, beat the *chamade*, and on the 31st withdrew his 4,500 survivors into the citadel under cover of a temporary armistice, whilst his 300 wounded were evacuated to Douai. The Allies strove to persuade de Surville to observe a further armistice until 5 September, and to capitulate on that date if not relieved, but when the terms of the proposed convention were referred to Versailles, Louis XIV refused to entertain them unless the armistice was linked to a general cease-fire throughout Flanders. This transparent subterfuge fooled nobody, so hostilities were at once resumed.

There now began one of the hardest-fought and least pleasant sieges of

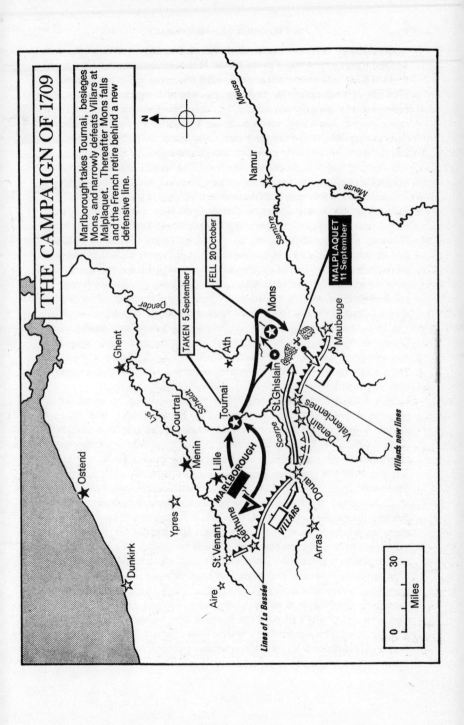

THE CAMPAIGN OF 1709

Marlborough takes Tournai, besieges Mons, and narrowly defeats Villars at Malplaquet. Thereafter Mons falls and the French retire behind a new defensive line.

N

TAKEN 5 September

FELL 20 October

MALPLAQUET
11 September

Meuse

Namur

Meuse

Sambre

Mons

Ath

Maubeuge

Dender

Ghent

St. Ghislain

Villars new lines

Tournai

Scheldt

Courtrai

Scarpe

Denain

Valenciennes

Menin

Lys

Lille

MARLBOROUGH

Ypres

Bethune

Douai

VILLARS

St. Venant

Ostend

Dunkirk

Aire

Arras

Lines of La Bassée

0   30

Miles

modern history. The five-bastioned citadel of Tournai, '. . . one of the best fortified places by Art that is in the World' in the opinion of brevet-Lt. Colonel Richard Kane, was no easy nut to crack, a fact reinforced by the presence within the walls of its designer. M. de Mesgrigny, one of the great Vauban's ablest colleagues. His speciality was mining, '. . . there being more works a great deal under ground than above, which made our approach very difficult; insomuch that we were obliged to carry great part of our works under ground, by which, and the springing (of) their mines, we lost great numbers of men.'[17]

Every yard had to be fought for. The two Allied 'attacks' made little progress against the combination of mines and sorties. Thomas Lediard quotes the newly-founded *Tatler* as reporting that 'the manner of fighting in this siege discovered a gallantry in our men unknown to former ages; their meeting with adverse parties under ground, where every step was taken with apprehensions of being blown up with mines below them, or crushed by the fall of earth above them, and all this acted in darkness, has something in it more terrible than was ever met with in any other part of a soldier's duty. However this was performed with great cheerfulness.'[18] The camp-follower, Mother Ross, also became personally involved in these perilous operations. 'Whenever my husband was ordered I always followed him, and he was sometimes of the party that went to search for and draw the enemy's mines; I was often engaged with their party underground, where our engagements were more terrible than in the field, being sometimes near-suffocated with the smoke or straw which the French fired to drive us out; and the fighting with pickaxes and spades, in my opinion, was more dangerous than with swords.'[19]

While this struggle continued, Villars persuaded Versailles to accept in principle his proposal to base the defence of the French frontier on the Scarpe-Scheldt lines, despite the exposure of his flanks, rather than to undertake a retreat to the River Lys as some advised. A number of Allied probes towards Marchiennes were successfully countered at this period. On other fronts, meantime, the war continued unevenly. In Spain there was little activity on either side. In Piedmont and on the Rhine Marlborough's hopes of a double attack to distract the French from Flanders foundered completely after the defeat of the Elector of Hanover at the action of Rummersheim (27 August). At sea, however, the Allied supremacy remained unchallenged.

Back at Tournai, the trenches crept towards the citadel. Mine and counter-mine exploded in devastating succession. To these abominable perils was soon added another—disease. 'The siege goes on slowly and in the dark underground . . .', wrote Blackader on 18 August, '. . . and a pestilence often treads upon the heels of famine so we are getting melancholy and alarming accounts of the plague. . . .'[20] On 5 August, 150 stormers were blown to oblivion. Three weeks later, a double-mine wrought fearful havoc, burying 300 men, but on the 31st, a grimly-determined Allied army stood prepared to storm the citadel.

Faced by this threat, de Surville agreed to treat, and after sundry fits and starts agreed to hand over the citadel 'and discover their mines' on 3 September. Two days later the Allies took formal possession, and the garrison was allowed to evacuate to France on parole, there to await exchange against the troops taken prisoner at Warneton. According to Millner, some 300 officers and 3,325 'centinels' (sic) were escorted to Condé. The siege had cost the French 41 officers and 1,668 men killed, besides a further 84 officers and 1,398 soldiers wounded. The Allies had lost all of 5,340 casualties during this costly 69-day operation.

After careful deliberation, the Allied commanders decided to march against the not very vital but strategically placed target of Mons, which offered the chance of a wider turning movement round the French lines and was closer at hand than St. Amand, the alternative objective considered. The overall aim was to maintain ceaseless pressure on the French, for once again peace negotiations were in progress (although these were doomed to founder once more over the 37th Article.)

Villars was favourably surprised by this unexpected decision, fearful as ever for Ypres. He waited warily near Denain, d'Artagnan on his left and Albergotti on the right, anticipating the need to fight a major engagement in the near future. 'The citadel of Tournai once gone', he had written to Voisin on 28 August, 'I do not hope long to avoid a battle.'[21] Nevertheless, the French King was appalled by the abrupt ending of the siege of Tournai—an unjust judgement on what had been an extremely pertinacious and active defence. As the Allies broke camp and marched on 3 September in a number of carefully protected columns towards Mons, Louis XIV sent urgent representations to Villars to the effect that 'should Mons follow on the fate of Tournai, our case is undone; you are by every means in your power to relieve the garrison; the cost is not to be considered; the salvation of France is at stake.'[22]

Such aid as was available was sent to the frontier. Despite his 65 years, Marshal Boufflers (recovered from his illness) hastened to join the army 'with his cuirass and weapons', willing to serve under the junior Villars in this hour of extreme national emergency. He brought with him the King's formal permission for a battle to be fought if deemed necessary.

The Allied advance was momentarily held up by the staunch defence of the small post of St. Ghislain on the River Haine, and the main army had to divert its march through Sirault. This delay notwithstanding, the investment of Mons was opened on 6 Sepetember—although not before a Regiment of Dragoons and four battalions of Spanish infantry had managed to join the garrison as Villars—intent on intervention if a favourable opportunity offered—moved to Quiévrain where he faced the Prince of Hesse-Cassel's cavalry, charged with covering the march of the main army.

The immediate theatre of operations destined to be the scene of the impending

battle of Malplaquet now requires description.* Four rivers effectively delimit
the overall area. Across the north runs the River Haine from Condé (where it
flows into the Scheldt) to the vicinity of Mons, newly invested. To the south-
east from Conde runs the Haine's tributary, the Hogneau, which finds its source
in the Wood of Lanières (and forms the western side of the rough quadrilateral).
To the south flows the Sambre, past Maubeuge; and to the east, from near
Mons, extends a network of streams running in a southerly direction, of which
the most significant is the Trouille. Bisecting the area thus enclosed there
stretched in 1709 four varying areas of dense woodland forming a rough arc,
the most northerly being the Bois de Dour (or Boussu), the next in line (and
largest) being the Bois de Sars (parts of which bear various local appelations)
including Taisnières and next the small Chaussée du Bois (or Wood of Tiry),
and lastly the far larger Bois de la Lanières which swept in a large arc to the
southwards, facing the Plain of Maubeuge at its limit. These woods extend over a
distance of some dozen miles, and are divided into their various parts by a number of gaps or *trouées*, those of Boussu (which divides the wood of that name
from the River Haine), Dour and Aulnois being the most significant in our
account.

Two major highways linked Valenciennes with Mons (via the Boussu Gap),
and with Maubeuge and Charleroi (via Bavai). Three lateral roads linked Quiev-
rain with Bavai, Mons with Malplaquet, and Mons with Maubeuge respectively.
To the west of the River Hogneau ran the lines recently extemporised by Villars'
army linking Condé with Maubeuge.

The ground near Malplaquet itself is undulating, being more even to the
west of the woodland belt than to its east, where in particular the Gap of
Aulnois was divided by numbers of gullies and small ravines, as the contemporary
map shows clearly. Numbers of villages, hamlets and large farmsteads dot the
plain, today as formerly. The Franco-Belgian frontier bisects the battlefield,
the Belgian customs-post standing almost exactly on the line of Villars' redoubts,
and the French Douane on the overlooking ridge some 600 yards up the road
where the massed French squadrons took up their position. Halfway between the
two stands the French memorial commemorating the battle. Today much of the
Wood of Lanière has been felled or thinned out, whilst that of Tiry has dis-
appeared save for a single line of trees.

As already mentioned, Villars was determined to intervene in the siege of
Mons. The best means to achieve this aim was to challenge a direct confrontation
with the covering armies. With this in mind he moved boldly over the Hogneau
late on the 7th, and placed his 80,000 men behind the Woods of Dour and Sars,
having Luxembourg's cavalry to the fore. From this position he could threaten
an approach to Mons along one of the Roman roads running through either the
Gap of Boussu or that of Aulnois, and use the intervening barrier of trees to

* See inset of map p. 255.

shield his movements. The Allies, who had crossed the Trouille south of Mons on the 6th, were soon alerted to his presence, and Eugene forthwith moved off to watch Boussu whilst Marlborough stood guard several miles away opposite the Gap of Aulnois, deliberately tempting Villars to fight. So matters stood through-out the 8th. That evening Villars decided in favour of the Aulnois Gap, and moved his army south-east to occupy it. On the 9th he advanced on Malplaquet in four columns, two of horse and two of foot. Marlborough was still dubious that Villars would accept his challenge, although a French general taken captive by cavalry frankly revealed that Villars had received direct royal orders to fight to save Mons. The Duke significantly took no steps to create lines of circumvalla-tion, which would have been normal if he had merely intended to cover the siege. Indeed, messengers were already spurring to St. Ghislain (newly taken) bearing orders of recall to General Withers and his corps, and also to Mons.

Some critics, particularly Feuquières, state that Villars should have attacked Marlborough early on the 9th whilst his army was still in considerable confusion, with many horses out at forage and his guns still on the road, and whilst Eugene was some miles distant with his wing of the army near Boussu.[23] It is true that such an attack might have gained the French a slight superiority of force, but Villars was no doubt aware of the danger of being taken in flank by the Imperial army had he adopted this course of action. He also realised that the Allies hoped to draw him beyond the sheltering woods on to the Plain of Mons, and accord-ingly refused to comply, but determined to make the most use of the natural advantages of the woodland areas, employing field defences to seal the gaps if time allowed.

On the other hand, it is also certain that Marlborough was correct not to force an immediate engagement. 'We had no guns come up', noted Lord Orkney,[24] many of his troops were still distant from the field, and Villars' final intention had only been divined at 9 a.m. that morning—and might still have proved a feint. As a result the afternoon passed with a desultory artillery bombardment (from 3.30 p.m.) whilst Villars' men delved like moles.

It is less easy to justify the Princes' decision to pass the whole of the 10th equally inactive. It is true that the Mons detachment of 1,900 men was still on the road, and that Withers' 19 battalions and 10 squadrons from Tournai and St. Ghislain had still to make an appearance, but Eugene had joined his colleague, the guns were in position, and the Allies clearly enjoyed considerable numerical advantage over the French, whose positions were still only half complete; but another day passed with only the exchange of artillery fire whilst detailed recon-naissances of the French position were carried out.

All that day and the succeeding night the French worked with intense energy. Under Villars' watchful and encouraging eye, the troops constructed five redans in the centre to dominate the open ground between the Wood of Sars and the approaches to the Farm of Blairon. To the right of these, Boufflers dug a line of continuous entrenchments along the line of a stream almost to the Wood of Tiry; thereafter, the line swept abruptly back, creating a salient. In a convenient re-entrant a concealed battery of 20 cannon was carefully sited— destined to wreak terrible havoc on the Dutch on the morrow—and then further entrenchments swept up the hill to the skirts of the Wood of Lanières, with extensions into the trees where *abattis* were constructed. Meanwhile, on the further western flank, General Albergotti was creating more positions along the forward edge of the Wood of Sars in such a way as to create an enfilading field of fire towards the Wood of Tiry, whilst other troops constructed obstacles amongst the trees to guard against an Allied incursion from the north. General Goësbriand prepared further trenches on the extreme left facing the near-side of the Wood and towards the hamlet of Chaussée du Bois and the Farm of La Folie. Late in the day an attempt was made to add a further support line some 300 yards to the rear of these positions, but the engineers had barely time to trace the outline of these fortifications and they were never constructed.

Villars had at his disposal 121 understrength battalions (averaging perhaps 300 men apiece), 260 squadrons and 80 cannon. He entrusted 63 battalions to Marshall Boufflers, designated commander of the right wing; 46 of these under Generals d'Artagnan and de Guiche were placed adjoining and within Lanières Wood, manning the prepared defences, supported by a battery of six guns in their centre and by the 20-gun concealed battery, already mentioned, on their left, which was placed so as to enfilade the ground to the front of the defences. Beyond this battery, de Guiche marched 18 battalions into the trenches facing Blairon Farm including the Swiss and the *Gardes Françaises*. The centre and left wing held a total of 55 battalions initially. Thirteen of these (including the Irish and Bavarian brigades) manned the five redoubts, with four more in close support. Three groups of guns, totalling almost 60 cannon, were deployed to the fore and on the flanks of the redoubts. Next, in the 'angle' of the Wood of Sars, the experienced Albergotti took command of 21 battalions amongst the trees and entrenchments overlooking the centre, with a battery of five guns in the centre. Finally, in the support line, General Goësbriand (who exercised, under Villars, overall command on the left) deployed the 17 battalions of the extreme left wing and reserve. To the immediate rear of the entire line, along a low but overlooking ridge on which stood the village of Malplaquet, stretched the horse-lines of General de la Vallière's horse and dragoons, together with the élite *Gendarmerie* and *Maison du Roi* under M. de Montesson. The Chevalier de Luxembourg was ordered to employ the reserve cavalry to watch the passages through the Bois de Longueville towards Maubeuge to the rear of the French right, in case the Allies tried to pass a force round the flank. No similar measures were taken to guard the extreme left, however. Finally, Villars established his headquarters close to Malplaquet.

Taken as an entity this comprised an extremely strong position. The centre

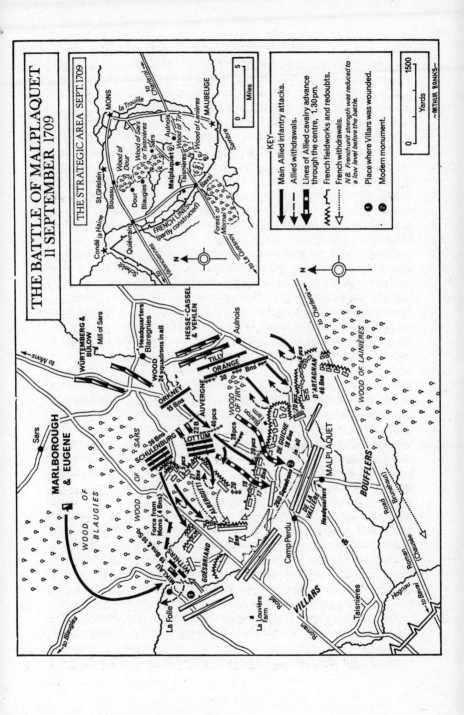

THE BATTLE OF MALPLAQUET
11 SEPTEMBER 1709

THE STRATEGIC AREA SEPT. 1709

MONS · la Trouille · to Charleroi

Boussu · Wood of Sars · Aulnois · Wood of Lanières · MAUBEUGE

St.Ghislain · Wood of Dour · Malplaquet · Wood of Sars or Taisnières · Sars

Condé · la Haine · Dour · Blaugies · Taisnières · Wood of Lanières

Quiévrain · FRENCH LINES (partly constructed) · Bavai · Sambre

Schaldt · Valenciennes · Forest of Mormal · to Le Quesnoy

N

0 — 5 Miles

KEY

Main Allied infantry attacks.

Allied withdrawals.

Lines of Allied cavalry advance through the centre, 1.30pm.

French fieldworks and redoubts.

French withdrawals.
N.B. French unit strength was reduced to a low level before the battle.

① Place where Villars was wounded.

② Modern monument.

0 — 1500 Yards

~ARTHUR BANKS~

N

---

to Mons

WÜRTEMBERG & BÜLOW · Mill of Sars

Sars · Headquarters Blaregnies

WOOD OF SARS · WOOD · HESSE-CASSEL & VEHLEN · Aulnois

MARLBOROUGH & EUGENE

WOOD OF BLAUGIES

ORKNEY 15 Bns · AUVERGNE · TILLY · ORANGE 30 Bns · to Charleroi

SCHULENBURG 36 Bns · LOTTUM 22 B · 40 pcs · 28 pcs · WOOD OF TIRY · Blairon · Bleron · D'ARTAGNAN 46 Bns · WOOD OF LANIÈRES

ALBERGOTTI 11 Bns · 21 · 20 · 19 · DE GUICHE 18 Bns · MALPLAQUET · BOUFFLERS

Force from Mons (4 Bns) · 17 · 260 Squadrons in all · DE LA VALLIÈRE · Headquarters · Road (Chaussée) Brunehal

GOESBRIAND · WITHERS · 17 Bns · Camp Perdu

MILLU 18 Bns & 10 Sqs · La Folie · VILLARS · Roman Road · Taisnières · Hognau · to Bavai

La Louvière Farm

N

was a veritable death-trap, against the approaches to which fire could be brought from three sides. It is possible that Villars and his staff, in designing their position, anticipated that this sector must attract the main enemy attack. It formed the only 'open' approach, and perhaps Marlborough's *penchant* for central attacks (as at Blenheim and Ramillies) had become appreciated. After channelling the Allied attack into the desired area, cannon and musketry fire would wreak a havoc which would be completed by the attack of the massed French cavalry, advancing through the gaps deliberately left between the redoubts, to engage the disordered Allied horse and foot on the fire-swept plain beyond. Perhaps too much faith was placed on the impassability of the defended woodland on each flank, but for the rest it was a soundly-based defensive plan, given the need to fight at all, and given the numerical disparity between the two combatants.

Following their reconnaissance, Marlborough and Eugene must have been aware of the problems they faced—although the concealed battery was not identified. Their plan was basically simple—and indeed a repetition of the scheme employed at Blenheim in 1704. Heavy attacks would be mounted against the flanks of the enemy line to induce Villars to weaken his centre which the Allies would then occupy before launching the *coup de grâce* through the centre with the massed cavalry. As always, much emphasis was laid on combined tactical support; horse, foot and guns were to work as a team on each sector according to the tactical possibilities and perils of each area. The disposition of forces for the implementation of this plan, however, underwent considerable adjustment before the battle opened. By the original scheme it appears (once again we have to work on incomplete evidence) that the disposition of the 110,000 men and 100 cannon* was as follows; on the Allied right, which was entrusted to Eugene's overall supervision, General Schulenburg was to lead 40 Allied battalions and some 20 guns into the main part of the Wood of Sars, supported by the contingent from Mons, whilst General Lottum on the inner flank (or right centre) led 22 battalions, including Argyle's British battalions, sustained by the fire of 40 massed guns and supported by the close presence of Auvergne's 30 Dutch squadrons, assaulted the 'angle' held by Albergotti. The centre—namely 15 battalions of troops, including 11 British formations—was entrusted to Lord Orkney, with the massed reserve strength of the Allied cavalry, some 179 squadrons in all, behind him. The left wing, as *originally* envisaged, would have comprised 30 Dutch battalions (including their famous Guards and the Scottish brigade in the Dutch army) *and* the 19 battalions of General Withers fresh from Tournai, supported by some 18 guns and the Prince of Hesse-Cassel's 21 squadrons, together with (presumably) the 10 squadrons of General Miklau who was accompanying Withers. The overall command of the left was entrusted

* The British contingent comprised 14 squadrons, 20 battalions and 40 guns, or some 15,000 men (Fortescue I. p. 527).

to the youthful Prince of Orange, seconded by Generals Tilly and Oxenstiern—and Withers. This was a balanced line of battle of standard type.

Circumstances, however, caused several important alterations to this order of battle. Mainly due to the late arrival of the forces from Tournai, who came up very weary on the afternoon of the 10th, a new element was built into the plan and dispositions which was to have important repercussions on the morrow. Instead of making Withers march three more miles through the main Allied camp (with the consequent confusion this might have caused) to take up his position with Orange on the further (left) flank, Marlborough decided to place the Tournai force on the *extreme right* of the Allied line—that is to say beyond the detachment from Mons originally forming Schulenburg's right flank. Furthermore, a special role was envisaged for Withers. The Duke hoped that this increase of strength, concealed from the French by the great Wood of Sars, would enable the Allied right to extend *beyond* the extremity of the French left; thus, after traversing the forest (hard though this would indubitably be), Withers and his men would suddenly debouch against the French left after outflanking it at a critical moment of the battle, and, hopefully, roll it up from west to east.

The final form of the plan, therefore, emerged as follows. Schulenburg and Lottum (under Eugene's general supervision) would open the attack, preceded by a heavy bombardment, and followed half an hour later by the Prince of Orange advancing against the Lanières' sector. These initial onslaughts against both French wings, would, it was hoped, induce Villars to weaken his centre to meet the threat to his wings as the Allies—particularly on the Sars sector—penetrated the woodland and threatened to debouch beyond. Orkney would then attack and take the central redoubts, prior to the advance of the massed Allied cavalry and the revelation of Withers's outflanking movement on the French extreme left. Caught between two fires, the Princes hopefully prophesied the disintegration of the last French army capable of obstructing their advance on Paris. The exact role foreseen for the Prince of Orange, with his greatly reduced strength, will be discussed later, but it may be that he failed to understand—or it was not made clear to him—that the attack on the Allied left must needs be restricted, in the final battle plan, to a subsidiary, containing role. 'Orders to attack the enemy tomorrow in the name of God', wrote Prince Eugene. 'My Lord Duke of Marlborough's armies, the Imperial troops and the corps from Tournai,* which is to make a special attack, are to be let loose upon the enemy. All attacks to begin at daybreak; the signal will be a salvo from the entire British artillery which will be taken up by the Dutch cannon.'[25]

Both armies passed the night heavy with thought and apprehension. Whatever the morrow would bring, it was not likely to be either quick or easy.

* The special emphasis on Withers' role in Eugene's letter emphasises its unusual nature; flank attacks of this type were not often encountered in the early eighteenth century. See p. 164.

The events that took place between 8 a.m. and 3 p.m. on 11 Sepetember 1709 were to shock the conscience of early eighteenth-century society. 'It was the most desperate and bloody attack and battle that had been fought in the memory of men ...',[26] recalled Richard Kane, in temporary command of the Royal Regiment of Foot of Ireland on that gory day.

The day dawned—as before both Blenheim and Ramillies—obscured by a dense mist, which hindered the initial Allied deployment. By 7.30 a.m., however, Colonel John Armstrong, commanding the British artillery, had his guns in position. Soon after the cannon opened fire, and shortly after eight the mist began to lift. About half-an-hour later, Marlborough, who had ridden forward from his headquarters at Blaregnies to a position slightly in rear of the 40-gun battery, ordered the firing of the arranged signal salvo.

Immediately the 83 battalions of the Allied right wing began to cross the 800 yards separating them from the ominously silent trees of the Wood of Sars. A single shot rang out, followed by a volley, and then all hell was let loose as Schulenburg's 40 battalions, three lines deep, stormed forward against the outlying French parapets. On his right, General Withers began his unopposed penetration in a double line into the depths of the forest, whilst his ten squadrons made an even wider detour on the outer flank, seeking a reasonable passage. On Schulenburg's left, General Lottum's 22 battalions, in triple line, marched forward over the ravine-dominated plain, skirting the wood beyond. Schulenburg was soon in trouble. His first line was checked by the intense fire of the brigades of Brittany and Provence, formed four ranks deep and firing by alternating lines at a range of merely 50 paces. Officer casualties were particularly severe—some Imperialist units being reduced at the very outset to merely two or three. Lottum fared little better. Brigadier-General de la Colonie, commanding the Bavarians in the central redoubts, watched whilst the French artillery commander, General St. Hilaire, rushed 14 guns to the front, whose fire 'carried off whole ranks at a time.' After advancing to within 500 yards of the redans, '... the column changed its direction a quarter right and threw itself precipitately into the wood on our left.'[27] A murderous hand-to-hand struggle began amongst the *abattis* prepared by Albergotti the previous day, and the terrible struggle for a triangular piece of woodland, barely 600 yards a side, forming the first major Allied objective of the day, had begun.

Thirty minutes after the opening of the battle on the right, the Prince of Orange led up his 30 Dutch and Scottish battalions to attack d'Artagnan's defences fringing the Wood of Lanières, part passing to the west of the Wood of Tiry. A terrible greeting awaited the main Dutch attack. When they had reached 100 paces from the parapets, the 20-gun battery suddenly leapt into thunderous action, hurling crippling salvoes of enfilading shot through the Dutch lines with remorseless accuracy and regularity. The five columns staggered, reformed, closed their ranks, and advanced again through the maelstrom of converging fire. Men fell in hundreds, General Oxenstiern being one of the first to be killed. Within 30 minutes of going into action, it is estimated that the Dutch sustained no less than 5,000 casualties, but on they came, time after time, in a suicidal demonstration of the greatest valour and intrepidity, led by their young Prince who curtly rejected all the pleas of his anxious staff that he should take up a less exposed position. The famous Blue Guards were decimated, and a second wave of attack fared no better than the first as Generals Spaar and Hamilton were shot down. At last flesh and blood could do no more; outnumbered by two to one on the sector, the Dutch attack, still in good order, rolled back, abandoning the hard-won Farm of Blairon on their right.

With a grim cheer, the veteran regiments of Navarre and Picardy sallied forth from their positions and formed up for a bayonet charge; but the watchful Hesse-Cassel spurred forward at the head of his 21 squadrons, and this threat caused the French to change their minds. Simultaneously, General Rantzau sent forward two of his four Hanovarian battalions from Marlborough's reserve to the south-western corner of the Wood of Tiry, where their battalion fire from the flank helped stabilise the situation, although at considerable cost. French commentators criticise Boufflers for not launching an all-out forward movement at this critical juncture, believing that this could have clinched the day on the Allied left, but there was no time to gain Villars' approval for such a move and Boufflers was never noted for brilliant extemporisations or daring initiatives, so the opportunity passed.

This notwithstanding, by 10 o'clock both Marlborough's initial attacks were repulsed or in dire trouble; but the day had hardly begun. Schulenburg and Lottum called for renewed efforts. 'The battalions which first attacked were entirely defeated', recorded Sgt. Millner, 'but being sustained by fresh troops the enemy were everywhere forced out of their entrenchments and pursued into the wood, through it, and from it into a plain.'[28] This masterly compression of several hours fighting into a simple sentence should not leave the reader with an impression of a one-sided struggle. By 10.30 a.m., for example, Lottum's renewed attack had been brought to a standstill, until he committed the Duke of Argyle's brigade (commanded by Sir Richard Temple) followed by two battalions (the Second Guards and one of the Royal Scots) sent over by Lord Orkney. As these fresh formations plunged into the wood on Lottum's left, they presented a tempting target for the enemy in the redoubts. General Chémerault prepared 12 battalions (including the Brigade of Champagne) for a counter-attack, but this did not go unnoticed by Marlborough, who promptly led up Auvergne's 30 Dutch squadrons to meet the threat. Villars, in turn, noticed this move, and promptly countermanded the proposed attack. Besides, he had a more pressing role for these formations. 'I saw that our infantry was losing ground in the wood (to Schulenburg's attack) and I posted these 12 battalions to receive them when they came out of it.'[29]

This was probably the climacteric moment of the battle, when the tide began to turn in the Allied favour. Villars' transfer of these 12 battalions implied two important developments; first, the abandonment by the French of the struggle to hold the triangle; second, the start of the denuding of the French centre to reinforce the left wing. At last, after three hours of fighting, Marlborough was beginning to assert his plan, and his opponent was being induced to comply with his foe's overall intentions.

Thus, by about 11 o'clock, Lottum at last found himself master of the stricken extremity of the Wood of Sars. It had required 30,000 troops to win this small area of woodland, and no less than 7,000 killed and wounded of all nations carpeted the ground. Marlborough, however, was not available to congratulate his subordinate on this costly success, for an even more stricken sector of the Allied line demanded his immediate attention. Summoned by an aide, the Duke was hastening over, accompanied by Prince Eugene, to visit the Prince of Orange. What he found there horrified him, but he arrived in time to countermand a third assault which the hot-headed Prince was about to unleash against Boufflers' positions.

Marlborough has been much criticised for not intervening to halt the suicidal Dutch attack at an earlier juncture. Other commentators—including C. T. Atkinson and Taylor—have accused the Prince of Orange of disobeying orders in a fit of pique, or simply of misunderstanding his instructions; a modern view suggests that he may have simply lost his bearings, and attacked the wrong sector—no difficult thing in the din and smoke of battle.[30] The truth will not be known, but Marlborough never suggested the least form of misconduct. 'Our left was the Dutch troops only, who beheaved (*sic*) themselves extremely well, but could not force the enemy retrenchment, so that their effort has suffered more than any other nation.'[31]

Of course, it was rarely Marlborough's habit to inform key subordinates that their operations were only secondary in importance; neither Cutts at Blenheim nor Orkney at Ramillies* were aware of their basically containing roles until the middle of the respective actions. The Duke preferred to leave all his options open for as long as practicable, and possibly felt that secondary attacks would lack credibility if his intentions were too fully appreciated. It is possible that Orange felt put out by the abrupt pre-battle reduction of his command to half its original size, and reacted by 'taking the bull by the horns' in an unrealistic if tremendously gallant fashion, attempting to improve on his orders by 'a quick breakthrough in that part of the French line which was closest at hand' (Bowen) instead of undertaking a more limited wood-clearing operation in the Bois de Lanières. If so, we may also conjecture that for once Marlborough's usually superb system of battlefield intelligence broke down, for it appears that he was not informed of the dire events on the Dutch sector until

* See pp. 145–6 and pp. 175–6 above.

shortly before 11 a.m., and in consequence could only reach Orange's head-quarters in time to forbid the third assault, rather than the second. This is pure conjecture, but the fact that Marlborough unquestioningly shouldered the responsibility for Orange's attacks should at least dispose of allegations of misconduct or blatant error on the part of the Prince of Orange.

By 11.15 a.m. the Duke was back at his headquarters in the centre, his attention newly focused on the fortunes of his right wing, now that the left had been necessarilly restricted to a containing role against Boufflers. Marshal Villars was also increasingly anxious about developments in the Wood of Sars. Although Withers needed all of two hours to traverse the forest, and his horse still further time, the French commander was far from satisfied. His troops were abandoning the Wood of Sars too rapidly, but where could he find troops to form a second line? His first thought was to appeal for aid from Boufflers' wing, but the brave Marshal was not prepared to weaken his defences, so impressed had he been by the fury of Orange's two onslaughts. Villars' sole recourse, therefore, was to weaken still further his centre, where everything remained quiet apart from the exchange of artillery fire. First he summoned the 'Wild Geese' from the right-hand sector of the redoubts, but 'by the time the Irish brigade had got well into the wood it was considered to be barely sufficient as a reinforcement by itself, and an order came to us to follow it', testified de la Colonie of the Bavarian brigade, 'although there was no one else to fill our place which would be left open to the enemy.'[32] His attempt to query the orders received a brusque rebuff, so that by 11.45 a.m. the French centre was almost wholly empty of troops as Villars set about massing some 50 battalions on his left wing preparatory to meeting the Allies as they emerged from the Wood of Sars with a telling counter-attack. Thus, as in two of Marlborough's earlier great battles, the foe was induced to weaken his centre prior to the launching of the critical attack. Villars, for all his skill and cunning, was being forced to comply with his greater opponent's will.

The Duke, accompanied by Eugene and his staff, were now summoned to visit Schulenburg. 'The wood being forced', that commander recalled, 'I found myself on the other side towards the enemy's lines, where I managed to bring up by a kind of miracle some big cannon which I had with me,* by which I did not fail to do great harm to the line of French cavalry.'[33] The centre of the French horse, exposed on a ridge beyond their foot and guns, soon drew back a short distance to better cover, whereupon the Imperialist artillery transferred its fire to the French entrenchments on this sector, taking several in enfilade. This fire indubitably assisted Orkney's impending attack on the central redoubts.

As the commanders surveyed the scene from the forward skirt of the wood, Prince Eugene was grazed by a musket-ball behind the ear, but typically refused to seek medical attention. Meantime, to revert from the general to the particular,

* In fact seven 12-pounders.

other stirring events were taking place amongst the trees and glades which
deserve attention. The celebrated encounter between the Royal Regiment of
Foot of Ireland with its opposite number in the French service has already
been described in an earlier chapter.* It will be recalled that this brief engagement ended decidedly in favour of the 18th Foot, demonstrating the superiority
of Allied platoon fire tactics. However, many subsequent historians have found
difficulty in deciding how and where this encounter, described so vividly (but at
secondhand) by Captain Robert Parker, could have taken place. It is strange that
neither Kane nor Millner, both of whom were present with the regiment,
mentioned the encounter, whilst Robert Parker, serving on a training mission in
Ireland gives it in such detail.[34] Perhaps the former two did not deem one skirmish amongst many that day worthy of attention, whilst the last-named had a
special interest in infantry tactics, and was therefore induced to cite the incident
as a case-study. This does not, however, explain the main difficulty the encounter
presents. The Irish 'Wild Geese' in the French service comprised five battalions
commanded by Colonels Lee, O'Brien, Dorington, O'Donnell and Galway;
they were sent into the Wood not far west of the 'triangle', and it is practically
certain they remained there, for General St. Hilaire records that at the moment
when Villars was wounded (see below) only the Irish brigade 'stood firm upon the
right of the French left wing.'[35]

Now, the 18th Foot, as all its regimental historians confirm, was part of
Withers' force marched up from Tournai, which would seem to place the
battalions on the extreme Allied right, and this would appear to be confirmed by
Parker, who records that 'the regiment happened to be the last of the regiments
that had been left at Tournai . . . and therefore could not come up until all the
lines were formed and closed so that there was no place for us to fall into. We
were ordered therefore to form up by ourselves on the right of the whole army,
opposite to the skirt of the wood of Sars.' If this was the case how could the two
Royal Regiments of Foot of Ireland have ever come into contact with one
another? Sir Winston Churchill surmises that the 18th Foot got lost in the forest
and wandered towards the sound of severe firing, presumably across the rear
areas of the rest of Withers' and Schulenburg's sectors, and happened upon its
opposite number in the French army. This does not seem wholly convincing.
Moreover, it disregards the testimony of Lieutenant-General Wackerbath commanding Schulenburg's front-line, that he positively identified Withers' 19
battalions fighting on his *left*, 'so that I became the right of the whole army.'[36]
This has, correctly in the main, been discounted as an error, even though Sautai
repeats it.

However, a new interpretation of the evidence may be cautiously entertained;
it is possible that Wackerbath had some grounds for his assumption after all. For
it is strange that Churchill and all other commentators seem to have ignored

* See pp. 92–3 fn above.

the evidence of Cpl. Matthew Bishop, serving with the 8th of Foot (later the King's Regiment). This witness, who fought in the desperate and gory struggle for the 'triangle' and is therefore unlikely to have been mistaken in the matter, is clear that Argyle's brigade which Sir Richard Temple led against the notorious 'triangle' in support of Lottum, comprised the 8th, 18th, 21st and 24th Foot,[37] and was placed on the 'extreme right' of the main *British* front line (drawn up in the centre under the command of Lord Orkney) which would indeed have placed the 18th 'opposite to the skirt of the Wood of Sars'. So, *pace* Sir Winston Churchill and Captain Parker *inter alia*, it would seem that part of Withers' command was in fact attached to Lottum's Prussians, and that the 18th Foot fought with it near the 'triangle' where it would almost certainly have encountered the Irish in the French service. This also helps explain Wackerbath's misconception; he probably identified the 18th Foot (which he knew belonged to Withers' command) on his left, and made the assumption that the whole, and not merely a part, of that general's command had somehow blundered through the woods to appear on his left. The evidence for this new interpretation is not conclusive, but it is borne out in part by Fortescue's list of British regiments serving at Malplaquet, which clearly brigades the 18th Foot (Royal Irish) with the 8th, 21st and 24th,[38] for the campaign of 1709. Perhaps we are closer, therefore to resolving one minor problem of military history relating to this vast and complex battle.

As Marlborough studied the scene presented by the French left, Schulenburg, aware of the weakness of the French centre, presumed to prompt his commander. 'Thus My Lord, the French having abandoned their entrenchments, I beseech you to have several battalions occupy them, along the reverse of course, as soon as possible.'[39] The Duke received this 'hint' with his usual equanimity, but did not delay sending off an urgent message to Lord Orkney, and warning orders to Hesse-Cassel and Auvergne to prepare their cavalry. 'It was about one o'clock that my 13 battalions got to the entrenchments, which we got very easily for as we advanced they quitted them and inclined to their right. We found nothing to oppose us. Not that I pretend to attribute any glory to myself, yet I verily believe that these 13 battalions gained us the day, and that without firing a shot almost.'[40] Thus wrote Lord Orkney of his crucial occupation of the central redoubts; this key operation had proved something of an anti-climax. The nearby French Guards made a single, half-hearted attempt to counter-attack, but then reprehensibly abandoned their own positions on Boufflers' left before a bold advance by a few intrepid Dutch battalions. The entire centre of the French army's first line thus passed into Allied hands, and the massed cavalry in their second line was also suffering heavy losses from direct and ricochet cannon fire. At once, Auvergne and Hesse-Cassel began to lead their squadrons forward to exploit Orkney's cheaply-won success.

At this juncture, two dramatic events took place towards the extreme French left. Marshal Villars was supervising the preparations for a 50-battalion counter-attack against the Wood of Sars, when he was approached by an anxious St. Hilaire, who reported the loss of the redoubts. Hardly had Villars heard the news than he was struck on the left knee by a musket ball. Despite this agonising wound, he gamely strove to retain command, but soon fainted, and was at once borne from the field in a sedan-chair. Almost simultaneously, General Chémerault dropped dead, and Albergotti fell seriously wounded. This loss of the commander-in-chief and two more senior generals at almost a single stroke had a paralysing effect on the French left, and the signal to advance was never given. The command on the left passed to General Puységur, but he was too bemused by his new responsibilities to order the attack which might have retrieved much of the fortunes of the day, for the Allied right wing was understandably weary.

That French morale was still of a high order is illustrated by the second incident—namely the rout of General Miklau's ten squadrons. This force, it will be remembered, had slowly filtered its way through the Wood of Sars on the extreme Allied right, as part of Marlborough's concept of mounting an out-flanking attack on the French battle-line at a critical moment. Miklau, after lengthy detours, had achieved the first part of his mission, but unfortunately when his squadrons appeared near the farm of La Folie and began to form into line, there were no infantry battalions of Withers' command within close supporting distance. For once Allied co-ordination had gone awry. M. de Rozel hastened to exploit this tactical error, and fell on Miklau's flank at the head of ten squadrons of carabiniers. Six Allied squadrons were cut to pieces, and the remainder fled into the woodland. This minor feat of arms cheered the French left, and made the Allied commanders on the right extremely chary about exploiting too far from the Wood of Sars. If the incident did little to help the French win the battle, at least it prepared the way for the successful retreat of their left wing—an idea that was already much to the fore in Puységur's mind.

Back in the centre, at 1.30 p.m., the first Allied squadrons began to filter between the redoubts held by Orkney, and to form up in the plain beyond, facing Malplaquet. Behind them, the dense masses of Allied cavalry—commanded by Generals Wood, Vehlen, von Bülow and the Prince of Württemberg, with Marlborough and Eugene themselves close at hand, advanced in column. Perhaps 30,000 horsemen were on the move.

This development evoked an immediate and spirited response from Boufflers. Newly informed that he was in supreme command, he placed himself at the head of the *Maison du Roi* and launched a telling attack against the deploying Auvergne. 'Before we got 30 squadrons out', recalled Orkney, 'they came down and attacked—and (there) was such a petty that I never really saw the like. Eventually we broke through them, particularly four squadrons of English; Jemmy Campbell at the head of the grey dragoons (*sic*) behaved like an angel, broke through both their lines. However, their attacks were sometimes so fierce

I really believe, had not ye foot been there, that the enemy would have driven our horse from the field.' Ten cannon dragged up from the newly-masked great battery also played a part in the eventual repulse of Boufflers—once again proving the importance of properly co-ordinated action by horse, foot and guns. The Scots Greys under Lt.-Col. Sir James Campbell, leading the van of Wood's supporting British cavalry, did much to turn the tables on the *Maison du Roi*, and de la Colonie also bore testimony to the valour of what he called 'the Scottish Guards of the Queen of England', but Boufflers, sword in hand, drove the Allies back no less than six times, only to be repulsed time after time by the deadly volleys of Orkney's men holding the redoubts.

In the end, however, numbers and freshness began to tell. Marlborough and Eugene led up more and more horsemen and fed them into the herculean cavalry struggle, so that after half an hour Boufflers was forced back onto the plain around Malplaquet, and the Allied horse had gained room to complete its deployment. For a further hour the cavalry battle raged on in the centre, without a clear decision being reached either way.

The fate of the day had, however, been decided on the flanks. Puységur, under renewed pressure from Eugene's battalions, ordered the French left to break contact and retire towards Quiévrain. On the right, a third advance by the Dutch carried them over three lines of entrenchments—at heavy cost—before their momentum ran out. This assault induced d'Artagnan to order a retreat in his turn, this time towards Bavai and Maubeuge. The embattled Boufflers could but comply with this general movement by his compatriots, and so he, too, ordered his wearying squadrons to fall back beyond the Hogneau river. The equally exhausted Allied cavalry followed-up this withdrawal to the banks of the stream causing fairly heavy casualties to the French, but beyond this limit they could not pass thanks to the intrepidity of Luxembourg and the French cavalry reserve, who fought to cover the general retreat, and only finally relinquished control over the Hogneau's left bank at midnight.

The main part of this dire struggle had come to an end shortly after 3 p.m. The Allies were too exhausted to pursue immediately, so camped on the battlefield. Marlborough rode back to his headquarters to write brief notes to Sarah, the Queen, Heinsius and the King of Prussia, which stressed his weariness, the rigours of 'a very bloody battle', and his conviction that 'it is now in our power to have what peace we please, and I may be pretty well assured of never being in another battle.'[41] Only the second wish would be fulfilled.

The cost of this technical victory in terms of human life was horrific. As Marlborough himself admitted, the battle '. . . has been more opinionatred (*sic*) than I have seen, so that it has been very bloody on both sides.'[42] Clear estimates of casualties are difficult to assess, but the Allies appear to have lost no less than 25,000 killed and wounded, and only 500 'hale' soldiers were taken prisoner. This small number of captives, together with the successful evacuation of perhaps 65 cannon, gives substance to the French claim to have conducted a highly successful retreat. Thus, if the French had been forced to concede the field, they shared in large measure the honours of the day, and were far from being either demoralised or rendered impotent by the massively superior Allied army. From his bed of pain at Le Quesnoy, Marshal Villars wrote to the King that 'the officers of all ranks and all Your Majesty's troops have done marvels, although your army is in retreat, it will become clear that it has lost less men than the enemy,'[43] something of an understatement for once from this flamboyant character given to extravagant claims. Marlborough made no attempt to conceal his admiration for the French performance. 'The French have defended themselves better in this action than in any battle I have seen', he wrote to Heinsius.[44] Yet his plan had been generally good, and his men had fought superbly well. Perhaps his error lay in somewhat underestimating his opponent prior to the battle, and delaying its opening until the 11th, although in the event he had certainly not controlled more troops than he needed to reap success. Perhaps, too, there were paradoxically too many men to permit the full exercise of his generally superb battle control—as the case of Orange might seem to demonstrate.

Louis XIV, once he had recovered from the initial shock of the news from the frontier, hastened to distribute largesse. Villars was named a Peer of France; Boufflers confirmed in command of the army; d'Artagnan appointed a Marshal; half a million livres were to be distributed amongst the troops. Such criticisms as were levelled at Villars included his failure to attack a disordered Marlborough on the 9th, an unrealistic assessment of the strength of his defences in the flanking woodland, and for over-extending his flanks, whilst Boufflers was taken to task for not exploiting his initial rout of the Dutch. St. Hilaire's enemies charged him with evacuating his guns too soon, but on his own evidence his gunners had fired all of 8,000 rounds during the day, and had had but 400 left when he ordered them to relimber. As for the victors, Marlborough's foes would make full use of the gory casualty lists to charge him with fighting an unnecessary battle, claiming a great decline in his skill; others would claim that he sheltered his British troops at the expense of his Allies; and there can be no doubt that the outcome of Malplaquet has served to dim the Duke's military reputation to a slight degree, though probably unjustly. He had stormed a strong position, and his revised plan had shown originality in its idea of an outflanking attack.

It did not, however, alter his basic humanity. After ordering the army to fall back to its original camp near Blaregnies on the 12th, Marlborough busied himself making the best possible arrangements for the wounded of all nations. According to Captain Peter Drake, the notorious turncoat, it was his personal plea to Marlborough that induced the Duke to send Cadogan to Bavai under flag of truce to concert arrangements with the French for the evacuation of their wounded,[45] but be that as it may, it was a humanitarian gesture. Slaughter and human suffering always affected him.

The campaigning season was already too far advanced to permit much more to be attempted that year. Both armies took steps to repair some of the gaps in their ranks, Marlborough drawing 30 battalions out of garrison duty and replacing them with his most battered units, the French sending detachments of 50 men from each of 42 garrison towns throughout the kingdom as reinforcements. While the Allies considered their next move, Boufflers, as in 1703, dissipated much of his remaining force to strengthen the towns and fortresses he deemed threatened, including three battalions into Mons (19th September). These successfully slipped through the token Allied forces investing the place.

After a period of recuperation and deliberation, on 20 September, the Allied army marched upon Mons, intent on completing unfinished business. The siege lines were commanded by the Prince of Orange, at the head of 30 battalions and as many squadrons, whilst Marlborough and Eugene camped on the River Trouille near Jemmapes to cover the siege, with an advanced force near St. Ghislain.

Mons possessed a garrison of 4,280 troops under the Marquis de Grimaldi, but was short of supplies from the outset. However, the early onset of the autumnal rains and various raids mounted by Villars from Condé, Maubeuge and Charleroi combined to hinder the early stages of the siege, but the 60 siege guns and 18 heavy mortars had arrived from Brussels by the 25th, and that same night the trenches were opened opposite the gates of Bartamont and Havre. One important casualty was the invaluable Cadogan, who received a bullet in the neck. 'I hope in God he will do well', wrote his anxious master to Sarah, 'for I can intierly (sic) depend upon him.' His wounding, he went on, 'will oblige me to do many things, by which I shall have but little rest.'[46] Fortunately the vital aide was soon out of danger.

French sorties on the 26th caused some damage, and wet weather again intervened, so that it was not until 1 October that the 30-gun siege battery could open fire. Thereafter the siege followed a regular course, stage following stage. On 16 October, the covered way of the hornwork protecting the Havre Gate was stormed, and lodgements made on three of its angles. The next day a similar operation took the defences protecting the Bartamont Gate.

The French, meantime, were wracking their brains for means of succouring Grimaldi. If Mons were to fall too quickly, the Court feared that Maubeuge or Le Quesnoy might follow suit before the Allies were forced into winter quarters; on the other hand, Boufflers was strictly enjoined not to risk another battle. The Marshal therefore had to content himself with strengthening the Lines of La Trouille. On the 18th, the Duke of Berwick, fresh from successes in Dauphiné, was sent to the front to make an independent assessment of the situation, but his report also advised against any direct attempt to relieve Mons, and suggested the concentration of the army around Maubeuge.

On the 20th, at midday, Grimaldi sought terms of capitulation. He was granted the honours of war and allowed to evacuate, less his cannon, to Maubeuge and Namur. During the 25 days of the full siege he had sustained 980 casualties, and inflicted over 2,000. The French marshals promptly split their field army into two, hoping to cover both Maubeuge and Condé. But the Allies were not willing to undertake anything further that year. On the 26th the army marched to Soignies, sending the siege train back to Brussels. Morale was not of the highest order, and a widespread epidemic of looting, arson and general indiscipline had to be firmly countered. By the 28th, the army began to split up for winter quarters around Brussels and along the Meuse—to the undisguised relief of the French army and Court.

'So ended a campaign', summarised General Pelet, 'which had begun under the most terrifying circumstances for France and the most difficult for the general charged with the defence of its frontiers. Without men or means, faced by a superior army accustomed to conquer, Marshal Villars, through his genius and activity, found the means to form an army out of nothing and resources in the midst of a general famine. His eye for ground led him to choose a position which his enemies respected, and which saved the kingdom. His valour and courage reanimated his troops, down-trodden though they were by despair and the lack of everything they needed. So, although forced to give way before the superiority of his foes, he was able to stop the exploitation of their victory and the execution of their vast projects, by denying them entry into the kingdom, and reducing them to the capture of two towns which did not belong to France.'[47]

Without doubt, many of the martial honours of the year belonged to Villars; against all expectations, the frontiers of France remained inviolate, and France still possessed an army capable of continuing the war. For the Allies, on the other hand, the military outcome had proved as disappointing militarily as diplomatically. The crucial decision had been to besiege Tournai at the outset of the active campaign. By thus sacrificing their mobility, the Allies made little use of their superiority of force, and afforded Villars sufficient time to prepare his scanty forces. The result had been the firm French stand at Malplaquet. The 'Two Princes' had done well to win the battle, given the natural strength of the position and the new-found determination of the French, and there are no signs, the high casualty lists notwithstanding, of any marked decline in their powers of generalship. It is true that they delayed the opening of the battle too long, erred in not checking Orange's costly attacks in time (perhaps an army of 110,000 was too large for the Duke's usual methods of control to operate properly), whilst Withers' 'special attack' was somewhat mishandled, being neither strong enough nor properly timed, but the real reason lay in the unexpected staunchness of Villars and his men, to whom, therefore, much credit is due.

For the Allies, the year 1709 ended in a flurry of discordant diplomatic activity. The Dutch were much concerned that Great Britain and Austria seemed agreed that the entire Spanish inheritance should pass to Charles III, heedless of the Republic's interests. The United Provinces desperately desired peace, for its economy was on the point of ruin, but the States-General would not buy this at the price of a bilateral pacification. They could, however, hint at such a possibility, and this proved sufficient to induce the Whig Ministry to offer considerable concessions to ensure full Dutch participation in the struggle and their guarantee of support for the Hanoverian succession. The result was the 'Treaty of Succession and Barrier', signed on 29 October, by which the Whigs agreed to cede a long list of fortresses, including Lille, Tournai, Condé, Maubeuge and disputed Dendermonde, together with Upper Guelderland, and a share in all trade and commercial advantages that might eventually be wrung from France and Spain, in return for unequivocal Dutch support for the Hanoverian right of succession to the British throne and British possession of Ostend. The Whigs were even prepared to hand Minorca to the Habsburg claimant— a term demanded by Dutch commercial interests in the Mediterranean. This sweeping agreement cut straight across secret agreements concluded in July 1707 with both the Emperor and Charles III, whilst it was notable that nowhere did the Dutch promise full military aid for the conquest of Spain although they did guarantee diplomatic support.

Although he had no alternative policy to suggest, it is significant that Marlborough would take no open part in these negotiations, but left them wholly to Townshend, being fully aware of all the trouble the terms would cause. He was privately convinced by now that France would never undertake the forcible removal of Philip V from the Spanish throne, and also knew that the Emperor would bitterly contest the loss of so many Netherlands fortresses from Charles's portion, and that the King of Prussia had strong pretensions to Upper Guelderland. He was also aware that the inhabitants of the Southern Netherlands dreaded nothing so much as a Dutch economic stranglehold, and that large sections of British public opinion, led by the Tories, would deem this agreement far too favourable to the Dutch, sacrificing the interests of all the other Allies including those of Great Britain itself. All this Marlborough knew, yet took no steps to declare his views. This might be deemed more of a sin of omission that one of commission, but the Duke compounded his error by, it appears, tipping off the Imperial and Prussian ambassadors of what was in the wind. These actions are hard to justify, and must be held to detract from his reputation as a statesman, as even Sir Winston is prepared to concede, although unwillingly.[48] Ostensibly, Britain stood at the peak of its power in Europe, but the Dutch would find their apparent success fatal to their chances of retaining the status of a European power. Their continuation in the war spelt ultimate betrayal and economic ruin within the space of four short years.

Marlborough returned to a country full of political disquiet. The Whigs were able to secure him a vote of thanks from Parliament for his services at Malplaquet, but his enemies were soon using the casualty figures to sully his repute.

This was inconsistent, for not only were the British losses relatively light, but the Tories had long complained that the Dutch—the most grieviously hit at Malplaquet—had never accepted their fair share of either blood or effort. Harley and the Tories also charged Marlborough with duplicity over the Barrier Treaty, accused him of corrupt financial profits in appointments to vacancies caused by the battle, and declared that he was largely responsible for the failure to achieve peace. There could be no denying that a strong desire for the end of the war was burgeoning throughout the country—corn was dear after two poor harvests, taxation on both land and purchased articles remained severe, and the compulsory recruitment of the unemployed for the army was highly unpopular—whilst rising costs had caused the economic burden of the war to double since 1703. However, the Whigs were as adamant as ever that 'peace without Spain' was unthinkable.

The Queen made little attempt to conceal her preference for Harley, Shrewsbury and other Tories. The headstrong Sarah's influence over the Queen was now a thing of the past, and the supremacy of Abigail Masham assured, whilst the Marlboroughs, amongst others of the Whiggish persuasion, had recently become the targets of the spiteful libels of Mrs. Manley's *New Atlantis*, which even charged Sarah with being Sidney Godolphin's mistress—with the connivance of the Duke.

Despite the unpropitious omens, including the opinion of his friend, Lord Chancellor Cowper, that such a post would be unconstitutional, Marlborough had insisted on renewing his claim to the Captain-Generalcy for life. He had exchanged several letters with the Queen on the subject during Sepetember and October, only to meet with a courteous but chilling royal rebuff. Although his main motive was his desire to raise the army's affairs above the level of party politics—or at least beyond the grasp of the Queen's Tory favourites—an element of personal ambition was indubitably also involved, for these letters reveal his feeling that he was receiving far less than his due, and in them he spoke once more of retiring from public life. Even worse, at the instance of an embittered Sarah, he unwisely charged his disappointments in these matters to the intrigues of Abigail Masham. This proved a most impolitic allegation; the Queen frigidly refuted the charge, and the whole underlying matter of the Captain-Generalcy provided his opponents with an ideal weapon to use against the Marlborough influence in both state and army. For once he had allowed his heart, and his wife's hatred for her rival, to rule his head, and before many months were out he would come to rue this lapse.

The Duke spent little time at court, but retired immediately to Blenheim with his wife and Godolphin to consider their further moves. The situation was extremely complex. The *Duumvirate* was under heavy fire from both the Tories and the extreme Whigs, and their influence with the Queen was clearly being rapidly eroded by the ceaseless propaganda of Harley and Mrs. Masham. The problems of treading a political *via media* were now insurmountable. Further-more, the extreme Whigs, emboldened by their success in November in forcing the Queen to bring Somers into the Ministry and to place Lord Orford at the head of the Admiralty, were anxious to demonstrate their new power and restate their principles. They found what they deemed to be a suitable occasion in the celebrated case of Dr. Henry Sacheverell. This Tory divine had preached on 5 November at St. Paul's a sermon on the text, 'In peril among false brethren', which was redolent with the High Church doctrine of 'Non-Resistance' and included a barely-disguised attack on Godolphin. This could be represented as a challenge to the validity of the Glorious Revolution and its settlement, and the Whigs, with the support of a greatly-piqued Godolphin, decided to impeach Sacheverell. By so doing, they had unwittingly prepared the way for their own downfall, and also, in the fulness of time, for that of the Captain-General.

Marlborough was inevitably embroiled in these bitter party controversies, but to cap them all, the New Year of 1710 brought a challenge to his military authority that he could not ignore. When Lord Rivers (prompted by Harley) applied for the post of Constable of the Tower on the death of the Earl of Essex, Marlborough returned an affable but unfavourable reply. Rivers thereupon applied directly to the Queen who, to Marlborough's stunned amazement, proceeded to confirm the appointment and award the colonecy of the Oxford Dragoons (also vacant) to Jack Hill, the brother of Abigail Masham, without any reference to her Captain-General. The slight was both obvious and deliberate—at least to Sarah—and inevitably bitterly resented. Deeming his authority within the army to be at stake, the Duke begged the Queen to rescind the appointments. Upon her refusal, Marlborough, shocked out of his customary urbanity, left Court in a rage for Windsor Lodge on 15 January, and proceeded to draft a demand for Mrs. Masham's immediate dismissal or his own. Despite Sarah's fiery advocacy, the letter was never delivered in its full format to the Queen thanks to Godolphin's caution and tact, but the gist of it was soon mooted abroad, and the Duke refused either to return to London or to wait upon the Queen. A period of intense negotiation followed, conducted through Lord Somers and Godolphin as go-betweens, but the crisis remained unresolved even though the Queen was induced to rescind the appointment of Colonel Hill as a sop to Marlborough's pride. Within a few months however, both Colonels Masham and Hill would receive commissions as Brigadier-Generals.

Induced by his anxious Whig colleagues to return to the capital on the 22nd, Marlborough set about persuading his friends to arrange a Parliamentary address for the removal of Masham and his own appointment to the Captain-Generalcy for life. Alerted to this development by Lord Somers, the Queen took swift action to prevent her hand being forced, mobilising all her influence in both Council and Parliament to block the move. The Duke of Argyle, long a bitter critic of Marlborough, offered 'whenever she commanded, to seize the Duke at the head of his troops and bring him away, whether dead or alive.'[49] This was bombast, but it showed how bold and bitter the opposition was growing, and Marlborough was forced to retreat. He was even reduced to denying—wholly unconvincingly—that he had ever planned to present an ultimatum or to seek special honours—such was the scale of his defeat.[50]

Sickened by the toils and convolutions of the political scene and shaken by this latest defeat, the Duke soon sought leave to return to the Continent. The Queen eventually notified her agreement and by the end of February, the Duke was back at the Hague. He thus missed the famous Sacheverell impeachment in Westminster Hall (27 February to 23 March O.S.) which ended, to the vociferous and riotous approval of the newly-Tory London mob (which at one tense moment threatened to storm the Bank of England), and to the relief of the mass of the population and the intense discomfiture of the Whigs, in a narrow vote of guilty and the imposition of a purely nominal sentence on the popular preacher, who was immediately lionised throughout the country. This massive Whig *débâcle* provided the Queen with a clear indication that the Ministry, apparently so secure only three months before, had forfeited the trust of the country at large. The moment for her revenge had almost come, and by the time the Duke next returned to English soil he would find a completely changed political firmament. The Tories—and most particularly Robert Harley—now sensed their opportunity; the stars of the Whig Junto, and of the Marlboroughs, were now decidedly on the wane.

The Final Rounds—Douai and Bouchain, 1710 and 1711

'Douai, Béthune, Aire, S. Venant and Bouchain underwent the same fate in two succeeding years. Their vigorous resistance could not save them. The army of France durst not attempt to relieve them. It seemed preserved to defend the capital of the monarchy.

The prospect of this extreme distress was neither distant nor dubious. The French acknowledged their conqueror, and sued for peace. . . .'

From the inscription on the Column of Victory,
Blenheim Palace (continued).

If the battle of Malplaquet brought intense grief to the United Provinces and bitter, if factious recriminations in London, at Versailles it was eventually hailed as an act of Providence. In Colbert de Torçy's opinion, the action 'raised the courage of the nation rather than weakened it', and Louis XIV was not slow to take advantage of the latest shifts in the wind, both at home and abroad, and seek once more the tortuous path towards an acceptable compromise peace.

Such a reaction was predictable. 'France', wrote Horatio Walpole to Boyle on 8 October 1709, '. . . imprudently believes she was victorious . . . and will have sufficient time to talk following the end of the campaign.'[1] Indeed, the French government could take comfort from the outcome on the Rhine front as well as in Flanders, for Marshal d'Harcourt had successfully repelled General Mercy's inferior army.[2] Even in Spain, despite the withdrawal of considerable numbers of French troops and the recall of the French ambassador on 2 September—moves dictated as much by diplomatic as by military policy—the overall situation remained reasonably stable, at least in the earliest months of the New Year.* There was a cautious feeling that the worst of the storm might even have been safely weathered.

* In fact the scale of the French withdrawal has often been exaggerated. Many garrisons remained in key fortresses and ports—including Pamplona.

Nevertheless, the *conseil d'en haut* remained divided on the best course for France to pursue. The Grand Dauphin still headed the war faction, which included Voisin; the Duc de Beauvilliers and the Duke of Burgundy were equally convinced that peace must be secured on any terms at the earliest possible moment—and their arguments were supported behind the scenes by the King's morganatic wife, Mme. de Maintenon. The King himself, with Torçy and Desmaretz behind him, pursued a *via media*, advocating a negotiated peace short of surrender.

The first attempts to reopen serious negotiations were hardly propitious, neither the Dutch nor the Duke proving receptive. Rebuffed, Torçy sought to create by hook or by crook an atmosphere more favourable to a meaningful search for a settlement. One means towards such an end was to demonstrate to the Allies that France was still capable of undertaking military initiatives. Supported by the convalescent Villars, Torçy resuscitated the idea of a Scottish diversion. For a time it appeared as if this might be attempted, and Marshal d'Estrées was appointed to the command, but the scheme eventually foundered on the usual twin rocks—men and money. Thwarted again, Torçy worked to strengthen the Franco-Bavarian alliance (for what this was worth), intrigued with the Northern Powers in the hope of securing an offer of mediation from Denmark, Russia and Poland now that Charles XII was in eclipse following his disaster at Pultava (28 June 1709)*, and investigated the possibility of bribing Victor Amadeus of Savoy into quitting the Grand Alliance. Above all, French diplomacy concentrated on attempts to suborn the United Provinces, but in this respect a whole series of secret enquiries made through Petkum bore little fruit, despite the French revelation that the British intended to retain Minorca as a permanent Mediterranean naval base—a sensitive matter affecting Anglo-Dutch commercial rivalries.

The crux of the problem of achieving a peace remained, as always, Spain. Louis XIV authorised Torçy to offer the Allies 'an exact neutrality in relation to Spain' and four cautionary towns in Flanders, if, in return, France could be released from any direct participation in the military reduction of Philip V's kingdom.[3] When this suggestion failed to elicit any response from the Allies, the French switched to the subject of possible compensation for Philip—suggesting various combinations of Mediterranean principalities. Once again the Allies' response was minimal, but at last in February 1710 they agreed to receive Abbé Polignac and Marshal d'Huxelles at the Hague to discuss the contentious Article 37.

In fact, the talks never took place at the Hague, but began at Moerdyke before being moved to Gertruidenberg on 8 March. There is no place here for an account of the long weeks of wrangling that ensued, and it must suffice to say that

---

* This concept collapsed in March 1710 when the Convention of the Hague blighted all French hopes of securing the neutralisation of North Germany.

no progress was made despite the good offices of the pacifically-minded Dutch plenipotentiaries, Buys and Van der Dussen. The Dutch thought the idea of compensation reasonable, and the British were prepared to waive the obnoxious Article if the Dutch would agree with the Emperor's suggestion of a separate peace being concluded with France, excluding Spain, but the remaining hurdles proved insurmountable, and in July 1710 the talks were broken off. It seemed as if French hopes of achieving anything through negotiations were again doomed, but the changes in Queen Anne's ministry which would come about a little later in the year were destined to offer them an ideal and largely undreamt-of opportunity. In the meantime, Torçy, suspecting the shift in the British political wind, spared no pains in tentatively wooing various sections of the Tories.

Meantime in France itself the achievements of Villars at Malplaquet were fast gaining almost legendary elaborations, and diplomats were repeatedly reporting a distinct improvement in the national morale as a whole. The true lesson of the battle was, of course, that whilst Villars could not defeat Marlborough and Eugene in the open field, he could nevertheless make their invasion of France prohibitively costly. The Marshal could not aspire to win the war for his monarch by feats of arms, but over the next two years it would be sufficient if he avoided losing it. After Malplaquet, Allied governments would prove as chary of allowing their commanders *carte blanche* in the matter of seeking major actions as the French monarch himself, and French strategy for the next years of the struggle would take the form of operating defensively on the north-east frontiers whilst launching circumspect offensives in Spain. Louis' advisers were well aware of the Allied doubts and dissensions, and the chances of the Grand Alliance falling apart remained real enough. In point of fact, the major military struggle (at least outside Spain) was now largely over, and the fight for the peace had begun. In this, the final phase of this long war, the French would emerge far more successfully than they had any reason to expect from the military evidence.

The Allied weakness lay at the grand strategical level. Spain and Naples had proved, and in the former case was still proving, a fatal diversion of both war aims and resources, and the net result had been to make it impossible for Marlborough and Eugene, for all their genius, to formulate strategic moves capable of winning the war outright. Allied disunity thus proved Louis XIV's greatest ally, and naturally enough proved extremely aggravating to the 'Twin Princes'. 'As the opportunities for a brilliant and decisive campaign were opening to the Allies', comments Dr. Sturgill, 'their ability to take advantage of them was dwindling.'[4]

The French prepared for the new campaign in considerably better heart than had been the case the previous year. Once again five armies were designated and commanders nominated; Villars, d'Harcourt, Berwick, Noailles and Vendôme prepared to return to the field in Flanders, on the Rhine, in Dauphiné, Roussillon and Spain respectively. The Spanish command was to be shared with the Marshal de Bay, and Marshal Montesquiou (as we must now term the promoted d'Artagnan) would exercise control in Flanders pending Villars' arrival. French troop levels in Spain were progressively reduced in the hope of lending credibility to Louis XIV's diplomatic declarations—also to permit rein-forcement of the army on the critical front—Flanders. Inevitably the north-east front received the lion's share of available resources. By early April it had been settled that 180 battalions and 280 squadrons should serve in Villars' field army (to include a detachment for the Meuse), beside a further 58 battalions and 85 independent companies in the garrisons.

This armament, however, was not so impressive in reality as it might appear on paper. Few battalions could boast more than 250 rank and file, and many squadrons were as much as two-thirds below establishment. Moreover, when Marshal Montesquiou carried out an inspection of the frontier fortresses in the early spring, he found their defences deplorably weak. His report led the King to order immediate reinforcements for the towns of Douai, Béthune, Aire and St. Venant, which he percipiently regarded to be most at risk, but he chose to disregard Montesquiou's strategic plan for a general withdrawal by the main army to a new line linking the Rivers Deule and Lys, favouring instead Villars' belief that the Lines of Cambrin would prove sufficiently strong. Louis XIV was adamant that a major action was to be avoided at all costs, and he enjoined a defensive strategy based upon holding the lines for as long as possible and thereafter the strong reinforcement of the key fortresses deemed to be at risk.

Enough has been said of the plans of Versailles. What of the Allied High Command? With 155 full-strength battalions, 262 squadrons and 122 cannon and howitzers at their disposal, Marlborough and Eugene appeared to be in a strong position. In numerical terms, this armament probably outnumbered Villars by as many as 40,000 men. In late March one much-debated course of action was a major attack along the Channel coast (yet another restatement of the plan originally shelved in August 1708), but once again this was put aside as likely to expose Brabant to a French counter-offensive. The decision was there-fore taken to drive in the French centre.

As both the Lys and the Scheldt were available for river transport, the Allies decided on an attack against Douai as their first major objective. If successful, this would open a path towards Arras and Cambrai, the very last line of the French frontier defences, and at the same time enable the Allies to cover both Brabant and the Spanish Netherlands. But Marlborough was, as almost always, plunged into the deepest sense of gloom immediately before the opening of the Campaign. 'I am so discouraged by everything I see', he confided to Sarah on 14 April, 'that I have never, during this war, gone into the field with so heavy a heart as I do this time.'[5]

During the last days of March, the Allies massed in two main groups opposite the Lines of Cambrin (or la Bassée) and the fortress of Denain. Smaller parties prepared to mount feints on more distant sectors, but Montesquiou hastened to call up troops from the Sambre and Meuse regions, and set to work to implement the King's orders. As a first step, a fresh garrison was sent post-haste into Douai on 10 April.

Marlborough instructed the Earl of Albemarle to execute *coups de main* against the towns of Mortagne and St. Amand on the Scheldt. In the former case, the town changed hands three times between 14 and 18 April before the Allies were able to establish their mastery, whilst St. Amand proved impregnable, protected as it was by inundations. Ignoring this minor setback to their preliminary plans, Marlborough and Eugene proceeded to mass their men at Tournai on the 18th, whilst French subordinate commanders scattered to their posts along the lines and rivers, Montesquiou in person leading up 58 battalions and 70 squadrons from Lens to occupy the Lines of Cambrin.

For the Captain-General, the immediate problem was to pierce the lines to his front. On the 19th, the Allies accordingly advanced over a 40 mile front in four columns, each some 10,000 men strong, and launched themselves against the lines and the bridges over the Deule. The moves were made with great rapidity, and within three days successful bridgeheads had been established at Pont-à-Vendin, Courrières and Saut, as Montesquiou fell back in accordance with his orders to avoid a major engagement, detaching parties to strengthen the neighbouring garrisons whilst the remainder reconcentrated around Cambrai. Only the post at Pont Auby successfully defied the Allies, but there was no denying that the French front had been seriously breached. The French had, in the main, been surprised by Marlborough's speed. 'The French, not apprehensive . . . , were mostly out that morning, in quest of forage, so that their generals had hardly any cavalry with them; and this likewise occasioned the loss of a good part of their officers' baggage, their servants being with the foragers.'[6]

Last light on the 22nd found Douai invested on three sides, whilst the main army moved on to camp near Vitry and Goeulzin on the Canal du Moulinet, the English, Dutch and Hanovarians gathering near the latter place. From these positions, they intended to cover the siege.

Within Douai, General Albergotti, 'an old and experienced officer', commanded a garrison of 7,500 men. The fortress itself was deemed well-constructed and adequately supplied, and since its first acquisition by France in 1667 its defences had been wholly reconstructed, the new works including a double-ditch and the outlying Fort Scarpe, built to protect the weakest sector on the north-eastern side. The French court expected Albergotti to fight a vigorous and protracted defence, and continual plans were under consideration for mounting diversionary operations with the main field army. As a preliminary to these, Montesquiou was ordered to redeploy the army between Arras and Péronne by 10 May, but was further enjoined to attempt no relief operations before the arrival of Villars to take over command.

The Allied pioneers were soon at work constructing the lines of circum-vallation. Engineers devised means for diverting the River Scarpe into the Sensée, thus largely draining the double-ditch around Douai and at the same time creating a large flooded area to the south of the city. A strong post, manned by 500 men, was established at Arleux to guard the approaches to the inundations. So well was the work pressed ahead that by the 28th the Allies were in a position to occupy the camp sites within the siege lines, and in the meantime their supply-convoys continued to roll in on schedule from Lille and Tournai. On the night of 4/5 May, the trenches were opened in two places against the northern defences, the right-hand attack being entrusted to the Prince of Anhalt-Dessau, the left-hand to the Prince of Orange. In all, 40 battalions were directly involved in prosecuting the siege, and on 9 May some 200 guns at last made their appearance on the scene. There was still no sign from the main French army.

In fact, Marshal Villars, accompanied by the Duke of Berwick, only left Versailles for the front on 11 May, The 'victor' of Malplaquet was still recovering from his serious wound, but insisted on reviewing troops on horseback, his shattered knee clamped in a special iron device which caused further excruciating pain.[7] Before leaving court, he had gained the King's permission for a bold advance towards the Allies before Douai, and had even obtained his unwilling leave to risk a battle if circumstances seemed to make it unavoidable. Arrived at the frontier region, Villars called a series of conferences at Peronne and Cambrai (14–19 May), and then ordered a review of the army to be held on the 23rd. Reputedly a total of 155 battalions and 272 squadrons were put through their paces under the eye of their commander-in-chief. Villars might boast of his invincible array of 160,000 men, but a more accurate figure would probably be 85,000, given the under-strength nature of practically every formation. Three days later the army marched in the direction of Arras, crossing the Scarpe over eight bridges on the 29th. The closer he approached the Allied army, however, the more the Marshal's ardour cooled, whilst Louis XIV ceaselessly bombarded his favourite general with cautionary advice.

Meanwhile the siege of Douai had been progressing satisfactorily, if slowly. The main Allied batteries opened fire on 14 May, and despite the explosion of mines and a number of strong sorties by the defenders, the siege proceeded stage by stage. Then, advised of Villars' approach, Marlborough moved his forces to block his path at Mont Saint Éloy, where they had constructed two new camps. 'I am this day three score', wrote the Duke on the 26th, 'but I thank God I find myself in so good health that I hope to end this campaign without being sensible of the inconvenience of old age.'[8] His spirits had evidently rallied with the prospect of imminent action. That same day the besieging forces pushed their works to within a few paces of the palisades protecting the covered-way of Douai, the engineers employing sap and gabbion. Another sortie was repulsed, and on the 29th the Allies were established on the glacis of the second counter-scarp.[9]

Early on the 30th, Villars ordered the issue of four days rations and the distribution of battle munitions, and with some panache the French paraded on to the Plain of Lens until they were within long cannon shot of the Allied army. There they camped some two miles from Marlborough and Eugene. 'He seemed determined to give the Duke battle', recalled Captain Parker, 'and began to cannonade us with great fury, and this brought Prince Eugene from the siege with as many men as could be spared. The cannonading held 'til night at which time he retired out of range of gun-shot, and there stood looking at us all the next day. Upon this we fell to throwing up a sort of entrenchment, to cover our men from his cannon; and then the Prince returned to the siege, and Villars retired to the plains before Arras.'[10]

Both Villars and Berwick had concluded that the Allied position was too strong to assault frontally, and the former informed Versailles that his new intention was to probe towards Vitry in the hope of interfering with Allied lines of communication connecting the siege with Lille and Tournai. At the same time, the Marshal proposed to strengthen the garrisons of Béthune, St. Venant, Aire and Ypres as a precaution against future possible developments. Louis XIV saw fit to approve this rather anti-climacteric change of plan, and decided to send Berwick to Dauphiné without further delay. Thus Douai was effectively abandoned to its fate.

The Allies were now more eager than ever to bring the siege to a conclusion. On 15 June they made themselves masters of the covered way, and re-sited their batteries to engage the four *demi-lunes* guarding the main *enceinte*. At this stage Albergotti smuggled out a message to warn Villars that he would soon be forced to sue for terms, and at noon on 27 June, after two days of negotiations, Douai and Fort Scarpe both passed into Allied hands, the garrison being permitted free evacuation to Cambrai. This success cost the Allies 8,009 casualties and the French 2,860 killed and wounded, 'all stations included', according to Sgt. Millner.[11] 'As I have nothing more at heart than the success of Your Majesty's army', wrote Marlborough to the Queen on the 27th, 'it is with the greatest satisfaction that I now sent Colonel Panton to give Your Majesty an account of the surrender. . . .'[12]

During these past three months, however, Marlborough's position with Queen Anne had been becoming ever more precarious, and the Duke's thoughts must have been as often filled with the problems of Whitehall as with the difficulties of Flanders. On 6 April the Queen had received Sarah for what proved to be her final audience. Following the decidedly chilly interview, the Duchess soon departed from Court for Windsor Lodge, still possessing her posts but definitely in royal disfavour. This disturbing, if predictable event, proved but the precursor of more important political upheavals. The Queen was now ready to

wreak her revenge upon the detested Whigs, and launched into a slow progressive series of dismissals and replacements designed to rid herself of her
troublesome servants. In mid-April the first to go was the comparatively
insignificant Marquess of Kent, replaced as Lord Chamberlain by the Earl of
Shrewsbury. Next and far more important, on 14 June Lord Sunderland gave
place to the Tory Lord Dartmouth as Secretary of State. The writing was now
on the wall for all to see, although the Queen instructed her envoys overseas to
reassure Britain's Allies that she had no intention of changing either her policy
or her Ministry. The question was widely asked, however, of how long could
Godolphin survive politically under the new conditions.

The dismissal of his son-in-law ruined all of Marlborough's satisfaction in
his capture of Douai. As he wrote to Heinsius on the 22nd, 'What I hear from
England gives me so much the spleen that I long extreamly (sic) to be out of all
publick business; you shall then be sure of my prayers.'[13] At distant Versailles,
an acute Torçy lost no time in instructing a trusted agent, Abbé Gaultier, to
contact the Tory Lord Jersey and through him sound out Harley, so clearly the
coming man, about the prospects for a bilateral peace.

Back at the front, the Allies lost no time in repairing the defences of Douai
and in considering their future moves. The French had found time to remove
all the forage from the vicinity of Arras, which effectively ruled out that town
as the next target, and the strength of their lines between Douai and Cambrai
was daunting, especially as the Dutch were now very unwilling to risk another
Malplaquet. 'I must then think of some other operations', mused the Duke,
'in which we may always be masters of not fighting, unless they give it under
great disadvantage.'[14] As a preliminary, the Duke and Prince decided to test
French reactions, and on 10 July they advanced boldly towards Vimy, taking
eight days rations with them. Heavy rain hindered the movement, and as the
French showed no sign of wishing to intercept the Allies they determined, on the
16th, to detach Generals Fagel and Schulenburg at the head of 28 battalions and
18 squadrons,[15] to besiege Béthune.

The fortress was close besieged from 17 July. It would be tedious to recount the
details of another siege, so it must suffice to say that Lt.-General de Vauban
(the younger) and M. de Roth defended the place obstinately, and that Allied
success was dearly bought. But as Villars was in no position to riposte, owing to
the priority he was according to the completion of his lines, the garrison was
induced to surrender on 29 August. This success had cost the Allies 3,365
casualties; the French were allowed free evacuation to St. Omer.

Nine days earlier perhaps the gravest possible blow had been dealt to the
Marlboroughs on the home front, with the dismissal of their closest friend and
confidant, Sidney Godolphin, 'the best man that ever lived' in Sarah's opinion.
Eight years of continuous unselfish public service were thus abruptly cast
aside with the promise of a pension of £4,000 a year that was, in fact, never paid.

It took urgent entreaties from Prince Eugene and Godolphin himself to prevent their afflicted friend from resigning with no more ado. 'I am afraid we must expect things to go from bad to worse in England so long as a woman is in charge', confided the misogynist Eugene to the Imperial ambassador at the Hague. 'She lets herself be led by many wrong-headed people. . . . I have spoken about it to the Duke of Marlborough and implored him not to despair but to wait and see what the next campaign brings forth.'[16] The Captain-General listened to these appeals. 'I leave you to judge by what you yourself felt at the dismission (*sic*) of Lord Godolphin . . . how much I must have been mortified and afflicted by so unexpected a blow . . .', wrote the Duke to Lord Halifax a little later. 'However, as I have told you already, I am resolved nothing shall lessen my zeal for the public, nor my endeavours to carry on the war with all possible vigour while I have the honour to command the army.'[17]

In England, the removal of Godolphin led to the complete eclipse of the Whigs. Lord Chancellor Cowper, despite repeated entreaties from both Harley (now become Chancellor of the Exchequer) and the Queen, insisted on following Godolphin out of office. By the end of Sepetember, Lord Somers, the Duke of Devonshire and Boyle, the second Secretary of State, had also been forced into resignation. In their places came in Lord Rochester, the Duke of Buckingham, and Henry St. John. Both the Treasury and the Chancellorship were placed in commission. The Harley star was now in the ascendant, and although he strove to follow a moderate line and control his extremist supporters he was not long able to withstand their pressure. On the Queen's personal insistence, Parliament was dissolved and new elections called for October (they resulted in a Tory landslide—no less than 320 supporters being returned to Westminster to the Whig 150 and 40 undecided), but there was as yet no serious suggestion or even desire to dispense with the services of Duke John. He was, however, utterly isolated politically. As the historian Klopp described it, 'the fearful carnage of Malplaquet . . . was less important to the development of the peoples of Europe than the bloodless change of the Ministry in England.'[18]

It was therefore a disheartened Marlborough who pressed—after the fall of Béthune—for a renewed advance along the Channel coast towards Calais. He was aware, however, that such a move would be unlikely to lure Villars out of his positions, and that in all likelihood it would expose the Allied flank and communications with Flanders to enemy raiding activities. In the end, a more prosaic policy was enunciated—namely an attempt to take the fortresses of Aire and St. Venant in order to secure the Allies unquestioned use of the River Lys and thus broaden the avenue of advance against the last fortress line protecting France. Both sieges were to run simultaneously.

The main army took up a position between the Lys and Lillers to cover these operations. The Prince of Orange took 20 battalions and 5 squadrons to besiege St. Venant, defended by Brigadier de Seloe with seven battalions. The defence was not particularly notable, and after a fortnight negotiations with the garrison began on 29 September, leading to the place's surrender on 2 October. Aire proved far more troublesome. The Prince of Anhalt-Dessau found M. de Goësbriand and his 15 battalions and 7 squadrons of dragoons a doughty opponent. Torrential rains and grave supply difficulties further hampered the besiegers, who suffered grievously amongst a sea of mud. A degree of relief was obtained from a most unlikely source, according to all the historians of the Royal Regiment of Foot of Ireland. Colonel Robert Sterne, for instance, recorded that 'During the siege of Aire provisions were very scarce; but one thing gave the soldiers relief and it is almost incredible—and it was the hoards of corn which the mice had laid up in storehouses in the earth, which our men found, and came home daily loaded with corn which they got out of these hoards.'[19]

Progress was slow, and the chances of French intervention grew daily. On one occasion the garrison of Ypres sortied forth to destroy an Allied convoy of barges on the Lys. However, Villars, impeded by a further deterioration in his health, was in no condition to plan bold initiatives, and in mid-September he was forced to hand over command of the French army to d'Harcourt; the new commander had no desire to launch an offensive. So Aire in its turn was left to its fate, and at length on 8 November, de Goësbriand sent out officers to negotiate the best terms obtainable. Evacuation to St. Omer was permitted by the Allies, who were only too glad to end this protracted siege, and so a fourth important town passed into their hands; its capture had cost 7,200 casualties, or a full quarter of the besieging force. The garrison had 1,400 killed and wounded.

This event ended the campaign of 1710. The year's activities had resulted in the capture of considerable tracts of country which certainly opened the way for an Allied onslaught towards the last line of French defences. But there was no disguising the fact that a further long campaigning season in Flanders had not ended the war, and the French had thus gained more time. Many vocal critics in England and Holland were claiming that the struggle was incapable of being satisfactorily brought to a military conclusion, and Marlborough's political position was now approaching its nadir, although he remained in command of the army. Moreover, news from the other major war fronts was far from comforting for the leaders of the Second Grand Alliance.

At one time during the year, the news from Spain had appeared most encouraging. The satisfactorily progressing repression of the Hungarian Revolt enabled the Emperor to send large-scale reinforcements to the Archduke Charles. Most action initially centred upon Aragon. Following two months of indecisive confrontation near Lerida, the Allies forced battle upon Philip V and his general, Villadarias, at Almenara on the River Noguera (27 July), and inflicted a sharp defeat. Placed under command of de Bay, the discomfited Spaniards retired on Saragossa, pursued by the victors. The resultant battle outside the city (20 August) cost the Spaniards another 7,000 casualties, and 'Charles III' made a triumphant entry the next day. This success effectively returned Aragon to Allied control, and temptingly opened the road towards Madrid.

Dissension returned to bedevil the Allies. Charles III was in favour of a move towards Navarre, there to sever the road links between France and Castile, but his generals and advisers induced him against his better judgement to undertake a direct advance on the capital. Meantime, an alarmed Louis XIV had authorised the return of substantial French forces over the Pyrenees, and by 17 September, Marshal Vendôme had joined Philip V and de Noailles at Valladolid. There they decided that de Bay should hold Estremadura against the Portuguese, whilst Vendôme advanced in the centre and de Noailles prepared to move from Roussillon.

During these developments and deliberations, the Allied army had been marching across the parched mountains and plains of Castile by way of Calatayud to reach Madrid, which was duly occupied on 28 September, Philip V having evacuated his capital some three weeks earlier. An uneasy two-month occupation ensued, but the unwavering hostility of the Castilian populace hindered the collection of food and forage. The approach of Vendôme's army soon spelt danger, and so, as in 1706, the Allies were forced in their turn to leave the city, the British and Dutch heading for Aragon, the Imperialists for Navarre. Philip V was back in his capital by 3 December, but Vendôme and 25,000 troops pressed hard on the heels of General Stanhope, and on the 8th succeeded in surrounding him at Brihuega, where he was compelled to surrender with 1,500 men. The next day General Stahremberg, rapidly retracing his steps from Cifuentes, engaged 20,000 French troops at Villaviciosa with only 14,000, and brought off a technical victory. This success was not in any way decisive, however, and the Imperial commander was soon in full retreat for Barcelona, much harassed by guerrilla operations, leaving Vendôme in unchallenged possession of the initiative. Thus the Marshal 'had permanently saved the cause of Philip V',[20] and the Franco-Spanish forces could once more undertake the reconquest of Aragon. By 15 December, de Noailles was besieging Gerona whilst Vendôme had reached Cervera. By 5 January, Charles III and Stahremberg were back in Barcelona, and their area of control was practically as limited as it had been in 1709. The Iberian struggle had taken its last turn.

The Allies had little reason for self-congratulation on any of the remaining fronts outside Spain and Flanders. In Dauphiné and Savoy, the year also ended in Allied disappointment and frustration thanks to the activities of Médavi and Berwick despite the initial advantages enjoyed by the Duke of Savoy and the later withdrawal of part of the French forces for service in Roussillon and Spain. Similarly, on the Rhine, Marshal de Bezons (despite desperate supply difficulties) had more than held his own against General Cronsfeldt and the Imperialists. All the year had to show, therefore, were a few towns conquered in Flanders; peace appeared as far off as ever. At least one more campaign if not more would be

needed to force an entry into France from the north-east. Only at sea did the
Allied supremacy remain real and unchallenged. But the cost of the war and its
seemingly endless character would soon induce the new Ministry in England to
hearken to Louis XIV's secret offers of peace.

* * *

After delaying his departure for the British Isles to complete outstanding
business, the Duke returned from the Hague on 6 January. He landed at Sole
Bay after a rough three-day passage, and we may surmise that his thoughts
dwelt on the naval battle of 38 years earlier where his conduct had earned him his
captaincy in the Admiralty Regiment. Driving to London, he found a vocifer-
ously enthusiastic crowd awaiting his arrival, but being aware of the delicate
atmosphere at court, and not wishing to arrive as a conquering hero in case this
should give his many opponents further ammunition, he turned aside from St.
James's Palace and visited Montague House.

His official audience with the Queen took place on the 10th. It was formal and
impersonal. After assuring her general that she was still desirous of employing
his services, Anne warned him not to seek any vote of thanks from Parliament.
The Duke duly signified his gratitude and compliance and withdrew. Over the
next days many influential men visited the Duke, but the cool attitude was
clearly apparent. Harley, in particular, was careful to demonstrate his independence, and made Marlborough apply for a formal audience. There is evidence
that the most extreme Tories were still hopeful that the Duke would be induced
to offer his resignation without compelling them to take the initiative in the
matter—which could be expected to have adverse repercussions both at home
and abroad. 'The Duke had a very cold reception last night', wrote Harley to a
confidant at the end of the month, '. . . How long he will keep his temper I
cannot tell.'21 Personally, the senior minister wished to avoid such a crisis, at
least in the immediate future, but he was aware that there were many Tory
M.P.'s baying for blood, whilst the Queen's quarrel with the Duchess was clearly
coming to a head.

Parliament with typical inconsistency chose to ignore recent failures in Spain,
and instead turned its critical attentions to the conduct of the war in the Iberian
Peninsula in 1707. The bitter calumnies of the Earl of Peterborough proved
ideal evidence for those politicians determined to vilify Generals Galway and
Stanhope over the issues of the defeat at Almanza and the fiasco outside Toulon.
In the Lords, Marlborough staunchly supported his unfortunate colleagues, but
the upshot was a vote of thanks for Peterborough and an equally undeserved
vote of censure for Galway. Another target for attack was Robert Walpole,
Treasurer for the Navy, practically the last Whig to remain in office—this
inconsistency being due to his widely-recognised abilities.

Henry St. John treated Marlborough to alternate scorn and condescending patronage. The Secretary's current brain-child was to launch an expedition against Quebec*—a reversion to the Tory maritime concept of strategy—and to gain the necessary men he was prepared to co-operate with the Captain-General. But behind the scenes moves against the Duke continued; plots to uncover evidence of any secret dealings with France and to implicate Marlborough in shady financial dealings continued apace. More openly, Ormonde proceeded to block the appointment of the Duke's friends to high positions in the army. If his foes could not yet complete Marlborough's fall, they could circumvent his authority. After his departure for Flanders, a special committee—the Board of General Officers—would be formed with powers to confirm or veto all military appointments. Its chief military members would be the Duke's foes, Argyle, Rivers and Erle.

The crowning humiliation was still to come. Some of the calumnies launched against the Marlboroughs in the Tory news-sheets were demonstrably false and trivial, but the crisis at court could no longer be ignored. As the Queen refused to grant Sarah an audience, in the end the Duke agreed to deliver in person a conciliatory letter from his wife. The fateful interview took place in mid-January. The Queen was not impressed by the missive, but demanded the return of Sarah's golden key of office. In despair the Duke went down on his knees to implore a reconsideration, but Anne remained obdurate. 'I will take no other business till I have the key. . . .' An unworthy interview descended to haggling. The Queen demanded Sarah's resignation within three days; the Duke pleaded for ten; Anne promptly reduced the period of grace to two, and further insisted that the Duke should return the key on his wife's behalf. Proud Sarah reputedly flung the key to the floor when she heard the news, and bade her spouse grovel once more to retrieve it. The humiliated Duke returned to the Palace, and the unsavoury episode came to a conclusion with the rejection by the Queen of yet another request for the Captain-Generalcy for life—an attempted facesaver. Mrs. Masham succeeded Sarah as Keeper of the Privy Purse, and the Duchess of Somerset was appointed Groom of the Stole. So ended the long and tempestuous association of 'Mrs. Morley' and 'Mrs. Freeman'.

Mollified by the eclipse of Sarah, the Ministry agreed to offer the high command to Marlborough for a further campaign, and secured a vote of six million pounds from Parliament for the furtherance of the war. That the Duke accepted can only be ascribed to his feeling for the Allied cause. 'I have been so out of humour ever since I came to England', he confided to Heinsius on 6 February, 'that I have troubled you with very few of my letters, but the Queen having now taken the resolution for my serving this next campaign as you will see by the next

* This expedition ended in failure (August 1711) and became a severe bone of contention between Harley and St. John. The latter indubitably made a personal profit from the fiasco.

post in Her answer to the States, I have write (*sic*) to Lord Cadogan that he should take with you at the Hague the necessary measures for the army's taking the field earlyer this yeare than the last. . . .'[22]

* * *

The Duke boarded ship at Harwich on 20 February 1711, and set out for what was destined to be his last campaign. His correspondence shows little sign of the mental strain he might have been expected to be suffering: perhaps he was only too pleased to escape from the intrigue-ridden Court of St. James's and return to the company of men he knew he could trust, namely his army. He reached the Hague early in March, and immediately busied himself with the necessary preparations for taking the field for this, his tenth campaign in as many years.

By the 22 April the Allies had almost 120,000 troops ready to march, namely 142 battalions and 269 squadrons in the vicinity of Douai, besides other garrisons and late detachments still on the road to the reporting areas. Marshal Villars was at the head of 160 battalions and 244 squadrons besides the garrisons of Ypres and St. Omer (perhaps 24 battalions); the great majority were drawn up in the vicinity of the redoubtable lines which the French engineers and peasantry had been at great pains to construct during the preceding months. This barrier—consisting of defended river lines, morasses (both natural and man-made), *abattis* of felled trees and small redoubts sited to dominate the causeways, and areas of scarped hillsides strengthened where necessary with palisades and earthworks—stretched all of 90 miles from the River Canche on the Channel coast to Namur on the Sambre, incorporating the rivers Gy, Scarpe, Sensée and Upper Scheldt in its various sectors, being anchored to or supported by a number of major fortresses of which Montreuil, Arras, Bouchain, Cambrai, Valenciennes, Le Quesnoy and Maubeuge were the most significant. Given the Allied presence in force near Douai, the most obviously threatened sector lay between Arras and Valenciennes, but the inundations associated with the rivers Scarpe and Sensée formed a strong bulwark, backed as they were by the mass of Villars' army.

Before operations opened, however, the death of the Emperor Joseph I (17 April) and the accession of Charles VI (hitherto the Archduke Charles) caused difficulties for the Allies. On the one hand it made the problem of the Spanish front more intractable than ever—posing the possibility of a huge Habsburg power-block the like of which had not been seen in Europe since the days of Charles V; on the other, it involved the withdrawal of considerable numbers of troops in the Imperialist pay, and, most important of all, of Prince Eugene in person, from the Flanders region. For some time Versailles had been planning a new offensive over the Upper Rhine into Germany, and the change of Emperors was the signal for its implementation. By late June, Villars had been constrained to release 35 battalions and 41 squadrons for service with the Elector of Bavaria on the Rhine, and this mounting threat resulted in the recall of Eugene (14 June) at the head of 16 battalions and 40 squadrons, much to Marlborough's disappointment and even alarm. At first he deemed this development to have ruined all chance of achieving anything that year. 'I send you enclosed the copy of Prince Eugene's letter ...', he wrote anxiously to Heinsius, '... As the conjuncture is now I fear we must not venture a siege.'[23] He was clearly apprehensive of the play his opponents might make of any protracted or enforced delay in opening the campaign.

As we have seen before, however, such pessimistic announcements were often the Duke's way in the early days of each year's operations, and as usual the reality was not to prove so grim as the omens. The first weeks of operations in 1711 saw little of real note; a French raiding party destroyed 30 barges of hay and corn and another group overwhelmed a fort near Ypres, but these were mere pin-pricks. Nevertheless they bolstered Villars' well-developed sense of self-esteem, and French 'notions of security ... proceeded, probably, from the inactivity in which the Confederate Army had hitherto remained, and the General was so fond as to believe they would not dare to attempt the passage of the Lines'.[24] This early example of what would, two-centuries later, be termed a 'Maginot complex' was due to lead to almost as great a shock to French prestige in 1711 as that suffered in 1940—but on the earlier occasion complete catastrophe would be averted. Busy though he was with plans, the duke found time to advise Sarah, furiously vacating her official appointments at St. James's, to remove her belongings as soon as possible. 'I beg you will not remove any of the chimney pieces'[25] he wrote on 24 May. Clearly Sarah was as redoubtable in defeat as she was intolerable in victory.

By mid-June, Marlborough had marched to the Plain of Lens. There he ordered his first offensive of the campaign, instructing the Governor of Douai to send 700 men to secure Arleux—a small town set slightly to the fore of the Lines which controlled the main approaches to the fortress of Bouchain. This operation was successfully carried through on 6 July, and the Duke—aware that a French reaction would be inevitable—ordered the engineer M. des Roques to fortify the place, whilst General Hompesch with 10 battalions and 12 squadrons of the Douai garrison was charged with covering the work from Fieren.

This was the first of a complex series of moves designed to fool the vainglorious but able Villars. Marlborough was aware that such an Allied position so close to the main enemy lines must surely act as a red rag to the susceptible Marshal whose habitual response to news of distant disasters was '*Je ne scaurois être partout*' ('I cannot be everywhere at once'). No such bravado would disguise his failings in 1711. The Gallic Bull obligingly lowered its head and charged. On the night of 11 July, a French force issued from their lines and making the

most, according to Sergeant Millner, of 'a prodigious great fog', surprised
Hompesch and routed part of his force before being repulsed. Marlborough
reacted to this demonstration by moving his main camp nearer to Arleux, and
simultaneously designated 600 men under Colonel Savary for the town's garrison.
Villars summoned the place to surrender, but Savary returned a defiant reply.
These indications of the Duke's serious interest in Arleux served as a second
flourish of the matador's cloak, and once again Villars obliged as soon as Marlborough's main army moved off to forage near Béthune and Aire. The French
advanced in force, and after a heavy bombardment of the newly-completed
defences, launched four assaults against Arleux.

'On the arrival of the express' (from Arleux announcing the French onslaught)
'he seemed very much cast down', noted Captain Parker, and the Duke lost no
time in sending off the trusted Cadogan at the head of 30 squadrons and a
picked force of grenadiers to the garrison's aid. Cadogan, it seems, had secret
orders to *festina lente*, and Arleux duly fell. On receipt of the news the Duke
gave a rare demonstration of public rage—we can guess for the benefit of the
French spies who he suspected to be at his elbow—intimating 'in a kind of
passion that he would be even with Villars'[26] for this 'affront'. Villars, meantime,
rubbed salt in the wound—or so he supposed—by razing Arleux's defences.
'This gave Villars another occasion of bouncing', continued Parker. He gave
the 'Court of France repeated assurances', stated Lediard, 'that these lines
were the *Non Plus Ultra* of the Duke of Marlborough.'* In actual fact the
Duke was laughing up his sleeve—because in order to be able to besiege Bouchain
—Marlborough's main intention—it was first necessary to secure the area around
Arleux before the main move took place. Marlborough had it in his power to
raze Arleux, as he had already demonstrated, 'but as soon as he was marched
from thence Villars would soon come and rebuild it, but should he pretend to
fortify it, then he expected as soon as he was marched away Villars would come
and retake it and demolish it'.[27] In other words Marlborough was playing an
expert game of trickery and deception to put the French off-balance before
revealing his main intention.

As if to show how determined he was to avenge the loss of Arleux, Marlborough
moved his camp forward to Villers Brulin and made every appearance of preparing an early attack against the Avesnes-le-Comte to Arras sector of the Lines—
patently the strongest. 'We may probably attempt to force his Lines before
two days are at an end', wrote Cardonnel to a Hanoverian contact on 3 August,
'all possible preparations being making for that end; tho' the weather is not

* Most authors, including Churchill, prefer *Ne to Non*—but Lediard and Atkinson and
several French sources employ the latter. The phrase was reputedly 'borrowed' by
Villars from the Duke's scholarly tailor, who astounded by a new red coat of particularly
dashing cut, exclaimed 'Non Plus Ultra' ('Nothing further is possible') apparently
parodying the motto of one of the Duke's many coats of arms.

the most favourable; it having rained continually to Day, (*sic*) from noon to this hour. ...'[28] Villars immediately concentrated every available man near the threatened area, confident in the strength of his positions. On 4 August Marlborough rode out heavily escorted to reconnoitre the French position, and everybody in both armies anticipated a terrible battle for the morrow. Unknown to all but a few confidants, however, secret moves were being made behind this ostentatious display. Already Brigadier-General Sutton, moving behind the natural cover afforded by Vimy Ridge, had set out with the guns and pontoons with orders to bridge the Scarpe near Vitry, and the bakeries of Lille had been instructed to prepare six days' rations. Attending the Duke's reconnaissance, Parker noticed 'General Cadogan steal out of the crowd attended by one servant only', but 'did not think much of this circumstance at that time.' In fact the trusted Quartermaster-General was soon riding at speed for Douai, there to join General Hompesch at the head of an extemporised force of some 20 battalions and 17 squadrons made up from the garrison of Douai and the escort of the trains, and various detachments from Lille, Tournai and St. Amand.

All this went unnoticed, and 'the grimace carried on so well' that the secret was still unknown to Marlborough's men even at dusk. 'Things had but a dismal aspect', recalled Parker, when suddenly the whole camp was stood to, and ordered to march off eastwards 'without beat of drum' (Kane), leaving their camp fires burning behind them. By 9 p.m. four columns were on the move, and it was two hours before Villars even suspected something was afoot, alerting his men against a possible night attack. So Marlborough—who was riding ahead of his infantry with the 50 squadrons of the left wing—gained five hours clear start on his opponent in what soon became the race for Arleux. By 2 a.m. on 5 August Villars had realised that he was being fooled, and instantly rushed off with a few troopers to head the Allies off, ordering his army to follow. But Marlborough had too long a start, even though he had more miles to cover and less suitable roads than the French. It was a fine, moonlit night, and the rear of the Allied Foot was soon marching in full view and half-cannon shot of the advance guard of the French army, both forces being separated by the Scarpe and Sensée.

Meanwhile, about midnight, Cadogan and Hompesch had stealthily descended upon Arleux, and found it and the Lines beyond deserted. By 3 a.m. the news had been brought to Marlborough near the bridges at Vitry. He at once passed the news back along the column, requesting every unit to step out. The troops responded willingly, and 'every regiment brought up as many men as they could without waiting for any that dropped behind.' However, the Duke had given orders that the cavalry rearguard of General Albemarle was to pick up behind their saddles as many men as possible. By dint of such improvised measures, the march proved a triumph. The 18th Foot covered 39 miles in 18 hours—'a great march for a foot soldier with all his luggage, computed to be near fifty pounds weight', and there is small wonder that Parker had to report that 'half

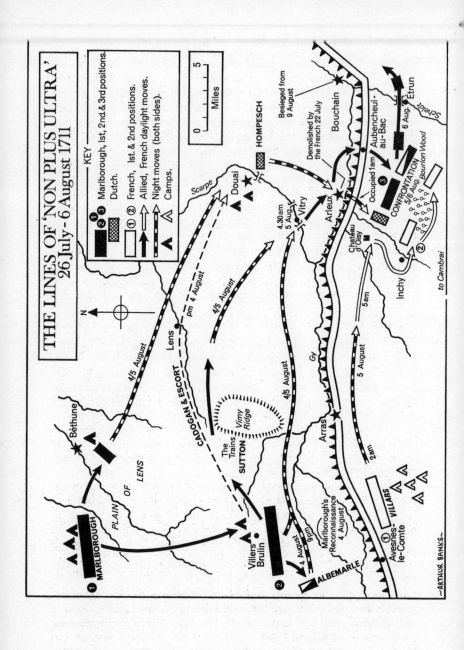

THE LINES OF 'NON PLUS ULTRA'
26 July - 6 August 1711

KEY

1 2 3 Marlborough, 1st, 2nd & 3rd positions.
Dutch.

1 2 French, 1st & 2nd positions.
Allied, French daylight moves.
Night moves (both sides).
Camps.

0 — 5
Miles

N

Béthune

MARLBOROUGH

PLAIN

OF

LENS

Lens

Scarpe

Douai

HOMPESCH

4/5 August

pm 4 August

4/5 August

CADOGAN & ESCORT

The Trains
SUTTON

Vimy
Ridge

Villers
Brulin

ALBEMARLE

4 August
9pm

4/5 August

Vitry

4.30am
5 Aug.

5 Aug.

Arleux

Demolished by
the French 22 July

Bouchain

Besieged from
9 August

Occupied 1am

CONFRONTATION
5/6 Aug.

Aubencheul-
au-Bac

6 Aug. Etrun

Scheldt

Bourlon Wood

Château
d'Oisy

Inchy

to Cambrai

5am

5 August

Gy

Arras

Marlborough's
Reconnaissance
4 August

2am

Avesnes-
le-Comte

VILLARS

~ARTHUR BANKS~

of our men dropped behind',[29] some taking three days to rejoin the colours.

By 8 a.m. the Duke and the cavalry were pouring through the vaunted lines near Arleux, the leading infantry reaching the crossing-place two hours later. As for the galloping Villars, near-frantic with rage and anxiety, he was almost taken prisoner at the Château of Oisy but escaped through a gap in the Allied forces that attacked his exhausted escort.

By mid-afternoon, Marlborough's army was formed up and ready to offer battle, but his position was too strong for Villars, and the French drew off to shelter beneath the walls of Cambrai. Somewhat untypically, Marlborough, too, decided not to force a major engagement in the days that followed. He has earned some criticism for this decision, but reasons can be suggested though not proved. In the first place, his avowed intention was to besiege Bouchain, and that, as we shall see, he now proceeded to do. As the Duke remarked to Sicco van Goslinga on 5 August; 'Now we shall make our siege, our hands are free. I shall use these five or six days which we need for the preparations in trying to bring the enemy to action.'[30] But his men were very tired after their exertions, and not a little disordered, whilst Villars had selected a strong position in his turn from which he refused to be lured. Thirdly, although he had demonstrated for all the world to see his superiority over Villars and his complete mastery of conventional warfare, Marlborough still bore some respect for his opponent as a battle commander. Doubtless memories of Malplaquet lingered, and the Duke must have been only too well aware that his tenuous position in the Court of Queen Anne could never survive the inevitable outcry that would be raised against another holocaust of the sort suffered in Sepetember 1709. Lastly, we may surmise that the great Duke was beginning to feel his 62 years, and possibly was slightly sickening of his trade after ten years of continuous campaigning. 'I must confess to you', he wrote on 7 August* 'the last six weeks have given me frequent and sensible remembrances of my growing old.'[31]

So instead of fighting, the weary warrior moved his troops to besiege nearby Bouchain. Like the bull-fighter who brings his adversary to a confused halt at his feet, he scornfully turned his back on Villars' superior army and set out to cap his marvellous feat of forcing the lines of *Non Plus Ultra* without the loss of a man to enemy action, by undertaking the siege of one of the most impregnable fortresses remaining to the French, daring Villars to do his worst. A second lesson in eighteenth-century warfare was about to be administered to the unfortunate

* Atkinson (p. 448) gives this famous extract with a footnote attributing its inclusion in Murray's *Dispatches*, Vol. V, p. 433. A check of the 1845 edition however, reveals no sign of this passage; the translation of the sentence (from the French) that appears at this reference is merely: 'I must confess to you that we must not lose any time, but press affairs as far as we can.' It is possible, however, that Murray left out part of the document, and that Atkinson, normally the most exact and precise of scholars, saw the original but overlooked to mention the discrepancy in a footnote.

Marshal, who was already sensible of his humiliation, 'to be thus visibly out-generalled' after all his bold claims of only a week earlier.

The Duke moved eastward with his 90,000 men from Aubencheul-au-Bac and crossed over the Scheldt near Étrun, intent upon besieging and taking the adjacent fortress of Bouchain situated at the confluence of the Rivers Scheldt and Sensée. This movement was carried through safely despite the presence of the stronger French army near Cambrai—only some ten miles away—and was completed by early morning on the 7 August.

The strategic significance of Bouchain lay partly in its position at the river junction as an anchor for the now defunct lines of *Non Plus Ultra*, and partly in the access its capture would afford the Allies to the countryside surrounding Cambrai, almost the last major French fortress protecting this sector of the French barrier. As Captain Robert Parker wrote, the fall of Bouchain would open 'a passage into the Kingdom of France.'[32] but in selecting this target, Marlborough had a political objective also in mind. Aware of his rapidly deteriorating position in England, he wished to provided a major demonstration of his military expertise, and in the process inflict a humiliating rebuff on Marshal Villars.

The proximity of Villars' 100,000 strong army was only one problem associated with this bold move; the nature of the fortress's defences and the surrounding countryside were also most daunting from a besieger's point of view. Bouchain was not particularly large as fortresses went, but it seemed to many Allied officers virtually impregnable. It consisted of an upper and a lower town, the latter defended by a huge hornwork with associated ditches and ravelins. The real strength of the place lay in its situation amidst very difficult marshland at the river confluence. Only to the south was the town overlooked by a hill holding the hamlet of Wavrechin, but this feature, as will soon be seen, the enemy took good care to deny to the Allies. Running through the marshes to link town and hill was a single track known as the 'cow-path' (eventually supplemented by a second passage).

To defend Bouchain, the Governor, M. de Ravignau, could deploy some 5,000 men, having received a timely reinforcement during the 7th in the form of M. d'Offry at the head of 800 grenadiers, two battalions of foot and two regiments of dragoons, besides 400 sacks of grain. The very next day, moreover, Marshal Villars advanced from the cover of Cambrai and encamped his army in a vast arrow-shaped formation in the space between the Sensée and the Scheldt; the apex of his position was at Étrun, hard by the marshes to the south of Bouchain, his extreme left being placed in the vicinity of the village of Entanglet and along the banks of the Scheldt respectively. Villars sited his headquarters in the hamlet of Paillencourt not far from Etrun, barely two miles from the walls of Bouchain. The same day he succeeded in making contact with the garrison through the marsh, and built a number of bridges over the Sensée, thus enabling General

Albergotti to occupy the key feature of Wavrechin hill on the left bank. By 10 August this energetic officer had surrounded his position with strong field fortifications including a deep ditch, and was eventually reinforced by the Marshal de Montesquiou and 45 battalions.

All things considered, Villars had justification for reasonable confidence about the siege's outcome. Although he still had no wish to undertake a major battle— so redoubtable was Marlborough's reputation—it was hard to see how the Allies could hope to take the place, given the facts that the southern approaches to the town were held by the French army in force, and that a strong entrenched camp had now been erected around Wavrechin. The French commander doubtless complimented himself on the grounds that he was following Vauban's preferred means of protecting a stronghold to the letter, namely by associating an entrenched camp *outside* the main defences with a strong garrison within the town.

By this time Marlborough had established his main encampment to the north and east of Bouchain, placing his headquarters at Avesnes-le-Sec. With the intentions of passing part of his army to invest the fortress from the westward, and of safeguarding his lines of communication with Marchiennes and Douai along the River Scarpe (the Allies were still of course awaiting the arrival of their heavy siege train from Tournai), the Duke ordered a number of bridges to be built over the Scheldt near Neuville and Denain, and sent General Dopf with 30 battalions and 40 squadrons to the west bank of the river. Owing to the need to prosecute the siege itself, no more than 70,000 Allied troops could be spared to cover this operation—and this obviously gave Villars a very decided superiority.

Nevertheless, the Duke was fully prepared to fight his opponent at this disadvantage if he could induce him to move in strength to the west of the Sensée. He hoped the activity at Wavrechin was a precursor to this, and built more bridges ready to move his main army over. This, however, Villars had no intention of doing. Although the obvious countermove was to cut the Allies' links with Douai, he was still anxious for the safety of Arras some 20 miles to the west, fearing that Marlborough's apparent preoccupation with Bouchain might be but another example of the Duke's famous sleight of hand.

As it became clear that the French were not going to be lured into a battle, the Allies concluded that it was time to complete the investment of Bouchain, but until the obstacle of the camp at Wavrechin had been eliminated (or its means of access to Bouchain severed) this could hardly be achieved. The first plan was to attempt an assault on Albergotti's position, now further defended by the siting of 26 large cannon. To this end General Fagel was sent over with 16 more battalions to reinforce the troops already west of the Scheldt (9 August).

The events of 10 August on this side of the river are best described by our eye-witness, Parker, whose Royal Regiment of Foot of Ireland was ordered to take part in the impending assault. 'When we approached near them (the enemy) we observed that they had entrenched themselves up to their eyes, and that they had a large deep fausse (ditch) before them, with a number of cannon mounted thereon. Villars seeing us advance, brought into the works as many men as they could contain: notwithstanding which, our generals made a disposition for attacking them. Our British grenadiers were ordered to march up to the top of the hill on the left of their works, in order to begin the attack on that side. Here we were posted in a large high grown field of wheat, about seventy or eighty paces from their works, expecting every moment when the signal should be given to fall on.

'I must confess I did not like the aspect of the thing. We plainly saw that their entrenchment was a perfect bulwark, strong and lofty, and crowded with men and cannon pointed directly at us; yet did they not fire a shot great or small, reserving all for us, on our advancing up to them. We wished much that the Duke might take a nearer view of the thing: and yet we judged that he chose rather to continue on the other side, in order to observe the motions of the enemy on that side, while we were attacking them on this. But while I was musing, the Duke of Marlborough (ever watchful, ever right) rode up quite unattended and alone, and posted himself a little on the right of my company of grenadiers, from whence he had a fair view of the greater part of the enemy's works. It is quite impossible for me to express the joy, which the sight of this man gave me at this very critical moment. I was now well satisfied. that he would not push the thing, unless he saw a strong probability of success; nor was this my notion alone; it was the sense of the whole army, both officer and soldier, British and foreigner. And indeed we had all the reason in the world for it; for he never led us on to any one action, that we did not succeed in. He stayed only three or four minutes, and then rode back. We were in pain for him while he stayed, lest the enemy might have discovered him, and fired at him; in which case they could not well have missed him. He had not been longer from us, than he stayed, when orders came to us to retire. It may be presumed we were not long about it, and as the corn we stood in was high, we slipped off undiscovered, and were a good way down the hill before they perceived that we were retiring; and then they let fly all their great and small shot after us: but as we were by this time under the brow of the hill, all their shot went over our heads, insomuch that there was not a single man of all the grenadiers hurt.'[33] In this incident Marlborough's personal leadership qualities are very evident.

The French were ill-advised enough to misconstrue the Allied withdrawal for a panic, and when their cavalry issued out of the works to exploit the situation, Marlborough contrived to lure them into a trap which caused heavy casualties before they could withdraw.

Convinced that Wavrechin could not be taken by direct attack without great loss, Marlborough consulted the engineers as to the practicability of continuing the siege. All except the loyal Cadogan, Quartermaster-General, and John Armstrong, were dubious, but Marlborough, 'who well knew the capacity of the man in that respect' accepted Armstrong's view and gave him the major share of the responsibility for continuing the siege operations.

Armstrong's first step was to use 5,000 men to construct an entrenched position opposite Wavrechin hill, capable of taking 24 large cannon, and managed to build this in a single night—a considerable achievement in itself.

Having thus neutralised Wavrechin to a large extent, the Allies set to and built a further series of lengthy lines of circumvallation to safeguard their positions against surprise. Urgent requisitions were sent off to the Dutch States requiring 6,000 workmen and 700 waggons to perform the work, which was started on the 12 August. By the 23rd no less than 30 miles of fortifications had been constructed. The main Allied camp, north-east of Bouchain, was protected by a line running from Haspre on the River Selle to Hordaing besides the Scheldt. Next, on the opposite side of the river, steps were taken to ensure free Allied access to Marchiennes roughly parallel to it. First Armstrong's redoubt, already mentioned, was extended to the west and north, until it reach the Scheldt not far from Neuville, and a camp for 30 battalions and 12 squadrons was established between this line of circumvallation and the approaches to Bouchain. This would safeguard the works that would have to be dug so as to attack the Lower Town. Next, two long 'lines of communication' (as contemporaries deemed them) were pushed out towards the Scarpe, and eventually stretched all the way from the Sensée to the environs of Marchiennes, enclosing between them 32 square miles of territory with a number of villages. Not only would this defended locality present the Allied army with a protected foraging area; it would also ensure the safe passage of the heavy guns still *en route* for Marchiennes and the siege beyond. These measures obviated to a large degree the peril of a major enemy sortie from neighbouring Valenciennes or various other enemy posts in the vicinity.

But the French had not been idle. Albergotti had used the lull in operations to carry on extending his own works, above all enlarging the two avenues of approach from Wavrechin to Bouchain running through the marshes. The *sentier des vaches* was reinforced and enlarged; 'a parapet was carried on with fascines, all the way to the town, from tree to tree, betwixt the willows and rushes which covered the inundation.'[34] If the French managed to complete this endeavour, it would be virtually impossible for the Allies to isolate Bouchain completely, which was of course at this juncture still imperfectly invested from the south. As Marlborough wrote on 17 August:

'We have not yet quite overcome our difficulties, though we have forced them from several posts; they have none left but a path called the Cow Path, through a great bog, at which they can only pass one in front (in single file).'[35]

That same day a special operation was mounted to sever the paths through the marshes. Four hundred picked grenadiers stood ready whilst the sappers and pioneers, supervised by the Duke in person, pushed numerous fascines into the outer parts of the marshes on both sides of the Scheldt and started to inch a rough parapet, yard by yard, through the watery mud towards their objective.

It soon became necessary to silence an enemy post situated to defend the Cow Path from just this sort of invasion. The grenadiers—drawn from eight battalions—entered the marsh, heedless of the fire being poured at them from three sides (from the redoubt, the town, and Wavrechin), and began to wade forward, 'up to the middle, and some up to the neck in the water, for several hundred paces.'

'An ensign of Ingoldsby's Regiment*, who was at the head of fifteen grenadiers of the same regiment, being very short of stature, seeing when they were advanc'd some part of the way, in the inundation, that he must either drown, or give up his share of the enterprise and return, chose rather to get upon the shoulders of one of his grenadiers, 'till they came to the parapet, where he was one of the first to jump into the enemy's works.'[36]

This desperate operation was crowned with deserved success. The four French Grenadier Companies holding the post only tarried to let off a single volley before taking to their heels. For the loss of six casualties, the Cow Path was seized, and Bouchain was very near to being completely cut off from the hope of any outside assistance.

By the 20th the two wings of the 'fascinades' had been linked by a bridge of hurdles, and the town was completely invested from that date. Several determined French sorties had in the meantime been driven back.

The very next day, with unusual precision, the siege train arrived in the Allied camp. Its tedious journey from Tournai had not been without critical moments, and on one occasion a strong party of Frenchmen from Valenciennes had waylaid the convoy near St. Amand. This attack was beaten off, however, and 50 heavy cannon and 30 mortars safely reached Marlborough's lines through Marchiennes.

On the night of the 22/23 August, the trenches were opened against the town of Bouchain. Three lines of attack were pursued, two against the defences of the upper town (undertaken by 31 battalions and 12 squadrons under General Fagel) one against the lower town (under Lieutenant-General Schwartzen). A further 20 battalions and 30 squadrons under General Withers supported Fagel's double-undertaking.

By the 30th, such progress had been made in the construction of parallels and approaches that the grand batteries could be mounted, and duly went into action intent on making a breach. Meantime Villars' batteries poured their fire against the Allied guns, which were thus threatened from two directions at once, but the French seem to have done little damage to the town's attackers.

There was still considerable fight left in Villars. On 1 September he sent out General Châteaumorant at the head of 6,000 horse to raid the Allied main encampment in the hope of recapturing the Cow Path and its defences. Crossing

* The 23rd Foot.

the Scheldt unnoticed, this force fell on a section of the Allied camp near Hordaing, and routed four battalions. The French followed up this success by capturing the bridge at Étrun, over which they proceeded to retire triumphantly to rejoin their own people—although the Cow Path remained in Allied hands. The main Allied army stood to in battle formation until evening, but nothing more developed.

Such alarms and excursions did little to hinder the relentless progress of Marlborough's trenches, or the ceaseless thunder of his breaching batteries. Attempting to create a new diversion, the French next sent 66 squadrons under d'Hautfort to camp on the left bank of the Scheldt near Marcoing, (4 September), but that very day the Allies successfully stormed the covered way and three *flêches* of the lower town. This success was followed on the night of the 6/7th by the capture of the right-hand counterscarp of the lower town, and two nights later the left-hand counter-scarp similarly fell.

Time was fast running out for the garrison of Bouchain, where sickness was raging, further reducing their capacity to resist. In a last desperate bid to avert the predictable outcome of the siege, on the night of 7/8 September, Albergotti and the Comte de Villars (son of the Marshal) led 5,000 men over the Sensée and headed in a desperate rush north-westwards in the hope of surprising the Allied garrison of Douai. Marshal Villars subsequently moved over the river at the head of the cavalry corps to support this venture, but the intended surprise was discovered in good time, and so the crestfallen French had no alternative but to return to their camp with all speed to avoid being intercepted by Cadogan and a strong force sent out from the Allied army.

The siege was now fast approaching its climax, and Villars was reduced to impotently awaiting the inevitable, still not daring to risk a battle. The bombardment reached a new intensity, and then, on 11 September, a storming party succeeded in capturing the detached bastion on the right of the lower town. The foe immediately evacuated the bastion on its left. Two breaches in the main defences were now deemed practicable for assault.

These events broke the will of de Ravignau, and the next day he beat a parley and offered to exchange hostages whilst staff officers discussed terms. The negotiations that followed have led to considerable dispute. The Governor claimed that a representative of General Fagel, one Colonel Pagnies, had promised on behalf of the Allied command that the garrison could evacuate the town with the full honours of war. Marlborough refused to admit any such undertaking, but insisted that the garrison must surrender as prisoners of war. Thereupon the French broke off the talks and the bombardment was reopened. The damage done was serious, and within an hour Ravignau 'beat the *chamade*' for a second time. The guns again fell silent. The French Governor agreed to surrender himself and his men as prisoners of war provided that they were immediately granted parole. Once more Marlborough refused to ratify such an agreement—and again the guns spoke. But the true hopelessness of the French situation was now apparent to all, and a few hours later Ravignau surrendered unconditionally. A main gate, 24 colours, and all arms were handed over on the 13th, and next day the garrison was marched off towards Holland. As Sir Winston Churchill described this moment of triumph: 'Marlborough was Master of Bouchain. It was his last conquest and command.'[37]

This success had cost the Allies between 4,000 and 5,000 casualties (the exact figure is in dispute); as for the garrison, it had been practically halved by fire and pestilence before the 3,000 survivors (and 229 officers of all ranks) surrendered under the circumstances described.

Although hopes that this success might silence the Duke's critics at home in England ultimately proved vain, Quarter-Master-General Cadogan's letter to Mr. Craggs at Whitehall, (dated 14 September 1711, from the Camp at Bouchain) is worth citing as a commentary on this great military achievement:

'I should make a great many excuses for the freedom I take in troubling you, were it on any other occasion than this of acquainting you with the happy conclusion of the siege of Bouchain, which has been attended by all the circumstances My Lord Duke's friends could wish for his Glory and Reputation. His Grace undertook it in sight of the enemy army, tho' superior to his by above 30 battalions, and commanded by a general that France looked on as its last hope and who, piqued even to rage by being duped in the Passage of the Lines, was resolved to leave nothing unattempted to repair his fault and relieve Bouchain. He indeed made a great many efforts towards it, but they all proved fruitless by the measures His Grace took to disappoint them, so that notwithstanding the French army's remaining within cannon shot of our approaches, yet our convoys of bread and artillery came regularly and safe, our communication was preserved with our great towns, and in 15 days after our batteries began to fire, the place was surrendered and the garrison consisting of eight battalions and a detachment of 600 Swiss (Guards) made Prisoners of War. I am sure you are not unacquainted with the difficulties most people foresaw in this enterprise, and I believe it was sufficiently made known in England *by some who intended My Lord no service* tho' as they have turned, their representations must add a lustre to the undertaking—the success of which is as honourable in the highest degree to His Grace . . . so tis no less advantageous in its consequences to the Common Cause of which the enemy's beginning to burn and destroy their own country in order to prevent our farther progress, is such a convincing proof as makes it unnecessary to say anything more on that article.'[38]

More lowly Allied soldiers were equally ecstatic. Captain Parker claimed that 'it crowned all the great actions of his life'. But Marlborough's foes were neither placated nor silenced. Swift dubbed Bouchain a 'dove-house' and great efforts were made to belittle the achievement on both sides of the Channel.

De Ravignau, after accusing the Allies of breaking faith, repeatedly turned his understandable wrath against Marshal Villars, 'who stood looking on with an army much superior to that of the Allies, and yet could suffer him to be drove to these dishonourable terms'.[39] Later French historians have blamed the Governor for being taken in, and great efforts have been made to challenge Marlborough's achievement—no small testimony to the way it rankled in French pride. Both *Père* Daniel and de Quincy insist that Marlborough dishonoured Fagel's firm undertaking, and a century later, A. Allent, writing the official history of the French *Génie* in 1805, dismissed the siege as follows: 'This little place, attacked from three sides at once, battered by 50 cannon and 30 mortars, wide open, was defended by a garrison which fire, fatigue and epidemic had conspired to destroy, resembling, as the historian of the siege said, "a hospital defended by sick and wounded men." It surrendered after 22 days.'[40] (In fact 34 days.) Matters seemed rather different at the time.

In conclusion, it is necessary to sum up Marlborough's showing in this remarkable campaign which in many ways proved a fitting climax, as well as the swan-song, of his long and varied military career. The pure military artistry with which he repeatedly deceived Villars during the first part of the campaign has few equals in the annals of military history. Rarely before had an enemy commander been so fooled and induced to make the very moves his opponent desired. Informed contemporaries were well aware of the supreme skill of the forcing of the Lines in 1711. 'This rais'd his character beyond all that he had done formerly', wrote one admiring biographer of Marlborough. 'The design was so well laid, and was so happily executed, that in all Men's opinions, it pass'd for a Masterpiece of military skill. . . .'[41] The subsequent siege of Bouchain, with all its technical complexities so dear to the eighteenth-century engineer's heart, was an equally fine demonstration of martial superiority, carried out, as it were, right beneath the nose of a chastened Villars and his larger army without them daring to try and call Marlborough's bluff. 'During the whole course of this Long War', enthused Thomas Lediard, '. . . there was not so critical an instance as this, in which the reputation of two great Generals was so nearly concerned, and their skill in the Art of War so fairly put to the test.'[42] The Duke's moral ascendancy over his opponent could not have been more convincingly demonstrated.

It is evident that Marlborough took great personal (although characteristically modest and unassuming) pride over his achievements in 1711. The walls of the state rooms at Blenheim Palace bear the evidence to this day. Although but two tapestries are devoted to the triumphs of 1704, which probably saw Marlborough's finest hours as a commander, no less than three commemorate the siege of Bouchain. The first of these is really misnamed as 'Bouchain I' as it shows the passage of the lines of *Non Plus Ultra* rather than the siege that followed, but the point is clear: Duke John was pleased to recall this culminating double-triumph. He was proud with good reason.

Marlborough—An Assessment of the Man and Soldier

> 'These are the actions of the Duke of Marlborough, performed in
> the compass of few years; sufficient to adorn the annals of ages. The
> admiration of other nations will be conveyed to latest posterity in
> the histories even of the enemies of Britain. The sense which the
> British Nation had of his transcendant merit was expressed in
> the most solemn, most effectual, most durable manner. The Acts of
> Parliament inscribed on this pillar shall stand as long as the British
> name and language last—illustrious monuments of Marlborough's
> glory and of Britain's gratitude.'
>
> From the inscription on the Column of Victory,
> Blenheim Palace (concluded).

While Duke John was giving what was to prove his last virtuoso performance in
Flanders, much secret activity was preparing the way for a bilateral agreement
with France. Throughout 1711, negotiations proceeded between Versailles and
London, entrusted in the main to Torçy and (from late April) Henry St. John,
and conducted through their intermediaries, Abbé Gaultier and Matthew Prior.
As Marlborough was not privy to these consultations and seems to have been kept
largely in ignorance of their progress, it will suffice to record that on 8 October—
just three weeks after the fall of Bouchain—preliminaries of peace were signed
between Great Britain and France. In due course three Conventions were
signed—two, affecting the United Provinces, Austria and Savoy being couched in
the vaguest terms, the third (affecting Great Britain) being very explicit.

In return for abandoning the Habsburg interest in Spain—never a popular
concern of the Tories, least of all following the succession of Emperor Charles VI
which would have led to a Habsburg supremacy hardly more acceptable than a
Bourbon one had the Spanish inheritance also gone his way—and at the price of
implicitly serving an ultimatum to the Allies, St. John gained highly favourable
terms for his country. France declared her preparedness to concede the *Assiento*

for 30 years besides other trade privileges, and to allow British possession of Gibraltar, Minorca, St. Kitts, Acadia, Newfoundland and Hudson Bay. For its part, the British government agreed to the calling of a general peace conference for New Year 1712, and acknowledged Philip V as rightful King of Spain.

These preliminaries ran contrary to several treaties concluded with the Allies during 1709—most especially the Barrier Treaty with the Dutch—but the Tories felt scant compunction about overthrowing Whig agreements, being quite prepared to doom the Second Grand Alliance to piecemeal collapse in return for British advantage. On the other hand, four years of negotiations had brought precious little prospect of any agreement to their predecessors in office, and the financial and social strains of the war could not be allowed to drag on indefinitely.

When the news was announced, however, there was an immediate outcry from the United Provinces, Austria and Hanover. The Dutch feared, with some reason, for their Barrier, as it now seemed that the Netherlands might be awarded to powerful Austria rather than weak Spain. The Emperor was scandalised to learn of the abrupt abandonment of the 'no peace without Spain' tenet which had long formed the most important principle of Britain's negotiating position. With the greatest finesse, St. John proceeded to play one party off against another, declaring one thing here, insinuating another there, until everybody was at loggerheads or in deep confusion. In October, Count Gallas, the Imperial ambassador, was forbidden the court for his furious remonstrations. Where the Dutch were concerned, St. John astutely calculated that they could not long withstand the pressures for peace, and in that case the Empire could not stand out alone against France indefinitely. He was to be proved right. During part of 1711 there had been signs of a *rapprochement* between Harley (newly created Earl of Oxford in June) and Marlborough—a development St. John was particularly eager to counter. He had little cause for anxiety, however, for the Duke's whole-hearted opposition to the idea of a separate peace was immediately evident after his return to England in late November. His exclusion from the secret rankled strongly. 'What hopes can I have of any countenance at home if I am not fit to be trusted abroad?'[1] he laconically enquired. Inevitably, he was soon drawn into the great political controversy and mounting crisis, and this ended for ever all chance of his coming to terms with the Tories.

The government turned to Swift's able pen in an attempt to gain wider public acceptance for the terms. His pamphlet, 'The Conduct of the Allies', hammered home the irrelevance of Spain to Britain's true interests, and stressed the disproportionate share of the war effort the country had been called upon to bear since 1702 by its selfish Allies. 'No nation was ever so long or so scandalously abused by the Folly, the Temerity, the Corruption, the Ambition of its domestic enemies; or treated with so much Insolence, Injustice and Ingratitude by its foreign friends.'[2] The Whigs were not unnaturally outraged, and stiffened by the well-publicised attitude of the Court of Hanover, as advertised by Count

Bothmar, proceeded to cause a major Parliamentary storm. The crisis reached a peak when the Whigs in the Lords won the support of Tory Lord Nottingham and his following by agreeing to support that ancient cause, the Occasional Conformity Bill. Within days of this sinister alliance, the London mob was burning Lord Oxford and his ministers in effigy.

The storm burst in Parliament on 11 December (O.S.), when what may be loosely termed the Whig 'opposition' in the Lords successfully moved an amendment to the Queen's address, introducing the peace proposals, by 62 votes to 54. Marlborough voted with the majority. Stung by this rebuff, the Queen considered calling a new ministry, but the Tories maintained their majority of 126 in the Commons, and the adaptable Oxford was far from despair. First, in the New Year, he persuaded his monarch to create 12 Tory peers to regain control of the Lords. Second, he now determined once and for all to encompass Marlborough's fall.

The means to achieve this had, in fact, been put in train several months before. In early November, whilst still in Flanders, the Duke had learnt that the Ministry had set up a Parliamentary 'Commission for the taking, examining and stating the publick accounts of the Kingdom', to study and report on alleged irregularities during the war years. The enquiries affecting Marlborough were two: first, an assertion that over nine years he had illegally received more than £63,000 from the bread and transport contractors in the Netherlands; second, that the 2½ per cent he had received from the pay of foreign auxiliaries had led to an irregularity of £280,000.

At first Marlborough was not alarmed at the news, and strove to assist the enquiry, encouraging such witnesses as Machado to give comprehensive evidence. He was used to routine accusations of financial malpractice, and he had faith in the validity of the defence put forward by Robert Walpole in his tract, 'The £350,000 Accounted For'. Concerning the first allegation, he claimed ancient precedent. In answer to the second, he could produce a Warrant signed by Anne in 1702, continuing the practice that had first been arranged during William III's reign, after proper consultation with all the Allied governments concerned, with the intention of providing the Captain-General with the means of creating a secret service fund.

These answers seemed foolproof—and Marlborough clearly deemed them so—but he miscalculated the political pressures mounting against him, particularly now that Oxford wished to use the financial charges to divert popular attention from the Peace issue. Consequently it was soon apparent when the Commission published its report on 1 January that the Ministry would be able to secure a majority against the Duke, however convincing his defence, in both Houses after the reassembly of Parliament. Oxford employed all his wiles with the Queen, and on 11 January (31 December O.S.) the Queen declared in Council that information against the Duke laid before her necessitated his immediate dismissal.

The decision taken, the Queen wrote a private and presumably insulting note to her long-time servant and former friend. Its contents will never be known, for so incensed was Marlborough that in a rare burst of passion he flung it straight into the fire. All his offices were at once forfeit. The Duke of Ormonde succeeded as Captain-General and also to the colonelcy of the First Guards. Lord Rivers became Master-General of the Ordnance. Thus fell the great Duke—the victim of political machination and court cabals. Once he had controlled the sources of power in late-Stuart England; now they were used against him. Thus the Earl of Oxford ensured his own survival by crushing the Lords and ruining the unofficial leader of the Whig opposition—if it is possible so to describe the unwilling Duke—within the space of a very few days.

Europe was astounded at the news. Marlborough's foes exulted, but in the army as a whole there was a grievous sense of both outrage and loss. Captain Parker denounced 'the little mercenary scribblers' who had helped encompass his hero's doom.[3] Lt.-Col. Richard Kane reviled the 'set of vile profligate men, who had insinuated themselves into the favour of the weak Queen.'[4] Corporal Bishop was astounded. 'Oh!' said I, 'must we part from such a man whose fame has spread throughout all the world ?'[5]

Versailles rejoiced—for Louis' ministers regarded Marlborough as the greatest threat to their peace plans, and saw his fall as their best possible guarantee of Tory intentions, whether or no they were supported by their Allies.

Into this atmosphere of uncertainty in London there stepped Prince Eugene, come to pay an official visit on behalf of his new Emperor. He came too late to succour his old friend and comrade, and too late to negotiate new terms which would keep Britain in the war, but he staunchly defended the Duke's reputation. When a derogatory pamphlet sneered at Marlborough, declaring that as a soldier he had been 'perhaps once fortunate', the Prince publicly retorted that this was the 'the greatest commendation that can be given, for he was always successful and this must imply that if he was in one single instance fortunate, all his other successes were owing to his conduct.'[6]

Eugene's visit also coincided with another burst of plot fever; a Jesuit, Plunket, even claimed that Marlborough and Eugene were in collusion, planning a *coup d'état*. This was too extreme a possibility to be given much credence, even by the Tories. So Parliament turned its attention in mid-February to that hardy annual subject—the failure of the Dutch to bear a fair share in the prosecution of the war.

Prior to this, however, late January saw the formal debate on the Report on the Public Accounts. After lengthy considerations, the Commons predictably dismissed Marlborough's defence that the army had been well-supplied with bread in Flanders, and voted 265 to 155 that his taking the commission on the bread-money was illegal. It was also resolved that the 2½ per cent on the payments to Allies 'should be accounted for', this despite the production of the Queen's Warrant of 1702, and the supporting evidence of Sir Charles Hedges (Secretary of State at the time) and of James Brydges, Paymaster-General. The Duke's claim that the money—averaging out at about £15,000 a year—had been wholly used 'for carrying on the secret service'⁷ cut no ice.

On 27 January, the loyal friend Walpole was sent to the Tower for an irregularity concerning a sum of £1,000, and the Queen eventually ordered the Attorney-General to prepare a prosecution against Marlborough. It was however, never pressed. Henry St. John was aware that an impeachment would be hopelessly compromised by the fact that the Ministry, with supremely cynical inconsistency, had already awarded Ormonde the percentage on the bread-money at his very first request. As for the second charge, the Secretary of State realised that the Duke had given excellent value for every guinea expended. 'He had served England as she had never been served before with the military intelligence he had bought, and by the splendid use he had made of it in so many glorious campaigns.'⁸

The story of the long and intricate negotiations at Utrecht is beyond the scope of this work.⁹ The Congress met on 29 January 1712. Many hazards were encountered, the most problematical being the refusal of Philip V to renounce his French rights after the cataclysmic series of deaths in the French royal household* which brought the Duc d'Anjou to only one step from the French succession. Even when the formal talks broke down in April, secret Anglo-French negotiations continued, and resulted in the notorious 'Restraining Orders' issued to Ormonde on 10 May. By these he was formally forbidden to use British troops in action against the French, and was further ordered to open conversations with Villars.

This somewhat infamous step ultimately ruined the Allied campaign of 1712 in Flanders. Ormonde refused Prince Eugene's orders to attack the French camp, but inconsistently agreed to share in and cover the Prince's siege of Le Quesnoy (8 June–4 July), which ended in success as Villars took no steps to interfere.

In the meantime Anglo-French talks continued, Henry St. John, newly created Viscount Bolingbroke in July, taking a leading and personal part in the talks. Louis XIV ultimately prevailed on his grandson, Philip V, to renounce his French rights after all, and gave further evidence of good faith by handing over Dunkirk —that nest of privateers—to an English garrison. Despite a stormy debate when the full terms were announced on 6 June, the attack on the Ministry being led by Marlborough, Godolphin and Nottingham in the Lords, Oxford and Bolingbroke pressed ahead and ordered a two-month armistice in Flanders. Ormonde was

* The Grand Dauphin died in April 1711, the Duke of Burgundy ten months later, and the Duke of Brittany in March 1712. This left a sickly two year old child as Louis XIV's heir.

now formally ordered to break contact with the Allies—and implemented his instructions on 16 July to the undisguised fury of his national troops. There was 'a great muttering in the army', and numbers of troops deserted to join Eugene's forces. 'The soldiers had nothing now to do but their Quarter-guard duty',' noted Parker, 'and from a rising ground in front of our camp had a fair view of that rich part of France, which they reckoned they had dearly earned the plunder of. . . . Here they often lamented the loss of the 'Old Corporal' . . . ; and to make the matter worse, through the carelessness of the contractors, their bread was so intolerably bad, that it was with great difficulty the officers could restrain them from mutiny.'[10]

Thus both the discipline and the supply of the army suffered from Marlborough's absence. Some very unsavoury incidents took place; the village of Molain was sacked, and its 400 inhabitants burnt in the church by troops out of hand. No nation has a monopoly of atrocities, and it is evident that the eighteenth century had its share of Badajozes, Oradours, and My Lais. Later in the season there were mutinies at Ghent and other garrisons.

At the Hague these developments inspired an atmosphere of fatalistic despair. Heinsius persuaded his colleagues to remain in the war alongside Austria for the present, and even to take over (and pay) many foreign formations until recently serving Queen Anne—but the effect would be ruinous.

Meantime, back at the front, Eugene was forced to undertake the siege of Landrecies covered by the Dutch alone. Villars sensed his opportunity— mounted a rapid attack and defeated Lord Albemarle and the Dutch at Denain on 24 July whilst the 12,000 strong British army remained confined to its camps. Even worse, the scale of the Dutch disaster was indubitably increased by the earlier insistence of Ormonde that a number of British pontoon bridges near Denain over the Scheldt should be removed not long before the French attack. This set-back proved the precursor of a string of Allied disasters, and by late October Villars had regained Marchiennes, Douai, Le Quesnoy and Bouchain. In all, over 50 Allied battalions—almost one third of the army—were casualties or prisoners. Once again, the effects of Marlborough's absence was severely felt. Eugene's 'inability to hold Villars may be some indication of what the British commander and the British contingent, for all its numerical weakness, had meant to the Allies.'[11] Thus for the Second Grand Alliance the war in Flanders moved towards its close on an unfortunate and unworthy note, and there is justification for French pride in Villars' undoubted achievements during these later months of full-scale hostilities in the major theatre of war.

After Denain, the Dutch realised that they could not stay in the struggle without Britain. All hopes of gaining the terms of the Barrier Treaty of 1709 were now abandoned, and the United Provinces were ready to accept second best. The number of towns the Dutch desired to feel secure would be halved, they would surrender all claims to Upper Guelderland (destined by Britain for

Prussia), and abandon all hope of an equal share in the Spanish trading concessions (except in the Netherlands). The new Treaty of Succession and Barrier was eventually signed on 30 January 1713.

Meanwhile Marlborough continued to attend the House of Lords, and make his views known. As 1712 drew on, however, it became increasingly evident that he would be well-advised to leave the country in his own interests.

His exact motives have been the subject of much speculation. In the first place he had no wish to become involved in the hurly-burly of the impending Parliamentary election of 1713. He needed rest and peace—and neither could be hoped for in faction-torn England. He had even less desire to remain the butt of faction, or the scapegoat for military irregularities. Thirdly there were grave financial problems involved in the building of Blenheim Palace which the government had ceased to support, whilst a writ had been issued in Queen's Bench aiming to recover at least part of the 2½ per cent paid over to him in Flanders— and if such suits proved successful they might release a flood of others and seriously impair the Marlborough fortune. Fourthly, there are signs that Oxford was highly desirous of removing this 'over-mighty' subject from the British political scene, and to this end may have laid his hands on some of the Duke's secret correspondence with France, before blackmailing Marlborough into leaving the country on pain of public revelation. Lastly, the death of his life-long friend, Sidney Godolphin at the Marlboroughs' house at St. Albans in September, was a great personal grief and sundered another tie. Godolphin's unobtrusive yet indispensable contribution had been noted many years before. 'King Charles gave him a short character when he was a page, which he maintained to his life's end, of being never *in* the way, nor *out* of the way.'[12]

For some or all of these possible reasons, the Duke requested formal leave to travel abroad, and in due course the Ministry granted him his passports dated 30 October (O.S.). Arrangements had also been privately made to transfer £50,000 of the Duke's money to the Hague. So, on 1/11 December 1712 Marlborough boarded the Dover pacquet-boat and sailed for Ostend, attended by only a few servants.

So began 21 months of exile. They were not a wholly lonely period. Cadogan resigned his military appointments to accompany his old master, and early in 1713 Sarah was permitted to join her husband. Moreover, wherever they travelled they were welcomed and fêted. A great deal of time was spent at Frankfort-on-Main, and a visit was also paid to Mindelsheim (destined to be returned by the Emperor to Bavaria at the peace without compensation to the Duke). Other visits were paid to Hanover, where Marlborough remained in great favour with the Elector. Nor did he neglect to keep in touch with his nephew Berwick, although there were few illusions left. 'There is no use to be got out of the Duke', reported Berwick, 'but it were as well to keep civil with him.'[13] He also managed to keep minutely informed of British affairs.

His absence abroad absolves the Duke from any responsibility for the Peace of Utrecht. The conference resumed in February 1713, and after a point-blank ultimatum from Bolingbroke to the temporising French the two definitive treaties affecting Great Britain were concluded during the next six months. On 11 April came the first, the Anglo-French agreement, followed the same day by a further series of treaties involving the United Provinces, Prussia, Savoy and Portugal. An anticipated Britain received the lion's share. Louis XIV accepted Philip V's renunciation of his French rights, and recognised the Hanoverian Succession, agreeing to expel the Old Pretender. France surrendered her 'favoured nation' status in terms of Spanish trade, and agreed to the permanent demilitarisation of Dunkirk. Louis also ceded St. Kitts, Hudson Bay, Acadia and Newfoundland (less a number of fishing rights). In return, the British government recognised Philip V, and agreed to abandon the Catalan rebels. The other Allies won minimal advantages. The United Provinces received a restricted Barrier and a share (with England) in the trade with the Spanish Netherlands. Prussia gained Upper Guelderland, and its ruler the title of King. Savoy received Sicily and an adjusted Alpine frontier, and Portugal minor concessions in South America along the Amazon.

The second major treaty was signed on 13 July, between Great Britain and Spain. In return for British recognition, Philip V accepted the Hanoverian Succession, conceded special trading rights in the Americas, and surrendered Gibraltar and Minorca in the Mediterranean.

As Winston Churchill wrote: 'For good or ill the Treaty of Utrecht was better than an indefinite continuance of a broken-backed war'.

Only Austria now remained in the war, wholly isolated, and the massing of Bourbon forces along the Rhine led to the recapture of Landau and the taking of Freiburg, Eugene proving incapable of mastering the victorious Villars. At last, after lengthy negotiations conducted by the two commanders-in-chief, the Peace of Rastadt was concluded on 7 March 1714. By it, the Emperor received Milan, Sardinia, Naples, and the Spanish Netherlands, and all territory on the east bank of the Rhine, but in turn conceded Strasbourg and Landau, and other west bank enclaves, and agreed to the full reinstatement of the Elector of Bavaria. The Empire formally adhered a short time later by the Treaty of Baden. Finally, with the surrender of Barcelona to Philip V by the Catalan rebels in September 1714, the long War of the Spanish Succession at last came to an end, and an exhausted Europe was at peace.

France emerged from the struggle far more advantageously than any statesman had even dreamed possible five years earlier at Gertruidenburg. Great Britain and Savoy had come off best of the powers of the Second Grand Alliance, and the United Provinces ultimately received an acceptable Barrier after the conclusion of a Treaty with Austria in November 1715. It may also be claimed that in several respects the war aims of the Grand Alliance had been achieved:

the Spanish inheritance had been partitioned, and the concept of a European balance of power had at last triumphed. The foundations for two centuries of British greatness had also been securely laid.

* * *

The months passed—not without incident—in Whitehall. Bolingbroke—furious at the slight (or so he interpreted it) of receiving only a Viscountcy instead of an Earldom—became increasingly hostile to Oxford. Aided by Abigail Masham, now equally disillusioned by her remote relation, he steadily under-undermined Oxford's credibility as leader of the Ministry with the Queen, whose health was deteriorating. In December 1713 the Queen was seriously ill, and influenced by Abigail and Bolingbroke Anne was supposedly moving towards an acceptance of the 'Old Pretender' as her heir. As usual, the Viscount played a crafty game, never wholly revealing his true colours, but at his insistence a purge of Whiggish pro-Hanoverian officers was carried out in the army. By January the Queen was considerably better, so the crisis passed for the time being, but two months later she suffered a relapse. June saw the death of the aged Electress of Hanover, which made George of Hanover the direct heir by the terms of the Act of Settlements but Anne refused to allow him to enter England.

Marlborough's friends—such as Stanhope—kept him fully informed of all these developments. The months of waiting weighed heavier on Sarah than on the Duke. He seems to have enjoyed his leisure—and the local plaudits of well-wishers. Amongst the many visitors when he moved to Antwerp in December was the Count of Mérode-Westerloo, a bitter critic of Marlborough in earlier years. 'Yet, although he had never done me anything but harm, I nevertheless wished to bestow some marks of my generosity upon him in his disgrace, and indeed to be numbered amongst his friends at a time when his power was gone. ... And indeed we showed one another a deal of friendship.'[14] About this time the waspish Sarah accused her spouse of being 'intolerably lazy.'[15]

The continued refusal of the Pretender to consider adopting the Protestant faith compelled Oxford and Bolingbroke publicly to support the Hanoverian claim. Relations between the two politicians steadily moved from bad to worse in the early months of the year. The recently-dismissed Lord Steward, the Duke of Buckingham had satirised the sorry state of British politics a few months earlier. ' "Good God" (says his Grace lifting up his hands) "How has this poor nation been governed in my time! During the reign of King Charles the Second, we were governed by a parcel of French whores: in King James the Second's time, by a parcel of Popish priests: in King William's time by a parcel of Dutch footmen: and now we are governed by a dirty chambermaid, a Welsh attorney, and a profligate wretch, that has neither honour nor honesty".'[16]

The 'rogues', as all Whigs saw them, were now open enemies. To humiliate

Oxford, Bolingbroke forced the intolerant Schism Bill through Parliament against his opposition. The Earl, not to be outdone, prepared evidence of Bolingbroke's corruption, particularly in respect of the profits he had drawn from the recent trade treaty with Spain, the Quebec expedition of 1711, and from his raids upon the Secret Service funds. Meanwhile the Whigs formed the Association, determined to fight a Civil War rather than accept a Catholic monarch, and organised their friends in London, the shires and Scotland. Marlborough, true to his anti-party views, refused to subscribe, but was kept up to date with all contingency plans. As usual he was playing his double game—seeking secret guarantees from Louis XIV in late 1713, and begging for the 'Old Pretender's' pardon in April the following year. But by interest and inclination his true proclivity lay with Hanover.

The Tories were principally concerned with Jacobite schemings and the divisions within their own ranks. On 9 July, Abigail induced the Queen, sick though she was, to prorogue Parliament—and thus earned Bolingbroke and herself a respite from Oxford's threatened revelations. By this time Anne was determined to be rid of her troublesome Lord Treasurer, and at a stormy Council meeting on 27 July indicated that he should surrender his white staff of office. A furious altercation took place between Oxford and Bolingbroke in the Queen's presence, and the distress this occasioned her probably brought on her final illness. By the 30th she was once more seriously ill. In the meantime, Bolingbroke was, briefly as it was to prove, unofficial master of the state. But instead of acting decisively he prevaricated between the Jacobites and Hanover. On the evening of the 28th he even held an extraordinary dinner-party for his most outspoken political foes, and continued to waver. Civil war was in the balance— but then, abruptly, on the 30th, Bolingbroke's bluff was called. After subtle manœuvrings in the council, Lord Shrewsbury, backed by the Dukes of Argyle and Somerset, was put forward by Bolingbroke himself to succeed Lord Oxford. On her deathbed, that evening the Queen handed the white-staff to Shrewsbury. This act was tantamount to accepting the Hanoverian succession. On 1 August, Queen Anne died.

Shewsbury and his friends took rapid action to secure George's position and avert all danger of civil war. Bolingbroke, now completely cowed, signed all necessary instruments placed before him as Secretary-of-State; the fleet was mobilised; the army alerted. The Whig Association swung into action. Count Bothmar produced his secret list drawn up by Elector George, appointing 25 Regents. Bolingbroke's name was not on the list; nor, more surprisingly, was Marlborough's.

Prior to these climacteric events, Marlborough and his Duchess had left their 'very inconvenient house' at Antwerp, and headed for Ostend. In late July, as they passed by Ghent, 'all the officers of both regiments [garrisoning the city] went without Antwerp port [gate] and drew up in two lines to pay him our compliments and show the respect we still retained for his Grace', recorded Robert Parker of the 18th Foot. 'He and his Duchess came up to us on horseback; they stopped and talked to us of indifferent matters about half an hour. . . .'[17] Arrived at Ostend, they awaited a fair wind for a week, desiring to complete the journey in a single day. It is clear that the Duke was determined to return to England whether the Queen was dead or no, for he only learnt of her death upon his arrival at Dover on 2 August.

His progress to London became something of a triumph. His arrival in the City was thus: 'First came about three hundred horsemen, three in a row, then a company of trainbands, with drums etc., his own chariot with himself, then his duchess, followed by sixteen coaches with six horses and between thirty and forty with two horses.'[18] Whigs cheered; Tories (more discreetly, we may guess) are said to have hissed.

Marlborough is supposed to have been somewhat put out by his name's omission from the list of Regents, but when King George 1 landed on 18 September he was instantly gracious to the Duke—'My Lord Duke', George is reputed to have said, 'I hope your troubles are now over.'[19] The very first patent the new monarch had signed in Hanover restored Marlborough to his posts of Captain-General, Master-General of the Ordnance and Colonel of the First Foot Guards. But although much was made of him at court—perhaps for propaganda purposes—it is clear that the Duke was never in a position of real power. He had influence and patronage at his disposal, but 'German George' seems to have had no intention of employing him in any but military capacities. Nevertheless, his sons-in-law did well enough: Lord Godolphin was appointed Cofferer of the Household, Bridgewater became Lord Chamberlain to the Prince of Wales, and Montagu received command of a regiment whilst his wife became a lady-in-waiting to the Princess of Wales.

Marlborough's roles in early-Hanoverian England were thus peripheral rather than central on the political plane (although he persuaded the disgraced Bolingbroke to flee abroad to save his head), but in the military sphere the Captain-General still had important contributions to make. First he became the champion of the 'foreign officers' (particularly those of Huguenot origin) during the debates in Parliament reducing the size of the army to its peace-time establishment. Then occurred the crisis of the Scottish Rebellion of 1715. Marlborough did not see fit to take command in person, but deputed Argyle to lead the British troops north, and Cadogan to command the 6,000 Dutch soldiers. When Argyle proved unwilling to press conclusions, the Duke was instrumental in having him replaced in the senior command by the reliable Cadogan.

One aspect of these events did not redound to the credit of either the Board of Ordnance or its Master-General. The Tower armouries were found hopelessly unprepared for the new challenge, and the train of artillery took all of six months to reach Scotland, by which time the Rebellion was all but over. It was evident that the Board's functions needed to be overhauled, and on 10 January 1716 Marlborough was pleased to approve the recommendations of his Principal Officers. Besides the effecting of important economies, the resulting measures led to the creation of the Royal Regiment of Artillery (27 May 1716), which in due course became a fully integrated part of the army.

This important administrative action was one of Marlborough's last practical services to the Britsh Army. As his health deteriorated, he applied to lay down the burdens of the Captain-Generalcy, but was persuaded to remain the titular head of the army by the King who dreaded lest the post should go to his loathed heir, the Prince of Wales. Ironically, therefore, an unwilling Marlborough virtually received the 'Captain-Generalcy for Life' for which he had once pressed so hard, and only finally laid down the office in 1721.

The Duke's last years were a tale of deteriorating health, sad personal losses, and devastating family rows, interleaved with periods of genuine contentment spent between his homes at Hollywell, Windsor Park Lodge, Marlborough House and Blenheim Palace, of which he lived to see one wing completed. The sudden death from tuberculosis of his favourite daughter Anne, countess of Sunderland, in April 1716, was a grave blow which probably led to his first paralytic stroke on the 28 May that same year. For a time he lost the power of speech, but then gradually recovered before suffering a second grave attack in November. Once again he regained most of his faculties, although his speech was permanently impaired. These physical burdens, together with the great strains engendered by Sarah's continuous and bitter arguments with her remaining daughters, Henrietta and Mary, tended to make him somewhat embittered—and he, for so many years the most urbane and forgiving of men, pressed his feud with the Earl of Oxford, over the latter's impeachment, to the point of vendetta.

The Duke continued to attend the House of Lords until November 1721, but formally retired from public life in the May of the same year. His health was again giving reason for acute concern, and after a number of relapses he finally died, at Windsor Lodge, on 16 June 1722, just as dawn was breaking.

*   *   *

On one occasion as his long life drew towards its close, Marlborough is reputed to have paused before his portrait by Kneller, painted when he was a young man, and to have made the rather sad remark: 'That was once a man.'[20]

Any attempt to assess or summarise John Churchill's contribution to the art and science of warfare must necessarily take as its starting point the man himself. A commander's character and personality, as well as being influenced by the strains of warfare, equally place a stamp on his particular brand of generalship. Many of Marlborough's traits have been mentioned in earlier chapters, but now it is time to draw together the varied threads—both golden and of darker hue— in the hope of producing an overall impression of him, as both man and soldier.

If the behavioural scientists are to be believed, the essential nature of a man is largely formed in childhood and adolescence. The genteel poverty and confused political atmosphere of his earliest years at Asche House indubitably left their mark.[21] His father's social pretensions and strong Royalist sympathies were clearly passed on to his eldest son, born 16 months after the execution of King Charles I. From these varied influences, the young Churchill learnt to revere the established church of the realm and the House of Stuart, to conceal his personal political feelings, and to be extremely careful in all matters pertaining to money. These traits we shall in due course return to.

We know relatively little about his mother's influence. Apart from the fact that she opposed her son's proposed marriage to Sarah (largely on financial grounds), and that she was decidedly 'peevish' when her daughter-in-law lived under her and Sir Winston's roof in 1680 (though Sarah must have been a redoubtable member of the family, even in youth)[22] Elizabeth Churchill remains in the shadows. John's maternal grandmother, on the other hand, was evidently of the strongest character and puritanical outlook, and doubtless applied the rod of discipline to the young boy when his father was lost in his genealogical research and his mother was wholly absorbed with the care of the rest of the family. There seems to have been little undue softness in Lady Eleanor Drake.

His schooling appears to have been conventional for the day, if somewhat dislocated by the family's frequent moves. However, the transition from the strict penury of Asche House and the intellectual discipline of St. Paul's School to the 'jovial times' and permissive atmosphere of the Court of Charles II must have given no small shock to the adolescent youth's system. Certainly he seems to have made the most of his opportunities, but the fact that he was not transformed into a voluptuary must be in large measure ascribed to his earlier upbringing. He had learnt from the earliest years to keep his own counsel and not to be taken-in by appearances. These qualities were to serve him well on many a long campaign in later years.

Two reasons may be suggested for his choice of a military career. First, the influence of Sir Winston Churchill, the sometime Captain of Royalist Horse, probably provided the original incentive. Secondly, the continued poverty of both John and his family after the Restoration must also have played a part. A young courtier with no money and even slenderer prospects could hope for no better way to improve his fortunes than to adopt the profession of arms—and earn preferment and notice by his gallant behaviour at the cannon's mouth. Churchill's ambition was not a development of later life, but was the main driving force from his youth. Of his poverty there can be no question: he relied on the gifts of his mistress, the Duchess of Cleveland, to procure his early steps, and it was only after five years of marriage that he could afford to buy a house of his own. Of his valour and reputation as a young soldier, we have already said enough in earlier pages.

Thus by his early twenties we have a young man already worldly-wise and experienced by the standards of his day, yet also noticed for his basic common-sense, willingness to learn, confidence in his own judgment, and his general good humour (rather than sense of humour, for to his life's end John Churchill seems to have been of a rather staid and serious temperament). His qualities as a husband and father were severely tested over the years—but some of the most likeable aspects of the man are those that relate to his life-long love for both Sarah and their children. The death of his son-and-heir in 1703 left a lasting scar, and that of his favourite daughter in 1716 hastened the collapse of his health. As for Sarah, in 1702 he wrote that her letters were 'so welcome to me' that he 'could not forebear to read them' even if he was 'expecting the enemy to charge me.'

From these general points drawn from his early life, we must pass to consider specific character traits which affected his skills as a general. First we must examine his ambition, for Churchill was driven by a ruthless daemon. He was avid throughout his life for wealth, power and social position. Fortunately for both himself and his country, his dreams were to a great degree matched by his talents, and although he suffered many disappointments and setbacks, and had to wait until his middle years for the realisation of most of his ambitions, he was tireless throughout his life (until the last decade, perhaps, when ill-health and a touch of disillusion appeared) in his quest for fame. In pursuit of his personal interests he could be unscrupulous—as his desertion of James II in 1688 bears evidence. On the other hand he could also display a strong streak of altruism and unselfishness—as his long loyalty to Queen Anne, which survived the decline of their friendship until 1712, or his refusal of the twice-proferred position of Viceroy of the Spanish Netherlands and his genuine concern for the interests of the Second Grand Alliance, provide incontrovertible witness. He became both a Duke and a Prince of the Holy Roman Empire, yet the passion for pre-eminent position (as well as political stability) could move him to press repeatedly and ill-advisedly for the award of the Captain-Generalcy for life during the years between 1709 and 1712. He was undoubtedly an opportunist.

This ambition was often concealed behind an urbane and polished exterior. His charm and outward gentleness were legendary even in his own time. On occasion he could revert to straightforward flattery—as during his visit to Altranstadt in 1707 when he assured Charles XII of Sweden of his desire to serve under his command to learn the last refinements in the military arts. It is re-corded of him that he never issued a harsher rebuke than to send a message to the culprit to the effect that 'My Lord Duke is surprised. . . .' The published correspondence, however, does occasionally give a sharper expression of phrase, and his private letters to Heinsius often reveal his unadorned feelings. Yet his good-manners in public were irreproachable and he could find time to write to persistent absentees amongst his officers entreating them to return to their duty 'for want of which the Queen's service doth suffer daily.'[23] He could refuse a request with considerably more grace than many another could muster to confer a favour. His consideration for Tallard, captured at Blenheim, is only one of many examples of his courtesy to his enemies, especially when vanquished or wounded—as after Malplaquet. His gentleness extended to the rank and file; he would give occasional lifts to tired and sweaty foot-soldiers in his coach;[24] he was ever-concerned for their welfare, and yet was genuinely surprised and elated when they responded with marks of affection—as at Elixhem in 1705 when he was cheered by his cavalry. '. . . This gave occasion to the troops with me to make me very kind expressions, even in the heat of the action, which I own to you gives me great pleasure, and makes me resolve to endure anything for their sakes.'[25] He had been similarly moved by the public rejoicing at his escape from the French in the barge incident of 1702. He liked popularity.

When occasion demanded it, however, he could be ruthless. On 16 July 1704 he coolly wrote to Godolphin as his army ravaged Bavaria: 'We are doing all the mischief we can to this country, in order to make the Elector think of saving what he cannot reach; for as we advance we burn and destroy; but if this should not make him come to a treaty, I am afraid it may at last do ourselves hurt for want of what we destroy.'[26] Not a word of compassion for the local populace— just the hard military realities, although we have every reason to believe from other occasions that the sight of wounded or suffering afflicted him. Indeed, he wrote to Sarah at much the same time that the destruction '. . . is so uneasy to my nature that nothing but an absolute necessity would have obliged me to consent to it.' Yet as a general he was prepared to burn 400 villages in the name of (to borrow Cromwell's reputed phrase), 'cruel necessity'.

This aspect of his personality contrasts markedly with the image of the solicitous and cosmopolitan Duke, who could ease his path through matters personal, diplomatic or military with the same deft courtesy—whether he was dealing with the touchy Württemberg in 1690, the cantankerous Baden in 1704 and 1705, the critical Goslinga or the mercurial Charles XII. A few were wholly untouched by his charm—including General Slangenberg; others refused to let it sway their judgement or ambitions—such as Robert Harley, and (latterly) the unscrupulous Henry St. John. The majority of men however, and not a few women, were deeply impressed by his manifest courtesy, poise and sound common sense. Many of his men adulated his memory. Corporal Matthew Bishop wrote that 'The known world could not produce a man of more humanity.'[27] It would be possible to quote similar testimony from a dozen other sources. His ability to inspire trust and confidence amongst his men of many nations is nowhere better evidenced than in Parker's celebrated passage describing an incident before Bouchain, already cited.* Yet it is possible that he was—his soldiers apart—rather admired than loved. As Professor Trevelyan aptly described it, 'the flame of his spirit served for light, not warmth.'

And yet this same paragon of virtue also had the reputation of being the meanest of men where money was concerned. One reason for this has already been suggested, but whatever the explanation there is no doubting that this avaricious streak existed. Not all the stories can have been apocryphal, and there was no lack of them, whether pertaining to his military or private life. In an age when generals were expected to keep open house for their subordinates, the Duke avoided entertaining in the field whenever possible.

It is true that he was a man of simple habits, but he went to some pains to 'drop-by' their quarters at appropriate times of day. 'There in my presence they were regulating the marches', wrote Lord Ailesbury of a visit to headquarters in early 1704, 'and my lord asking what general officer would be, of the day, as they term. And then asked is such and such had a good cook, as that they should treat him at supper after the marches. . . .'[28] He was similarly averse to spending good guineas on hiring suitable accommodation for part of the winter season, if an alternative could be discovered. Early in 1709 he persuaded a Dutch general to take a modish and sizeable residence at the Hague, and then moved into half of it with his suite as an unpaying and largely uninvited guest. Once in Bath, after losing some money at cards, and needing to hire a sedan-chair to carry him home, he borrowed a coin from General Pulteney for the fare. On reaching the door, however, the canny Duke decided to walk after all, but not before bidding ceremonious good-night to his host—and pocketing the sixpence! Years later he had his campaign tent pitched in the garden of one of his houses, and opened it to visits by the public, but (in anticipation of numerous modern and certainly more impecunious lords) exacted a considerable admission-fee for the privilege. He is even reputed to have commented approvingly of Prince Eugene's supposed failure to dot his 'i's in letters, that the habit 'would serve to save the ink.' All great men have their quirks of character, and Duke John was no exception. But if he hoarded his guineas he was equally careful with his men's lives—a trait of which they thoroughly approved. And he could be generous—with Sarah and the family always; and occasionally he is known to have paid for the promotion of some deserving but impecunious junior officer.

His personal courage—both moral and physical—was also legendary from at least the Maastricht episode of 1672 if not earlier. Yet he was certainly never over-confident or unduly sanguine. We have seen him set out for almost every campaign 'with a heavy heart', burdened with the sense of responsibility and strain that are the inescapable concomitants of high command. He was frequently very depressed and even physically ill over the days immediately preceding

* See Chapter 14, p. 294 above.

battle—as before both Blenheim and Oudenarde. His comments after the latter battle reveal how aware he was of the risks he undertook in crossing the Scheldt that July day—but he also knew that 'nothing else would make the Queen's business go well.'* His personal interventions, sword in hand, in the cavalry engagements at both Ramillies and Elixhem, provide testimony to his continued gallantry in action.

Given his age on first assuming high command, Marlborough must have been endowed with a remarkably strong constitution to have survived so well the rigours of ten successive campaigns with barely a break. We know that he relied upon hard riding every day to keep himself fit, and the abstemious side of his character and his preference for simple living on campaign were undoubtedly of assistance. By any standards he was remarkably tough for a middle-aged man. At Ramillies he spent 15 hours in the saddle planning and controlling the battle; he led at least two charges, was 'rid over' and almost captured once, and narrowly avoided being killed by a cannon-ball—and yet was still capable of pursuing the enemy for 12 miles before at last snatching a few hours sleep on the bare ground, wrapped in his general's cloak, which, with typical thoughtfulness (and perhaps a cunning awareness of the opportunity for a theatrical gesture) he invited the critical Dutchman, Colonel Goslinga, to share.

On the other hand he was frequently the victim of severe migraines and 'dizziness in my head'. It is clear that these attacks were often brought on by the relentless strains of politics and war, and always lurked in the background at times of maximum crisis and stress—as, for instance, before Oudenarde. In the end these headaches may have led to the strokes that killed him. There is also some evidence to be culled from his letters that on occasion he suffered from insomnia; the utterly calm and composed aspect of the Duke on days of battle— so admired by his soldiers—was partly a deliberate act and reveals his great degree of self-control. He appears never to have vented his rage on any human being, but most probably his bottled-up emotions, frustrations and 'silent rages' were a major contributory factor to his migraines. His chaplain, Dr. Hare, noted that 'the Duke does not say much, but no one's countenance speaks more.' By 1710 he was becoming 'sensible of the inconvenience of old age', and during his last campaign he was mentioning 'frequent and sensible remembrances of my growing old.' By that time he was over 60, and it is amazing that his capabilities, both mental and physical, were still so unimpaired. Perhaps the ceaseless activity of his wonted life was one good reason. In Winston Churchill's opinion, 'he was a greater worker than man.'[29]

There is no denying that he was a life-long intriguer of a most cunning disposition. Thirty-five years of close association with the convolutions of Stuart courts had inevitably bred a complex personality with a strong instinct for personal survival. His continued contacts with the courts-in-exile of James II

* See Chapter 11, p. 222 above.

and his son were as much a matter of insurance as one of convenience. Both William III and George I had some reason for mental reservations in regard to the Duke. His desertion of his old master and patron in 1688 might have helped clinch the 'Glorious Revolution', but no monarch (except possibly Anne) could wholly trust so powerful a subject thereafter. Of Marlborough's strongly Anglican religious convictions there can be no doubt, and his determination to see the development and maintenance of an equitable balance of power in Europe would also seem to have been firmly established, but many of his other attitudes appear somewhat enigmatic and ambiguous. In this he was very much a man of his time, and perhaps it is therefore unjust to judge him by any other standards.

It seems distinctly improbable that he was venal—as his enemies so often strove to prove. He certainly took pleasure in the legitimate perquisites attached to his high rank and station, and indubitably collected every penny he considered his fair due (it is estimated that in his hey-day he was worth £60,000 a year in the values of the time) from the sale of commissions and other offices in his gift; but it is nonsense to assert that he sought 'to prolong the war in order to further his advantage.'[30] He was to a considerable extent the butt of lesser men and the public enemy of the envious. He and his Duchess were the victims of 'scurrilous pamphlets and malicious invectives' (Parker); the 'little mercenary scribblers' and even the great Jonathan Swift certainly did their best to sully his name and bring him down.

On the other hand, there was a little fire beneath all the smoke of party and factional vituperation. As we have seen, he was fully aware of the value of his services to Queen and country, and was determined to gain his fair share of recognition, honours and other rewards. This is understandable. But it was one thing to maintain a clandestine correspondence with St. Germain and Versailles as a means of gaining political and military intelligence and of dispensing a little fallacious or out-dated information in return (as in the case of the Camaret Bay letter), and quite another to use these channels to make it clear that he expected a *douceur* of several million gold *livres* in return for good offices in securing an amelioration of peace terms at the conference table—as happened in 1708 and 1709—or again to seek Louis XIV's personal guarantee for the security of the Marlborough fortune—as happened in 1713.

It is clear that his sense of pride and personal integrity were capable of adjustment to meet the needs of the hour. If a little flattery and sinuosity are acceptable and even amusing in his handling of Charles XII in 1707, it is difficult to reconcile the scourge of the French army with the abject lordling who could plead on his knees for his wife's continued employment about the Queen in 1710. Yet this same man was capable of long and genuine friendships with such men as Godolphin and Cadogan, and was in his wife's view tolerant and forgiving to a fault where others were concerned—even when, like Henry St. John, they owed much yet served him false. As the Duke once wrote to Godolphin, he had a great belief in 'patience that can overcome all things.' In sum, here was a most complex and multi-sided personality that largely baffles final analysis. If, as was most certainly the case, there was both good and bad in the man, all that we can say is that the gold far outweighed the dross.

To conclude this character assessment, it is worth citing perhaps the most percipient contemporary view which has survived—that of Colonel Sicco van Goslinga. A politician as well as a soldier himself, he knew he was describing no ordinary man. 'His mind is keen and subtle, his judgement both clear and sound, his insight quick and deep, with an all-embracing knowledge of men which no false show of merit can deceive. He expresses himself well, and even his very bad French is agreeable: he has a harmonious voice, and as a speaker of his own language he is considered amongst the best. His address is most courteous, and while his handsome and well-graced countenance engages every one in his favour at first sight, his perfect manners and gentleness win over even those who start with a prejudice or grudge against him. He has courage as he has shown on more than one occasion: he is an experienced soldier, and plans a campaign to admiration. So far his good qualities. Now for the weak points which I consider I have discovered in him. The Duke is a profound dissembler, all the more dangerous that his manner and his words give the impression of frankness itself. His ambition knows no bounds, and an avarice that I can only call sordid, guides his entire conduct. If he has courage—and of this there is no question, whatever may be said by those who envy or hate him—he certainly lacks that firmness of soul which makes the true Hero. Sometimes on the eve of an action, he is irresolute or worse; he will not face difficulties, and occasionally lets reverses cast him down: of this I could give several eye-witness accounts [Goslinga was at Oudenarde]. Yet I saw nothing of the kind either at Ramillies or Malplaquet, so that it may be that some constitutional weakness, unfitting him to bear fatigue, has something to do with it. He is not a strict disciplinarian, and allows his men too much rein, who have occasionally indulged in frightful excesses. Moreover he lacks the precise knowledge of military detail which a Commander-in-Chief should possess. But these defects are light when balanced against the rare gifts of this truly great man.'[31] This, it should be remembered, was the view of a critic.

The complex kaleidoscope of early eighteenth-century war can, for convenience of study, be divided into five closely inter-related levels. At the apex comes 'Grand Strategy', the formulation of national policy and war aims, the creation and preservation of alliances. Next comes 'Strategy', the planning of campaigns and series of operations with the intention of carrying out the Grand Strategic objectives. Third are 'Grand Tactics'—the devising of battle plans and the outlines of operations to profit from the situations the strategy has made possible or encouraged to develop. Fourth are 'minor Tactics'—the actual fighting methods employed at unit level to gain a local success, which, together with a dozen or more similar engagements, go to make up a victory. Lastly, but in fact involved at every level, come logistics—an immense field involving every aspect of military administration and support, especially the movement, equipment and feeding of armies in the field. None of these strata are self-sufficient: the dividing line between 'Strategy' and 'Grand Tactics', for instance, becomes blurred and indistinct, whilst logistical considerations affect 'Grand Strategy' as vitally as 'Tactics'. The planning, organisation and waging of an armed struggle is thus a cumulative process, and probably the most daunting test a country, government and its armed forces and populace can be called upon to face.

Many soldiers of distinction have been directly involved in each successive level as they proceed up the military tree. Very few have been called upon to be intimately concerned with all strata at the same time, but one such was John Churchill in the years between 1702 and 1712.

In considering Marlborough's showing at the level of Grand Strategy, it is first necessary to devote a few words to the machinery that formulated policy. In the case of Great Britain, the Queen, as advised by her ministers, controlled foreign and war policy, but Parliament had a considerable say through control of the purse, and since 1700 had exerted a demand to approve proposed treaties. In the case of the United Provinces, the key figure was the Grand Pensionary, answerable in varying degrees to the States-General. The Emperor, on the other hand, was master within his own domains, advised on matters of military policy by the *Hofkriegsrath*; in the case of the Holy Roman Empire, however, he found it politic to consult the various Electors and member states and in effect negotiate with them. Apart from the occasional conference, the conduct of the affairs of the Grand Alliance was entrusted to ambassadors and special envoys—and this could involve long delays in negotiations concerning policy. At best, therefore, the Alliance was governed by a 'discordant committee'; at worst, the individual members followed only their own interests.

The Bourbon powers, by comparison, were far more centralised in terms of both geography and institutions. Louis XIV, advised by his ministers and the *conseil d'en haut*, but responsible to nobody but his conscience, was able to dictate policy on many occasions to his confederates. Philip V and the Spanish government were rarely in a position to contest the decisions of Versailles on account of family, economic and military considerations. From 1704 both Bavaria and Cologne had fallen into Allied hands, and their rulers were little more than ciphers. In sum, therefore, the French had the advantages of relatively centralised war direction.

In the final analysis, the Grand Strategic issues were simple. France and Spain were basically committed to the defensive, desiring to preserve the *status quo*—both in terms of the will of Charles II of Spain, and, in the case of France, those territories that had been gained by marriage and war since 1648.

The powers of the Grand Alliance, on the other hand, shared only two aims in common at the outset of the struggle, namely the restriction of the ambitions of Louis XIV and a fair division of the Spanish inheritance to maintain the balance of power. For the rest, their interests tended to be divergent, selfish and conflicting. All the main Allied aims involved offensive action in one way or another, as the Bourbons would not consider (before 1706) any significant concessions.

Marlborough played a vital part in this potential imbroglio. He was one of the few influences working towards genuine unity. He alone, after 1704, had the prestige that could sway international decisions. Even earlier, he had been William III's vital deputy during the formulation of the original treaties. His role as preserver of the Alliance was no less crucial, as was proved during the crises of 1704, 1705 and 1707. His methods were threefold. First, his ever more redoubtable military reputation inspired his Allies, some of whom were further sustained by regular and sizeable subsidies. Between 1701 and 1711 England and the Dutch paid over £8 million, two-thirds of which came from London.[32] Secondly, there were the Duke's frequent personal visits to heads of state, often made during the winter months. And thirdly we must mention the combination of his charm and gifts for dissimulation, which he lavishly employed to avoid head-on clashes of interest.

Doubtless this determination to avoid major confrontations forms one vital pre-requisite in the head of a far-flung alliance, but in Marlborough's case it led in one vital instance to a grave error of policy. The extension of the war aims to include the replacement of Philip V as King of Spain proved a fatal mistake. This decision developed over a number of years. From the first, the Emperor had formally demanded such a clause, but this was regarded as little more than a negotiating position by both England and the United Provinces—and without the support of these two powers Austria could not hope to force the issue. The accession of Portugal in late 1703 had occasioned the 'writing-in' of this concept, however, and by 1706 the Whigs in Great Britain had become enamoured of the proposal, whilst the States-General offered scant resistance. Marlborough too, as we have seen, had early hopes of achieving peace through Spain and Italy. Following the disasters of 1707, however, the chances of victory in Spain became increasingly remote, and Marlborough stands charged with not pressing his private grave doubts on this subject. The Allies would have been wise to cut their losses after Almanza, and close-down the Spanish front. Instead, they insisted on reinforcing failure—and thus created an incessant and hopeless drain of men, money and material which ultimately also prejudiced their chances of complete success in Flanders. Marlborough—for possibly understandable political and diplomatic reasons, including the sanctity of treaties——never spoke out, and for this he must bear the full responsibility. Spain proved as poisonous and debilitating an ulcer for the Second Grand Alliance as ever it became for Napoleon a century later.

Of course there were moments when the policies of the Alliance, however ill-conceived, came very close to achieving victory. In both late 1708, and early 1709 and 1710, Louis XIV was on the point of accepting humiliating terms; but as we have seen the Allied statesmen insisted on imposing conditions of increasing severity, until even Marlborough found himself in secret sympathy with the King of France.* By then, although Marlborough's political influence at home had practically disappeared, he still possessed vast prestige abroad; but he does not seem to have communicated his innermost convictions to either his Allies or to his political masters. To this extent, then, he must bear responsibility for the continuation of the war beyond its logical limits.

There can be little doubt that Marlborough's weakness lay in his relationship to the English political scene. With so much else to claim his attention, it is amazing he found any time—as revealed by his letters—to devote to the endless convolutions of British politics. Even so, here after 1707 lay his Achilles' heel, and the occasion of his fall. Marlborough was never desirous of selling himself, body and soul, to any single party or faction, preferring a *via media*. His personal convictions were moderate-Tory; those of his wife strongly Whig; but whilst he and Godolphin enjoyed full royal support Marlborough's non-partisan policy enjoyed considerable success. Once Anne's favour was turned elsewhere, however, the Duke's political isolation was manifest, and he became little more than a political cipher, the servant of the Whigs and then the victim of the Tories. In sum, he failed to secure his political base, just as Godolphin, for all his financial acumen, failed to find any solutions other than the imposition of ever higher taxation and the seeking of more expensive loans to meet the mounting costs of the war.† As a result, when the delicate system of checks and balances was disturbed, both men fell from both favour and office.

In finally assessing Marlborough as a grand strategist, we find a man with a rare grasp of the broad issues and problems involved. From the start of the war, he could see the struggle as a whole, and if his judgment of the Spanish front was blurred after 1707, he proved remarkably prescient and competent in other areas. Few, if any, contemporaries shared this attribute, and so non-existent was the general appreciation of the rudiments of strategy that in 1704 it was possible for serious politicians to fear that he had 'stolen the army' when he left the Netherlands for the Danube.[33] Marlborough's 'over-view' (if such it may be termed) is well exemplified that same spring by his willingness to detach four prized English battalions from his army in Flanders for service with Rooke's fleet in the Mediterranean on the very eve of his own risk-taking march.

He was unique amongst his fellow-soldiers in his appreciation of the part

* See p. 244 above.

† Public expenditure averaged out at £8,500,000 p.a. between 1702 and 1714. Some 40% o f this was spent on the army, and 35% on the navy. Subsidies to allies amounted to about £500,000 p.a. (1701–1711).

sea-power could play in support of a Continental war. He never subscribed to the emerging 'blue water' school of thought,* but adhered to William III's concept of a continental approach to European and naval strategy. His experiences aboard the fleet in his early career and the influence of William III had convinced him of the value of a navy deployed in support of a large native army fighting in Europe, employing such operations as coastal raids, the capture of bases (particularly in the Mediterranean) and the threat of landings to distract enemy resources, once command of the seas had been secured by the defeat or blockade of his fleet, and the free passage of the Allied merchant 'trades' from the depredations of squadrons and privateers had been assured. If this policy had its failures (Cadiz, 1702 and Toulon, 1707, or the heavy losses of merchant ships suffered at the hands of the Dunkirk and St. Malo privateers), it also had its successes (the winning of Malaga and capture of Gibraltar in 1704, and the taking of Minorca in 1708). His abortive plan for exploiting Oudenarde in late 1708 further demonstrates his ability to coordinate naval and military forces in single enterprises, and so do the arrangements made to support the siege of Lille. His influence over naval matters was exercised for many years through his friendship with Prince George of Denmark, Lord High Admiral, and with the rather less valuable assistance of his brother, Admiral George Churchill.

As a strategist, Marlborough proved inspired, despite the limitations imposed by doubting governments and hesitant allies. Only in 1704, when he deliberately fooled friend and foe alike, did the Duke wage a campaign wholly of his own devising, and even then he was bound to a basically defensive concept by the circumstances of the day. Passing his ten campaigns in review, it is difficult to escape the conclusion that the Duke was at his best in a strategically defensive role. His first two campaigns, together with those of 1704 and 1708, were largely fought to neutralise enemy gains and retrieve lost ground. His offensives—as in 1705, 1707, 1709 and 1710—tended to lead to less dramatic results, but that of 1706 reveals his greatness in exploiting an unanticipated battle success to the very limit. Unfortunately a similar opportunity after Oudenarde had to be abandoned in favour of a more prosaic and conventional approach—namely the siege of Lille. But in judging Marlborough's showing it cannot be stressed too much that he never enjoyed true freedom of action. His Allies proved late in reporting—as was the case with Baden in 1705—or insisted on mounting irrelevant campaigns—for example the Austrian attack on Naples in 1707. The Dutch were obsessed with their national security, or concerned to keep casualties and expenditure as low as possible—even at the expense of vetoing promising military operations. Marlborough suffered greatly from the restrictions imposed by Dutch field deputies or obstructive generals. Under the circumstances it is amazing that he achieved so much. One factor, however, other than his genius,

* See p. 58 above. The Tory interest in the 'blue water' approach is typified by St. John's expedition against Quebec in 1711 and the terms of the Peace of Utrecht.

consistently operated in his favour. The French problem was diametrically opposite to his own. If the Duke had to carry his Allies with him and frequently accept compromises in order to ensure their cooperation, the proud marshals rarely dared to change or even vary a plan without time-consuming reference to Versailles. King Louis XIV kept his generals on a very tight rein, and however desirable a rigid centralisation might be in the formulation of general policy, it proved a grave complication in the waging of day-to-day warfare. The disadvantages of the two systems therefore tended to cancel one another out: what Marlborough conceded by way of shelved schemes in the interests of Allied unity, the French Marshals lost in terms of delays and hesitation.

Marlborough's abilities as a general in the Spanish Succession War largely relate to his showing in the Netherlands and Flanders regions. Only twice—in 1704, and (briefly) in 1705, did he lead his armies elsewhere—to the Danube and Moselle respectively. In 1706 he planned to march to Italy, but circumstances intervened. The 'Cockpit of Europe', therefore, absorbed most of his military attention.

There were good reasons for this. The theatre's proximity to both the United Provinces and to England was one major advantage. The area was the most convenient rallying point for the forces supplied by Denmark and the princes of North Germany, whilst the sea-link from Harwich to the Hague was the principal life-line for English reinforcements, remounts and munitions. Secondly, the region enjoyed a superior communications system—rivers and canals—which eased movement and encouraged a high relative level of fertility, which helped solve the perennial problems of supply. It also held large towns and a prosperous population, which offered both strategic defensive advantages and the alluring prospects of booty. Again, the perennial Dutch fears for security were largely quieted by his presence at the head of the main English army, and after the shocks of 1704 the States-General virtually insisted upon his remaining in the region.

Some commentators have tended to criticise Marlborough as a strategist for allowing himself to be restricted to a single front in this way. His critics claim that this doomed him to an unimaginative war of sieges, removing one by one the great fortresses blocking the roads towards Paris and victory. There can be no denying that his campaigns did become siege-dominated after 1706, nor that he found this irksome (*vide* his plan, first produced in 1708 and resuscitated at least twice, based upon a sea-supplied 'hook' round the fortress region to the River Somme). It cannot be contended that he was, in fact, attacking the best-defended sector of the French frontiers. At the same time, however, there are convincing arguments for the wisdom of such a course. Apart from the geographical and supply advantages already mentioned, the region represented the most important strategic sector blocking the approaches to northern France (and thence to Paris) and to the United Provinces and North German Plain respectively.

Furthermore, the importance the French laid upon the region made it the ideal area for a war of attrition. If the Allies would not give Marlborough a free hand in devising a rapid war-winning strategy, at least Flanders enabled them to deploy their superior resources under a proved leader, at a point that must, magnet-like, attract the steadily diminishing French reserves year by year. In other words, Flanders can be likened to the role accorded to Verdun by the Germans in 1917—a deliberate attempt to bleed the French white, both in terms of men and money—and thus ultimately destroy the will and the ability of Louis XIV to offer further resistance to the Allied demands. But for the fatal counter-attraction exerted by Spain, this strategy of attrition might well have proved successful: we have seen how limited were French resources by early 1709 and 1710. As it transpired, however, the Allies were just not strong enough to clinch their mounting advantage, and Flanders became the scene of first a strategic stalemate, and then, after Marlborough's removal from the scene, for the eleventh-hour French recovery.

So much for overall considerations of strategy. Marlborough's methods as a strategist have been listed on earlier pages: his preference for battle as the sole means of achieving long-term advantages, if at a heavy immediate price; his consequent distaste for slow-moving siege warfare.* It is estimated that his genius created all of 18 battle situations, but only one third were actually fought. On five occasions he found enemies more or less willing to fight (at the Schellenberg, Blenheim, Elixhem, Ramillies and Malplaquet); on one (Oudenarde), he forced the issue. At Wynendael, General Webb defeated an over-confident enemy. On perhaps six occasions he was thwarted by Allied hesitations or obstruction, twice his own ardour cooled and once he refused to force battle (after Bouchain); the French escaped him twice.[34] Time and again he used ruses and speed to conceal his intentions, and the corollary was his own skill at divining enemy intentions through the superior intelligence activities masterminded by Cadogan.

In sum, as a strategist he proved far-sighted and able to grasp essentials, and he was often far-ahead of his contemporaries in his conceptions. His aim was generally clear and maintained—except in those instances when considerations of Allied unity induced him to change his plans. Aided by his expert staff, particularly Cadogan, he was a master at calculating time and distance, at assessing marching capacity, reinforcement prospects and his own men's and the foe's characteristics in action, and at allowing for the interaction of weather and terrain. Above all, he could convert theory into practice. As Hilaire Belloc wrote, 'The test does not lie so much in the general conception as in the execution of a plan.'[35]

At the level of Grand Tactics—the planning of the general nature of an operation—Marlborough was again extremely adept. His objective in battle was to defeat the enemy, inflicting the maximum damage in the process. His method,

* See p. 63 above.

as we have seen, was invariably to seize the initiative and keep it throughout. Under his command, the Allies invariably attacked—in interesting contrast to later years when the British generally awaited the foe before counter-attacking. This offensive posture was also good for morale, gave him in some degree the choice of time and place, and the chance to exploit both. After employing surprise to commit the enemy to action whether he desired it or not (rapid advances under cover of darkness were the chosen means before both Blenheim and Oudenarde; at the Schellenberg, he achieved surprise by pressing a major attack late in the afternoon), the Duke invariably conducted a minute personal reconnaissance of the enemy position, seeking indications of structural weaknesses in their dispositions, or of helpful characteristics of terrain.

Next, having thrown the foe off-balance by the abrupt precipitation of the crisis, Marlborough would launch initial probing attacks designed to draw enemy reserves into action, whilst his own forces completed their own battle formations. These were often unusual in design—as at Blenheim, where the left was six lines deep and the centre all of four or, at Oudenarde, where a battle-line was gradually assembled, the troops arriving over the Scheldt being rushed straight into action as the encounter-type engagement developed.

At all stages of a battle, the Duke was insistent that infantry, cavalry and cannon should cooperate closely in what today would be termed combat groups. At the same time, he invariably made a point of keeping a strong force of cavalry in reserve ready to deliver the *coup de grâce*, or (it never proved necessary) cover a retreat. The action developed from probing attacks to stronger onslaughts on selected points—designed to draw in the remaining enemy reserves, and, ideally, to induce the foe to weaken the sector by now chosen for the main attack. Then, after containing the induced amalgamations of enemy troops with a minimum of his own forces, the Captain-General would carefully assemble a decisive superiority of force opposite the predetermined point, and unleash his devastating blow. The enemy line once sundered, the battle was *ipso facto* won, but it still remained to convert the foe's defeat into rout. Marlborough was unusual in his belief in immediate pursuit. After Ramillies the follow-through was relentless; after Blenheim, the pursuit was delayed for a day by the need to cope with the mass of wounded and prisoners; after Malplaquet there were no fresh troops available. Strategic exploitation of success was even rarer in this age, but it was certainly achieved in May and June 1706, when the whole of the Spanish Netherlands was overrun in the weeks after Ramillies.

The pressure in a Marlburian battle was relentless—pauses being brief and only countenanced when necessary to re-order the line of battle, which was regarded as sacrosanct on land as at sea. A major problem was the imposition of overall control over a battle area that might be several miles in extent, with the scene almost wholly obliterated by the dense clouds of black-powder smoke. Marlborough was famed for his ability to overcome the problems of distance and obscurity, and for his knack at appearing at critical points to rally the men as if guided by superhuman knowledge. As has been mentioned elsewhere, his secret was the use of carefully-selected *aides-de-camp*, who were trained to report on what was taking place on every sector using their own judgement. These 'eyes' served the Captain-General well.

If there was a weak side to Marlborough's Grand Tactics, it lay in their becoming a trifle predictable. Although on three occasions he experimented with tactical outflanking movements that interestingly foreshadowed Napoleon's later practice, his basic method remained the combination of secondary attacks against the enemy's flanks followed by the break-through attempt in the centre. Thus were Blenheim and Ramillies won, and also Malplaquet—but only at grave cost, for by 1709 Villars had learnt what to expect. Oudenarde was the exception that proved the rule. In 1708 the Dutch outflanking attack round the Boser Couter was the clinching move, but the other outflanking attempts—at the 'unfought Waterloo' in 1705 and against the French left at Malplaquet, were either not put into execution or mistimed.

Considerations of timing and use of ground were of the very essence. Marlborough was generally extremely skilled in judging the former, and he had a sure eye for terrain. It was use of dead-ground at both Ramillies and Oudenarde that materially assisted the winning of the day.* He would also use fog and mist to conceal the moves before battle, but several times heavy rain reduced his mobility and thwarted his schemes. His flexible mind and complete confidence in the instrument ready to his hand made him a formidable opponent. It would be wrong to assert that he advanced into battle with a complete plan fixed in his mind (save, possibly, at Malplaquet), but it is equally certain that he had a broad scheme already considered which he adapted to suit revealed circumstances. In his conduct of each battle there were unique factors, but the general principles became well-established and identifiable. In the case of his sieges, he was more bound by convention and the rigid practices of the time, but the skill with which he covered the sieges of Lille and Bouchain were outstanding examples of the military art.

Fourthly, at the tactical level, he also had a determinant influence to exert. At a time when there were no intermediary staffs at corps or divisional level (these formations lay in the future, although the battle-lines did provide a rough command structure), and even brigades were largely extemporised, it was not uncommon for the army commander to issue orders directly to his colonels of foot and horse. Command in battle was thus a very personal affair. Marlborough's tactical concept of coordinated all-arms attacks has already been referred to; he was equally insistent on the broad type of tactics each arm was to adopt. For the foot, he insisted on the use of the platoon-firing system, and ensured that the necessary drills were frequently practiced, even during the winter season.

* See pp. 176 and 270 above.

He did not originate the system (which evolved from Swedish and Dutch practice), but he did insist on its implementation.

Where the cavalry was concerned, he taught the importance of shock action. Twin-squadron charges, four ranks deep, delivered at the fast trot (the charge *à l'outrance* was discouraged as too likely to lead to confusion) was his formula for success. That it worked well is illustrated by Palmes' charge at Blenheim and the final attack, as well as the great cavalry actions at Ramillies and Malplaquet.

As Master-General of the Ordnance, Marlborough was more interested in the artillery than most commanders-in-chief of his day. He took a personal part in the siting of his batteries, and implemented the re-siting of the cumbersome pieces at the height of battle. The two medium pieces that accompanied the Dutch Guards in their early attacks against the French extreme right at Ramillies form one notable example. The Duke was also insistent that two light pieces should accompany each infantry battalion to afford it close fire support in action. Once again, this was originally a Swedish practice, but Marlborough grasped its advantages, and applied them.

The ways in which these practices contrasted with those in vogue in the French and Spanish armies have been analysed in an earlier chapter.* Suffice it here to say that Marlborough's predeliction for fire and movement, and his making the fullest use of the various arms, lay at the root of each of his great battlefield successes.

As an administrator, he was also without peer. First we must mention his skill at choosing a capable and dedicated team of assistants to run his staff. Without the aid of Cadogan, Cardonnel, or Davenant, Blood and Armstrong, few if any of his great projects could have come to fruition. My Lord Duke had an unerring instinct for a capable and loyal subordinate to whom he could safely delegate responsibility. The Duke also had a great eye for detail. He worried about the daily fluctuations in the price of bread, or the provision of adequate shoe-leather for his infantry as much as he was concerned about the movements of the enemy army. His grasp was all-embracing. On the larger plane he could devise complete new systems of communications (as in 1704); on the smaller, he could insist of the adoption of two-wheeled munitions and rations carts in the interests of mobility, or the issue of hand-mills to every battalion in preparation for the proposed march to Italy in 1706. He supervised the bread and transport contractors with an eagle eye, and checked many of their fraudulent practices. Aided by Godolphin, he did his best to keep the military chest well-provided with gold: his army paid its way. It was one of his proudest claims that that the army had never gone short for bread during his eight campaigns in Flanders, yet paradoxically it was charges of malversation of the bread-money that helped *inter alia* to bring him down in 1712. In every way he had the 'faculty

* See Chapter 5, p. 91.

for command' that is the indispensable attribute of a successful general. His soldiers were aware of his concern for them, and dubbed him 'the old Corporal' in recognition of his efforts on their behalf. As Matthew Bishop wrote in 1708, 'The Duke of Marlborough's attention and care was over all of us.'[36]

Marlborough's basic strengths as an administrator were the following. He was from the first aware that wars are concerned with human beings. His humane attitudes have frequently been mentioned, and need no further elaboration here. Second, he was able to distinguish the essentials in an administrative problem—often the provision of food, forage, transportation and gold. At the same time, and thirdly, he had a minute eye for detail. Fourthly, he had a distinct gift for making existing systems work well or at least adequately; he on the whole eschewed innovations, and thus avoided much confusion. It is true that the administrative systems he inherited were often inefficient and rudimentary, but close supervision of the responsible authorities kept such bread contractors as Solomon and Moses Medina and Vanderkaa up to the mark, or revealed the fraudulent practices of the less scrupulous who included Machado and Solomon Abraham. At the same time, he tried to gain them a fair deal in terms of government payments of contracted sums—not always successfully, however. Fifthly, he appreciated the importance of well-trained and well-disciplined officers as the very basis of an efficient and battle-worthy army.

To achieve a good response from officers and men requires, *inter alia*, a commander with evidence of full support from the highest authorities, who is endowed with proper powers of reward and punishment, and noted for providing steady yet unobtrusive backing for deserving subordinates. Until 1709 Marlborough was secure on all three counts. He had the favour of the Queen and the assistance (rather less demonstrably in later years) of her ministers—even if this advantage must be balanced against the obstruction encountered from certain of his allies. His promotion lists were for long automatically implemented; his recommendations on disciplinary grounds accepted. The Duke was never noted for great severity as a disciplinarian—and was invariably plagued by officer-absenteeism, pay and supply irregularities, and instances of plundering (as his frequent minatory pronouncements testify). Yet until 1710 his prestige and personal example kept these problems to manageable proportions. Thereafter, however, he lost control of appointments and promotions, which became increasingly political, and prepared the way for his fall. He proved incapable of securing a key post in his Board of Ordnance for even so trusted a colleague as Cadogan—basically because he was his friend. Yet he never deserted his subordinates, or the unfortunate (he found time to care for the interests of widows and orphans by improving the system of 'widow's men' on regimental establishments), although he could not achieve perfection. Even our friend Parker, Marlborough's greatest adulator, '. . . never lay under any private or personal obligations to his Grace; on the contrary he once did me injustice by putting a captain over my head. This however I knew he could not well avoid sometimes, for men in power are not to be disobliged.'[37] The rash of minor mutinies that followed his fall provides some evidence of the importance of his personal grip on matters of discipline and administration. During his years at the head of the army, his care for his men's well-being resulted in an outstanding response from his rank and file, including 'that lively air' Prince Eugene noted in the faces of the Duke's cavalrymen at their first meeting in 1704.* After Blenheim, for example, Marlborough insisted that Commissioners for Sick and Wounded should henceforth accompany the army to organise the care of the victims of battle: such attentions to detail were greatly appreciated by the men. 'He secured the affection of his soldiers by his good nature, care for their provisions, and vigilance not to expose them to unnecessary danger', wrote Lediard in a just summary, 'and gained those of his officers by his affability; both one and the other followed him to action with such a cheerfulness, resolution, and unanimity as were sure presages of success. ... The poor soldiers who were (too many of them) the refuse and dregs of the nation became tractable, civil, orderly, and clean, and had an air and spirit above the vulgar.'[38] As a noted modern authority on Marlborough's army has commented: 'What more could any officer ask?'[39]

The morale factor cannot be overrated, for here, if anywhere, lay the ultimate secret of Marlborough's success. Leaders and led alike acknowledged his pre-eminence. The trust he engendered enabled him to make calls on their endurance that few others would dare contemplate, as during the forced marches before Oudenarde or during the *Non Plus Ultra* operations of 1711. Marlborough's characteristics as both man and soldier provided him with the *charisma* that caused him never to forfeit the confidence, loyalty or affection of his rank and file. His unique military reputation, his humanitarian concern for their welfare, and his willingness to share their perils and discomfitures in battle and on campaign, earned the Captain-General his special place in his soldiers' affections. Above all, as Wellington noted, 'He was remarkable for his clear, cool, steady understanding.'

Of course, this was not a one-man achievement. We have mentioned his debt to his staff. He was equally fortunate in the great majority of the generals who served beside him. Pre-eminent amongst these stands the imposing figure of Prince Eugene. His complete dedication to the profession of arms and his single-minded cooperation with Marlborough made him the perfect colleague. If he proved less successful in fighting the French than the Duke (as the events of 1707 and 1712–13 demonstrate), his reputation earned fighting the Turks both before and after the War of the Spanish Succession caused Napoleon to nominate him one of the seven great commanders of all time. On a somewhat lower plain were such competent soldiers as Marlborough's brother, Charles, Lords Cutts and Orkney, the Dutchmen Overkirk, Goor and Fagel, Saxon

* See p. 123 above.

Schulenburg and Danish Württemberg, not to forget such faithful regimental officers as Kane, Parker or Sterne. If the Duke was a pre-eminent leader, he was indubitably fortunate in the calibre of a significant number of the officers and men he led.

It can also be argued that the Duke was fortunate in the foes he was called upon to face. There can be little denying that Tallard, Marsin, Villeroi and Boufflers were not particularly gifted commanders. On the other hand, Vendôme and Villars were generals of high calibre, and although neither proved capable of mastering Marlborough and Eugene acting in concert both proved the equal of, or superior to, Prince Eugene as Vendôme demonstrated in Italy (1705 and early 1706), and Villars in Flanders and Germany during the last years of the war. Even the great Duke was given some nasty scares by Vendôme in early July 1708. It is therefore not possible to explain Marlborough's success in terms of his opponent's ineptitude to any large degree.

Nevertheless, the showing of the marshals invites telling criticism. Tallard, Villeroi, Vendôme and even Villars displayed a disinclination to make personal reconnaissances. The first-named proved a weak controller of his subordinates; the second permitted Louis XIV to influence even his tactical decisions; the third was incapable of close cooperation with the Duke of Burgundy in 1708; whilst the last, for all his undoubted talent, was too full of bravado and did not always have the courage of his convictions. Almost all French commanders preferred adopting the defensive in battle, thereby sacrificing the tactical initiative time after time. At the level of strategy all, except possibly Villars, remained totally subservient to Versailles, and proved singularly incapable of discovering Marlborough's intentions early in a campaign, or of reacting successfully when all was at last revealed. In justice to Vendôme, however, it must be recalled that he skilfully avoided battle near Ninove in 1708—one of the few occasions when Marlborough was completely fooled.* In terms of Grand Tactics, the French commanders generally devised orders of battle of sound but highly conventional design, failed to appreciate the tactical revolution that had accompanied the changes in infantry weapons, and proved far inferior to Marlborough in their ability to control a major engagement, once joined. No French commander ever came near to equalling Marlborough's moral supremacy or mystique over the common soldier (although both Vendôme and Villars were popular with their men), and none approached his skill at field administration. Their troops fought with great gallantry and considerable self-sacrifice, but before the genius of Marlborough and the fury of his onslaughts they had little chance of victory. 'Monsieur Malbrook' came to enjoy the type of legendary reputation amongst his foes that would accrue in later wars to the names of Napoleon and Rommel.

What, then, should we conclude was the achievement of Marlborough? His reputation rests more on his record as a soldier than as a statesman or courtier—

* See p. 213 above.

that much is evident. As a commander, he was an 'experienced and dedicated professional rather than a brilliant amateur.'[40] He was the product of half a century of military experience rather than a human phenomenon of the type of Napoleon. For ten consecutive campaigns he produced 'the constant display at their highest of those qualities which are necessary to victory,'[41] overcoming in the process the grave limitations hampering the conduct of effective warfare, with the occasional, brief lapse caused by illness or fatigue. He raised the reputation of British arms to a level which had not been known since the Middle Ages, and inaugurated a period of British prominence, both in Europe and overseas. It is fitting to turn to Robert Parker for a last salute and tribute to this commanding figure. '. . . As to the Duke of Marlborough (for I cannot forbear giving him the precedence) it was allowed by all men, nay even by France itself, that he was more than a match for all the generals of that nation. This he made appear beyond contradiction, in the ten campaigns he made against them; during all of which time it cannot be said that he ever slipped an opportunity of fighting, when there was any probability of coming at his enemy: and upon all occasions he concerted matters with so much judgement and forecast, that he never fought a battle, which he did not gain, nor laid siege to a town which he did not take.'[42]

England has never produced a greater soldier.

Appendices, References, Bibliography & Index

Appendix A:
Marlborough's Major Engagements

Year	Battle or action	Date (New Style) (except where indicated as O.S.)	Opponents	Forces in Action
1685	Sedgemoor	6 July (O.S.)	(a) Feversham	3,000 Royal troops
			(b) Monmouth	4,000 Rebels
1689	Walcourt	25 August	(a) Waldeck	35,000 Allies (only part engaged)
			(b) d'Humières	24,000 French
1704	The Schellenberg	2 July	(a) Marlborough and Baden	25,000 Allies
			(b) d'Arco	10,000 Bavarians
	Blenheim	13 August	(a) Marlborough and Eugene	52,000 Allies
			(b) Tallard, Marsin and Max Emmanuel of Bavaria	56,000 Franco-Bavarians
1705	Elixhem (Passage of Lines of Brabant)	18 July	(a) Marlborough	14,000 Allies (initially)
			(b) Hornes, d'Alègre and Caraman	3,000–15,000 Franco-Bavarians
1706	Ramillies	23 May	(a) Marlborough	62,000 Allies
			(b) Villeroi and Max Emmanuel of Bavaria	60,000 French, Spaniards and Bavarians
1708	Oudenarde	11 July	(a) Marlborough and Eugene	80,000 Allies
			(b) Vendôme and Burgundy	85,000 French, Spaniards and Bavarians
	Wynendael	28 September	(a) Webb	6,000–8,000 Allies
			(b) La Motte	23,000 French and Bavarians
1709	Malplaquet	11 September	(a) Marlborough and Eugene	110,000 Allies
			(b) Villars and Boufflers	80,000 French and Bavarians
1711	Non Plus Ultra (Passage of Lines)	5/6 August	(a) Marlborough	85,000 Allies
			(b) Villars	90,000 French and Allies

Guns	Extent of battlefront (in yards)	Casualties	Result
16	880	(a) 300	West Country rebels
4	880	(b) 1,000 killed & 500 prisoners	routed; collapse of Monmouth's rebellion
approx. 28	3,500	(a) 100 & 30 prisoners	Sharp repulse for the French
approx. 20	3,500	(b) 600–2,000	
	2,200	(a) 5,041	Allied storming succeeds; they take Donauwörth
	2,200	(b) 5,000 & 16 guns	and gain bridges over Danube
60	7,000	(a) 12,883	Major Allied victory which saved Vienna
90	7,000	(b) 20,000 & 14,190 prisoners 60 guns	
n.d.	1,640	(a) 50–200	Allied tactical success but
18	1,500	(b) 3,000 & 18 guns	strategically indecisive
120	5,300	(a) 3,620	Major Allied victory
70	8,300	(b) 12,000 & 7,000 prisoners 54 guns	leading to the conquest of the Spanish Netherlands
32	7,000 (eventually)	(a) 4,000	Major Allied victory which retrieved the
50	5,000 (exclusive of disengaged left wing)	(b) 6,750 & 8,250 prisoners 25 guns	initiative
6	800	(a) 940	Allied success which
19	800	(b) 2,500 & 500 prisoners 19 guns	enabled the siege of Lille to continue
100	9,000	(a) 24,000	Allied technical victory which led to the capture of Tournai and Mons only
60	8,500	(b) 9,000 & 3,000 prisoners 16 guns	Mons only
45	not applicable	(a) unknown, but few	Allied strategical success
n.d.		(b) unknown, but few	which led to the siege of Bouchain, but no battle

Appendix B:
Marlborough's Major Sieges

Year	Place	Dates (*New Style*)*	Duration, Defender (*And Strength*)†		
1691	Cork	4–8 October (O.S.)	4 days	Macgillicuddy	(6,000)
	Kinsale	8–25 October (O.S.)	17 days	Scott	(2,000)
1702	Kaiserswerth	18 April–15 June	27 days	Blainville	(5,000)
	Lüttich	13 June–17 October	122 days	Tilly	(8,000)
	Venlo	29 August–25 September	28 days	Varo	(1,100)
	Stevenswaert	25 September–2 October	11 days	Castellas	(1,500)
	Ruremonde	26 September–6 October	10 days	Hornes	(2,400)
	Liége & Fort Chartreuse	13–29 October	16 days	Viollane & de Millon	(7,200)
1703	Bonn	27 April–15 May	18 days	d'Alègre	(3,600)
	Huy (1st)	15–26 August	11 days	Millon	(7,500)
	Limburg	10–27 September	17 days	Reignac	(1,400)
1704	Trarbach	4 November–20 December	46 days	not known	(?600)
1705	Huy (3rd)	6–11 July	6 days	St. Pierre	(600)
	St. Leau	29 August–6 September	8 days	Dumont	(?400)
	Santoliet	23–29 October	6 days	not known	
1706	Ostend	19 June–9 July	20 days	La Motte	(5,000)
	Menin	22 July–22 August	31 days	Caraman	(5,500)
	Dendermond	27 August–9 September	13 days	Vallé	(2,000)
	Ath	16 September–1 October	15 days	not known	(2,000)

Besieger (& Strength)†	Casualties (Killed & Wounded)†	Result
Marlborough	(11,500) Allies–appx. 80/Irish–no details	Garrison made prisoners of war.
Marlborough	(11,000) Allies–appx. 250/Irish–400	Garrison made prisoners of war.
Nassau-Saarbrücken	(22,000) Allies–2,900/French–1,000	Garrison capitulated.
Marlborough	(40,000) Allies–no details/French–3,000	Garrison capitulated on terms.
Marlborough & Nassau	(30,000) Allies–1,100/French; 839	Garrison allowed to evacuate to Antwerp.
Marlborough & Nassau	(30,000) Details uncertain	Garrison allowed to evacuate.
Marlborough	(25,000) Allies–60/French 40–50	Garrison allowed to evacuate to Louvain.
Marlborough	(25,000) Allies–1,034/French–not recorded	Garrison capitulated & disarmed; a few allowed to go to Namur.
Marlborough	(40,000) Allies–c.600/French–860	Garrison allowed to evacuate to Luxembourg.
Marlborough	(42,000) Allies–c.60/French–1,200	Garrison made prisoners of war. Town regained by French, 10 June 1705. (2nd siege)
Marlborough & Hesse-Cassel	(16,000) Allies–100/French–60	Garrison made prisoners of war.
Hesse-Cassel	(20,000) Allies–1,000/French–350	Garrison made prisoners of war.
Scholten (strength uncertain)	Not known/French–700	Garrison made prisoners of war.
Dedem	(9,000) Allies–60/French–40	Garrison made prisoners of war.
Noyelles (strength uncertain)	Allies–100/French–50	French surrender.
Marlborough	(20,000) Allies–1,600/French–800 (Naval inc.)	French capitulated; Spaniards join Allies.
Marlborough	(30,000) Allies–2,620/French–1,101	Garrison allowed to evacuate to Douai.
Marlborough	(6,000) Not known/Not known	Garrison made prisoners of war.
Overkirk	(21,000) Allies–800/French–60	Garrison made prisoners of war.

Year	Place	Dates (New Style)*	Duration	Defender (And Strength)†	
1708	Lille (city & fortress)	12 August–10 December	120 days	Boufflers	(16,000)
	Ghent	18 December–2 January	15 days	La Motte	(15,000)
1709	Tournai (city & fortress)	27 June–3 September	69 days	Surville	(7,000)
	Mons	9 September–20 October	44 days	Grimaldi	(4,280)
1710	Douai (1st)	23 April–25 June	63 days	Albergotti	(7,500)
	Béthune	17 July–29 August	43 days	Vauban (the younger)	(4,000)
	St. Venant	5–29 September	17 days	de Seloe	(3,000)
	Aire	6 September–8 November	64 days	Goësbriant	(7,000)
1711	Bouchain (1st)	9 August–12 September	34 days	Ravignau	(5,000)

* Siege dates are, as a general rule calculated from the investment of a fortress to the date its commander agreed to capitulate. New style dates have been employed except in the cases of Cork and Kinsale.

† Casualty and strength figures need treating with care; the main sources from which they have been drawn are Millner, Lediard, Pelet, Bodart and Atkinson (see bibliography).

Besieger (& Strength)†	Casualties (Killed & Wounded)†	Result
Eugene (35,000)	Allies–15,000/French–7,000	Garrison allowed to evacuate to Douai.
Marlborough & Eugene (40,000)	Allies–4,800/French–4,000	Garrison allowed to evacuate to Dunkirk.
Marlborough (40,000)	Allies–5,400/French–3,800	Garrison repatriated for exchange.
Orange (10,000)	Allies–2,300/French–980	Garrison allowed to evacuate less cannon.
Marlborough & Eugene (60,000)	Allies–8,009/French–2,860	Garrison allowed to evacuate to Cambrai.
Schulenburg (31,000)	Allies–3,365/French–1,200	Garrison allowed to evacuate to St. Omer.
Orange (9,000)	Allies–960/French–400	Garrison allowed to evacuate to Arras.
Anhalt-Dessau (28,000)	Allies–7,200/French–1,400	Garrison allowed to evacuate to St. Omer.
Marlborough (30,000)	Allies–4,080/French–2,500	Garrison made prisoners of war.

References

Chapter one: 1650–1684 (pp. 1–11)

1 Robert Parker, *Memoirs of the Most Remarkable Transactions from 1683 to 1718*, London 1747; recently republished, edited by David Chandler, as *Robert Parker and the Comte de Mérode-Westerloo*, London 1968, p. 126. This edition has been used *passim*.

2 Sir John Creasey, *The Fifteen Decisive Battles of the World*, London 1948 (edn.), p. 271.

3 Octave Aubry, *Napoléon*, Paris 1964, p. 117.

4 Dr. H. Felton, *Dissertations on Writing the Classics*, London 1719.

5 A. L. Rowse, *The Early Churchills*, London 1956, pp. 9–10 and 26–7.

6 Cited by W. S. Churchill, *Marlborough, his Life and Times*, London 1967 (paperback edition), Vol. 1, pp. 44–5 and f.n. p. 14. This edition has been used *passim*.

7 *The Pauline*, June 1892, p. 117.

8 *The Dartmouth Papers* (Historical Manuscripts Commission—hereafter *H.M.C.*) 1887, Vol. 5, p. 61.

9 *Calendar of State Papers* (hereafter *C.S.P.*) *Ireland 1669–70*, p. 91.

10 *The Hatton Correspondence*, edited Thompson, The Camden Society, 1878, Vol. 1, p. 92. See also C. Dalton, *English Army Lists and Commission Registers*, London 1898, Vol. 1, p. 146.

11 Cited by Churchill, *op. cit.*, Vol. 1, p. 101.

12 Viscount G. J. Wolseley, *Life of Marlborough to the Accession of Queen Anne*, London 1894, (3rd edition), Vol. 1, p. 146.

13 *La correspondance politique—Angleterre*, tome 120 C, folio 231.

14 Alan Wace, *The Marlborough Tapestries at Blenheim Palace*, London 1968, p. 131.

15 *Letters of Sir J. Vanbrugh*, ed. G. Webb, Vol. 4, p. 170.

16 *Correspondance politique . . . op. cit.*, tome 120 C, folio 206.

17 Wolseley, *op. cit.*, Vol. 1, p. 213. See also Churchill, *op. cit.*, Vol. 1, p. 133.

18 Churchill, *op. cit.*, Vol. 1, p. 153, citing the Spencer Manuscripts at Althorp.

19 Wolseley, *op. cit.*, Vol. 1, p. 256.

Chapter Two: 1685–1688 (pp. 12–25)

1 Gilbert Burnet, *History of His Own Time, 1660–85*, Vol. 3, p. 269.

2 Dalton, *op. cit.*, Vol. 1, p. 301.

3 *The Northumberland Papers* (*H.M.C.*) 1872, Vol. 3, p. 99.

4 *Ibid.*, p. 97.
5 *The Book of the Axe* (Axminster Town Records), p. 347.
6 Edward Hyde, Earl of Clarendon, *Correspondence and Diary*, London 1828, Vol. 1, p. 141.
7 Wolseley, *op. cit.*, Vol. 1, p. 306–7.
8 Blenheim Palace Papers, Vol. 5, p. 304.
9 From papers deposited in Hoare's Bank, London. A second version of the map is displayed in Weston Zoyland parish church, Somerset.
10 *The London Gazette*, 8 July (O.S.) 1685.
11 *State Trials*, Vol. 2, p. 593
12 Sir John Dalrymple, *Memoirs of Great Britain and Ireland*, London 1773, Vol. 2, p. 62.
13 Cited by Wolseley, *op. cit.*, Vol. 2, p. 12.
14 *War Office Papers* 55/424, folios 13 and 13a.
15 Thomas Bruce, Earl of Ailesbury, *Memoirs*, London 1890, Vol. 1, p. 184–5.
16 *C.S.P.* (*Domestic*) *William III*, 1689, and also the Blenheim Palace Papers.

Chapter Three: 1689–1691 (pp. 26–44)

1 Ailesbury, *op. cit.*, Vol. 1, p. 245.
2 Sicco van Goslinga, *Mémoires* (*1706–9 et 1711*), Paris 1857, p. 42.
3 A. L. Rowse, *op. cit.*, p. 171.
4 An excellent and succinct account is to be found in the *New Cambridge Modern History*, Cambridge 1970, Vol. 6, chapter 7, by Sir G. N. Clark.
5 C. Walton, *History of the British Standing Army*, London 1894, p. 61.
6 *C.S.P.* (*King William's Chest*), 8–5, folios 40 (dated 26 June), 44 (28 June) and 124 (18 Sept.).
7 *Additional Manuscript* (hereafter Add Mss.) 29878, *The Diary of William Cramond, 1688–9*; see also *C.S.P.* 8–5 folio 82, for Waldeck's letter to William III dated 6 August.
8 Anon., *An Impartial Account of ye Campagne* (*sic*) *of 1689*, London 1690, p. 17.
9 Add. Mss. 29878 *op. cit.*,; entry under 15 August (O.S.); also *An Impartial Account* . . . , p. 14.
10 *C.S.P.* 8–5 *op. cit.*, folio 96.
11 Sir Charles Petrie, *The Marshal Duke of Berwick*, London 1953, chapter 2 *passim*.
12 Admiral A. T. Mahan, *The Influence of Sea-Power upon History*, London 1890, p. 187.
13 Cited by Wolseley, *op. cit.*, Vol. 2, p. 133.
14 Archdeacon W. C. Coxe, *Memoirs of John, Duke of Marlborough*, London 1820, Vol. 1, p. 189.
15 Wolseley, *op. cit.*, Vol. 2, p. 158.
16 Dalrymple, *op. cit.*, Vol. 3, p. 128.
17 Petrie, *op. cit.*, p. 80.
18 Cramond Diary, *op. cit.*, folios 28b–34 relate to the siege of Cork.
19 *Ibid.*, entry for 28 September (O.S.).
20 Wolseley, *op. cit.*, Vol. 2, p. 111.

21 *Cramond Diary, op. cit.*, entry for 12 October (O.S.).
22 *Ibid.*, entry for 17 October (O.S.).
23 Cited by Churchill, *op. cit.*, Vol. 1, p. 283.

Chapter Four: 1692–1701 (pp. 45–60)

1 S. H. Baxter, *William III*, London 1966, p. 299.
2 *The Buccleuch Papers*, (H.M.C.), 1903, Vol. 2, p. 647.
3 Churchill, *op. cit.*, Vol. 1, p. 432.
4 Baxter, *op. cit.*, p. 370.
5 Spoken by Castel des Rios, Spanish Ambassador to Versailles, not by Louis XIV.
6 Cited by Churchill, *op. cit.*, Vol. 1, p. 447.
7 Baxter, *op. cit.*, p. 390.
8 Churchill, *op. cit.*, Vol. 1, p. 446.
9 *Ibid.*, p. 453.
10 Stowe Manuscripts 58, folio 25.
11 Cited by Churchill, *op. cit.*, Vol. 1, p. 476.
12 *The Correspondence, 1701–11 of John Churchill and Anthonie Heinsius*, ed. B. van
   'T Hoff, The Hague 1951, No. 17, p. 8. (Hereafter Van 'T. Hoff.)
13 See D. Coombs, *The Conduct of the Dutch*, London 1958.
14 See Iris Butler, *The Rule of Three*, London 1967, for a perceptive and sympathetic
   analysis of Queen Anne's character, and David Green, *Queen Anne*, London 1970,
   for a full treatment.

Chapter Five: The Art of War (pp. 61–93)

1 See C. V. Wedgwood, *The Thirty Years War*, London 1944, p. 512–13.
2 Coxe, *op. cit.*, (1820 edn.), Vol. 1, p. 250.
3 Quoted in H. Weygand, *Histoire de l'Armée Française*, Paris 1938, p. 155.
4 T. Lediard, *Life of John, Duke of Marlborough*, London 1736, Vol. 1, p. xxiii.
5 R. E. Scouller, *The Armies of Queen Anne*, Oxford 1966, p. 82, and Appendix B.
6 H. Kamen, *The War of Succession in Spain*, London 1969, pp. 59 and 70.
7 J.-F. Puysegur, *L'art de la guerre par principes et par règles*, Paris, 1748, Tome 1.
8 Weygand, *op. cit.*, p. 155.
9 Add. Mss. 23,642, f. 33—The Tyrawly Papers.
10 See *New Camb. Modern History, op. cit.*, Vol. 6, ch. XXII, pt. 2, pp. 763–5.
11 See G. Farquhar, *The Recruiting Officer*, (play), 1707.
12 S. Burrell and P. Jordan-Smith (Ed.), *Amiable Renegade—the Memoirs of Captain
   Peter Drake*, London 1960.
13 De la Colonie, *Chronicles of an Old Campaigner* (ed. C. Horsley), London 1904,
   p. 159.
14 Parker, *op. cit.*, (1968 edn.), p. 103.
15 *Parliamentary History*, Vol. 6, p. 1088.
16 R. E. Scouller, *Marlborough's Administration* in *The Army Quarterly*, Vol. 95,
   p. 110.
17 Lediard, *op. cit.*, Vol. 1, p. xx.
18 Parker, *op. cit.*, p. 57, and Add. Mss. 23,642, f. 26.

19 Duc de St. Simon, *Mémoires*, Paris 1873, Vol. 1, p. 5.

20 Add. Mss. 23,642, f. 23.

21 D. Defoe, *An Essay upon Projects*, in *The Earlier Life and Chief Earlier Works of Daniel Defoe*, London 1889, p. 135.

22 The Earl of Orrery, *A Treatise on the Art of War*, 1677, p. 15.

23 See Vauban, *Traité sur l'attaque* . . . and *Traité sur la défense des places*, The Hague, 1779 edition.

24 Vauban, *Traité sur défense des places, op. cit.*, p. 301–3.

25 Parker, *op. cit.*, p. 23.

26 Turpin de Crissé, cited by G. B. Turner, *A History of Military Affairs in Western Society*, New York, 1953, p. 24.

27 See D. G. Chandler, *The Campaigns of Napoleon*, London 1967, Pt. III *passim*.

28 Brigadier-General R. Kane, *The Campaigns of King William and Queen Anne*, London 1745, p. 110.

29 The Papers of Lord Orkney, *English Historical Review*, Vol. 19, p. 308.

30 Parker *op. cit.*, p. 88–9.

Chapter Six: 1702–1703 (pp. 94–122)

1 *Archives du dépôt de la guerre*, tome, 1528, Pt. 2, Sect. 2, f. 278.

2 *Ibid.*, tome, 1552, f. 180.

3 *Ibid.*, tome, 1528 as cited, f. 293.

4 Parker, *op. cit.*, p. 17.

5 See Van 'T. Hoff, *op. cit.*, No. 30, p. 14.

6 See *ibid.*, pp. xii–xiii, and Burton *op. cit.*, p. 46–7 on this subject.

7 *Ibid.*, No. 32, p. 15; also see Coombs, *op. cit., passim.*

8 C. T. Atkinson, *Marlborough and the Rise of the British Army*, London 1924, p. 166.

9 Van 'T. Hoff, *op. cit.*, No. 35, p. 17.

10 *Archives . . . de la guerre, op. cit.*, tome 1554, ff. 200, 221 and 240.

11 *Ibid.*, tome 1528 as cited, f. 323.

12 Van 'T. Hoff, *op. cit.*, No. 38, p. 19. See also Sir Geo. Murray, *Letters and Despatches of John Churchill, First Duke of Marlborough*, London 1845, Vol. 1, p. 11 f.n.

13 Parker, *op. cit.*, p. 19.

14 Marshal the Duke of Berwick, *Mémoires*, Paris 1779, Vol. 1, p. 170.

15 Atkinson, *op. cit.*, p. 168.

16 Burton, *op. cit.*, p. 34 and ref. 10 above, refer.

17 Atkinson, *op. cit.*, p. 169, and Murray, *op. cit.*, Vol. 1, p. 25.

18 J. G. Pelet et le F. E. de Vault, *Mémoires militaires relatifs à la succession d'Espagne sous Louis XIV*, Paris, 1836–42, Vol. 1, p. 104. (Hereafter Pelet & Le Vault.)

19 Van 'T. Hoff, *op. cit.*, No. 41, p. 21.

20 *Ibid.*, No. 57, p. 33.

21 Parker, *op. cit.*, pp. 22–3.

22 Van 'T. Hoff, *op. cit.*, No. 61, p. 35.

23 See also Churchill, *op. cit.*, Vol. 2, p. 161; also see Murray *op. cit.*, Vol. 1, p. 54–5 f.n.

24 Van 'T. Hoff, *op. cit.*, No. 69, p. 39.

25 Ailesbury, *op. cit.*, Vol. 1, p. 558

26 Van 'T. Hoff, *op. cit.*, No. 81, p. 48.

27 *Ibid.*, No. 106b, p. 65.

28 *Ibid.*, No. 94, dated London 16/27 February, p. 55-6.

29 *Ibid.*, No. 101; see also addendum to No. 114; pp. 61 and 71.

30 *Ibid.*, No. 104, p. 63.

31 Coxe, *op. cit.*, Vol. 1, p. 273; and see van 'T. Hoff No. 124 for the Duke's thoughts of resignation expressed in mid-June.

32 *Archives . . . de la guerre*, tome 1651 f. 2, and Pelet & Le Vault, *op. cit.*, Vol. 3, p. 77-8.

33 Coxe, *op. cit.*, Vol. 1, p. 189, and Murray, *op. cit.*, Vol. 1, pp. 129-133.

34 Van 'T. Hoff, Nos. 126 & 128, pp. 77 & 78.

35 *Ibid.*, No. 141, p. 88.

36 *Ibid.*, Nos. 135 & 136, p. 85-6.

37 *Archives . . . de la guerre*, tome 1640, p. 99.

38 Van 'T. Hoff, *op. cit.*, No. 151, p. 95,

39 Murray, Vol. 1, p. 163-4.

40 *Ibid.*, No. 120, pp. 73-4.

41 M. Ashley, *Marlborough*, London 1939, p. 41.

Chapter Seven: 1704 (pp. 123-50)

1 Dr. Hare's *Journal*, cited by Churchill, *op. cit.*, Vol. 2, p. 291; large parts of the Journal are also to be found in Murray, *op. cit.*, Vol. 1, pp. 332-8 & 394-409.

2 Pelet & Le Vault, *op. cit.*, Vol. 4, pp. 370-2.

3 Coxe, *op. cit.*, Vol. 1, p. 306.

4 J. W. de Sypesteyn, *Het Leven van Menno Baron van Coehoorn*, Leeuwarden, 1860, p. 64.

5 G. M. Trevelyan, *England Under Queen Anne*, Vol. 1, (*Blenhiem* paperback edn.), London 1965, p. 354.

6 Sloane Mss. 3392—the Strafford Papers—f. 11.

7 Coxe, *op. cit.*, Vol. 1, p. 320.

8 Parker (1968 edn.) *op. cit.*, p. 30. See also Murray, *op. cit.*, Vol. 1, pp. 251-2 & 285 f.n.s.

9 Churchill, *op. cit.*, Vol. 2, p. 273, Pelet & Le Vault, *op. cit.*, Vol. 4, pp. 470-2 and van 'T. Hoff, *op. cit.*, Nos. 175 and 177 for Allied preparations to return to the Rhine.

10 *La campagne de Monsieur le Maréchal de Tallard en Allemagne*, 1704, Amsterdam 1763, tome 1.

11 Add. Mss. 22,196—the Correspondence of Cadogan and Lord Raby, 1703-10, entry dated 30 May 1704.

12 Parker (1968 edn.), *op. cit.*, p. 31.

13 D. Defoe, (ed.) *The Life and Adventures of Mother Ross*, London, 1929, p. 54.

14 Comte de Mérode-Westerloo, *Mèmoires* (edited version by D. G. Chandler), London 1968, p. 160.

15 Murray, *op. cit.*, Vol. 1, p. 311, and Churchill, *op. cit.*, Vol. 2, pp. 294-6, and 304.

16 Add. Mss. 22, 196—dated from Mainz.

17 Add. Mss. 4,742—the Correspondence of Henry Davenant, Vol. 3—entry dated 19 June 1704.

18 Mérode-Westerloo (1968 edn.), *op. cit.*, p. 163.

19 *Archives . . . de la guerre*, tome 1731, lier partie, lier Section, p. 16.

20 De la Colonie, *op. cit.*, pp. 185–191; see also Hare's *Journal*, Murray, *op. cit.*, Vol. 1, pp. 332–8.

21 Add. Mss. 4747, f. 8. Other estimates vary in detail, but totals roughly tally. c.f. Sgt. J. Millner, *A Compendious Journal . . .*, London, 1733, p. 98.

22 Van 'T. Hoff, *op. cit.*, No. 194, p. 118; Add. Mss. 4747, f. 9, and see Churchill, *op. cit.*, Vol. 2, p. 329.

23 Mérode-Westerloo (1968 edition), *op. cit.*, p. 161.

24 Pelet & le Vault, *op. cit.*, Vol. 4, pp. 547–9.

25 Van 'T. Hoff, *op. cit.*, No. 204, p. 123, and the *Blenheim Archives*, cited by Churchill, *op. cit.*, Vol. 2, p. 349–50.

26 Mérode-Westerloo (1968 edition), *op. cit.*, p. 166.

27 *Ibid.*, p. 167.

28 *La Campagne de Monsieur le Maréchal de Tallard en Allemagne*, 1704, *op. cit.*, Vol. 2, p. 140, and Pelet & le Vault, *op. cit.*, Vol. 4, p. 556.

29 Mérode-Westerloo (1968 edition), *op. cit.*, p. 164; R. G. Burton, *op. cit.*, pp. 68–9.

30 Pelet & le Vault, *op. cit.*, Vol. 4, p. 573.

31 Mérode-Westerloo, *op. cit.*, p. 172.

32 Orkney, *op. cit.*, *E.H.R.* Vol. 19 (1904), p. 308.

33 *Ibid.*, p. 308.

34 C. T. Atkinson, *op. cit.*, p. 233.

35 WO 4/5 f. 106, the *Blenheim Roll* (reproduced in Dalton, *op. cit.*, Vol. 5), Millner, *op. cit.*, pp. 126–8, and Murray, *op. cit.*, Vol. 1, pp. 409–10.

36 Parker (1968 edition), *op. cit.*, p. 44.

37 Mérode-Westerloo, *op. cit.*, (1968 edition), p. 174.

38 The Atholl Papers, *op. cit.*, *HMC*, Vol. 1, p. 62.

39 Van 'T. Hoff, *op. cit.*, No. 206, p. 125.

40 As displayed at Blenheim Palace.

Chapter Eight: 1705 (pp. 151–65)

1 Pelet & le Vault, *op. cit.*, Vol. 5, p. 14.

2 Van 'T. Hoff, *op. cit.*, No. 273, p. 171 and Murray, *op. cit.*, Vol. 2, p. 55 (letter dated 27 May).

3 Van 'T. Hoff, *ibid.*, No. 280, p. 174–5; also cited by G. M. Trevelyan, *op. cit.*, Vol. 2—*Ramillies*, p. 67.

4 Murray, *op. cit.*, Vol. 2, pp. 82–3.

5 Churchill, *op. cit.*, Vol. 2, p. 433.

6 Pelet & le Vault, *op. cit.*, Vol. 5, p. 451.

7 Van 'T. Hoff, *op. cit.*, No. 289, p. 182 for Heinsius's summons dated 13 June; *ibid.*, No. 293, p. 184 for Marlborough's reply.

8 Add. Mss. 469—the Stowe Papers—f. 6a.

9 Parker (1968 edn.), *op. cit.*, p. 52.

10 Pelet & le Vault, *op. cit.*, Vol. 5, p. 37.
11 De la Colonie, *op. cit.*, pp. 293–4.
12 *Archives . . . de la guerre, op. cit.*, tome 1836 N. 224.
13 *E.H.R.* April 1904, p. 312.
14 National Army Museum Mss. 6909/4, f. 10.
15 Pelet & le Vault, *op. cit.*, Vol. 5, p. 579.
16 *E.H.R.*, *op. cit.*, p. 312.
17 Churchill, *op. cit.*, Vol. 2, p. 459.
18 Murray, *op. cit.*, Vol. 2, p. 217 and Van 'T. Hoff, *op. cit.*, No. 324, p. 203.
19 Parker, (1968 edition), *op. cit.*, p. 57.
20 Pelet & le Vault, *op. cit.*, Vol. 5, p. 607.
21 See Chandler, *Campaigns of Napoleon*, Part 3, ch. 16.
22 Mérode-Westerloo (1968 edition), *op. cit.*, p. 194.
23 Murray, *op. cit.*, Vol. 2, p. 224 and Van 'T. Hoff, *op. cit.*, p. 203, f.n. 2 for Marlborough's strong letter to the Secretary of the Council of State at the Hague.
24 Murray, *op. cit.*, Vol. 2, p. 293.
25 Atkinson, *op. cit.*, p. 278.

Chapter Nine: 1706 (pp. 166–83)

1 Van 'T. Hoff, *op. cit.*, No. 367, p. 224; and see Burton, *op. cit.*, p. 97.
2 H. Kamen, *The War of Succession in Spain, 1700–15*, London 1969, citing A. D. Ortez, *La Sociedad Espanole en el Siglo XVIII*, Madrid 1955, p. 368, f.n. 9.
3 Cited by Churchill, *op. cit.*, Vol. 3, p. 74–5.
4 Parker, (1968 edition), *op. cit.*, p. 58.
5 Murray, *op. cit.*, Vol. 2, pp. 494–5.
6 Pelet & le Vault, *op. cit.*, Vol. 6, p. 18.
7 Murray, *op. cit.*, Vol. 2, p. 517.
8 Pelet & le Vault, *op. cit.*, Vol. 6, p. 19.
9 De la Colonie, *op. cit.*, p. 311.
10 *E.H.R.*, April 1904, p. 315.
11 *Ibid.*
12 De la Colonie, *op. cit.*, p. 313.
13 Peter Drake—cited by Trevelyan, *op. cit.*, Vol. 2, p. 133.
14 Lediard, *op. cit.*, Vol. 2, p. 27.
15 *Ibid.*, pp. 42–3.
16 Pelet & le Vault, *op. cit.*, Vol. 6, pp. 40–1.
17 Coxe, *op. cit.*, Vol. 2, p. 365.
18 Cited by C. T. Atkinson, *op. cit.*, p. 298.
19 Add. Mss. 23,642, f. 20.
20 Pelet & le Vault, Vol. 6, p. 65.
21 *Archives . . . de la guerre, op. cit.*, tome 1939, No. 36.
22 Add. Mss. 22,196, letter dated 17 August 1706.
23 Sgt. Millner, *op. cit.*, p. 186.
24 Murray, *op. cit.*, Vol. 3, p. 160.
25 Coxe, *op. cit.*, Vol. 1, p. 460.

Chapter Ten: 1707 (pp. 184–200)

1 Churchill, *op. cit.*, Vol. 3, p. 203.
2 Coxe, *op. cit.*, Vol. 2, p. 57.
3 A. L. Rowse, *op. cit.*, p. 260.
4 Coxe, *op. cit.*, Vol. 3, p. 117.
5 Churchill, *op. cit.*, Vol. 3, p. 202.
6 For example, see Pelet & Le Vault, Vol. 7, and Mérode-Westerloo, (1968), pp. 198–200.
7 Murray, *op. cit.*, Vol. 3, p. 195.
8 *Ibid.*, p. 286.
9 *Ibid.*, pp. 268–9.
10 *Ibid.*, p. 249.
11 R. M. Hatton, *Charles XII*, London 1968, p. 224.
12 Lediard, *op. cit.*, Vol. 2, p. 165, citing M. de la Mottroye's account.
13 *Ibid.*, p. 166. Lediard was present at Altranstadt and is regarded as a credible witness.
14 Hatton, *op. cit.*, p. 224.
15 Parker (1968 edn.), p. 66.
16 Kamen, *op. cit.*, p. 19.
17 Coxe, *op. cit.*, Vol. 3, p. 207 *et seq.*; see also van 'T. Hoff, *op. cit.*, No. 512, p. 310.
18 Murray, *op. cit.*, Vol. 3, p. 390.
19 *Archives . . . de la guerre*, tome 2015, Pt. 1, Sect. 1, f. 10.
20 Coxe, *op. cit.*, Vol. 3, p. 262.
21 *Archives . . . de la guerre*, tome 2015, Pt. 1., Sect. 1, f. 18.
22 Coxe, *op. cit.*, Vol. 3, p. 202.
23 The Bath Papers, *H.M.C.*, Vol. 1, p. 173.
24 Goslinga, *op. cit.*, pp. 34–5.
25 Murray, *op. cit.*, Vol. 3, p. 549.
26 Prinz Eugen, *Feldzüge*, 1st Series, Vol. 9, supplement, p. 182.
27 Pelet & le Vault, *op. cit.*, pp. 54–5.
28 N. P. Henderson, *Prince Eugene of Savoy*, London 1964, p. 150.
29 *H.M.C.*, Portland Mss. Vol. 4, p. 144.

Chapter Eleven: 1708 (pp. 201–22)

1 Klopp, *op. cit.*, Vol. 13, p. 10.
2 Add. Mss. 23,642, f. 33 (the Tyrawly Papers, Miscellaneous, 1679–1759).
3 Trevelyan, *op. cit.*, Vol. 2, p. 349.
4 Rowse, *op. cit.*, p. 261.
5 Van 'T. Hoff, *op. cit.*, No. 593, p. 362.
6 Add. Mss. 5132, ff. 123–143 inclusive.
7 J. M. Deane, *A Journal of the Campaign in Flanders, 1708*, London 1846, p. 4.
8 Add. Mss. 5132, f. 137.
9 Parker (1968 edition), *op. cit.*, p. 70.
10 Lediard, *op. cit.*, Vol. 2, p. 242.

11 Coxe, *op. cit.*, Vol. 4, p. 154.
12 *Ibid.*, Vol. 2, p. 216.
13 Mérode-Westerloo (1968 edition), *op. cit.*, p. 143; see also D. Flower fed.) *Saint-Simon at Versailles*, London 1953, p. 136.
14 Berwick, *op. cit.*, Vol. 2, p. 7.
15 Mérode-Westerloo (1968 edition), *op. cit.*, p. 201.
16 Millner, *op. cit.*, p. 212.
17 Churchill, *op. cit.*, Vol. 3, p. 337.
18 A short, useful study of the battle has been recently published by Eversley M.G. Belfield '*Oudenarde, 1708*' in Charles Knight's Ltd. *Battles for War-Gamers* series.
19 Lediard, *op. cit.*, Vol. 2, p. 282.
20 St.-Simon, *op. cit.*, Vol. 6, p. 56.
21 Lediard, *op. cit.*, pp. 267-8.
22 Add. Mss. 5132, f. 228 *et seq.*—the Dutch State Papers.
23 Pelet & le Vault, *op. cit.*, Vol. 8, p. 38.
24 Belfield, *op. cit.*, p. 66.
25 *Archives . . . de la guerre*, tome 2081, f. 78.
26 *Ibid.*, f. 170 *et seq.*
27 Coxe, *op. cit.*, Vol. 4, pp. 153-4.

Chapter Twelve: Lille (pp. 223-39)

1 Pelet & le Vault, *op. cit.*, Vol. 8, p. 38-9.
2 *Ibid.*, p. 400-1 & *Archives . . . de la guerre*, Vol. 2075, Part 1, Section 1, No. 25.
3 Murray, *op. cit.*, Vol. 4, p. 147.
4 Lediard, *op. cit.*, Vol. 2, p. 303.
5 Mérode-Westerloo (1968 edition), *op. cit.*, p. 204-5; and Lediard, *op. cit.*, Vol. 2, p. 302.
6 Pelet & le Vault, *op. cit.*, Vol. 8, p. 68.
7 Murray, *op. cit.*, Vol. 4, p. 144.
8 Pelet & le Vault, *op. cit.*, Vol. 8, p. 68.
9 Murray, *op. cit.*, Vol. 4, p. 204.
10 *Ibid.*, p. 218-9.
11 Murray, *op. cit.*, Vol. 4, p. 237.
12 Coxe, *op. cit.*, Vol. 4, p. 243, and van 'T. Hoff, *op. cit.*, No. 670, p. 402.
13 Add. Mss. 23,642, f. 35; reprinted in part in Parker, (1968 edn.), *op. cit.*, p. 8.
14 Lediard, *op. cit.*, Vol. 2, p. 338.
15 Pelet & le Vault, *op. cit.*, Vol. 8, pp. 100-1.
16 *Ibid.*, pp. 100 and 444-9 (La Motte's report). *S.A.H.R. Journal*, 1956, pp. 26-31.
17 Murray, *op. cit.*, Vol. 4, p. 243.
18 Burton, *op. cit.*, p. 140, citing Marlborough.
19 Parker, (1968 edn.), *op. cit.*, p. 80.
20 Mérode-Westerloo, (1968 edn.), *op. cit.*, p. 207; also Parker, *ibid.*, p. 80; Lediard, *op. cit.*, Vol. 2, pp. 333-6, and Pelet & le Vault, *op. cit.*, Vol. 8, pp. 107-8 and 456-9.
21 Cited by Lediard, *op. cit.*, Vol. 2, p. 336.
22 *Archives . . . de la guerre*, tome 2083, Nos. 173 and 195.

23 A. J. Veenendaal's chapter in the New Cambridge Modern History, Vol. 6.
24 Murray, *op. cit.*, Vol. 4, p. 269 and Coxe, *op. cit.*, Vol. 4, p. 261.
25 Murray, *ibid.*, pp. 268–9 and 271–2.
26 See, *inter alia*, van 'T. Hoff, Nos. 693 and 695 (pp. 413 and 414).
27 *Ibid.*, No. 703, p. 419.
28 Iris Butler, *The Rule of Three*, London 1967, p. 205.
29 Private Deane, *Journal of a Campaign in Flanders, 1708*, London 1846, cited by Churchill, *op. cit.*, Vol. 3, p. 308.

Chapter Thirteen: 1709 (pp. 240–72)

1 Mérode-Westerloo, (1968 edn.), *op. cit.*, p. 206.
2 Legrelle, *La Diplomatie Française et la Succession d'Espagne*, Vol. 5, p. 385.
3 Pelet & le Vault, *op. cit.*, Vol. 9, p. 5.
4 Van 'T. Hoff, *op. cit.*, No. 724, p. 429, letter dated 8/19 March 1709.
5 Churchill, *op. cit.*, Vol. 4, p. 61.
6 See *History Today*, July 1969, pp. 575–485 for an account of the siege of Alicante.
7 Van 'T. Hoff, *op. cit.*, No. 754, p. 445.
8 Coombs, 'The Augmentation of 1709', *E.H.R.*, 1957, pp. 642–61.
9 Dangeau, *Journal*, Vol. 12, p. 412.
10 Churchill, *op. cit.*, Vol. 4, p. 82, citing *La vie de Villars*, 1784, Vol. 2, p. 30.
11 M. Sautai, *La bataille de Malplaquet*, Paris 1910, p. 14.
12 *Ibid.*, p. 22, citing *Archives . . . de la Guerre*, Vol. 2151.
13 *Ibid.*, p. 5–6.
14 Millner, *op. cit.*, p. 260.
15 Van 'T. Hoff, *op. cit.*, No. 740, p. 436–7.
16 *Archives . . . de la guerre*, tome 2146, Pt. 1, Sect. 1, No. 56.
17 W. Kane, *Campaigns of King William and Queen Anne 1689–1712*, London 1745, p. 83.
18 Lediard, *op. cit.*, Vol. 2, p. 482.
19 D. Defoe, *The Life and Adventures of Mother Ross* (ed. Sir J. Fortescue), London 1929, p. 128.
20 Blackadder, *op. cit.*, p. 343.
21 Sautai, *op. cit.*, p. 35.
22 Pelet & le Vault, *op. cit.*, Vol. 9, p. 86.
23 A. M. de Pas, Marquis de Feuquières, *Mémoires*, Paris 1775, Vol. 4, pp. 34–8.
24 *E.H.R.*, 1909, p. 317.
25 *Feldzüge*, *op. cit.*, Series 2, Vol. 2, p. 101.
26 Kane, *op. cit.*, p. 851.
27 De la Colonie, *op. cit.*, p. 338.
28 Millner, *op. cit.*, p. 275.
29 Claud-Louis-Hector, Duc de Villars, *Mémoires*, Paris 1883, Vol. 3, pp. 70–1.
30 See Trevelyan, *The Peace*, p. 50; Atkinson, p. 402, and Taylor, Vol. 2. Also *S.A.H.R. Journal*, March 1962 for article by H. G. Bowen, 'The Dutch at Malplaquet' for the stated view.
31 Add. Mss. 9107, f. 38.

32 De la Colonie, *op. cit.*, p. 339.

33 J. M. Schulenburg, *Leben und Denkwurdigkeiten*, 1834, Vol. 2, p. 417.

24 See Parker (1968 edn.), pp. 7–8.

35 Sautai, *op. cit.*, p. 129, citing St. Hilaires's letter to the Duc de Maine, 12 September 1709.

36 Churchill, *op. cit.*, Vol. 4, f.n. p. 133, citing Wackerbath's account.

37 Mathew Bishop, *Life and Adventures*, London 1744, p. 207, and K.M. Moir, '*Corporal Bishop s'en va-t-en Guerre*', privately printed 1952, p. 33.

38 Sir J. Fortescue, *History of the British Army*, London 1899, Vol. 1, p. 527.

39 Schulenburg, *op. cit.*, Vol. 2, p. 417.

40 *E.H.R.*, 1909, p. 317, *et seq.*, for this and subsequent quotations from Orkney at Malplaquet.

41 Coxe, *op. cit.*, Vol. 5, p. 70.

42 Add. Mss. 41178, f. 65.

43 *Archives . . . de la Guerre, Tome* 2152, No. 170.

44 Van 'T. Hoff, *op. cit.*, No. 789, p. 463.

45 Peter Drake, *op. cit.*, p. 190 and Murray, *op. cit.*, Vol. 4, pp. 596 and 599.

46 Murray, *op. cit.*, Vol. 4, pp. 605–6 and Churchill, *op. cit.*, Vol. 4, p. 151.

47 Pelet & le Vault, *op. cit.*, Vol. 9, pp. 114–15.

48 See Churchill, *op. cit.*, Vol. 4, p. 159.

49 Swift, *Memoirs relating to that change which happened in the Queen's Ministry*, in the *Collected Works* (ed. H. Davis), Vol. 8, pp. 112–13.

50 For the best modern analysis of this issue, see the *S.A.H.R. Journal* for 1967, pp. 67–83: article by H. L. Snyder.

Chapter Fourteen: 1710–1711 (pp. 273–99)

1 State Papers 84/233 Pt. 1 f. 258 (reverse).

2 See Marlborough's letter to Mercy, Murray, *op. cit.*, Vol. 4, p. 660.

3 H.M.C., Round Mss, p. 344–5.

4 Sturgill, *op. cit.*, p. 101.

5 Coxe, *op. cit.*, Vol. 3, p. 39.

6 Lediard, *op. cit.*, Vol. 3, p. 31.

7 Dangeau, *Journal*, Vol. 13, pp. 153, 156 ff.

8 Coxe, *op. cit.*, Vol. 5, p. 194.

9 See Murray, *op. cit.*, Vol. 5, p. 194.

10 Parker (1968 edn.), *op. cit.*, p. 91.

11 Millner, *op. cit.*, p. 299.

12 Murray, *op. cit.*, Vol. 5, p. 58.

13 Van 'T. Hoff, *op. cit.*, No. 857, p. 499.

14 *Ibid.*, No. 860, p. 501.

15 Murray, Vol. 5, p. 69 & van T' Hoff No. 870, p. 586.

16 Henderson, *op. cit.*, p. 181, citing A. Arneth, Vol. 2, p. 477.

17 Murray, *op. cit.*, Vol. 5, p. 139.

18 O. Klopp, *Der Fall des Hauses Stuart*, 1884, Vol. 13, p. 440.

19 R. Cannon, *Regimental Histories of the British Army*, London 1835, Vol. 18, p. 38 f.n.

20 Kamen, *op. cit.*, p. 23.
21 H.M.C., the Portland Papers, Vol. 2, p. 224.
22 Van 'T. Hoff, *op. cit.*, No. 936, p. 538.
23 *Ibid.*, No. 942, pp. 540–1.
24 Lediard, *op. cit.*, Vol. 3, p. 138.
25 Coxe, *op. cit.*, Vol. 5, p. 417.
26 Parker (1968 edn.), *op. cit.*, p. 99.
27 Kane, *op. cit.*, p. 89.
28 Cited by Lediard, Vol. 3, p. 149.
29 Parker (1968 edn.), p. 103.
30 Goslinga, *op. cit.*, p. 132.
31 Atkinson, *op. cit.*, p. 448, citing Murray, Vol. 5, p. 433.
32 Parker (1968 edn.), *op. cit.*, p. 106.
33 *Ibid.*, pp. 107–9.
34 Lediard, *op. cit.*, Vol. 3, p. 170.
35 Coxe, *op. cit.*, Vol. 6, pp. 79–80.
36 Lediard, Vol. 3, p. 170.
37 Churchill, *op. cit.*, Vol. 4, p. 374.
38 Stowe Mss. 246, f. 10.
39 Parker (1968 edn.), *op. cit.*, p. 111.
40 A. Allent, *Histoire du Corps Impérial du Génie*, Paris 1805, pp. 592–3.
41 Cited by Lediard, *op. cit.*, Vol. 3, p. 154.
42 *Ibid.*, p. 167.

Chapter Fifteen: 1712–22 (pp. 300–31)

1 Coxe, *op. cit.*, Vol. 3, p. 255.
2 H. Davis (editor), *Political Treatises*, Oxford 1951, p. 15.
3 Parker (1968 edn.), p. 114.
4 Kane, *op. cit.*, p. 102.
5 Bishop, *op. cit.*, p. 266.
6 Atkinson, *op. cit.*, p. 467.
7 *History of Parliament*, Vol. 6, p. 1088.
8 Trevelyan, *op. cit.*, Vol. 3, p. 221.
9 See *New Cambridge Modern History*, Vol. 4, ch. 14, and *E.H.R.*, April 1971, p. 264.
10 Parker (1968 edn.), pp. 120–1.
11 Atkinson, *op. cit.*, p. 467.
12 G. Burnett, *A History of My Own Time*, Vol. 2, ch. 2, citing the Earl of Dartmouth.
13 Stuart Mss, Vol. 1, p. 313.
14 Mérode-Westerloo (1968 edn.), p. 225.
15 *Letters of Sarah, Duchess of Marlborough, at Madresfield Court*, London, 1875, p. 74.
16 Parker (1968 edn.), pp. 129–30.
17 *Ibid.*, p. 9, citing the 1745 edition, p. 254.
18 Swift, *Collected Works*, Vol. 16, p. 178.
19 Cited by Churchill (paperback edition), Vol. 4, p. 522.
20 S. J. Reid, *John and Sarah, Duke and Duchess of Marlborough*, London 1914, p. 413.

21 See Chapter One above.

22 Wolseley, *op. cit.*, Vol. 1, ch. XXIX, p. 226.

23 Young and Lawford, *The British Army*, London 1970, p. 27.

24 Defoe, *Mother Ross*, *op. cit.*, p. 54.

25 Coxe, *op. cit.*, Vol. 2, p. 146.

26 *Ibid.*, Vol. 1, p. 371.

27 Bishop, *op. cit.*, p. 267.

28 Ailesbury, *op. cit.*, Vol. 12, p. 570.

29 Churchill (paperback edn.), Vol. 4, p. 25.

30 Mérode-Westerloo, (1968 edn.), p. 211.

31 Goslinga, *op. cit.*, pp. 43–4.

32 *House of Commons Journals*, Vol. 17, p. 48.

33 J. R. Wolf, *The Emergence of the Great Powers, 1685–1715*, New York 1962, p. 67.

34 See Burton, *op. cit.*, pp. 196–8 for a full analysis.

35 Belloc, *op. cit.*, p. 48.

36 Bishop, *op. cit.*, p. 194.

37 Parker (1968 edn.), p. 115.

38 Lediard, *op. cit.*, Vol. 1, pp. xix and xx.

39 For an admirable summary of Marlborough's gifts as a field administrator, see R. E. Scouller's article in *The Army Quarterly*, Vol. 95 (1967–8), pp. 197–208 and 102–13.

40 Burton, *op. cit.*, p. 199.

41 Belloc, *op. cit.*, p. 5.

42 Parker, (1968 edn.), p. 125.

Bibliography

A. Manuscript Sources

British Museum: Add. Mss.: 22196 (the Cadogan-Raby correspondence)
                         23642 (the Tyrawly Papers)
                         29878 (Diary of William Cramond)
                           4742 (Correspondence of Henry Davenant)
                           4747 (Casualty and strength estimates)
                           5132 (Dutch State papers)
            Stowe 58 & 469 (Richards' diary, 1705), 742, 825
            State Papers 84/233
Public Records Office: Calendar of State Papers (Domestic), James II 1686.
                     Calendar of State Papers (Domestic) 1689.
                     Calendar of State Papers Series 8-5, King William's Chest.
                     Calendar of State Papers (Ireland), 1669-70.
                     War Office Papers 4/5 (the Blenheim Roll), 55/424, Flanders etc.

B. Printed documentary sources and works of reference

Archives du dépôt de la Guerre, tomes 1528, 1552, 1554, 1640, 1651, 1371, 11751, 1836, 1939, 2015, 2081, 2108

Axe, the Book of the (Axminster records)

Blenheim Palace Papers

Bodart, G., *Militär-historisches Kriegs-Lexicon, 1618–1905*, Vienna & Leipsig, 1908

Delbruck, H., *Geschichte der Kriegskunst*, 4 vols., Berlin 1900–20

English Historical Review, April 1904 (XIX)—(the correspondence of Lord Orkney . . .)

Eugen von Savoyen, *Feldzüge*, 20 vols., Series One and Two, Vienna 1876–92

Gazette, the London for 1685, . . . 1712 etc.

Hoff, B. van 'T. (editor), *The Correspondence, 1701–11, of John Churchill and Anthonie Heinsius*, the Hague 1951

Hatton Correspondence, the, Camden Society 1878, Vol. 1.

Historical Manuscripts Commission: *Atholl Papers* (1891)
                                      Buccleuch Papers (1903)
                                        Bath Papers (1904)
                                        Dartmouth Papers (1887)
                                        Northumberland Papers (1772)
                                        Portland Papers (1930)
                                        Spencer Papers (1871)

Legrelle, A., *La Diplomatie Française et le Succession d'Espagne*, 6 tomes (2nd edn.) Braine-le-Comte, 1895–1900

Murray, General Sir George (editor), *The Letters and Dispatches of John Churchill*, 5 vols., London 1845

National Army Museum Papers, 6909/4 (account and map of Elixhem, 1705)

Pohler, J., *Bibliotheca historico-militaris*, Munich 1890

Raa, F. J. G. ten and Bas, F. de, *Het Staatsche Leger Band* 7, The Hague 1950 *Correspondance politique, Angleterre, La*, Quai d'Orsai, Paris

Snyder, H. L., *The Marlborough-Godolphin Correspondence 1701–11*, 3 vols., Oxford 1975

C. Published Works

Alison, Sir A., *Life of John, Duke of Marlborough*, London 1852
Allent, A., *Histoire du Corps Impérial de Génie*, Paris 1805
Anon., *A Journal of the several sieges of Kaiserswaert, Landau and Venlo*, London 1702
Anon., *The Lives of the Two Illustrious Generals*, London 1713
Arneth, A., *Prinz Eugen von Savoyen*, 3 vols., Vienna 1858–64
Ashley, M., *Marlborough*, London 1939
Atkinson, C. T., *Marlborough and the Rise of the British Army* (2nd Edition), London 1924
Atkinson, C. T., articles in the *Journal for the Society for Army Historical Research: Marlborough's Sieges* (1933); *The cost of Queen Anne's War* (1955); *Wynendael* (1956); *Ramillies Battlefield* (with Col. Wijn, 1960)—amongst many others.
Aubry, O., *Napoléon*, Paris 1964
Baxter, S. B., *William III*, London 1966
Barnett, C., *Marlborough*, London 1974
Belfield, E., *Oudenarde 1708*, London 1972
Belloc, H., *The Tactics and Strategy of the Great Duke of Marlborough*, London 1933
Bengtsson, F. G., *Life of Charles XII, King of Sweden*, Stockholm 1960
Berwick, J. Fitz-James, Duke of, *Memoirs*, 2 vols., London 1779
Bishop, M., *Life and Adventures of Matthew Bishop from 1701–1711*, London 1744
Blackmore, H. L., *British Military Firearms, 1650–1850*, London 1961
Blomfield, Sir R., *Sebastien le Prestre de Vauban*, London 1938
Boulanger, J., *Le Grand Siècle*, Paris 1949
Bowen, H. G., The Dutch at Malplaquet, *S.A.H.R. Journal*, 1962
Burnet, G., *History of my own Time, 1660–85*, 3 vols., London 1823
Burrell S., (editor), *Aimiable Renegade: the Memoirs of Captain Peter Drake*, London 1960
Burton, I. F., *The Captain-General*, London 1968
Butler, I., *The Rule of Three*, London 1967
Cambridge Modern History, the New, Vol. 6, London 1970
Cannon, R., *Historical Records of the British Army*, Vol. 18, London 1835
Chandler, D. G., *The Campaigns of Napoleon*, London 1967
———, (editor) *Robert Parker and the Comte de Mérode-Westerloo*, London 1968
———, 'The Campaign of 1704' and the 'Siege of Alicante', in *History Today*, 1964 and 1969, and 'The Old Corporal,' 1972
Childs, C., *The Army of Charles II*, London 1976
Churchill, Sir W. S., *Marlborough, his Life and Times*, 4 vols., London 1933—8 and paperback edition, London 1967
———, Sir W. S., *History of the English Speaking Peoples*, Vol. 2, London 1956.
Clark, Sir G. N., *The Seventeenth Century*, Oxford 1947 (revised edition)
———, *The Later Stuarts*, Oxford 1934
Clausewitz, C. von, 'On War', 3 vols., London 1903
Coombs, D., *The Conduct of the Dutch*, Amsterdam 1958
———, *The Dutch at Malplaquet*, article in *S.A.H.R. Journal*, 1962
Coxe, Archdeacon W. C., Memoirs of John, Duke of Marlborough, 6 vols., London 1820

Crichton, A., (editor), *Life and Diary of Lt. Col. John Blackadder* ..., Edinburgh 1824

Creasey, Sir John, *The Fifteen Decisive Battles of the World*, London 1948 (edn.)

Crockatt, J. H. *Marlborough*, London 1971.

Dalrymple, Sir J., *Memoirs of Great Britain and Ireland*, 2 vols., London 1773

Dalton, C., *English Army Lists and Commission Registers, 1661-1714*, 6 vols., London 1898-1904

Dangeau, P. de, *Journal*, 10 tomes, Paris 1857

Deane, Pte. John, *A Journal of the Campaign in Flanders, AD MDCCVIII*, London 1846

Defoe, D., *The Life and Adventures of Mother Ross* (Ed. Sir J. Fortescue), London 1929

————, *An Enquiry upon Projects*, in 'The Earlier life and Works of D. Defoe', ed. H. Morley, London 1889

Dickinson, H. T., articles: *S.A.H.R. Journal*, 1970-71 on the Craggs - Raby Correspondence

Dutems, J. F. H., *Histoire de Jean, Duc de Marlborough*, revised by Duclos, Paris 1806

Farquhar, G., *The Recruiting Officer* (play), London 1707

Felton, Dr. H., *Dissertation on writing the Classics*, London 1719

Feuquières, A. M. de Pas, Marquis de, *Mémoires*, 4 tomes, Paris 1775

Flower, D. (Editor), *St. Simon at Versailles*, London 1953

Fortescue, Sir John, *History of the British Army*, Vol. 1, London 1899

Geikie, R., and Montgomery I. A., *The Dutch Barrier, 1702-15*, Cambridge 1930

Goslinga, Sicco van, *Mémoires*, Paris 1857

Green, D., *Sarah, Duchess of Marlborough*, London 1967

————, *Queen Anne*, London 1970

Hare, Dr. F., *Journal*, included in part in Coxe, *op. cit.*, and Murray, *op. cit.*

Hatton, R. M., *Charles XII*, London 1968

Henderson, N. P., *Prince Eugen of Savoy*, London 1964

Hill, C., *The Century of Revolution, 1603-1714*, London 1967

Horsley W. C. (Editor), *The Chronicles of an Old Campaigner (J-M de la Colonie)*, London 1904

Hyde, Edward, Earl of Clarendon, *Correspondence and Diary*, Vol. 1, London 1828

Kamen, H., *The War of Succession in Spain*, London 1969

Kane, Brig. Gen. R., *The Campaigns of King William and Queen Anne, from 1689-1712, also a new system of Military Discipline* ... London 1745

Klopp, O., *Der Fall des Hauses Stuart*, 14 vols., Vienna 1875-88

Lazard, P., *Vauban, 1633-1707*, London 1934

Lediard, T., *Life of John, Duke of Marlborough*, 3 vols., London 1736

Mahan, Admiral A. T., *The Influence of Sea-Power on History*, London 1895

Mérode-Westerloo, *Feld-Maréchal, Comte* de, *Mémoires*, 2 tomes, Brussels 1840

Millner, Sgt. John, *A Compendious Journal* ... *1701-1712*, London 1733

Moit, K. M., 'Corporal Bishop s'en va-t-en Guerre', privately printed 1952

McKay, D., *Prince Eugene of Savoy*, London 1977

Ogg, D., *Europe in the 17th Century* (5th edition), London 1948

Orrery, Earl of, *A Treatise on the Art of War*, London 1677

Parker, Capt. Robert, *Memoirs of the most remarkable Military Transactions* ... *1683-1718*, (2nd edn.), London 1741

Parnell, Sir A., *The War of Succession in Spain* (2nd edition), London 1905

Pauline, the, June 1892

Pelet, J. J. G. and Le Vault, F. E. de, *Mémoires militaires relatifs à la Guerre de la Succession d'Espagne*, 11 tomes & atlas, Paris, 1836–42

Petrie, Sir Charles, *The Marshal Duke of Berwick*, London 1953

Philips, T. R. (editor), *Saxe's Reveries on the Art of War*, Harrisburg 1944

Puysegur, Maréchal J. F. de, *L'art de la guerre par principes et par règles*, 2 tomes Paris 1748

Reid, S. J., *John and Sarah, Duke and Duchess of Marlborough*, London 1914

Rogers, H. C. B., *The British Army of the 18th Century*, London 1977

Rousset, C., *Histoire de Louvois*, 4 tomes, Paris 1862–3

Rowse, A. L., *The Early Churchills*, London 1956

Sautai, M., *La bataille de Malplaquet*, Paris 1910

Saint-Simon, Duc de, *Mémoires*, 40 vols., Paris 1881–1907

Schulenburg, J. M., *Leben und Denkwürdigkeiten*, 2 vols., Vienna 1834

Scouller, R. E., *The Armies of Queen Anne*, Oxford 1966

———, *Marlborough's Field Administration*, two articles in the Army Quarterly, Vol. 95, 1967–8

Snyder, H. L., *Marlborough's request for the Captain-Generalcy for Life*, S.A.H.R. *Journal*, 1967

Swift, Jonathan, *Memoirs relating to that change which happened in the Queen's Ministry*, in 'Collected Works' (ed. H. Davis)

———, *The Conduct of the Allies*, London 1712

Sypesteyn, J. W. de, *Het Leven van Menno van Coehoorn*, Leewarden 1860

Tallard, Maréchal, *Campagne de M. le M. de Tallard en Allemagne, 1704*, 2 vols., Amsterdam 1763

Taylor, F., *The Wars of Marlborough, 1702–9*, 2 vols., Oxford 1921

Trevelyan, Sir G. M., *England in the Reign of Queen Anne*, 3 vols., London 1930–4 paperback edition, London 1965

Turner, G. B., *A History of Military Affairs in Western Society*, New York 1953

Vauban, Simon le Prestre, Seigneur de, *Traité sur l'Attaque des Places* and *Traité sur la Défense des Places* (edition), Paris 1779

———, ed. G. R. Northrock, *A Manual of Siegecraft and Fortification*, Michigan 1968

Veenendaal, A. J., 'The opening phase of Marlborough's campaign of 1708' in *History*, 1958

Villars, Claud-Louis-Hector, Duc de, *Mémoires*, (ed. by de Vogüé), Paris 1887

Wace, Alan, *The Marlborough Tapestries at Blenheim Palace*, London 1968

Walton, C., *History of the British Standing Army, 1660–1700*, London 1894

Wedgwood C. V., *The Thirty Years War*, London, 1944

Weygand, H., *Histoire de l'armée française*, Paris 1938

Wolseley, Field Marshal Viscount, G. J., *Life of Marlborough to the Accession of Queen Anne*, (3rd edition), 2 Vols., London 1894

Young, P., *The British Army, 1642–1970*, London 1967

Young, P. and Lawford J. (editors), *A History of the British Army*, London 1970

Index

Note: Ranks and titles indicated below are usually the highest held by individuals.

Holland, Province of, 13, 190 (and see *United Provinces*)
Holstein-Beck, Prince of, 146
Hompesch, Lt.-Gen., Count, 287, 289
Hop, Jakob, Dutch Field Deputy, 116
Hornes, the Comte de, 103, 159, 161
Hudson Bay Company, the, 27, 46
Huguenots, in Allied service, 66, 72, 112, 167, 183, 221
Hull, 23
Humières, French Lt.-Gen. Louis-Humières, Duc de, 31, 32
Hungarian Revolt, 112, 154, 200
Huy, town and sieges of, 97, 105, 115, 116, 118, 119, 156, 158, 193, 195, 196, 209, 211
Huysse, Heights of, 215, 221

Ingoldsby, Lt.-Gen. Richard, 159, 296
Ingolstadt, siege of, 133, 140
Ireland, 14, 33, 35
Italy, North, 55, 95, 107, 120, 124, 153, 154, 165, 166, 168, 169, 185, 189, 190, 195

James II, Duke of York and King of England, friendship for M., 5, 12; M.'s growing doubts about; 11, 22, 23; and desertion of, 24, 25, 313; flees abroad, 24, 30, 35; in exile, 28, 46; death, 57; mentioned, 8, 10, 11, 13, 14, 22, 23, 33
James III, the Old Pretender (Chevalier de St. George), 23, 57, 206, 308
Jeffreys, Capt, Richard, 193
Jeffreys, George, 1st Baron, Lord Chief Justic, 21, 22
Jennings (or Jenyns), Frances, Duchess of Tyrconnel, 8
Jennings (or Jenyns), Sarah, Duchess of Marlborough, 8; character of, 8, 9, 311; political views of, 107, 186, 204, 270; love for M., 11, 47; relation with Q. Anne, 12, 24, 28, 58; loses favour, 152, 186, 204, 238, 270, 271; dismissed the Court, 279, 285; mentioned, 10, 11, 149, 183, 265, 267
Jersey, Edward Villiers, 1st Earl of, 59, 126
Joseph I, Archduke and Emperor, 51(fn), 154, 157, 164, 169, 185, 205, 269, 286
Joseph-Ferdinand, Electoral-Prince of Bavaria, 51, 52
Judoigne, 172, 178
Juliers, 96, 100
Junto, the Whig, 241, 272, 280. See also the *Whigs*

Kaiserswerth, town and siege of, 29, 94, 96, 97, 98, 101
Kane, Gen. Richard, 92, 250, 258, 262, 303, 330
Kehl, 112, 136
Keppel, Arnold Joost van, 1st Earl of Albemarle, 27
Keynsham, 16
Killiekrankie, battle of, 33

Kinsale, siege of, 33, 36, 37, 41
Kirke, Lt.-Gen. Percy, 14, 26, 38

Lamotte, French Gen. Louis-Jacques, Comte de, 231, 232, 234, 237,
Landau, city and sieges of, 100, 120, 127, 133, 151, 153, 183, 307
Landen, battle of, 47, 157
Landrecies, siege of, 305
Launsheim, 132
Lauzun, Antoine, Comte de, 34, 36, 37
Lavingen, 140, 141
Leake, Admiral Sir John, 238
Léau, town and siege of, 119, 158, 161, 164, 170
Lech, River, 141
Lediard, Thomas, 63, 76, 178, 250
Lee, River, 38, 39, 40
Leffinghe, siege of, 231, 234, 236
Leopold I, Emperor, 50, 52, 53, 111, 113, 121, 154
Lerida, siege of, 191
Lessines, 213, 214
Liége, Bishopric, city and siege of, 29, 53, 95, 104, 105, 112, 114, 156, 157, 193
Lille, city and siege of, 65, 116, 120, 180, 181, 182, 206, 213, 223-39 *passim*, 242, 245, 322
Lillenroot, M., Swedish Ambassador, 56
Lille St. Hubert, 101
Limburg, siege of, 104, 119
Limerick, siege and town of, 36, 37
Lisbon, 167, 202
Londonderry, 34
Lords, House of, 22. See also *Parliament*
Lorraine, Leopold, Duke of, 52
Lottum, Gen. and Count, 219, 220, 222, 232, 256, 257, 258, 259, 260, 263, 330
Louis XIV, King of France, 6; negotiations with William III, 51, 52; and the Spanish Succession, 50-4; accepts the will, 53, 54; war plans of, in various years, 53, 95, 112, 114, 153, 170, 190-1, 211, 229, 245, 248, 276; ambitions of, 51-4; willingness to make peace, 187, 205; relationship with his marshals, 65, 69, 100, 133, 150, 266, 330; M. and, 10, 12, 163, 241, 309; inspires French resistance in 1709, 245; and negotiations of peace, 241, 242-3, 244, 248, 273-5, 321; negotiations with Tories, 275, 284, 307; mentioned, 22, 28, 30, 34, 64, 66, 97, 118, 120, 168, 170, 193, 197, 206, 227, 235, 237
Louvain, 161, 175, 179, 194, 196, 209
Louvois, François, Marquis de, French Minister of War, 29, 70
Low Countries, the, 120, 121, 190, 202
Lumley, Gen. Henry, 220
Lutzingen, 142, 144, 147
Luxembourg, Lt.-Gen. Christian-Louis, Chevalier and Duc de, 234, 235, 254
Luzzara, battle of, 107
Lyme Regis, 13, 14

READ MORE IN PENGUIN

In every corner of the world, on every subject under the sun, Penguin represents quality and variety – the very best in publishing today.

For complete information about books available from Penguin – including Puffins, Penguin Classics and Arkana – and how to order them, write to us at the appropriate address below. Please note that for copyright reasons the selection of books varies from country to country.

In the United Kingdom: Please write to *Dept. EP, Penguin Books Ltd, Bath Road, Harmondsworth, West Drayton, Middlesex UB7 ODA*

In the United States: Please write to *Consumer Sales, Penguin Putnam Inc., P.O. Box 12289 Dept. B, Newark, New Jersey 07101-5289*. VISA and MasterCard holders call 1-800-788-6262 to order Penguin titles

In Canada: Please write to *Penguin Books Canada Ltd, 10 Alcorn Avenue, Suite 300, Toronto, Ontario M4V 3B2*

In Australia: Please write to *Penguin Books Australia Ltd, P.O. Box 257, Ringwood, Victoria 3134*

In New Zealand: Please write to *Penguin Books (NZ) Ltd, Private Bag 102902, North Shore Mail Centre, Auckland 10*

In India: Please write to *Penguin Books India Pvt Ltd, 11 Community Centre, Panchsheel Park, New Delhi 110017*

In the Netherlands: Please write to *Penguin Books Netherlands bv, Postbus 3507, NL-1001 AH Amsterdam*

In Germany: Please write to *Penguin Books Deutschland GmbH, Metzlerstrasse 26, 60594 Frankfurt am Main*

In Spain: Please write to *Penguin Books S. A., Bravo Murillo 19, 1° B, 28015 Madrid*

In Italy: Please write to *Penguin Italia s.r.l., Via Benedetto Croce 2, 20094 Corsico, Milano*

In France: Please write to *Penguin France, Le Carré Wilson, 62 rue Benjamin Baillaud, 31500 Toulouse*

In Japan: Please write to *Penguin Books Japan Ltd, Kaneko Building, 2-3-25 Koraku, Bunkyo-Ku, Tokyo 112*

In South Africa: Please write to *Penguin Books South Africa (Pty) Ltd, Private Bag X14, Parkview, 2122 Johannesburg*

INSPECTION COPY REQUESTS

Lecturers in the United Kingdom and Ireland wishing to apply for inspection copies of Classic Penguin titles for student group adoptions are invited to apply to:

Inspection Copy Department
Penguin Press Marketing
27 Wrights Lane
LONDON
W8 5TZ

Fax: 020 7416 3274

E-mail: academic@penguin.co.uk

Inspection copies may also be requested via our website at:
www.penguinclassics.com

Please include in your request the author, title and the ISBN of the book(s) in which you are interested, the name of the course on which the books will be used and the expected student numbers.

It is essential that you include with your request your title, first name, surname, position, department name, college or university address, telephone and fax numbers and your e-mail address.

Lecturers outside the United Kingdom and Ireland should address their applications to their local Penguin office.

Inspection copies are supplied at the discretion of Penguin Books

READ MORE IN PENGUIN

PENGUIN CLASSIC MILITARY HISTORY

 This series acknowledges the profound and enduring interest in military history, and the causes and consequences of human conflict. Penguin Classic Military History covers warfare from the earliest times to the age of electronics and encompasses subjects as diverse as classic examples of grand strategy and the precision tactics of Britain's crack SAS Regiment. The series will be enjoyed and valued by students of military history and all who hope to learn from the often disturbing lessons of the past.

Published or forthcoming:

Corelli Barnett	**Engage the Enemy More Closely**
	The Great War
David G. Chandler	**The Art of Warfare on Land**
William Craig	**Enemy at the Gates**
Heinz Guderian	**Panzer Leader**
Heinz Höhne	**The Order of the Death's Head**
Anthony Kemp	**The SAS at War**
Martin Middlebrook	**The Kaiser's Battle**
Philip Warner	**Sieges of the Middle Ages**
Cecil Woodham-Smith	**The Reason Why**